THE COLONIAL IRONSIDES

English Expeditions under the Commonwealth and Protectorate, 1650–1660

Jonathon Riley

'This is the Century of the Soldier', Fulvio Testi, Poet, 1641

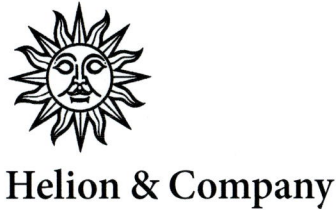

Helion & Company

Helion & Company Limited
Unit 8 Amherst Business Centre
Budbrooke Road
Warwick
CV34 5WE
England
Tel. 01926 499 619
Email: info@helion.co.uk
Website: www.helion.co.uk
Twitter: @helionbooks
Visit our blog http://blog.helion.co.uk/

Published by Helion & Company 2022
Designed and typeset by Serena Jones
Cover designed by Paul Hewitt, Battlefield Design (www.battlefield-design.co.uk)

Text © Jonathon Riley 2022
Photographs and images © as individually credited
Maps drawn by George Anderson © Helion & Company 2022

Every reasonable effort has been made to trace copyright holders and to obtain their permission for the use of copyright material. The author and publisher apologise for any errors or omissions in this work, and would be grateful if notified of any corrections that should be incorporated in future reprints or editions of this book.

ISBN 978-1-915070-37-1

British Library Cataloguing-in-Publication Data.
A catalogue record for this book is available from the British Library.

All rights reserved. No part of this publication may be reproduced, stored in a retrieval system, or transmitted, in any form, or by any means, electronic, mechanical, photocopying, recording or otherwise, without the express written consent of Helion & Company Limited.

For details of other military history titles published by Helion & Company
Limited, contact the above address, or visit our website: http://www.helion.co.uk

We always welcome receiving book proposals from prospective authors.

Contents

Acknowledgements	v
Introduction	vi
A Note on Dates	ix
A Note on Colonial Activity in the East Indies	x
1. France, Spain and the Netherlands: Great Power Relations in Europe, 1564–1654	11
2. Cromwell's Design: Commonwealth Foreign Policy After the End of the Civil Wars	23
3. Recovering the Royalist Enclaves, April–December 1651	32
Appendix I to Chapter 3: Blake's and Ayscue's Squadrons for the Scilly and Channel Islands Expeditions	54
Appendix II to Chapter 3: The Commonwealth Invasion Force and Garrison, Isle of Man	56
Appendix III to Chapter 3: Royalist and Commonwealth Forces in the Channel Islands	60
Appendix IV to Chapter 3: Royalist and Commonwealth Forces in the Isles of Scilly	68
4. The Expedition to Subdue the West Indies, 1651–1652	71
Appendix to Chapter 4: Military Forces in the Barbadoes, 1651–1652	79
5. The Expedition to New Amsterdam, Saint John and Port Royal, 1654	81
Appendix to Chapter 5: Order of Battle for the expedition to New Amsterdam, Saint John and Port Royal, 1654	95
6. Virginia, Bermuda and Maryland During the Civil Wars and the Protectorate	97
Appendix to Chapter 6: Military Forces in Maryland	113
7. Mounting the Expedition to Hispaniola	115
Appendix I to Chapter 7: English Navy Lists of the Expedition to Hispaniola	127
Appendix II to Chapter 7: English Army Lists of the Expedition to Hispaniola	129
8. Penn and Venables' Attack on San Domingo, 1655	137
Appendix to Chapter 8: Spanish Army Lists of Forces in Hispaniola	160
9. The Capture of Jamaica	163
Appendix I to Chapter 9: The Cromwellian Garrison in Jamaica, 1657–1662	183

Appendix II to Chapter 9: Spanish Order of Battle, Jamaica, 1655–1660	190
10. General-at-Sea Blake's Naval Operations in the Mediterranean and Against Spain	191
Appendix to Chapter 10: English Navy Lists of Blake's Expedition to the Mediterranean	204
11. Charles II, the Prince of Condé and the Spanish Army of Flanders	206
Appendix to Chapter 11: Royalist Regiments in Spanish Flanders, 1656–1660	221
12. Cromwell's Expeditionary Brigade and the French Army of Flanders	227
Appendix to Chapter 12: Cromwellian Regiments of Foot in Flanders, 1657–1658	233
13. Opening Moves: the Sieges of Montmédy, St-Venant and Ardres, June–September, 1657	237
Appendix to Chapter 13: The Garrison of Ardres	250
14. The Siege and Occupation of Mardyck, September 1657–April 1658	251
15. The Siege of Dunkirk and the Battle of the Dunes, June 1658	261
16. The Capture of Furnes, Bergues, Dixmüde and Gravelines, June–August 1658	284
Appendix to Chapter 16: The Garrisons of Dunkirk and Mardyck, 1658–1659	291
17. Oudenaarde, Ypres and the Defeat of the Prince de Ligne, September–October 1658	295
18. The Peace of the Pyrenees and the Death of Cromwell, September 1658–May 1660	305
19. The Restoration and Aftermath, May 1660–April 1663	314
Appendix to Chapter 19: Army Lists of the Dunkirk and Mardyck Garrisons after the Restoration May 1660–April 1663	320
Notes to the Text	334
Bibliography	360
Index	368

Acknowledgements

I would like to acknowledge with thanks for their help and patience the following people and organisations: first, to Professor John Childs who without knowing it, inspired this book as the successor to my earlier work, *The Last Ironsides*. Mr Philip Abbot and the library staff of the Royal Armouries in the Tower of London; the staff of the National Archives, Kew; the staff of the British Library; the staff of the Bodleian Library in Oxford; the House of Commons Library; and the University of Manchester Library. To the Royal Historical Society, in particular for permission to reproduce material relating to the expedition to Hispaniola, the exact details of which are noted on the maps and illustrations concerned. To Wienand Drenth for information on the wars in the Low Countries from the Dutch point of view; for proof-reading and correcting many of the chapters; and for permission to use many of his maps and illustrations from *The First Colonial Soldiers* as acknowledged in the chapters. To Mr Nick Keyes who has also done much proofing and supplied information on the Spanish side of events in the seventeenth century. Last to my partner Clare for all her encouragement, help and inspiration.

Introduction

Sir John Seeley once said in a lecture in 1883 that Britain acquired her empire in a fit of absence of mind. Neither is true, for what Seeley intended to convey was that the earliest objective of colonial settlement – trade – turned into political conquest because of circumstances rather than through calculation. It was through trade that the English, late comers to the business of colonial expansion, set out to emulate, compete against and ultimately surpass those who had first set out to capture the wealth of the Caribbean and the Americas. The initial motivation of money only later turned into a quest for possessions. This financial motivation extended to merchants, to pirates and buccaneers, to adventurers and indeed to kings – for at home, a king had to battle with parliament for funds whereas possessions overseas brought a more direct stream of revenue – as the King of Spain could show.

Following Columbus's rediscovery of the Americas, the Pope issued a bull in 1493 allocating the Indies and China to Portugal and the Americas to Spain – ignoring the presence of other empires such as those of Muscovy, China, the Ottomans and the Mughals. But after 1530, neither the English nor their other rivals, the Dutch, were minded to obey His Holiness. Indeed, as Protestantism took hold, there grew up a belief among the reformers that it was their duty to promote the Protestant religion abroad among the heathen and to confront Catholicism wherever it could be found. By the 1580s, Grenvile, Drake, Raleigh and others had all begun to make attempts at settlements in the Americas, but with small success. As a result, rather than trade or establish colonies, the English turned for the next 30 years or more to plunder, attacking Spanish treasure ships and settlements. From piracy it was a small step to privateering, the licensing by government of private men-of-war through letters of marque to attack enemy shipping.

Individual groups of settlers, with varying motivation, did however begin to establish a footprint in the Americas that was not solely founded on predation. On the North American mainland this was motivated in part by religious and politically motivated migration (the two being impossible to separate at this period), but as time went on, the trade in furs and tobacco and the fishing grounds off Newfoundland became hugely significant. By the outbreak of the Civil Wars in the three kingdoms, the English colonial presence was well established in North America and the Caribbean. With the exception of Maryland and the Barbadoes there was no fighting in these colonies although in some cases, such as Virginia and Bermuda, the colonies declared for the King until obliged by the arrival of Commonwealth forces to conform to the new Republican order.

The successful establishment of these colonies signalled huge demographic changes. The population of Massachusetts, for example, tripled in 30 years, the result partly of immigration but also partly procreation: unlike New Spain, where there were relatively few Spaniards and the bulk of the population remained native American, the population of New England was just that: English. Between 1600 and 1714, 750,000 people left England for her new colonies out of a total population of just over five million. No other country sent out such a proportion of its population, not even the Norse migrations of the 8th, 9th and 10th centuries. It was a migration that changed the world.

As has been noted, religion, especially its Protestant expression, played a significant role in the foundation of much of colonial New England. For many extreme Protestants, the Elizabethan settlement was a compromise and a halfway house. They saw the Reformation as the chance to establish the new Jerusalem in England, but the maintenance of an Established Church with bishops, tithes and a recognisably Catholic order, was a betrayal. The New World was therefore an opportunity to strike out and raise the third Jerusalem – a fourth there would never be. Thus came the foundation of the Puritan or Quaker colonies like Plymouth Bay, Massachusetts Bay, Rhode Island and Pennsylvania. Maryland was different, being an attempt to establish religious toleration for Catholics – a scheme which the builders of the new Jerusalem did all they could to destroy. The Puritans initially sought the friendship of the native people and the Massachusetts colony in particular wanted nothing more than to be left alone, so that in its earliest years, there was virtually no need for a strong military system. The friendship with the native people was, however, short–lived. Within 10 years the Puritans had come to regard the native people as Philistines threatening their New Jerusalem. They did not see themselves as invaders, but as God's chosen people for whom the new land had been prepared and which they would expand without limit. Like the Jews of old confronting the Philistines, the colonists confronted the native people: 10 years after the Puritans landed, those at Boston had developed a formidable military system.

It is not surprising therefore that the desire to export Protestantism from England reached its apogee under the Puritan Protectorate of Oliver Cromwell and was the motivation for his war against Spain in the Americas – the Western Design – and for his alliance with France (another Catholic power) in Europe. Spanish trade, and her treasure convoys from the New World, had already been attacked in the Mediterranean by Admiral Blake. It was Cromwell's wars, first with the Dutch and then with Spain, that initiated the disastrous expedition to Hispaniola – which, having been easily taken by Drake, seemed an obvious target – and after it, the settlement of England's first substantial colonial presence in the western hemisphere outside the North American mainland, in Jamaica. A substantial presence indeed, but it must be noted that a number of smaller colonies like the Somers Islands, the Barbadoes, Antigua, Nevis and St Christopher had been established during the reigns of James I and Charles I and were already a source of friction with Spain.

Ideology and money from raw materials were the spurs to Cromwell's colonial expansion, in spite of the horrible climate and the accompanying diseases that killed nine white men in 10. In the West Indies, sugar could be grown, and sugar was England's biggest single import from the early seventeenth century until the early nineteenth, when cotton overtook it.

Cromwell had no scruples about attacking French colonies in the New World, using the forces that were to have seized New Amsterdam to attack what is now Nova Scotia; yet three years later, the Protectorate was allied with Catholic France against Spain, fighting a war in Europe that established an English colonial presence on the mainland, at Dunkirk, for the first time since the loss of Calais in 1558. Here, as also in Maryland, the last acts of the Civil Wars in the Three Kingdoms were played out as Cromwell's contingent in the French army in Flanders confronted not only the Spanish, but also the small army of English Royalists, Scots and Irish that followed Charles II in exile.

This book seeks to survey the whole gamut of Cromwell's expeditionary wars under both the Commonwealth and the Protectorate, with the exception of Ireland, since that island already formed part of the three kingdoms. It also includes the first essays in the islands around Britain which continued to be held for the King – Jersey, Guernsey, Man and the Scillies. It also deals with naval operations against Royalist privateers, the French and Spanish as well as the naval support to expeditionary operations on land. It goes on to examine the expeditions to the New World, both in subduing colonies inclined to royalism and the attempts to establish new ones through conquest, before returning to the war in Continental Europe. It was inspired by my earlier work, *The Last Ironsides*, which told the story of some of the men from Dunkirk and other old soldiers of both the armies of the Civil Wars after the Restoration. When I wrote that book – the first time it had been researched in any real detail – it was always in my mind that I would at some point have to explain how it was that English troops went to Portugal from a colony at Dunkirk. From there, it was a short step to embracing the whole notion of expeditionary operations under the Commonwealth and Protectorate: a form of warfare for which the English armies of the time were simply neither prepared nor equipped. The result was the dismal failure of Hispaniola; however, the successes in Jamaica, the Mediterranean and the Low Countries more than offset this. Cromwell was, therefore, perhaps far more successful than he or his army deserved to be. But success depends as much on the relative quality of the opposition as on one's own preparations and if Cromwell was going to take risks, he probably realised that these risks were lower against the Spanish than any other European opponent.

A Note on Dates

In the mid seventeenth century, the Julian Calendar was still in use in England and Wales, Scotland, Ireland and the Channel Islands; as well as by the English colonies in the Americas and the Caribbean. It was also in use in the Netherlands and most of Germany. It was at this time 10 days behind the Gregorian Calendar introduced by Pope Gregory XIII in 1582 (it rose to 11 days in 1700). Any dates given in the Julian Calendar are usually referred to as *Old Style* (O.S.). The Gregorian Calendar was used in Spain, Portugal and their territories and was not adopted in Great Britain and its colonies until 1752. Dates given in the Gregorian Calendar are generally referred to as *New Style* (N.S.). Moreover, in the Julian Calendar, the New Year began not on 1 January, but on 25 March – the Feast of the Annunciation of the Blessed Virgin Mary. This leads to the complicated side-effect that dates before 25 March, but after 1 January, are noted in contemporary accounts by the date of the preceding year, or else by a fractional notation. For example, 8 March 1658 or 8 March 1658/59 would in today's reckoning be 8 March 1659 – or indeed 18 March 1659 if the disparity between the calendars is taken into account. These discrepancies have the potential to cause huge confusion when trying to disentangle the dates in various campaigns and actions when reviewing the accounts of two sides using different calendars. I have therefore put all dates into New Style except where indicated and have started the New Year on 1 January.

A Note on Colonial Activity in the East Indies

This book is primarily concerned with the wars of the Protectorate against Catholic Spain. However, the Protectorate was as likely to fight fellow Protestants as Catholics if vital interests were at stake, as the First Anglo-Dutch War proved. Rivalry was especially fierce in the East Indies where the Dutch East India Company (the V.O.C.) was established in 1600 and it was they who began to build the first factories in what is now Indonesia; but behind this lay a major three-way struggle for control of the riches of the world between the Dutch and the English, the Dutch and the Portuguese; the Dutch and English against initially the Spanish but later the French. The first English East India Company was founded in 1602, two years after the Dutch Company, and made an early foothold at Bantam in Java. Here, however, the Dutch were too strong, both in militarily and mercantile resources, and it was this that drove the later development of the English Company on the mainland of the Indian sub-continent rather than in the islands further east. English settlements such as Bantam in Java were attacked and eventually extinguished. To confront the Dutch in the Americas and the West Indies (it was too late to do so in the Far East), the English began rapidly to expand their naval strength and thus came the first Anglo-Dutch War and the aborted expedition against New Amsterdam; there would be two more wars after the Restoration of Charles II and the ruinous effects of this confrontation were not dealt with until the accession of William III as King of England in 1688. Because colonies in the Far East were established as trading posts, under the aegis of the Honourable East India Company and not of the State, they are not considered further in this book.

Jonathon Riley
Llanllwni, Carmarthenshire
December 2021

1

France, Spain and the Netherlands: Great Power Relations in Europe, 1564–1654

By the middle of the seventeenth century, mighty imperial Spain, the world's superpower, had been drained by her long wars over the previous hundred years. She was short of men, money and capable generals. However, Spain possessed a reputation at this time as the most formidable military power in Europe, if not the world; her territories stretched from northern Italy, throughout western Europe, to the Low Countries. She also possessed valuable colonies in the Americas, from whence flowed gold, silver, sugar and food. But with their heavy commitments from the 1560s onwards caused by revolts in Europe, the Spanish had faced a manpower crisis caused by the coincidence of maximum military pressure combined with plague in the Iberian Peninsula: there were wars in Languedoc and Brittany in support of insurrections inside France;[*] simultaneous campaigns in Lombardy, Franche-Comté, the Low Countries and Germany and at sea.

The costliest of Spain's wars was the Eighty Years' War, the long and grinding struggle from 1568 to 1648 in several of the Seventeen Provinces, also known as the Low Countries or the Spanish Netherlands, fought for their independence. The revolt that led to the Eighty Years' War and eventually to the establishment of the independent Republic of the Seven United Netherlands – usually referred to in short-hand as the Dutch Republic – resulted partly from the religious upheavals of the time, but also from secular resistance against attempts by the government of Philip II of Spain and his lieutenants throughout the empire to introduce by force a more centralised state, such as that achieved later in the period by Louis XIV in France; and with it, inevitably, a centralised system of public taxation, revenue and

---

[*] During the War of the Catholic League, 1590–1598, Phillippe Emmanuel de Mercoeur, Governor of Brittany, sought to have himself proclaimed Duke of Brittany and allied himself with Spain; in 1632, Henri de Montmorency, Governor of Languedoc, joined the rebellion of Gaston d'Orléans against Cardinal Richelieu's land tax.

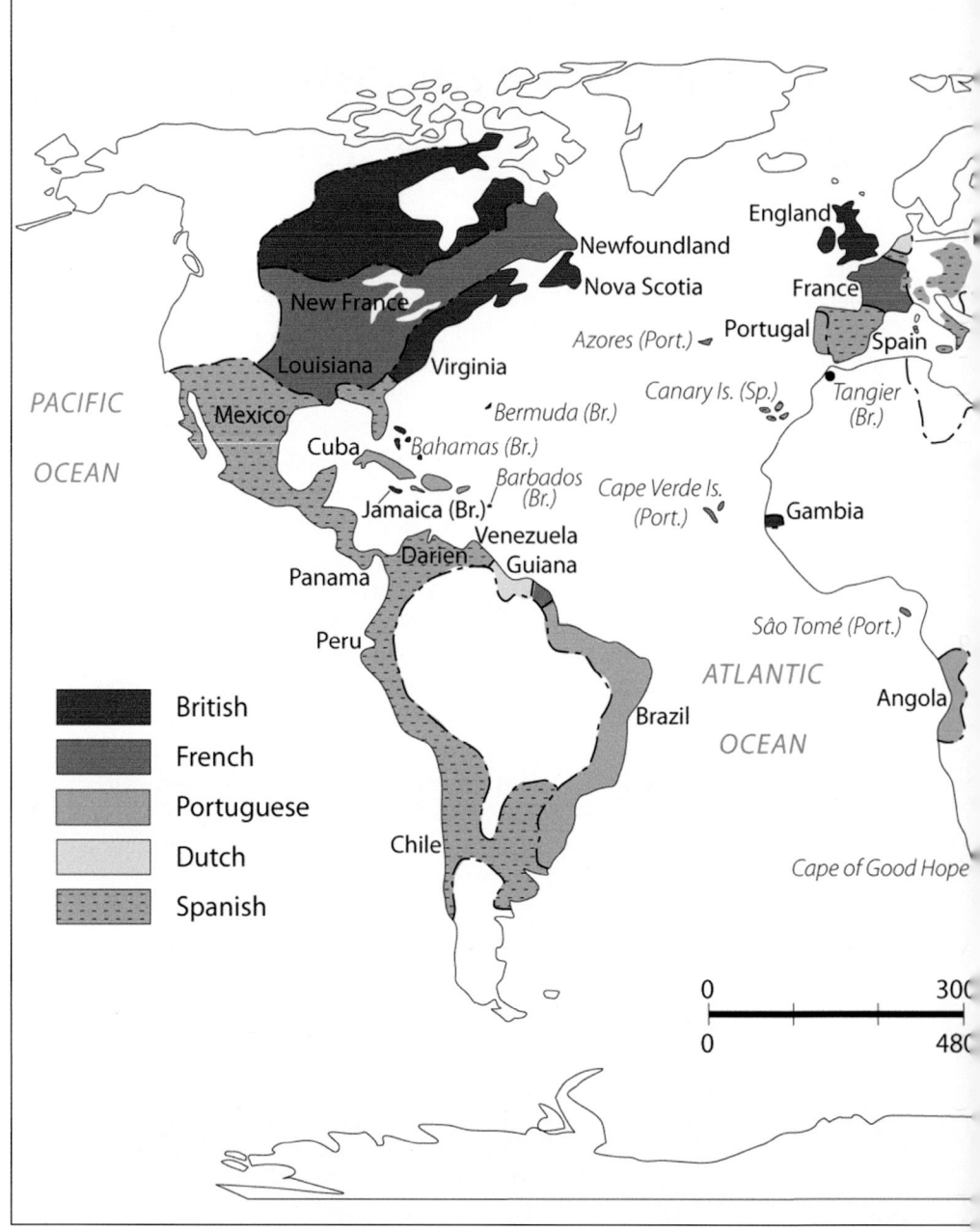

FRANCE, SPAIN AND THE NETHERLANDS: GREAT POWER RELATIONS IN EUROPE, 1564–1654

The European Empires, c. 1660

COLONIAL IRONSIDES

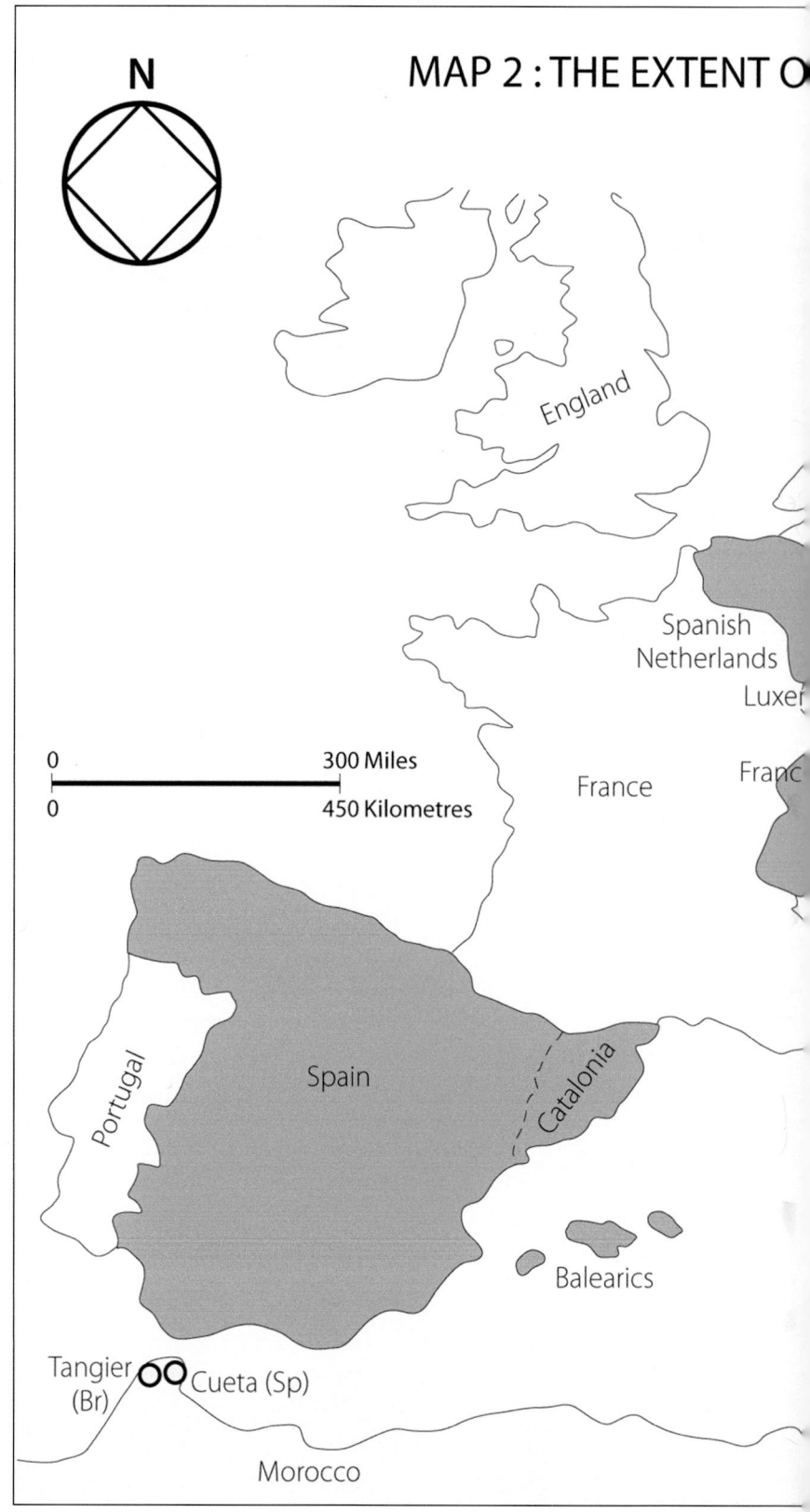

FRANCE, SPAIN AND THE NETHERLANDS: GREAT POWER RELATIONS IN EUROPE, 1564–1654

HABSBURG DOMINIONS IN EUROPE 1667

The Extent of Habsburg Dominions in Europe, 1667.

finance. The Dutch, on the other hand, aimed at a markedly decentralised state and financial system. It is ironic, therefore, that it was the Spanish government that made the fiscal reforms that gave the Dutch provinces the means to conduct a war of independence. From the 1540s, the Hapsburg Emperor Charles V urgently needed to borrow money in order to finance his many wars. He had, therefore, to introduce reforms that would ensure that public debt could be properly serviced and so avoid bankruptcy. In 1542, the president of the Habsburg Council of State, Lodewijk van Schoor, proposed a number of taxes in the Spanish Netherlands: for example, on income from property and private loans; and excise duties on beer, wine, and wool.[1] These taxes, collected by each province, would oblige those provinces to find subsidies for the imperial government. Bonds were also to be issued, secured by the capital provided by these taxes. These bonds would in turn finance extraordinary levies in time of war. The law of unintended consequences being what it is, these reforms strengthened the position of the provinces, especially the Dutch, because it placed the power to raise and then disburse revenues in their hands rather than the hands of the imperial government.

The Dutch, especially in the province of Holland, could now establish their own credit and issue their own bonds at moderate interest rates. This created a market for credit that had not previously existed. The same advantages did not accrue to central government and after the accession of Philip II, it was the tensions in this system that brought about the crisis that caused the Revolt, exacerbated and underpinned by the rise of Calvinist Protestantism in the northern provinces of the Spanish Netherlands – a faith which was by its nature opposed to Catholicism and therefore to his most Catholic Majesty, the King of Spain.

The first phase of the war began with the suppression of Calvinist anti-Catholic violence during 1566: the *Beeldenstorm*, or Great Iconoclasm. After a failed attempt at compromise and religious toleration, the uprising was put down by the Spanish regent, Margaret of Parma, who executed at least 1,000 prominent Protestants. The struggle moved eventually to the separation of the northern and southern Netherlands as the Unions of Arras and Utrecht, by the end of 1590, and to the formation of the Dutch Republic. In response to the growing turbulence, Philip sent a new regent, the Duke of Alba,[*] with an army that successfully put down revolt, rooted out heresy and forced the Dutch leaders including Prince William of Orange to seek service and sanctuary with the French. As well as military repression, Alba also tried to bring in yet more, centrally directed, taxes but without consultation or agreement in the provinces.[2] Executions were widespread, with perhaps 9,000 opponents of Spanish rule, including the Counts of Egmont and Hoorne, being killed. The first phase of actual war, rather than revolt, began with two unsuccessful invasions of the provinces by mercenary armies under Prince William I of Orange in 1568 and 1572; and raids by the *Guezen*, originally *de guezen*, or *les Gueux*, or in English simply beggars. At first, they were Dutch nobles opposed to Philip II but later the term was applied to

---

[*] Fernando Álvarez de Toledo, 3rd Duke of Alba (1508–1582).

FRANCE, SPAIN AND THE NETHERLANDS: GREAT POWER RELATIONS IN EUROPE, 1564–1654

irregular soldiers fighting the Spanish. In April 1572 the Guezen captured Den Briel (Brielle) and Vlissingen (Flushing). This encouraged other towns to declare for revolt with eventually Holland and Zealand, which had been converted to Calvinism, joining. It was ultimately ironic that the Dutch were able to carry on their war for so long and with such success because of the financial system introduced by their former overlords. On this system was built not only Dutch military power on land, but also their powerful navy, their merchant fleet and their rapidly expanding empire overseas which produced yet more revenue to finance the war.

After Holland and Zealand, Friesland and Utrecht joined in the revolt in 1576, and William of Orange was considered stadholder. No general union was formed at this time there than the Pacification of Ghent, in which provinces agreed on religious toleration and a joint effort against Spain. In 1579 the union was badly undermined by the declaration of loyalty by the Roman Catholic Walloon provinces to Spain and the formation of the Union of Arras. This provoked the formation of the Union of Utrecht in response. The Act of Abjuration (*Acte van Verlantinghe*) in 1581 can be seen as the formal declaration of independence by the northern provinces. There were several attempts to find a sovereign to replace Philip II, including the Duke of Anjou and the Earl of Leicester, but when these failed, it was decided in 1587 to continue as a republic with sovereign powers vested in the States General.

By 1588 the Spanish, under Alessandro Farnese, Duke of Parma, had reconquered the southern Low Countries and seemed poised to destroy the infant Dutch Republic. However, Spain's parallel conflicts with both England and France allowed the Republic to survive and then move to a counteroffensive. By the time of the Twelve Years' Truce, which began in 1609, the Dutch frontiers were secure. Fighting resumed in 1621 and the campaign was subsumed into the more general religious struggle of the Thirty Years' War which devastated Europe. After 1625 the Dutch, under Prince Frederick Henry of Orange,[*] scored significant victories.

The Dutch empire overseas was largely built at the expense of the Portuguese, now also subject to Spanish overlordship until the Portuguese, too, revolted. Far from making common cause, however, the Dutch gradually seized control of the most profitable Portuguese colonies and trading stations through the great militant mercantile entities, the Dutch East and West India Companies. The Dutch attacked Portuguese interests from the Brazils to the Azores, Madeira and Tangier; from West Africa to Angola and Mozambique; from Bombay in India to China and Japan. Development of the Dutch base at Batavia (later Djakarta) in Java threatened the Portuguese position at Malacca and their operations in the Moluccas were all but eliminated. Between 1629 and 1636, nearly 150 Portuguese ships were lost to the Dutch in Asian waters alone.[3] These predations continued even after Portugal and

---

[*] Frederick Henry (1584–1647) was Prince of Orange and stadtholder of Holland, Zeeland, Utrecht, Guelders, and Overijssel from 1625 until his death in 1647. From 1640 he also was the stadtholder of Groningen. As the leading commander of Dutch forces against Spain, his most notable victory was the siege and capture of 's–Hertogenbosch in 1629. This well–fortified town was the main Spanish base and was strongly garrisoned.

the United Provinces signed a treaty of defensive and offensive alliance against Spain, known as the Treaty of the Hague, on 12 July 1641.[4]

As well as growing financial strength in the Netherlands, foreign intervention was also a repeated factor in the longevity of the war. William of Orange had originally invaded the Spanish Netherlands from Germany and subsequently, assistance came from France, England and from Scots mercenaries. The involvement of the French stemmed from their wider wars with Spain; the involvement of England was more complex. The English government had been sensitive to the problems of trading with the Netherlands almost from the start of the Eighty Years' War. Between 1558 and 1562, it had tried to secure and confirm the position of English merchants in the Low Countries, since they were a vital source of revenue. Moreover, the flight of many Protestant cloth workers from Spanish territory to England had raised the standard of English exports to the Continent, making them much more saleable. In Spanish eyes, these English merchants were the agents of the heretic Queen, Elizabeth: depriving England of her Netherlands trade would bring the country to its knees – and maybe, with the application of military force, back to the fold of the Catholic faith. Another faction in Spain, headed by the Duke of Alba, felt that fighting England was a distraction at best and at worst would push England into open alliance with France.

Alba's arrival with the Spanish Army in the Netherlands in 1567 caused considerable consternation in England. Not only would a military rule in the Netherlands deprive her of her markets there, but also the presence of 50,000 Spanish troops, the striking force of the Spanish Empire, was a strategic threat to the British Isles – at its closest, the Spanish Army was only 100 miles from London. Even though the English government was not well disposed to Calvinists, Secretary Cecil concluded that war with Spain was inevitable sooner or later. He therefore began a covert policy of unofficial intervention as the best way of preventing the Spanish from securing invasion ports.[5] In April 1572, Captain Thomas Morgan's company of 300 mercenaries was the first to begin this policy, shipping to Flushing with the support of the English government.[6] From then until 1585 there was a series of English military bodies, on both sides, in the Netherlands.[7]

The belief in 1585 that the Spanish Army, now under the Duke of Parma, had so far succeeded in subduing the Netherlands that it would soon be free to embark for England brought a change in the policy of the English government. A treaty was signed with the United Netherlands, the Treaty of Nonsuch, followed by the despatch of an English army of 10,000 men under the command of Robert Dudley, Earl of Leicester.[8] Leicester was named in the Treaty as Governor General of the Dutch provinces – who were, as already discussed, looking for a sovereign. It was this open policy of opposition to Spain, as well as the execution of Mary, Queen of Scots, by the English that directly triggered the despatch of the Spanish Armada in 1588. English and Scots troops remained in the Netherlands, in Dutch service, after peace was concluded in 1648and even until after the Restoration of Charles II of England in 1660. Even so, the Dutch successes in commerce and empire–building brought about war with their former allies, the English, in 1652. (See Chapters 2 and 10).

FRANCE, SPAIN AND THE NETHERLANDS: GREAT POWER RELATIONS IN EUROPE, 1564–1654

Even while Spain's struggle with the Dutch Republic and England was in progress, in 1580, the army of Philip II of Spain had marched into Portugal in response to a succession crisis. It had quickly defeated Portuguese troops and then occupied and sacked Lisbon. Philip is reputed to have said of Portugal: 'I inherited it, I bought it, I conquered it.'[9] In 1640 a revolt broke out, while the Spanish armies were heavily committed to fighting against France in one of the many episodes of the Thirty Years' War, while at the same time having to deal with the revolt in Catalonia[10] which became known as the Reapers' War. The revolt eventually ended with the re-establishment of Portugal as an independent country after military intervention by France and England, in 1668.[11] This Spanish–Portuguese war was complicated by the fact that by 1640, the Portuguese like the Spanish had also been at war with the Dutch for nearly 40 years, as already noted.

By the 1650s, there were over 20,000 Spanish troops in Extremadura because of the Portuguese war and another 27,000 in Flanders. Between 1649 and 1654, almost 30 percent of Spanish military expenditure – around six million ducats* – was directed towards fighting Portugal. Spanish governments had no alternative but to raise taxes to pay for the war through levies on other Habsburg territories, especially in Spain itself, to supplement the income from the Americas. This led to an enormous increase in the size of the Spanish national debt and was ultimately the driving factor in the acceptance of accept Dutch independence in 1648.[12]

Military pressures were exacerbated by natural disasters. Between 1598 and 1602, around eight percent of the population of Spain was killed by plague, exacerbated further by a sequence of failed harvests throughout the 1590s. The overall effect of plague and emigration reduced Spain's population from eight million in the early sixteenth century to seven million by the mid seventeenth century – a turning-point in the demographic history of Castile in particular. Land was taken out of production for lack of labour and the incentive to develop it, and Spain, although predominantly agrarian, depended on imports of foodstuffs. No wonder that this period has been characterised by historians as the decline of Imperial Spain.[13]

Military expenditure had, moreover, done little to stimulate the domestic economy: silver from her South American mines passed through Spain like sand through a sieve to pay for troops in the Netherlands, Germany and Italy, to maintain the Emperor's forces in Germany and ships at sea, and to satisfy consumption at home. The amount of precious metal brought from the Americas and spent on Spain's military establishment quickened inflation throughout Europe, left Spaniards without sufficient specie to pay debts, and caused Spanish goods to become too overpriced to compete in international markets. Nor could American bullion alone satisfy the demands of military expenditure. Domestic production was heavily taxed, driving up prices.[14] As her supply of specie decreased in the seventeenth century, Spain was neither

---

* The ducat became a standard gold coin throughout Europe, especially after it was officially imperially sanctioned in 1566. Its weight is 3.4909 grams of .986 gold, which is 0.1107 troy ounces. The ducat remained sanctioned until 1857. There was also a silver ducat minted in many European countries. The Royal Dutch Mint still issues silver ducats with a weight of 28.25 grams.

able to meet the cost of her military commitments nor to pay for imports of the manufactured goods that could not be produced efficiently at home. The costs of war caused Spain to be technically bankrupt on three occasions in 1607, 1627 and 1647; and there were 50 mutinies over arrears of pay in the Army of Flanders between 1570 and 1607. How to export military costs was therefore a major preoccupation; the best way to do this was to extract contributions of food and money from enemy or conquered territory, and especially to go into winter quarters on an opponent's territory, forcing his population to bear the costs of the army.[15]

Bad as the situation seemed to the Spanish government, matters were not especially rosy when seen from the point of view of Spain's most determined enemy, France. Warfare on the scale of that in progress throughout Europe in the early seventeenth century was only possible through the organisation of a centralised state. The ultimate expression of this idea was that which emerged in France during the reigns of Louis XIII and XIV. Louis XIV, when he came of age in 1652, harnessed the largest block of national population in Europe and directed its energies towards centrally controlled policies and strategies, under great military captains like Turenne, Condé and later, de Saxe. The large military establishment that resulted was necessary to fight the costly and exhausting war in which France had been embroiled with Spain since 1635, an extension of the European Thirty Years' War which had not been included in the general peace of 1648. France felt encircled by Spanish territories from the Netherlands to Italy, running down the 'Spanish Road';[16] the enmity this created was further exacerbated by Spain's involvement with French rebels against the regency government of Anne of Austria (during Louis' minority) and Cardinal Mazarin. Even so, as early as 1640, Cardinal Richelieu, chief adviser and minister to King Louis XIII, knew all too well that France was operating militarily at the limits of her power. She was at war with Spain on four fronts: in Lombardy, in the Pyrenees, in the Spanish Netherlands and in Franche–Comté on the eastern border with Switzerland, the latter two regions being Spanish territories. She also faced rebellions within France that were supported and financed by Madrid. Seen from Paris, Philip IV of Spain controlled considerable territories in Italy, where he could, whenever he chose, further stretch French resources by opening a fourth front against French-controlled Savoy, where Christine Marie of France[*] ruled as regent on behalf of her young son, Charles Emmanuel II, Duke of Savoy.[†]

Richelieu therefore decided that the best way to relieve pressure on France would be to force Philip IV to divert military resources to other theatres of war – and he sought to do this by creating internal problems for the Spanish. The Portuguese revolt was one opportunity to do just that: a treaty of alliance between the two countries was concluded in Paris on 1 June 1641 and a large contingent of French troops was sent to serve in Portugal. The treaty endured for 18 years, until Richelieu's successor, Cardinal Mazarin, broke it

---

[*] Christine Marie of France (1606–1663), sister of Louis XIII and Duchess of Savoy by marriage. At the death of her husband Victor Amadeus I in 1637, she acted as regent of Savoy.
[†] Charles Emmanuel II (1634–1675) was the Duke of Savoy from 1638 to 1675 and under regency of his mother until 1663.

FRANCE, SPAIN AND THE NETHERLANDS: GREAT POWER RELATIONS IN EUROPE, 1564–1654

and abandoned his Portuguese and Catalan allies to sign a separate peace with Madrid.

From 1635, France managed to campaign against her enemy simultaneously on four fronts: Lombardy, the Pyrenees, Franche-Comté and the Netherlands, thus keeping Spanish armies in a state of permanent overstretch throughout the Portuguese revolt. A Spanish attack into France in 1636 to relieve pressure elsewhere failed. Yet in 1643 the captain-general of the Army of Flanders, Don Francisco de Melo, Marquis of Tor de Laguna, decided to invade France: with Richelieu dead and Louis XIII in terminal decline, France seemed headed for civil war. Active intervention against France had long been an established credo; in 1558, for example, Philip II observed that 'I am well aware that it is from the Netherlands that the King of France can best be attacked and forced into peace.'[17] So rather than compromise with the Dutch and let his French enemy disintegrate, de Melo intervened: with 19,000 foot and 8,000 horse he invaded France and besieged Rocroi, a small fortress that commanded the routes from Rheims and Soissons, respectively, to Paris. The French pulled together and sent a relief army of 17,000 foot and 6,000 horse under the 22-year-old Prince of Condé. In the ensuing defeat, the Spanish lost 7,000 casualties and 8,000 prisoners;[18] but more than that, the invincible reputation of the Spanish army was lost. De Melo was recalled in disgrace.

French armies and the Dutch navy now cut off the Spanish Netherlands from all outside assistance. In July 1644, Philip IV informed his ministers that peace should be concluded on all fronts as rapidly as possible, first and foremost with France: but France had no advantage to gain after Rocroi by making peace. French armies conquered Spanish towns in the south of the Netherlands and again beat the Spanish field army at Lens in August 1648. But Philip's initiatives elsewhere were not without some success, for in January 1648, a peace was at last made with the Dutch, ending the Eighty Years' War and recognising a Dutch sovereign state. In October of the same year, the Thirty Years' War was also concluded in Germany with the Peace of Westphalia. Spain ceded Alsace to France, thus severing the great Spanish Road, the corridor that connected the Spanish provinces in the Low Countries with Lombardy and allowed for the rapid movement of troops and supplies between the two.

The French victory at Lens did not, however, stop the threatened slide into civil war in that country. The Edict of Nantes in 1598 had given the Protestant Huguenots a great deal of autonomy, which after 1627 the government sought to undo – with considerable success. However, this engendered not only the enmity of England under Cromwell, but also renewed violence inside France. In January 1649 the *Fronde* revolt broke out and the French government fled Paris. The *Fronde* is the collective name given to the series of civil wars in France between the end of the Thirty Years' War in 1648 and 1653. They took place during the Franco–Spanish war that had begun in 1635 and were supported by the Spanish government. During this series of wars, Louis XIV faced the combined opposition of the princes, the nobility, the *parlements*, and many of the French people chiefly over taxation, but he and his drive towards a centralised state triumphed. The

Fronde was divided into two major campaigns, the *Fronde* of the *parlement* and the *Fronde* of the Princes; the latter led by the great general Louis II de Bourbon, Prince of Condé, known as le Duc d'Enghien before his father's death.* As a result of this series of wars, Louis XIV reorganised the French armies under a chain of command that was responsible to, and controlled by, the monarch. Richelieu's successor Mazarin mishandled matters early on but gained eventual control of the country on the King's behalf, bringing to a close the last attempt of the French nobility to curb the power of the King, and overseeing the humiliation of his opponents.[19]

Presented with this opportunity to recover territory and prestige, Spain proved slow at regaining either. Some towns were recovered, but the manpower and money to invade and punish France were simply not there. As well as the Portuguese revolt, in 1647–1648 there were serious revolts in Naples and western Sicily, which took almost a year to quell; riots inspired by near-famine conditions in Andalusia; and a virulent outbreak of plague in Valencia and western Spain. The revolt in Catalonia was still raging but without French support, the revolt was brought under control until 1652.

As if matters were not bad enough, a new threat emerged in the mid 1650s as relations with England deteriorated. At first, the English appeared a threat only to Spanish interests in the Americas and Spanish diplomacy vied with that of France to secure an alliance with England (see Chapter 2). However, by 1655, only seven years after making peace with the Dutch, these efforts had come to nought and another enemy was added to the list of Spain's still formidable opponents.

---

*   Louis II de Bourbon, Prince of Condé and Duc d'Enghien (1621–1686).

2

Cromwell's Design: Commonwealth Foreign Policy After the End of the Civil Wars

The execution of Charles I on 30 January 1649, and the subsequent declaration of a republic in England, marked the start of the period of English history known as the Commonwealth. It did not, however, spell the end of the Civil Wars, nor of the House of Stuart. On 5 February, Charles's eldest son was proclaimed King of Scots in Edinburgh, and later King of Ireland. In the summer of 1649, the Commonwealth sent an army to Ireland under Oliver Cromwell's command. Cromwell defeated the royalists and reduced the Irish. With no help coming from Ireland, it was clear that Charles's best chance of engaging Scots' help would be to embrace the Covenants, of which there were two: the first was the National Covenant of 1638 which rejected the religious practices of the Anglican church under Charles I and Archbishop Laud, as being crypto–Catholic. This not only reaffirmed Protestant doctrine and practice, but also urged loyalty to the King. The second was the Solemn League and Covenant of 1643 which was an agreement between the English Parliamentarians and the Scots to forge a civil and religious union. Under its terms, the Scots had sent troops into England and it was to them that Charles I had surrendered in 1646. The Covenant, although accepted by Parliament and indeed by Charles I, was never honoured on the English side.

Charles had initially sworn that he could not accept either of these agreements but in the end, he had no choice.[1] In May 1650 he concluded the Treaty of Breda with the Scottish Covenanters and on 23 June signed both the National Covenant and the Solemn League and Covenant. In later life Charles reflected on the endless preaching and humiliating lectures to which he was subjected – so much so that in October 1650 he attempted to escape and rode north to join with a pro–Royalist force known as the Engagers, an event which became known as 'the Start'. Within two days, however, the Presbyterians had caught up with him. In the long term, signing the Covenants probably harmed Charles in the eyes of many people in England and may have contributed to his failure to raise supporters during the campaign in 1651.

COLONIAL IRONSIDES

Oliver Cromwell, Lord Protector of England, between two pillars, 1658. (Wienand Drenth)

CROMWELL'S DESIGN: COMMONWEALTH FOREIGN POLICY AFTER THE END OF THE CIVIL WARS

Meanwhile, the Commonwealth Council of State in England decided to mount a pre-emptive invasion of Scotland and when Fairfax refused the command, Cromwell was again appointed. The English army marched north and the battle of Dunbar followed in September – an emphatic and decisive victory for Cromwell. However, Charles was crowned King at Scone in 1651 and the Scots invaded England. Cromwell followed and, a year to the day from Dunbar, Cromwell smashed Charles's army at Worcester. Charles fled to France; Scotland and Ireland remained occupied by Republican troops – in Ireland with considerable brutality, forced evictions and the resettlement of many areas by English and Scottish Protestants. By March 1652, the Commonwealth army and navy had subdued the majority of royalist privateering under Prince Rupert, all the colonial authorities in North America and the West Indies, as well as the Channel Islands, the Scillies and the Isle of Man, that were sympathetic to the Stuarts.

Cromwell was now the dominant force in the politics of the Three Kingdoms: the Rump Parliament was broken up on 20 April 1653, an act of open force for which many Parliamentarians, no lovers of the Stuarts, never forgave Cromwell. The nominated Parliament of the Saints was followed in December 1653 by England's first written constitution, the Instrument of Government (probably written in large part by John Lambert), which came close to introducing monarchical government but under a different form from that of the Stuarts.[2]

Oliver Cromwell assumed power as Lord Protector under the Instrument in December 1653. To protect, enforce and extend his rule, a powerful standing army and navy were absolute requirements. Charles II and his followers were a force in being under French protection; there were constant fears over Royalist uprisings; and unwilling subjects in Scotland and Ireland, of which Cromwell was also Lord Protector, to be kept down. The military establishment therefore remained a major burden on the exchequer throughout the Protectorate. It also created widespread opposition and the fear of a harsher tyranny than that of Charles I during the period of regional government by Cromwell's Major-Generals from 1655 to 1656.

The standing army of the Protectorate (including garrisons in the Channel Islands, Isle of Man and Scillies, but not Ireland) comprised 15 regiments of horse, each of six troops of 60 men, of which seven were in England, seven in Scotland and one was the Protector's bodyguard; a regiment of dragoons; 18 regiments of foot, each of 10 companies of 100 men, of which six were in England and 12 in Scotland; a train of artillery; and guards and garrisons in all the major castles and fortresses.[3] In Ireland there were another 10 regiments of foot, some dispersed in garrisons, one of dragoons and six of horse. Because of continued tension with the Dutch, the threat from Spanish ships and privateers in the colonies, and the activities of Royalist privateers closer to home, the Navy stood initially at 35 capital ships and 5,000 seamen, but trebled in size during the Protectorate. The cost of this force was estimated in December 1654 at £2,626,537 per annum out of a total government expenditure of £2,877,079; the annual revenue was approximately £1,586,175, leaving a deficit equivalent to a full year's income from taxation.[4] Although impressment ended in 1651, the armed forces could not be substantially reduced after peace was signed with the Dutch and more men had to be raised as volunteers to deal with Penruddock's Rebellion. Throughout the Protectorate, therefore, and particularly by the summer of 1658, Cromwell's standing was always high abroad, but he was in financial trouble at home. By this date, C.H. Firth calculates that the army consisted of about 10,000 men in England, not counting the guards and garrisons; 10,400 in Scotland; 14,000–15,000 in Ireland; and 1,500 in Jamaica – a total of about 43,000 if the troops later sent to Flanders are also included.[5]

A large military establishment was not, as is often thought, a wholly reliable instrument, dedicated to Puritanism and the Republic. Extremists like the Levellers had to be weeded out; and there was trouble in the Navy over the decision to go to war with the Spanish in 1656. This was a navy that had previously mutinied and gone over to Charles Stuart, albeit briefly, in 1648. Nor was the army, unlike the navy, organised or equipped for expeditionary operations outside the British Isles. Nevertheless, the possession of a large and capable army and a powerful navy made England a power to be reckoned with, to be courted by both France and Spain, in a way that Stuart England had never been.

Under the Instrument of Government, Cromwell was obliged to summon parliaments at least every three years, if only to raise revenue for the maintenance of his military forces. Three were called between 1654 and 1657, the first refused his demands for money for a large military establishment and rejected his control of the militia. The second, although also angry with Cromwell's militaristic style of government, offered the 'Humble Petition and Advice', including the Crown, to Cromwell in March 1654. John Evelyn wrote in his diary on 29 March that: 'The Protector Oliver, now affecting Kingship, is petitioned to take the title on him by all his new-made sycophant lords, but dares not for fear of the fanatics not thoroughly purged out of his rebel army.'[6] Cromwell indeed refused, but was made Protector for life and permitted to name his successor. More to the point, the Parliament also endorsed his approach to relations with France, Spain and the Netherlands.

The chief interest of English foreign policy in Europe during the early years of the Protectorate lay in keeping those two most powerful nations of the Continent, France and Spain, at war with each other. Only if thus distracted would either, or both, be unable to support an invasion of England in support of the exiled Charles Stuart. However, as time went on, France appeared to be the more attractive ally and therefore it suited the Protectorate to have Charles Stuart in the Spanish camp. Spain, with its Inquisition and recent history of aggression towards England, not to mention its war with England's fellow Protestants, the Dutch, was easier to paint as the Devil's child.[7] The French were not popular in many quarters, however, for it was felt that they had been the prime movers in Charles II's invasion in 1651 and the subsequent third phase of the Civil Wars.

In 1652, the Commonwealth had also gone to war with the Dutch, with whom England had, since the reign of Elizabeth I, been allied as fellow Protestants, during the Eighty Years' War between the Netherlands and Spain. The Netherlands, by the 1650s, as discussed in Chapter 1, had become the pre-eminent trading nation of the world, remarkable when considering their size, and the envy of other nations including England. The war was fought over trade with the Americas and the West Indian colonies following the passing of the English Navigation Acts in 1651 and consequent seizures of Dutch shipping. It was fought entirely at sea between the navies of the two protagonists.* Although the English Navy won most of the battles, it was only able to exercise sea control effectively in the waters around England; after the English victory at Scheveningen, the Dutch turned to smaller warships and the use of privateers to prey on English merchant shipping.[8]

By November 1653, on the eve of the establishment of the Protectorate, Cromwell was willing to make peace, provided the House of Orange was excluded from the office of Stadtholder, or elected head of state in the Dutch Republic. Cromwell also attempted to create a monopoly on trade between England and her colonies for English merchant shipping. Peace was declared on 15 April 1654 with the signing of the Treaty of Westminster. The *Acte van Seclusie*, which kept the House of Orange from office, was a secret annex to the treaty. The peace was no more than a truce, however, for war with the Dutch was to be a recurring theme of the next two decades.

War with the Dutch was an inconvenient, if pressing, necessity; war with either France or Spain was more a matter of choice. Popular and governmental enthusiasm for an anti–Catholic crusade by Cromwell's New Jerusalem on the continent of Europe was a factor in policy formation, but not perhaps as great as is sometimes believed.[9] Protestant rebellions inside France, like the *Fronde* (see Chapter 1), might be thought to have been obvious candidates for English support and indeed appeals for help were considered by Cromwell.[10] Indeed, in April 1653 Cromwell considered assisting the *Fronde* leader, *Le Grand Condé*, and his Spanish sponsors in south–western France.[11] The rebels at Bordeaux even offered to surrender the city to English rule, before reconsidering.[12] In fact, Cromwell was highly pragmatic in maintaining relations with Spain, rather than being swayed by religious fervour, throughout 1654. King Philip IV, in spite of Cromwell's credentials as a regicide, kept Don Alonso de Cardenas as resident ambassador. Cardenas had been in London since before the opening of the Civil Wars, from 1640, and had kept contact with both parties throughout; influenced, perhaps, by the fact that Charles I had married Henrietta Maria, a French Bourbon princess.

The Commonwealth's representatives, including Cromwell himself as Lord General, had negotiated with both France and Spain since 1651, and Cromwell continued to do the same as Protector during 1654. Various offers were made by both powers to enlist English support: the Spanish offered England the return of Calais if Cromwell's army and navy would join a Spanish offensive in Flanders;[13] Mazarin, on the back foot because of Bourbon links to the Stuarts – up to and including armed support – and his initial unwillingness to recognise the Commonwealth, made a counter–offer of the fortress and port of Dunkirk, which had been taken by the Spanish in 1652.[14] This was an attractive offer, for Dunkirk had long been a major

---

* For more details, see Chapter 10.

base for privateers operating against English trade. The French occupation had suppressed this, but the Spanish conquest opened the doors for the Dunkirkers to be a threat once more.[15]

It was also apparent that Cromwell's Council of State had different views.[16] Cromwell was required, but not obliged, to consult the council on matters of foreign policy under the terms of the Instrument of Government. One faction, led by Major-General John Lambert, at that point probably the second most important man in England, urged alliance with Spain against Charles Stuart and his French allies; another, led by Sir Gilbert Pickering, was for France; and a third, led by Secretary John Thurloe, held that direct entanglement in war should be avoided, but that the Franco–Spanish war should be kept alive since a state of dynamic instability, that tied up the resources of the two major Continental nations, was to England's benefit. Thurloe also believed that Cromwell should be much more forceful in putting himself forward as champion and leader of Protestants in Europe and oppose any Catholic power which was oppressing Protestants.[17] This role appeared, in 1654, to pit England against France because of the latter's treatment of the Huguenots; and in April 1655 French participation in the massacres of the Vaudois by Savoyard troops under the Marquis of Pianezza in Piedmont. John Milton, Cromwell's Latin Secretary, wrote his Sonnet XV, *On the late Massacre in Piedmont*, in response to the attack in Piedmont.[18]

Negotiations with both Spain and France continued during 1654. The Marquis of Cardenas acted for Spain, assisted by the Prince of Condé's emissary Henri de Taillefer de Barrière; the new French ambassador, Antoine de Bordeaux–Neufville, was assisted by Philippe de Castelmore, Baron de Baas. Baas was the brother of the model for Alexandre Dumas's musketeer, D'Artagnan. Cromwell confronted Baas after concluding that he had been involved in the Royalist Gerard Plot of June 1654 and expelled him;[19] Mazarin, however, promoted him rather than punishing him. The Spanish were unable to capitalise on this situation because their straitened exchequer could not raise the subsidy of £100,000 initially, rising to £240,000 per year, which Cromwell demanded as the price for any English expedition to Flanders.[20] The inability of the Spanish to find money provoked Cromwell to other demands: if a projected joint siege of Calais were to succeed then he would expect Dunkirk in exchange – an object which had clearly been in Cromwell's mind since late 1651. This was, however, probably no more than an attempt to gain time for the arrangement of matters with the French.

Thus, the end of the rebellions in France coincided with Spain's inability to finance an English alliance; and Cromwell could raise no money at home without recalling Parliament – and the Protector had had no better relationship with Parliament than had Charles I. Disputes, however, continued with the French too – over trade, compensation for seized shipping, and the like. Neither an expedition to Flanders nor assistance to French Protestants appeared possible; and Cromwell's eyes turned elsewhere. The need for money underpinned any expedition, and the obvious target in this regard was the gold–laden Spanish empire in the Americas. The Council of State debated the issue in April 1654, considering the choice of either attacking France, or attacking Spain, or maintaining peace with both

– but on the understanding that subsidies from both might be forthcoming. Attacking France was thought too difficult after the failure of the rebellions.

On the other hand, Spanish threats to the fledgling English colonies of Providence (which had been captured), St Christopher, Nevis and the Barbadoes in the West Indies invited retaliation, especially as efforts had had to be made to recover them from their allegiance to the exiled English Crown; although the Spanish Viceroys of Mexico and South America were hardly directed from Madrid, deciding on local action of their own accord. Moreover, the booty taken by the likes of Drake and Hawkins from the Spanish galleons of the Spanish Plate Fleet, as they carried the gold and silver from American mines to the Spanish exchequer, made an attack there look like 'the most profitable in all the world'.[21] Cromwell himself, according to Thurloe, was 'for war, at least in the West Indies, unless assurances were given and things well settled for the future'.[22] Because the Protectorate Army was not organised for expeditionary warfare abroad, it was decided that a major operation would be too difficult and – above all – too costly. A new colony would therefore be established on a Spanish–held island in the Caribbean, to which several thousand troublesome Royalists could be transplanted from Scotland and Ireland, as indentured servants, to work the new lands.

Plundering Spanish colonies and fleets in the Americas as envisaged by Cromwell did not necessarily mean war with Spain in Europe. Thurloe later recorded that: 'Cromwell intended not to meddle with anything in Europe until the Spaniards should begin, unless the Plate Fleet should be met with, which was looked on as a lawful prize.'[23] Quite how Cromwell thought that he could pick a quarrel with Spain in the Americas and yet avoid war in Europe is open to question; certainly Pickering's faction pressed for the logical conclusion of open war with Spain and alliance with France, arguing that this would keep the Franco–Spanish war in being. Lambert, on the other hand, argued that England would lose the Spanish trade, especially in wool, and English ships passing through the Straits of Gibraltar to trade in the Levant would be blocked from the Spanish naval base of Cadiz. Still, Cromwell insisted on restricting military action to the Americas, where Spanish breaches of earlier treaties with the Stuarts in 1604, which had concluded the 19–year Anglo–Spanish war; and in 1630 ending English support for Protestants in the Low Countries, provided excuses for retaliation. Cromwell summed up matters to General Robert Venables, when he appointed him to the command of the expedition: 'Either there was peace with the Spaniard in the West Indies or there was not. If peace, they had violated it, and to seek reparation was just. If we had not peace, there was nothing acted against articles.'[24]

The result was the Western Design and its method, the expedition to Hispaniola and Jamaica which are covered in Chapters 7, 8 and 9 of this book. The Spanish Council of State soon heard of Cromwell's design but did not withdraw Ambassador Cardenas before this rumoured attack became a fact, as this would push Cromwell into open alliance with France. This was the key consideration that allowed Cromwell to press ahead with the Western Design while still continuing negotiations with both France *and* Spain. Cromwell gave a long, almost rambling, explanation of his reasoning, stressing not only the practical desirability of the move but also the religious dimension:

> And the Spaniard is not only our enemy accidentally, but he is providentially so; God having in his wisdom disposed it to be so ... the Spaniards design became, By all unworthy, unnatural means ... to seek the ruin and destruction of these Kingdoms ...
>
> ... when they [the Long Parliament] asked for satisfaction for the blood of your poor people unjustly shed in the West Indies ... when they asked liberty of conscience for your people who traded thither, satisfaction in none of these things was given, but was denied.
>
> Now if this be so, why, truly then here is some foundation laid to justify the War has been entered upon with the Spaniard![25]

He failed, however, to convince General John Lambert who, in particular, cited distance, expense, the harsh environment, the inability to enlist existing colonists and the need, at some point, to explain matters to Parliament.[26]

In May 1655, Cromwell sent a fleet under Admiral Blake with orders to operate against Spanish shipping in the eastern Atlantic and Mediterranean,[27] a considerable escalation (see Chapter 10) since it turned into an interdiction of Spanish resupply or reinforcement to the West Indies – not that the Spanish were in any position to carry this out, being deeply committed to military operations in Europe. Philip IV's chief minister, Don Luis de Haro, sent a second ambassador, the Marquis de Leda, to London in the same month, but with nothing new to offer. But at the same time, the French massacres in Piedmont, mentioned earlier, caused outrage in England, especially among extremist Protestant preachers and in the Army. Cromwell therefore held back from further negotiations with the French.

The logic of a French alliance, however, had become inescapable.[28] Attacks on the Spanish colonies in the New World and seizures of shipping simply could not be reconciled with a Spanish alliance. There was, too, another factor: the sanctuary given to Charles II by Louis XIV. Once an alliance was in place between the Protectorate and France, the Stuarts would be forced out. The focus of Cromwell's war with Spain now swung back from the Americas to Europe and the Mediterranean – and in particular, to Flanders.

In October 1655, a commercial treaty was concluded with France, which included the expulsion of Charles II. In December 1655, Cromwell sent his ambassador, Sir William Lockhart of Lee, to Paris to conclude matters. Lockhart had served in the French army in the 1630s and then in various appointments with the Covenanter army against the English Parliamentarian forces. After a dispute with Charles II in 1650, he withdrew his support from the Stuart cause. While on a visit to London, he met Cromwell and on 18 May 1652 he was appointed one of Cromwell's commissioners for the administration of justice in Scotland and a Scottish privy councillor. Matters were further cemented when Lockhart married Cromwell's widowed niece, Robina Sewster, in February 1656. Perhaps because of his marriage, it was not until April 1656 that Lockhart set out for Paris.

CROMWELL'S DESIGN: COMMONWEALTH FOREIGN POLICY AFTER THE END OF THE CIVIL WARS

In the meanwhile, the Spanish had made the choice of an ally easy: Philip IV declared war on England in March 1656. Initially, war was prosecuted in Jamaica and by sea in the Americas, the Mediterranean and the eastern Atlantic. On 23 March 1657, England and France concluded the Treaty of Paris.[29] Under the terms of this treaty, Cromwell would supply a force of 6,000 men to serve in the 20,000-strong French army in the Low Countries under the command of the great Marshal Turenne.* Once victory had been secured, England would receive the port of Dunkirk – and with it, an end to the ravages of the Dunkirk privateers – and the great fortress of Mardyke. England would have a foothold on the continent of Europe for the first time since Mary Tudor had lost Calais.

---

* Henri de La Tour d'Auvergne, Vicomte de Turenne (1611–1675), His 50-year military career which had begun in service with the Dutch against Spain and continued in the service of France earned him a reputation as one of the greatest generals in modern history.

3

Recovering the Royalist Enclaves, April–December 1651

In early 1650, the new republic of England faced a series of enemies close at hand. After the execution of Charles I, Scotland and Ireland had both proclaimed Charles II and an army from either neighbour could appear in a relatively short space of time. Then there were the Dutch, French and Spanish to consider, as discussed in Chapter 2. The authority of the Commonwealth would have to be asserted in the English colonies in North America and the Caribbean, but before that, there were Royalist enclaves much closer to home: the first of which was the problem of Royalist privateers led by Prince Rupert of the Rhine, operating from Royalist-held islands around Britain. To deal with this, and probably too the Dutch, new ships had to be built or taken and existing ones refitted – and renamed, since the old royal names would not do in republican times. A new leadership was also required and to this end, the Commonwealth appointed three Generals–at–Sea – the rank of admiral did not exist. These three were Edward Popham, Richard Deane and Robert Blake. It was Blake who would take the lead in dealing first with Rupert and then with the Royalist garrisons in the Isles of Scilly, the Isle of Man and the Channel Islands.

Blake's career up to this point had been remarkable enough. Born in 1598, he was elected as the M.P. for Bridgewater in the Short Parliament of 1640 but was not re-elected to the Long Parliament that followed. When the Civil War broke out in England, Blake began his military career on the side of the Parliament, in spite of having no experience of military or naval matters – a common enough situation at the time. He was granted a commission as captain in Alexander Popham's Regiment of the New Model and distinguished himself at the siege of Bristol in July 1643, after which he was promoted to Lieutenant-Colonel. After holding Lyme Regis throughout the siege of April 1644 he was promoted to colonel. He then also held Taunton in 1645 and succeeded in capturing Dunster Castle in November 1645.[1]

Blake was appointed General-at Sea in 1649 and he was also a commissioner of the navy and a member of the Council of State of the Commonwealth.[2] Blake is sometimes referred to as the 'Father of the Royal Navy'. He was at least in part responsible for rapidly building the largest navy the country had known up to that time, more than a hundred ships of all rates. He was also instrumental in writing the Navy's first regulations, *The Laws of War and Ordinances of the Sea*, with 20 provisions, which were approved by Parliament in March 1649.[3] The regulations were published in 1652 as *The Laws of War and Ordinances of the Sea (Ordained and Established by the Parliament of the Commonwealth of England)*, listing 39 offences and their punishments – mostly death. The subsequent *Instructions of the Admirals and Generals of the Fleet for Councils of War*, issued in 1653 by Blake, George Monck, John Desborough and William Penn, instituted the first courts martial in the English navy.[4] Blake also developed new tactics for blockades and landings using ships' boats. His *Sailing Instructions* and *Fighting Instructions* were the bedrock of English naval warfare throughout the age of sail; the *Fighting Instructions*, issued in March 1653, were the first of any nation to order the use of the line–ahead battle formation.[5]

In January 1649, not long before the execution of Charles I, Prince Rupert had taken eight ships to try to prevent Parliament from taking control of Ireland. Blake blockaded Rupert's fleet in Kinsale from 22 May, allowing Cromwell to land his army at Dublin on 15 August. Blake could not, however, attack Rupert's ships close under the guns of Kinsale and although the initial naval campaign had begun with the squadrons of all three Generals–at–Sea, Popham and Deane withdrew, leaving Blake with his flagship the *Triumph* and three other warships. In Kinsale, Rupert's privateers,[*] deprived of the prizes for which they had taken service, were growing mutinous, to the extent of threatening him with death. On 16 October, the garrison of Cork declared for the Commonwealth and this left Kinsale exposed – however a storm forced Blake to run for shelter in Milford Haven and by the time he returned Rupert had broken out with the *Constant Reformation*, *Swallow* and *Convertine*, all powerful privateers which had deserted Parliament during the Downs revolt in 1648 although no match for Blake's warships. Rupert's force also included a number of prizes, former naval ships and smaller vessels among which were the *James, George, Culpepper, Roebuck, Blackamoor Lady, Ambrose* and *Charles*.[6] Rupert made first for Spain and then to Lisbon in Portugal, where he had negotiated with King John for a base.

Blake put to sea with 12 ships in February 1650 and anchored off Lisbon. Here, unable to get past the formidable shore batteries, he conducted negotiations lasting two months with the Portuguese for the expulsion of Rupert. Two French ships, briefly detained by Blake, joined Rupert (the French were at this time supporting the Royalist cause) and a further four ships under Edward Popham – *Liberty, Constant Lion, Assurance* and *Increase of London* – arrived to join Blake, bringing with them a letter of authority from Parliament to attack the Portuguese if necessary – indeed it was clear

---

[*] Privateers were licensed by governments and carried letters of marque distinguishing them from pirates. Their ships were often well armed and manned by large numbers of highly competent seamen. Their purpose was not to engage the enemy's warships, but to destroy his trade. In doing so, the value of the prizes they took accrued on the basis of shares by rank to the privateers themselves.

COLONIAL IRONSIDES

An engraving showing the Star Castle and the Garrison on St Mary's. Tresco is to the right and it can be seen how easily a battery there could dominate the harbour, the fortifications and Hugh Town. (Author's collection)

that Rupert could only be attacked in Lisbon at the cost of war. Authority was also given to sink or capture French ships that sided with Rupert.

Blake meanwhile had seized nine English merchant ships which the Portuguese had hired. King John, already embroiled in a long war of independence against Spain and another in the colonies with the Dutch, prepared for war with yet another adversary. Rupert tried twice to break through the blockade, supported by Portuguese ships that turned for home rather than fight. Blake then fought an engagement with the inbound Portuguese Brazil convoy, capturing seven valuable prizes and sinking one. These he carried to Cadiz for repairs and thence to England, escorted by his vice-admiral, Richard Badiley. Returning once more to Lisbon, Blake found that Rupert had gone: King John had found him a guest whose expense he could no longer bear.

Rupert was now without a base, but he was determined to do as much damage as possible. He disguised his largest ship as the *Triumph*, took two prizes and burned other English ships in Spanish ports. Blake caught up with Rupert, now with six ships, on 3 November near Málaga and took one of his ships, the *Roebuck*. Two days later Rupert's other ships were driven ashore while attempting to escape from Cartagena and were forced to discharge their guns and stores before being burned. This series of actions secured the Commonwealth's supremacy at sea and was instrumental in gaining the recognition of the new government by European states, including France and Spain. Only Rupert and Prince Maurice escaped with a single ship and took refuge at Toulon. Rupert patched up a force of five ships but by 1653 he was reduced once more to one ship and had no choice but to leave the Mediterranean.[7]

Blake returned home to a rapturous welcome, but he had little time to relish his triumph, for the Council of State was now determined to stamp out

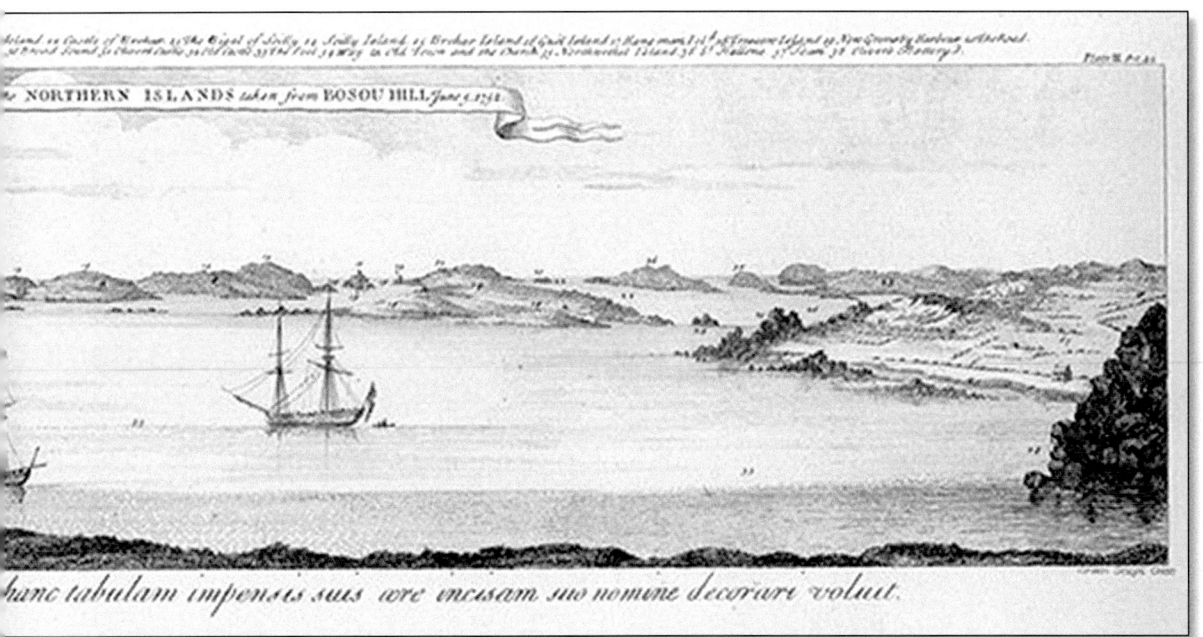

the remaining Royalist enclaves close to home, which had provided bases for Rupert as well as defiance of the Commonwealth, in the Scilly Isles, the Isle of Man and the Channel Islands. Blake was charged with conveying the force for the Isle of Man with his flagship, the *Phoenix*, some frigates and two armed merchantmen. Before he could complete preparations to sail, however, word reached London that the Dutch Admiral Maarten Tromp was on his way with a force of ships to attack the Scillies and destroy Royalist privateers there, who were taking Dutch prizes. The Council feared that the Dutch intended to secure the islands from the Royalist Governor, Sir John Grenville, and use it as a base for their own privateers. On 10 May, therefore, Blake was ordered to sail at once for the islands. There he was to take under his command a squadron of five ships under Sir George Ayscue[*] which was intended to subdue the Barbadoes (see Chapter 4) but had been diverted by this more pressing problem.[8] Blake was to find out what the Dutch intended – the Council had no objection to the Dutch recovering their own prizes – and forestall any attempt by Tromp to establish a base by destroying the Royalist garrison and the privateers there.

The Isles of Scilly are an archipelago of small islands – the biggest no more than two square miles – about 25 miles (40 kilometres) off the south-western tip of Cornwall, and form part of the historic Duchy of Cornwall. The principal inhabited islands are St Mary's, Tresco, St Martin's and Bryther.

---

[*] Sir George Ayscue (c. 1616–1672) later rose to the rank of Admiral of the White. He was Governor of the Scilly Isles in 1647 and nominally Governor of the Barbadoes from 1650 to 1652. He received his first naval command in 1646. In 1648, while serving as a captain in the navy of Parliament, he prevented much of the fleet from defecting to the royalists and was promoted to general-at-sea after the death of Edward Popham. In 1649 he was appointed Admiral of the Irish Seas.

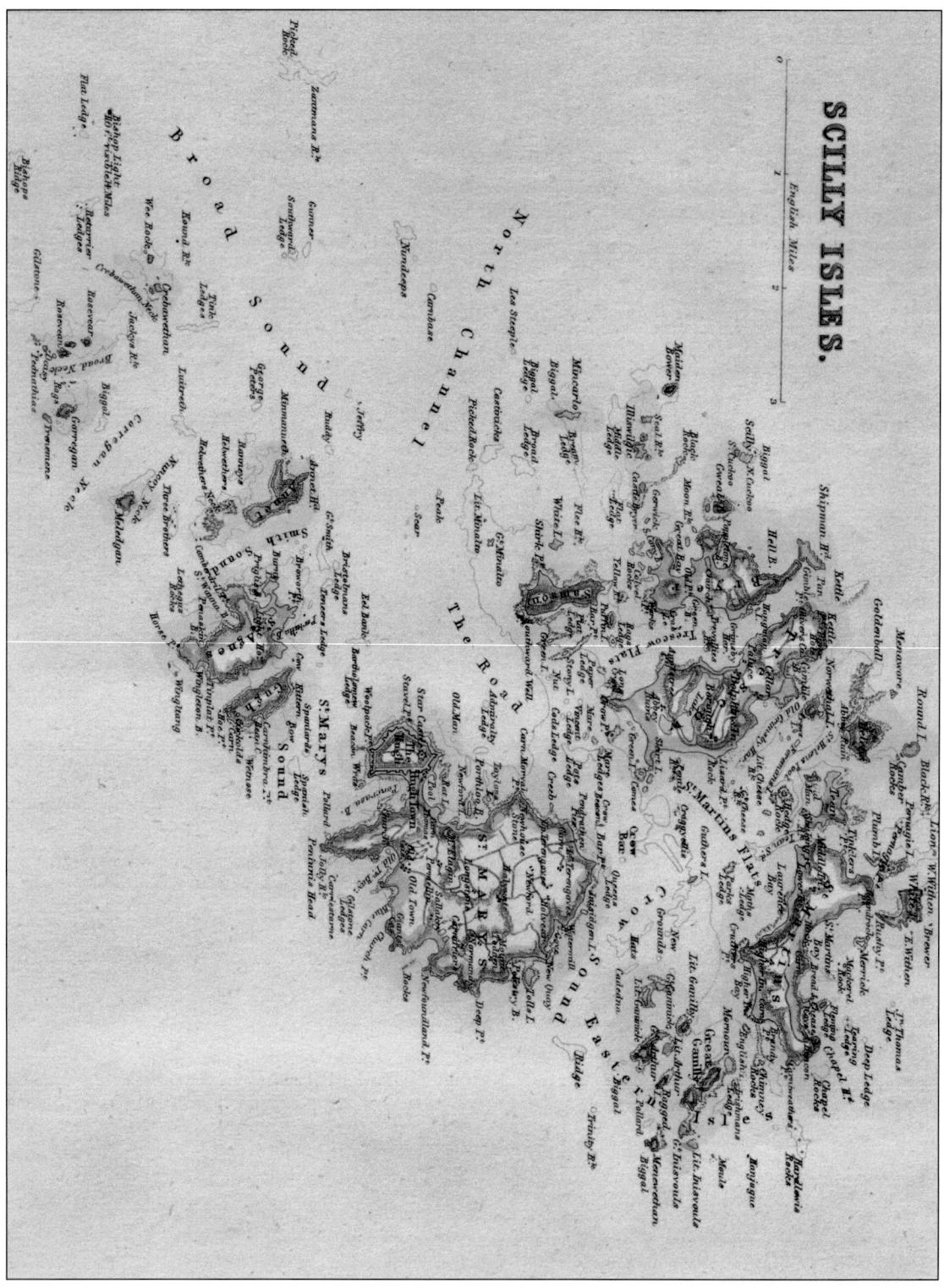

Smaller islands are Samson, Annet, St Helen's, Teän and Great Ganilly; there are also 45 rocks or islets. The islands' position produces contrasting weather conditions. On the one hand, the effect of the sea means that there is rarely frost or snow and the growing season for crops is a long one. On the other hand, exposure to the Atlantic results in spectacular storms and gales. Hugh Town on St Mary's is the largest settlement on the islands, and their capital.

Before 1548, the only fortification in the islands was Ennor Castle, overlooking Old Town Bay on St Mary's, which probably dated from the thirteenth century. Almost nothing remains of this today. In 1548, work commenced on Tresco Castle, later renamed King Charles' Castle, a polygonal artillery fort for five guns located on Castle Down on the west side of Tresco, where it guarded both New Grimsby harbour and the northern maritime approach to St Mary's. At the same time, work commenced on a blockhouse on the east coast overlooking Old Grimsby harbour.

The main harbour of St Mary's Island is situated on St Mary's Pool, on the western side of the island, facing Tresco. During the 1550s, construction began on a modern artillery fort which dominated the eastern side of the harbour. Known as Harry's Walls, it was never completed. In 1570, Queen Elizabeth I leased the islands to Francis Godolphin, who, in 1593, during the period of war with Spain, built the Star Castle, an eight-pointed star-shaped fort on the Hugh, a prominent headland or isthmus to the west of St Mary's harbour. In the first years of the seventeenth century, Godolphin built a mole for the harbour as well as a curtain wall across the neck of land joining the Hugh to the rest of the island. This began both the fortification of what became known as 'The Garrison' and the growth of Hugh Town as the capital of the islands.

By the 1620s, Scilly's defences had fallen into disrepair. New earthworks were built around King Charles' Castle and a magazine was also constructed. Development of the defences continued until 1651, particularly when the islands were held by the Royalists, who placed batteries to cover all the main approaches.

During the Civil Wars, the first period of Royalist occupation lasted until 1646 under the Governorship of Sir John Godolphin, grandson of the earlier Francis who had built Star Castle. From the islands, Royalist privateers operated against English merchant ships operating on behalf of the Parliament. Following the final surrender of Royalist forces in the south-west of England in March 1646, Charles, Prince of Wales, fled to the islands for a short time before moving on to Jersey with Prince Rupert. A Parliamentarian naval blockade was then put into effect by Sir George Ayscue which resulted in the surrender of the islands in September 1646. Ayscue held the islands until Colonel Anthony Buller was appointed as the Parliamentarian governor with a garrison drawn from part of Fortescue's Regiment of Foot.[9]

In 1648, with the outbreak of the Second Civil War, the garrison rebelled against the governor and declared for the King, a rebellion precipitated by the arrival of a considerable force of 21 Royalist privateers led by Prince

Facing page: John Bartholomew's map of the Scilly isles. (Author's collection)

Rupert and Vice-Admiral John Mucknell.* Rupert sailed from Kinsale having embarked a body of Irish troops.[10] Having landed the troops, Rupert left Mucknell in charge of the islands and went off with 10 ships to rescue Charles, Prince of Wales, from the Isle of Wight and take him to Jersey. Buller was held prisoner but treated with kindness before being released; he later commanded a regiment in the expedition to Hispaniola and Jamaica (see Chapters 7, 8, and 9). The Council of State in England ordered Sir Hardress Waller to have 400 men ready to embark for the islands in October, but the mutiny in the Parliamentarian fleet meant that no action could be taken.[11] Charles then appointed Sir John Grenville, eldest son of the famous Sir Bevile Grenville, who was killed leading his regiment at the Battle of Lansdowne in 1643, as Governor. Mucknell remained in support of Grenville, as well as carrying out privateering operations against English and Dutch vessels in the Western Approaches – an important source of money for Charles II, especially once he was forces once more abroad after the defeat at Worcester.

Grenville commanded a garrison consisting of '300 Irish, 120 English' soldiers according to the report by Blake at the end of the operation; there also appeared to be a large number of refugee Royalist officers: 13 colonels, four Lieutenant-Colonels, one bishop, two doctors, two parsons and two Popish priests'. The troops therefore included many Royalist officers serving as reformadoes, or gentlemen-at-arms, deserters from the Parliamentarian garrison and the Irish troops from Kinsale. The Irish, under the terms of an ordinance issued by Parliament in October 1644, could expect execution if they were captured on English soil.

Tromp arrived off the Scillies on 30 March 1651, but with only three ships, having been separated from the rest of his squadron by bad weather. Tromp demanded the return of all Dutch ships held by the Royalists, or compensation, which Grenville refused: he did release two batches of prisoners taken from the ships,[12] glad no doubt to relieve himself of extra mouths to feed. Grenville had already sold many prizes and their cargoes and so could not return what he did not have but in any case, he seems to have believed that he could defy both the Dutch and the Commonwealth from his base in St Mary's Island. Tromp, incensed, went so far as to declare war on Grenville – a state of affairs that existed between the Netherlands and the islands for more than 300 years.

Tromp departed in search of the rest of his squadron and shortly afterwards, the combined force of Blake and Ayscue arrived having sailed on 12 April.† Ayscue, being familiar with the Scillies, knew that the vital ground was the island of Tresco. If this island was held, store ships could take shelter from the Atlantic gales in the channel between Tresco and Bryther while a close blockade was put in place on St Mary's. Privateering would become impossible; so too would resupply or reinforcement from outside. Grenville would have no choice but to surrender or face an assault from the sea.

---

* John Mucknell (1608–?) was originally a captain in the service of the East India Company. As a Catholic, he rejected the Puritan rule of the Commonwealth and became a pirate. He was knighted, appointed as a vice-admiral and licensed as a privateer by Charles, Prince of Wales.

† There is a list of Blake's and Ayscue's ships in the appendices to this chapter.

Most of Grenville's troops were on St Mary's, but two companies and a number of gunners held King Charles' Castle on Tresco, with men detached to the blockhouse at Old Grimsby. Guns and gunners had also been taken from two frigates, the *Michael* and the *Peter*, which guarded the approaches to the channel, and used to reinforce the land defences; the channel itself was narrow and easily dominated and therefore the frigates could anchor and employ the guns of one side only, sparing the guns of the inward side for the land batteries. Blake, being both a soldier and a sailor, looked for an indirect approach and found it: he decided to attack Old Grimsby on the eastern side of Tresco. Lieutenant-Colonel John Clarke was in command of the troops embarked in Ayscue's squadron for service in the Barbadoes. These men appear to have been five companies drawn from each of Hardress Waller's New Model Regiment of Foot,[13] and James Heane's and Robert Bennett's Regiments, 15 companies in all, perhaps 1,500 men:

> Council of State to the Army Committee. To the end the forces in Scilly may be supplied with provisions, they should have three months' pay beforehand, out of which their provisions may be bought, and we have written Major General Desborow to take order accordingly. This advance may be made by advancing one months' pay on account to the three regiments out of which those forces are drawn, viz., Sir Hardress Waller's, Col. Heane's, and Col. Bennett's, who may, out of the same, advance the three months' pay to those companies that are in Scilly ...[14]

Waller's was certainly at hand in the west country as it was required to find the garrisons for Dartmouth castle and Salcombe Fort;[15] Heane's was at Weymouth,[16] but the whereabouts of Bennett's is not known.

Because of unfavourable winds, it was not possible to attempt a landing until 17 April. The troops under Clarke's command were divided into two assault columns and were to make their attempt under cover of the guns of the fleet. The first column was led by Lieutenant-Colonel Richard Bowden and the second by Clarke himself. Bowden's party encountered rough seas and strong currents and his locally engaged pilots and oarsmen ran for the small islet of Northwithiel, claiming that they could not make it to Tresco. Clarke, who was with Ellis's party, also went astray. Coming ashore on Tresco, his men, inexperienced in amphibious operations, came under heavy fire from Royalist musketeers deployed from the blockhouse. Some men got ashore on a rocky part of the coast but were driven back to their boats. Clarke had no choice but to abandon the attack and withdraw to the islet of Teän. Both parties spent a cold, wet night on their rocks. At dawn next day, Blake sent food and ammunition along with Captain Lewis Morris and 200 seamen from the fleet, more boats and more oarsmen; these men were to lead a second attempt that night.

As darkness fell, fires were lighted, and 80 men left on Northwithiel to deceive the Royalists and create a smokescreen. The assault moved off between 11.00 p.m. and midnight on 18 April and the troops were not observed by the Royalists until they were halfway to Tresco: the alarm was raised, and fire was opened. Morris kept his boats close together and landed the seamen successfully; they held the beach until more soldiers arrived. The

A modern photograph of the blockhouse showing part of the landing area at Old Grimsby. (Richard Croft, Blockhouse Point 2010)

Royalists put in a strong counter–attack, pushing the redcoats and seamen back to the waterline, however enough of Clarke's troops arrived to turn the tide. After an hour's close combat with sword, pike and clubbed musket, the Royalists pulled back, having lost 15 men for the loss of four redcoats; 167 other Royalist solders were taken prisoner. Morris was later voted 100/– (£5.0s.0d) by Parliament as a reward for his service: about £700 at today's values in terms of purchasing power – £22,000 in terms of the income value.[17]

Grenville had come to Tresco in person to direct the defence. Seeing that the Commonwealth force was ashore in strength he decided to evacuate what was left of his troops back to St Mary's. The evacuation did not go well, and another 40 men were drowned. With the fall of Tresco, the two Royalist frigates surrendered; Bryther was also secured and with both islands in his hands, Blake brought his ships into the safety of the anchorage. This was just as well, as bad weather continued until 25 April.

On that day, Blake sent Grenville a summons to surrender; Grenville agreed to negotiations and both sides appointed commissioners who met on Samson Island on 2 May. Agreement could not be reached. Blake then ordered the construction of a battery on the very southern point of Tresco and within range of St Mary's, where guns were taken from the fleet and mounted. Blake and Ayscue arrived at the battery to watch the bombardment and had a lucky escape from death: a culverin, probably overcharged, exploded, injuring the crew and several other observers. A new gun was ferried ashore, however, and the bombardment began from the battery and from the ships of Blake's and Ayscue's squadrons.

There was no hope of relief or reinforcement for Grenville: his men knew this and quickly lost hope. On 23 May, Blake again offered terms, this time more generous, knowing that an assault on Star Castle and the garrison would be costly. Grenville would be interned in Plymouth until the Council of State had ratified the surrender, after which he would be given free passage to the Continent with any that wished to follow him. The English soldiers in the garrison would be free either to compound with the Commonwealth or go to Scotland to join Charles II. The Irish would be returned to Ireland. All Royalists would be granted indemnity, and this was extended to 13 privateers at sea and a number of named individuals. Grenville was even compensated for the guns he left on the island. These terms were indeed generous, given that both the English troops, as deserters and mutineers, and the Irish, could well have been liable for execution. On these terms, Grenville agreed to surrender his remaining 300 officers and men on 2 June. Blake also freed three officers from the Commonwealth army in Ireland, Colonels Daniel Axtell, Thomas Saddler* and Richard Le Hunt, and Captain James Jennings,[18] who had been captured while taking ship to London.[19] The detailed terms agreed by the Council of State laid down that:

> That the islands and Castle of St. Mary and Agnes, with all the fortifications, 50 barrels of powder, with match proportionable, two thirds of the shot, and all the ordnance that was found there upon the arrival of Sir Jno. Grenville to the government, shall be delivered to such person as the contracting parties shall appoint, for the use of Parliament, on Monday, 2 June next, by 10 a.m., wind and weather permitting, or at any time before, if Sir Jno. Grenville shall think fit, notice being given to Admiral Blake and Col. Clarke thereof …
>
> That Sir John Grenville, the governor, with all officers and soldiers by sea or land, commissioned or reformed, civil or military, clergy, gentry, and others residing in the said isles of St. Mary and Agnes, with their money, plate, and merchandise, together with their arms and horses, with beat of drums, sound of trumpets, colours displayed, and matches lighted at both ends, and all the rest of the powder, ammunition, and utensils of war, with the ordnance not excepted in any other articles, together with all the victuals and provisions, and particularly the corn and wine, shall, at or before the said day of surrender, be embarked to be transported in the ships and vessels belonging to Sir Jno. Grenville, or any under his command, and in one other vessel to be provided by Admiral Blake and Col. Clark, if need shall require, with furniture and mariners, and safe passes and protections; and that all the English and strangers, officers and soldiers, with their arms, ammunition, provisions, bag and baggage, be transported to Galloway in Ireland …
>
> That no ship or vessel belonging to Sir John Grenville, and now abroad upon employment, shall molest, trouble, or do violence to any of the ships, boats, or goods belonging to any of the commonwealth of England … That an Act of Indemnity be procured from Parliament, to all the persons comprehended in these articles, for all acts committed in time and place of war, to be effectual in all the Parliament quarters for 12 months ensuing the surrender …[20]

It was a rapid and successful reduction, at very little cost. On 12 June, Admiral Tromp returned and sent Captain Cornelius Evertsen aboard Blake's flagship. Blake told Evertsen that the islands had already surrendered to him and Tromp, realising that there was nothing more he could do, departed.

Blake returned to England on 28 June and Sir George Ayscue, with his seven ships and the five companies under Clarke, returned to Plymouth on 19 June.[21] They sailed again for the Barbadoes on 5 August. The Commonwealth's new Governor, Lieutenant-Colonel Joseph Hunkin,[22] was

---

*   Saddler was infamous for his cruelty in Ireland and it is a wonder that the Irish troops did not discover his identity and take revenge on him.

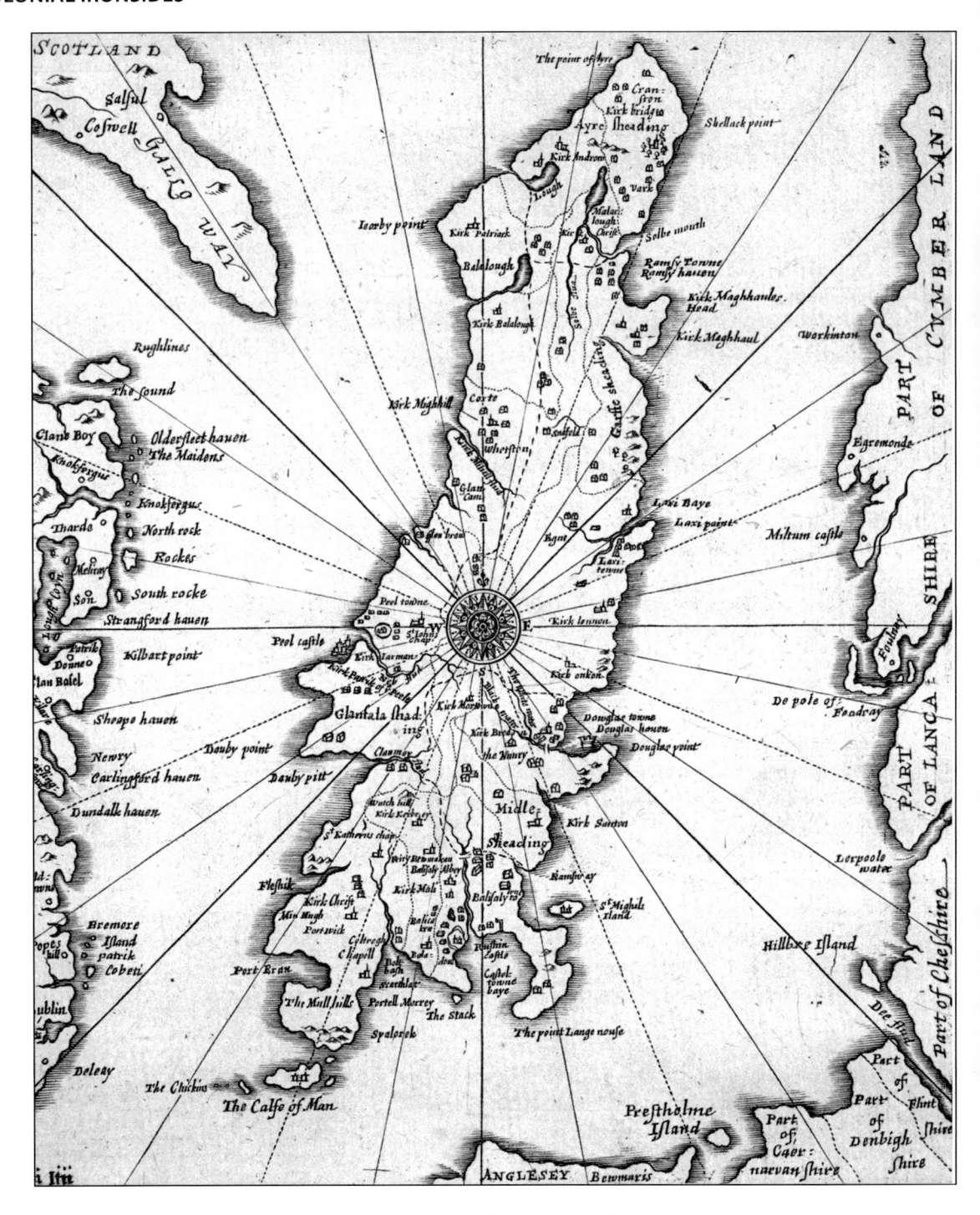

The Isle of Man. (Wienand Drenth)

appointed on 2 July and on his arrival in the Scillies began to improve the island's defences further, particularly against another move by the Dutch. Of note, he built Cromwell's Castle, a gun fort using materials salvaged from King Charles's Castle. A garrison was approved on 11 July, to consist of five companies of foot, each of 120 men besides officers, and a staff which included a commissary of stores, chaplain, surgeon, marshal, master gunner, two gunners and four mates, and 20 matrosses.[23] In June the following year, James Heane, Governor of Jersey, was ordered to send 300 muskets and pikes and 100 bandoliers to Scilly to equip the garrison.[24] The composition of the garrison is not recorded, however the original force had consisted of companies drawn from the regiments of Hardress Waller, Heane and Bennet. Given that Heane's and Waller's regiments were embarked at full strength of 12 companies for the attack on Jersey later in the year, Waller's having raised more men to compensate for the five companies that remained with John Clarke for the expedition to the Barbadoes, it seems likely that Bennet's provided the troops – it had been due for disbandment in July 1651, but was ordered to be extended, at least for three months.[25] After the Restoration, three companies were established on the islands: one under Sir Francis Godolphin, the new governor, as captain, with Lieutenant Henry Noye as lieutenant and John Crudge as ensign; the second under Captain Francis Godolphin, a cousin of the governor, with William Painter as lieutenant and John Allen as ensign; and the third with Sir Arthur Bassett, later a captain in Tangier, in command, with John Bluet as lieutenant and John Reskimer as ensign – who went with Bassett to Tangier.[26]

War with the Scots was, however, still in progress in spite of the victory of Dunbar in 1650. In early August, in a move expected by the Commonwealth government, the Scots invaded England with Charles II at their head. Blake was sent to take command on land of the forces in the western counties; however only 12 days later he returned to sea, taking command of the squadron left vacant by the death of his old friend, Edward Popham. In the aftermath of the defeat of the Scots at Worcester on 3 September 1651, Blake's former task of subduing the Isle of Man was undertaken by others.

The Isle of Man is located in the northern extremities of the Irish Sea; it is 32 miles (52 kilometres) long and, at its widest point, 14 miles (22 kilometres) wide. It has an area of around 221 square miles (572 square kilometres). Man was and is a self-governing Crown dependency with its own Parliament, the Tynwald. Much of the history of Man derives from its settlement by Norsemen; in 1266 the island became part of Scotland; it then alternated between English and Scottish rule until it became subject to the English Crown in 1399. It has never become part of the United Kingdom and like the Channel Islands is not subject to the British parliament. At the time of the Civil Wars, Man was ruled on behalf of the King by the Lord of Man, James Stanley, Seventh Earl of Derby. A Governor carried out the day-to-day duties of administration of the island under the authority of the Lord. There were various fortifications on the island of which the most important were Peel and Rushden Castles. Each of these had a small regular garrison under a Constable. Peel Castle was located on St Patrick's Isle and was connected to Peel itself by a causeway. Rushden was located in Castletown, the historic capital of the island. In addition, there were lesser forts at Douglas, Ramsey and Derby which were held by small bodies of militia.

Throughout the Civil Wars, Stanley had sided with the King and held the island for him; to do so, he had kept a force of troops in the island, in part at least to overawe the Manx as well as to support the King's cause. This force consisted of the garrisons of the major fortresses, a regiment of 250 foot and a troop of 60 horse. By the late 1640s, Stanley was in sore need of money and he tried to raise funds by reforming the inheritance and tenancy laws on the Isle of Man. These changes to the old feudal system of property ownership, termed the *tenure of the straw*, were to be one of the grievances that would cause rebellion later among people already financially strained by the effects of the Civil Wars: Stanley had made repeated requisitions of food, fodder, fuel and money to arm and feed his troops. Growing dissatisfaction over these reforms and rumours of revolt led by a member of one of the island's most prominent families, William Christian, known by his Manx name of Illiam Dhone (or 'Brown William'), prompted Stanley to return to the Isle of Man from England in 1643.

To try to neutralise the plot and buy support, Stanley appointed Dhone as Receiver-General in 1648. Stanley then left the island again in August 1651 to join Charles II's Scots army, taking with him his regular troops and 170 additional militiamen levied from the parishes. He left his wife, Charlotte Stanley, Countess of Derby, at Rushden Castle under Dhone's guardianship. Stanley also left the island's militia under Dhone's command. Stanley's troops took part in the Battle of Wigan Lane in Lancashire on 25 August 1651. Here, Stanley was badly defeated and his troops suffered heavy losses; a list published after the battle records 41 officers and reformadoes and 460 soldiers killed or captured.[27] Stanley himself was also taken captive.

In his final letter to his wife in October he instructed her to broker his release by negotiating for the surrender of the Isle of Man with Colonel Robert Duckenfield, the Commonwealth's Governor of Chester, who had been ordered by Cromwell to raise forces to invade and secure the island. Duckenfield was a Cheshire man who had defended Stockport Bridge against Prince Rupert and conducted the siege of Wythenshawe:

> The governor of this place [Chester], Colonel Duckenfield, is general of the forces which are going now against the Isle of Man, and however you might do for the present, in time it would be grievous and troublesome to resist, especially those that at this hour command three nations; wherefore my advice, notwithstanding my great affection to that place is, that you would make conditions for yourself, children, servants, and people there, and such as came over with me, to the end you may go to some place of rest where you may not be concerned in war; and taking thought of your poor children, you may in some sort provide for them.[28]

The Governor of the Isle of Man, Sir Philip Musgrave, with several members of the Tynwald's House of Keys, drew up proposals which were sent by Lady Stanley to Duckenfield; however, these came to nothing and Stanley was executed on 15 October 1651. At the same time, however, Dhone was also negotiating with the Commonwealth, supported by many in the

The execution of James Stanley, Earl of Derby, at Bolton on 15 October 1651, by James Taylor. (Author's collection)

House of Keys who feared that the Stanleys would save themselves at the expense of the islanders.

The force being assembled by Duckenfield originally consisted of his own regiment; that of Oliver Cromwell – a new regiment raised in Lancashire and commanded by Lieutenant-Colonel Charles Worsely;[29] and the regiment of Colonel Valentine Walton.[30] The regiment of Thomas Birch was then added – the House of Commons voted thanks on 6 November 1651 to Birch and his officers and men for their part in the taking of the Isle of Man.[31] Birch did not at this time actually command a regiment of foot; he was Governor of Liverpool from 1644 to 1655. In March 1651, Duckenfield had been instructed to raise 10 companies from the militia of Cheshire, Lancashire and Shropshire; six of these companies were to replace troops in garrisons and four were to be sent north to Scotland.[32] It appears likely that some of Duckenfield's levies made up his own regiment, which was therefore not a standing regiment, and others replaced Birch's garrison troops in Liverpool so that these companies, plus those in Chester and Shrewsbury, could form also part of the expeditionary force as a composite regiment under Birch. What is certain is that Cromwell's instructions to Birch on 30 September required him to assist in the reduction of Man.[33] According to the *Dictionary of National Biography*, Birch held joint command of the expedition.

A note in the Minutes of the Council of State also says that the regiment of 'Major-General [Richard] Deane'[34] also took part in the attack. Deane* had been given the regiment of Maleverer on 17 June 1650 and it had fought

---

* Deane was killed in the sea battle with the Dutch off the Gabbard on 2 June 1653.

Peel Castle seen from the east, by Daniel King, between 1643 and 1651. (Author's collection)

at the Battle of Worcester.[35] It seems that it was this regiment that was sent to Duckenfield, for Deane departed for Scotland in December 1651 without his regiment, which is otherwise unaccounted for but which followed him later. Its presence in the Isle of Man in late 1651 therefore solves this particular puzzle. Two troops of horse were allocated to Duckenfield: those of Valentine Walton, commanded by Major William Packer; and that of his son, Robert Duckenfield. Finally, there was a small train of artillery under Colonel Morgan.*

Dhone and Musgrave agreed to defend the island from invasion until favourable terms for a settlement were arranged with the Commonwealth. However, the negotiations were merely a cover by Dhone to gain time. On the same night that the proposed terms of surrender were sent to Duckenfield, Dhone led an uprising against the lordship of the Stanleys. Dhone summoned the captains of all the parish companies and ordered them to seize the major fortresses. Around 800 men answered the call and soon took all the smaller forts but could not take the two major castles of Rushden and Peel.[36]

Bad weather caused a delay in the arrival of the Commonwealth force and it was not until 30 October that Duckenfield landed,[37] carried in the ships of the Irish Sea squadron.† It was quickly arranged that the Commonwealth would take control of the island, subject to the restoration of the rights that Stanley had tried to overturn. In Rushden Castle, the Countess did not learn of the death of her husband until probably early November, for on 8 November she received a letter from Duckenfield demanding her surrender, which she answered saying that she could not give up the castle without orders from Stanley himself. After

---

* Son of Robert Morgan of Llanrhumney and Governor of Gloucester; knighted by Richard Cromwell in 1659.
† *Portsmouth*, *Swiftsure*, *Concord*, *Fellowship*, *Hector* and an unrecorded number of merchant ships as troop carriers.

Castle Rushden seen from the south-south-west, by Daniel King, between 1643 and 1651. (Author's collection)

only a few more days, however, she realised that she could no longer rely on her few troops and on 13 November she surrendered, being given safe passage with her family and followers through England and on to Europe. It is said that it was Colonel Thomas Birch who led the siege of Rushden and, after the island surrendered, had charge of 'the countess being conveyed to Liverpool Castle and subsequently to Chester for greater security'.[38]

Once the Commonwealth had secured the island and the considerable amount of ordnance and stores in its fortresses,[39] most of the troops were withdrawn. Cromwell's Regiment went to London; Duckenfield's Regiment was disbanded, with five of its companies sent under Lieutenant-Colonel Simon Finch to complete Hardress Waller's Regiment for service in Ireland.[40] Deane's Regiment was disbanded in late 1651 and Walton's reduced to five companies at the same time.[41] Birch's Regiment appears to have been broken up immediately and returned to garrison duties in Cheshire and Lancashire.

In their place, the Council of State established a garrison in 1651 which consisted of two large companies each of 240 men, besides officers. In January 1652 this was reduced to two companies of 120 men, besides officers, and an additional company of 60 men under a third captain with only two sergeants and a drummer.[42] The cost of the whole establishment came to £12/6s/6d per day. The governor was to be captain of one of the companies and he was to have £1/6s/– per day, 16s as governor and 10s as captain.

In June 1652, the establishment was again reduced to two companies of 80 men and one of 70 men, besides officers, under the command of Colonel Charles Worsley and Lieutenant-Colonel William Mitchell.[43] The garrison was further reduced in October 1653 to two companies each of 100 men besides officers.[44] This garrison remained in place until the Restoration. The Commonwealth administration also took charge of the 22 militia companies on the island, each commanded by a captain, and appointed a major of

COLONIAL IRONSIDES

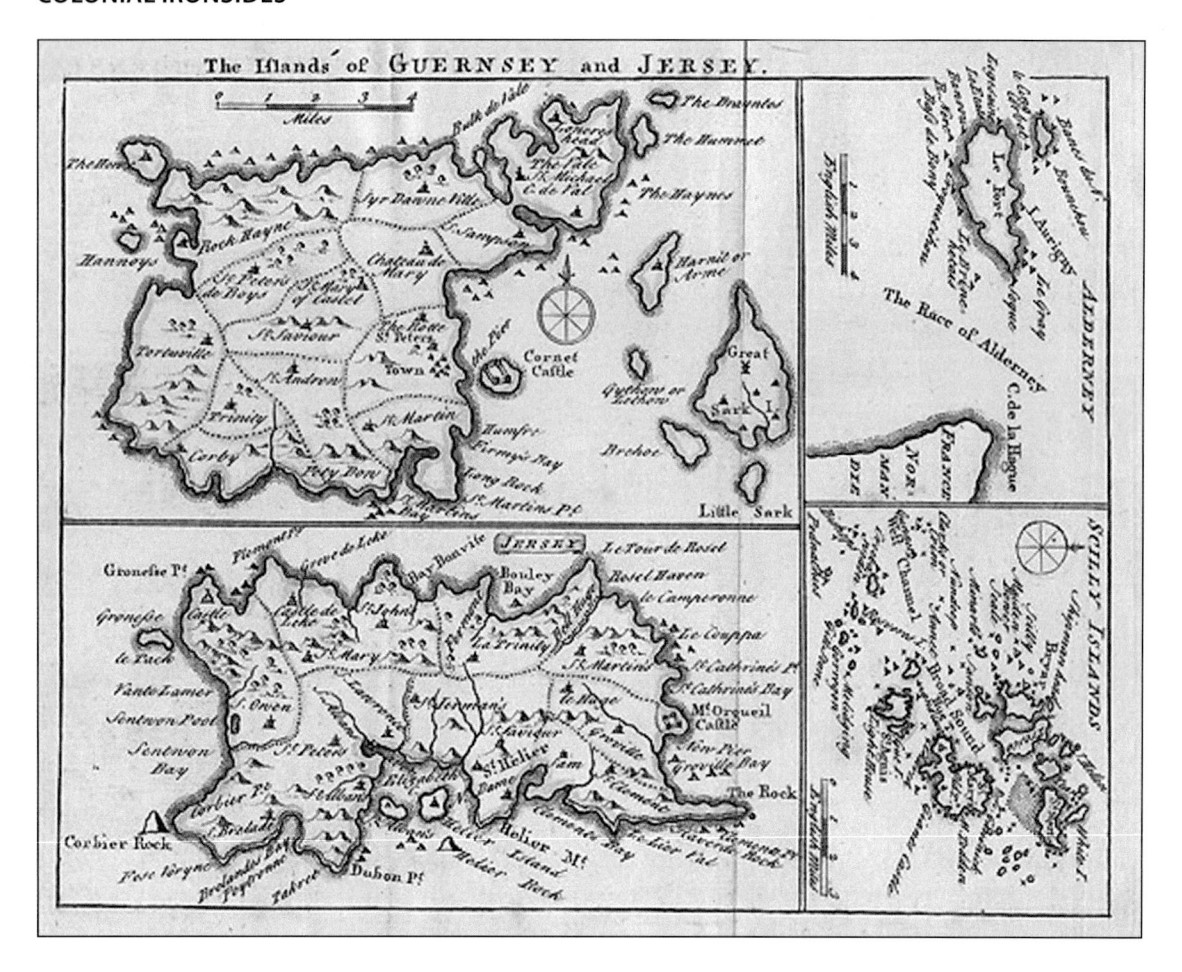

The Channel Islands (Wienand Drenth)

militia to oversee their training and readiness under the authority of the governor as captain-general.

Dhone, for his services to the Commonwealth, became governor from 1653 to 1659, under the Lordship of Sir Thomas Fairfax. With the fall of the Protectorate, he fled to London. There he was arrested and although he was released and returned to the Isle of Man, he was once more arrested, tried for treason and executed by shooting on 2 January 1663.

One final Royalist enclave remained to be dealt with and the task was once again entrusted to General–at–Sea William Blake. This task was the subjugation of the Channel Islands, notably Jersey. The Channel Islands – Jersey Guernsey, Alderney, Sark, Herm, Jethou and Brechou – lie just to the south of the Cotentin peninsula of Normandy and within sight of the French coast. Originally, they formed part of the Duchy of Normandy and when Duke William conquered England, the kingdom and the duchy were united. In the reign of King John, Normandy was conquered by France, but the islands preferred to stay with the England: they therefore owed their allegiance to the English crown, but not to the English government.

The principal islands are Jersey and Guernsey, where an obscure dialect of medieval Norman French was spoken at the time of the Civil Wars. Each was governed by a parliament known as the *Etats*, under a Bailiff, with

Castle Cornet in Guernsey. (Author's collection)

the monarch represented by a Governor. Protestantism took hold in the islands strongly and at an early date, further distancing the islanders from France, and it was not surprising that many people therefore took the part of Parliament during the early years of the Civil Wars. The royal governors, however, remained staunch, holding the fortresses of Elizabeth Castle and Mont Orgueil in Jersey, Castle Cornet in Guernsey, and a number of smaller forts.

In 1629, Lord Danby had surveyed the defences of the islands because of fears of an attack by France or from the United Provinces. He found that the artillery of the fortresses had been issued with new carriages. He reviewed the landing places and their defences, after which he gave 'directions for additional entrenchments.'[45] Improvements were put in hand at all the major fortifications including Sark, which had only been fortified in 1627. Two companies of foot were recruited in Devon and Cornwall, each of 100 men besides officers, one company for each of Jersey and Guernsey.[46] Each company based 20 men in the major castles and the rest were quartered around the island, billeted on the local people, amid general dissatisfaction. As well as the regular garrisons of the fortresses, both islands had a sizeable militia, formed into companies based on the parishes and commanded by a captain who was often the local lord, or *seigneur*. Danby reviewed the militia and 'found them ill armed and worse in order.'

In 1644 Sir Henry Jermyn, Earl of St Albans, was appointed governor but did not take up residence. Sir George de Carteret,* *Siegneur* of St Ouen's, had inherited the deputy-governorship from his uncle in 1643 and in 1647 he landed at Gorey in Jersey, quickly rallying the island to the Royalist cause – the two major castles had been held for the King by their captains and Carteret greatly strengthened the garrisons. By 1650, there were also two companies of fusiliers each of 120 men;[47] a troop of horse and another of dragoons; and a garrison of 442 officers and men at Elizabeth Castle made

---

* Vice-Admiral Sir George de Carteret, 1st Baronet (*c.* 1610–1680) later served in Clarendon's ministry after the Restoration as Treasurer of the Navy. He was one of the original lords proprietor of Carolina and New Jersey.

49

up of 20 English regulars supplemented by Irish, Scots, French, Danish, Swiss and Germans, chiefly mercenaries, and a number of militiamen. Mont Orgueil had about 20 English soldiers and 47 militia, under the command of Lady Phillippe de Carteret. Carteret governed with considerable severity, imprisoning Commonwealth supporters and confiscating their property; he also sponsored privateering operations against English shipping.

Parliament had, however, appointed a rival governor, Colonel Leonard Lydcott. Lydcott arrived with three captains, six soldiers and a handful of followers, relying perhaps on the enthusiasm of the militia for the cause of Parliament. He was forced to take refuge in St Aubin's Fort until evicted by Carteret in 1647. His small force was replaced by 10 English and Irish soldiers and 12 militiamen.

In Guernsey, where the governor was also responsible for the smaller islands, there were fewer Royalists. In 1643, a Parliamentarian commission took control of the island with the Earl of Warwick as governor and Lieutenant-Colonel Russell as his deputy. However, the Royalist lieutenant-governor, Sir Peter Osborne, refused to submit and held on to Castle Cornet with a garrison of 55 soldiers, supplied by sea from Jersey. In 1647, Osborne was replaced by Sir Bernard Wake, who disappeared in 1649 and was in turn replaced by Sir Roger Burgess. Burgess's tenure did not last long. In 1650, a Commonwealth force of ships carrying seven companies of Colonel Alban Coxe's Regiment arrived and invested the castle by sea and land. Burgess surrendered on 19 December 1651. Coxe became lieutenant-governor until Cromwell's nominee, Colonel John Bingham, arrived in 1653.

Charles II made his first visit to Jersey between April and June 1646 as Prince of Wales, after he had left the Scilly Isles. When he moved on to France, he left behind Sir Edward Hyde. He returned after the execution of his father in October 1649. On 31 October 1649, Charles reviewed the entire military establishment of the island, less the garrisons of the castles, on the sands at St Aubin's. This consisted of the English and Irish regular troops, and the militia. The latter comprised 12 parish companies of foot, grouped into three regiments, along with gunners and drivers. Each company mustered 238 officers and men.[48] There was also one troop of horse, making a total of at least 3,200 men; a number of untrained recruits and pikemen also seem to have formed part of the parade.[49] On leaving to join his mother in France ahead of the Second Civil War, Charles appointed his brother, James, Duke of York, as Governor with Carteret as Deputy.

The Commonwealth had long planned to force Jersey to submit and as early as 1646 it had appointed Colonel Edward Aldrich to command the force.[50] It was not, however, until after the Royalist's final defeat at Worcester in September 1651 that the fleet under Blake was assembled to deal with the Royalist enclaves.[51] Blake's ships embarked a body of troops commanded by Colonel James Heane, consisting of 12 companies of his own regiment, 12 companies of Sir Hardress Waller's Regiment, four troops of horse and a train of artillery – a total of at least 3,000 men. Two companies of Alban Coxe's Regiment were also ordered to join the force from Guernsey, however only one arrived.

RECOVERING THE ROYALIST ENCLAVES, APRIL–DECEMBER 1651

Mont Orgueil Castle, from the Earl of Dartmouth's survey in 1680. (Author's collection)

Having dealt with the Scilly Isles and refitted, Blake's fleet of 17 ships sailed from Weymouth on 17 October. Blake was at first forced back by storms and did not appear off St Ouen's Bay on the west coast of Jersey until midday on 20 October. However, as in the Scilly Isles, the sea was still too rough for the troops to land from boats and the alarm was quickly raised. Governor de Carteret assembled 2,000 militia, a troop of horse and another of dragoons, his own company of fusiliers and six small field guns which were formed up on the five-mile stretch of sand forming St Ouen's Bay. The militia companies of St Helier, St Saviour, and St Clements were mustered to oppose a possible landing in the bay of St Helier; the militia company of St Brelade was mustered to guard its own bay and two batteries there; the company of Grouville was ordered to remain on the east of the island; and all other companies – St Mary, St Peter, Trinity, St Lawrence, St Martin and St Ouen's – were mustered with the regulars at St Ouen's Bay under the Lieutenant-Colonel of the St Ouen's militia, Edward Bosvill.

The next morning, Blake sent a trumpeter by boat, demanding the island's surrender. Carteret seems to have had little faith in the militia, in spite of their numbers; the fusiliers therefore fired a warning volley, and the boat withdrew. Blake then sent several frigates close inshore to bombard the Royalists. The fire was kept up for several hours, but the Atlantic rollers did not abate. Blake therefore moved the fleet around to St Brelade's, on the south–west corner of the island. Carteret followed by land. Unable to put his troops ashore, Blake sailed his fleet up and down the coast, forcing the

COLONIAL IRONSIDES

Elizabeth Castle, by Wenceslaus Hollar. (Author's collection)

Royalists to shadow him. After several days, worn out with marching, soaked by rain, and cowed by constant fire from the ships, the militiamen were close to open mutiny.

The weather finally slackened on the night of 22 October. At 11.00 p.m., troops were put ashore. When Carteret tried to counter-attack, he found that most of the militia horse had deserted and only the St Ouen's militia, his own personal command, had stayed firm. Colonel Edward Bosvill led the remaining regular horse to attack the ironsides on the beach, while Carteret held the militia in reserve with his fusiliers. Bosvill's attack drove the landing party back to the shoreline, inflicting some casualties. Another charge was about to be made when Bosvill was shot and wounded, disheartening the Royalists and giving a breathing space for Heane to land more troops. Under a heavy fire from Heane's men, the Royalists broke off the action and withdrew to Elizabeth Castle.

Heane then advanced unopposed to St Helier. On 24 October, he summoned Carteret to surrender Elizabeth Castle, but was, according to the code of honour of the day, refused. The castle could only be approached across a causeway at low tide as rocks and shoals prevented ships from coming close inshore. Heane therefore left part of his force to invest the castle, while he himself marched east to Mont Orgueil at Gorey. On 25 October he summoned Sir Philip and Lady de Carteret to surrender. Although the Carterets were defiant, the little garrison would not stand, even though it had been reinforced, and negotiations were opened for a surrender. The terms offered were generous: Sir Philip was allowed to keep his estates in Jersey and the garrison was granted indemnity. Sixty men who wished to do so were permitted to join Sir George de Carteret in Elizabeth Castle; the rest (mostly foreign mercenaries) were given free passage to Europe.

During the last week of October, a battery of six 36-pdr guns was established on high ground above St Helier and the bombardment of Elizabeth Castle began. The fire, however, had little effect. Six more guns and three mortars were added to the battery at the beginning of November. On 9 November, a direct hit by a mortar shell blew up a magazine in the crypt of the medieval priory that formed part of the castle. This explosion killed six men, buried or injured another 40 and caused significant structural damage. Many in the garrison began to lose heart and a number deserted, but Carteret remained defiant even after Charles II sent a messenger giving him permission to surrender. Carteret ordered the evacuation of all the women in the castle to France by ship as provisions were running low and an effective blockade by Blake's ships meant that there was no possibility of resupply.

On 8 December, Carteret opened a parley for terms of surrender. Generous terms were again offered: Carteret himself was given free passage to France with his property and as many of his followers as wished to go. The castle was surrendered to the Commonwealth force at noon on 12 December 1651. As recounted earlier, Sir Roger Burgess surrendered Castle Cornet on Guernsey on 17 December under the same terms, thus completing the Commonwealth's conquest.

Once the operation was brought to a conclusion, the company from Coxe's Regiment returned to Guernsey and Hardress Waller's Regiment was taken back to the west of England. Three companies of Heane's Regiment also returned to England and were disbanded,[52] along with two troops of horse which were not disbanded. Another three companies of Heane's Regiment were sent to Ireland, leaving six companies and two troops of horse. In January 1652, the Council of State ordered a new establishment for Jersey consisting of the Governor's staff, a troop of horse and six companies of foot; these appear to have been drawn from the troops already there with Heane. Three companies of Coxe's Regiment had remained in Guernsey, the others having been sent to Ireland and to Weymouth. When the new establishment for Jersey was settled, five companies were allowed for Guernsey, although it seems that only two or three were actually present.[53] In January 1652, only the companies of Colonel Helsham, Captain Samuel Clarke and Captain Symcock were present.

Heane remained as Governor until 1653 when he left to form a new regiment for service in the West Indies (see Chapter 7). He was replaced by Colonel Robert Gibbon, who had served in Philip Skippon's Regiment at Naseby. Gibbon was a truculent character who despised all civilians and became the focus of the islanders' hatred. The end of the Protectorate brought the recall of Gibbon and his replacement with an Anabaptist, Colonel John Mason; however, in January 1660, Monck replaced him with Colonel Carew Raleigh. After the Restoration, Lord Henry Jermyn resumed his post as Royal Governor.

The conquest of Jersey meant that the rule of the Commonwealth extended over the entire British Isles – England, Ireland, Scotland and Wales, as well as Man, the Scillies and the Channel Islands. The Council of State now turned its attention to the colonies further afield, in the Americas and the Caribbean.

Appendix I to Chapter 3

Blake's and Ayscue's Squadrons for the Scilly and Channel Islands Expeditions[1]

Phoenix	General Robert Blake	32 guns	150 crew
	Captain John Wadsworth		
Providence	Captain John Pearse	30 guns	120 crew
Fox	Captain John Seaman	22 guns	80 crew
110th Lyon's Whelp*	Unidentified	11 guns	
Mayflower	Captain John Cole	28 guns	120 crew
Hind	Captain John Sherwin	18 guns	
Truelove	Captain Robert Vessey	14 guns	30 crew
Convertine	Captain Thomas Allen	40 guns	
Old President	Captain Thomas Sparling	34 guns	80 crew
Constant Warwick	Captain Owen Cox	32 guns	140 crew

Unnamed hoy, or supply barge (probably carrying powder and shot)
Two armed merchant ships as troop carriers

Detached to the Irish Sea

Portsmouth	Captain William Brandley	34 guns	150 crew
Swiftsure	Captain John Gilson	46 guns	260 crew
Concord	Captain Thomas Penrose	24 guns	70 crew
Fellowship	Captain Robert Nixon	28 guns	
Hector	Captain Edmund Curtis	22 guns	70 crew
President frigate	Captain Anthony Young	34 guns	180 crew

---

*   The last of a series of war pinnaces built for George Villiers, 1st Duke of Buckingham around 1628 by Robert Tranckmore of Shoreham and employed as privateers. She was a Royalist ship until captured in 1645. She was fitted out as a fireship for Blake's pursuit of Prince Rupert but not used, and thereafter used for convoy and troop-carrying duties.

APPENDIX I TO CHAPTER 3

Sir George Ayscue's Squadron[2]

Rainbow	Colonel George Ayscue	52 guns	280 men
Amity	Captain Michael Pack	36 guns	150 men
Success	Captain Edward Witteridge	30 guns	90 men
Ruth	Captain Edward Thomson	30 guns	80 men
Brazil frigate	Captain Thomas Heath	24 guns	70 men
Malaga armed merchantman	Captain Henry Collin	30 guns	90 men
Increase of London	Captain Thomas Varvell	36 guns	100 men

NOTES

1. Rev. J.R. Powell, 'Blake's Reduction of the Scilly Isles in 1651', in *Mariner's Mirror*, vol. 17, no. 3 (1931). Ship details from <www.threedecks.org>, accessed 20 November 2020.
2. Commons Journal, vol. vi, August 1651, p.70.

Appendix II to Chapter 3

The Commonwealth Invasion Force and Garrison, Isle of Man

Command and Staff
Colonel Robert Duckenfield
Colonel Thomas Birch
Lieutenant-Colonel Isaac Birkenhead
Engineer-General John Roseworm
Chief Engineer __ Morgan
Major of Militia __ Fox

The Lord General's Regiment

Colonel Charles Worsley	Lieutenant-Colonel Francis White	Major __ Huntingdon
Major George Drury	Major Roger Sawtry	Captain John Hodgson
Captain Oliver Edge	Captain John Jewell	Captain James Priest
Captain John Wigan	Captain __ Jenkins	Captain __ Middleton
Captain John Reynolds	Captain __ Blackwell	Captain Clement Keane
Captain William Bland	Captain George Baldwin	Ensign (to Worsley) Charles Bolton

Major-General Deane's Regiment

Lieutenant-Colone Denis Pepper	Major John Pitman	Captain George Bradshaw
Lieutenant William Sadlington	Lieutenant William Carpenter	Lieutenant __ Whitby
Ensign Benjamin Waters	Ensign Richard Saunderson	
Captain Richard Wisdome	Captain Henry Watson	Captain Thomas Cooke
Lieutenant William Harrison	Lieutenant Gabriel Ewood	Lieutenant John Pearson
Ensign Mathew Harland	Ensign George Noble	Ensign Roger Cooke
Chaplain Thomas Warde	Captain Michael Bacon	Captain Thomas Bourchier
Lieutenant Thomas Waters	Lieutenant Thomas Spratt	Lieutenant Moses Leniger

Ensign Edmund Howson   Ensign John Reeves   Ensign Thomas Dawson

Captain George Wesbie
Lieutenant Jervice Hardstaffe
Ensign William Staniford

Staff
Chaplain Thomas Moore
Surgeon John Swadlin
Quartermaster & Marshal Allen Stileman

Colonel Robert Duckenfield's Regiment[1]

Colonel Robert Duckenfield	Lieutenant-Colonel Isaac Birkenhead	Major Symon Ffinch
Captain James Stockport	Captain Thomas Partington	Captain Jo. Corbet
Captain Henry Greene	Captain Jonathan Rudge	
Phillip Eyton		

Colonel Thomas Birch's Regiment

Colonel Thomas Birch	Lieutenant-Colonel Alex Standish	Major William Emmett
Captain Robert Marsden	Captain Roger Tattersall	Captain Thomas Ebersall
Captain Thomas Boardman	Captain James Haworth	

Colonel Valentine Walton's Regiment*

Colonel Valentine Walton*	Lieutenant-Colonel William Mitchell	Major John Disbrowe
Captain John Fox	Captain Edward Scotten	Captain John Blackmore
Captain Joseph Wallington	Captain __ Jenkins	

Troops of Horse

Captain Robert Duckenfield	Major William Packer
Lieutenant William Shipley	Lieutenant Jervis Bonner
Cornet John Griffith	Cornet __ Walton
Quartermaster M. Gardner	Quartermaster Obadiah Crisp

Militia Companies in 1650–1651

Rushden	Captain William Gawne
Peel	Major Woods, Captain of the Castle
Castletown	Sir Thomas Armstrong, Captain of the Castle
Douglas	Lieutenant Robert Calcott
Ramsey	Captain Ingram, Captain of the Castle

---

* Walton married Oliver Cromwell's sister, Margaret, and was one of the Regicides. He died in Flanders in 1661.

COLONIAL IRONSIDES

Patrick	Captain Samsbury Radcliffe[†]
Loyal Fort	Major Thomas Stanley
German	Captain Thomas Taubman
Michael	Captain John Channell
Ballaugh	Captain Thomas Thompson
Jurby	Captain John Teare
Lonan	Captain Phillip Moore
Conchan	Captain Edward Christian
	Lieutenant James Banks
Andreas	Captain John Sayle
Bride	Captain David Christian
Lezayre (North)	Captain John Christian
Lezayre (South)	Captain Ewan Curghy
Maughold	Captain John Christian
Braddan	Captain Robert Moore
	Robert Calcott (1651)
Santon	Captain John Moore
Marown	Captain John Moore(?)
Malew	Captain William Huddleston
Arbory	Captain Richard Stevenson

The Commonwealth and Protectorate Garrison

Staff
Provost Marshall
Chirurgeon
Master Gunner
Storekeeper
2 Gunner's Mates
6 Matrosses

1st Company	**2nd Company**	**3rd Company**
Captain (the Governor)	Captain	Captain
Lieutenant	Lieutenant	
Ensign	Ensign	
2 sergeants	2 sergeants	2 sergeants
3 corporals	3 corporals	
drummer	drummer	drummer
80 soldiers	80 soldiers	60 soldiers

---

[*] One of the leaders of the 1651 revolt, he besieged Peel Castle. His estates were confiscated in 1662.

APPENDIX II TO CHAPTER 3

On 17 October 1653, the Establishment was again reduced.[2] The staff remained unchanged, but the foot was reduced to two companies of 100 men in each company with officers and NCOs as per the June 1652 Establishment. The following officers have been identified:[3]

Colonel Charles Worsley to 1652	Lieutenant-Colonel William Mitchell to 1652	
Captain Robert Duckenfield 1651	Captain Robert Smith 1651	Captain George Bradshaw 1651
Captain William Christian 1652	Captain Mathew Cadwell 1652	Captain Francis Duckenfield 1652
Captain James Chaloner* 1652–1660	Captain __ Wade 1653	
Lieutenant __ Whitby 1651	Captain Samuel Rose 1659	Ensign John Sharples 1653
Ensign John Hathorne 1653	Lieutennant Mathew Scot	Ensign Robert Gaye

NOTES
1. TNA SP 25/119, Commissions Register 12 September 1650, f.11.
2. Commons Journal, vol. vi, 17 October 1653.
3. Commons Journal, various dates; TNA CSPD Interregnum, 1649–1660.

---

* Later governor in 1659.

Appendix III to Chapter 3

Royalist and Commonwealth Forces in the Channel Islands

JERSEY

The Commonwealth Invasion Force

Staff
Colonel James Heane
Colonel James Stockall
Captains Daniel Norman and Michael Lemprière
Thomas Wright, chief engineer and commanding the train of artillery

Colonel James Heane's Regt of Foot (12 companies)
Colonel James Heane
Lieuetnant-Colonel __ Joyce
Major Hugh Harding*
Captain-Lieutenant Richard Ashby
Captain William Heane
Captain Kympton Hilliard
Captain William Yeardley
Captain __ Dover
Captain __ Awder
Captain __ Hughes
Captain John Hunt[1]
Captain Edward Botsford[2]
Lieutenant Pigeon

Sir Hardress Waller's Regt of Foot (six companies drawn from those of:)
Major Philip Ebsery
Captain John Lane
Captain Richard Aske

---
*   Ensign in Fairfax's Regiment in 1642.

Captain (Thomas?) Chamberlain
Captain __ Thomas
Captain Richard Hodden
Captain __ Howard
Captain __ Wade
Captain John Gorges
Captain Philip Desborough
Captain Nathaniel Chute

Troops of Horse

Captain Stephen West	Lieutenant Thomas Smith	Cornet Dober
Captain Ralph Margerum[‡]	Lieutenant Thomas Roper	Cornet Boalry
Captain Norris		Cornet Brockenhurst
Captain William Fleetwood[3]		

Two companies of Alban Coxe's Regiment were ordered from Guernsey but only one arrived, under the command of Major James Harrison, and retuned to Guernsey immediately after the conquest of the island.

The Royalist Garrison

Troop of Horse (150 men)
Captain Dumaresq

Troop of Dragoons (150 men)
Captain Le Hardy

Two Companies of Fusiliers (each 120 men)

Captain Simon Canham	Lieutenant William Blake	Ensign John Collins
Captain Robert Johnson	Lieutenant John Coates	Ensign __

Elizabeth Castle
442 officers and men made up of about 20 regular English soldiers, supplemented by Irish, Scots, Frenchmen, Danes, Swiss and Germans and a number of militiamen. Organised into three companies.

Captain of Elizabeth Castle (for the King)
Seneschal – Hungerford, 1644[4]
Chaplain – Mr Durel

First Company – Carteret, Capt Paulet
Second Company – 'the Lieutenant-Colonel of the Germans'
Third Company – Major Collins

---

* Ralph Margerum (1592–1653) was the original 'plain russet–coated captain' in Cromwell's famous rebuke. He raised a troop of horse in Suffolk in 1643. The established strength of his troop was one captain, one lieutenant, one cornet, one quartermaster, two trumpeters, three corporals and 112 troopers (TNA SP 28 (1645))

COLONIAL IRONSIDES

Mont Orgueil Castle
Twenty regular English soldiers plus a contingent of militia under Lady de Carteret. The castle had been extensively remodelled as an artillery fort during the sixteenth century, but work was abandoned in 1593 when the decision was made to concentrate effort on Elizabeth Castle.

Captain of Mont Orgueil (Gorey) Castle (for the King)
Captain Richard Legge, 1644–1645 and 1650–1651[5]
Lady de Carteret, 1645–1650

St Aubin's Fort
Ten English and Irish regular soldiers. Twelve militiamen were added in 1651 at a rate of pay of 50 *sous* per man per day.

Captains of St Aubin's[6]
Major Leonard Lydcot (for Parliament), deputed to Lieutenant __ Brand, 1643–1647
Captain John Deane, appointed by Sir G. de Carteret, 1647–1651, deputed to Lieutenant Manuel Clement.
Captain __ Sausmarez, 1651, deputed to Lieutenant Manuel Clement
Lieut Jasper Brand

Militia
The militia mustered a total of 27 companies of foot and one troop of horse from the 10 parishes and was described by the Royal Commissioners Conway and Bird in 1617 as being drilled three or four times every year, the men wearing red coats and each parish possessing two or three brass field pieces, mustering 2,657 officers and men in total. The estimated population of the island at that date was around 9,000.[7]

Colonels[*]
Jean Dumaresq, Colonel of the East Regiment (for the King) 1643–1650[8]
Philip de Carteret II, Colonel of the West Regiment (for the King) 1643–1650
Amias de Carteret, Colonel of the North Regiment (for the King) 1643–1650

Commander of the Horse
Colonel Edward Bovill[9]

Militia Companies	Captains[§]	Lieutenants
St Ouen's	Edward Bosvill	Jean Dauvergne
St Helier	Jean Dumaresq	Edouard Dumaresq
St Martin	__ de Rossel	Abraham Le Maistre
St Peter	Helier de Carteret	Edward de Carteret
St Saviour	__ de Rossel	Etienne Antoine
St Lawrence		Guille de Gruchy
St Clement	__ de Suamarez	Helier Dumaresq
St Mary	Jean de Carteret	Philippe Le Couteur

---

[*] Full Militia Lists for Jersey and Guernsey are in Drenth and Riley, vol. i.

Trinity	Amias de Carteret	Edouard Romeril
Grouville	__ de Suamarez	Jean Cooper
St John	__ Dilamen	Jean Esnouf
St Brelade	Helier de Carteret	John Seale

The Commonwealth Garrison, Post 1651

From 4 December 1651 in Jersey, Colonel Heane's Regiment with Lieutenant-Colonel Joyce, Major Philip Ebzery and six companies, and the troops of captains West and Margery. Captain Henry Hatsell appointed Agent and Commissary.

January 1652 – The undermentioned companies from Jersey are to be sent to England and reduced:
Captain Dover's – 100
Captain Heath's – 100
Captain Hughes' – 100

2 troops of horse are to be returned to England but not reduced; 2 troops are to remain in Jersey.[10]

3 companies from Jersey are to be sent to Ireland:
Capt Awder – 100
Out of the Coll's company to go with Awder as recruits [to reinforce other regiments]
From the Colonel's Company [Heane's] – 80
From the Lt-Col's company – 80
From Major Harding's Company – 40

30 January 1652 – Captain Norris and Cornet Brockenhurst mentioned
27 February 1652 – Thomas Wright mentioned as Fire-Master in Elizabeth Castle on Jersey

The Commonwealth garrison from 1652 after the conquest of the island was reduced to a company of foot and a troop of horse. In March 1694 the Protector was petitioned to repair Elizabeth Castle and improve the accommodation for the garrison,[11] to which Cromwell agreed the following year.[12]

An Establishment for the Isle of Jersey to commence the 8th Day of March 1651[13]
The Governor besides Coll of a company
Chaplaine
Master Gunner and Storekeeper
Three Gunner's Mates
Eighteen Matrosses
Commissary of provisions
Assistant Commissary
Chirurgeon
Provost Marshall
Gunsmith
Boatman

---

* Some captains were responsible for more than one company.

COLONIAL IRONSIDES

A troop of horse consisting of the captain, lieutenant, cornet, quartermaster, two trumpeters and three corporals, 60 troopers.

Six companies of foot consisting of a colonel, major, six captains, six lieutenants, six ensigns, 12 sergeants, eight corporals, 12 drummers, six gentlemen of armes and 600 private soldiers.

Isle of Guernsey
Surgeon's mate
Gunsmith
Commissary of provisions
Five companies of foot each 100 soldiers besides officers

Staff
Governor of Jersey: Colonel James Heane
Colonel Robert Gibbon, 1653
Colonel John Mason, 1659
Major __ Harding
Commissary, Captain Henry Hatsell
Firemaster in Elizabeth Castle Thomas Wright

Companies of Foot

Captain James Heane	Captain William Heane	Captain Kympton Hilliard
Captain William Yeardley	Captain Heath	Captain Ashby
Ensign Watson		

Troop of Horse

Captain William Fleetwood	Lieutenant __	Cornet __ Brockhurst[14]

Changes

Militia
Colonels
James Stockall (for the Commonwealth and later the Protector), 1651
John Mason, 15 June 1659 (for Parliament)[13]

Captain-Major & Adjutant
Daniel Norman (for the Commonwealth), 1651

Companies	**Captain****	**Lieutenants**
St Ouen's	Philippe LeFebvre	Jean Ricard
St Helier	Jacques Lemprière	André le Vavasser
St Martin	Jean de la Rue	Thomas Bandinel
St Peter	John Le Hardy	Nicolas Le Boutillier

---

* Full Militia Lists for Jersey and Guernsey are in Drenth and Riley, vol. i.

	Simon Le Sebinel (1655)	
St Saviour		Clement Gallie
St Lawrence		Elie Le Gros
St Clement	Henry Dumaresq	Jean Dumaresq
St Mary		Aaron Journeaux
Trinity	Elias Dumaresq	Jean Maret
		Philippe Le Boutellier (1653)
Grouville	Richard du Parq	Clement Dumaresq
St John	Thomas Le Merinel	Thomas Esnouf
St Brelade		Edouard Anley

The Restoration Garrison

Captain William Victor's Company, with Lieutenant Henry Fincher from Portsmouth in June 1662. August 1662, two companies detached from Lord Wentworth's Guards at Dunkirk, pending the arrival of garrison companies:
Captain Ralph Sydenham, Lieutenant Philip Paramore (to Portsmouth)
Captain Herbert Jeffreys, Lieutenant William Sanderson, vice Victor's company which under Captain Fincher was then disbanded.

Succeeded by companies under:
Captain Henry Jermyn, Earl of St Albans (Governor), Lieutenant George Raleigh, Ensign Richard du Shamell
Captain Sir Thomas Jermyn Lieutenant Francis Carteret, Ensign William Hopkins. This company disbanded in the autumn of 1662.

GUERNSEY

The Royalist Garrison, Castle Cornet
Fifty-five regular soldiers under Colonel Sir Peter Osborne, 1643–1647 and Major Harrington. Succeeded by Colonels Sir Bernard Wake, 1647–1649, and Sir Roger Burgess, 1649–1651. Others named at the time of surrender were:

Major John Burgess	Major John Hamilton	Captain John Clarke
Captain Henry Geach	Thomas Byng	John Yackesley
Richard Johnson	Edmund May	John Plunkett

Commonwealth Invasion Force and Garrison

Colonel Alban Coxe's regiment of Foot (7 Companies)

---

*   Some captains were responsible for more than one company.

COLONIAL IRONSIDES

Reduced to one company in 1652 when the remaining companies sailed for Weymouth and Ireland.[14]

Colonel Alban Coxe
Lieutenant-Colonel Arthur Helsam
Major James Harrison
Captain-Lieutenant __ May
Captain Samuel Clark
Captain James Symcock
Captain Thomas Howell
Captain __ Lacey
Captain John Clarke

Parliamentary Garrison from 1643 (not including Castle Cornet)

Lieutenant-Colonel Robert Russell	Lieutenant Walter Rendall	
Captain Henry Fabian	Benjamin Temple	Ensign Francis Fabian
Captain Thomas Howell		Ensign Thomas Howell (jnr)

Commonwealth Garrison from 1651

Governor
Commissary of Provisions
Surgeon's Mate
Gunsmith

Five companies of foot, each 100 soldiers besides officers
Those of Lieutenant-Colonel Arthur Helsham, Captain Samuel Clark and Symcock known to served in Guernsey; those of Harrison and Lacey went to Ireland; Coxe's and John Clarke's went to Weymouth.

Garrison Company from 1652

Lieutenant-Colonel Barrett Lacey
Ensign Nicholas Roberts
Captain Waterlouise, named as Lieutenant-Governor of Guernsey under the Protector, 1649.[15]

Others mentioned in various sources in Guernsey 1652–1659:
    Captain __ Sharpe
    Lieutenant Charles Waterhouse (probably the 'Waterlouise' named above)
    Lieutenant Richard Wyne
    Ensign Nicholas Roberts
    Ensign Thomas Cromwell

Chaplain Increase Mather*
Surgeon and Commissary Samuel Bradshaw.

The Restoration Garrison

August 1662: Captain Robert Walters' company of Lord Wentworth's Regiment of Guards, from Dunkirk. Temporary detachment until the arrival of the garrison company: Captain Sir Hugh Pollard (governor), Lieutenant Nathaniel Darell, Ensign Charles Waterhouse.

SARK

John Le Gros appointed to command the militia by Waterlouise, 1649.[16]
Company of Foot detached from the Guernsey Garrison in 1643 under Lt Nicholas Ling

ALDERNEY

In 1647, Captain Pierre le Febure was sent from Guernsey by Parliament to take control of the island militia and expel all Catholics.

NOTES
1. TNA CSPD 25 April 1656.
2. From Ingoldsby's Regiment. TNA, CSPD 25 April 1656.
3. TNA SP 25/97, f. 86.
4. F.J. Ellis, *Société Jersiaise*, 1937.
5. F.J. Ellis, *Société Jersiaise*, 1967.
6. Norman Rybot, 'The History of St Aubin's Fort', in *Annual Bulletin of the Société Jersiaise* (1948).
7. Jason Nicolle, 'The Population of Jersey in the 17th and 18th Centuries', in *Annual Bulletin of the Société Jersiaise* (1991).
8. Blanche B. Elliott, *Jersey, An Island of Romance* (St Helier, 1923), Chapter XIV.
9. Philip Falle.
10. TNA, SP 25/97 f. 86, Letter Book 1651.
11. Thurloe vol. ii, 9 March 1654.
12. Thurloe vol. ii, 13 March 1655.
13. TNA. SP 25/66 f.284 (Council of State Order Book).
14. Commons Journal, 1656.
15. Saunders, *Jersey in the 17th Century* (Jersey: Bigwood, 1931).
16. *Mercurius Politicus*, 25 March to 1 April 1652..
17. J. Bertrand Payne, *Armorial of Jersey*.
18. J. Bertrand Payne, *Armorial of Jersey*.

---

* Increase Mather (1639–1723) was a Puritan minister and an important figure in the early history of Massachusetts. He was chaplain in the Channel Islands from 1659 to 1661 and went to America following the Restoration. There he became involved in the administration of Harvard University and in the politics of the Massachusetts Bay colony. In 1687 or 1699 he travelled to London to petition the King on the revocation of the colony's charter. He later also became involved with the infamous Salem witch trials.

Appendix IV to Chapter 3

Royalist and Commonwealth Forces in the Isles of Scilly

The Commonwealth Invasion Force, 1646

Sir George Ayscue, governor September 1646–1647 with his flotilla of ships as listed

The Commonwealth Garrison, 1647–1648

Colonel Anthony Buller, governor 1647–1648

Colonel Richard Fortescue's Regiment (part) from Pendennis (four companies)
Lieutenant-Colonel Ralph Cobbett
Fortescue's company (under the Captain-Lieutenant)
Major John Jennings
Captain William Farley

The Royalist Invasion Force and Garrison, 1648–1651

Admiral Sir John Mucknell, Governor 1648–1649
Sir John Grenville, Governor 1649–1651

300 Irish soldiers, 120 English and approximately 100 reformadoes formed into five companies with two companies and gunners in King's Castle, Tresco and the remainder at St Mary's

The Commonwealth Invasion Force, 1651

Lieutenant-Colonel John Clarke
Lieutenant-Colonel Richard Bowden

APPENDIX IV TO CHAPTER 3

Sir Hardress Waller's Regiment of Foot (5 companies under Clarke) (see Appendix III)

James Heane's Regiment of Foot (5 companies) (see Appendix III)

Robert Bennett's Regiment of Foot (5 companies)
Bennett was Governor of St Michael's Mount and St Mawe's Castle in Cornwall and detached companies to the Scillies from there. His regiment was composed as follows:

Colonel Robert Bennett	Lieutenant-Colonel William Hinder
Captain-Lieutenant Richard Gerry	Lieutenant William Rawlings
Ensign Henry Squire	Ensign Edmund Croft
Major __	Captain Samuel Kekewick
Lieutenant Hannibal Simian	Lieutenant Ferdinando Wallis
Ensign Richard Silkwood	Ensign Richard Hammitt
Captain Francis Vivian	Captain Digory Cloake
Lieutenant Philip Coombes	Lieutenant Francis Terrafusis
Ensign Mathew Vivian	Ensign Richard Porter
Captain William Keade	Captain Francis Langdon
Lieutenat John Randall	Lieutenant William Rieble
Ensign __ Hambly	Ensign __ Radolf
Captain Christopher Hewer	Captain William Parker
Lieutenant __ Flaminoke	Lieutenant Symon Slope
	Ensign John Williams

The Commonwealth Garrison, 19 June 1651–1660

Lieutenant-Colonel Joseph Hunkin as Governor

Staff
Commissary of Stores Francis Barnes
Surgeon Symon Paynter
Chaplain
Marshal Ezekias Barry
Master Gunner
Two gunners and four mates
20 matrosses

Five companies each 120 men from Robert Bennett's Regiment of Foot (as above)

COLONIAL IRONSIDES

The Royalist Garrison, Post 1660

Sir Francis Godolphin as governor
The companies of captains Ashton and Wise of the King's Guards were designated to serve at Pendennis and in Scilly but neither appears to have reached the islands.

Three garrison companies:

Sir Francis Goldolphin	Captain Francis Godolphin[*]	Captain Arthur Bassett[†]
Lieutenant Henry Noye	Lieutenant William Painter	Lieutenant John Bluet
Ensign John Crudge	Ensign John Allen	Ensign John Reskymer

---

[*] Son of Sir William Godolphin and cousin of the Governor.
[†] Afterwards a captain in Tangier.

4

The Expedition to Subdue the West Indies, 1651–1652

After the surrender of the Royalist enclaves close to home, the attention of the republican government in London turned towards the New World, for here, in spite of distance, the rivalries of the Old World were being played out. The first acts in this drama were enacted in the Caribbean, or West Indies. Here, European colonisers had exploited the production, refining and export of sugar, along with its by-products of rum and molasses, to great financial benefit. In the early years, the mainstay of the colonial economy in the Caribbean had been the growth and export of tobacco, but tobacco prices fell from the 1630s as Chesapeake production expanded. The introduction of sugar cane from Dutch Brazil completely transformed society and the economy.[1] From about 1625, the Dutch carried sugar cane from the territories they had conquered from the Portuguese in South America to the West Indies, where it was grown from the Barbadoes to the Virgin Islands. Contemporary sources compared the worth of sugar to other valuable commodities like musk, pearls and spices. Production grew everywhere in the eastern parts of the Americas but the Caribbean rapidly became the largest area of production in the world, with the lowest prices.

From 1640, the West Indies attracted over two-thirds of English emigrants to the New World. By 1650, there were 44,000 English settlers there, compared with 12,000 in the Chesapeake Bay area and 23,000 in New England. Most of these emigrants were indentured servants who, after five years as effectively white slaves were given freedom dues of about £10, usually in goods. Until about 1635, they were also given a land grant, but this ceased when land ran out. During the Commonwealth and Protectorate, a number of English, Irish and Scots Royalists were also transported to the West Indies as convicts or were sent as exiles. Some of these, like Guy Molesworth, Christopher Codrington and Humphrey Walrond, were experienced soldiers who refused to compound with the Commonwealth.

The scourge of life here was disease. Malaria and yellowjack were an ever-present scourge, the result of humidity, warmth, bad drainage and abysmal sanitation, and they killed men and women by the thousand. Parish registers

COLONIAL IRONSIDES

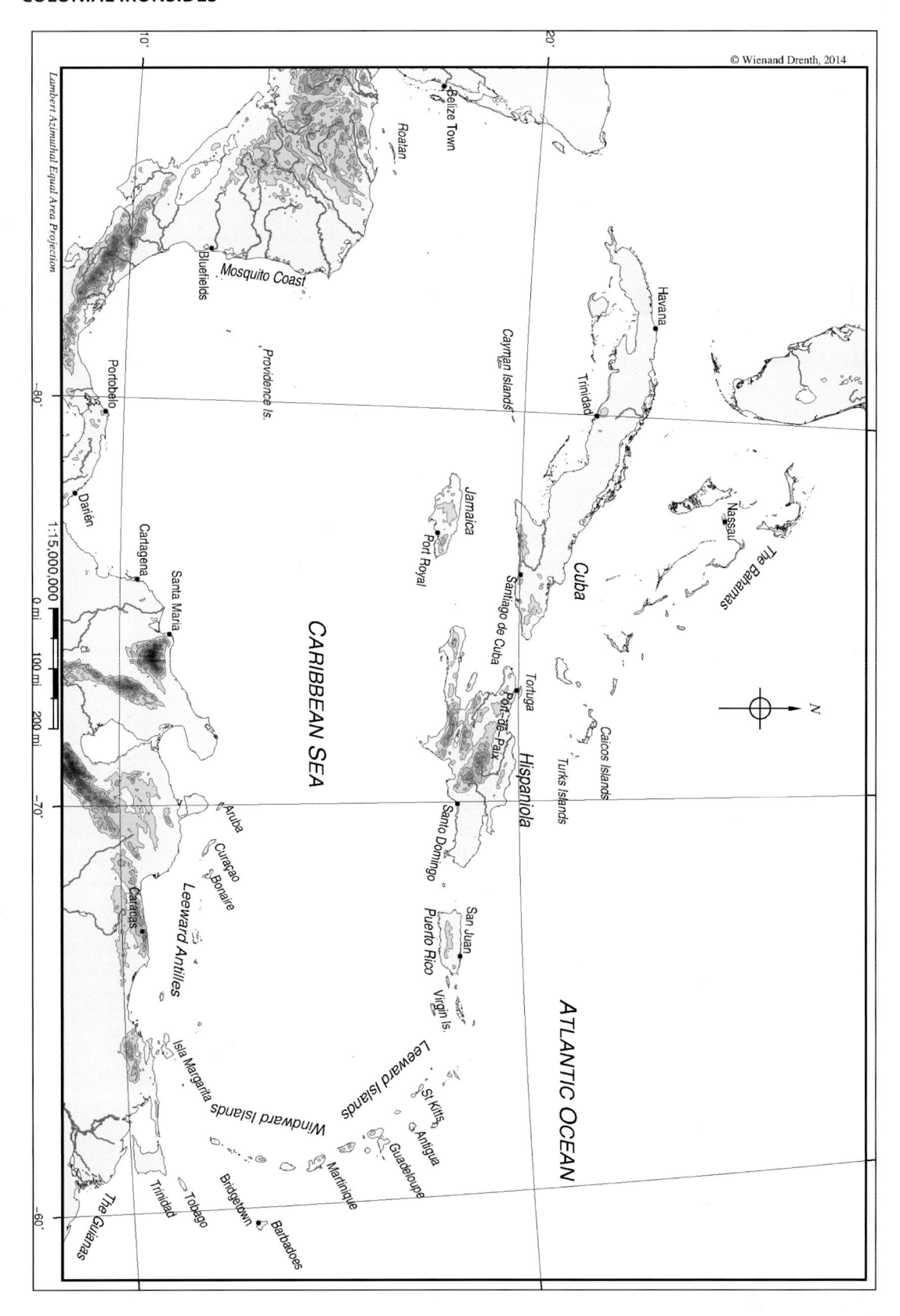

THE EXPEDITION TO SUBDUE THE WEST INDIES, 1651–1652

in the Barbadoes from the 1650s, for example, show four times as many deaths as marriages.

The most significant of the West Indian colonies at the time of the defeat of Charles I and the ascent of the Commonwealth was the island of Barbados, or the Barbadoes as it was then known. Barbados lies off the north–east coast of what is now Venezuela, at only 13 degrees north of the equator. Its climate is tropical, with a steady temperature of about 27 degrees centigrade all year with over 70 percent humidity. Its wet season is from June to October. Its climate was therefore tolerable for Europeans, but malaria and yellow fever were prevalent there as elsewhere in the Caribbean.

Although Spanish and Portuguese sailors had likely visited the Barbadoes, the first English claim on the Barbadoes dates from 1625, although an earlier claim may have been made in 1620. James Hay, 1st Earl of Carlisle, was a director of the Virginia Company and a patentee and councillor of the plantation of New England. Carlisle also had an interest in the Caribbean. On 2 July 1627 Carlisle obtained from the King a grant of all the Caribbean Islands, including the Barbadoes, confirming a concession already given by James I. A colonial plantation venture in Barbados, as a proprietary colony, was led in 1628 by Marmaduke Roydon, a prominent City of London merchant and one of Carlisle's major creditors, funded by Sir William Courten, a City of London merchant. Courten later lost his share of the title to Carlisle, in what was called 'the Great Barbados Robbery'. The Barbadoes quickly grew to become the third major English settlement in the Americas after Massachusetts and Bermuda due to its prime eastern location. The first colonists were actually tenants and much of the profits of their labour returned to Courten and his company. By 1650, the population of the Barbadoes was estimated at 30,000, of whom about 800 were Africans and the remainder mainly planters and their indentured servants of English descent, and Scots Royalists transported by the Commonwealth.

Under the Carlisle proprietorship, the Barbadoes and the other Leeward Islands, so called because the prevailing trades, blowing from the north–east to the south–west, did not bring ships immediately to their shores, were grouped together. The English colonies in the Leewards at this point also included Antigua, St Christopher, a colony since 1628, Nevis and Montserrat, both established in 1632.[2] St Christopher had originally been an independent colony, the first to be established by the English in the Leeward Islands in 1625, before the settlement of the Barbadoes, and as a result it had been attacked and all but destroyed by the Spanish. Thereafter, Sir Thomas Warner had been Governor until 1649, during which time he had had to put down an internal rebellion on the island brought about by commercial rivalries, with the aid of the French. A colony on Providence Island, established by Puritans, became a haven for privateers attacking Spanish trade until it was destroyed by the Spanish.

Perhaps inevitably, the effects of the Civil Wars and the Interregnum in the Three Kingdoms spilled over into the royal colony of the Barbadoes, although the island was not directly involved in the war until after the execution of Charles I. At this point, the island's government fell under the control of

Facing page: English, French and Spanish colonies in the Caribbean. (Wienand Drenth)

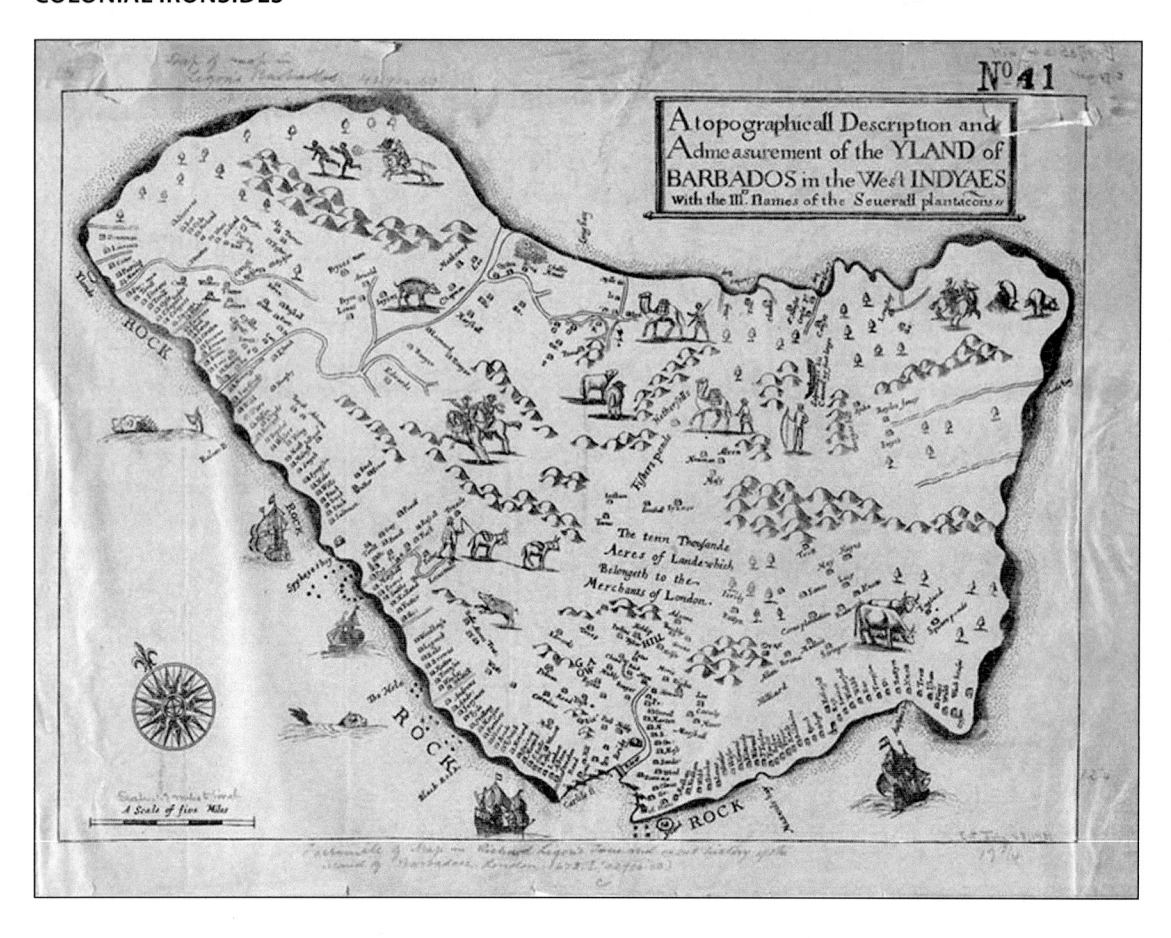

The Barbadoes. (Wienand Drenth)

royalists. The governor, Philip Bell,* sided with the Parliament, while the Barbadian House of Assembly generally supported Charles II. Factions slowly formed on the same lines as in England. Bell himself maintained neutrality and therefore the Commonwealth faction took the local notable, Colonel James Draxe,† as its leader and among the principal men with him, who held positions in the island's militia, were Colonel John FitzJames, Major William Fortescue, Captains Richard Alleyne and Thomas Middleton, and Lieutenants Thomas Rous and John Johnson.[3] The Royalists were led by two brothers, Humphrey and Edward Walrond, and as Parliament's cause prospered in England, so the Walronds moved to secure the Barbadoes for the King. Draxe and his supporters were strong enough to prevent a proposed alliance with the Bermudas which, after the execution of Charles I, declared for his son, but Edward Walrond engineered a bill in the Assembly requiring an oath of allegiance by all citizens to Charles II.

---

* Philip Bell (1590–1678) was Governor of Bermuda, or the Somers Islands, from 1626 to 1629, of the Providence Island Colony from 1629 to 1636, and the Barbadoes from 1640 to 1650 During his terms of office in Providence and Barbados, the colonies moved from using indentured English servants to black slaves imported from West Africa.

† Sir James Draxe, or Drax (*c.* 1609–1662) was a plantation owner who accumulated huge wealth as a pioneer of the sugar trade and was one of the first to use imported slave labour from Africa.

THE EXPEDITION TO SUBDUE THE WEST INDIES, 1651–1652

The island's militia had been reorganised during the 1640s into two regiments of horse and four of foot, with regular training, and thus the Royalists were able to arm themselves rapidly. On 19 April 1650, Governor Bell issued a demand for disarmament but this came too late: the Walronds embodied the militia regiments of Colonels Henry Shelley and Edmund Reade, at which point Bell turned to Draxe and asked him to raise troops. Draxe was, however, only able to find 20 horse and about 100 foot: the result was total Royalist control of the government, the magazine and the arsenal, and a declaration of loyalty to Charles II. Draxe and his associates were all declared disturbers of the peace, delinquents, and were severely fined for their allegiance to the Parliament.[4]

At the end of 1650, Charles II appointed Francis, Lord Willoughby,* as Governor. However, at the same time, news of the state of the island, and of St Christopher, Nevis and Antigua, reached London, brought by Colonel James Draxe and Captain Reynold Alleyne who had fled the colony. To try to bring the colonies to heel, the Commonwealth Parliament revoked their royal charters and passed the Non–Intercourse Act on 3 October 1650, which prohibited trade between England and the island, and because the island also traded with the Netherlands, Navigation Acts were passed forbidding any but English vessels from trading with Dutch colonies. These acts were a direct cause of the First Anglo–Dutch War.

In the January 1651, a fleet of seven ships was sent to subdue the Barbadoes, under the command of Sir George Ayscue;† the fleet did not sail from Plymouth until 5 August however, having been diverted first to support Blake's subjugation of the Scilly Isles (see Chapter 3). Ayscue carried a commission appointing him as the Commonwealth's Governor, his squadron now augmented by six merchant vessels.[5] Powder and other stores had been completed in July.[6] Troops were again embarked under Clarke; whether these were the same men as had undertaken operations in the Scillies is uncertain. The troops for the Barbadoes seem to have been in nine companies, five of which were once more drawn from what had been Hardress Waller's New Model Regiment of Foot, which had raised more men to complete its 12 companies for the attack on Jersey. The rest may have come from Ingoldsby's Regiment, which was moved to London after the Battle of Worcester, frequently tasked with finding men for sea service, supplemented by recruits and men from other regiments in the west country to make up

Francis, Lord Willoughby, Governor of the Barbadoes. (Wienand Drenth)

---

* Francis Willoughby, 5th Baron Willoughby of Parham (*c*.1614–1666) was twice governor of the Barbadoes, the second time after the Restoration of Charles II.

† There is a list of the initial seven ships under Ayscue, later increased to 13, in the appendices to Chapter 3.

the numbers.[7] A declaration made by Cromwell and the Council of State on 11 June 1651 states that a garrison of 1,200 men will be forced on the island.[8] The fleet sailed first for Lisbon and then to Cape Verde for water, where a large number of valuable Dutch merchant ships were seized as prizes. Ayscue arrived off the Barbadoes on 26 October 1651.

By now, Lord Willoughby could field around 5,000 horse and foot from the militia and had fortified the major landing places on the island. Ayscue immediately forced a passage into what was then the chief harbour in Speight's Bay and there took another 12 Dutch merchantmen as prizes. Ayscue reported in a letter home that he:

> has not lost one man by sickness. Made the island of Barbadoes overnight, and the next morning surprised in the bay 15 sail, most of them Dutch. Went within half musket shot of the chief fort; very free with their shot, which was as readily answered; but one man slain in all the fleet. They are in a confused trouble manning the prizes.[9]

Next morning, 27 October 1651, he sent a summons to Lord Willoughby, requiring him to submit to the authority of Parliament. Willoughby answered, boldly, that he knew no such authority, that he had a commission from King Charles II and that he would keep the island for His Majesty's service at the hazard of his life. On receiving this rebuff, Ayscue decided not to risk a landing immediately as this would show the relative weakness of his troops in terms of numbers. He did, however, receive word of the defeat of Charles II and the Scots at Worcester, which considerably strengthened his hand. He therefore summoned Willoughby a second time, sending with his summons a copy of an intercepted letter from Lady Willoughby containing an account of the Battle of Worcester. In spite of this, Willoughby continued to hold firm.

In December, a squadron of 15 ships under Captain Robert Dennis arrived.[10] These ships were bound for Virginia, to subdue the Royalists there, but Ayscue presented their arrival as a reinforcement. In addition to Clarke's Regiment, Ayscue put together a second body composed of 400 seamen drawn from the two squadrons and 159 Scots who had been captured at the Battle of Worcester and were bound for the colonies as indentured servants. This provisional regiment was placed under the command of Francis Allen. Allen was Major of Ingoldsby's Regiment, indicating that at least some of the troops embarked were from that corps.[11] Ayscue, pondering how best to bring about the submission of the island, decided on a series of amphibious raids using ships' boats. On the night of 22 November, the first of these was launched when 200 seamen and soldiers under the command of Captain Lewis Morris,* who had led the assault on Tresco during Blake's campaign in the Scilly Isles, came ashore in a surprise attack on the Royalist fort at Holetown. The fort was overrun, its guns spiked and 30 prisoners taken. The Commonwealth landing party got away without loss.

---

* Morris appears to have remained on the island as a planter as he later helped raise D'Oyley's Regiment for service in Hispaniola (see Chapter 7).

THE EXPEDITION TO SUBDUE THE WEST INDIES, 1651–1652

Another body of troops was landed on 17 December and this time found the Royalists well entrenched in a fort at Speightstown, which held around 1,200 men and four troops of horse under Colonel Gibbes: they were well aware of the impending attack. The Royalists, issuing from their fort, advanced against the landing force. After a brief struggle on the beach, the Royalists fled, abandoning the fort, believing the Commonwealth force to be stronger than it was – not surprisingly, given that most of Clarke's men were experienced redcoats from the New Model against whom an untried militia force was unlikely to stand. Around 30 Royalists were killed and 80 taken prisoner, including Lieutenant-Colonel William Bayley. The Commonwealth troops suffered around 60 casualties, including Allen who was killed during the landing, Major Andrewes and Captain Morris. The seamen and Scots could not be persuaded to remain ashore and so rather than tie down regular troops in a garrison, the redcoats razed the fort and took away four heavy guns, 500 stand of arms and the colours of the fort.

In spite of his success in raiding, Ayscue did not have enough troops to invade and subdue the island. He therefore tried subversion, treating Royalist prisoners well, informing them of the situation in England and then releasing them. Two were hanged by Willoughby for spreading sedition. Ayscue also established contact with Colonel Thomas Modyford,[*] who commanded the Windward Regiment, and who was thought to be lukewarm in his support for Willoughby and the Royalist cause. A meeting was arranged with Captain Michael Pack, Ayscue's vice-admiral; after several such meetings, Modyford agreed to press Willoughby and his Council for a treaty of submission. Modyford laid these proposals before Willoughby who as a result himself opened talks with Ayscue; but Willoughby came to the view that Ayscue's forces were not strong enough to compel him to surrender and he broke off negotiations. It was expected that Modyford would now declare for the Commonwealth; but on 31 December, Modyford's contacts with Pack were betrayed by a deserter and Modyford was denounced as a traitor.[12] Discovery forced Modyford's hand. On 3 January 1652, he brought 500 of his own regiment and 120 horse to relieve the main guard, whereupon he made a speech urging acceptance of the Commonwealth. Before long, he could count on around 2,000 foot and 120 horse; Ayscue himself went ashore to address them at their headquarters and camp, Austin's Fort in the bay of the same name. However, it was found that Willoughby had drawn up a force of 2,000 foot and 400 horse only 400 yards from the Windward Regiment's encampment.

Willoughby called a council of war, taking the line that the Royalists should attack with their strongest arm, their horse; but as the council was sitting, a cannonball from the fleet crashed through the door of the room, taking off the head of the sentinel posted in front of it. This had a marked effect as the Royalists abandoned their plan of attack – which would have brought them under the fire of the guns of the fleet – and withdrew about two miles inland,

---

[*] Colonel Sir Thomas Modyford, 1st Baronet (*c.* 1620–1679) was later Governor of Jamaica from 1664 to 1670.

leaving picquets on all the routes leading from the shore. Ayscue immediately ordered all his land forces on shore, as if preparing an assault.

At this point, heavy rain began and continued until 9 January, so that slow match could not be kept alight and powder could not be kept dry. Once the rain had ceased, another attempt was made to persuade Willoughby to give in, but he would have none of it.[13] This was but a brief defiance, however, for clearly most of the Royalists had lost their nerve. A trumpeter arrived at the Windward Regiment's camp with a message agreeing to negotiations and appointing Sir Richard Pearce, Colonel Thomas Ellice, Major William Byam and Mr Charles Pym as commissioners for Lord Willoughby. Ayscue already had nominated commissioners for the Commonwealth in the shape of Captain Michael Pack, Mr Daniel Searle and Colonels John Colleton and Thomas Modyford – the latter two being Barbadians.

On 17 January, articles of rendition were agreed, which were generous. Lord Willoughby was granted indemnity and the possession of his estates, as were all the other leading Barbadians in return for submission to the authority of the Commonwealth; the conditions of surrender were incorporated into the Charter of Barbados under the Treaty of Oistins. Willoughby soon after returned to England. Ayscue's men took possession of the major fortifications, including the castle of St Phillip's; some 70 pieces of ordnance of all calibres, 900 barrels of powder and 4,500 muskets, carbines and pistols. The islands of Nevis, Antigua and St Christopher were also included in the surrender; no fighting took place on any of these islands. Ayscue, his commission completed, returned to England with 36 prizes, representing a huge sum in prize money and leaving Daniel Searle as the Commonwealth Governor. The fleet arrived in Plymouth on 25 May 1652, discharging the troops, who rejoined their regiments.

Appendix to Chapter 4

Military Forces in the Barbadoes, 1651–1652

Island Militia

Lieutenant-General Francis, Lord Willoughby
Commissary-General John Parrault

Colonel Henry Shelley's Regiment of Foot Lieutenant-Colonel __ Guy Major William Byam[*] Captain __ Jarmin Captain __ Boucher Captain __ Usher	Colonel Humphrey Walrond's Regiment of Foot	Colonel Thomas Modyford (the Windward Regiment; changed sides to the Commonwealth) Lieut-Colonel William Birch Captain Robert Hooper
Colonel __ Ellis's Regiment of Foot	Colonel Gibbes's Regiment of Horse	Colonel Edmund Reade's Regiment of Horse

Commonwealth Forces

Lieutenant Colonel John Clarke's Regiment (9 companies drawn from Sir Hardress Waller's, Ingoldsby's and other regiments in the West Country)

Lieutenant-Colonel John Clarke
Major __ Andrewes

Provisional Regiment (400 seamen from the fleet, 159 Scots prisoners)
Lieutenant-Colonel Francis Allen
Captain Lewis Morris

Known Commonwealth adherents who had been named as 'Disturbers of the Peace' under the Walronds:
Colonel John Fitz James

---

[*] Byam was banished until 1653 and went to the newly founded colony of Surinam.

COLONIAL IRONSIDES

Lieutenant-Colonel James Draxe[*]
Major William Fortescue
Captain Henry Ferris
Captain Richard (or Reynold) Alleyne
Captain Thomas Middleton
Captain George Briggs
Captain David Bix
Captain John Hockerdige
Captain Peter Edney
Lieutenant Thomas Rous
Lieutenant John Johnson

---

[*] Draxe and Alleyne had returned to England and came back to the Barbadoes on Ayscue's ships.

5

The Expedition to New Amsterdam, Saint John and Port Royal, 1654

Although the focus of Cromwell's Western Design was Spain, the first expeditionary operations in the New World were not directed against the Spanish at all, but against first the Dutch and later the French – ironic, since the Dutch were Cromwell's co-religionists and opponents of Catholic Spain; and the French would become his major allies on the continent of Europe.

By the time of the formation of the Protectorate, English colonies were well established in North America: Virginia became a Royal Colony in 1624; while proprietary colonies had been established in Maryland and Carolina (which included the island of Bermuda); and in the various enclaves that formed New England: Massachusetts Bay, Plymouth, Connecticut, New Haven, and Rhode Island. Settlements were also established on Long Island (later New York) and further north in Newfoundland. In the Caribbean, English colonies had been established as described in earlier chapters. Finally, there was a foothold on the coast of South America, at Surinam.

The Dutch had first established colonies in what is now New York State as early as 1614 at Fort Nassau (later Albany); and at Fort Orange (later Beverswyck) in 1652. However, the major centre of New Netherland was New Amsterdam, at the tip of Manhattan Island. Construction had begun in 1625 and settlers from elsewhere were moved here. The following year, Peter Minuit, the Director, or Governor, of New Netherland negotiated the purchase of Manhattan Island from the Lenape people for 60 guilders worth of trade goods – a sum in keeping with what Europeans paid each other for land in the same region.[1] During the Anglo–Dutch War, construction of an inland fortification was undertaken by Peter Stuyvesant,* the then governor, but this was never put to the test.[2]

---

* Peter Stuyvesant (1611 or 1612–1675) was Dutch director-general of New Netherland from 1647 until it was ceded to England in 1664, after which it was renamed New York. He was a major figure in the early history of New York City, was highly influential in its politics, religion,

COLONIAL IRONSIDES

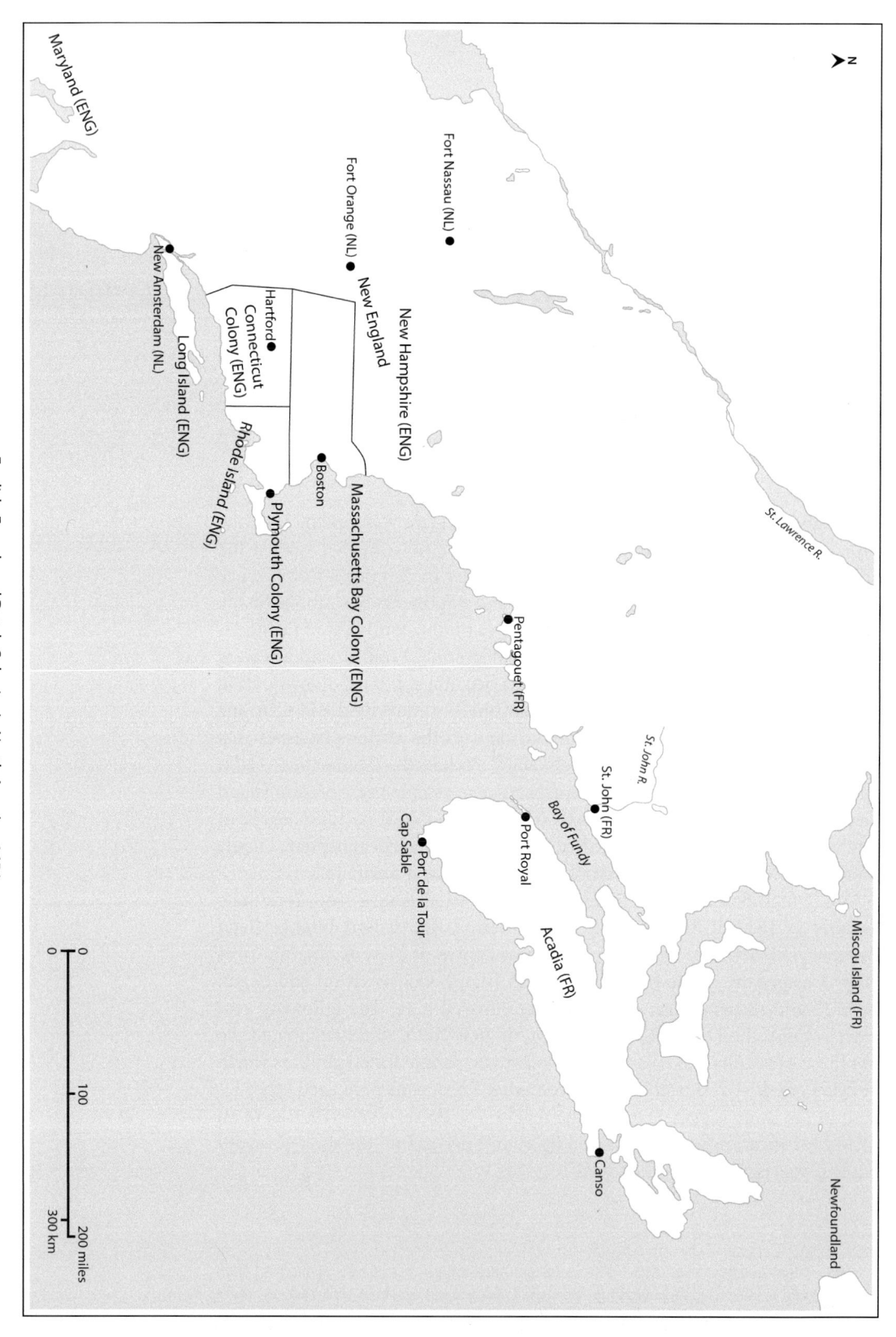

English, French and Dutch Colonies in North America, 1654.

THE EXPEDITION TO NEW AMSTERDAM, SAINT JOHN AND PORT ROYAL, 1654

In 1652 the first Anglo–Dutch War broke out (see Chapters 1 and 2). Its complex causes and course in Europe and the Mediterranean are not relevant here. Suffice to say that although the war was prosecuted by both sides at sea, Cromwell determined to strike a blow at the Dutch in North America, in an area that England also claimed, based on the exploration of John Cabot. The Treaty of Hartford in 1650 had demarcated colonial boundaries in the region, but the agreement was never ratified in London.

When news of the war reached them, the English colonists in New Haven, Plymouth, Connecticut and Massachusetts Bay, who were highly apprehensive of the Dutch as well as the French and the native people, made approaches to Cromwell both for approval to attack New Amsterdam and for the means to mount such an attack. Governor William Hooke sent a letter to Cromwell by the hand of Captain Ashwood which was received after Hooke's death, in December 1653, in which he complained that Massachusetts was not fully committed to action, but others were, and he set out the position:

> … our cure is desperate if the Dutch be not removed, who lie close upon our frontier westward (as the French do on the east) interdicting the enlargement of our borders … our danger also from the natives is greate, to whom these ill neighbours have traded … multitudes of guns with powder, shott and weapons … [3]

Hooke went on to ask for two or three frigates to protect the coasts and also that Cromwell compel Massachusetts to join in any operations against the Dutch, French and native people.

In London at this time was Robert Sedgwick, although it is not clear if Sedgwick had been sent in pursuit of the Colonies' demands to Cromwell or was caught up in the business while there. Sedgwick was a Puritan who had left England for Massachusetts in 1636.[4] Here he held several political offices, and, having served in the London Train Bands, helped form and train the Massachusetts Militia as captain of the Charles Town company in 1637. He became Major-General of the colony in 1652.[5] His commission from Cromwell to go to the aid of the North American colonies was originally dated 17 February 1652,[6] but that of 8 February 1654[7] appointed him general of the fleet and commander-in-chief of all the New England coast with authority to wage war on the Dutch and the French – the latter in reprisal for the incursions of French privateers on English maritime trade, commissioned by Charles II in exile and by Prince Rupert.[8] 'Being come to the Manhattoes [Manhattan]', wrote Thurloe, who drafted the commissions:

> you shall, by surprise, open force, or otherwise, endeavour to take the place. You have power to give fair quarter in case it be rendered upon summons without opposition. If the Lord give his blessing, you shall not use cruelty to the inhabitants, but encourage those who are willing to remain under the English government, and give liberty to others to transport themselves to Europe.[9]

---

and relations with the native people and other Colonial powers. Today, many landmarks in the city are still named after him.

Cromwell provided a force of four ships, the *Black Raven*, a 38-gun ship that had been captured from the Dutch; the 34-gun *Hope*; and two armed merchant ships as troop carriers, *Augustine* and *Church*. However, the small fleet was delayed by bad weather and on reaching Fayal it was decided to send the *Black Raven* home, as she was not fit to make the Atlantic crossing.[10] There was clearly some drunkenness and disorder on board this ship which was described by Sedgewick as: 'a bad ship and a wicked crew'.[11] In the ships was a body of 200 soldiers in two companies each of 100 men drawn from standing regiments in England.[12] The troops appear to have come chiefly from the Regiments of Ingoldsby and Goffe, each of which had been increased from 700 to 1,000 men the previous year,[13] although there may have been volunteers from other standing regiments in England. Sedgwick complained on 3 March that when embarking the troops: 'the soldiers came on board without arms, those had from the Tower must suffice…'[14] Ingoldsby's Regiment had been ordered to supply 500 men to the fleet for sea service in February 1653,[15] and another 270 in April;[16] as they had lost some men at sea while fighting the Dutch, the draft for service with Sedgwick probably represented what was left of the regiment, supplemented by those from Goffe's Regiment which had also sent men to the fleet.[17] There are no surviving lists of the officers, however some appear in other documents and others can be inferred. Captain Richard Salmon, who had served in Lambert's Regiment of Foot in 1649, signed the surrender document later at Port Royal. The Calendar of State Papers, Colonial Series, contains a list of petitions for arrears or relief by widows and families, of officers and men who served in the expeditions to America and the West Indies. Comparing the officers' names in that list with those known to have served in the West Indies, some other names from Sedgwick's expedition can be postulated.[18] These are first, Captain Edward Spry. It is possible he remained in America as another member of his family, William Spry (later a Lieutenant-General during the American Revolutionary War) purchased land in Nova Scotia and established the town of Spryfield. The others are Lieutenants Thomas Trafford Hugh Jones and Lieutenant Nathaniel Rockwell, who appears to have been a Leveller and may have been anxious to leave England,[19] interesting, given that Levellers had inspired Ingoldsby's Regiment, hitherto quiet, to join their revolt in September 1649.[20] In January 1655, Leverett wrote to Captain James Garrett arranging passage back to England for a group of 18 officers and men from Ingoldsby's and Goffe's Regiments 'who were with Major Sedgwick when he took St John', and for which £90 was paid at the rate of £5.00 per man.[21] Named on the list are Lieutenants John Whitlosse and James Hangley of Ingoldsby's, and Ensign Edward Hellny of Goffe's. These men were the first English regular troops to be sent to North America as a formed body, rather than through individual emigration.

Carrying Sedgwick and his troops, the small fleet arrived at Boston on 1 July 1654.[22] Here, assisted by his son-in-law Captain John Leverett, he began the task of assembling more troops for the expedition. Leverett had moved to Massachusetts with his parents in 1633. He joined the Ancient and Honorable Artillery Company in 1639 and continued as a member of it for 32 years. He commanded the 4th Boston militia company in 1652 and also held command, simultaneously, of the Suffolk Troop of Horse.[23] He became a freeman of Boston in 1640. Four years later he went to England, where he received a commission as a captain in the Parliamentarian regiment of Thomas Rainborowe: several other New Englanders also held commissions in this regiment, including Israel Stoughton of Dorchester, Massachusetts, who was the Lieutenant-Colonel; and Nehemiah Bourne, the major.[24] The connection may have come from Rainborowe's sister, Martha, who was married to John Winthrop, colonel of the Suffolk Regiment of Militia in Massachusetts and later governor. Leverett returned to Boston by 1648. In 1651 he was elected to the General Court and became one of the selectmen of the town of Boston.[25]

The additional troops for the expedition were to be raised in New England would be found from the militia, which was based on the Elizabethan militia model in England. It is widely believed that in Britain, there has only been conscription in the two world wars and for a period afterwards – but this is very far from the truth. For most of English history, the largest component of her military force on land has been the militia and the militia was always based on compulsory service. How this principle was put into practice overseas differed widely from colony to colony, but everywhere the militia had two coercive elements. First, it enrolled every able–bodied male between certain ages (usually 16 to 60), with few exemptions: it was unlike regular service therefore in that it was based on compulsion.[26] In England, the authority to call out the militia had rested with the Crown, which delegated it to the Lords Lieutenant and its employment was restricted to its own county. By 1654, control of the militia was firmly in the hands of the Protector and his Major-Generals. In the colonies, delegation of authority usually went to the governor although in many North American colonies, the issue of commissions and the control of the militia in peacetime were exercised by colonial assemblies which enacted militia laws.

Militiamen either bought their own arms, powder and shot, or were armed by their commanders. There is no evidence of the militia being provided with uniforms, although early in the period, armour was often provided. Some militiamen were often mobilised or even employed as locally enlisted regulars at times. It is important to emphasise that although not trained to the same standard as the regular forces, the militia was the largest military force in the Three Kingdoms and it is no surprise, therefore, that control of the militia by the Crown as opposed to Parliament had been one of the prime causes of the Civil Wars. This struggle for control played out in America, too. As well as finding their own arms and equipment, colonial governments required those enrolled to muster for regular training; failure to attend resulted in a fine.

The second coercive element was the mobilisation of the militia for active service on expeditionary operations, even though the militia had been raised for local defence. Only in emergency, and only for as short a period as possible, would a militia district deploy its whole available manpower, even at home. Normally, when a colonial government called out its militia, it would set quotas for each district. The districts would then try to fill the quotas with volunteers; or encourage volunteering by the offer of

COLONIAL IRONSIDES

New Amsterdam in the 1630s, a Dutch woodcut. (Wienand Drenth)

bounties. However, if insufficient volunteers were forthcoming, the districts would meet their quotas by draft. Generally, the only legal ways of avoiding such drafts were by either paying a fine or hiring a substitute. Colonial governments were not generally empowered to send drafted militiamen outside the colony and the conscript's term of service was usually limited to three months. Consequently, if colonial governments planned long military expeditions, they generally relied upon militia volunteers who contracted specifically for such expeditions. This explains why some colonies therefore established locally enlisted regular forces independent of the militia,[27] such as the Maryland Rangers or the Virginia Dragoons.

Colonial governments nonetheless made frequent recourse to militia drafts during the wars against the Dutch, the Spanish and native people. If necessary, they passed special legislation removing all restrictions on the militia draft, or they directly impressed men not on the militia rolls, but from the lowest levels of society – as was commonly done in Britain. In addition, the militia functioned as a police force. The New England colonies, for example, merged the militia with the night watch. Within this fundamentally coercive system, a volunteer component did emerge. Alongside the common militia was what came to be called the volunteer militia, consisting of privately recruited military units. The earliest such unit in North America was the Ancient and Honorable Artillery Company of Boston, organised in 1636 and still in existence.

Troops from the militia were to be raised under the New England colonies' unified defensive plan – the New England Confederation of 1643

– for they had placed their militias under this authority. The Confederation was primarily a military organisation for collective security which included of New Plymouth, Massachusetts, Connecticut and New Haven. This was essentially the same area as the later Dominion of New England. Delegates met in Boston and adopted a written constitution which formed 'The United Colonies of New England'. The confederation appointed, or approved the appointments of, officers and it designated an overall commander-in-chief as required.

Usually, Confederation troops were commanded of the most senior officer of the colony in which the troops were to be deployed.[28] When the council of the Confederation met to consider the matter of the expedition against the Dutch it was presented with Cromwell's instructions by Sedgwick:

> At a meeting held at Charles-Town, June the seventeenth, 1654. with Major [Major-General] Robert Sedgwicke, and Captain John Leverett, commissioned by his highness Oliver, protector of England, Scotland, and Ireland, as by his highness's letters, directed unto the general courts in the four colonies, may more fully appear, for the carrying on a design against the Dutch on Hudson's River, and at the Manhatoes.[29]

The council then began to consider 'what number of soldiers might be requisite, if God called the Collonies to make warr against the Dutch'. Major John Masson and Captain John Collett appeared on behalf of Connecticut, producing commissions dated 13 June 1654. Mr. William Leet, and Mr. Thomas Jordan appeared on behalf of New Haven and showed their commission dated 9 June 1654. Sedgwick noted that Plymouth had sent two unnamed agents and was ready to find troops, but the agents had no authority to conclude a formal arrangement and had returned, 'more fully to understand the mind of the general court, concerning what and how many persons they would furnish for the design.'[30]

The Council named John Leverett as captain-general of its forces, and approved a force not exceeding 500 men, subject to the agreement of each of the individual colonies: 300 from Massachusetts Bay (although it had originally hoped for 500), 200 from Connecticut under Captain Aaron Cooke;[31] and 133 from New Haven under Captain Robert Seeley. Plymouth's contribution was to be determined but was likely to be small; it was eventually 50 men under Captain Myles Standish.[32] All the contingents were to be assembled, equipped, victualled and ready to march for embarkation on 27 June. However, Massachusetts Bay refused to join a war against the Dutch, a position which had earlier caused the petition to Cromwell already mentioned, and this had to be resolved, for without its men and money, the rest of the Confederation could not operate. A large part of the problem was the principle of voluntary service away from home, discussed earlier. No government, it was argued, could force soldiers to serve beyond the boundaries of their own colony, and only rarely beyond their own region.[33] Militia districts filled their quotas by a combination of volunteers, draftees, substitutes and hirelings, with volunteering being the preferred method. To spur volunteering from among the men in the trainbands, governments usually offered volunteers a bounty.

Sedgwick reported on the raising of troops to Cromwell:

> As soone as wee arived, we imeditly sent your highnes letters to the severall governers of the New–English colloneys, and had a full concureinge from them all to assist against the Dutch, the Massachusetts only excepted, who so farr did concure as to give us libertye to your rasing of five hundred vollenters amongst them: the rest of the colloneys sent commissioners to joyne with us in consultation for the carring on the designe; so that in fourtene days wee had fitted and victualled our shipps, and soe farr in readines, as within six dayes after that, to have advanced with about nyne hundred foote, besides one troope of horse …[34]

Eventually Massachusetts agreed to provide 170 men under Captains William Hathorne, Richard More, Thomas Lathrop and Lieutenant Edward Raymond.[35] Hathorne was Captain of the Salem Militia; More had been one of the original passengers on the *Mayflower*; Lathrop and Raymond were also officers of the Salem Militia. With the concurrence of Massachusetts, it seemed on 20 June that, 'there appeared a competent number to the satisfaction of all the commissioners, being met at Boston, in further consultation about the manner of managing the design with all vigour and expedition.'[36]

However, that same day, a ship arrived from England carrying news that peace had been made between England and the Dutch Republic. Sedgwick had assembled a force and was now faced with the prospect of a humiliating climbdown. He took refuge in the permissions in his loosely worded commissions that he might also pursue the French: 'If tyme permit and opertunitye be presented, you are to proceed to the gaineing in any other places from the Enemie …' This accorded with the desires of the American colonists to remove at least one threat. Leverett therefore reported to the Protector that:

> The major Sedgwicke haveing received commission and instructions from the honorable generalls of the fleet and the comissioners of the admiralty, for the seizeing upon the shipps of any of the subjects of the French king; by vertue of which, and the other considerations afore–mentioned, major Robert Sedgwicke is this day set sail with a fair wind to the French coast, haveing the Augustine, Church, Hope, and a small catch …[37]

Leverett stayed awhile, with the task of completing the fitting out of the expedition, while Sedgwick went ahead to scout the coast. That Leverett did not accompany Sedgwick immediately is known from a letter by Leverett written in Boston on 8 September 1654.[38] He meanwhile arranged supplies and a cargo of masts to be taken back to England in due course by the ships as ballast.

Sedgwick's three ships embarked the two companies of English redcoats and 170 men from Massachusetts Bay, formed into three companies, and sailed from Nantasket for the Saint John River, in French Acadia, on 4 July.

THE EXPEDITION TO NEW AMSTERDAM, SAINT JOHN AND PORT ROYAL, 1654

Given the small numbers, the lack of a threat from cavalry and the likely nature of the fighting – siege warfare – it seems probable that this was an all-musketeer force with no pikemen. The Acadians were in a poor posture to resist an attack, having themselves been engaged in a civil war since 1634 and Sedgwick clearly meant to take advantage of this even though France and England were at peace. This civil war was fought between the two competing governors of the French province of Acadia. Governor Charles de Saint-Étienne de La Tour, a Protestant, had been granted one area of territory by King Louis XIV, and Charles de Menou d'Aulnay, a Catholic, had been granted another. However, the two territories were badly delineated and they overlapped. The dispute was intensified by personal enmity between the two governors. The centres of the two territories were Port Royal (present-day Annapolis Royal), where Aulnay had his seat; and Saint John, 45 miles away in present-day New Brunswick, which was held by La Tour.

In New England, the popular opinion was with La Tour since he was a Protestant, but also because he permitted free fishing and lumbering in and along the Bay of Fundy. D'Aulnay, by contrast, demanded payment for these concessions. When news came to La Tour that d'Aulnay was preparing attack on his fort and fur-trading operation at Saint John, La Tour went to Boston to ask Governor John Winthrop for help. Winthrop arranged for several merchants to advance loans to La Tour to pay for men and material to defend the Saint John River fort from d'Aulnay's attack.

In spite of this, d'Aulnay defeated La Tour at Saint John in 1645, unifying Acadia. From his capital of Port Royal d'Aulnay administered an area that included settlements or trading posts at La Have, Nova Scotia; Pentagouet (now Castine, Maine); Canso, Nova Scotia; Cap Sable (now Port De la Tour, Nova Scotia); the Saint John River (Bay of Fundy) and Miscou Island. He died in 1650, leaving the governorship of Acadia vacant, and prompting La Tour to return. He married d'Aulnay's widow in 1653.[39]

Another threat to La Tour emerged almost at once with the arrival of the trader Emmanuel Le Borgne, who claimed to be owed a large debt by d'Aulnay and who meant to saddle his widow with the debt. La Tour had spent the preceding months in France, where he had reached an agreement with the Duc de Vendôme. Under his patronage returned to Port Royal in 1654 in the ship *Châteaufort*, laden with 75,000 *livres* of merchandise, provisions and munitions, and carrying more than 100 men, to enforce the Duc's claim to Saint John and Saint-Pierre and establish himself as governor. Le Borgne tried and failed to capture the Saint John fort and La Tour before his operations were interrupted by the unexpected arrival of Sedgwick. Le Borgne departed on 13 July for Port Royal; Sedgwick arrived the following day. Le Borgne was later accused of favouring the New Englanders, since he refused to supply La Tour with needed provisions and munitions once the threat from the English became known, and of having maintained a treasonable correspondence with Sedgwick.[40]

Sedgwick, not surprisingly, took full advantage of the dispute between Le Borgne and La Tour. He at once laid siege to Saint John, a fortification with four bastions and a half-moon battery in front, whose garrison of 70 men and 19 guns was under La Tour's personal command. After a few

COLONIAL IRONSIDES

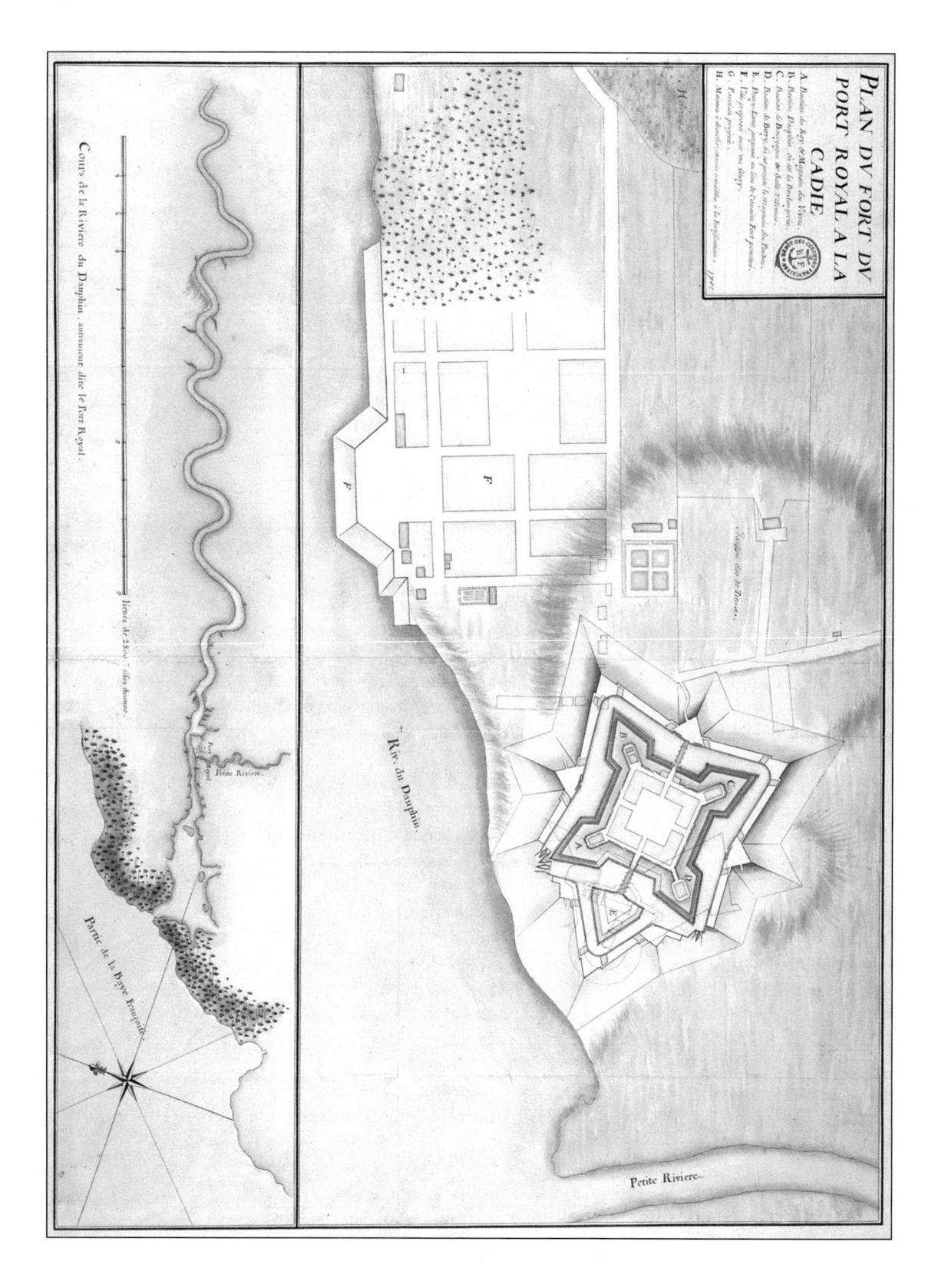

THE EXPEDITION TO NEW AMSTERDAM, SAINT JOHN AND PORT ROYAL, 1654

Port Royal in 1612. (Project Gutenburg)

Facing page: Arcadia. (Wienand Drenth)

days, with entrenchments in progress and guns disembarked from the ships, Sedgwick summoned the garrison to surrender in keeping with the practice of the time. Faced with the firepower of three ships and a force perhaps seven times his own in size (if the sailors from the ships are included), the French raised the white flag having made enough of a resistance for honour to be satisfied. Sedgwick plundered the fort, taking furs and skins which were later reckoned to be worth 200,000 *livres*, or £10,000 sterling (£1.7 million at today's prices).[41] Captain Mark Harrison of the ship *Church* sent a report on the capture of the fort on 21 July:

> it hath pleased the Lord to give into our hands from the French the fort commonly called St. John's Fort; in it were near ninety persons, about seventy men, nineteen pieces of ordnance, 16 'bases and murderers', with other arms enough for three times as many men, not much beaver, but a considerable quantity of skins. The terms upon which they surrendered were that they should be transported to France, have their clothes and single arms, forty days' victuals, and march out of the Fort with colours flying and match burning at both ends, and drum sticks. The Major intends with speed to go for Fort Royal, ten leagues from this place; it is a considerable place, but not so strong as is already taken.[42]

The garrison became prisoners and were embarked in the expedition's ships. Leaving a replacement garrison of 18 English regular troops from Ingoldsby's Regiment and an unknown number of Massachusetts Bay men

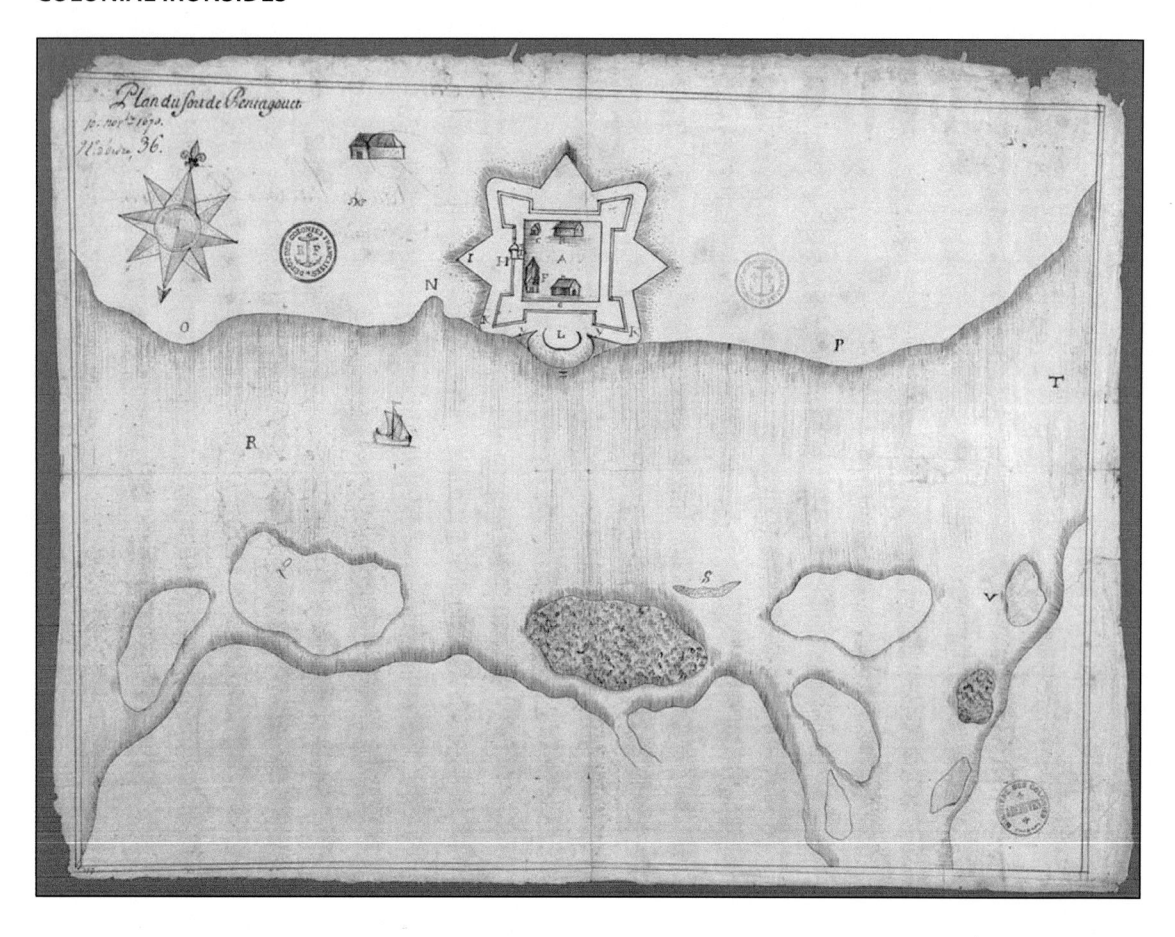

Fort de Pentagouet en 1670. (Archives Nationale d'Outre-Mer, France)

under their Captain, Hathorne, to hold Saint John,[43] Sedgwick sailed on to Port Royal, where he found Le Borgne. In a direct reference to the English redcoats, Harrison wrote to the Navy Commissioners, saying that:

> … in taking Fort Royal they lost one man outright, and 6 wounded, while marching up to the fort, by an ambush. They fired at our men before they saw them, but our Old England soldiers gave them no more time to load, but ran upon them and put them to the route, killed 5, wounded divers, and quite disheartened them from coming out of the fort any more although they had as many men as we.[44]

Le Borgne surrendered after a short siege on 8 August: he was treated with kid gloves, underlining the suspicions of him by other Acadians:

> … it hath pleased God to give us the fort commonly called Fort Royal, which they took the 8th inst. In it were 113 men, twenty-three great guns besides others, arms for 500 men, 50 barrels of powder, and shot proportionable, and a great quantity of provisions; also a ship of about 200 tons and 16 guns [the *Châteaufort*], partly laden with brandy, French wines, &c. The ship was given them to carry the Frenchmen taken in the fort to France, only the guns, powder, and shot were taken out. Are now at Penobscot, where the French have a small fort yet in their

possession, but expect it from them daily; it is a place of good trade with the Indians. Not any more French inhabiting this coast.[45]

On 2 September the isolated fort of Pentagouet was also captured; it had been held by the English until 1635 and indeed lay on the boundary between New England and the French territories. Sedgwick described as 'a small Fort, yet very strong and a very well composed peece with eight peece of Ordnance one brass, three murthers [mortars], about 18 barrels of powder, and eighteen men in garrison.' The commander, Captain La Verdure, was allowed to march out of the fort with his 'soldiers and domestics … with their arms, drums beating, flags displayed, fusil on shoulder…'[46] Archaeology at the fort has uncovered the remains of muskets and ammunition used by the garrison, but no swords or armour.[47] Having marched out with the honours of war, these French men and women went into captivity before being returned to France.

John Leverett was then appointed as Governor of Acadia, endorsed as such by Cromwell in a letter of 3 April 1655 as 'Commander of the Forts lately taken from the French' and was urged to use 'your utmost care and circumspection, as well to defend and keep the forts above said.' He continued to be regarded as commander until the forts were delivered up to Colonel Thomas Temple on 1 May 1657, although Leverett had been appointed colonial agent in England on 13 November 1655. Several of Leverett's petitions for compensation for his expenses as commander in Acadia were among the many presented to the Council of State during the years that followed; he complained in July 1655, for example, that he had spent £2,500 on provisions and pay for the English and Colonial troops.[48] Leverett was still petitioning for his expenses into the 1670s.[49]

From Pentagouet, Sedgwick returned to Boston, leaving redcoat garrisons in all the captured forts. Here, the General Court of Massachusetts ordered a thanksgiving on 20 September. From Boston, Sedgwick returned England, carrying La Tour, La Verdure and the other prisoners with him along with what remained of the 200 redcoats. Some of these men sailed with Captain James Garrett on the *Hopewell*.[50] In addition to the three officers already mentioned there were 15 soldiers named: unusual for this time when records of the names of private men appear only if they petitioned over a grievance, or were miscreants, or as in this case were embarked in ships. The men named in Ingoldsby's regiment were John Sims, William Hale, Nicholas Hicks, Ralph White, Richard Denis, jnr., Powell, Richard Davis, snr., William Pound, William Hughs, John Langford and Patrick Larry. From Goffe's, those named were Richard Howe, Thomas Smith and Patrick Smythe.[51]

Cromwell welcomed Sedgwick because possession of Acadia provided additional bargaining power in his negotiations with France (see Chapter 1). The Protectorate agreed to recognise La Tour's title to Nova Scotia, if he would undertake to reimburse Sedgwick for the cost of the expedition, nearly £1,800 (£300,000 at today's prices).[52] Much of this sum appears to have been the arrears of pay for the troops drafted from the Army in England.[53] This led La Tour to sell his rights to Sir Thomas Temple and Colonel William

Crowne, who became proprietors of Nova Scotia for the next 14 years until the territory was returned to France in 1667:

> Orders of the Council of State. Approving report upon petition of Mons. Delatour, concerning the forts of St. John, Port Royal, and Pentecost, in Acadia, and the lands purchased by him of the Indians, together with the country called Nova Scotia; representing their opinion that Delatour be permitted to enjoy the same, and the whole trade and traffic there, upon certain conditions, set forth in 13 articles, which being performed, a patent may be granted to Chas. St. Stephen, Lord Delatour, Thos. Temple, and Wm. Crowne, their heirs and assigns.[54]

Port Royal was recaptured by the English in 1690 but again returned to France; Acadia as a whole was finally subjected to permanent English rule in 1710. Sedgwick was made a commissioner of the expedition in Jamaica as a reward for his services and his story continues in Chapter 9 of this book.

Appendix to Chapter 5

Order of Battle for the Expedition to New Amsterdam, Saint John & Port Royal, 1654

Command

Major-General Robert Sedgwick
Lieutenant and Captain-General of the New England Forces, Captain John Leverett

English Troops

Two companies each of 100 men drawn from the Regiments of Ingoldsby and Goffe[1]
Captain Richard Salmon
Captain Edward Spry
Lieutenant Thomas Trafford Hugh Jones
Lieutenant Nathaniel Rockwell
Lieutenant John Whitelosse
Lieutenant James Hangley
Ensign Edward Hellny

Ships *Church, Hope* and *Augustine*: Captain Harrison

New England Troops

Massachusetts Bay
Two companies, total 170 men
Captain William Hathorne
Captain Richard More
Captain Thomas Lathrop
Lieutenant Edward Raymond

COLONIAL IRONSIDES

New Haven Company
133 men
Captain Robert Seeley
Lieutenant John Nash
Ensign Richard Baldwin

Connecticut Company
200 men
Captain Aaron Cooke
Lieutenant Thomas Bull
Ensign Thomas Wheeler

Plymouth Company
50 men
Captain Myles Standish
Lieutenant Matthew Fuller
Ensign Hezekiah Hoare

NOTES
1 TNA CSP Colonial Series 1574–1660, vol. cv, Interregnum Order Books, 16 December 1656 and 10 June 1658; TNA SP 29/61 f. 157 (State Papers online).

6

Virginia, Bermuda and Maryland During the Civil Wars and the Protectorate[1]

While attention in military matters in the Americas was largely focused on the expeditions to Acadia, Hispaniola and Jamaica during the middle years of the Protectorate, there was also turbulence on the mainland of North America. The various colonies had largely kept out of the Civil Wars in Britain even though their sympathies lay largely with the cause of Parliament and religious Puritanism. This they were able to so because of the nature of their governance. These colonies had been set up under Charters granted by the Crown, but which gave them self-government. Some colonies, like Pennsylvania and Massachusetts, were based on a strictly regulated Protestant way of life to live under which the inhabitants had forsaken the British Isles. Their sympathies, and their unwillingness to become embroiled in the affairs of the old world, is thus understandable.

When news of the execution of Charles I and the establishment of the Commonwealth reached the New World, six colonies – Antigua, St Christopher, Nevis, the Barbadoes, the Somers Islands (Bermuda) and Virginia – proclaimed Charles II as king and declared allegiance to the Stuart monarchy. In Virginia, laws were passed to restrict supporters of the Commonwealth – for the Governor, William Berkeley, was a firm supporter of the monarchy. Trade also played a part, as under the Commonwealth, trade goods could only be carried in English or colonial ships and this would badly affect Virginia's commerce with the Dutch. There were also fears that land grants would be revoked by the Commonwealth.[2]

The Commonwealth reacted in 1650 by placing an embargo on trade with the Royalist colonies in the Non-Intercourse Act of 19 September and revoking their royal charters. In the autumn of 1651, a fleet of 13 ships was sent to the Barbadoes under the command of Sir George Ayscue; while a fleet of 15 ships went to Virginia under Captain Robert Dennis.[3] No list of the ships survives but they included the *John*, *Guinea* frigate, *Gillyflower* and *Thomas*. The fleet sailed first for the Barbadoes where it paused on 8 December to reinforce the blockade of the colony established by Ayscue, who had been himself delayed when he was diverted to help subdue the Royalist garrison in the Scilly Isles. After a lengthy blockade and some fighting in the Barbadoes (see Chapter 4), surrender terms were agreed and Dennis's fleet then passed on to Virginia. Only four of the ships reached James City in January 1652, however: the rest sank having encountered severe storms in the Atlantic.

Commissioners were appointed to compel or negotiate the colony's submission; a summons was sent to Governor Berkeley on 19 January 1652. As well as Dennis, these were Richard Bennet, Thomas Stagg and Captain William Claiborne,[4] however both Dennis and Stagg were drowned when the *John* foundered. Edward Curtis, captain of the frigate *Guinea*, had been deputed by Parliament to act in Dennis's place should he die. The arrival of the fleet, and the expected advent of more ships and possibly troops, clearly alarmed the colonial council. News had also arrived of the defeat of Charles II and the Scots at Worcester, as had word of the submission of the Barbadoes, leaving Virginia as the only colony holding out for the King. Around 1,200 militia men had been embodied in James City and these were immediately sent home, as a token of goodwill.

After some negotiations, in which George Ludlow, a wealthy merchant, played the same role as that of Modyford in the Barbadoes, a surrender was agreed on 12 March 1652. The terms were generous: an indemnity was granted to all who had supported the King; free trade was permitted as an exception under the Navigation Act of 1651; and permission was granted to retain the Anglican Book of Common Prayer. Permission was also granted for Berkeley to travel to Charles II's court in exile to explain the capitulation. Thus, no fighting took place, no blood was shed and a show of force was all that was needed to bring Virginia to heel.[5]

The Bermudas were also brought to submission without violence. Originally a dependency of Virginia, the Bermudas are a group of over 300 islands, coral reefs and sandbanks, lying in the Atlantic Ocean 700 miles from Halifax, Nova Scotia and about the same distance from New York. They are often wrongly thought of as part of the West Indies when in fact they lie off the coast of North America, 800 miles north of the Caribbean. Because of their physical structure, the islands contain excellent anchorages with tortuous channels into the ocean, giving excellent security. Tobacco cultivation was tried early on but was not successful; thus, the main commerce and business of the islands was in servicing and victualling shipping plying between Europe and North America; and later in shipbuilding and ship repair.

The islands were named after the Spanish navigator Juan Bermudez who first sighted the islands in 1505. However, they were first colonised by the English under Sir George Somers, who was shipwrecked there in 1609 on his way to Virginia and for some years the name of the islands was changed to the Somers Islands. The first permanent settlers arrived in 1612, the islands having been included in the charter of the Virginia Company. By 1623 the inhabitants numbered between two and three thousand. Some black slaves were introduced early in the colony's history but as agriculture did not take root, white indentured servants remained the chief source of labour. Representative government was allowed to the colonists in 1620 by a charter

VIRGINIA, BERMUDA AND MARYLAND DURING THE CIVIL WARS AND THE PROTECTORATE

New England, New Netherlands, New France, Virginia and Maryland. (Wienand Drenth)

given to the Somers Islands Company by King James I in 1615, making it independent from Virginia.

By 1650, the Bermudas were already the most heavily fortified English colony in the Americas. Several of the islands strung across the south entrance of Castle Harbour were fortified in the early days of the territory. The first permanent town, St George's – then called New London – was placed on the north side of St George's Harbour. This harbour, too, was quickly fortified and garrisoned by a standing militia. King's Castle is, today, the oldest surviving English fortification in the New World. This is due primarily to the fortifications, as elsewhere in the islands, being constructed of stone, whereas contemporary English fortifications on the North American continent were generally built from timber and earth. In 1614, King's Castle, held throughout the period of the Commonwealth and Protectorate by Captain Wilkinson,[6] famously repulsed the Spanish attack on Bermuda. Other forts built at the south of Castle Harbour included Devonshire Redoubt (1620) and the Landward Fort on Castle Island; Southampton Fort (1620) on Brangman's Island (originally known as Moore's Island and Southampton Island), at the east side of Castle Roads; Old Castle, or Charles' Fort (1615), on Goat Island; Pembroke Fort on Cooper's Island; and Fort Bruere, on the main island of Bermuda.

When news of the execution of Charles I reached the Somers Islands, the governor, Thomas Turner, was in favour of the Commonwealth. Many other prominent citizens, however, backed by the majority of the islands' militia, were for the King. Turner was deposed and replaced by John Trimingham, who declared for the King. This marked a growing divide between the islanders and the governing body in England. Finding themselves a minority on the islands, a group of Puritans under former governor William Sayle, known as the Eleutheran Adventurers, who had tried once before to establish a new colony, left the islands to establish a settlement in the Bahamas on 8 November 1650.[7]

In England, the Board of the Somers Island Company was reviewed by the Council of State; John Danvers, the Governor of the Company, was required immediately to take the oath along with other members of the council. Josias Forster was appointed Governor of the Colony, with authority to appoint a new council and to replace all 'captains and commanders within the islands'.[8] The new council immediately sent word to the islands which, while not explicitly demanding an oath of allegiance to the Commonwealth, presumed their loyalty. This was soon followed by a formal demand for acquiescence. In September 1650, the Non–Intercourse Act was passed, and the Somers Islands included in it; this bit the colony hard as the islanders had begun to build ships to carry trade goods rather than rely on vessels from Europe and North America. The Commonwealth also ordered the transportation of 900 Scots and English Royalist prisoners taken at Dunbar; the ship *Unity*, carrying the men, touched at Bermuda but went on to Massachusetts. A year later, after the Royalist defeat at Worcester, more Scots soldiers were ordered for transportation. On 8 November 1651, the *John and Sarah* left England with 300 men on board. 272 of them survived to reach Bermuda, where some were dropped off, the rest going on to Charlestown, Carolina. They were followed by other English Royalists and later, Irish men and women.

VIRGINIA, BERMUDA AND MARYLAND DURING THE CIVIL WARS AND THE PROTECTORATE

Government House, Bermuda, 1612. (<www.bermuda-online> accessed 17 November 2020).

In due course Forster, with several other representatives of the Commonwealth appointed as Commissioners, including Colonel Owen Rowe, Sir Thomas Wroth and Cornelius Holland, were sent to the islands. They returned a report to the Council of State in October 1653 which summarised the state of the colony thus:

> Recapitulate the patent granted by King James I. in 1615, and the commission superseding it, granted on 23 June 1653, by the Council of State, because of the misgovernment of the Company in England and the disposition of the governing power in the islands "to invite Charles Stuart's interest to take possession" thereof. The islands for the most part naturally fortified or otherwise secured by four forts, with 60 guns, and five companies; 1,500 men able to bear arms, and the commands in good hands. About 3,000 inhabitants with but one minister. The charges of government amount annually to 500*l.*, and the duties from tobacco to 800*l.* per ann. Recommend that the government of the Company should be again vested by patent in certain select persons approved by his Highness and the Council of State; that the government remain at present in the hands of those in power; fitting ammunition be forthwith sent; and a duty of 1*d.* per pound levied upon all tobacco from thence.[9]

In effect, when confronted with the representatives of the Commonwealth and being well aware of what had happened to Virginia and the Barbadoes, any idea of standing firm for Charles II fizzled out. Trimingham was

COLONIAL IRONSIDES

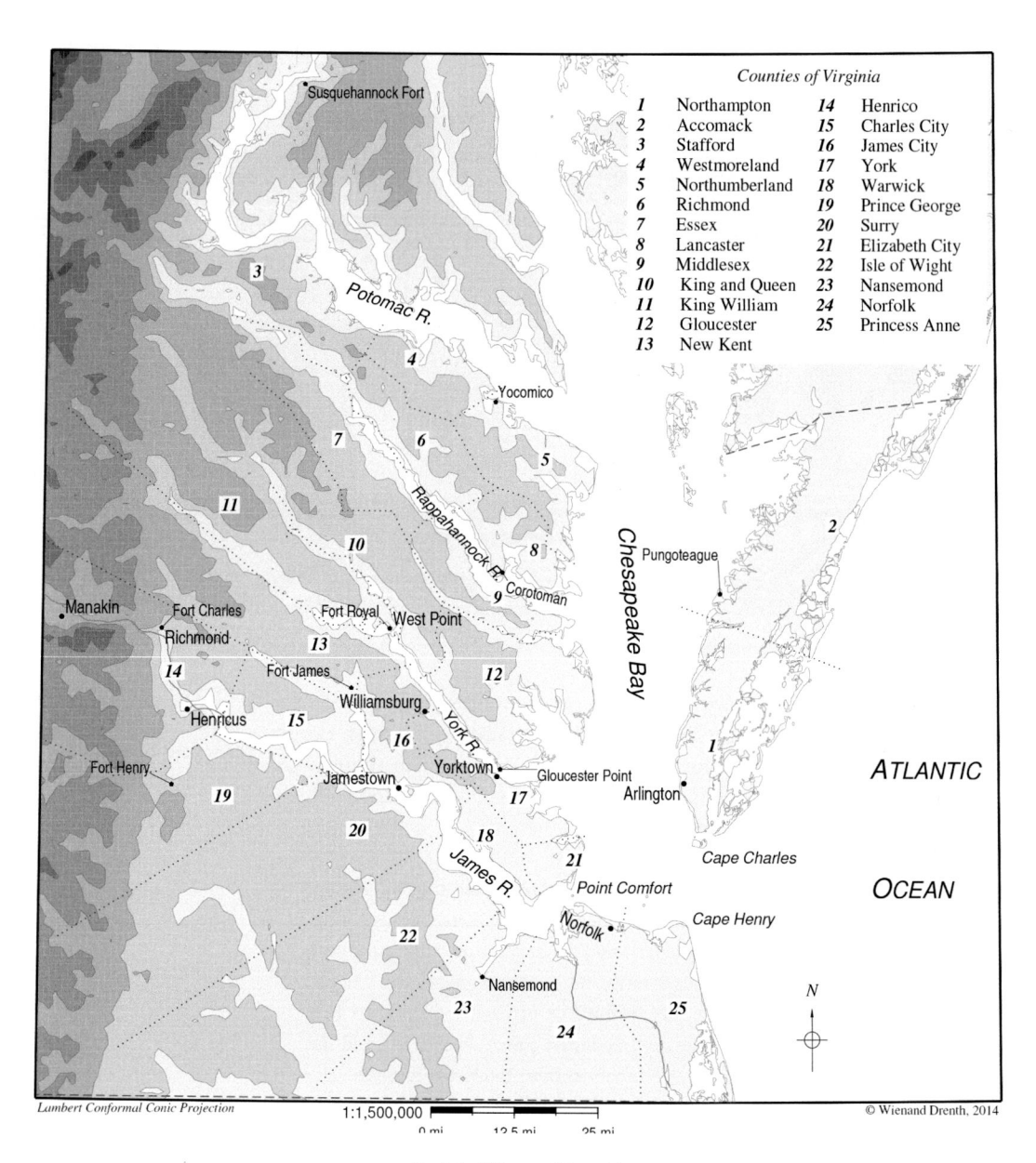

Virginia. (Wienand Drenth)

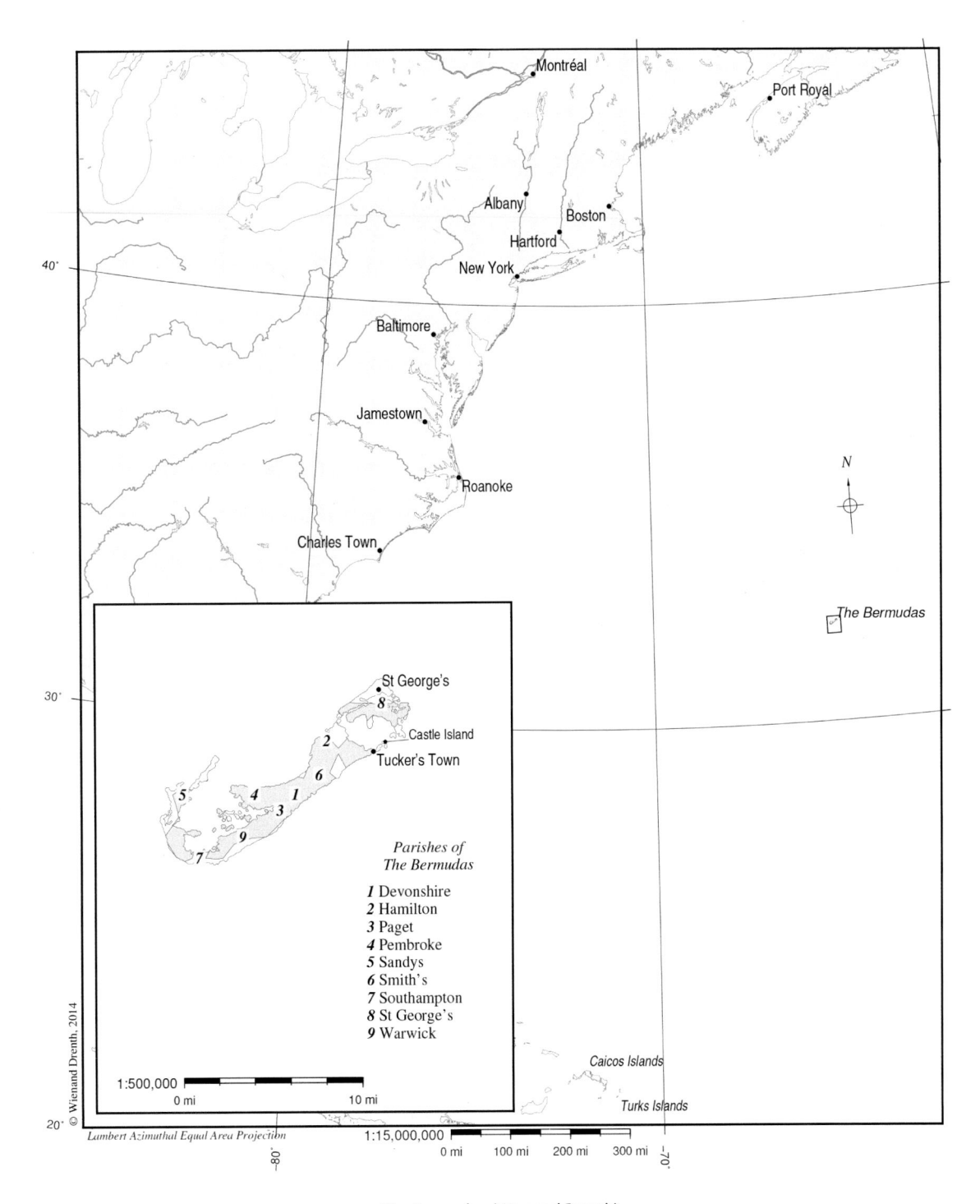

VIRGINIA, BERMUDA AND MARYLAND DURING THE CIVIL WARS AND THE PROTECTORATE

Parishes of The Bermudas

1. Devonshire
2. Hamilton
3. Paget
4. Pembroke
5. Sandys
6. Smith's
7. Southampton
8. St George's
9. Warwick

The Bermudas. (Wienand Drenth)

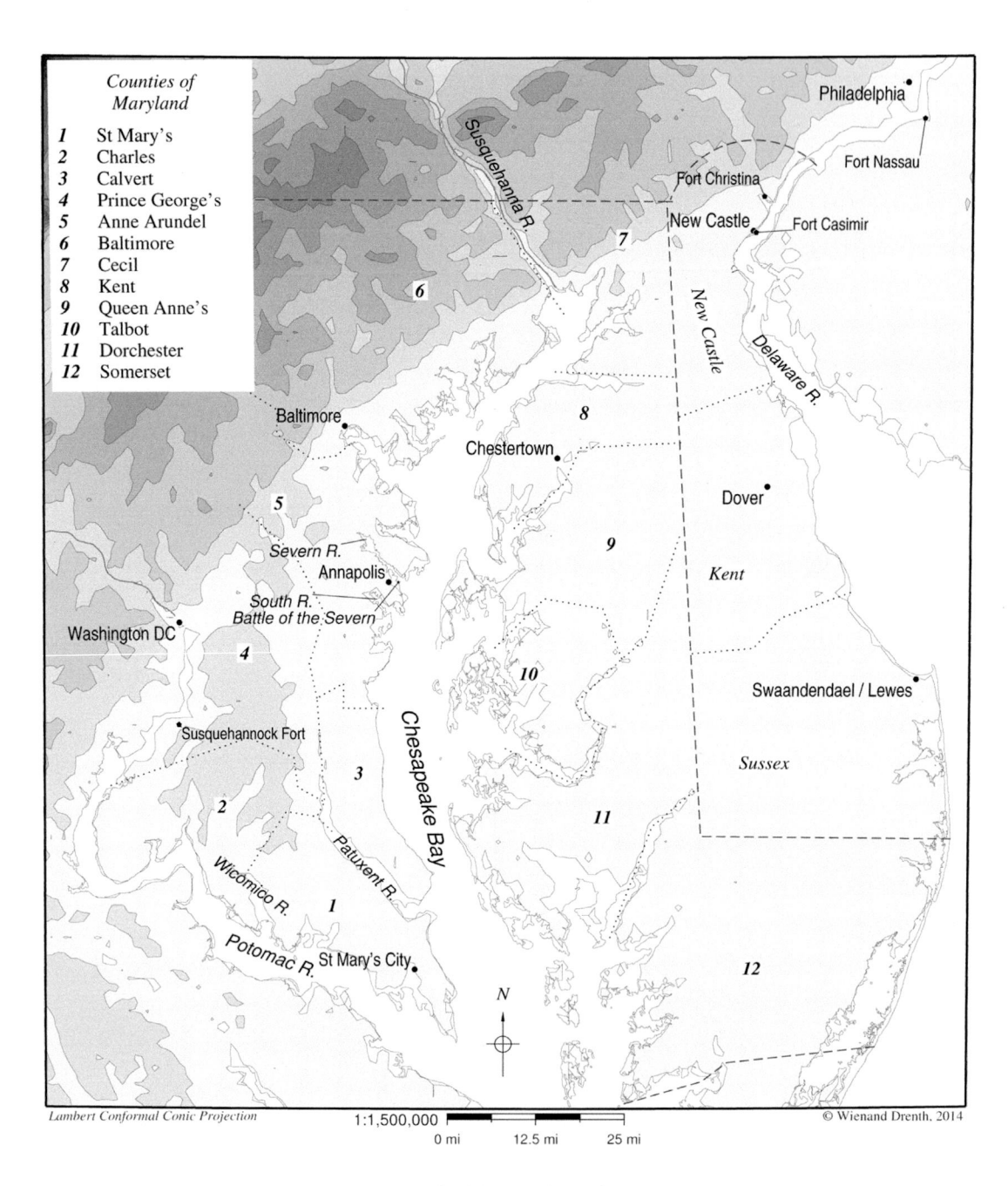

COLONIAL IRONSIDES

Maryland. (Wienand Drenth)

replaced by Forster, with Rowe as Deputy Governor. Royalism remained a present force throughout the Protectorate but seems generally to have been overlooked in favour of maintaining the status quo and the profits from trade. The only uprising was one by Irish prisoners and black slaves in 1656, which was discovered, after which the importation of the Irish was ended. The leaders were executed, and any freed slaves thought to have been involved were sent to the Bahamas.[10]

The only fighting in the Americas during the period took place in the colony of Maryland, whose foundation was of a very different nature from that of Virginia or Bermuda. In 1524 Giovanni da Verrazzano passed the mouth of Chesapeake Bay. It was mapped for the first time in 1564 by the Spaniards Estêvão Gomes and Diego Gutiérrez. In 1608 the English explorer John Smith entered explored the area. Following this, George Calvert, 1st Baron Baltimore, applied to Charles I for a royal charter for what was to become the Province of Maryland. Calvert, however, died in April 1632 and the charter for 'Maryland Colony' was granted to his son, Cecilius (Cecil) Calvert, 2nd Baron Baltimore, on 20 June 1632. The new colony was named in honour of Queen Henrietta Maria, although the specific name given in the charter was *Terra Mariae, anglice*, or English Maryland.[11]

The King had very good reasons for creating a colony north of the Potomac River. The Dutch colony of New Netherland specifically claimed the Delaware River valley and its border with Virginia remained debatable. Charles rejected all the Dutch claims on the Atlantic seaboard and was therefore anxious to bolster English claims by formally occupying as much territory as possible. Colonial Maryland was considerably larger than the present–day State of Maryland. The original charter granted the Calverts a loosely defined swathe of territory north of Virginia and south of the 40th parallel, comprising perhaps as much as 12 million acres in all. In the 1670s, Maryland lost some of this territory to Pennsylvania when Charles II granted that colony a tract overlapping the Maryland grant. It was not until the Mason–Dixon Line was drawn in 1767, however, that the boundary was finally settled.

Led by Leonard Calvert, Cecil Calvert's younger brother, the first settlers sailed in two small ships, the *Ark* and the *Dove*. In Maryland, Baltimore sought to create a haven for English Catholics and to demonstrate that Catholics and Protestants could live together in harmony. Cecilius Calvert was himself a convert to Catholicism, a considerable political handicap for a nobleman in seventeenth–century England. However, like other aristocratic proprietors, he also hoped to make money from the new colony. This first group of colonists consisted of 17 mainly Catholic gentlemen and their ladies, and about 200 others of both religions, mostly indentured servants who could work off their passage. The party landed on 25 March 1634 (appropriately enough, the feast of the Annunciation of the Blessed Virgin Mary and at that date, New Year's Day) at St Clement's Island. This was the site of the first Catholic Mass said in the English Colonies, celebrated by Father Andrew White.[12]

Land was purchased from the Yaocomico people and the small town of St Mary's was established. Maryland became one of the few predominantly

Catholic provinces among the English colonies in North America – although for most of its colonial history, Protestants of various sorts were the majority of its inhabitants. It was also one of the major destinations for the transportation of English convicts. The first government was feudal and, meeting resistance, Leonard summoned the first colonial assembly in February 1635. In 1638, the Assembly forced Calvert to govern according to the laws of England and the right to initiate legislation therefore passed to the assembly.

The first fortifications were erected to guard the seaward approaches to the colony. These were Fort Kent, at or near Kent Point which was the first English settlement in the colony. Fort Craford was built in 1634 on Craney Creek; a double row of palisades stretched across the island on both sides of this fort. St Mary's Fort, a 120–square–foot palisaded fort with four bastions, or blockhouses, which fell into disrepair around 1640. St Ignatius Fort, also known as St Inigo's Fort, was erected on Fort Point in 1644 after Fort St Mary's had fallen into disrepair. It was dismantled in 1655. Fort Conquest was built on Garrett Island by Maryland troops after the seizure of the island from the Virginian William Claiborne.

Several forts were erected inland to provide garrisons and safe haven against attacks by the native people. Mattapany Fort was a stockade built in response to the attack by native warriors and the destruction of the Jesuit Mission in 1636. A manor house was built here in 1663 which later became the governor's house and provincial arsenal until 1684. Pawtuxunt Fort was erected at about the same time. Other forts were at Christina, Thomas Sterman's House in St Michael's Hundred and Thomas Weston's House in St George's Hundred.

As was usual, the royal charter gave Calvert, as Proprietor, the title of commander of forces by land and sea, with the authority to appoint all military officers in the province. Thus, officers were not elected by the men, as they were elsewhere in North America, but appointed. Militia Bills came before the Assembly in 1638 and 1639 but did not become law. The earliest militia force recorded was the trained band at St Mary's in 1638, which mustered 120 men. From about 1640, the Provincial Assembly appointed a captain for every hundred men. By 1658 the militia was formed into two regiments, the Northern and the Southern. Able–bodied men between 16 and 60 were to hold arms and attend monthly musters. There was also a Governor's Company, not part of either regiment.

In 1638, Calvert seized a trading post on Kent Island that had been established by William Claiborne. In 1642, Maryland went to war with the native Susquehannock people. The Susquehannock, with the help of the colonists from New Sweden, defeated the Marylanders in 1644. The Susquehannock remained in a state of war, albeit inactive, until peace was concluded in 1652. Records from this period are poor and accounts of these early conflicts are sparse.

In April 1643, with the Civil Wars raging in Britain, Leonard Calvert left Maryland to consult his brother Cecilius Calvert, leaving Giles Brent as acting governor in his absence. During this time, St Mary's City was visited by Captain Richard Ingle, an ardent supporter of the Parliamentarian side in the Civil Wars,* who was placed under nominal arrest for making disloyal comments concerning the King, but who was allowed to escape. When Leonard Calvert returned home, he discovered that Ingle had joined forces with Claiborne and they were planning an invasion of the colony.[13]

In February 1645, Ingle arrived in the ship *Reformation* and launched a surprise attack on Fort St Inigoes before the militia could be called out. He then captured St Mary's City, burning and looting the houses of leading citizens and, especially, Catholics. At the same time, Claiborne recovered Kent Island, forcing Calvert to seek refuge in Virginia, which had remained loyal to King Charles. What followed became known as the Plundering Time, a period of almost two years during which Ingle and his companions roamed the colony, robbing at will and sending two Jesuit priests back to England as prisoners. Ingle and his men constructed a fort around the home of Governor Calvert. At the time, Calvert's house was one of the largest buildings in the Chesapeake. The fort was around 200 feet long and 120 feet across, constructed of logs with a ten–foot–wide external ditch. The fort consisted of three bastions and was certainly capable of mounting cannon. Ingle left Nathaniel Pope, a Marylander, in command of the fort and for this reason it became known as 'Mr. Popes Fort'.

Calvert returned at the head of an armed force in 1646, reasserted Proprietary rule, took Pope's fort, recaptured St Mary's City and restored order. In the aftermath, the Maryland Toleration Act, issued in 1649, was one of the first laws that explicitly defined tolerance of different manifestations of Christianity and has been considered a precursor to the First Amendment of the Constitution of the United States. Most of Ingle's men were granted amnesty but Ingle himself was executed as a pirate in 1653.

In 1649, following the execution of Charles I, Captain William Stone was appointed as governor. Stone appears to have served in Lord Hopton's Dragoons in 1642,[14] and possibly later in the Regiment of Colonel Talbot.[15] In 1651, rumours began to circulate indicating that Lord Baltimore would lose his charter. Parliament had appointed two Commissioners, one of whom was none other than Claiborne, to force Maryland to submit to Parliamentarian authority. In March 1652 they removed Stone as Governor, only to reinstate him in June 1652. On 16 December 1653, Oliver Cromwell established the Protectorate, dismissing Parliament. Following the news of this, on 2 March 1654, Stone decreed that although he was faithful to the Commonwealth, all writs should 'run in the Proprietary's name as heretofore'.[16]

When Anglicanism had become the official religion in Virginia around 1642, a band of Puritans had left for Maryland; here they founded the settlement of Providence, later renamed Annapolis. These Puritans, who had been given toleration and safe haven under the laws of Maryland by Stone, showed their ingratitude and their own views on toleration on 3 January 1654, by stating formally to the commissioners that they objected to the oath of fidelity to Baltimore as a Roman Catholic. On 20 July 1654 Stone resigned

---

* No record has been found of Ingle's having served as an officer in the armies of Parliament or the Protectorate.

as governor under duress. The Commissioners became *de facto* governors of the colony and the first general assembly under their authority was held on 20 October 1654. Roman Catholics and any other individuals who had borne arms against the Parliament could not be members – effectively limiting the membership to Puritans. Among the 44 Acts passed under this junta were a repeal of the Toleration Act and another act forbidding Catholics from practicing their religion. During this period Puritan mobs burned down all the original Catholic churches of southern Maryland.

On 31 January 1655, the merchant ship *Golden Lyon*, commanded by Captain Roger Heamans, arrived in Maryland. Stone told Heamans that he was no longer gGovernor, having been superseded by the Commissioners. At about that time, another ship, *The Golden Fortune*, arrived in the colony with a personal letter from Cromwell, addressed to Captain Stone, Governor of Maryland. Using this as evidence of official recognition, Stone challenged the authority of the Commissioners, seized back the records of the colony, and raised a force of 225 men in St Mary's County to deal with the Puritans.

Detailed accounts of the fighting that followed have been reconstructed by Robert Giglio and Peter Cottrell, cited in the sources for this chapter, and these form the basis of the following description. On 20 March 1655, Stone left St Mary's for Providence with his militia, a distance of about 60 miles to the north. On the way, he planned to collect more men. He was supported by a flotilla of small craft to carry supplies and to ferry the men across the watercourses that flowed into Chesapeake Bay. Meanwhile, the Puritans in Providence evacuated all women and children to safety in the merchantman *The Golden Lyon*. A war council was then convened which appointed Captain William Fuller of the Puritan settlers of Providence, as its leader. Fuller claimed to have been a New Model officer, although no record of this can be found, and a veteran of the expedition to the eastern shore as well as the wars in England.

Fuller, warned of Stone's approach, called out the Providence militia of Ann Arundel County on 23 March. This numbered about 150 men. On 23 March, the council issued a warrant to Captain Heamans of the *Golden Lyon* to serve as a counsellor. The following day, Heamans' ship fired on Stone's sloops and boats heading towards his ship, forcing their retreat. Heamans then ordered an armed two–gun sloop under Captain John Cutts to bar their escape by blocking Spa Creek, the inlet of the Severn to which Stone's forces had retreated.

In the late afternoon of 24 March, Stone's force rounded Horn Point, with the intent of calling for the surrender of Providence. They were, however, met by gunfire from the *Golden Lyon*. Stone's small craft, unarmed as they were, stood no chance against an armed ship. They therefore turned into Spa Creek to escape. Cutts's sloop then moved in and forced Stone further upstream. The water approaches were now secure and Stone was cut off from the Severn and the Chesapeake Bay. With no other options open to him, Stone landed on the Peninsula opposite Providence and camped for the night.

Fuller led the Providence militia across Spa creek, upstream of the Royalists. When dawn broke on 25 March (the anniversary of the first landing in the colony) Stone formed his force for a land approach towards

VIRGINIA, BERMUDA AND MARYLAND DURING THE CIVIL WARS AND THE PROTECTORATE

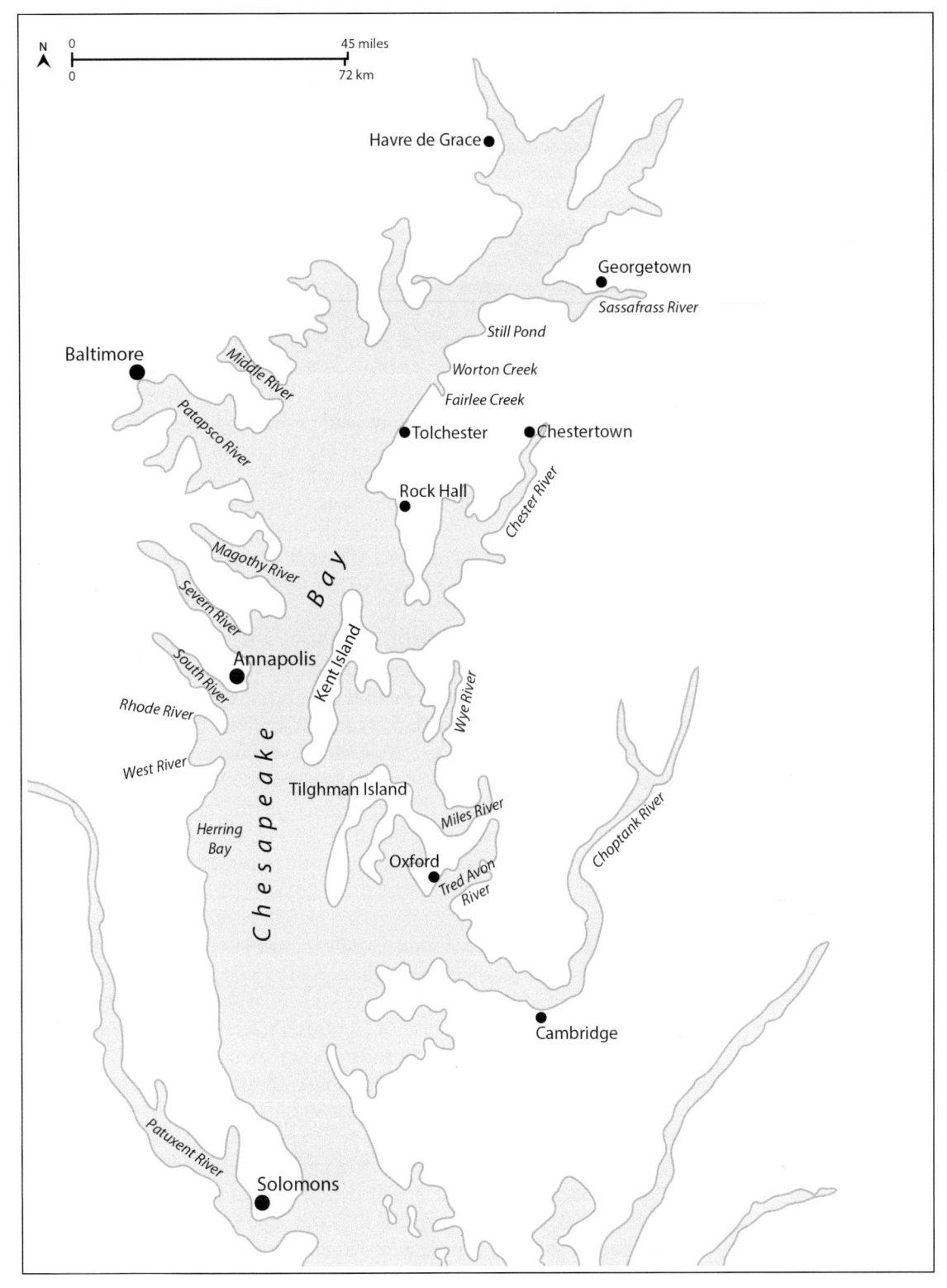

The Chesapeake Bay Area

Providence, the waterway having been denied to him by the enemy. Fuller, however, was already in a position to block Stone's line of advance.[17]

Although composed of militia, both forces had a number of veterans of the fighting in Britain among their ranks. There were also veterans of the Susquehannock war and fighting with New Sweden. Stone's St Mary's force had several Royalist veterans and, possibly, a number of German professionals. The Providence militia under Fuller had a substantial number of New Model Army veterans and, according to Giglio and Cottrell, citing a contemporary source, they were wearing their red coats. Both forces were therefore well trained but Cottrell suggests that Fuller's was more proficient in firing and drill. It also seems likely that, with the absence of cavalry or dragoons, both were all–musket forces rather than a mix of pikes and muskets.[18]

The battlefield which became known as the Severn lies near Horn's Point, a small peninsula across Spa Creek to the south of Providence. This battle, the Battle of the Severn, was the first battle ever fought between American soldiers on American soil and, with those fought in the Low Countries, among the last of the Civil Wars of Great Britain: it was the only battle in America in which the flag of the Commonwealth of England was flown. The battle was also the first in which the Provincial flag of Maryland was flown.

The Royalists formed up facing south–west as the Commonwealth force advanced towards them. The Royalists' boats were moored to their right and rear, effectively blockaded by the armed merchantmen at the mouth of Spa Creek. Cottrell proposes that the St Mary's militia was trained in older musketry practices and was therefore drawn up six deep. This allowed the front rank of each division to fire and then move to the rear, while the next rank took its place to give fire. Thus, a continuous fire, rank after rank, could be kept up. Because Fuller was a New Model veteran and had a significant number of similarly trained veterans available, Cottrell argues that the Providence militia would have been trained in the newer, Dutch, 'salvo' tactic rather than the rolling fire by ranks, favoured by Gustavus Adolphus. For this, the musketeers were drawn up in three ranks, allowing all to fire simultaneously as they closed with the enemy in a devastating mass of projectiles.[19]

The Providence militia continued to advance and were met with a Royalist volley at extreme range, which killed the ensign carrying the Commonwealth colour. It was quickly picked up, and with discipline holding firm, the Puritans continued their advance. At 50 yards, Fuller's whole force delivered their salvo, killing perhaps 20 Royalists. They then immediately clubbed their muskets and charged. Although some of the St Mary's militiamen stood their ground, most had had enough and turned to flight, casting away their weapons as they did so. One body of men probably under Governor Stone, fell back behind a large fallen tree and began an accurate fire which, one Commonwealth soldier said, 'galled us, and wounded divers of our men'. However, the long Commonwealth line was able quickly to envelop the Royalist flanks. Stone, now wounded, had little choice but to ask quarter, was given it and surrendered. The actual engagement probably lasted less than a half hour, with 17 of Stone's men killed, including Thomas Hatton, secretary

VIRGINIA, BERMUDA AND MARYLAND DURING THE CIVIL WARS AND THE PROTECTORATE

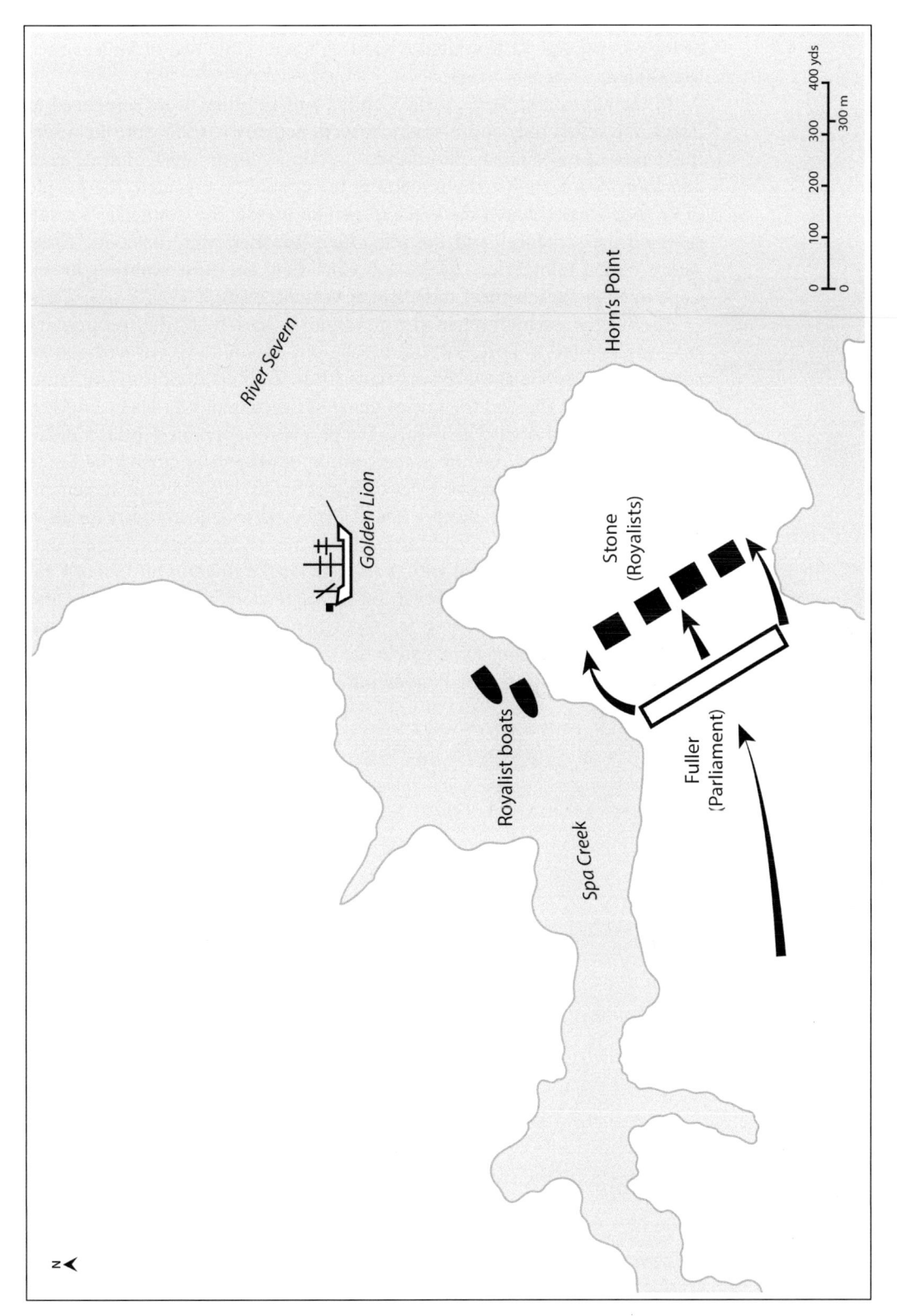

The Battle of the Severn

111

of the colony, and 32 wounded, including Stone. Only two of Fuller's men were killed.

In the aftermath, Stone, Josias Fendall and 10 others were sentenced to death. However, only four sentences were actually carried out, including those passed on William Eltonhead, Captain William Lewis,* John Legatt, and John Pedro. Before the remaining men could be executed, the people of Providence petitioned the War Council for mercy. The Council as a result reversed the sentences and the remaining prisoners were released. These were Colonel John Price,† Major Job Chandler,‡ the Hon. Robert Clarke,§ Captain Nicholas Gwither¶ and Captain William Evans.**

The Puritan assembly retained powers until 27 April 1658, when proprietary rule was restored to Lord Baltimore, religious freedom was ensured and an agreement of general amnesty was made. Thus, Lord Baltimore kept his lands and powers and avoided the fate of many of his contemporaries in England during the period of the Civil Wars. The proprietor appointed Josias Fendall to succeed Stone as governor in recognition of his loyalty during the Battle of the Severn. The Claiborne grievance was finally settled by an agreement reached in 1657. Lord Baltimore issued Claiborne with an amnesty for all of his offences, Virginia laid aside any claim it had to Maryland territory, and Claiborne was compensated with land grants in Virginia for his loss of Kent Island. Governor Fendall, however, soon disagreed with Lord Baltimore and a bloodless revolution followed in 1659 whereby he and Fuller reorganised Maryland's government to resemble the Commonwealth's. The Restoration of Charles II in 1660 forced Fendall into exile and restored proprietary rule once more.[20]

---

* Served in Colonel Henry Wentworth's Regiment against the Scots in 1640.
† *c.* 1607–1660. Had served in Prince Charles's Regiment of Foot.
‡ d. 1659.
§ *c.* 1611–1664.
¶ *c.* 1626–1666.
** d. 1668.

Appendix to Chapter 6

Military Forces in Maryland

Governors of Maryland

Proprietary Governors
The Hon Leonard Calvert, 1634–1647
Thomas Greene, 1647–1649
Colonel William Stone, 1649–1656[*]
Lieutenant-General Josias Fendall, 1657–1660

Military Organisation

The Battle of the Severn, 25 March 1655

Royalist Force	Puritan Force
Colonel William Stone	Colonel Edward Lloyd
Lieutenant-Colonel Josias Fenton	Captain William Fuller
Lieutenant-Colonel John Price	Captain Peter Knight
Major Job Chandler	
Captain William Lewis	
Captain Nicholas Gwither	
Captain William Evans	

Fort Inigo Commander
Captain John Price (1646–1652)

Provincial Regulars
In April 1650 the provincial Assembly of Maryland authorised a full-time garrison of six men under a captain for the fort in St Inigo harbour.

---

[*] William Stone (*c.* 1603–*c.* 1660).

The Militia by Companies and Regiments

Command and Staff
Colonel John Price (1647–1650)
Colonel Thomas Dent (1650)
Major-General Edward Gibbon (1658)
Colonel William Evans (1658–1659)
Muster-Master Thomas Baldridge (1642)

Governor's Company
Captain __ the Governor

Northern Regiment
Colonel Philip Connor (1652–1658)
Major Nicholas Sewall

Baltimore Company (1659)
Not identified

Kent Island Company (1637)
Captain William Braithwaite (1638)
Captain Robert Evelyn (1639)
Captain Giles Brent (1642–1644)
Captain Robert Vaughan (1645–1660)

Ann Arundel County (Providence) Company (1650)
Captain George Puddington
Captain William Fuller (1655)
Captain John Norwood (1655–1661)

Ann Arundell 2nd Company (1654)
Captain Richard Ewen (1654–1658)
Captain Thomas Howell (1658)

Calvert County Company (Patuxent) (1654)
Captain John Smith (1654)
Captain Peter Johnson (1655)
Captain Woodman Stockley (1656)
Captain Philip Morgan (1656)

Southern Regiment
Colonel Giles Brent, 1643

St Mary's Company (1638)
Captain Giles Brent
Captain William Stone (1645)
Captain Edward Hill (1646)

Captain-General Thomas Greene (1647)
Captain Thomas Cornwallis (1652–1675)

St Mary's 2nd Company (1654)
Captain Josias Fendall (1654–1657)
Captain George Reed (1658–1665)

St Mary's 3rd Company (1654)
Captain Richard Hodskey (1654–1655)
Captain Nicholas Gwither (1655)

St Mary's 4th Company (1654)
Captain John Sly (1654–1655)
Captain William Evans (1655)

Dorchester County Company (1668)
Captain Henry Tripp (1676)
Charles County Company (1658)
Captain Thomas Cornwallis (1658)
Captain Gerard Fowkes (1658)
Captain John Jenkins (1658–1660)

Charles 3rd Company
Captain Nicholas Gwither (1658)
Captain James Langworth (1659–1661)

Expeditionary Forces

The Expedition Against Claiborne, 1638
Colonel Thomas Cornwallis

Expedition to the Eastern Shore, 1652–1654
Captain William Fuller

7

Mounting the Expedition to Hispaniola

If it was to be carried through to success, the Spanish Design, described in Chapter 2, needed a specific objective and a large naval and military force to obtain that objective. With the various expeditions against recalcitrant Royalists and the French either completed or in hand, Cromwell's Council had discussed the matter of the Western Design, and of Hispaniola in particular, on 20 July 1654 and in spite of misgivings, especially by John Lambert, Cromwell had forcibly carried the day.[1] The Protector's subsequent instructions directed the expedition towards the island of Hispaniola and its capital and port, San Domingo. The capture of the port was considered important for supply purposes, but also because from there, Spanish treasure fleets from South America could be intercepted – a reversion from the idea of colonisation towards the Elizabethan model of raiding and plunder. San Domingo was thought to be poorly fortified and defended and therefore easy to take. An alternative objective was San Juan (St John's) on the island of Porto Elico (now Puerto Rico), just to the west of Hispaniola. With one of these as a base, the expedition could thereafter capture Havana on the island of Cuba: '[it is] the back door of the West Indies and will obstruct the passing of the Spanish Plate Fleete into Europe.'[2] A more radical alternative suggestion was a landing 400 miles (620 kilometres) south of Hispaniola, between the mouth of the Orinoco River and Porto Bello on the peninsula of Panama, with Cartagena mentioned as a possible base. It was, however, left to those in command to decide which objective should be taken.

This was in keeping with the general tone of the instructions, which were very general in nature.[3] They stated that the expedition was made necessary not only because of the threat to English colonies in the West Indies, but also to free people in North America from 'the cruelties, wrongs and Injuries done and exercised upon them by the Spaniards … Miserable Thraldome and Bondage, both Sprituall and Civill … the Popish and cruel Inquisition … bringing in the light of the Gospel and power of true Religion and Godliness into those parts.' The object of the expedition was: 'to gain an interest in that part of the West Indies in the Spaniard … for the effecting whereof we shall not tye you up to a method by any particular instruction, but only

General Robert Venables. (<britishempire.co.uk> accessed 29 December 2019)

communicate to you what hath bin under our consideration.' That different objectives were suggested, as described above, but not directed, was both helpful in giving freedom of action, but unhelpful in that Cromwell's intention remained opaque.[4]

Cromwell's intention may have been influenced by the idea of a West Indies Company, considered as early as the 1620s. Cromwell was certainly connected with several men who set up the Providence Island Company in the 1630s to found a private colony in the Caribbean as a base for attacks on Spanish shipping. They included his cousin Oliver St John, Lord Saye and Sele, John Pym, and the future admiral, John Rich, 2nd Earl of Warwick.[5] It is possible that the Protector saw a colony in Hispaniola, or indeed on the South American mainland, as being in keeping with those ideas and the instructions were vague enough to allow his commanders considerable leeway. Cromwell may also have believed that because of the ease with which Sir Francis Drake had conquered Hispaniola 70 years before (see Chapter 8), that the task would be easy, although a raid like Drake's was a quite different proposition from the capture and running of a colony which demanded an expeditionary operation to seize the territory and then a security operation to hold it. He was also further influenced by two men who had knowledge of the place: Colonel Thomas Modyford of the Barbadoes who recommended an attack on Cartagena in Guiana; and Mr Thomas Gage. Modyford had been instrumental in the subjugation of the Barbadoes in 1652 (see Chapter 4). Gage had been in the West Indies as a member of the Dominican Order but had returned to England in 1641 and become a Protestant minister. In 1654 he suggested to the Protector that the conquest of the thinly populated island of Hispaniola, and indeed other islands, would be easy. It was Gage's advice that Cromwell had accepted,[6] and Cromwell appointed Gage as chaplain to the general commanding the expedition.

Preparations for the Caribbean expedition had begun immediately after the Council had agreed to the scheme and initially 14 ships were identified for it.[7] Security in England being bad, it was not long before the Royalists at home and abroad knew the destination.[8] The information was passed on to the Spanish and the Council of State duly discussed it, concluding that 'the English have some hankering after the island of Santo Domingo', and put preparations in order for its defence.[9] Although the Spanish knew what was intended, they could not, because of the war with France, afford to withdraw Ambassador Alonso de Cardenas before the attack became a fact, for to do so would push Cromwell into open alliance with France. This was a critical factor in allowing Cromwell to push ahead with plans for the expedition and at the same time, continue talks with both France and Spain. It should be remembered that the despatch of a government expedition to the Americas was something new in English foreign policy. Elizabeth and the Stuarts had both been content to leave the founding of colonies to groups of individuals or chartered companies and there was, therefore, no national policy on colonisation until now.

In part at least because this was a new departure, a special commission was assembled on 18 August 1654.[10] The two most important military figures on this committee were General Robert Venables, who had been commissioned to command the land forces; and General-at-Sea William Penn, who was to command the fleet. Venables had served in Cheshire and Lancashire from 1642 to 1648. In 1649 he had commanded a foot regiment during the reconquest of Ireland under Cromwell and remained in Ulster until May 1654 in command of the English army.* He had returned to England to represent the views of his officers about the settlement of Ireland and the allocation of land, and while in London, Cromwell offered him the command of the expedition against Spain. Venables accepted. Reports on Venables' character and capabilities are mixed. Scoutmaster Isaac Berkenhead said that he was:

> so justly and temperately discreet and active, so conscionably just and careful to relieve the oppressed … he lays his shoulders so much to the work in hand that we are sometimes afraid lest he overturn himself; for his rest is hardly four hours most nights.[11]

He was to show no want of personal courage later in Hispaniola – so necessary a quality in any field commander of the period whatever his rank. Other members of the expedition called him godly, valiant, discreet, wise, prudent and unwearied.[12] On the other hand, among his chief subordinates, Richard Holdep was damning with faint praise, and Edward D'Oyley roundly condemned his generalship, as did Anthony Buller.[13] There were frequent complaints that he did not consult and called few councils of war – two before the landing on Hispaniola and two during the operation. He was also criticised for taking his wife, Elizabeth Aldersey, on the expedition. Venables countered the accusation by saying that the object of the expedition was to settle new territories, for which families were needed, and moreover that wives would be able to act as nurses during the campaign.[14]

William Penn, father of the founder of Pennsylvania,† had fought in the Civil Wars on the side of Parliament, being himself member for Weymouth and Melcombe Regis. He commanded a ship in the Irish Sea squadron where the service was hard and called for energy and good seamanship. In 1648, he was arrested and sent to London, probably on suspicion of corresponding with the Royalists. He was, however, soon released, and sent back to the

---

* Robert Venables (*c.* 1613–1687). After the Restoration he became governor of Chester, but largely retired from public life.
† William Penn (1620–1670) continued to serve in the Navy after the Restoration with mixed fortunes. See in particular Granville Penn, *Memorials of the Professional Life and Times of Sir William Penn* (2 vols, London, 1833).

Irish Squadron as rear-admiral in the *Assurance*. After 1650, Penn served as commander-in-chief of the southern fleet in the Atlantic and in the Mediterranean in pursuit of the Royalists under Prince Rupert. After an action at Macroom in County Cork, Ireland he was rewarded with a grant of land and a seat at Macroom Castle. During the First Anglo-Dutch War, he had commanded squadrons at the battles of the Kentish Knock (1652), Portland, the Gabbard and Scheveningen (1653). In 1654, he was again in correspondence with the Royalists, offering to carry the fleet over to Charles II in exile. Penn was certainly a man with a foot in both camps, but he remains a figure of considerable importance in English naval history, if somewhat overshadowed by Blake. As Admiral and General-at-Sea, he helped in 1653 to draw up the first code of tactics provided for the English navy. It became the basis of the 'Duke of York's Sailing and Fighting Instructions',[15] later adapted by Nelson, which continued for many years to be the basic tactical manual of the Royal Navy. Penn was an early advocate of fighting in line ahead, in order to bring as much firepower as possible to bear on the enemy.[16] Samuel Pepys knew him later when Clerk of the Acts to the Navy Board. Pepys speaks of him regularly and usually – but not always – in admiring tones, writing on 5 April 1666: 'To the office, where the falsenesse and impertinencies of Sir W. Pen would make a man mad to think of.'[17] However it is certain that he was an excellent seaman and a good fighter who later succeeded in maintaining his position at the Restoration, probably as a result of his covert correspondence during the Protectorate. Pepys wrote in July 1666, giving a long account of Penn's analysis of what was to be learnt from the Four Days' Battle at sea against the Dutch, ending with the comment: 'He did talk very rationally to me, insomuch that I took more pleasure this night in hearing him discourse then I ever did in my life in anything that he said.'[18]

The other members of the Commission were first, Edward Winslow, who was born in 1595 and had been one of those who sailed for America on the *Mayflower* in 1620. He was Governor of New Plymouth from 1633 to 1646 when he returned to England to support the Parliamentarian cause. In 1650 he was appointed as one of the Parliamentarian commissioners who compounded with Royalists. He was frequently consulted on colonial matters. He was clearly trusted by the Protector and from a letter to Thurloe in March 1655, it is clear that he was expected to give 'an impartial character of all things' to Cromwell.[19] Secondly, Daniel Searle, an American planter who was Governor of the Barbadoes from 1652 to 1660; he did not accompany the expedition but his position as governor was to be of great importance. Thirdly, Captain Gregory Butler, who had served under the Earl of Essex, William Waller and Major-General Sir Edward Massey. He seems to have had some knowledge of the West Indies, and was considered by Wilmslow and others as honest but of little use: 'the unfittest man I ever knew employed', wrote Wilmslow to Thurloe.[20]

The expedition suffered from the very beginning from a divided command and oversight by a committee. Venables was the land commander and Penn the fleet commander and this led to dissention throughout the expedition. So too did the requirement to accept joint management of matters of common interest, including policy, and Venables complained regularly about interference with his command.[21] He complained even more frequently about dissention between himself and Penn.[22] In particular there were quarrels about precedence. Penn was jealous of Venables and Cromwell knew this, seeking to placate him by telling him in a letter that:

> I have full assurance of you, notwithstanding I have had some knowledge of a little dissatisfaction remayneinge with you, which I hope by this tyme will be removed, and I desire you it may be so ... You have your owne command full and entire ... the command at land is also distinct, and there the generall at land must exercise his authoritye ...[23]

A fleet of 60 ships, including transports, was to be assembled to transport the expedition, the details are contained in the appendix to this chapter. The core of the land force was to be a corps of six regiments of foot and a troop of 100 horse.[24] Instead of designating entire formed regiments, with their own officers, Cromwell directed that new regiments were to be assembled from drafts drawn from the standing regiments in England – the Lord General's, Goffe's, Ingoldsby's, Lambert's, Farley's, Howard's and the Tower Regiment. Venables wanted volunteers, or at least, drafts drawn from the regiments in Ireland who were used to tough living conditions and hard fighting. This, however, was refused and it seems that regimental colonels were only too happy to unload the very worst of their men onto Venables in the form of drafts: 'hectors and knights of the blade, with common cheats, thieves, cutpurses and such like lewd persons.'[25] Another account said that 'The soldiers were the refuse of the whole army.'[26] These drafts were 500 short of the required total and the numbers were made up with raw recruits: 'the riff-raff of the London streets.'[27] Not only Venables, but all the field officers complained of the quality of the troops;[28] and things were not helped by the speed at which the expedition was put together. There was no time for a general muster at Portsmouth, where Venables was directed to assemble the force and rendezvous with the fleet, nor any training before embarkation. Even worse in the eyes of self-righteous Puritans, there were Catholics: 'Among those thus entertained were diverse papists, in particular sixteen, and four of them Irish, and one a priest ... out of the Tower Regiment.'[29]

According to the practice of the time, and the organisation of the New Model, each regiment was to consist of 10 companies – although that of the general might have an extra company. About two-thirds of the men would be armed with the matchlock musket and one-third with the pike.[30] The pikemen, who still wore back and breast armour and pot helmets, were to protect the musketeers during the vulnerable periods when they were reloading; and to repel bodies of enemy horse. That the English regiments on this expedition wore armour is recounted in a Spanish account, that of Captain Pallano.[31] Although the effectiveness and number of musketeers had increased from the beginning of the century, the pike was still held to be the more honourable weapon: in *Henry V*, written in 1599, William Shakespeare has Pistol ask the disguised Henry, hearing that he is a 'gentleman of a company', 'Trailest thou the puissant pike?' (Act IV Scene 1). Each company would number 100 men, although in the general's and Major-General's

A horseman of the period, detail from Henry Hexham *Principles of the Art Military* (<https://digi.ub.uni-heidelberg.de> accessed 1 January 2020).

regiments, their own companies could be up to 200 men and those of the Lieutenant-Colonel 160 and the major, 140. Each company had 12 officers: a captain, lieutenant, ensign – whose duty was to carry the company colour – two sergeants, three corporals, two gentleman-at-arms, or reformadoes, and two drummers.[32] The regimental staff consisted of the colonel and Lieutenant-Colonel, adjutant, chaplain, paymaster, surgeon and mate, armourer and mate and quartermaster. Gentlemen-at-arms, or reformed officers, or reformadoes as they were known, were usually officers without employment who might be enlisted by relatives in the chain of command for some pay and rations. Their duties would include being 'a sort of store-keeper for the regimental arms and ammunition; he was responsible for the marking, presentation and repair of all arms.'[33] In addition to the regimental staffs, Venables had a small staff of his own to administer and command the army – adjutant-general, commissary-general, surgeon-general, provost marshal and so on – a list of which is included in the appendix to this chapter.

The regiments assembled were, first, those of Venables himself, de facto commanded by the Lieutenant-Colonel, Edward D'Oyley and not to be confused with Venables' earlier regiment which had served in Ireland. It mustered 10 staff officers, 120 officers, non-commissioned officers (NCOs) and drummers, and 912 men.[34] The second regiment was that of the Major-General, second in command to Venables, James Heane. Heane was a brave and competent officer, a Puritan, who had served under Massey as Major of Fitzjames's Regiment of Horse in 1645–1646.[35] He was Governor of Weymouth in 1647 and then with his regiment had been engaged in the capture of Jersey in October 1651 (see Chapter 3). The efficiency with which he had carried out this task had recommended him to the Protector. His regiment also should not be confused with his earlier command; it numbered 10 staff, 120 officers and NCOs, and 1,058 men in 10 companies. Next was the regiment of the experienced Colonel Richard Fortescue. Fortescue had been a Lieutenant-Colonel under the Earl of Essex in 1644, promoted to colonel in the same year, and given command of a regiment in the New Model in 1647. In the dispute between Parliament and the Army he had sided with Parliament and been cashiered; he had remained unemployed until offered a command on Venables' expedition. It was said that he did so because he needed money to pay off his debts.[36] His regiment mustered 10 staff, 120 officers and NCOs, including Lieutenant-Colonel Richard Holdep, and 1,052 men in 10 companies. The regiment of Colonel Anthony Buller also mustered 10 companies, with 10 staff, 120 officers and NCOs and 916 men. Buller was rumoured to have Royalist sympathies. He had served with the Army in the West and was governor of the Isles of Scilly in 1646 where his men mutinied and declared for Charles II;[37] he had been imprisoned but released and sent back to England (see Chapter 3). It appears he was approached by a French agent named Theodore Naudin in the spring of 1654, who suggested that he raise mutiny in the army in England, but Buller revealed the plot and was rewarded with a command on this expedition.[38] His Lieutenant-Colonel, Francis Barrington, had served in Okey's Dragoons and in Ireland under Henry Cromwell. Finally, there was the regiment of Colonel Andrew Carter which mustered 10 staff, 120 officers and NCOs, and 834 men in 10 companies. Not much is known of Carter other than that he had served as Lieutenant-Colonel in Lambert's Regiment during the invasion of Scotland but had retired under something of a cloud in 1651. Full lists of the officers, as far as they can be ascertained, are included in the appendix to this chapter.

In addition to the foot regiments, a troop of horse was raised in England, under Captain Henry Jones, consisting of 12 officers and NCOs, and 65 troopers. There was also a Scoutmaster General's Company of 60 men under Captain Isaac Berkenhead, responsible for scouting, screening, guarding the

The Tower of London, from a contemporary woodcut. Note the cannon barrels on the wharf: Tower Bridge did not then exist and the land on the Southwark bank was largely waste; guns were therefore fired from the wharf by the Tower Armouries for proofing. (Author's collection)

flanks and gathering intelligence. A small train of artillery was assembled under Captain Hughes, consisting of 50 gunners, matrosses and artificers with an unspecified number of pieces. There is no evidence that any large siege artillery was issued and we must presume that it was intended that the guns of the fleet would be used to support the army ashore, either by firing from the sea or else, as was not unusual, by dismounting guns and their crews from ships and employing them on land from earthworks. A company of 12 officers and 120 men armed with the flintlock, or firelock, also formed part of the force under the command of Captain Pawlett of the General's Regiment. The flintlock, or fusil, could be used at sea where matchlocks were useless. They were also used to guard the artillery since lighted match and gunpowder can be an unhappy combination in the wrong circumstances. The company could also be used as a force of shock troops, or to guard against the unexpected, as the rate of loading and firing of the fusil was greater than that of the matchlock – three rounds per minute as opposed to two, or even one. Finally, there was a complete company of reformadoes consisting of two officers and 100 gentlemen. Their most likely task seems to have been to act as the advance guard, or 'forlorn hope' of the army.[39] The whole force numbered 78 officers and NCOs with an additional 85 staff, and 5,067 men. In addition, the ships' crews numbered 3,265.

Among the staff and the regimental officers there was a considerable number of veterans, but equally there were many 'lazy and dull officers that have a large portion of pride, but not of wit, valour nor activity'.[40] The want of good officers, who might have been able to form the mass of indifferent soldiery into something resembling an army, showed up strongly in the want of discipline – usually a marked characteristic of the New Model and post-New Model Protectorate forces: 'There was no discipline at all', wrote Penn, 'but every one doth what he lists, and the officers as bad as the men.'[41] The hasty march from points of assembly to Portsmouth, where the army was to embark, caused further confusion as officers, men and baggage became separated.

The great haste evident in assembling the expedition and getting it to sea, which accounted for the lack of cohesion and training among the troops, was due in large part to the knowledge that the main season of rain in the Caribbean, in which very heavy falls could be expected, began in late May and lasted until early December; there was also the question of hurricanes, which were most prevalent in those same months. It was felt imperative, therefore, for the expedition to arrive before that time. This haste inevitably meant that the equipment and supply of the expedition was of very uncertain quality. This had been placed in the hands of Major-General John Desborough,[42] Cromwell's brother-in-law, one of the four generals-at-sea who was also a commissioner of the army and navy. Desborough had shown considerable talent during the Civil Wars, but the preparation of this expedition was not his finest hour. Venables later asserted deliberate neglect or corruption by Desborough – a dangerous course of action against a member of the Protector's family.[43] The situation was not helped by the fact that the Army of the Protectorate was not organised for expeditionary operations outside the British Isles. The campaigns in Scotland and Ireland had been difficult enough in terms of supply, but this was to be something quite outside the experience of all except a few veterans of service on the Continent.

The first consideration was how to feed the army. Most professional soldiers of the period agreed that a satisfactory ration for a soldier consisted of about 2 lb of bread, one pound of meat and a gallon of drink per day of which the most important ration item supplied to troops was bread: wheat, barley or rye, in loaves of 1, 1½ or 2 lb. The minimum daily ration was usually 1½ lb (0.7 kg) per man per day, paid for by stoppages of pay. This had to be supplemented by meat or other protein, and beer or wine since water was seldom safe to drink unless sterilised by alcohol. Based on sixteenth-, seventeenth- and eighteenth-century figures for requisition, a force of men of the size sent against Hispaniola – eventually 9,000 strong – would consume 18,000 lb (8,160 kg) of bread, 9,000 lb (4,080 kg) of meat, salted fish, cheese or dried peas and 18,000 gallons, or 375 hogsheads of small beer *per day*.[44] If rum was issued at the rate of one pint per man per day, this would require 47 hogsheads per day. These figures would apply whether on land or embarked in ships and do not, of course, include the rations for the seamen, apart from those forming the additional regiment raised from the fleet. These huge quantities of stores would have to be loaded on Penn's fleet – or at least a sufficient part to carry the force as far as the West Indies. The constant complaints during the campaign about the scarcity of rations, especially flour for bread, indicates that nowhere near these amounts was provided, a situation made worse by several store ships being left behind when the fleet sailed. Shortages of food and other supplies were to be a constant problem throughout the campaign that followed. There was not enough brandy or grog,[45] necessary to stiffen the sinews of reluctant heroes as well as to sweeten bad water.

When on land and in enemy territory, as the army would be once disembarked, organised plunder was the general rule. Martin Van Crefeld has calculated that given the population density and agricultural practice in Europe at the time, an army of 30,000 people could be comfortably supplied with food by a strip of country measuring 65 miles by seven miles and would consume only 15 percent of the available food as it passed through this corridor.[46] It is however important to understand that this would not be a uniformly distributed slice of 15 percent, which would make the peasant farmer's life more difficult but still tolerable: in reality, some farms would be stripped bare while others would escape untouched: the effects of war were therefore patchy, tended to cluster around the more accessible areas, and produced extreme hardship in some localities. In the West Indies, however, this situation would be unlikely to apply as there was nothing in the way of cereal production. Agriculture was focused on cattle, sugar, tobacco and citrus fruits with some potatoes or yams – but these last would not be recognised by European soldiers.

Because of the quantities needed, local supplies of animal fodder were the most important resource for a pre-modern army. A horse required a daily ration of about 20 kg (50 lb) of green forage, or 4 kg (10 lb) of hay, plus (2.5 kg) 6 lb of oats and 1.75 kg (4 lb) of wheat or barley in its stead in winter – and three bundles of straw every week. Horses could graze on the march but in camp, foraging was required every third or fourth day. It was every army's insatiable appetite for green forage that restricted the campaigning season to the growing season, and at least Venables, with his small number of horses, was relieved of this problem.

Medical supplies and equipment were also in very short supply. Worse still, the quantity of arms and ammunition was wanting: only about 1,600 men were properly armed with matchlocks or fusils;[47] most of the pikes and half-pikes were wanting pikestaffs and there were in any case too few even of these. There was insufficient powder, ball, lead and slow match; there were no tents or camp stores, few smiths' tools and – a deficiency later to be much regretted – no water bottles for the troops. This was, therefore, a thoroughly ill-prepared expedition, perhaps the worst manned and equipped that has ever left the shores of Britain. Venables' later defence of himself is therefore, at least in part, justified. After his experiences in the early period of the Civil Wars, with the Eastern Association and with the New Model, one would have thought that Oliver Cromwell, of all people, might have known that assembling an armed mob is not the same thing as fielding an army.

* * *

The first squadron of Penn's fleet sailed on 20 December 1654, the remainder following on Christmas Day, less two store ships which failed to arrive in time. On 29 January 1655, the fleet dropped anchor in Carlisle Bay in the English colony of the Barbadoes, which had earlier been recovered from its allegiance to the exiled House of Stuart by Sir George Ayscue's expedition in 1651–1652 (see Chapter 4). Here it was planned to raise additional troops; however, its potential as a recruiting ground was questionable, for the Barbadoes and indeed the Windward Islands in general were, according to one participant in the expedition: 'the dunghill whereon England doth cast forth its rubbish'.[48]

The arrival of the fleet caused an unwelcome interruption to the trade between the settlers and the supposed enemies of the England, the Dutch. A number of Dutch ships were impounded and as a result, cooperation between the expedition and the colonists was problematic. In particular, Venables expected to make up the lack of numbers in his existing regiments, and indeed raise new regiments, from the colonists. Somewhere between half and three-quarters of the colonists in the West Indies at this time were indentured servants who had pledged their labour for a term of years after which they would be free and could hope for some grant of land, as discussed earlier in Chapter 4. Mortality in the hot, humid climate with its plethora of diseases killed up to 80 percent of the workforce in the Barbadoes between 1650 and 1670 and it was this that later turned the labour market to black African slaves.[49] In the short term, it was from these labourers that Venables intended to recruit and given the conditions of their service, the alternative he offered, especially with the prospects of plunder, were bound to be attractive. Such was the opposition of the landowners through their governor, the Commissioner Daniel Searle, however, that the Commissioners had to agree to recruit only free men, or those who had less than nine months of their term of indentured service left.[50] Even this compromise left some landowners with no staff at all to work their farms.

As well as filling the gaps in his existing regiments and bringing each of them up to a strength of 1,000 men, Venables formed a sixth regiment, the Barbadoes Regiment, which mustered 830 men with 120 officers, NCOs and drummers, and 10 staff in 10 companies under the command of Colonel Lewis Morris, who had taken part in the subjugation of the island in 1652 and had stayed on, assisted in the raising of this regiment and was offered command of it, but at the last minute declined to go to Hispaniola, leaving the command to D'Oyley. The Barbadoes also supplied two small troops of horse with a total of 10 officers and 56 men under Captains Philip Carpenter and Heane, son of the Major-General. These were needed as the original troop under Henry Jones had been driven in its ship to Ireland by contrary winds and so did not reach the Barbadoes with the rest of the expedition. Not only the horse, but also the small amount of artillery had been left behind. The Barbadoes could supply only a small mortar and two drakes, small guns of a type developed in the 1620s to allow more guns to be carried on ships. They usually fired a 4 lb cast iron ball.[51]

At least in appearance, the army was now impressive, mustering 6,973 men on 21 March 1655.[52] In quality, however, these new men were no better than the old: 'most fearful, only bold to do mischief, not to be commanded as soldiers, nor to be kept in any order; being the most profane debauched persons that we ever saw, scorners of religion … so cowardly as not to be made to fight.'[53] The expedition was further increased by raising a seventh regiment from the island of St Christopher and throughout the Leeward Islands; this regiment was picked up as the fleet sailed for Hispaniola.[54] Commissioner Butler, Captain Edward Blagge of the *Marston Moor* and Lieutenant-Colonel Richard Holdep were sent in February, raising 80 men from Montserrat, 300 from Nevis and 800 from St Christopher. Holdep was given the command in spite of the objections of some officers, for Holdep had experience as governor of a colony in Surinam.[55] The eighth regiment was formed from seamen of the fleet under Vice-Admiral Goodson. The total troops available to Venables therefore, including the seamen, numbered 9,700.

Although this number was impressive, the quality was, as we have noted, poor. Increasing numbers also added to the problems of equipment and supply and it must be asked why Venables continued to recruit men he could barely feed, never mind arm. The provisions carried by the fleet were eaten up more quickly than had been planned; dissension arose over allegations that the best food was reserved for the sailors and the worst rations served out to the soldiers. Some food was bought on the island but this was generally poor stuff – salt meat, cheese and flour in wooden barrels – sent out by the Navy Commissioners and left to spoil in the climate of the West Indies. Weapons were also still in very short supply. Armourers' tools were not to be had and the timber on the island was of poor quality, making it impossible to fashion proper pikestaffs to fit the heads brought from the Tower. The resulting weapons were less than half the usual length of 12 feet and far inferior to the Spanish pikes which could be as long as 16 feet, or indeed to the shorter Spanish lances which were to prove deadly during combat in close country; nor would Penn release any arms from the fleet. Moreover, many were little more than half-pikes fashioned from the ribs of the palm fronds from the native trees, sometimes referred to as 'cabbage', because the inside of the trunk resembles cabbage and can be eaten as such. It had been expected that 1,500 muskets would be collected in the Barbadoes but these weapons were only to be had by withdrawing them from the island's militia regiments.[56] There was still too little powder, match and ball. There was little time, therefore, for the army to be mustered and drilled under arms.

On two matters at least, Penn and Venables were agreed. The first, decided at a council of war in the Barbadoes,[57] was that the object of the expedition should be San Domingo on the island of Hispaniola. The second, which caused much dissension later, was that all plunder from official or government buildings should be placed in a common pool and divided among the expedition members; and more strictly that the plundering of private dwellings, property, livestock and wealth should be prevented by the officers.[58] This was done because of the intention of founding a colony rather than ravaging the city – which given the quality and motivation of the troops was the most likely outcome. It was a policy opposed by the other Commissioners and later the cause of a near mutiny. The rag-tag army embarked once more in the ships of Penn's fleet on 20 March and sailed first for St Christopher, where Holdep's Regiment was taken into the force, and from thence for Hispaniola.

Appendix I to Chapter 7

English Navy Lists of the Expedition to Hispaniola

A fleet of 60 ships sailed from London to the Barbadoes in 1655 under the command of General-at-Sea William Penn:

Swiftsure	General-at-Sea William Penn / Flag Captain Jonas Poole	60 guns	350 crew and 30 soldiers
Paragon	Vice-Admiral William Goodson	54 guns	300 crew and 30 soldiers
Torrington	Rear-Admiral George Dakins	54 guns	280 crew and 30 soldiers
Marston Moor	Captain Edward Blagge	54 guns	280 crew and 30 soldiers
Gloucester	Captain Benjamin Blake	54 guns	280 crew and 30 soldiers
Lion	Captain John Lambert	44 guns	230 crew and 30 soldiers
Mathias	Captain John White	44 guns	200 crew and 30 soldiers
Indian	Captain James Terry	44 guns	220 crew and 30 soldiers
Bear	Captain Francis Kirby	36 guns	150 crew and 30 soldiers
Laurel	Captain William Crispin	40 guns	160 crew and 30 soldiers
Portland	Captain Richard Newberry	40 guns	160 crew and 30 soldiers
Dover	Captain Robert Sanders	40 guns	160 crew and 30 soldiers
Great Charity	Captain Leonard Harris	36 guns	150 crew
Heartsease	Captain Thomas Wright	30 guns	70 crew, 150 soldiers
Discovery	Captain Thomas Wills	30 guns	70 crew and 160 soldiers
Convertine	Captain John Hayward	30 guns	75 crew and 200 soldiers
Katherine	Captain Willoughby Hannam	30 guns	70 crew and 200 soldiers
Martin	Captain William Vesey	12 guns	60 crew
Half-Moon	Captain Bartholomew Ketcher	36 guns	Transport – 130 crew
Rosebush	Captain Richard Hodges	32 guns	Transport – 130 crew
Golden Cock	Captain William Garrett	32 guns	Transport – 140 crew

COLONIAL IRONSIDES

Gillyflower	Captain Henry Fenn	24 guns	Transport – 120 crew
Adam and Eve	Captain William Coppain	Unarmed	Storeship – 30 crew
Arms of Holland	Captain Samuel Hawkes	34 guns	Transport – 140 crew
Crow	Captain Thomas Thompson	30 guns	Transport – 140 crew
Marigold	Captain Humphrey Felsted	20 guns	Transport – 100 crew
Sampson	Captain John Hubbard	20 guns	Transport – 140 crew
Westergate	---	34 guns	Transport – 140 crew
Cardiff	Captain John Grove	36 guns	Transport – crew unknown
Tulip	Captain Jeffrey Dane	32 guns	Transport – 180 crew
Falcon	Captain Thomas Fleet	28 guns	Flyboat – 80 crew
Falcon	Captain William Tickell	10 guns	Fireship – crew unknown
Hound	Captain Richard Rooth	28 guns	100 crew
Falmouth	Captain Thomas Wright	28 guns	100 crew
Adventure	Captain Robert Mills	32 guns	120 crew

2 ketches, 1 hoy, details not recorded

TOTALS   **1,118 guns**   **5,105 crew**

1,830 soldiers, less those in transports

38 horses

Appendix II to Chapter 7

English Army Lists of the Expedition to Hispaniola

5,320 officers and men embarked for the expedition under the command of Robert Venables. In the Barbadoes he recruited a further 3,600 men from the freemen and indentured servants on the island, who were joined by further detachments from St Christopher, Nevis and Montserrat to form eight regiments of foot for the attack on Hispaniola.

Command and Staff

General Robert Venables	Controller of the Ordnance Thomas Hughes	Judge Advocate John Cudworth
Major-General James Heane	Clarke Edward James	Provost Marshal Mark Fowler
Major-General Richard Fortescue	Richard Povey, Commissary of Stores	Provost Marshal Thomas Goodfellow
Adjutant-General Thomas Jackson*	Quartermaster General John Rudyard	Deputy Provost Marshals William Deane, Luke Hill, Thomas Bossey, Edward Rich
Adjutant-General James Butler	Marshal General John Dean	Paymaster General Robert Wadeson
Adjutant-General Phillip Warde	Commissary Richard Fleetwood	Muster Master John Laughton
Chaplain Thomas Gage	Assistant Commissary __ Murford†	Deputy Muster-Master Richard Scott
Secretary John Daniel	Gunsmith George Varley	
Treasurer Thomas Wadeson		
Secretary __ Temple†		

---

*   Cashiered in Hispaniola.
†   Killed in Hispaniola.

COLONIAL IRONSIDES

Venables' Regiment

This regiment was raised in England in 1654 and had no connection with Venables' earlier Irish regiment. It mustered 10, possibly eleven companies with a strength of 10 staff, 120 officers and NCOs and 912 men. The regiment suffered severely at Hispaniola in 1655, losing five of its 10 or 11 colours, three captains killed and many men killed or captured. After this engagement, the regiment numbered only 245 fit men, with another 238 sick.

Captains	Lieutenants	Ensigns
Colonel Robert Venables	Captain-Lieutenant Henry Potter	Ensign Robert Minshin
Lieutenant-Colonel Edward D'Oyley	Captain-Lieutenant Chad Mattersley	Ensign Henry Skepworth
Major Francis Mercer	Lieutenant John Lloyd (to D'Oyley)	Ensign Henry Goddard
Captain Francis Disney‡	Lieutenant Lewis Ashton	Ensign Thomas Elendre
Captain Thomas Hancock§	Lieutenant __ Ballard	Ensign Thomas Breres (to Cooke)
Captain George Butler§	Lieutenant John Barrell (to Hancock)	Ensign James Burey (to D'Oyley)
Captain Obadiah Hinde§	Lieutenant Thomas Fuller	Ensign Robert Don (to Hancock)
Captain __ Pawlett§	Lieutenant Ralph Swinnerton	Ensign William Simons (to Butler)
Captain George Parsons	Lieutenant Henry Ferrobosco (to Disney)	
Captain John Cooke	Lieutenant Tate Howell (to Cooke)	
Captain __ Paris	Lieutenant Andrew Peter (to Hinde)	
Captain Henry Davis	Lieutenant Edward Sackfield (to Parsons)	

Staff
Provost Marshall Nathaniel Flick
Gentleman-at-Arms William White (to Cooke)
Surgeon Richard Duckenfield‡
Surgeon's Mate William Armstrong
Surgeon's Mate William Fisher
Apothecary William Drew
Chaplain Thomas Cage
Quartermaster John Frampton
Gentleman-at-Arms Henry Ramsey

D'Oyley's Regiment, or the Barbadoes Regiment

This regiment was formed as the Barbadoes in 1655 and mustered 830 men with 120 officers, NCOs and drummers, and 10 staff. Morris did not accompany the regiment when it left the Barbadoes, resigning the Colonelcy in favour of D'Oyley.

Colonel Lewis Morris	Captain-Lieutenant James Berry
Lieutenant-Colonel Edward D'Oyley	Lieutenant John Fisher

---

*   Served in Hammond's Regiment 1645–1646. Died during the voyage.
†   Killed at Hispaniola.
‡   Possibly a relative of Colonel Robert Duckenfield, who had raised a regiment for service in the Isle of Man.

APPENDIX II TO CHAPTER 7

Major John Reade
Captain Richard Stevens
Captain Robert Smith
Captain Theobald Thornhill
Captain __ Noell
Captain __ Vavaster
Captain Augustine Thornhill
Captain __ Downes
Captain __ Madison**
Captain __ Fenn**

Lieutenant Humphrey Groves
Ensign Robert Stephens

Buller's Regiment
Raised in England by drawing drafts from the standing regiments, Buller's consisted of 10 companies with a strength of 10 staff, 120 officers and NCOs and 916 men.

Captains	Lieutenants	Ensigns
Colonel Anthony Buller††	Captain-Lieutenant Thomas Allen	Ensign Thomas Smith
Lieutenant-Colonel Francis Barrington‡‡	Captain-Lieutenant Thomas Sprey	Ensign John Barrow
Major Michael Bland	Lieutenant Henry Middleton	Ensign Samuel Greene
Captain Vincent Corbett	Lieutenant Peter Parry (to Cooper)	Ensign Anthony How
Captain Christopher Cooper	Lieutenant Abraham Pegg (to Bingham)	Ensign John Eyton (to Minne)
Captain Edward (Adam) Baynard	Lieutenant Charles Glapthorne (to Corbett)	Ensing John Hooke (to Bland)
Captain __ Throgmorton	Lieutenant Randall Kettell (to Baynard)	Ensign Richard Weld (to Baynard)
Captain John Minne	Lieutenant Benjamin Larkin (to Minne)	
Captain John Poulton	Lieutenant Jonathan Penkeville (to Arundell)	
Captain Stroud Bingham	Lieutenant Ralph Garth (to Throckmorton)	

Staff
Chaplain John Vaughan
Gentleman-at-Arms James Bland (to D'Oyley's Regiment)
Gentleman-at-Arms William Wosley
Quartermaster Isaac Berkenhead (moved to command the Scoutmaster's company)
Surgeon James Winter
Gunsmith George Varley

---

* Died May 1656, CSPC Addenda, 1656.
† Rumoured to have Royalist sympathies; blamed for miscarriage of the attack on Hispaniola, later encouraged 'murmuring' the army.
‡ Served in Okey's Dragoons and in Ireland under Henry Cromwell. Died in 1660.

COLONIAL IRONSIDES

Carter's Regiment

The regiment was raised in England by drawing drafts from the standing regiments. Before leaving the Barbadoes it mustered 10 staff, 120 officers and NCOs and 834 private men in 10 companies.

Captains	Lieutenants	Ensigns
Colonel Andrew Carter[§§]	Lieutenant John Filkins[¶¶]	Ensign William Blanch (to Halford)
Lieutenant-Colonel Theobald Bushell	Lieutenant Thomas Totty (to Bushell)	Ensign James Herbert (to Filkins)
Major John Ferguson	Lieutenant Robert Hanny (to Ferguson)	Ensign Gabriel Huntley (to Bowers)
Captain John Filkins	Lieutenant Richard Baker (to Filkins)	Ensign George Watts (to Blunt)
Captain __ Colbourne	Lieutenant Thomas Clayton (to Bowers)	
Captain Nathaniel Bowers	Lieutenant Orwin Powell (to Halford)	
Captain Abraham Fincher	Lieutenant George White	
Captain Daniel How		
Captain Nicholas Halford		
Captain Winkfield Blunt		
Captain Thomas Salkield[‡‡‡]		
Captain-Lieutenant Richard Wilbraham		

Staff

Gentleman-at-Arms William Johnson
Surgeon Walter Barefoote
Chaplain William Chidley
Quartermaster William Blewfield
Gunsmith Lasen Jenkins
Gunsmith's Mate John Palmer

Fortescue's Regiment

Raised in England by drawing drafts from the standing regiments. This regiment mustered 10 staff, 120 officers and NCOs in March 1655 in 10 companies.

Captains	Lieutenants	Ensigns
Colonel Richard Fortescue[†††]	Captain-Lieutenant William Hambleyne	Ensign David Douglas
Lieutenant-Colonel Richard Holdep	Lieutenant Thomas Hill (to Hill)	Ensign William Hall

---

* Died in 1655.
† Captain in March 1656.
‡ Possibly a relative of Sir William Salkield.
§ Died in October 1655.

Major William Hill	Lieutenant John Bray (to Leverington)	Ensign Thomas Freeman
Captain Thomas White	Lieutenant James Rudiard	Ensign James Bates (to Edwards)
Captain Henry Bartlett	Lieutenant __ Debben	Ensign William Carman (to White)
Captain Samuel Leverington‡‡‡	Lieutenant Benjamin Gordward	Ensign Thomas Dowing (to Keene)
Captain Bartholomew Davis§§§	Lieutenant Thomas French (to Wells)	Ensign William Denis (to Bartlett)
Captain Richard Kenne	Lieutenant Henry Hurst (to Edwards)	Ensign Thomas Howell (to Davis)
Captain Richard Wells	Lieutenant Edward Mallinson (to White)	Ensign Richard Lawrence (to Wells)
Captain Obadiah Edwards	Lieutenant Thomas Ethon (to Davis)	Ensign James Peake (to Holdep)
Captain Thomas White		Ensign Henry Kent (to Leverington)
Captain __ Douglas		

Staff
Quartermaster Ralph Hardwick
Gentleman-at-Arms Thomas May (to Fortescue)
Gentleman-at-Arms John Poulton (to Buller)
Gentleman-at-Arms Thomas Edwards (to Edwards)
Surgeon John Henry Hilsman
Surgeon's Mate Edward Stapleton
Chaplain Nathaniel Lane

Heane's Regiment
Heane and his regiment had been engaged in the capture of Jersey in 1651 and the efficiency with which he had carried out this task had recommended him to the Protector. This regiment seems to have been a new unit raised by drawing drafts from the standing regiments in England. The regiment consisted of 10 companies with a strength of 10 staff, 120 officers and NCOs and 1,058 men.

Captains	Lieutenants	Ensigns
Colonel James Heane¶¶¶	Lieutenant __ Marshall	Ensign __ Farris (to Heane)
Lieutenant-Colonel John Clarke¶¶¶	Lieutenant Andrew Houncell (to Heane)	Ensign William Hopkins (to Barry)
Major Samuel Barry	Lieutenant William King (to Barry)	Ensign John Clarke (to Clarke)
Captain Thomas Walters¶¶¶	Lieutenant William Wandell (to Heane)	Ensign George Rivers (to Walters)
Captain Henry Archbold	Lieutenant William Rivers (to Archbold)	Ensign Thomas Boys¶¶¶

---

* Severely wounded at Hispaniola.
† Died in October 1655.
‡ Killed at Hispaniola.

COLONIAL IRONSIDES

Captain Richard Younge   Lieutenant William Huntley
                                                         (to Younge)

Captain Richard Bamford   Lieutenant George Faulkner
                                                         (to Willett)

Captain Gregory Toms

Captain Edward Willett

Captain Daniel Smith

Captain Robert Taylor

Staff
Gentleman-at-Arms Richard Clearke
Gunsmith William Fudge
Surgeon's Mate John Frankling
Surgeon's Mate Jesse Wharton
Quartermaster Bartholomew Jackson
Chaplain Roger Manners

Holdep's, or the St Christopher's Regiment
This Regiment was raised in St Christopher and the Leeward Islands during February and March 1655. Between 800 and 900 men came from St Christopher, 300 from Nevis and 80 from Montserrat making a total of 1,200 men. The regiment was placed under the command of Richard Holdep, Lieutenant-Colonel of Fortescue's Regiment in the Barbadoes, who had been governor of Surinam.

The regiment sailed to join the expedition to Hispaniola, where half the men were landed, with Buller's Regiment and took part in operations against the fort of St Jeronimo. After the failure of the expedition the regiment sailed for Jamaica. The St Christopher's Regiment was disbanded in June 1655.

Colonel Richard Holdep
Lieutenant-Colonel Michael Bland
Captain Giles Clapthorne
Captain John Cox[*]
Captain __ Bounty[†]
Ensign James Bland
Lieutenant John Otter

The Sea Regiment
Raised from the seamen of the fleet. It consisted of 1,000 men in 10 companies and was probably the best fighting unit in the army.

Vice Admiral William Goodson as Colonel
Lieutenant-Colonel Benjamin Blake
Major Edward Blagg
Captain Bartholomew Ketcher
Captain David Catts, or Kats[‡]

---

[*] From St Christopher. Killed at Hispaniola.
[†] From St Christopher.
[‡] Killed in Hispaniola.

Captain Humphrey Fleshed
Captain William Tickle
Captain Francis Kirby
Captain Robert Mill
Captain John Molam
Captain-Lieutenant Thomas Blackman

Troop of Horse (raised in England)
Because of contrary winds, the ship carrying this troop did not reach Hispaniola in time to take part in the campaign. Two small troops of horse were raised in the Barbadoes to take its place.

Captain Henry Jones
Lieutenant John Josse
Cornet Samuel Bedlington
Quartermaster William Brigham
Surgeon Thomas Lugg
12 officers and NCOs, 65 men.

Troop of Horse (raised in the Barbadoes)
Captain __ Heane[*]

Troop of Horse (raised in the Barbadoes)
Captain Philip Carpenter
10 officers and NCOs, 56 men between the two troops.

Scoutmaster General's Company
Captain Isaac Berkenhead
60 men

Traine of Artillerie
Captain John Hughes
50 gunners, matrosses and artificers

Company of Fusiliers or Firelocks
Captain __ Pawlett[†]
Captain __ Johnson
12 officers and NCOs, 120 men

Reformadoes
Captain __ Jennings, one other officer and 100 gentlemen.

Peter Blenen	Edward Powell
James Baker	Henry Rudyard

---

[*] Son of Major-General Heane.
[†] From Venables' Regiment. Killed in Hispaniola. Possibly Thomas Pawlett who had served in Colonel Thomas Glemham's Regiment in 1640 (Peacock, p.80).

COLONIAL IRONSIDES

John Dolaners	Stanley Stephenson
Thomas Fisher	John Sharpe
Francis Fairfax	Roger Sheere
Benjamin Francis	Robert Terrill
John Hill	Thomas Walded
George Howard	Samuel Sutton
George Herbert	John Wilson
Edward Hayd	Robert Warde
William Kidwell	Richard Cutts
Peter Murford	William Mordaunt
William Owin	Richard Blake

NOTES

1 See especially *The Narrative of General Venables*, in Thurloe, vol. iii, Appendix B for lists of the officers; and CSP Colonial Series, North America and the West Indies, Addenda 1574–1674, pp.90, 91, 105; and Firth and Davies, vol. ii; and 'A particular list of persons paid their first month's pay for their Respective qualities under the command of general Venables in the west indies, December 1654', in *Caribbeana*, vol. II, citing CO5/32, f.16.

8

Penn and Venables' Attack on San Domingo, 1655

Hispaniola, the object of Penn and Venables' expedition, is the second largest of the Caribbean islands after Cuba, with an area of 29,418 square miles (76,192 square km). Cuba lies 50 miles (80 km) to the north-west across the Windward Passage; 120 miles (190 km) to the south-west lies Jamaica, separated by the Jamaica Channel. Puerto Rico lies 80 miles (130 km) east of Hispaniola across the Mona Passage. Because of its mountainous topography, Hispaniola's climate is varied; the predominant winds northeast trades. These winds drop their moisture on the northern mountains and create a rain shadow on the southern coast, where some areas receive as little as 16 inches (400 millimetres) of rainfall, and have a semi-arid climate for much of the year, the wettest period being from late April to October during which hurricanes can be experienced, especially August to October. Droughts are common when hurricanes do not develop.

It was on Hispaniola that Christopher Columbus first landed on 6 December 1492, at a small bay he named San Nicolas, on the north-western coast. He was given a friendly welcome by the indigenous people, the Taino. Trading with the natives yielded much gold and Columbus was led to believe that much more would be found inland. Before he could explore further, his flagship, the *Santa Maria*, ran aground and sank in the bay on 24 December. With only two smaller ships left to make the voyage home, Columbus built a fortified encampment, La Navidad, and left 21 men to await his return the following year. Colonisation then began in earnest when Columbus brought 1,300 men to Hispaniola in November 1493 with the intention of establishing a permanent settlement. They found that the encampment at Navidad had been destroyed and all the men left behind killed by the Taino. Columbus decided to look for a better site and in January 1494 he established La Isabela, named after the Queen of Spain. In 1496, it was destroyed by a hurricane. As a result, the town was rebuilt on the opposite side of the Ozama River and called renamed Santo Domingo. It is therefore the oldest permanent European settlement in the Americas.

In reprisal for the murder of Columbus's men, the Spanish instituted a harsh regime of slavery and ethnic cleansing of the Taino, while bringing

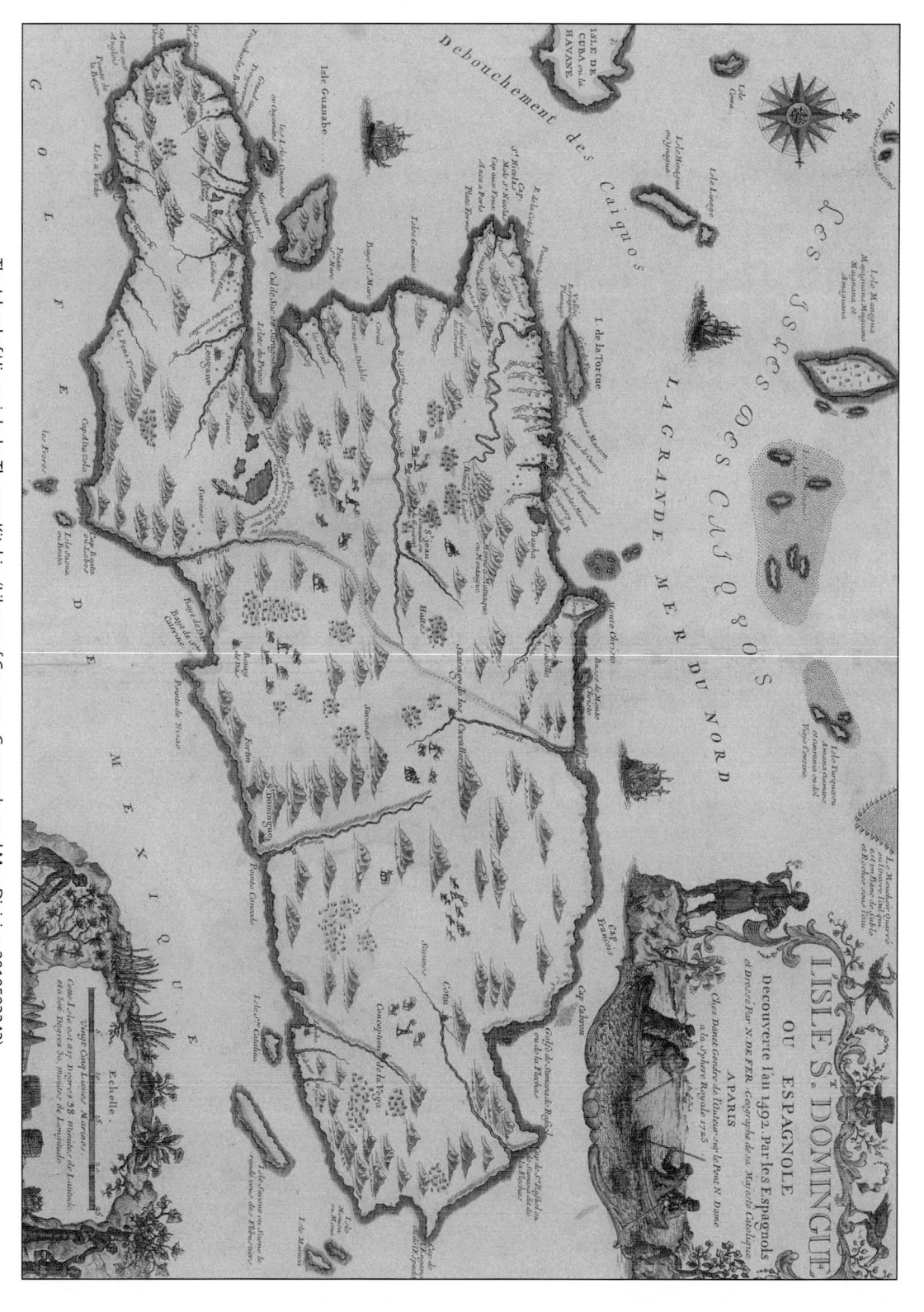

The Island of Hispaniola, by Thomas Kitchin. (Library of Congress, Geography and Map Division 2010593343)

African slaves to develop the agriculture of the island which focused on sugar, tobacco, cocoa, fruit and cattle. A census of 1574 reported 1,000 Spanish and 12,000 African slaves on the island, a figure which had grown by the time Venables and Penn arrived.

On 1 January 1586, as a consequence of Queen Elizabeth I's war with Spain, Hispaniola was attacked by an English force led by Sir Francis Drake, during his Great Expedition to raid the Spanish Main. English soldiers and sailors occupied the city for over a month and captured much booty along with a ransom of 25,000 gold ducats, paid by the Governor, Don Cristobal de Ovalle, as the price of their departure on 1 February. They left behind 20 ships in the harbour burned or sunk, and three other vessels seized by Drake to replace three of his that had been abandoned as unseaworthy. Two-hundred and forty guns and quantities of merchandise were moved into the holds of the English ships, and the ranks were bolstered by scores of liberated galley slaves. One-third of Santo Domingo lay in ruins and it took many decades for the city to recover from Drake's attack. For the Spanish it was a major blow to their prestige, but a huge triumph for the English.[1]

San Domingo by Allain Mallet, *Les Traveaux de Mars* (<https://digi.ub.uni-heidelberg.de> accessed 2 January 2020>).

The Island was described as being: 'Fruitful and pleasant … it abounds in cattle, as beeves and hogs, tame and wild … there are also sheep, and goats and delicate fowls … their maine trade is hides, sugar, tobaccos and chocolate.'[2] The city of San Domingo, according to Venables' instructions, was 'not considerably fortified' and would 'probably be possessed without much difficulty'. It was described in detail as follows:

> … scituate [sic] on a plaine, next the seaside, in a bay to the westward of a river running by the eastward part thereof [the river Ozama], a most safe and convenient harbour … The towne is walled to the westward, hath the river on the eastward, the sea to the southward: but to the northward it hath only a lime hedge growing thick about it … [the] castle, forts and the towne walls believed to have 100 pieces of ordnance, 11 or 12 churches, in form about 2 miles in circumference.[3]

This was a very fair description, as can be seen from the sketch map on p.140, which is taken from Spanish accounts of the campaign.[4] The contemporary map with its notes (pp.146–147), shows the investment made by the Spanish in the aftermath of the attack but it should not be supposed that the fortifications were anything like as formidable as those prevalent in Europe. The Spanish, as we know, had been alerted to the likelihood of an English attack. A new governor and captain-general, Don Bernardino de Meneses Bracamonte y Zapata, 1st

COLONIAL IRONSIDES

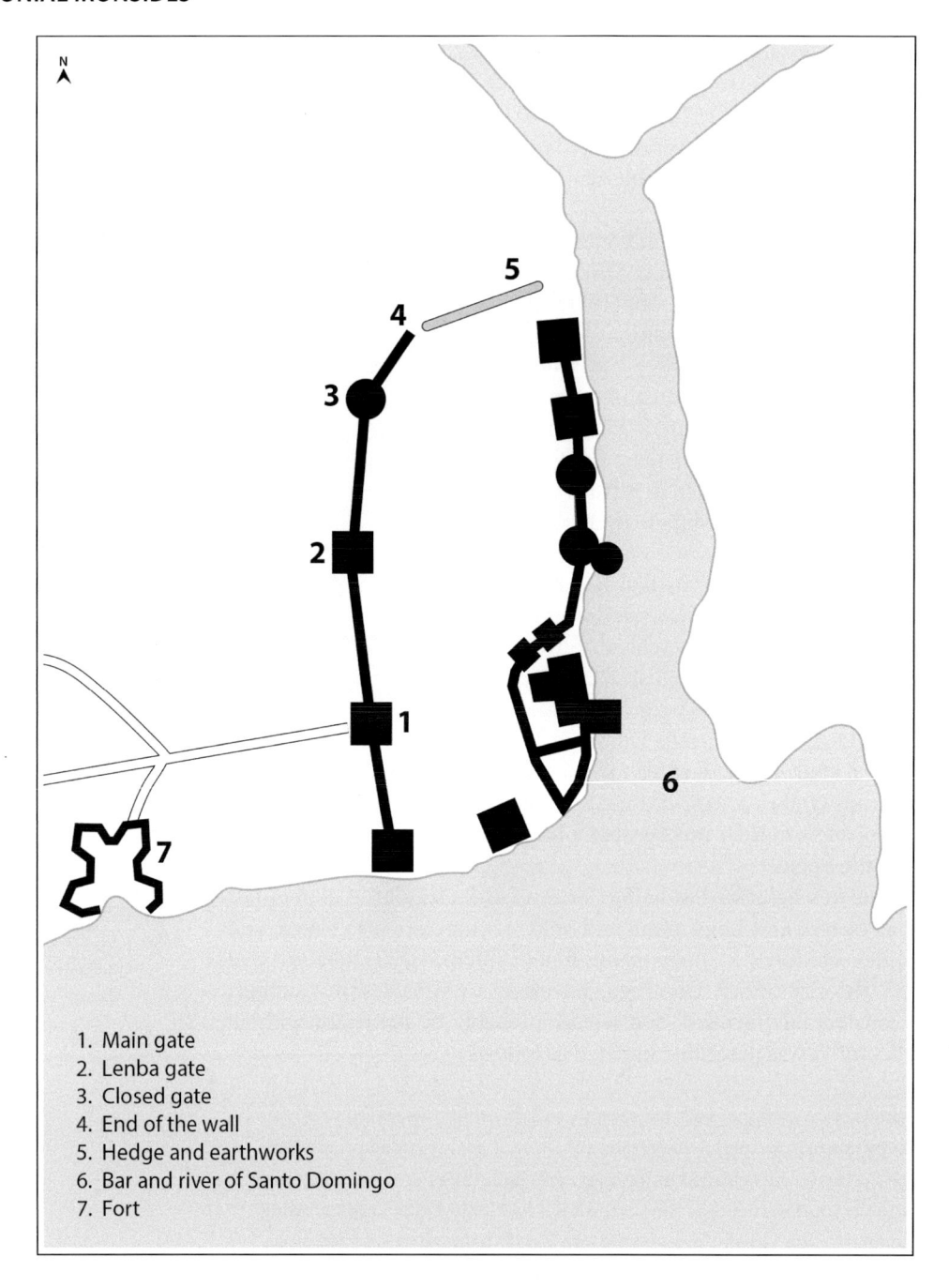

1. Main gate
2. Lenba gate
3. Closed gate
4. End of the wall
5. Hedge and earthworks
6. Bar and river of Santo Domingo
7. Fort

Sketch map of the fortifications of San Domingo as they appeared in 1655, drawn from an original in *Spanish Narratives of the English Attack on Santo Domingo 1655*, reproduced by kind permission of the Royal Historical Society.

Notes

This plan shows the walls and fortifications of the city of Santo Domingo as they were when the Count de Peñalva arrived and the English attacked in April 1655, It differs in many details from the contemporary map on p.146, which incorporates improvements made after the attack had been repulsed.

Extreme lower left is the Fort of San Geronimo and the road junction where the English were ambushed; compare with to see the changes that followed the walling up of the Main gate, or Puerte Grande.

Count de Peñalva,* had been despatched and he arrived only a few days before the English. Peñalva found that only 170 of the 300-strong garrison were fit for service.[5] He had also brought 200 arquebusiers as reinforcements with him; he reformed and reinforced the existing companies and even formed a new company from the passengers on the ship in which he had arrived, the *La Conception*,[6] so that once the militia was mobilised, and contingents called in from other settlements like Santiago and Azua, he could field a force of 1,200 to 1,500 – outnumbered on paper at least by the English to the tune of seven to one.[7] The Governor ordered a rapid increase in the amount of food stored in the city which was, however, well supplied with water, arms and ammunition. The outlying forts were also supplied with more powder, shot and slow match. All foreigners were immediately locked up and a curfew initiated.[8] As well as sending out warnings to outlying settlements and calling in the militia, the Governor also sent warning of the arrival of the English to his counterparts at Cartagena, Puerto Rico, Cuba and Tortuga.

All males over the age of 14, regardless of their ethnic origin, were ordered to report for duty in the militia and a proclamation issued to all runaway slaves who reported for duty, that they would be freed.[9] Many of the militia, perhaps 300, appear to have been found from among a part of the population who hunted the wild cattle with long lances, selling the meat, hides and tallow. These men were described as:

> … a sort of Vagabons that are saued from the gallows in Spaine and the king doth send them heare; These go by the name of Cow killers, and indeed that is theyer trad, for they lieu by killing of Cattille for the hides and tallow. Thes are those that done all the mischief … when you have fired at them they will fall doun vpon thayer right knew, and when you have fiered then they will come most desperate. But if you keep them out, then they flie for it; but if they come within you, then stand cleare … these lances are longer than a halfepicke.[10]

They and other troops of the militia were armed with a fearsome weapon which caused them to be described as 'lancers', as Captain Manuel Pallano graphically described them:

> These lances are the most effective weapons which cruel industry has yet invented against the human kind … these lances do not wound – they kill. Although the enemy be numerous, two lance-thrusts are as quickly given as one. Although they come on in armour … one two-handed stroke lays them low, and the throat or lower abdomen are exposed, so that if the man did not die of the first thrust, he is made a corpse by the second. Each lance head is the size of a man's fist, and they make as big a hole entering as leaving. They are handled by men who use no other weapons, and with them they may face a bull or a bear – fierce animals! I prefer a hundred lancers to a thousand firearms, because with lancers, coming hand-to-hand, in the time it takes to say two *credos*, not a man will be left alive out of a whole army.[11]

---

*   Born *c*. 1625 in Talavera de la Reina, died 30 January 1656 in Cartagena de Indias. He is also described as President of the Royal *Audencia*, a superior court with extensive jurisdiction and from which appeal could only be made to the Council for the Indies in Spain.

A seventeenth-century army on the march from Henry Hexham, *Principles of the art militarie*. (Folger Digital Image Collections <https://luna.folger.edu> accessed 1 January 2020)

What followed is recounted in detail from the English side in *The Narrative of General Venables*, with its several annexes including the journal of Lieutenant-Colonel Whistler; in *Memorials of* Penn; and in various letters to Secretary Thurloe by officers of the expedition. On the Spanish side, the beautifully written account of Captain Manuel Gonzalez Pallano is a prime source, already cited; so too Count Peñalva's report, the Notorial Account and the Treasurer's Report. All these appear in translation in *Spanish Narratives of the English Attack*, found in the *Archivo General de Indias* in Seville and edited by Irene A. Wright in 1923. There is a remarkable degree of agreement between the sources.

The fleet approached San Domingo on 13 April and on this day the proclamation against plunder and the rules on prize distribution were issued. The orders, no surprise to Venables himself, led to an outcry, little short of actual mutiny. Commissioner Winslow had already written to Thurloe from the Barbadoes complaining of the prize regulations and suggesting that Penn, who was noted at this time for extreme prickliness, was attempting to embezzle the proceeds of any prizes by withdrawing control from the Commissioners.[12] As the fleet closed with the coast on 14 April, around noon,[13] the inhabitants could be seen running for refuge in the city. A council of war of the commissioners, senior staff officers and the regimental colonels had been convened on 20 April to decide on where to land,[14] as Colonel Holdep recalled:

> ... it was put to the vote which way the army should march; and it was pressed by the Generall and Fortescue to march intirely with the army by way of Geronemoe [Fort San Geronimo, to the west of the city close to the coast]; but the Major Generall, Colonel Buller and myself, with Lieutenant Colonel Clarke, were for dividing the armey, and marching to the north-west of the citty; but the generall ... and some others overvoted us.[15]

The Commissioners therefore ordered that the landing should take place close to Drake's landing place, near the mouth of the Jaina river. This was close enough to the city for the troops to close rapidly with the objective but far enough for concealment. The surf was, however, heavy and a lee shore caused Penn to refuse to risk his ships' boats.[16] Venables suggested in his *Narrative* that he had urged Penn to land the force close to San Domingo but that Penn had refused, citing a boom across the River Ozama – which according to Spanish sources was not there, but the river mouth was blocked by two ships, sunk there by Captain Vincente Duran on the orders of the governor;[17] The guns of the city appear also to have had plenty of powder and shot and commanded the entrance comprehensively. There is mention of a special platform having been erected for bronze guns, which would fire heavier shot to greater ranges than iron guns.[18] Landing thus under the guns of the city and in a harbour which was unsounded was anyway an unsafe method of operations and Penn would take no advantage from the failure of the operation. Penn himself said that he was prepared to land there, once soundings had been taken.[19] It is certainly clear, too, that there was a good deal of confusion in the orders issued to the various transports.

Whatever the reason, the main body of the army was landed much further west at the mouth of the River Nizao and according to Venables consisted of his own regiment; those of Heane, Fortescue, Carter and D'Oyley; five companies of the regiment of Holdep; the Sea Regiment under Goodson; the reformadoes; two troops of horse raised in the Barbadoes; the Scoutmaster's foot troopers; and Captain Pawlett's fusiliers. The regiment of Buller, with the remaining five companies of the regiment of Holdep (some 1,500 men, therefore), were put ashore to the east of the city, on the far side of the River Ozama, which therefore cut them off from cooperating easily with the main body.[20] The Spanish were well aware that the fleet had divided as this is mentioned in several accounts and had been reported by fishermen.[21]

The main body landed without opposition on 14 April, just over 20 miles by road from the Jaina River and another 10 miles from there to San Domingo. Three days' rations were supposed to have been issued. It appears, however, that the sailors held back part of the stores to fill their own wants, leaving the soldiers on very short commons. The missing store ships, noted earlier, did not in fact arrive until after the expedition had left; the Spanish beached them, wrecked them, looted them and burned them.[22] Quarrels over stores were, from here on, a frequent fact of life.[23] Water was also short, although the rivers and streams, at the end of the dry season, did maintain some flow. It was at once apparent that the want of leather water bottles, or flasks, noted earlier, was a serious problem.

On the first day the army marched at around 1.00 p.m. with no guide: the reformadoes led as advanced guard or forlorn hope, followed by the scouts and with Pawlett's men on the flanks to protect against ambush. Next came D'Oyley's West Indians followed by the remaining foot regiments and the horse. The march covered three or four miles through open savannah in which a few Spaniards fired shots at the forlorn hope before making off. Night came early and the army camped for the night without water or tents and the temperature fell rapidly so that little sleep was to be had.

After morning prayers, the march continued on Sunday, 15 April in hot weather, with no surface water to be found. The way again led through grassland, which the Spaniards had burned after having driven off their cattle. After marching some 10 miles they came around noon to a river, probably the Agua Dulce, which had almost dried up although some water was found.[24] The army then turned south and marched a mile to the sea. Here the advanced guard surprised a small body of Spaniards and drove them into the woods, exchanging musketry fire during which Captain Thomas Allen and a trooper of the scouts were killed. Here the army rested during the heat around noon. The afternoon march covered around seven miles along a country road lined with citrus trees and the soldiers did not hesitate to eat their fill – so much so that many suffered from diarrhoea; this in turn induced dysentery and a fever from which men soon began to drop and then die.[25] In the late afternoon another Spanish ambush was encountered and beaten off with the loss of one man killed and another wounded from the scouts, who were, it appears, mounted.[26] The army camped for the night close to a small watercourse, having marched 18 miles.[27]

On the following day, 16 April, the army set off at 6.00 a.m. led by the forlorn hope with Fortescue's Regiment taking up the lead position in the main body. Less than half a mile on the road, the forlorn hope stumbled into a Spanish farm and sugar factory which the scouts had failed to identify the previous evening: there was water, sugar, fruit and pigs. Shortly afterwards the soldiers found and wrecked a Catholic chapel half a mile short of the Najallo River, which was crossed. A mile or so further on, the Sinagua River was also crossed beyond which several farms were passed and plundered.

That evening, its rations exhausted, the army reached the Jaina River. Here, a man was seen on the far side and so one of the forlorn hope who could swim, crossed the river and spoke to the man. He turned out to be a soldier from Holdep's Regiment who had been left behind, sick, when the fleet had landed Buller's force. From him, Venables learned that Buller had not after all landed to the east of the city but had come ashore to the west, close to a small fort, 'breast works of bush and sand',[28] which commanded the landing beach. Peñalva had placed 200 men there, under Captains Damian del Castillo Vaca* and Don Alvaro Garabito de Aguilar. When news of the landing was received in San Domingo, a further 100 men under *Maestre de Campo* Don Juan Morfa Geraldino were sent to reinforce the position and to reconnoitre as far out as Nisao.[29] Geraldino was in fact an Irish Catholic émigré, a former privateer, who had joined the Spanish Army in 1633; he is identified, interestingly, in Venables' narrative as an Irishman.[30] It was this force that had ambushed the main body on the 15th and from their prisoner, the Spanish had learned the size of the English force. The fort at Jayna was reinforced to a strength of 400 but once the main body of the English closed up, the garrison withdrew to the city.[31]

---

* In 1662, Castillo petitioned for requital of services against the English; his letters and account of the action in the West Indies Library, Institute of Jamaica, agree with the account of Captain Pallano.

PENN AND VENABLES' ATTACK ON SAN DOMINGO, 1655

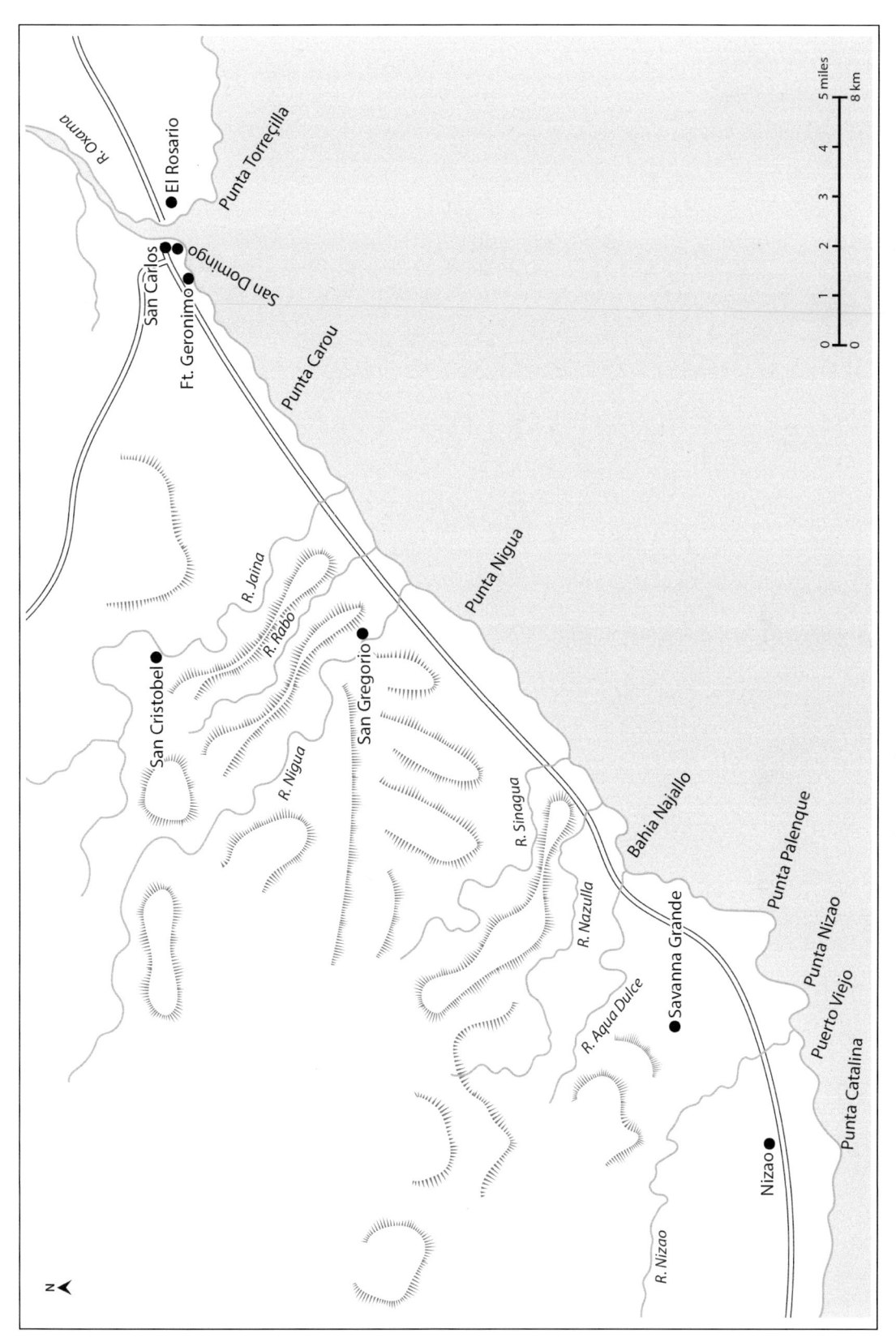

The route of the English Army to San Domingo

COLONIAL IRONSIDES

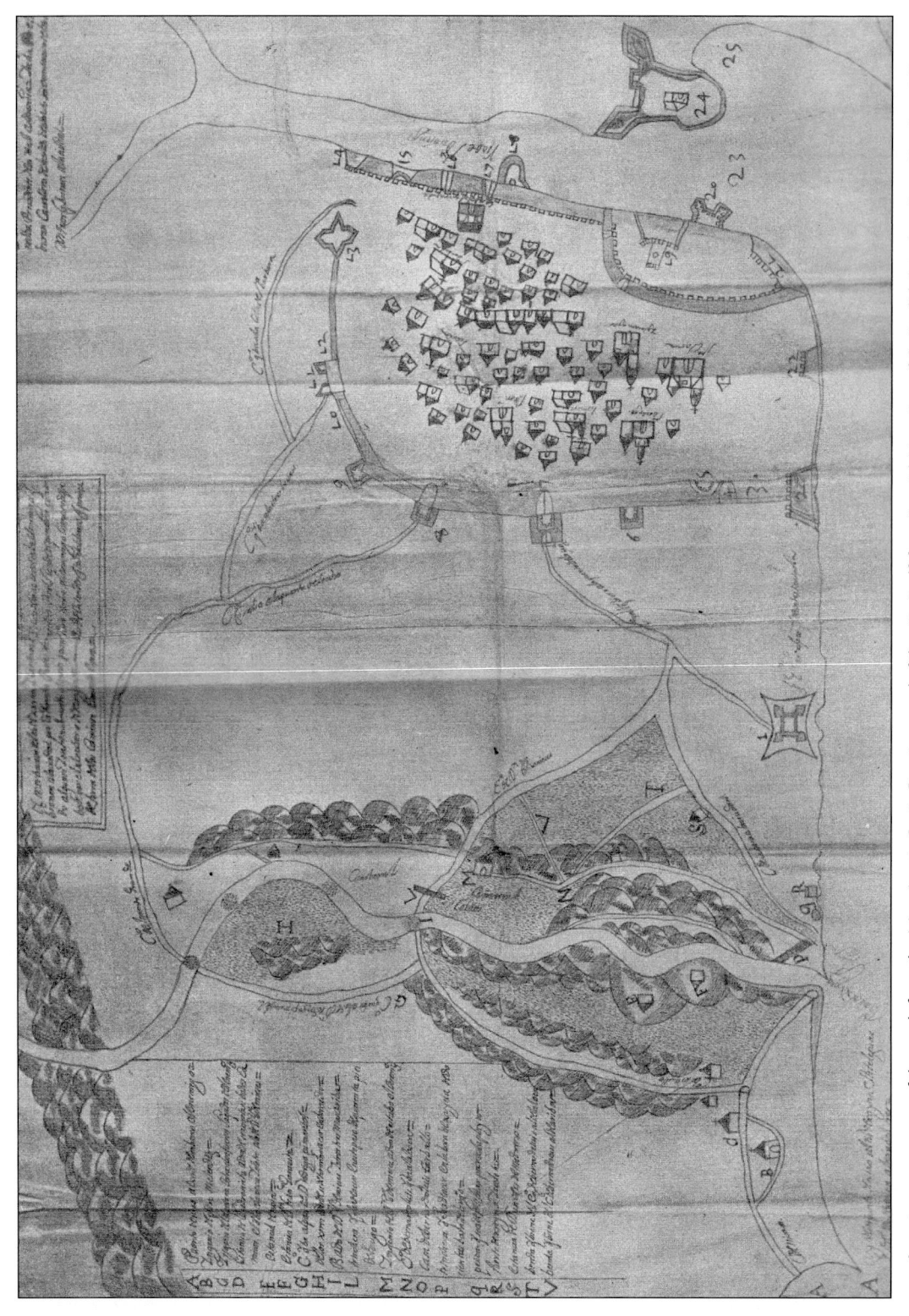

A contemporary map of the roads from the Jaina river to Santo Domingo, and of the city itself, from *Spanish Narratives of the English Attack on Santo Domingo 1655*, reproduced by kind permission of the Royal Historical Society.

Key to Contemporary Map (above)

(From *Spanish Narratives of the English Attack on Santo Domingo 1655*, edited and translated by I.A. Wright for the Royal Historical Society. Camden Miscellany vol. xiv, London, 1926).

II. Map of Jaina river and roads that come up to the city by different routes from Nisao, where the enemy landed; closed some, and built trenches at various places to receive the enemy, as is indicated in the lettered explanation in the margin. It is to be understood that all the white part, except the roads, is thick bush. Drawn by Francisco Vincente Duran, 1656 and accompanying Count de Peñalva's letter of April 3, 1656.

A. Port Nisao, where the enemy landed. From Point Nisao to the Jayna river, seven leagues; and from Jayna river to the city, three.
B. From fort San Geronimo, a third of a league; and from the river mouth to San Geronimo, two and two-thirds.
C. Pedro Melendez' sugar mill.
D. The depositary's mill. Both were sacked by the enemy.
E. Don Pedro Nieto's farm, where the two roads divide – one leading to the river mouth and the other to Don Juan de Mieses' property. Tapia's farm.
F. Don Francisco Garabito's farm.
G. Road that leads to Don Rodrigo Pimentel's ford.
H. Belonging to the free blacks, where it has been decided to lay an ambuscade.
I. Don Juan de Miseses' ford, and three others, above it.
L. Trench to be thrown up at this ford, forty feet long.
M. Don Juan de Mieses' sugar mill, where the enemy was.
N. Bernado Luis' road to the river mouth.
O. Bernado Luis Caraballo's house.
P. Trench to be built at Boca de Jayna, 200 *varas* long.
Q. Hill to be fortified, to protect the beach.
R. Jayna fort and small harbour.
S. Don Andres Medrano's farm.
T. Trail, from Bernardo Luis' road to the river road.
V. Trail, from Bernardo Luis' road to the upper road.

Roads:
Nisao Road
Balsiquillo Road.
Road that leads to Don Rodrigo Pimentel's property.
Monte Grande Road (see B.)
Road that formerly led to the Lenba Gate.
Road to Tres Cruces [Three Crosses]
Road to Santa Barbara Street.

NOTES

A is Nisao where the bulk of the English army landed; B and C are the sugar factories which they came across and sacked.

It is stated that the distance from Nisao to Boca de Jayna (the harbour at the mouth of the Jaina river, where Buller and Holdep landed), is seven leagues, or twenty-one miles, and three leagues, or nine miles, from Jaina to the city. These distances agree with the figures given by the English accounts.

Of interest is the comparative position of M in the centre right, which is Don Juan de Mieses' sugar factory, where the main body of the English rested on 27 April before advancing into the first ambush and battle; they retired there at dawn the next day.

III. Plan of the city of Santo Domingo, fortified by Count de Peñalva, president of its royal *audienca*. And drawn by Captain Francisco Vicente Duran, knight of the Order of Christ; with map of the river Jayna and roads leading to the city.

(Within the walls)
Santa Clara.
Santo Domingo (Dominican convent).
The principal church (cathedral).
La Merced. (Mecedarians).
San Francisco. (Franciscan convent).
S. Anton.
Santa Barbara.

Table explaining the Plan of the city and its fortifications:
1. Fort San Geronimo, which battered the English.
2. Slaughterhouse fort, and end of the wall added, and suitable for eight pieces of ordnance which command the sea and countryside.
3. Wall added and newly built.
4. Main gate, which was closed because it was advisable that our forces be able to go out of the city without being seen from the sea.
5. Fort, newly built into the wall.
6. Santiago fort, newly built.
7. Gate called the Closed gate and now called Count's gate, because it was ordered opened by the Count, with a fine bulwark for its defence.
8. Lenba gate, which it was considered advisable to close; with a bulwark to permit a cross fire along the wall.
9. Bulwark at the old gate in the wall: with the same purpose.
10. New wall, built as far as Tres Cruces.
11. Fort which is being built on Tres Cruces hill.
12. Earth work which continues the line of the walls.
13. Fort which is being built on Santa Barbara height.
14. Bulwark at the end of the wall which faces the river.

PENN AND VENABLES' ATTACK ON SAN DOMINGO, 1655

15. Another bulwark, facing the river.
16. Dock and waterhouse gate.
17. Sea gate.
18. Fort Sant Alberto, opposite the bar.
19. The city's principal fortress.
20. New platform, facing the bar.
21. Casemate and end of the bar.
22. Schoolhouse fort.
23. Mouth of Santo Domingo river.
24. Royal fortress which was built on the other side of the river, with 32 pieces of ordnance which command the bar and the country; most important to the defence of the city and island.
25. Bay and beach by way of which the enemy might easily have taken this city, for the point which was fortified overlooks our fortifications and the city.
26. Small tower, demolished.

NOTES

Lower left is Fort San Geronimo with a moat, which it did not have when the English attacked.

2 and 22, the Slaughterhouse and Schoolhouse forts, which fired on the English attack.

3, this portion of the wall did not Exist at the time of the attack.

4, the Main gate, closed later.

5, the point from which possibly the English were fired on from the wall.

Within the walls, observe *la iglesia mayor*, the principal church and cathedral, where the Spanish gave thanks for their victory and deliverance.

19, the fortress, Count de Peñalva's headquarters.

20, the platform with bronze ordnance.

COLONIAL IRONSIDES

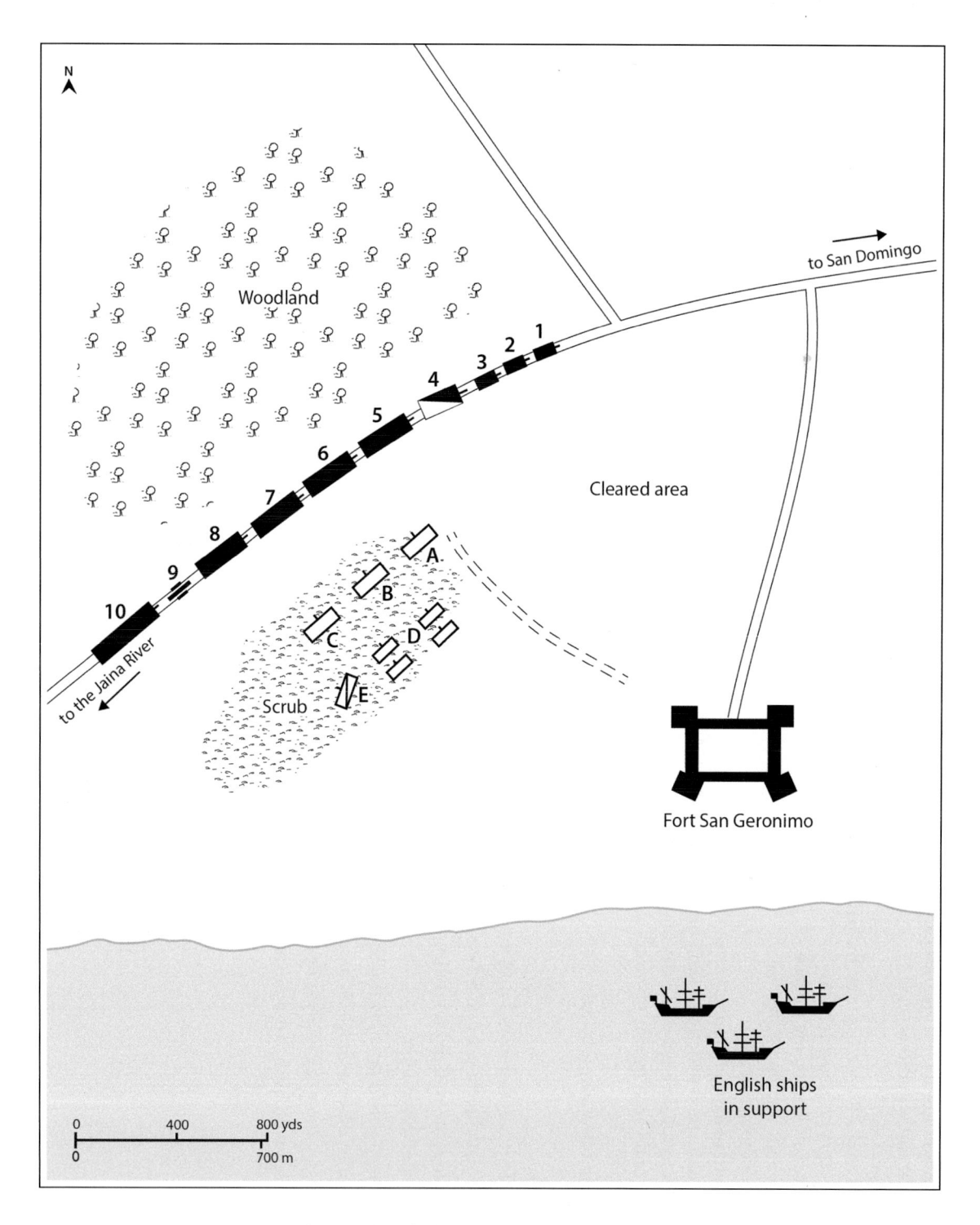

The Spanish Ambush, 25 April 1655 (see key opposite)

Map Key: Spanish Ambush, 25 April 1655

English army:

1. The forlorn hope (50 men from each regiment, total 500)
2. The Reformadoes (55 men)
3. Pawlett's firelocks, or fusiliers
4. Captain Carpenter's two troops of Barbadian horse
5. Heane's Regiment
6. Venables' Regiment
7. The Sea Regiment (Goodson)
8. D'Oyley's Regiment
9. The mortar and two small drakes
10. Regiments of Buller, Carter, Fortescue and Holdep (order of march not known)

Spanish Force:

A. Company of lancers, La Vega militia (Captain Torralba)
B. Arquebusiers and lancers, City (Captain Bueno)
C. Foot company, Santiago militia (Captain Tirado)
D. Foot companies including firelocks, City (Captains Guzman, Barroso, Garabito and de Castro)
E. Troop of Horse, City (Captain Nuñez)

NOTE: The position of the English scoutmaster's company under Captain Berkenhead is not mentioned in any account.

Venables had told Buller not to advance on the city without the main body, but to secure the 'fort and trench' at the landing site only.[32] However, Buller had ignored his orders and moved towards San Domingo, taking with him the only guides, a Captain Cox from St Christopher and a Mr Bounty. Cox had for some time been the gunner in the castle of San Domingo and so knew the area well. Venables clearly felt that Buller had alerted the defenders to their danger and thus put the expedition in peril.[33] One officer subsequently wrote to Venables suggesting that Buller had sent a party out next day under Major Michael Bland to identify the Fort San Geronimo and then remain there gathering information – they were seen by the defenders. Buller would have done better to identify a ford across the river and stockpile whatever food could be obtained; for want of either, the main body spent many hours searching for a crossing place, without success. The army camped for the night on the western side of the river without tents or food – but at least with water.

The search was resumed at dawn on 17 April and a ford was found at some distance from the river mouth and a very short time later, a large plantation was reached where some food including sugar and cocoa was discovered; this was the sugar mill of Don Juan de Mieses Ponce de Leon.[34] That afternoon the march was resumed, led by a captured Irishman who offered to lead Venables to a point on the Ozama river north of San Domingo where there was good water and from which the city could be attacked on its weakest side.

This march proved even more difficult than those of previous days.[35] There were no streams and the wells had been destroyed on Peñalves' orders.[36] The road was no longer shaded by trees, but in full sun. The troops demanded frequent rest halts and could not be made to resume by their officers until they were pleased to do so. Early in the march the leading regiment came upon a deserted monastery. An image of the Virgin and child was torn from the chapel and stripped of the gold and gems which decorated her robe. The image was then pelted with oranges. Eventually, a fork in the road was reached. The left-hand turning led towards San Domingo but the Irish guide persuaded Venables to take the right turn, which passed through woodland in front of a fort called San Geronimo, commanding the seaward approach to the city.[37] Quite why Venables took the advice of an Irishman, given that any Irishman or woman would seek in some way to repay what Cromwell had done in Ireland, is remarkable. It is also remarkable that Venables did not establish communication with the fleet before going any further, both to supply provisions and to coordinate the fire of the fleet with any land attack.

Venables clearly did not feel threatened. He had 9,000 men at hand even though food and water were short. Few if any inhabitants had been seen and there was no evidence that the Spanish intended to fight. The country anyway was thinly populated, mostly by so-called cow killers, whose fighting potential was not yet understood. Venables was himself suffering from dysentery at this point but nevertheless, he went forward with the Irish guide and another man who had been collected on the way, a black man from St Christopher who had been captured by the Spaniards and put to work as a slave. He was accompanied by the forlorn hope – 100 reformadoes – and his engineer officer, probably Thomas Hughes, since fortification and artillery were at this time the same science. At about 4.00 p.m. they met Buller's force. After a short conference, Venables went forward to reconnoitre Fort San Geronimo. Penn with the fleet, meanwhile, had, it appears, tried to buoy a route into the port, but the marker had been quickly removed by the Spanish; he did indeed also bombard the city; the Spanish forts replied but the range was long and neither side seems to have done the other much harm.[38]

As the English approached, the Spanish garrison was working hard on improving the defences of the city; every day, reinforcements arrived from outlying settlements. Peñalves had personally been out and seen all the arrangements on 17 April and had also sent detachments of troops out, both to round up their own stragglers and to locate the advancing English. One large detachment consisting of 100 foot from the city garrison under Captain Joseph Gutierre de Meneses y Luna, and a troop of horse under Captain Alonzo de Jaques Carvajal, was based at a small fort called Pozo del Rey (King's Well), between Fort San Geronimo and the city. Scouting forward, Caravajal's horsemen and a detachment of foot under Captain Manuel Pallano, the author of the *Narrative*, found that: '… the enemy was advancing, beating drums and firing shots … marching three abreast.'[39] A few shots were exchanged without effect. As a result, Pallano urged that the garrison should attack the English before they closed up to the city. Further reports from scouts told the Spanish of the progress of Venables' force and accordingly an ambush was prepared by Captain Alvaro Garabito on

Peñalves' personal instructions,[40] close to Fort San Geronimo, with 200 men from the city companies; Gabarito sent word to the Governor that if he failed to stop the English, then he would expect to be beheaded.[41]

Here the road was reported to be 14 or 15 paces wide; Venables at the head of the column was marching straight into the ambush laid by Garabito, who had been joined by Pallano and some horsemen, an ambush described as being the length of two horse races – about 800 yards. Garabito's 30 arquebusiers fired a volley, which was answered by Pawlett's fusiliers, but before the English could reload, the Spanish foot soldiers armed with the same short lances as the cow-killers rushed from the ambush position, broke through the fusiliers, who ran, causing disorder among the forlorn hope. The reformadoes, however, recovered and stopped the attack until the Sea Regiment came up. Lieutenant-Colonel Whistler of Fortescue's Regiment recalled the scene:

> There did fly forth of the woods a party of the enemy which did lie in ambush upon our forlorn, and General Venables being one of the foremost, and seeing the enemy fall on so desperately with his lances, he very nobly ran behind a tree; and our sea regiment … did fall on most gallantly and put the enemy to fly for their lives.[42]

Whistler was not, however, present and made a number of errors in his letter: his account seems calculated only to do mischief to Venables' reputation. Another letter explained that Venables emerged from the woods after the repulse of the ambush, having gone too far and been cut off by the enemy.[43]

In the city of San Domingo, the garrison had stood-to in case of an assault. Spanish reinforcements of 50 arquebusiers were also sent forward with Captain Pallano,[44] These arquebusiers fired two volleys, then a third which killed Captain Jennings of the reformadoes, but which the Sea Regiment answered with such effect that the Spanish rapidly pulled back in some disorder, covered by the fire of the fort.[45] The Sea Regiment pursued the Spanish through the woods to an open plain in front of the city. Here, between Geronimo and the city, was the small fort called Pozo del Rey, which the Spanish largely evacuated, although some gunners remained, continuing to fire on the Sea Regiment.

That evening, Venables was able to view the walls of the city on the south-western side – probably its strongest aspect. The Council of War had determined that San Domingo should be summoned to surrender and if this was refused, the place would be stormed and put to the sack. But Venables had neither siege gear nor artillery and his men were dropping from hunger and thirst. In spite of objections, he ordered a retreat back to the sugar plantation which the army had left that morning. The Spanish reported killing at least 70 of the English, 'not counting those we afterwards found dead along the Esperilla road and in the bush, who were many'.[46] Their own losses were reported as seven wounded.

Spanish scouting parties of horse and foot followed the English withdrawal. Their account records that all along the withdrawal route they found:

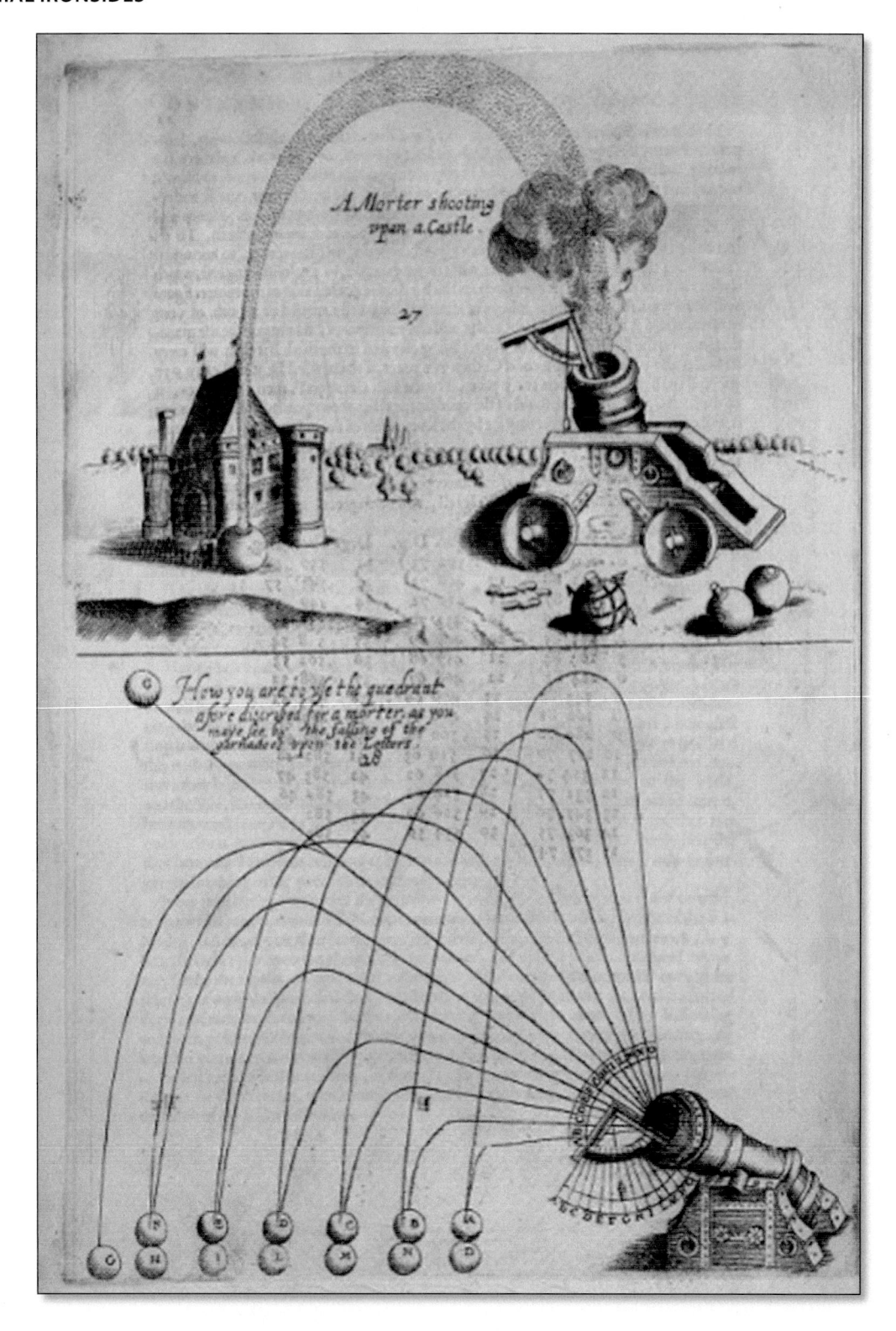

A siege mortar of the type used by the English at San Domingo in Henry Hexham, *Principles of the art militarie*. (Folger Digital Image Collections, <https://luna.folger.edu> accessed 1 January 2020)

… vestiges of a great army. The ground was covered with orange peels, and elsewhere there were oranges that they had squeezed, drinking the juice in their thirst. There was sugar they had found at the mills between Nisao and Jaina; and tobacco; and knapsacks, some full of clothing, others of biscuit; others of meat; and many strings of plucked fowls; squashes; little barrels and small kegs in which they carried water; some pikes and implements; a great quantity of books, like prayerbooks; white paper; and many shoes, some not worn …[47]

The troops had again despoiled a Catholic chapel dedicated to the honour of St Anne, cutting off the head of the image and then removing the lips, ears and nose; even giving: 'two thousand wounds in her sacred face'.[48]

But the Spanish main body too had withdrawn, to the city, causing confusion to their own reserves in so doing – probably the new arrivals believed them to be Englishmen – and also meeting a foot company commanded by Captain Juan de Lugo and Caravajo's troop of horse.[49] Had this whole body turned around and followed up the English, who knows what might have been the result? Alternatively had the English main body rallied and pursued they would have greatly outnumbered this force, which represented the bulk of the regular Spanish garrison, potentially being able to storm the city immediately. The what-ifs of history are fascinating, if ultimately fruitless.

After noon the next day, 18 April, the English army marched two miles to the sea where Buller had landed and found a depot of food from the fleet, which allowed a half-ration to be issued. Communication was now established with the fleet and arrangements were made to land stores either near the mouth of the Jaina or in boats to the next halting place.[50] Venables himself went on board the *Swiftsure* to recover from his dysentery and be nursed by his wife, a move which drew jeers from the many soldiers who were also suffering from this sickness. The ravages of fever increased when, somewhat earlier than anticipated, the rainy season opened and men could not keep warm or dry. To make matters worse, the Spanish, wisely in view of the force ratios preferring *guerrilla* tactics, mounted a major sortie from the city on 20 April which killed a number of men who were foraging. The reformadoes and Pawlett's fusiliers were acting as a guard force and their fire repulsed the attack with the loss of the Spanish captain and six or seven men.[51]

A new council of war was held at which it was revealed that the two guides, Cox and Bounty, had been killed, along with Captain Catts of the Sea Regiment who had been in command of the forlorn hope, Mr Temple, the General's secretary and Mr Murford, the assistant commissary. It was also found that there were no siege ladders or artillery, little food and almost no slow match. As a result, on 24 April, more supplies began to come ashore as did a small siege mortar with its crew under John Hughes and a quantity of bombs and powder. Ships from the fleet, among them the *Martin*, anchored off the city and the Fort of San Geronimo. Their fire seems to have done little damage, however: either because the range was too long or the gunnery too bad. Carrying the mortar, the two small guns brought from the Barbadoes and six days' food at a half-ration per day – a heavy load given that there were no draught horses, mules, donkeys or carts – the army once more set off, making only two miles before dark.[52] At least the rain let up for a time during the night.

On the next morning, 25 April, the English army resumed its march on exactly the same route as before, with as many as 17 ships from the fleet in position to give covering fire off San Geronimo. The order of march was first, the forlorn hope, made up of 500 men drawn from every regiment and commanded now by Adjutant-General Thomas Jackson; the reformadoes; Pawlett's fusiliers; Captain Carpenter's troops of horse; Major-General Heane's Regiment; Venables' Regiment; the Sea Regiment; D'Oyley's Regiment and then the remaining foot regiments with the siege artillery. Marching three abreast, the column would have covered well over a mile (1.6 km). In spite of the experience of ambush a week before, Venables had given no orders for flank security – and neither Pawlett of the Fusiliers nor Scoutmaster Berkenhead seem to have felt it necessary to do their duty in the absence of specific direction, even given the hard experience of the previous days' ambushes.

Spanish scouting parties had been on watch for any move by the English army and as it passed a farm belonging to Don Andres de Medina, at about 11.00 a.m., a new ambush was laid, just as before, but the troops were organised as a *tercio* and commanded by *Maestre de Campo* Don Juan Morfa Geraldino. The left-hand third of the ambush was formed by the company from Santiago commanded by Captain Luis Lopez Tirado; in the centre was a force of arquebusiers with more lancers to support them under Captain Francisco Bueno; and on the right was a company of lancers from the militia of La Vega under their captain, Don Juan de la Vega Torralba. To the rear were companies of lancers and firelocks from the militia of Azua and from the city, under Captains Don Garcia de Guzman, Captain Antonio Barroso, Don Francisco Garabito and Don Pedro de Castro, and a troop of horse under Captain Melchor Nuñez. The whole force amounted to around 300 men.[53] The dead of the earlier battle were still lying on the field but the Spanish had cleared the brush to open the fields of fire from San Geronimo castle: 'our ambush began at this clearing', reported Captain Pallano.[54]

About 1.00 p.m., the van of the English army was reported to be approaching, marching 10 deep this time, and the Spanish soldiers were ordered to lie flat. As the column passed San Geronimo, the fort could clearly be seen. The fort commander had orders to let up to 70 files pass and it was not until the forlorn hope, the reformadoes and the fusiliers had passed that the fort opened fire across the cleared area, with seven rounds of round shot loaded over case shot, a devastating combination at close range but one that apparently did little damage.

The arquebusiers then fired a volley, which the English answered, killing several Spanish officers and several men. Before they could reload, the Spaniards, armed with their fearsome lances and supported by Nuñez's horse and other lancers who mounted riderless English horses, rushed from the trees and charged the head of the column. Neither the short pikes of the English, nor renewed musket fire, could stop the attack and in any case, the English troops were not drilled and trained to do so and the Spanish were more experienced in the use of staff weapons in close country.[55] The forlorn hope under Jackson turned and fled, so too did Pawlett's fusiliers, leaving the reformadoes standing: of the 55 men left in the company, only 18 survived the day. As Captain Pallano reported: 'All our people having come out of the ambush, in the time it takes to say "Jesus!" not an Englishman was left alive of all who had walked into the ambush.'[56] The fleeing mass of men disordered the troops of horse and the regiments of Heane and D'Oyley, with it: '… soe that the enemie with their lances killed until they were wearie of killing, falling chiefly among the bravest of our men.'[57]

Major-General Heane charged with some of the horse, who were engaged by artillery fire from the fort. Heane then dismounted, armed only with a sword, doing his best to stop the rout: '"Stand but 10 men and we shall beat them"', he is said to have cried, but 'none but 3 would stand with him … against whom a big fellow issued from the fort on horseback', who, bringing a number of men with him, attacked Heane and his companions. Isolated among the enemy and with only two other officers with him, Captain Thomas Walters and Ensign Thomas Boys, he was mortally wounded by a man the Spanish identified as Lucas Hernandez. Boys, who had wrapped the colours of the colonel's company around him, was also killed.[58] So perished the general whom men called the best soldier in England. The Spanish captured eight colours: those of the reformadoes, the fusiliers, five of Venables' Regiment and one of Heane's.[59] As well as Heane and Walters, the Spanish killed Lieutenant-Colonel John Clarke, an unnamed major and Captains George Butler, Obadiah Hinde, Thomas Hancock and Pawlett – evidence that the officers at least had stood firm while the rank and file broke. There is no record of how many men died: the Spanish reported that prisoners said that 1,500 had been killed although this figure is probably an exaggeration as reports of mass graves indicated between 600 and 800 killed.[60]

The Spanish showed no mercy and of those killed, the few who did stand, like Heane, were the best officers of the army. Venables too, weakened by dysentery and needing help to stand, did his best to rally the troops. It was again the Sea Regiment under Vice-Admiral Goodson that saved the day, opening its ranks to let the fleeing rabble through and swiftly closing again, supported by four files of Venables' Regiment, forcing the attackers back into the woods.

The Spanish eventually broke off the fight and pulled back. Venables ordered a composite force of 100 men from each regiment to act as rearguard: 'We marched up within musket shot of the fort, and were there commanded to stay, and waited, in expectation of orders to march forward to the town of Sto. Domingo till next morning at 7 of the clock …'[61] all this time, fire from the Fort 'swept away our men by eight or nine at a shot.'[62] The mortar was brought up to try to neutralise the fire from the fort but this simply attracted concentrated Spanish fire and more slaughter. Seeing that the English did not move, the Spanish reformed and brought up reinforcements from the city under Captain Lazaro Franco de Robles so that their force numbered 600, and exchanged fire with the rearguard, of which the English had the best.[63]

The main body of the English army, meanwhile, withdrew after dark, burying the mortar shells. The noise of this was heard by the Spanish who took it for entrenching; however, the next day they uncovered the bombs, 'bigger than water bottles', as well as the burned carriage of the mortar. The whole army, it was said, apart from the rearguard, was in great disorder. All the men were suffering from thirst and when they reached the river Jaina they threw themselves down and drank, causing many to develop the flux. Most of the food and all the tools and equipment for a siege, such as there were, had been flung away in the rout and these too were recovered by the Spaniards.[64]

Such was the state of mind among the soldiers that the appearance of two black slaves caused further panic as the troops believed the Spanish had again come upon them. Many ran, others jumped into the river, where they were drowned. The army camped for the night in the rain, without food or shelter.

After this, an attack on the city was abandoned. The troops had no confidence in their general; the General and many of his officers knew that the army was no more than a rabble and would never force a defended fortress: 'ten of the enemy would see off 100 of ours, leaving the officers to be killed'.[65] In spite of the example of Heane, many officers had fled with the men, prominent among them the Adjutant-General, Thomas Jackson who was cashiered and sent in irons to work on the hospital ship (which ship it was remains unclear), swabbing decks and attending to the wounded. He was not the only officer to be broken, but discipline, if it had ever existed among such a mob of the sweepings of the English army and the Barbadoes, was too far gone to be restored.

Penn offered whatever assistance the fleet could give, including urging a third advance during which he would bring the fleet close in, batter the city Fort San Geronimo with gunfire to clear the way for the army and land seamen in numbers on the harbour at San Domingo – but to no avail;[66] and in any case there was no trust between soldiers and seamen, at any level.[67]

On 28 April Penn, with Commissioners Winslow and Butler, recorded the opinion reached during a council on the *Swiftsure* that the army: 'will never be brought to march up to that place [San Domingo] again.'[68] Winslow had at first argued for a third attempt at the city but in the end it was decided that an attempt to capture Jamaica would be more likely to succeed and therefore the army should be re-embarked. It was difficult to keep the army together in the days before the embarkation. Even the noise made by land crabs at night was believed to be the rattling of the ammunition bandoliers of an advancing enemy. Parties sent out to forage for food were killed without compunction and little difficulty by small groups of Spaniards, who had sent out strong reconnaissance parties.[69] The tropical rains fell in streams, food was again short and the few horses which could not be embarked were slaughtered for meat, 'as a great delicate'.[70] The men ate dogs, rats and whatever fruit they could find, including guava and mayas, or canistel; but also yucca or cassava root, which is poisonous unless properly cooked, leading to more deaths: 40 a day at least were dying.[71] Venables blamed Penn for not providing more supplies, but Penn could not land what he did not have.[72]

The Spanish commanders were sure that Venables would again attempt to attack the city and strong advanced guards of horse and foot were deployed on the roads leading westward. New bodies of militia continued to arrive to strengthen the garrison: 100 men from Santiago, for example, and others from San Juan and Guaba which was some 200 miles from the city. Their alarm gradually abated, however, as it became clear that the English were remaining close to the fleet, with launches plying back and forth. On 2 May, their scouts reported that the English were re-embarking.[73]

At about 8.00 a.m. on Friday 4 May, the embarkation was completed and the fleet sailed away, carrying with it the remains of the army. The Spanish found many dead on the beach, as well as horses both dead and alive, one of the small cannons, and a few deserters who surrendered themselves. Thereafter, they celebrated the day with an annual festival of rejoicing. Captain Pallano, writing his account for the King of Spain, was in no doubt about whose side God, at least, was on: 'The fortunate arms of your Catholic and royal majesty triumphed (as over heretics they are wont to do) in one of the greatest victories of the present century.'[74]

The English had indeed left behind several hundred weapons and much equipment, as well as their many casualties. Venables initially underestimated these, recording a muster on 5 November 1655 at which 2,194 able men were on parade while 2,316 were sick. This gave a total of 4,510. By this time, however, Venables had received 790 reinforcements. The actual number of survivors was therefore 3,720. If 1,000 men of the Sea Regiment are added, then the balance, either killed or abandoned in Hispaniola, was 4,280 – close on half the force.[75] More importantly, however, it destroyed the reputation of the Ironsides as an unbeaten, and unbeatable, force. 'Never', wrote one survivor, attributing the failure to the ungodliness of his men, 'were men more disapoynted than some of us, nor did the hearts of English men faile them more than in this attempt.'[76]

The blame for the failure cannot be laid at the door of Penn, in spite of Venables' accusations, nor at those of the other commissioners. Venables could well be reproached for a lack of vigour and for several tactical mistakes – but no more. The real cause of failure lies in the shockingly bad quality of the troops; overconfidence amounting to arrogance about the relative fighting qualities of the Spanish; ignorance in matters related to warfare in the tropics; and the appalling supply and equipment arrangements. These dead dogs must be placed on the doorstep of none other than the Protector himself. He had forced the idea of the expedition through his Council and its failure hurt him deeply. The news reached him on 24 July 1655 and it said he locked himself away for an entire day, brooding over the disaster.[77] He had aimed at establishing mastery over enough of North America and the West Indies as to dominate the trade routes but instead, his reputation and that of England were badly damaged. The episode certainly contends for the title of the most shameful episode in the history of British arms; Cromwell had placed his faith in God, but God had taken the other side, and for once Cromwell had not taken his own advice – he did not keep his powder dry.

Appendix to Chapter 8

Spanish Army Lists of Forces in Hispaniola[1]

Command and Staff

Governor and Captain-General Don Bernardino de Meneses Bracamonte y Zapata, 1st Count de Peñalva
Mastre de Campo Don Juan Morfa Geraldino*
Sargento Mayor Lucas de Verroa
Chaplain Fr Juan Berrosano

City Garrison
Commander
Don Gabriel de Rojas Valle y Figueroa
Aide, Reformado Pedro de Bustos

Governor's Company
Captain Don Gregorio de Castro

Artillery Companies
Captain Don Nicolas Coronado
Captain Gonzalo de Frias
Captain Antonio Ortiz de Sandoval

Foot Companies
Captain Don Garcia Guzman, Reformado Don Juan de Lugo, Reformado Don Lope Lopez de Morla, Reformado Franciso del Hoya
Captain Pedro Velez Mantilla, succeeded by Captain Antonio Martin Barrosco
Captain Don Francisco Garrabito, Reformado Don Pedro de Castro
Captain Francesco Bueno (killed in action)
Captain Manuel Pallano, Ensign Hernandez de Cuellar
Captain Lazaro Franco de Robles, Reformado Don Juan de Cabiedes

---

* An Irish emigré. His real name was John Murphy Fitzgerald.

APPENDIX TO CHAPTER 8

Captain Damian del Castillo Vaca

Militia Companies
Captain Don Alvito de Garabito de Aguilar, Reformado Don Fernando de Morenta y Fuenmayor
Captain Don Joseph de Alvarez, Ensign Sebastian Sanpayo
Captain Lazaro Franco
Captain Don Juan de Viloria y Quiñones
Captain Don Pedro Verdugo
Captain Don Rodriguo Pimentel

Troops of Horse
Captain Melchor Nuñez
Captain Alonso de Jacques Caravajal, Reformado Don Alvaro Otañez

Garrison of Fort San Geronimo
Artillery company (not identified)
Company of Foot (not identified)

Garrison of Fort Pozo del Rey
Company of Foot
Captain Joseph Guttiere Meneses y Luna
Sargento Diego Rodrigues Tirado

Garrison of Caucedo
Captain Don Juan Alvarez Piñero, Reformado Don Juan de Rojas

Militia of Santiago
Commander and captain of a company of foot
Captain Fernando Nuñez

Alcalde Mayor
Don Juan Maldonaldo y Montijo

Company of Foot
Captain Luis Lopez Jurado (wounded in action)
Lieutenant Thomas Gillen
Reformado Juan Francisco
Reformado Don Alonso Estevez de Figuero (killed in action)

Militia of Azua
Company of Foot
Captain Gonzalo Fagoso

Militia of La Vega
Company of Foot
Captain Don Juan la Vega Torralba

COLONIAL IRONSIDES

Militia of Baraguana
Company of Foot
Captain Esteban Pegero
Reformado Don Miguel de Villafranca
Reformado Esteban Liranso

NOTES
1   Compiled from the accounts published as *Spanish Narratives of the English Attack on Santo Domingo 1655*, edited and translated by I.A. Wright (London: Royal Historical Society, 1926).

9

The Capture of Jamaica

Jamaica, with a land area of just over 4,000 square miles, is the third-largest island of the Greater Antilles and the Caribbean after Cuba and Hispaniola. Jamaica lies about 90 miles (145 kilometres) south of Cuba and 120 miles (191 kilometres) west of Hispaniola. Originally inhabited by the indigenous Arawak and Taino peoples, the island came under Spanish rule following the arrival of Christopher Columbus in 1494. Many of the indigenous people were either killed or died of diseases to which they had no immunity; and the Spanish thereafter brought in large numbers of black African slaves to work the land.[1]

The interior of Jamaica is mountainous and forested, but the coastal plains are fertile. Its climate is similar to that of its neighbour, Hispaniola. Like Hispaniola, its agriculture in 1655 supplied plenty of beef, fruit, sugar, spices, cotton, tobacco and root vegetables, with fish from the coastal waters: the Spanish called it 'the garden of the Indies.'[2] It was a far easier proposition to conquer and colonise Jamaica than Hispaniola, with just as much, or more, potential – but Venables seems not to have made this clear to the Protector other than saying: 'We effected what we were sent about: the fixing of a Colony, tho' we failed in the place.'[3] This may have been on account of his ill health, or else he was ashamed of his failure and did not wish to seem to be making excuses.

The Spanish population numbered no more than 1,500, of whom 600 at most were soldiers or militia men. There were in addition probably around 4,000 black African slaves. The capital, and only town, Santiago de la Vega – now Spanish Town – lay inland from the main anchorages on the southern coast and consisted of around 1,000 houses. The harbour was described as: 'one of the Best in the Wordell: in it may ride 500 sayle of ships from 50 fadham water.'[4]

During the short voyage from Hispaniola, on 7 May, Commissioner Winslow had died of sickness – on top of the death of Heane, this was a serious blow, for Winslow was one of the very few men in the expedition who knew how to found and develop a colony. Land was sighted on 9 May; Penn's fleet arrived in Caguaya Bay, now Cagway Bay, on 11 May 1655 but as they rounded Point Morant, they were, as at Hispaniola, sighted by Spanish fishermen who took a report to the governor, Juan Ramírez de Arellano. The islanders and the governor were caught completely off guard in spite of warnings sent out from San Domingo. Penn transferred from his 60-gun ship *Swiftsure* to the 12-gun galley *Martin* and led a flotilla of smaller craft to land troops; these were used because the innermost part of the bay was exceptionally shallow. Even so, some of the flotilla, including the *Martin*, grounded briefly before moving on. Soon, an exchange of shots began between the English and a fort covering the inner harbour.

The fort, Passage Fort, on the western side of the anchorage, was 'strong and cannon-proof', and mounted eight guns.[5] It and two smaller fortifications containing only musketeers were bombarded by the *Martin*: the garrison, around 300 men, quickly fled with the galley firing on them as they ran.[6] The English troops were much encouraged at this, especially after their experiences in Hispaniola, throwing their hats in the air, but no pursuit was permitted. Venables, who was still far from well, did not land with the troops. Instead, he: 'watched the landing from on board, muffled in his cloak, with his hat slouched over his face, not deigning to cast a glance on the men to whose misconduct he attributed his failure.'[7]

A council of war was held that evening, at which it was decided to advance and occupy Santiago de la Vega. This lay about six miles (9.6 km) inland. The army was to advance at once, but Venables countermanded the order and the troops moved the next morning, 12 May. The army marched first through thick woods, finding another small fort which was abandoned, and another about one mile from Spanish Town. This last mile was across the grasslands and as the army broke into open country, a party of about 20 Spaniards approached under a flag of truce, carrying a message for a parley with the governor. It seems likely that they believed the English had come merely for victuals. Venables explained that the English came as colonists and asked for a supply of food, demanding that Spanish negotiators should appear to surrender the island: 'Military officers in active service, or the governor, or the maestre de campo … If the Governor would come in, he should be received and treated with the honours of captain general …'[8] The Spaniards left to report to the governor and the army then marched on and entered the town; all the people had fled, carrying their goods with them.

The next day, 13 May, an officer and a priest appeared with six other Spaniards. It was clear that unlike the Spaniards in Hispaniola, those in Jamaica had no immediate intention of offering resistance. It was agreed that a truce should come into force and that 200 cows per day, and bread, would be supplied. In further negotiations, Venables, announcing that from now on, Jamaica was to be annexed to the Commonwealth of England, gave the Spanish hard terms for their surrender: they were to leave the island within 10 days with what they could carry, abandoning their land and buildings, all arms and military equipment, and all ships and stores – or else face death and the seizure of all their property. These were the same terms that the Spaniards had given to English colonists on Providence Island, when they captured it in 1641.* They were also in keeping with the terms usually offered to the vanquished, as Venables would have known very well from his service in Ireland.[9] Spanish civilians were not to be harmed, but would, if they chose, be taken to San Domingo by 16 June. The Spanish governor was to

---

* Providence Island lay off the north-east coast of what is now Nicaragua and had been established by English Puritans in 1631.

THE CAPTURE OF JAMAICA

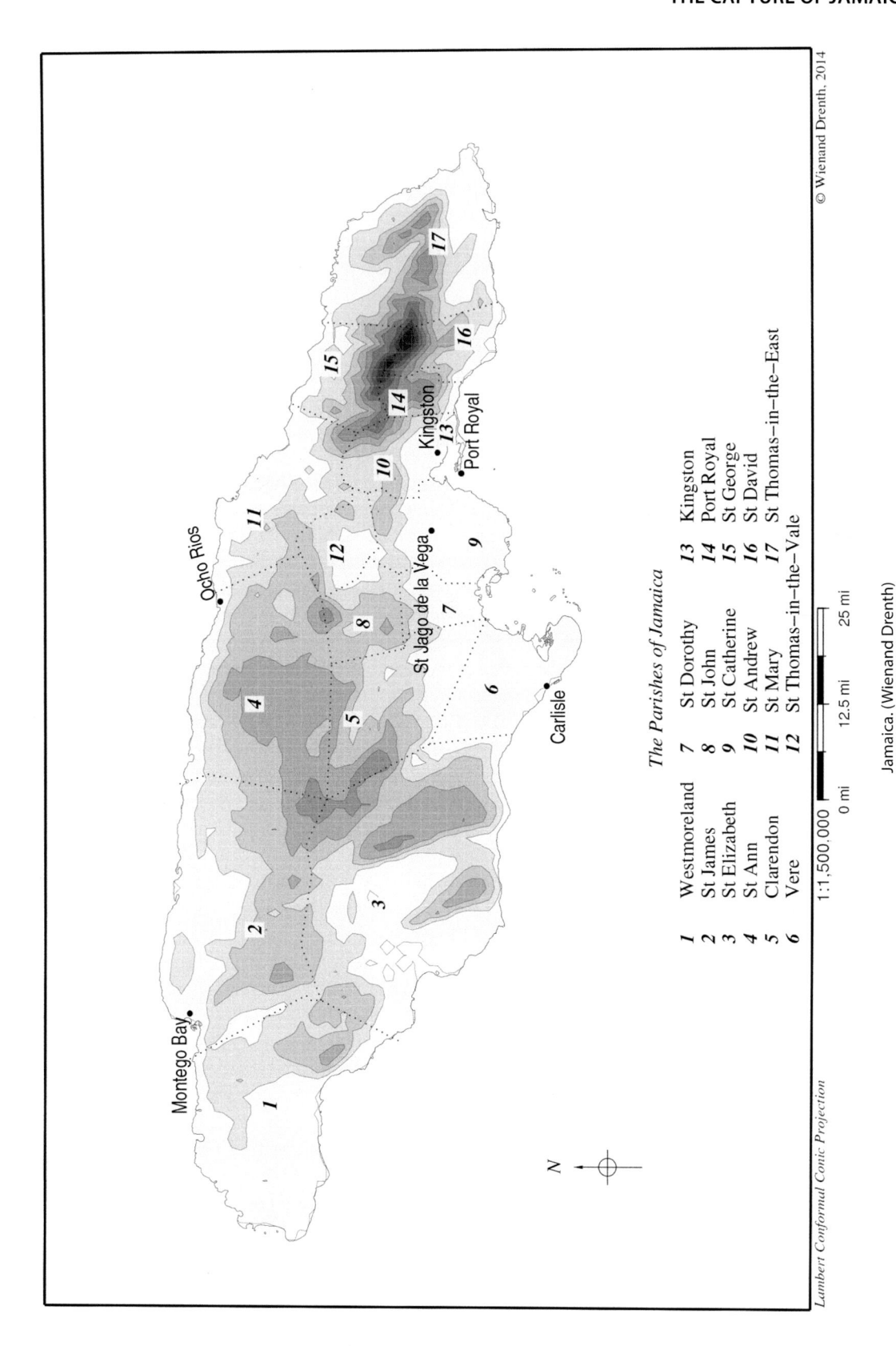

The Parishes of Jamaica

1	Westmoreland	*7*	St Dorothy	*13*	Kingston
2	St James	*8*	St John	*14*	Port Royal
3	St Elizabeth	*9*	St Catherine	*15*	St George
4	St Ann	*10*	St Andrew	*16*	St David
5	Clarendon	*11*	St Mary	*17*	St Thomas–in–the–East
6	Vere	*12*	St Thomas–in–the–Vale		

Jamaica. (Wienand Drenth)

surrender himself as a hostage for the compliance of his people on 15 May; the evacuation was to commence on the 22nd.

On 14 May, Venables met a large delegation of Spaniards,* accompanying the governor, who was being carried: '… in a hannacka [hammock] between to Negors upon a pole with to men a horsback to wait one him: But the Governor was soe iloten, and soe much eaten out with the pox, that he could neither goe, nor stand, nor seat, nor well lie …'[10] The English Army was drawn up in its 66 companies, each with a volour, to pay the respects due to the governor and must have appeared an intimidating array. At the end of the negotiation, the alleged Spanish governor was allowed to depart on parole and it was agreed that the supplies of beef and bread would be delivered; the terms of the capitulation were not, however, signed.

It was soon clear that the pox-ridden old man was not the governor, but rather an elderly man of no standing, who had been made to impersonate the real governor in order to buy time. Ramírez himself temporised for two more days but eventually signed the surrender on 27 May. Shortly thereafter he sailed for Campeche in Mexico, but died before he reached his destination. Not all the Spaniards were prepared to follow Ramírez, however, and many collected their livestock and withdrew into the wooded, hilly interior of the island. Venables' delays had given them just enough time to put this scheme into effect.[11] Thereafter the daily supply of meat vanished. After evacuating many non-combatants from northern Jamaica to Cuba, *Maestre de Campo* Francisco de Proenza, who had been governor until 1651, established his headquarters at the inland village of Guatibacoa, in the centre of the island. The Spanish also freed their slaves, who fled into the mountainous forests of the interior. Here they joined many other former slaves who had fled over the years, to a degree intermarried with the remaining native inhabitants, and established free and independent communities. They became known as 'Maroons', derived from the Spanish *cimarrón*, meaning wild, or free. Their leaders, Juan de Bolas (or Lubolo) and Juan de Serras, allied with the Spanish to begin a *guerrilla* war against English occupation.

The English regiments were quartered around Spanish Town and began to forage for food, rather than construct fortifications. The island could supply large quantities of beef from the herds of cattle grazing the savannah grasslands, but there was no corn and therefore no bread – the basis of the day's ration for a soldier. Penn sent as much biscuit ashore as could be spared and on 19 May, two store ships at last arrived from England carrying at least some flour. However: 'The bread they brought is so inconsiderable it will but serve the army 22 days at half allowances.'[12] The soldiers hunted the cattle and killed them by the dozen, but there being no proper butchers and no means of preserving the meat, many carcases were left to rot and were wasted. 'The army was starving in a cook's shop', wrote Lieutenant-Colonel Barrington, with much truth.[13] The soldiers were reduced once more to eating such fruit as they could find along with dogs, mules and rats. Sanitary conditions were also poor and not surprisingly, disease flourished. 'The plague is very much feared here,' wrote Barrington, 'and

---

* Venables' account says 2,000 but given the population of the island this is highly improbable – 200 would be more likely.

doubtless … will come in sore amongst us, for the scents we have here are so noisome that in some parts of this town a man is not able to walk … we offend our quarters very much by our nastiness and throwing the garbage of our cattle in inconvenient places.'[14] Another officer wrote of the conditions that:

> Wee have a sevanno or plaine neere us where some of the souldiery are buried soe shallow that the Spanish dogs, which lurk about the towne, scrape them up and eate them. As for the English dogs they are most eaten by our souldiery; not one walkes the streets that is not shott at, unless well befriended or respected. We have not only eaten all the cattle within neare 1, 2 miles of the place, but now alsoe almost all the horse, asses, mules …[15]

On 7 June another council of war was held, attended by Penn and Venables; Commissioner Butler; Colonels Fortescue, Buller, Carter, D'Oyley and Holdep; Lieutenant-Colonels Barry, Rudyard and Berkenhead; and Major Smith. It was clear that a colony would have to be established, both to feed the troops and to deny the island and its resources to the Spanish. In the short term, however, the food situation had to be mitigated: a ship was to be sent to New England to ask for help; and all the larger warships and transports were to be sent home, to reduce the number of men to be fed. The 12 frigates were left to guard the maritime approaches and to look for prizes. With the ships was to be sent a representative to report to the Protector on the condition of the Army and ask for reinforcements and for help in establishing the colony: clothing, tools, instruments, flour and corn, oatmeal, brandy, medicines, arms and armour and timber for building were all needed. In addition, farmers, mostly from Scotland, were needed to establish the agriculture of the island. Finally, land allotments would be made to the officers and men, but Cromwell was asked for a code of laws.[16]

Penn, on bad terms with Venables and ashamed of the failure at Hispaniola, decided to return with the capital ships and make his report to the Protector, appointing Vice-Admiral Goodson to command what remained. The fleet left on 25 June, and with it also went Venables, now very sick, and Buller – the latter presumably as insurance should Venables not survive the journey. Venables turned over his command to Fortescue, who had taken Heane's place as Major-General – in spite of the objections of Commissioner Butler (not surprising since Butler had been Heane's aide under General Massey during the Civil Wars); but his objections were overruled, for Fortescue had a good record, was liked by Cromwell and was respected by his officers and men. Moreover, Butler had a bad name for drunkenness and idleness. Cromwell acknowledged Fortescue's command, sending him and Goodson instructions on how to proceed.[17]

A letter from Venables reached the Protector on 4 August, telling him of the capture of Jamaica. Penn arrived at Portsmouth on 1 September along with a rumour that Venables was dead.[18] On 10 September, however, Venables reached Plymouth and then went on to Portsmouth, again writing to the Protector to announce his arrival.[19] On 20 September both were summoned to face an angry Protector and his Council, charged with desertion. Penn was in a dangerous place, for his justification for leaving was weak – it could well be argued that his prime responsibility was the defence of the new colony.

Venables had slightly more cause, being seriously ill – but many of his officers and men had died and were dying of disease, without the ability to use their rank to escape. However, even if Venables had stayed at his post, it is highly unlikely that he would have lived long enough to accomplish anything.

In front of the Council Venables claimed that his return had been agreed by all his subordinates; there is no record of Penn's defence. A furious Cromwell replied: 'Have you ever read of any general that had left his army, and not commanded back?' (That is, without having been ordered to do so from above). Venables struggled but gave the example of the Earl of Essex from Ireland in 1599, which Cromwell dismissed as: 'A sad example!'[20] Both men were sent under arrest to the Tower until such time as they publicly admitted their guilt and surrendered their commissions – in the case of Venables, not only the command in America, but also his regimental, governor's and general's commissions in Ireland. Penn did so on 25 October; Venables held out until the 31st.[21] Penn went on to a further career in the Navy after the Restoration; Venables was briefly Governor of Chester in 1660 and at the Restoration, retired from public life.

Even before the arrival of Penn and Venables, the Protector, having heard of the disaster, appointed Major-General Robert Sedgwick, who had led the expedition against the French in Acadia (see Chapter 5), as a commissioner.[22] Cromwell clearly trusted Sedgwick and relied on his knowledge to help put matters on a better footing. Sedgwick left England in the ship *Marmaduke* on 21 July 1655 and reached the Barbadoes on 6 August.[23] Here it was reported that Venables had captured Hispaniola. Sedgwick therefore sailed on, approaching the harbour of San Domingo. He reported seeing:

> … the Spanish colours upon the castle, and ships in harbour, and we sent a wherry in less than sacker [saker] shot of the towne, who took a survey of it, plainly the people, in armes, and men hard at work in building a new castle on the south side, some shot being made of them in the mean while.[24]

Sedgwick therefore sailed on for Jamaica, arriving on 10 October. Here he found Fortescue, the acting Major-General and governor, seriously ill; he died a few days later. Carter was also dead and although for a short time the command had fallen on the capable Holdep, Sedgwick reported to the Protector that: '… the Command of the Army naturally fel upon Coll. D'Oyley, and indeed the man most capable, & the best fitted for ye employ whom we invested with the Command of the Army, and settled a Council of War …'[25] D'Oyley convened a council of seven officers to assist him. Holdep was probably the best qualified officer to govern the new colony and indeed his regiment's plantation was already flourishing; however, D'Oyley and the English officers were clearly jealous. Holdep was accused of embezzlement, deported from Jamaica, and his regiment of colonists from St Christopher broken up. His accusers took his land and his men for themselves.[26]

When Sedgwick arrived at Jamaica, he found the troops dying fast, everything in disorder and necessaries of every kind wanting. 'You must in a manner begin the work over again' was his message to Cromwell; but, though inwardly in some uncertainty about the future of the colony, with his help, and the energy of D'Oyley, matters began to improve. Sedgwick had brought a group of settlers from Nevis to augment the colony, but these people rapidly died from disease. He also wished to recruit settlers from New England and sent Captain Daniel Gookin to Massachusetts Bay; to no avail, for already Jamaica had a bad reputation.[27] Only the Governor of Nevis, Luke Stokes, produced some settlers. 1,600 of the poorest colonists were sent to Jamaica – for the first time, whole families – and went to Port Morant; within three months, two-thirds of them were dead, including Stokes himself.[28]

Sedgwick had three clear priorities for the new colony: fortification and planting being the first two and opposition to piracy the third[29] – not that the army officers would take orders from a mere Colonial like Sedgwick. Cromwell, on the other hand, rewarded his zeal by sending him a commission as Major-General and commander-in-chief, which reached Jamaica early in May 1656. However, Sedgwick never took up the command nor dealt with his opponents, for he, like so many others, died, on 24 May 1656.

Cromwell had indeed taken heed of the requirement to augment the new colony, sending a reinforcement at the beginning of October 1655 in the shape of a new regiment under Colonel John Humphry.[30] This had been raised in England and was largely composed of veterans; among the officers were a number of men who had served in the New Model: Humphrey himself; Lieutenant-Colonel Christopher Ennis, who had raised and led a troop of 100 horse; Major William Pelham; Major Martin Van Alfen; Major Edward Tyson; and Captain Thomas Fairfax, the son of Sir William Fairfax.* The regiment actually embarked 700 men and made up its strength to 831 in the Barbadoes and St Christopher.[31] By 5 November 50 of them were dead and the colonel, Lieutenant-Colonel, and five other officers were among the seriously ill. A muster taken during the month showed only 335 men well, with only four officers fit, and 455 men sick.[32]

Cromwell then instructed Major-General George Monck to assemble 500 men from the regiments in Scotland and another 700 from those in Ireland, in two regiments, under the command of Major-General Edward Brayne, who was to assume command of the garrison from D'Oyley. More care was to be taken in the drawing of troops than in the original venture. Cromwell instructed Monck that:

> … forasmuch as there is very pressing occasion that all expedicion bee used in prepareing of these forces, and putting them under good conduct in respect of officers, and that choice be made of such soldiers as have given good testimony of their courage, resolucion, and obedience …'[33]

The first regiment, that of Brayne himself, was raised in Scotland by drawing 42 men from each of the 12 regiments garrisoned there, making a total of 504. It was sent to Jamaica in November 1655 and, being mostly composed of veterans, was of far better quality than the troops already there. However, 200 men drowned when the ship *Two Brothers* foundered on the coast of Ireland. The dead included Lieutenant-Colonel John Bramston and

---

* Fairfax survived the Restoration and commanded a regiment in Ireland until 1687 when he was displaced by Tyrconnell. He was restored under William III and died a brigadier-general in 1715.

his son William and three other officers. Brayne reached Jamaica on 14 December 1655 and the remains of his regiment followed a week later, with part of a second regiment, that of William Moore.

Moore's Regiment was assembled from drafts of the regiments in Ireland and assembled at Carrickfergus from May 1656. It sailed on 3 October but the ship *Sapphire*, with Moore and 260 men, was driven back by a storm. Five hundred men reached Jamaica with Brayne in December 1656; Moore then waited for the next spring before sailing. Moore himself immediately made a nuisance of himself, petitioning Brayne for permission to go home. Brayne threated him with trial by court martial,[34] but he was permitted to return to England in the summer of 1658.

On arrival, bringing with him not only troops but money, tools, provisions and weapons amassed over the past year for this purpose,[35] Brayne assumed command from D'Oyley – not only of the forces in Jamaica, but over also all military forces and matters in the Americas. He dismissed the council of war and ignored the Commissioners, running matters as a military command in cooperation with Goodson. He immediately turned his attention to the business of establishing the agriculture of the new colony, which he found very backward, in order to make the place self-supporting. Venables had early given orders for 1,000 men to begin planting, on the basis of what had been done in Ulster. Each regiment was placed in garrison and given area of cultivation under a field officer: it was plant or starve. Brayne's view, which accorded with that of Monck and others at home, was that Jamaica should be a self-supporting station, from which war could be exported to the Spanish possessions and treasure ships.[36] It was also expected that the New England colonies and elsewhere in the Caribbean would help to establish the new plantation, in response to the call from 'their head and Centre'.[37] However, most of the soldiers were against becoming farmers and were encouraged in this by some of the officers. There were a few wives and children, who might help to found the colony, and the wives were being allocated one-quarter of their husband's pay; single men were getting almost nothing. Brayne advised that paying the single men might help stimulate the local economy and that their arrears should be made up. Brayne gave a description of the garrison that was not encouraging: the soldiers did not care how they lived, so long as they did not have to work; they were in arrears of pay; they neglected their military duties. Brayne therefore reported that he had:

> … given libertie to the most discontented and uselesse officers to returne for England, of which I finde the benefit already; for now the soldiers goe cheerfully to worke. Besides, there being a necessity of reducing the regiments to a lesser number, I thought it better to suffer the officers to depart of themselves, then be forced to reduce them hereafter. I have placed Scottish and Irish parties about Port Morant [on the south-eastern corner of the island] …[38]

In March 1657 Brayne reported the declining state of the garrison's numbers due to sickness; death from disease rapidly diminished the ranks of officers and men; the places of the capable ones were most difficult to fill. Sedgwick and Goodson had reported to the Protector in January 1656 that: 'We cannot but be sensible of the state and quality of the commanders in general, men of no great high natural parts, and by much long sickness, parts and qualities both impaired and weakened.'[39]

The St Christopher Regiment was broken up in June 1655 and the Sea Regiment's manpower returned to the fleet. An abstract of the Regiments, 'the General's regiment, the Major-General's, Col. Carter's, Col. Buller's, Col. Doyle's, Col. Holdippes and Col. Humphere's', on 14 November 1655 in Jamaica gives a strength of 2,194 well, 2,316 sick, and 172 women and children.[40] The breakdown for each regiment is given for December 1655:[41]

Regiment	Well	Sick	Women and Children
Venables' (General's)	245	238	38
Fortescue's (Major-General's)	359	356	42
Carter's	277	365	18
Buller's	361	217	27
D'Oyley's	269	461	35
Holdep's (late Heane's)	340	455	30
Humphrey's	335	455	0
TOTALS	2,186	2,547	190

By June 1656 Humphrey's Regiment numbered 312 all ranks and by September of that year only 276. Even the well men were of little use: when put to work manning a new fort, Fort Cromwell, at the mouth of the anchorage, they proved, according to Sedgwick, useless and had to be replaced with seamen from the fleet.[42] The arrival of Brayne's and Moore's, Regiments in December 1655, already much understrength., had brought the nominal total of regiments to nine. By October 1657 the strength of Moore's Regiment had declined to only 160 men who were incorporated into the other regiments of the garrison, although some may have returned to Ireland.[43]

Faced with declining numbers of men and indifferent officers, Brayne had no choice but to effect a radical reorganisation. He removed the worst officers, as already noted, giving them leave to return home. He then reduced the regiments, making each as far as possible fully manned, to four, by October 1657: these were Ward's Regiment (formerly the General's), Burrough's (formerly Buller's) Regiment, D'Oyley's Regiment and Barry's Regiment (formerly Holdep's); the regiments of Fortescue, Carter, Brayne, Moore and Humphrey being reduced and incorporated into the new ones. The resulting regiments, leavened by better quality officers and men who moreover had in many cases survived the various tropical diseases and developed some immunity, proved far more capable than the original expedition force when put to the test of combat.

The difficulties of equipping the troops and of feeding them until agriculture became established that had bedevilled the original expedition to Hispaniola, continued. Much of the supply from England was in the hands of Alderman Martin Noell and Thomas Povey, who had been appointed as the army's commissioning agents; Povey had his brother Richard made

COLONIAL IRONSIDES

A Spanish Captain of the American Colonies. (Alamy Image ERG02E)

commissary with the army. It seems clear that they were at best inefficient and at worse, thieves, for arms and ammunition sent over by them continued to be insufficient, the food scanty and often rotten.[44]

It was as well that Brayne's reforms had strengthened the English army, for disease was not the only killer. There was hard fighting to come against the Spanish and the Maroons over the next five years. The Spanish soldiers who had gone into the interior repudiated the terms of the treaty with the English, brought to them by Don Geronimo Tello at Banducu, where they had assembled to consider the terms, led in doing so by Proenza and *Sargento Mayor* Don Cristobal Ysassi Arnaldo.[*] In March 1656 an expedition was mounted from Cartagena by the Governor, Don Pedro Zapata, which landed at Pozo de Ayron, a small haven on the south coast. Ysassi, who had, it appears, been in Cuba, returned and was sent south by Proenza with the rank of *Teniente Maestre de Campo*.[45]

The arms brought from Cartagena were mostly lances and machetes and these had been distributed, along with rations of salt, wine, maize, vinegar and cassava. There was also a quantity of powder, shot, lead and slow match. Ysassi therefore began an offensive campaign with his small force of 45 men of whom 30 were Spaniards and 15 Maroons, using a stockade as their base.[46] Until now, the Spanish had given little trouble to the English garrison, besides killing a few stragglers and foragers. Now, however, they became a positive menace which threatened to undermine efforts to persuade farmers to settle in Jamaica. Ysassi and his followers were, according to Sedgwick who wrote numerous letters of complaint, 'bold and bloody: a people that know not what the laws and customs of civil nations mean.'[47] Ysassi's own letters and the Castilla narrative give a colourful summary of raids and sack by the guerrillas: Ysassi's campaign, as he describes it, carried him to the very doors of Brayne's headquarters, where he showed himself in the light of the houses he had set on fire.[48]

Throughout 1656, therefore, Brayne was obliged to seek out Ysassi by land and sea with his reorganised army, assisted by the ships of the fleet which gave him mobility, while the Spanish sought only to maintain a force in the field to harass the English and await better times – a true economy of force operation. Ysassi's letters reached the King's Council in Madrid and so impressed King Philip with his energy, loyalty and religious zeal, that he appointed Ysassi governor in succession to the late Don Juan Ramírez. Proenza was quietly dumped.[49] There is some evidence that Proenza had gone blind as a result of disease, for sickness in Jamaica was no respecter of nationality and affected the Spanish as well as the English.

The significance of Jamaica was becoming apparent to both sides, for it sat in the middle of the trade routes on which Spain relied – just as Cromwell had foreseen. Admiral Goodson's ships raided Spanish colonies and took prizes, especially around Cuba, in waters that were already infested with pirates – for it was the late seventeenth century that was the heyday of Caribbean piracy. Brayne had begun to build up the town of Cagway and to fortify the harbour with an inland wall and batteries of guns to protect the anchorage; The result was the

---

[*] Ysassi's father was Captain Don Cristobal Sanchez Ysassi; Don Blas Ysassi Arnaldo, the lieutenant-governor of Cuba, was his brother. He and Proenza were related by blood, or marriage, or both: there was a high degree of intermarriage among the Spaniards of Jamaica.

rapid growth of the town of Fort Cromwell, later Port Royal, which in due course became the capital of the island. Agriculture was developing quickly around Liguani and Morant, in particular, to feed this new settlement. He also pushed offensive operations along the north coast, from ships, and in the south-west. Already his combined force had come a long way from the chaos of Hispaniola. However, no attempt seems to have been made to enlist the support of the Maroons who were the bulk of the manpower available to the Spanish.

In October 1656, a renewed Spanish effort began to recover Jamaica. Orders were issued for the assembly of men, equipment, supplies and money under the authority of the Viceroy of Mexico, the Duke of Albuquerque,* from Puerto Rico, Cuba, Santo Domingo and Mexico. Concentration was ordered at Santiago de Cuba and from thence the force would be moved by sea to Jamaica.[50] Because Spain was heavily entangled in European wars, King Philip advised Albuquerque that: '… circumstances do not permit the despatch of a regular fleet, with forces of the regular army, to disembark and operate by land, and so attempt the restoration by regular methods …'[51] Albuquerque at once put in hand the concentration of troops that had been ordered; he also sent Captain Rodriguez de Vera to make contact with Ysassi at his camp on the north coast of Jamaica in April 1657. De Vera reported to the Duke in late July that a frigate loaded with stores had reached the small harbour of Santa Ana (also known as La Maguana) in northern Jamaica; The supplies did not reach Jamaica until November. Four more ships carrying 120 men under Captain Salinas with money and supplies had also reached Havana in Cuba in late March or early April. Had they but known it, the English were in crisis. The last stores of provisions brought from England by Brayne had been issued in March and by mid April, most of their troops were dispersed for hunting and foraging. Hunger was everywhere and discipline nowhere. They were rescued by the arrival of ships bringing provisions in late April, enough to tide them over until the harvest. The Spanish had missed their window of opportunity.

They missed it because the assembly of troops and supplies took time. Some money was appropriated by the governor of Santiago de Cuba, Don Bayona Villanueva, for his own garrison – a dangerous course of action in the face of a royal order; the 120 men under Salinas at Havana did not reach Santiago in time to join the main force;[52] another company of 100 men under Captain Don Cristobal Añues arrived at Santiago on 23 April, but appeared to have been improperly armed. Other contingents came from Puerto Rico – Captain Juan de los Reyes with about 30 men; and Captain Don Domingo da Silva with about 100 men from Santo Domingo, who were said to be unfit for the task. Two companies of refugee Spanish Jamaicans were also formed: one under Captain Don Francisco Cartagena de Leiva and the other under Captain Lucas Borrero Vardesi. All these men, around 400 in total, embarked for Jamaica and sailed on 6 July 1657.[53]

The royal order had instructed the Governor of Santiago to send the troops: '… to Don Cristobal Ysassi, by way of the safe port and landing places

---

*   Francisco Fernández de la Cueva y Enriquez de Cabrera, 8th Duke of Albuquerque, 6th Marquess of Cuéllar, 8th Count of Ledesma (1619–1676) was Viceroy of New Spain from August 1653 to September1660. He was also Viceroy of Sicily from 1668 to 1670.

which Don Cristobal names in his letter [of 3 April 1657]'.[54] The Viceroy had also reinforced this intention. Ysassi preferred a landing on the south coast as this was closer to the English base and to this end, he had prepared caches of stores with his Maroon allies. However, Villanueva overruled this choice and ordered the ships to Santa Ana in northern Jamaica – another example of interference with royal orders which was bound to have a bad effect on the expedition. The force arrived, unseen by the English, on 7 July 1657.

Ysassi, having received a further resupply on the south coast, marched north to meet the new arrivals. After a council of war, he sent the force southwards with Captain Juan de los Reyes as *Maestre de Campo* and Domingo de Silva as lieutenant; he himself followed a few days later. The long march south proved arduous for Ysassi's inexperienced and poorly equipped force, which was soon beset by exhaustion and sickness, as had the English in Hispaniola. At a higher level, jealousies and prejudice against Ysassi, who was of mixed race, meant that as much effort was put into internal fighting as should have been directed towards the English. By the time the little army had reached Los Bermejelas the men were mutinous; a large number had to be allowed to return to Las Chorreras with Reyes. From there, having picked up horses and a small force of 50 men under Captain Pavon, they were to go to Baycani – orders which Reyes disobeyed.[55]

Brayne, who had received word of the Spanish intention of mounting an expedition,[56] did not hear of the actual landing for nearly two months. Ysassi had been mounting a *guerrilla* campaign with some success using his small band of followers in the areas which later became the parishes St Catherine, Clarendon, Manchester, St Elizabeth and Westmoreland; but with less success in St Andrew and St Thomas.[57] But Brayne's reorganised and reinvigorated army was now actively seeking out the *guerrillas*. Not long after Ysassi had left for the north, the English made a successful raid, seizing all his pack animals – a stroke which Ysassi was unable to rectify.

Ysassi meanwhile pressed on with about 170 Jamaican exiles and Maroons, and most of the company of Don Cristobal de Añues. They met and defeated a small body of English troops and by late August were established in the Guatibacoa area, west of Spanish Town, where meat was plentiful.[58] At about this time, Brayne, who had been ill for much of the time, died on 2 September 1657. Edward D'Oyley once again took up the command and held it until the Restoration in 1660. D'Oyley sent out a troop of 60 to 80 horse which found Ysassi at a place known as Santa Ana gully – an uncertain site and not to be confused with Santa Ana on the north coast. In the encounter – hardly a battle – the English were beaten and lost heavily, but the Spanish lost even more heavily and seem to have been thoroughly disheartened in spite of their victory.[59] A few days later, Ysassi sent out a scouting party towards Cagway which was seen by the English. Most of them were killed and the rest of his men began to melt away. By the end of October, he had only 20 men left.

Meanwhile in the north, Reyes was doing all in his power to destroy the enterprise, encouraging quarrels and disloyalty; and wasting stores. D'Oyley at last learned from a prisoner, possibly a deserter, that Ysassi had received reinforcements and he determined at once to pursue him.[60] By the beginning of November, D'Oyley had driven what remained of Ysassi's force out of Guatibacoa to Los Bermejelas, where Ysassi was:

COLONIAL IRONSIDES

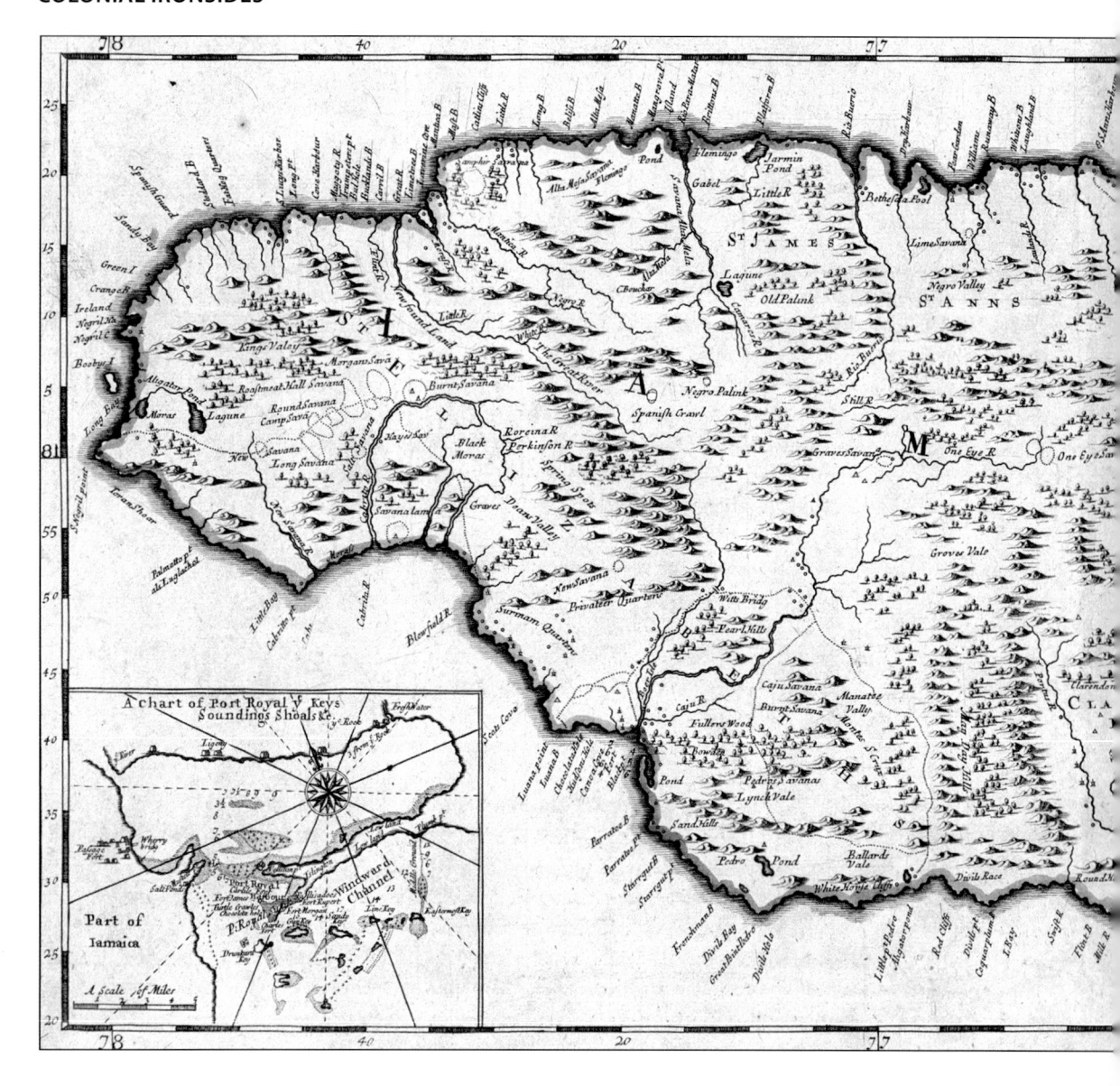

Jamaica by Philip Lea, showing the parish boundaries and settlements. (Wienand Drenth)

… making my headquarters in the negro stockade, since it is the strongest situation in all the island, where, with 100 men, though 1,000 attack, I can defend it. In order not to be beaten off by the enemy, I want to make all the king's munitions safe. Then, from there, I will set out on the campaign…[61]

D'Oyley was not going to repeat Brayne's mistake of allowing the Spanish to make free in his own courtyards. He established a new headquarters in what had been the Spanish capital, surrounded by the quarters of three of the four garrison regiments[*] with stockades to prevent raiding, storehouses, magazines and a church; and he also recruited a force of horsemen as his

---

[*] See the appendices to this chapter for a breakdown of the regiments' garrison areas.

bodyguards – the only mounted force on the island – which was also to make regular mounted patrols.⁶²

The naval squadron was reinforced by frigates from England under the redoubtable naval captain, Christopher Myngs,* Myngs, who was viewed as a pirate by the Spanish and at one time was seems to have been a privateer, assembled the ships *Marston Moor*, *Hector*, *Coventry*, *Blackamoor* and *Cagway*, embarking 300 soldiers from the garrison for a raid on Cuba; taking part in the raid were two Captains who later succeeded D'Oyley as governor – Henry Morgan and Thomas Lynch.⁶³ Myngs first looked into Havanna but then sailed

---

* Later Vice-Admiral Sir Christopher Myngs (1625–1666). He served in the Royal Navy after the Restoration and died as a result of wounds received at the Four Days' Battle in 1666.

to Tolú, which was sacked. He then sailed north-east, landing the troops and marching 12 miles inland, re-embarking three days later. He returned after 10 weeks carrying three prizes and a quantity of plunder. Myngs made another raid in January 1659, this time in company with several privateers. D'Oyley allowed this as he had little choice, needing to ally with the privateers (if not the pirates) to keep the Spanish at bay. This time Myngs sailed to Cumana on the north coast of Brazil, seizing and sacking the port. Puerto Cabello received the same treatment. Myngs seized large quantities of gold bullion, perhaps as much as £300,000 worth (£40 million at today's values),[64] although the Protectorate agents believed that much of the money never made it back to Jamaica. Myngs was forced to abandon further operations on land when he was attacked by numbers of Spanish mounted militia. The alliance with the freebooters was to have unintended consequences, including the encouragement of the piracy that became a scourge in the Caribbean after the Restoration.

D'Oyley also learned the location of Reyes' camp on the north coast and sent 300 men under Major Richard Stevens, of his own regiment, by sea. The business of naval reconnaissance and cooperation with land forces had made huge strides since Hispaniola. Stevens divided his command and advanced on the Spanish at Las Chorreras from two directions. Many of the Spaniards seem to have been dispersed, building boats in which they would return to Cuba. No opposition was made, therefore, to the landing. As the English approached the small stockade, Captain da Silva went forward with a forlorn hope which fired a single volley and then fell back. The English immediately attacked, rushing the wooden walls, firing through the gaps and hacking down the palisades with axes. killing at least 120 of the Spaniards and taking the stores and equipment as well as a number of prisoners, including *Maestre de Campo* Proenza. English losses were about 20.[65] This attack put a halt to Spanish raids on the English settlements from the north for a good while.

Shortly afterwards, Governor Villanueva, having heard news of the mutiny, sent a ship to Jamaica, to persuade the men to return to obedience. It arrived shortly after the defeat. Reyes, with the wounded da Silva and other survivors left in it for Cuba, leaving Añues in command of what remained – and promising reinforcements. Añues also fled to Cuba soon afterwards, with most of his men. Ysassi remained in the bush with his Maroon allies, learning of the defeat from an English prisoner. His supposed subordinates did all they could in Cuba to blacken his name and pin the blame for the fiasco on him – but the Duke of Albuquerque saw through the smokescreen and reported accordingly to the King.[66]

The Duke had in fact assembled more men at Vera Cruz, forming what became known as the *Tercio de Mexico* of 557 officers and men, under Captain Don Alvaro de la Raspuru. The soldiers were not only native Spaniards, but also black Africans, native Americans or boys, and well suited to warfare in the climate and conditions of the Caribbean; but they were poorly equipped and Raspuru was already sick; there were also too many captains and therefore a divided command. These men arrived in Havana on 9 November 1657. From here, Governor Villanueva sent word to Ysassi; but Villanueva again ordered the troops to land on the northern coast of Jamaica. Having no choice, Ysassi agreed to meet the expedition.

Hardly had he done so than D'Oyley's troops found him by using tracker dogs and horsemen and attacked his camp at Oristan on the south coast from land and sea. Among those taken prisoner was Captain Don Francisco de Cartagena de Leiva, who knew all the details of the new Spanish expedition. Ysassi decided, unsurprisingly, that the rendezvous should be changed, and sent a message to Villannueva recommending Baycani, which was not far from Las Chorreras.

On 30 January 1658 the *tercio* arrived in Santiago de Cuba. Goodson's frigates were watching the port but even so, the troops were embarked in three ships and on 15/16 May 1658 they sailed for Rio Nuevo, about six miles (10 kilometres) east of Santa Ana. Here, Ysassi had arranged to receive the troops and stores but when the expedition landed, they found that the Maroon's camp had been attacked by the English. Ysassi, however, soon appeared. Six artillery pieces were landed along with the troops, who, with Ysassi's followers, now numbered about 650 and included 31 captains – a huge proportion of the force, even if half (as seems likely) were reformadoes), 31 ensigns, 28 sergeants and 467 soldiers, along with around 50 maroons. Even if half the captains held a command with the other half acting as lieutenants, a company would have been no more than 30 men. Preparations were made to fortify an encampment at Rio Nuevo.

Goodson had probably been shadowing the Spanish ships for an English frigate soon appeared and opened fire. It was driven off but reappeared with reinforcements. They were again driven off, but Ysassi ordered the Spanish ships to slip away. Next day, five English ships, including merchantmen acting as troop transports, appeared and landed soldiers under cover of fire from the ships; they were, however, once more forced to withdraw. But this was only a preliminary, for D'Oyley was well aware of the Spanish landing and on 11 June, after a week at sea, he personally led an embarked force of 700 troops bound for the north coast. The troops were in excellent condition: D'Oyley's reforms had allowed the ration to be doubled; the men were given a regular rum ration – counterbalanced by a diet of Puritan preaching of course – and their morale was much improved. There is no record to show the regiments from which the men were drawn but given the strength of the garrison, the force was probably made up of as many fit men as could be mustered from all four regiments, leaving aside the need for work details in the fields and on the fortifications. On 26 June they made an opposed landing and laid siege to the Spanish encampment.[67]

D'Oyley demanded that Ysassi surrender, offering quarter and safe conduct, and wasting an entire day in negotiation; but surrender was refused. The English were in fact buying time to make scaling ladders and fill hand-grenadoes. The next day, D'Oyley sent part of the naval squadron further down the bay with a portion of the troops to make a feint on the far side – probably the south-west. D'Oyley then led the rest of the troops into the forest, crossing the Rio Nuevo upstream from the fort, encountering a party of Spaniards as they did and killing them. After a pause to drink and recover themselves, the troops stealthily approached the fort from the inland side, seeing that the fortifications were not finished.[68] D'Oyley, dressed in the full uniform of a Protectorate general then exhorted the troops:

telling the soldiers that a great deal of England's honour lay at stake, and therefore hoped they would consider it and carry themselves accordingly, going himself from party to party, and following the rear of the forlorn in a very signal habit. His gallant behaviour was answered both by officers and soldiers with a silent cheerful obedience, and through God's gracious goodness there was found such a joint unanimous willingnes to the work that the truth is it was of God and it hath exceedingly endeared us one to another since we came here.[69]

The Spanish meanwhile taunted the English with cries of 'Santo Domingo': 'which inflamed the English troops with rage'.[70] The redcoats then charged into the Spanish musket fire, rallying at the angles of the makeshift bastions to throw their grenadoes into the fort. They then scaled the walls with their ladders and came to close quarters with the Spaniards – who were by no means shy.

Fighting lasted only 15 minutes and was so fierce that: 'This gallant action repaired the honour of the [English] army, which had sustained some injury at St Domingo.'[71] The Spanish were forced out of the fort and pursued down the steep escarpment to the sea where they were trapped between the redcoats and the English ships from where the sailors: seeing them run along the rocks, came out with their boats and killed many of them.'[72] The English killed at least 300 Spaniards, took the fort, the Royal Standard of Spain, 11 company colours and all the stores. They left having destroyed what they could not carry and levelling the fortifications, taking with them 100 prisoners including six captains whom D'Oyley sent home to England with his report, which was well publicised. The six captured Spanish guns and stores were used to improve Fort Cromwell. D'Oyley lost about 30 men killed and around the same number wounded; among the dead were Captain Wiseman of the horse; and Mears, Walker and Robinson, all originally from Humphrey's Regiment. Ysassi tried to rally the survivors but on 17 July it was decided to ship back to Santiago de Cuba all but 50 men, who would remain with Ysassi to keep a foothold on the island and preserve the Spanish claim.[73] In retrospect, however, this battle was probably decisive.

No further action followed, but Ysassi continued to send intelligence on English activities to Morales until the Duke of Albuquerque heard of the defeat. In consequence, Reyes was imprisoned and Villanueva was removed from his governorship. Don Pedro de Morales became Governor of Santiago and Captain Don Juan de Tabor was made *Sargento Mayor* of Jamaica but told to acknowledge Ysassi as his superior.[74] One hundred men were sent from Spain, to be equipped by the governors of provinces close to Jamaica. Albuquerque also ordered what was left of the *tercio* to return to Jamaica along with ammunition and stores that he provided.

News of Cromwell's death had by now reached both Jamaica and New Spain and the duke probably hoped that the English would lose heart and withdraw. By the end of the year, there were once more around 600 Spanish troops in Jamaica. Mostly on the north coast. However, all the governors of the neighbouring provinces were advising both the Viceroy and Madrid that nothing short of a major *armada* of Spanish regular troops and ships would shift the English. An offer of money was made to D'Oyley, in exchange for his garrison's departure, but without result. It was better, thought the governors, to abandon Jamaica than to keep on with useless *guerrilla* warfare: only Ysassi disagreed. Hungry, ill-equipped and all but abandoned, he stubbornly hung on.

February 1660 found Ysassi, *Sargento Mayor* de Tabor and his troops back at Las Chorreras. Here, he received alarming news. D'Oyley had succeeded in persuading one of the leaders of the Spanish Maroons, Juan Lubolo, known as de Bolas to the English, to switch sides and join him, along with his warriors. Lubolo had, it seemed, lost faith in Ysassi's ability to support the alliance and had therefore approached the English with offers of information in exchange for peace terms:

> Last week a party with Lieut.-Col. Tyson went out to seek the negroes; came to their plantation, and three of the chief came to Port Cagway to wait on the General. Our party remained with the rest, with whom questions not but they shall agree very well; they are to bring their wives and children to remain with us for conditions. Major Fairfax gone with another party to make conditions with them. They promise to carry our men to the Spanish Governor's quarters and to bring him in. Are now so intermixed with them and have possession of all their provisions that should they offer to go back we can with ease destroy them …[75]

The offer had been accepted: More bad news followed: Lubolo and a force of English troops under Lieutenant-Colonel Edward Tyson had attacked and destroyed another stockade manned by Maroons loyal to Ysassi. On 26 February, Tyson, at the head of a force from Burrough's Regiment, surprised Ysassi at a new camp:

> … the enemy having proffered their friendship and delivered up twelve hostages to make good their promise; and they, with our men, routed and destroyed two settlements of other negroes and then took them to the Spanish camp where of about 140 we killed and took about 80. Desire of the Spanish Governor for peace. Intelligence that a bark would arrive with relief from Cuba, which was trepanned and fell into their hands, and the Spaniards not dreaming of the cheat were surprised by our men who lay in ambush. About four days since another settlement was destroyed where 30 negroes were taken. Though the number of these was inconsiderable yet their advantages were so great that it is God's mercy a man of our regiment was left alive.[76]

The Spanish lost many men, including de Tabor, leaving only 175 left alive. Tyson left letters for Ysassi tied to trees, offering quarter and safe passage; but even before this, Ysassi himself had asked for terms.[77] Negotiations dragged on – probably because D'Oyley realised that Ysassi's situation was so bad, he need not offer terms. Eventually, Ysassi was reduced to building two large canoes in which he and his remaining men departed Jamaica on 3 May 1660, after four long years of warfare. On arrival in Santiago, Ysassi received much the same cold treatment that had been meted out to Venables in England.

In spite of the triumph over the Spanish, by 1660 the English troops had become mutinous, possibly under the encouragement of civilians who sensed the end of the Protectorate and dictatorship with it. This was, perhaps, their chance to overthrow D'Oyley and establish a republic before monarchy was restored.

> Finding their legs, and able to stand by themselves ... they became more refactory, and head-strong, and of a lesse bounded discipline: acknowledging but small homage where they received so small pay ... their discontents heated them so a touchinesse, that they were ready to take fire on all occasions.'[78]

Under the encouragement of Lieutenant-Colonel Thomas Raymond, a veteran of service in Ireland, a rising was planned. However, when the moment came, the soldiers deserted their leaders, leaving Raymond and Edward Tyson to be tried by court martial and shot.[79] After the Restoration and the arrival of a new, royal, governor, the old regiments were disbanded.

This book is about expeditionary operations, not about colonisation; suffice to say that throughout the period of the Protectorate, strenuous efforts had been made to populate the new colony. Cromwell had issued a proclamation in October 1655 giving encouragement: 'to such as shall transplant themselves to Jamaica.'[80] Every soldier was given 30 acres of land and every civilian male immigrant was allocated 20 acres; if accompanied by a wife and child they received an additional 10 acres. Some 1,400 colonists made the journey to Jamaica from many different places: some came from Caribbean islands like the Barbadoes, or from Bermuda further north, to find land to grow the increasingly profitable crop of tobacco. The Quakers of the Barbadoes moved en masse in order to escape compulsory service in the militia. There were also Dutch who had been expelled by the Portuguese from Brazil as a result of colonial warfare between Portugal and the Netherlands: Dutch Jews were particularly keen to avoid the Portuguese, and with them the Inquisition, and saw Cromwell's Parliamentarian government as benign in the aftermath of Cromwell's decision to readmit Jews to England. The Dutch also brought expertise from Brazil in growing sugar cane, which was becoming highly profitable. Indentured labourers from Scotland were sent to Army officers in Jamaica as servants, in lieu of arrears of pay. Cromwell agreed a plan to send 2,000 Irish boys and girls, all under the age of 14, to the island as indentured servants in December 1655, but this plan was never carried out.[81] In addition, the Sheriffs of Scotland were ordered to transport convicted vagrants and thieves to help populate the island. Appeals to the Puritan colonists of New England went largely unanswered. In spite of these efforts, disease and malnutrition eroded the population faster than the dead could be replaced. By 1661, although 12,000 people, not including the original expeditionary force, had come in, the population of the island had reached only 3,500, of whom just over 2,000 were soldiers and another 514 black slaves.[82] A return dated 31 January 1659 gave the total strength of the English garrison as 2,041, including '4 Colonels, 3 Lt-Colls, 4 Majors, 24 Captains, 2 chaplaines, 7 surgeons, a troop of horse of 70' and 1,541 privates.'[83]

Over the years that followed, however, the agriculture was developed, piracy was eventually suppressed after a period of ascendancy, a militia replaced the old redcoated regiments of the Protectorate and Jamaica became a highly valuable colony. Perhaps Cromwell's ghost permitted itself a wry smile.

Appendix I to Chapter 9

The Cromwellian Garrison in Jamaica, 1657–1662[1]

The eight regiments which had sailed under Venables were subsequently reduced to five and a troop of horse in Jamaica: those of Venables, Heane, D'Oyley, Carter and Buller, the surviving troops from St Christopher, Nevis and Montserrat having returned home. An abstract of the Regiments, 'the General's Buller's Doyle's, Holdippes and Humphere's', on 14 November 1655 in Jamaica gives a strength of 2,194 well, 2,316 sick, and 172 women and children.[2] Buller's Regiment was quartered at Guanaboa in Jamaica;[3] Holdep's (formerly Heane's) was stationed at Liguanea;[4] D'Oyley's and the General's, with the horse, were in garrison in Kingston. Carter's was down to 302 all ranks in November 1657 and although retained as the fifth regiment after the initial drawdown, it was disbanded soon afterwards, reducing the five regiments to four. A return dated 31 January 1659 gives the total strength of the garrison as 2,041, including '4 Colonels, 3 Lt-Colls, 4 Majors, 24 Captains, 2 chaplaines, 7 surgeons, a troop of horse of 70.'[5] Three other regiments were sent from England as reinforcements, those of Brayne, Moore and Humphreys. Disease also reduced these in numbers and they were incorporated in the four regiments remaining at the time of the Restoration.

Where possible, the regiments are given by company.

Staff

General Edward D'Oyley	Controller of the Ordnance Thomas Hughes	Judge Advocate John Cudworth
General William Brayne (December 1656)	Clerk of the Ordnance Edward James	Marshal General John Deane
General Edward D'Oyley (second appointment, September 1657)	Commissary of Stores Captain __ Bunn (1656)	Provost Marshal Mark Fowler (1655)
Adjutant-General James Butler	Commissary of Stores Richard Povey (1657)	Provost Marshal Thomas Goodfellow (1656)
Adjutant-general Thomas Walters (1656)	Quartermaster General John Rudyard	Provost Marshal Thomas Povey (1657)
Adjutant-General Phillip Warde (1657)	Commissary Richard Fleetwood	Deputy Provost Marshal William Deane (Keane), Luke Hill, Thomas Bossey, Edward Rich
Chaplain Thomas Gage	Gunsmith George Varley	Paymaster General Robert Wadeson

COLONIAL IRONSIDES

Secretary John Daniel
Treasurer Thomas Wadeson
Muster Master John Laughton
Deputy Muster-Master Richard Scott

General's (D'Oyley's, or Barbadoes) Regiment (later Barrington's)

Colonel Edward D'Oyley
Colonel Francis Barrington (1657)
Colonel Thomas Lynch (*c.* 1660)
Lieutenant-Colonel Francis Mercer
Major Robert Smith
Major Richard Stevens (April 1657)
Captain-Lieutenant James Berry
Captain John Fisher
Captain Augustine Thornhill (to Jan 1657)
Captain George Smithsby (Jan 1657)
Captain __ Noell
Captain __ Downes
Lieutenant Humphrey Groves
Unplaced
Lieutenant Ralph Hardwick

Holdep's Regiment (formerly Heane's, later Barry's)

Colonel Richard Holdep	Lieutenant-Colonel Samuel Barry (colonel in 1656)	Major Richard Hope
Captain-Lieutenant Andrew Houncell	Lieutenant William King	Major Richard Bamford (April 1656)
Lieutenant William Wandell	Ensign William Hopkins	Lieutenant __ Marshall
Ensign __ Farris		
Captain George Audley	Captain Henry Archbould	Captain Richard Younge
Ensign John Clarke	Lieutenant William Rivers	Lieutenant William Huntley
Captain Richard Bamford	Captain Gregory Toms	Captain Edward Willett
Ensign George Rivers		Lieutenant George Faulkner
Captain Daniel Smith	Captain Richard Bamford	Captain Robert Taylor

Staff
Gentleman-at-Arms Richard Clearke
Gunsmith William Fudge
Surgeon's Mate John Frankling
Surgeon's Mate Jesse Wharton
Quartermaster Bartholomew Jackson
Chaplain Roger Manners

APPENDIX I TO CHAPTER 9

Fortescue's Regiment

This regiment mustered 120 officers and NCOs in March 1655 but was reduced to 351 all ranks by November 1657. It was therefore disbanded.

Colonel Richard Fortescue*	Major William Hill	Captain Thomas White
Captain-Lieutenant William Hambleyne	Lieutenant Thomas Hill	Captain Henry Bartlett
Ensign James Peake		Ensign William Denis
Gentleman-at-Arms Thomas May		
Captain Samuel Leverington†	Captain Bartholomew Davis*	Captain Richard Kenne
Lieutenant John Bray	Lieutenant Thomas Ethon	Ensign Thomas Dowing
Ensign Henry Kent	Ensign Thomas Howell	
	Gentleman-at-Arms John Poulton	
Captain Richard Wells	Captain Obadiah Edwards	Captain Thomas White
Lieutenant Thomas French	Lieutenant Henry Hurst	Lieutenant Edward Mallinson
Ensign Richard Lawrence	Ensign James Bates	Ensign William Carman
	Gentleman-at-Arms Thomas Edwards	

Captain __ Douglas

Unplaced
Lieutenant Ralph Hardwick
Lieutenant James Rudiard
Lieutenant __ Debben
Lieutenant Benjamin Gordward
Ensign David Douglas
Ensign William Hall
Ensign Thomas Freeman

Staff
Quartermaster Ralph Hardwick
Surgeon John Henry Hilsman
Surgeon's Mate Edward Stapleton
Chaplain Nathaniel Lane

---

*   Died in October 1655.
†   Severely wounded at Hispaniola.

COLONIAL IRONSIDES

Ward's Regiment (formerly Venables', later Ballard's)

Colonel Philip Ward	Lieutenant-Colonel Thomas Ballard	Major Robert Smith
Colonel Thomas Ballard (1661)	Lieutenant John Ballard	Major Richard Wilbraham (1661)
Captain-Lieutenant Henry Potter	Ensign James Burey	Lieutenant Lewis Ashton
Ensign Robert Minshun		
Captain Henry Ferrobosco	Captain Edward Sackwell (Sackfield)	Captain Ralph Betts
Lieutenant John Barrett	Lieutenant William Willoughby	Ensign Thomas Elendre(?)
Ensign Robert Don	Ensign William Simons	
Captain John Cooke	Captain Henry Davis	Captain Abraham Peg
Lieutenant Tate Howell	Lieutenant Thomas Archbould	Lieutenant Andrew Peter
Ensign Thomas Breres		

Unplaced
Lieutenant Ralph Swinnerton
Lieutenant Thomas Huddlestone
Lieutenant Thomas Fuller
Ensign Henry Goddard

Staff
Surgeon Henry Hilliard

Burroughs' (formerly Buller's) Regiment

A muster of this regiment in 1656 showed that it numbered 578 men, of whom 217 were sick; there were 27 women and children attached to it; a muster after the reduction of the original regiments to four new ones showed it to number no more than 400.

Colonel Cornelius Burroughs	Lt-Col Francis Barrington‡	Major __ Smith
	Lt-Col Henry Archbould (1659)	Major Christopher Cooper (1656)
	Lieutenant Robert Taylor	Lieutenant Henry Middleton
		Ensign Anthony How
Captain	Captain John Minne	Captain Stroud Bingham (Brigham)
Lieutenant Randall Kettel	Lieutenant Benjamin Larkin	Lieutenant Peter Parry
Ensign Richard Welde	Ensign Thomas Eyton	Ensign Thomas Smith
Captain Jonathan Penkeville	Captain __ Fry	
	Lieutenant Matthew Paine	

---

*   Served in Okey's Dragoons and in Ireland under Henry Cromwell. Died in 1660

Unplaced
Lieutenant Lewis Prothero
Lieutenant Thomas Trafford

Staff
Chaplain John Vaughan

Barry's (formerly Holdep's) Regiment

A muster of the regiment in November 1655 showed that it numbered 572 men, of whom 224 were sick, with 30 women and children attached. In April 1656 it numbered 428.

Colonel Samuel Barry	Lieutenant-Colonel Michael Bland	Major Richard Bamford
Lieutenant William Wandell	Lieutenant Andrew Houncell	Major Francis Fairfax (1659?)
Ensign __ Farris	Ensign John Clarke	Lieutenant William King
		Ensign William Hopkins
Captain George Audley	Captain Gregory Tom	Captain Edward Willett
		Lieutenant George Faulkner
Captain Richard Yonge	Captain Daniel Smith	
Lieutenant William Huntley		
Ensign George Simpson		

Unplaced
Lieutenant James Bedlow (Bellewe)
Lieutenant George Rivers
Ensign John Pollard

Brayne's Regiment

This regiment was raised in Scotland by drawing 42 men from each of the 12 regiments garrisoned there, making a total of 504. It was sent to Jamaica in late 1655 and was the best of the regiments there, being mostly composed of veterans, however half the men drowned when the ship *Two Brothers* foundered on the coast of Ireland. By 1660 it had been incorporated into the four remaining regiments of the garrison.

Colonel William Brayne[§]	Lieutenant William Godfrey	Ensign William Bramston[¶]
Lieutenant-Colonel John Bramston[¶]	Lieutenant Thomas Petty	Ensign James Williams
Captain James Dorrell[¶]	Lieutenant William Wood	Ensign Hugh Norman
Captain Edward Boone	Lieutenant Moses Rayner[¶]	Ensign William Webley[¶]

---

* Died 2 September 1657.
† Drowned on the *Two Brothers*.

Humphrey's Regiment

This regiment was raised in England and consisted of around 700 veterans, reinforced in the Barbadoes and at St Christopher. Although it originally consisted of better-quality men than many of the other regiments, the climate of the West Indies soon took its toll. By the Restoration it had been incorporated into the four remaining regiments.

Colonel John Humphrey
Lieutenant-Colonel Christopher Ennis[*]
Lieutenant-Colonel William Fleetwood (July 1656)
Lieutenant-Colonel Edward Tyson (September 1656 – executed for mutiny in 1657)
Major William Pelham[§]
Martin Van Alfen (April 1656)
Major Thomas Fairfax (1657)
Captain Samuel Barry
Captain John Filkins
Captain Robert Smith
Captain Henry Jones[†]
Captain Martin Van Alfen
Captain William Fleetwood
Captain Edward Tyson
Captain Thomas Fairfax[‡]
Lieutenant __ Mears (Captain by 1658, killed in action against the Spanish)
Lieutenant __ Walker (Captain by 1658, killed in action against the Spanish)
Lieutenant __ Robinson (Captain by 1658, killed in action against the Spanish)

Moore's Regiment

The regiment was assembled from drafts of the regiments in Ireland and assembled at Carrickfergus in May 1656. It did not arrive in Jamaica, due to shortage of shipping and bad weather, until December. Moore himself then waited for the next spring before sailing. It rapidly diminished in strength from 500 to 160 and was disbanded by 1657. No lists of the regiment exist.

Colonel William Moore
Lieutenant-Colonel __ Brumpston[§]
Captain __ Fry
Lieutenant Matthew Paine

Troop of Horse

Captain Henry Jones
Captain __ Wiseman (1658)[¶]
Lieutenant John Josse

---

[*] Died in Jamaica.
[†] Died 30 May 1656.
[‡] 1633–1712. He was the son of Sir Thomas; he survived the restoration and the Dutch invasion of 1688. He was later Brigadier-General and Governor of Limerick.
[§] Possibly William Bramstom.
[¶] CSPC Addenda, 1658; killed in action against the Spanish in 1658.

Cornet Samuel Bedlington
Quartermaster William Brigham
Surgeon Thomas Lugg

Unplaced

The following appear by name in D'Oyley's journal in late 1656 but disappear thereafter; they may have died, returned to England or else been reduced. Alternatively, they may be the officers of Moore's Regiment.

Major Throgmorton
Captain Hodforde
Captain Winkfield Blunt
Captain Pattison
Captain Howlett
Captain Colbourne
Captain Archer
Captain Ryley

NOTES
1. CSPC 1656, 1657 and 1658; TNA Entry Books (Protectorate) vol. 106. (1656), 107 (1657) and 108 (1658), BL Add MSS 12423
2. TNA CO 5/32 f.40.
3. Firth & Davies, vol. ii, pp.709–710.
4. Firth & Davies, vol. ii, pp.719–721.
5. TNA CO 5/33 f.52.

Appendix II to Chapter 9

Spanish Order of Battle, Jamaica, 1655–1660

Governor and Captain-General
Juan Ramírez de Arellano (1655)
Franciso de Proenza (acting, 1655)
Don Cristobal Ysassi Arnaldo (1656)

Maestre de Campo
Franciso de Proenza

Sergeant-Major General
Don Cristobal Ysassi Arnaldo (1655)
Don Juan de Tabor (1659)

Expedition of October 1656

400 Spanish and Jamaican exiles, 50 Maroons
Captain Rodriguez de Vera
Company of Spanish troops – Captain Don Cristobal de Añues
Company of Spanish troops – Captain __ Salinas
Company of Jamaican exiles – Captain Don Francisco Cartagena de Leiva
Company of Jamaican exiles – Captain Lucas Borrero Vardesi
Detachment from Puerto Rico – *Maestre de Campo* Juan de los Reyes
Detachment of Horse – Captain __ Pavon
Lieutenant Domingo da Silva

Tercio de Mexico
31 captains, 31 ensigns, 28 sergeants and 467 soldiers; six field pieces; 50–60 Maroons and Jamaican exiles
Captain Don Alvaro de la Rasparu

Maroon Irregulars
Juan de Bolas (Lubolo)
Juan de Serras

10

General-at-Sea Blake's Naval Operations in the Mediterranean and Against Spain

While William Penn sailed for the West Indies with one English fleet, another under General-at-Sea Robert Blake sailed for the Mediterranean. Although it was well known that Blake had sailed, his precise instructions remained unclear to both friend and foe.

Blake's early career has been covered in Chapter 3 and as well as his reforms in discipline and fighting methods, he is also remembered for his command during the First Anglo-Dutch War. The war began with a skirmish between the Dutch fleet of Maarten Tromp and the English under Blake, off Folkestone on 29 May 1652, known as the Battle of Goodwin Sands or in the Netherlands as *Slag bij Dover*. War began in earnest, however, in June with the English campaign against the Dutch East Indies, their Baltic trade, and their fishing fleet. Blake commanded around 60 ships. On 5 October 1652 Dutch Vice-Admiral de With tried to attack Blake in bad weather but failed: the Dutch were then attacked by Blake on 8 October in the Battle of the Kentish Knock, or *Slag bij de Hoofden*. The defeated Dutch ran for home. Assuming the war to be won, the Commonwealth government reduced Blake's fleet in order to send ships to the Mediterranean under Captain John Appleton, leaving Blake with 42 capital ships. Unsurprisingly, he was attacked and decisively beaten by nearly 90 Dutch ships under Tromp on 9 December 1652 in the Battle of Dungeness, or *Slag bij de Singels*, as a result of which control of the English Channel passed to the Dutch. Meanwhile, the fleet sent to the Mediterranean had also been defeated by the Dutch under Commodore Jan van Galen, at the Battle of Leghorn, or Livorno.

Blake demanded that the Navy Commissioners should rapidly expand the fleet and carry out major reforms to correct the patchy performance against the Dutch, especially at Dungeness. Among those introduced as a result were the *Articles of War*, which firmly established the authority of the General-at-Sea over his captains and tightened up discipline generally. Blake put to sea with around 75 ships, engaging Tromp with a roughly equal fleet in the Battle of Portland. The battle, which lasted from 28 February until 2 March 1653, ended inconclusively but with the English in the ascendant; Tromp escaped under cover of darkness.

At the Battle of the Gabbard on 12 and 13 June 1653, Blake, along with the squadrons of Generals Richard Deane and George Monck, decisively defeated the Dutch, sinking or capturing 17 ships without loss. The Channel and the North Sea were now under English control and the Dutch fleet blockaded in ports until the Battle of Scheveningen, in which Tromp was killed, ended the series of major fleet actions with England holding the initiative.[1]

With the Dutch confined to their ports and reduced to using small craft to carry on hostilities, Blake was ordered to the Mediterranean in October 1654 with 24 ships to pursue Cromwell's Mediterranean strategy.* His precise instructions remain unclear – indeed there may never have been any – but Cromwell's intentions can be discerned.[2] First, Cromwell was still playing off France against Spain, and at this point, leaning towards an alliance with Spain, even though he was pursuing their colonies and commerce in the West Indies. A naval presence in the Mediterranean would halt any attempt by the French to attack the Spanish territories in southern Italy. It was known that Cardinal Mazarin was attempting to raise a revolt against the Spanish in Naples and at the same time, preparing a military expedition under Henry II, Duke of Guise, at Toulon. This force was to be transported to Naples in the French fleet under Admiral Nieuchèse, which would have to sail from Brest on the Atlantic coast to make rendezvous. Secondly, the defeat at Leghorn could be avenged and English prestige restored. Thirdly, English merchant ships could be protected. Fourthly, aid might be given to the Venetians, resisting the incursions of the Muslim Turks. And last, the activities of the Algerine pirates, or Barbary Corsairs, might be curbed. On 5 August, Cromwell wrote to King Philip of Spain, informing him of Blake's despatch and begging the protection of his ports;[3] Given Blake's record of success against Spain's enemies, the Dutch and the Portuguese, he was likely to be welcomed.

Blake hoisted his flag in the *George* (60 guns), with Richard Badiley as his vice-admiral in the *Andrew* (54) and Joseph Jordan as rear-admiral in the *Unicorn* (54). The French soon learned of Blake's mission; Louis wrote to Cromwell demanding the details of Blake's commission;[4] he also warned Nieuchèse that he should make rendezvous with Guise before Blake's fleet arrived in the Mediterranean. Given heavy French commitments against the Spanish, they could not countenance a war with the English at sea and Mazarin was therefore desperate to maintain at least the semblance of peace with Cromwell and would therefore tolerate a great deal of provocation. It was not until 4 November that Blake appeared off Cadiz, on the south-west coast of Spain, where the Spanish governor sent word that he was welcome. Blake did not linger but made for the Straits of Gibraltar, where he was able

---

* See the appendix to this chapter for details.

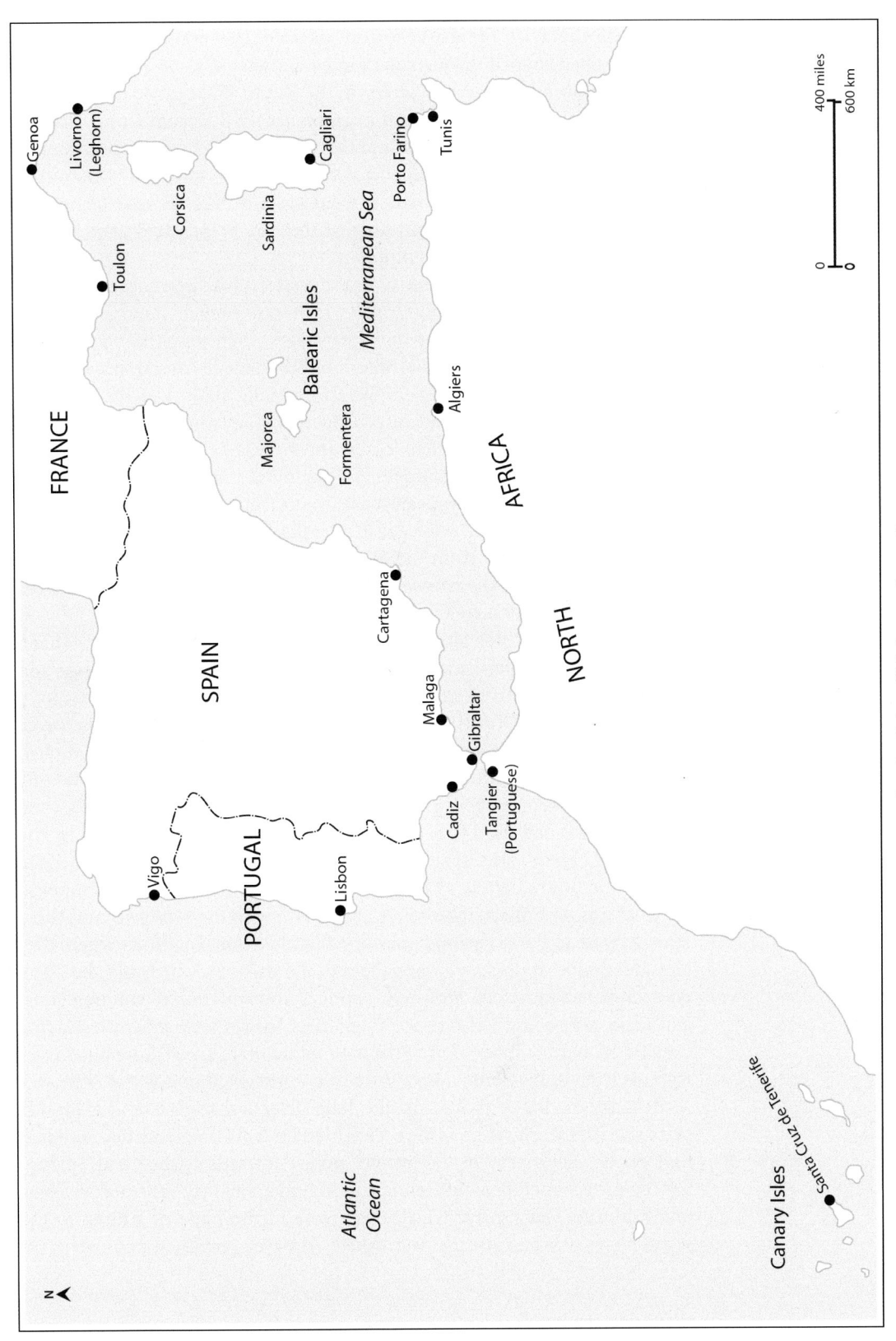

GENERAL-AT-SEA BLAKE'S NAVAL OPERATIONS IN THE MEDITERRANEAN AND AGAINST SPAIN

General-at-Sea Robert Blake's area of operations

to prevent the main French fleet from passing. However, four days before, nine ships had slipped through and joined Guise.

On 21 November, leaving a screen in the Straits, Blake sailed in pursuit via Málaga, Alicante and Cagliari and from thence on 8 December for Naples.[5] He arrived three days later but found that Guise, having seized Castellamare and Torre Annunciata, had failed to storm the city, and had withdrawn.[6] Blake sailed for Leghorn (Livorno), relations with the Genoese being very good, to take on provisions,[7] but learned that the French had gone back to Toulon and were unlikely to venture out.

Blake had achieved sea control in the western Mediterranean with little effort.[8] He then detached four frigates to harass French trade around the Balearic Islands and suppress their privateers, then prepared to sail with the rest of his force against the Algerines. The North African provinces of Tunis, Tripoli, Sallee and Algiers were nominally subject to the Ottoman Sultan in Constantinople, but in practice their deys had a high degree of autonomy. From their fortified bases, their corsairs preyed on European merchant shipping, seizing cargoes and taking slaves for their galleys. They were known to raid the European coasts, venturing as far as Cornwall, South and West Wales and the west coast of Ireland. Blake's intentions were to demand compensation from the Tunisian ruler for the seizure of the ship *Princess* and to secure the release of English, Irish, Welsh and Scottish slaves,[9] a requirement under a treaty signed by the Dey of Algiers and Sir Edward Casson in 1646.[10] It was also rumoured – wrongly as it turned out – that a Barbary fleet was concentrating at Tunis for an attack on the Venetians and this Blake was anxious to stop.[11]

Blake arrived off Tunis on 8 February 1655 and laid his demands before the Dey, who refused them on the grounds that an English captain, Mitchell, had agreed to transport a company of Tunisian troops to Smyrna in 1651, but had sold them as galley slaves to the Knights of Malta; although the English consul had tried to secure their release, the price demanded by the Knights – £10,000 – was too high.[12] The Dey was, however, prepared to make a treaty for future conduct but was not prepared to offer any recompense for what was past. Blake then sent Captain Hill with the *Worcester* and three other frigates to Porto Farino (Ghar-al-Milh), just north of Tunis, where they blockaded nine of the Dey's war galleys in the harbour, which was the Dey's new naval headquarters. However, supplies and water were running short and Blake was obliged to run for Cagliari in Sardinia to replenish, leaving Captain Richard Stayner of the *Plymouth* to maintain an offshore blockade[13] with the frigates *Plymouth*, *Kent*, *Newcastle*, *Foresight*, *Taunton* and *Mermaid*.

At Cagliari, Blake picked up the four detached frigates and a French prize, *La Persée*. Here, he also received letters from England that updated him on developments in Cromwell's policy towards France and Spain.[14] Having provisioned here, at Genoa and Majorca, the fleet returned to Tunis on 18 March, leaving five frigates to cruise in the hope of adding to the seven prizes that had already been taken.* The Dey remained unmoved: 'We

---

* *Langport, Hampshire, Diamond, Maidstone* and one other unknown.

GENERAL-AT-SEA BLAKE'S NAVAL OPERATIONS IN THE MEDITERRANEAN AND AGAINST SPAIN

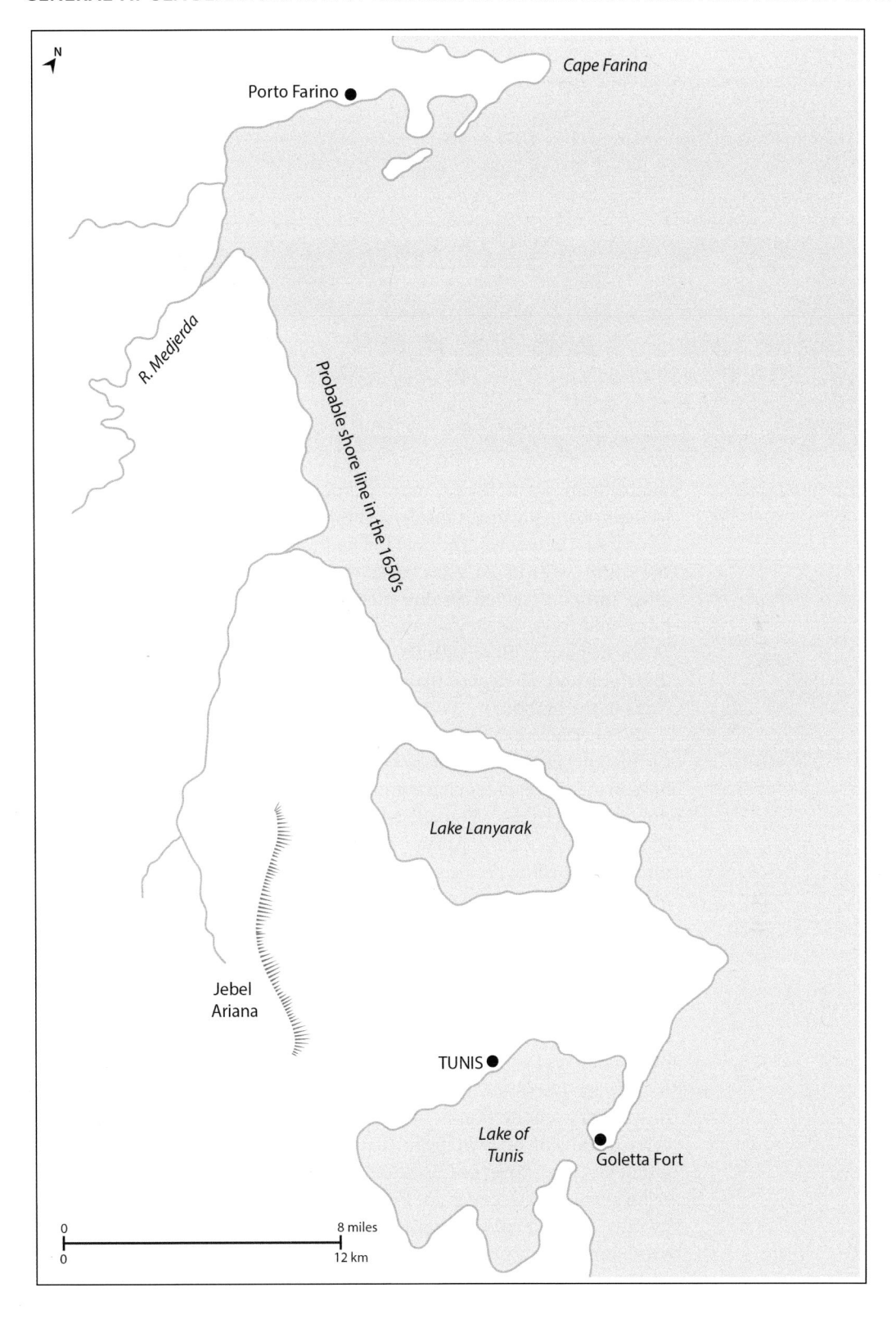

Tunis and Porto Farino

COLONIAL IRONSIDES

A modern photograph of Porto Farino. (Ghar-al-Milh)

found them', wrote Blake, 'more wilful and intractable than before, adding to their obstinacy much insolence and contumely, denying us all commerce of civility.'[15] Moreover, the corsairs had anchored their ships under cover of the castle, with its 24 guns, strengthened shore batteries with another 36 guns and constructed an entrenched camp occupied by several thousand horse and foot: the Dey's troops were ordered to open fire on any attempt by the English to close with the shore; the galleys had in the meantime been disarmed and de-rigged. Blake made up his mind to take and burn all the ships in the harbour.

It is certain that the shoreline in 1655 was different from that of today, for the entrance to the bay is now so narrow that Blake's fleet could never have made entry; older charts show the shoreline as it was.[16] As a ruse, Blake drew the fleet off to Trapani where he took on more water, but returned to Porto Farino on 3 April.[17] He began his attack at dawn the following morning, dividing the fleet into two squadrons. Captain Nathaniel Cobham of the *Newcastle* led the smaller warships – *Foresight, Amity, Princess Maria, Pearl, Mermaid, Merlin, Ruby* and *Diamond* against the Tunisian galleys; Badiley in the *Andrew* took the heavier ships in close against the castle and the fortifications: he was followed by the *Plymouth*, Blake's flagship, the *George, Worcester, Unicorn, Bridgewater* and *Success*; then the six second and third rate ships.[18] Blake had not embarked any soldiers for sea service as was often done and so relied on the firepower of his guns and boarding parties of seamen. The ships dropped anchor 50 yards from the castle and opened a heavy and accurate fire. Fortunately, the wind was blowing onshore, which carried the smoke away from the fleet and into the faces of the Tunisian gunners. Under cover of this cannonade, Cobham sent his boats, loaded with sailors armed with cutlasses, flintlocks and pistols, to board the galleys one by one. As the English approached, the Tunisian sailors panicked, jumped overboard and swam for the shore; the troops in the outworks also panicked and fled into the castle. The galleys were boarded one after another and burned. By 8.00 a.m., every ship was ablaze, and the shore batteries had been silenced. With the wind onshore, the English could not sail out of the bay but had to warp clear – something that would have been impossible had the enemy continued firing. Blake had lost around 20 men killed and 80 wounded, almost all from the boats' crews. This action is generally held to be the first successful naval attack on a fortified port by coming to anchor close inshore and silencing the batteries by weight of fire.[19]

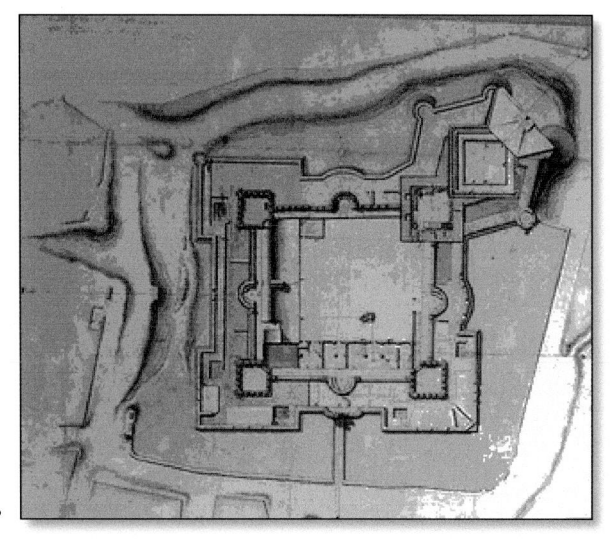

Even after this victory, with no troops to put ashore, Blake was unable to oblige the Dey to give in to his demands; the Dey went so far as to tell Blake that he would have to account to the sultan in Constantinople for the destruction of the galleys. Blake therefore sailed first for Cagliari, and then for Algiers where the Dey, learning of the action at Porto Farino, was willing to negotiate the release of all British slaves in return for a payment of their value as slaves; 40 Dutch slaves were also redeemed by subscription from the sailors of the fleet. Blake was received with marked respect and supplies of food and water, so great was the effect of the action at Porto Farino.[20]

The fortress of Sanlucar at Cadiz. (Author's collection)

From Algiers, Blake sailed for Formentera, the smallest and most southwesterly of the Balearic Islands. Here, in mid May, he appears to have received letters from England with the intimation at least that Cromwell intended war against Spain rather than France. Before this situation developed further, Blake used his good standing with the Spanish to land at Cartagena and recover the guns left by Prince Rupert in 1650,[21] which was done with much courtesy from the Spanish – ironic, as Penn's fleet was by this time active against them in the West Indies. The main objective of English maritime power from then on became the capture of the annual Spanish treasure fleet from South America.[22] The loss of bullion would bankrupt the Spanish treasury and cripple their war effort, while at the same time finance English expeditionary war against them. It was also necessary for Blake to prevent Spanish reinforcements setting sail for the West Indies.

As described in Chapter 2, Cromwell concluded a commercial treaty with France which included the stipulation that Charles II and his followers be expelled from French territory; the declaration of war by Spain followed in March 1656. The fleet had returned to England for the winter and as it prepared to return to the Mediterranean in the spring of 1656, because of Blake's poor health, the Protector's protégé, Edward Montagu, joined the fleet in January 1656.* Montagu was appointed to the joint command with Blake, the foremost naval commander of the day, even though he had never before commanded a fleet: his was clearly a political appointment.[23] Manning the fleet proved difficult in the extreme, and there was discontent about the coming war with Spain; Captains Hill and Lyons were relieved of their

---

* Edward Montagu, later 1st Earl of Sandwich KG (1625–1672).

Cadiz in 1590, by George Hofnagel. (Author's collection)

commands for complaints that, first, the Protectorate did not take sufficient care of the seamen and their families; and secondly that there was no proper reason to make war on the Spanish.[24] A similar fate befell John Lawson, who had been appointed as Blake's deputy. Lawson had been appointed captain of the 40-gun *Centurion* in the Commonwealth navy in 1650 and after supporting Cromwell's campaign in Scotland he had been sent to support Penn in the Mediterranean, seeking Prince Rupert. Rupert had evaded an engagement but Penn and Lawson took 36 French and Portuguese prizes by March 1652. In October 1654, Lawson had endorsed a petition calling for the end of the impressment of seamen, provision for widows and the address of various grievances – it is indeed possible that Lawson was the author of the petition. As a result of all this, Lawson was popular with the officers and ratings of the navy but regarded with suspicion by Cromwell. Cromwell could not easily dismiss Lawson, so he appointed the inexperienced Montagu as general-at-sea over him; Lawson duly resigned and was replaced once more by Badiley, whose health was little better than Blake's. On his return to England, he was suspected of dealings with Levellers and the Fifth Monarchy Men on one hand and the exiled Charles II on the other and was imprisoned by Cromwell in the Tower. He was shortly thereafter released and banished to his home at Scarborough in East Yorkshire.

Blake's fleet returned to Cadiz in April, this time mounting a full blockade. While Blake was absent, a Spanish fleet had arrived in Cadiz, but the port was too well defended to be attacked from the sea. An assault on Gibraltar was contemplated, as a base for operations in the Mediterranean and against the Plate Fleets. Montagu was sent in the *Naseby* to reconnoitre. He thought the best method of attack was to land on the narrow isthmus with a force strong enough to cut communication with the mainland and hold the position until the garrison was starved into surrender. This, he believed, would need 4,000 to 5,000 men, soldiers not seamen. Blake and Cromwell accepted this view but there were, even now, no troops available.[25] A Spanish fleet left Cadiz on 12 August and took station off Cape St Vincent but war having not been declared, no confrontation took place. By the autumn, the English fleet was badly in need of refit; Blake himself was ill and, after sending for permission to return home and this being granted,[26] Blake's fleet anchored in the Downs, off the Kentish coast, on 6 October 1655.

Blake and Montagu then sailed for Tangier to take on water and supplies. From Tangier, Blake himself sailed briefly to Lisbon to attend the ratification of a treaty between Portugal and England: the two countries had been at war between 1652 and 1654 and Blake himself had defeated the Portuguese fleet; but peace had been concluded on 10 July 1654 and the Treaty of Westminster agreed.[27] Even so, King John of Portugal was unwilling to ratify the treaty and a payment of £50,000 had not been made. Cromwell therefore despatched Philip Meadowe as special envoy. Meadowe offered terms that, for Cromwell, were far too generous, promising not to molest the Brazil fleet (on which Portugal's finances depended), but also making concessions on the rights of the papal authorities to convert English deserters. The presence of the fleet was necessary to make the reluctant King change his mind, by intimating that the Brazil fleet would be seized if the treaty was not immediately ratified.[28] This business concluded, Blake returned to the blockade on 28 July. The Spanish made no attempt to break out, which allowed Blake to send ships to raid other Spanish ports, including Vigo on the north coast and Málaga in the south, where nine Spanish ships were sunk.

In July, 10 of Blake's 40 ships were recalled to England and the rest sailed once more for Lisbon first, to replenish supplies, then for the Mediterranean. Blake left a squadron of eight ships under Richard Stayner to maintain the blockade: these were the *Speaker, Tredagh, Plymouth, Bridgewater* and

COLONIAL IRONSIDES

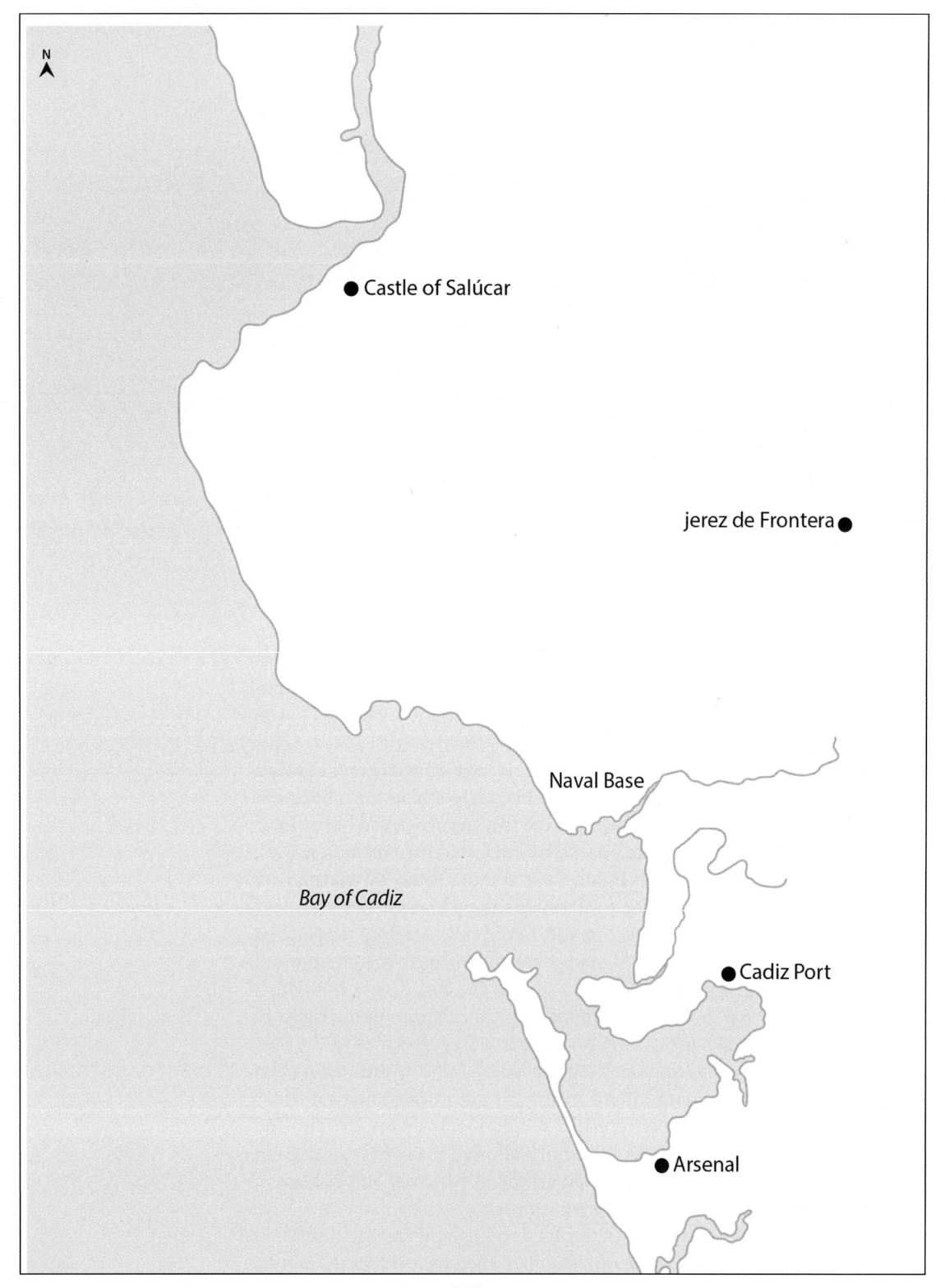

Cadiz.

Diamond, all first or second rates, and three frigates. On the evening of 8 September, the squadron sighted one of the two annual Spanish treasure fleets, under the command of Marcos del Puerto, formed of two galleons – *Victoria*, and *Jesus, Maria y Jose*; three merchantmen *San Francisco Javier*, *Profeta Elias* and *Rosario*; two armed cargo ships – *San Francisco y San Diego* and *Patache*; and a captured Portuguese merchantman. Because of Blake's blockade, the convoy had had to sail from Havana without an escort.

In the darkness of night and gloomy weather, the Spaniards mistook the English squadron for fishing boats and took no evasive action. As dawn broke on the morning of 9 September, three of the English ships engaged the Spanish: Stayner aboard the *Speaker* attacked and captured the *Jesus, Maria y Jose* under the command of Rear-Admiral Juan de Hoyos. Its cargo consisted of 45 tons of silver, 700 chests of indigo, and 700 chests of sugar. Captain Anthony Earning of the *Bridgewater*, meanwhile, engaged the *Victoria* under the command of Vice-Admiral Juan Rodriguez Calderón. After a long battle, the crew set the galleon on fire and abandoned ship. There were many Spanish casualties, including Francisco López de Zúñiga, 2nd Marquis of Baides, the retiring Governor of Chile. The *Plymouth* sank the *San Francisco Javier*, losing 60,000 gold pieces with the ship. Captain John Harman of the *Tredagh* captured the *Profeta Elias* intact with all its cargo. The third merchantman, *Rosario*, was beached, while the Spanish Admiral Marcus de Puerto escaped on the *San Francisco y San Diego* to Cadiz harbour with *Patache* and the Portuguese prize.[29] The English took nearly £1,000,000 worth of cargo, another £250,000 in silver. With the bullion lost in the sea the total loss to the Spanish was perhaps £2,000,000 all told, or £330,000,000 at today's values.[30] It was, however, Montagu not Stayner who had the credit for the victory since it was he who carried the plunder back to England in the *Naseby*. By the time the treasure was delivered to the Tower, half of it had been embezzled.[31]

With the coming of winter, Blake decided to maintain the blockade, supported by victuallers from Lisbon, the first time the fleet had stayed at sea all year. Troops were asked for from home, but Cromwell was by now preparing the expedition against Dunkirk, and there were none to spare. This finally put paid to any idea of attacking Gibraltar.[32] At this point, Cromwell's Mediterranean strategy became no more than an adjunct to the Western Design and the actions in the Spanish Netherlands, although it was maintained by Cromwell and Mazarin with vigour until the Protector's death.

In February 1657, Blake again left a small squadron of two ships to continue the blockade at Cadiz while the main fleet sailed to intercept the 1657 treasure fleet, for Blake had received intelligence that the convoy from Mexico was on its way across the Atlantic. Rather than search for the fleet, Blake kept his fleet concentrated until he could be sure of its location; he also took on much-needed supplies sent from England at the end of March. When news of the whereabouts of the Spanish fleet came in from merchant ships, Blake sailed on 23 April to attack it where it had docked, at Santa Cruz de Tenerife in the Canary Islands, awaiting an escort to Spain – once again, no escort had been available when the fleet had left Havana because of Blake's blockade.[33]

Blake's fleet arrived off Santa Cruz on 29 April. Santa Cruz lies in a shallow bay of deep water on the craggy volcanic coast of Tenerife, at the northern end of the island; the anchorage falls away directly from the heights. Its harbour was defended by the Castle of San Cristobal, which mounted 40 guns, and by a several smaller forts with an interconnecting system of breastworks for troops. Blake planned an attack very similar to that at Porto Farino: 12 frigates under Stayner in the *Speaker* would enter the anchorage and attack the treasure galleons, while Blake in the *George* would lead the main fleet close inshore to suppress the castle and the shore batteries.[34]

The attack began at 9.00 a.m. on 30 April. Stayner's squadron came close alongside the Spanish ships, using them as shelter from the shore batteries. Stayner held his fire until the squadron had dropped anchor and then opened up with broadsides. Blake's heavy warships then commenced the bombardment of the castle and the batteries: Blake had given orders that no prizes were to be taken and that the Spanish fleet was to be utterly destroyed.[35] Most of the Spanish ships were small armed merchantmen and were quickly silenced by Stayner's frigates, but the two galleons fought on for several hours until their crews set them alight and abandoned ship. Blake's squadron destroyed the breastworks and smaller forts where, as at Porto Farino, smoke from the burning ships worked to the advantage of the English by obscuring the Spaniards' view.

Around noon, the flagship of the Spanish admiral, Don Diego de Egües, caught fire and then blew up as her powder magazine ignited. Blake's seamen then took to their boats to board other Spanish ships and set them on fire. By 3.00 p.m., all 16 Spanish ships in the harbour were sunk, on fire or taken. Contrary to orders, the *Swiftsure* and four other frigates each took a prize and attempted to tow them out of the harbour. Blake immediately signalled that they were to be burnt, repeating his order three times before the reluctant captains obeyed.[36]

Having achieved its objective of destroying the Spanish vessels, the English fleet was faced with the hazardous task of withdrawing from Santa Cruz. According to several accounts, the wind shifted suddenly and almost miraculously from the north-east to the south-west, to carry Blake's ships out; the truth, however, is that as at Porto Farino, the fleet warped clear. The *Speaker*, which was the first ship to enter the harbour and last to leave, was badly damaged, but no English ships were lost. No treasure was taken, of course, and as things turned out, the treasure had already been unloaded. With no soldiers, Blake could not seize it; the Spanish of course could not spend it, but they could draw credit based on it. Eventually, Egües transported the treasure to Spain, arriving at Cadiz on 28 March 1658.[37]

Blake, his work now completed, returned home with the fleet. As noted, he had been ill for some months and he died in Plymouth Sound as the fleet came in, at the peak of his career. He was given a full ceremonial funeral in Westminster Abbey. The command of the Commonwealth Navy, and that of the Restoration, was left to Monck, Montagu and Penn.

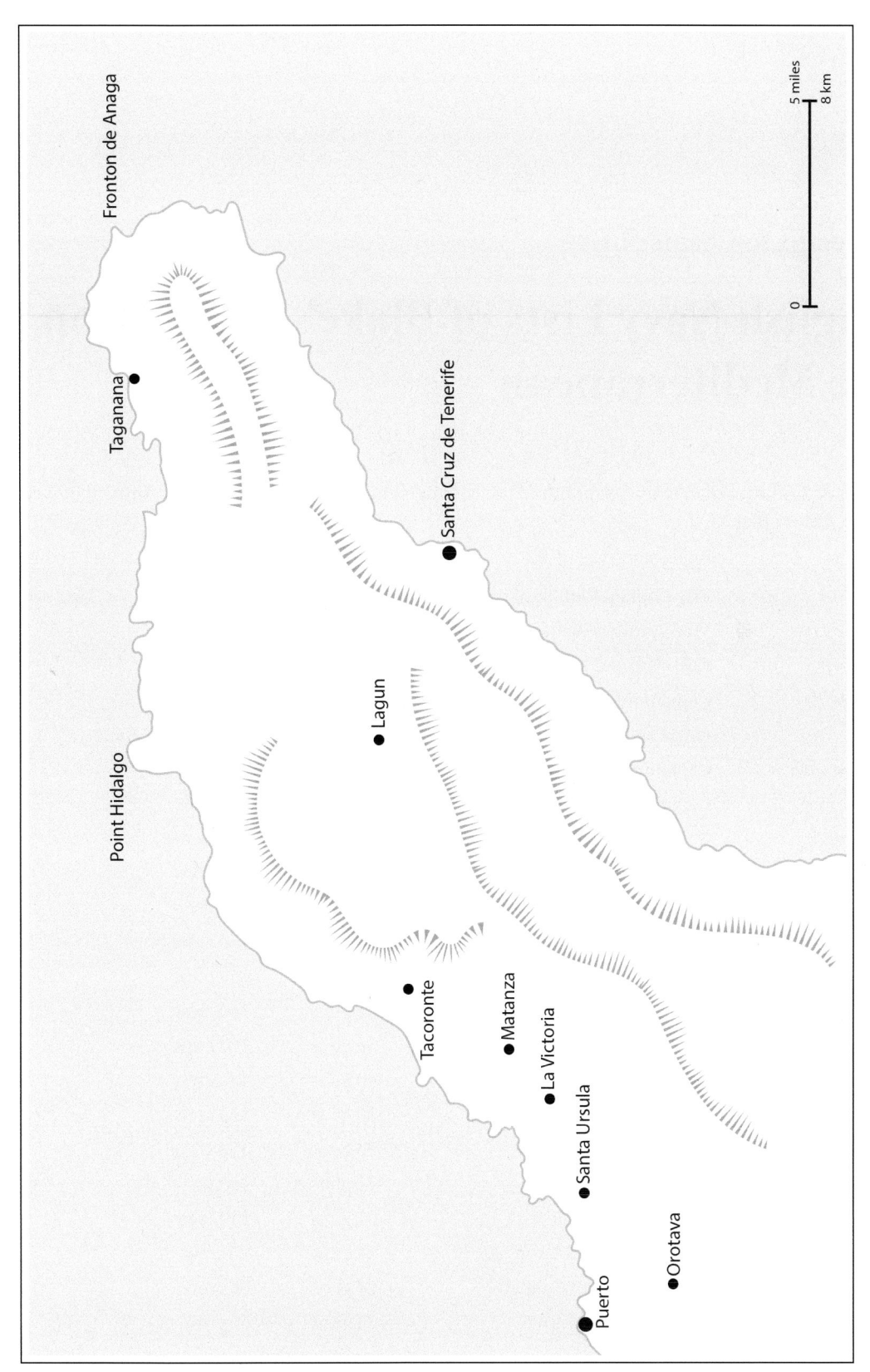

GENERAL-AT-SEA BLAKE'S NAVAL OPERATIONS IN THE MEDITERRANEAN AND AGAINST SPAIN

Appendix to Chapter 10

English Navy Lists of Blake's Expedition to the Mediterranean

A fleet of 24 ships sailed from Plymouth to the Mediterranean in 1645 under the command of General-at-Sea Robert Blake:

George	General Robert Blake	60 guns	350 crew
	Flag Captain John Stokes		
Andrew	Vice-Admiral Richard Badiley	54 guns	300 crew
Unicorn	Rear-Admiral Jos. Jordan	54 guns	300 crew
Langport	Captain Roger Cuttance	50 guns	260 crew
	John Coppin, 1656		
Bridgewater	Captain Anthony Earning	50 guns	200 crew
Worcester	Captain William Hill	46 guns	240 crew
Plymouth	Captain Richard Stayner	50 guns	260 crew
Hampshire	Captain Benjamin Blake	34 guns	160 crew
Foresight	Captain Peter Mootham	36 guns	160 crew
Kent	Captain Edward Witteridge	40 guns	170 crew
Taunton	Captain Thomas Valley	36 guns	160 crew
Diamond	Captain John Harman	36 guns	160 crew
Ruby	Captain Edmund Curtis	36 guns	160 crew
Newcastle	Captain Nathaniel Cobham	40 guns	180 crew
Amity	Captain Henry Pack	30 guns	120 crew
Maidstone	Captain Thomas Adams	32 guns	150 crew
Princess Mary	Captain John Lloyd	34 guns	150 crew
Elias	Captain John Symonds	32 guns	140 crew
Mermaid	Captain James Ableson	24 guns	90 crew
Success	Captain William Kendall	24 guns	60 crew
Sophia	Captain Robert Kirby	24 guns	60 crew

ENGLISH NAVY LISTS OF BLAKE'S EXPEDITION TO THE MEDITERRANEAN

Hector	Captain John Smith(?)	16 guns	35 crew
Dolphin	Captain John Smith	16 guns	45 crew
Nonsuch	Lieutenant Thomas Bowry	8 guns	35 crew

TOTALS 880 guns 3,590 crew

Ships added in 1656/7:

Naseby	Captain Roger Cuttance	80 guns	500 crew
Resolution*	Captain Anthony Young	50 guns	210 crew
Phoenix	Captain Thomas Whetstone	38 guns	180 crew
Sapphire	Captain Robert Clay	38 guns	140 crew
Happy Entrance	Captain John Hayward	32 guns	150 crew
Bristol	Captain Thomas Penrose	50 guns	200 crew
Jersey	Captain John Simons	40 guns	140 crew

Five fire-ships and victuallers

TOTALS 428 guns 1,470 crew

GRAND TOTAL 1,308 guns 5,060 crew

---

* Renamed, was the *Tredagh*.

11

Charles II, the Prince of Condé and the Spanish Army of Flanders

Cromwell's alliance with France in pursuit of his war against Spain, as outlined in Chapter 2, meant that the involvement of Commonwealth troops in a European war was not only inevitable, but also intended. Such an involvement would mean, too, that Commonwealth troops would come into direct contact with troops loyal to the exiled Charles II. Fleeing the Parliamentarian advance during the Civil War in the west of England in 1646, Charles had first taken refuge in the Scilly Isles and then in Jersey, where he remained until June with a group of about 300 supporters including Edward Hyde. Following Charles I's surrender to the Scottish Covenanters, the Prince had joined his mother at the French court. In April 1648 they were joined by his brother James, Duke of York. Amid abortive plans for a Royalist invasion of England, Charles then went to his sister Mary, Princess of Orange, in the Hague. Here, on 4 February 1649, he received the news that Parliament had executed his father. Although the English Parliament abolished the office of King, and subsequently made it illegal for anyone to claim the title, Charles II was proclaimed King by the Scottish Parliament on 5 February; he was soon afterwards also proclaimed King in Ireland.

Charles then began a phase of wanderings, moving to Antwerp, Brussels and Saint-Germain-en-Laye near Paris. After another residence in Jersey, which prompted the Commonwealth to invade and subjugate the Channel Islands (see Chapter 3), he returned to Breda in the Netherlands for negotiations with the Scots emissaries with whom he had determined to come to terms as the price of returning to the British Isles. In June 1650 he arrived in Scotland; in January 1651 Charles was crowned King of Scots at Scone which was followed by Cromwell's invasion and the defeat at Dunbar. In the summer of 1651, Charles led the Scots Army into England – only to meet with defeat at Worcester on 3 September (see Chapter 2).

After Worcester, Charles was on the run for 43 days, hunted all the while by Parliamentarian troops, until he was able to cross the English Channel from Shoreham to Fécamp in Normandy. He returned to Paris

CHARLES II, THE PRINCE OF CONDÉ AND THE SPANISH ARMY OF FLANDERS

but as Mazarin embarked on negotiations with Cromwell he embarked on a series of visits to Cologne and Spa as the guest of princes of the Holy Roman Empire. Mazarin's negotiations with Cromwell had certainly made his position in France highly uncertain. On 30 June 1654 Charles finally left Paris to visit his sister Mary at Spa,[1] having decided to move the seat of his exile away from France.[2] When smallpox broke out at Spa he moved to Aachen where he was joined by his father's old Secretary, Sir Edward Nicholas.[3] Nicholas had been deprived of office by the enmity of Queen Henrietta Maria but was now reinstated.[*]

Throughout the second half of 1654, Charles was in constant communication with his supporters in England – he had by this time given up on any idea of support from any of the German princes. However, the likelihood of any sort of restoration coming from internal opposition to Cromwell evaporated when a planned rising by the Sealed Knot failed in early 1655, followed by the suppression of Penruddock's rising in the west in March.[4]

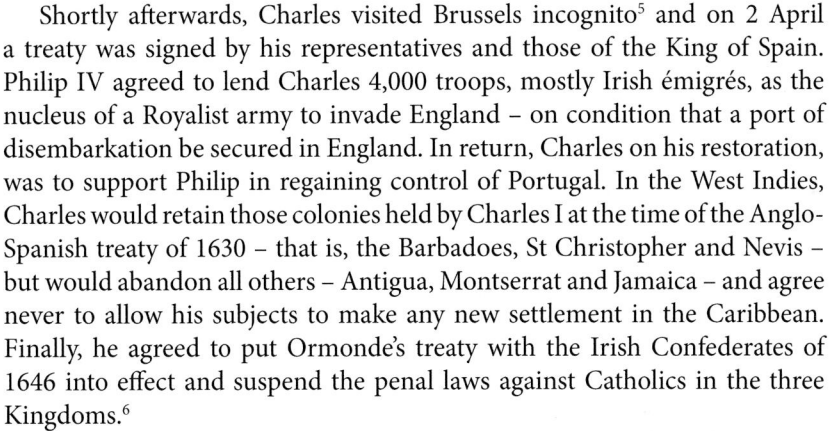

Charles II, King of England. (Soham Roots)

Shortly afterwards, Charles visited Brussels incognito[5] and on 2 April a treaty was signed by his representatives and those of the King of Spain. Philip IV agreed to lend Charles 4,000 troops, mostly Irish émigrés, as the nucleus of a Royalist army to invade England – on condition that a port of disembarkation be secured in England. In return, Charles on his restoration, was to support Philip in regaining control of Portugal. In the West Indies, Charles would retain those colonies held by Charles I at the time of the Anglo-Spanish treaty of 1630 – that is, the Barbadoes, St Christopher and Nevis – but would abandon all others – Antigua, Montserrat and Jamaica – and agree never to allow his subjects to make any new settlement in the Caribbean. Finally, he agreed to put Ormonde's treaty with the Irish Confederates of 1646 into effect and suspend the penal laws against Catholics in the three Kingdoms.[6]

The Spanish did not set much store by this treaty, for without the support of General-at-Sea Robert Lawson to neutralise the Commonwealth navy, there was no chance of crossing the Channel – and Lawson was out of favour and confined to his home. A request from Charles to King Philip to take up residence in Spanish Flanders was reluctantly agreed and Charles was

---

[*] Sir Edward Nicholas (1593–1669) had served as Secretary of State to Charles I. He also sat in the House of Commons at various times between 1621 and 1629. He supported the King throughout the English Civil War and accompanied the court into exile, however from 1649 to 1654 he lived in poverty until Charles II restored him to the position of Secretary of State, which he maintained after the Restoration.

allowed to go to Bruges and granted a pension.[7] Given that Cromwell's treaty with the French excluded him and 17 named supporters from France, his agreement with the Spanish was timely. Only his mother, Henrietta Maria, being by birth a French princess, was allowed to remain in France.

In Flanders, Charles assembled a small army of exiles, around 2,500 strong, formed around some of his principal supporters. These included, first, his brother James, who had joined Louis XIV's army against the *Fronde* and against the Spanish under the command of Marshal Turenne; He served in five campaigns with the French in the Low Countries and had been offered the command of all French troops in Italy.[8] Secondly, Edward Hyde, later Earl of Clarendon. Hyde had served as political adviser to Charles I until 1646 when the enmity of Queen Henrietta Maria caused him to accompany the Prince of Wales to Jersey. He remained with the Prince in exile and was appointed Lord Chancellor in 1658.[*]

Philip IV, King of Spain by Diego Velàzquez

Next came the erratic George Digby, 2nd Earl of Bristol. Digby had sat in the House of Commons from 1640 until 1641 when he was raised to the House of Lords. He supported the Royalist cause in the English Civil War but his personal ambition and instability caused a series of disputes and problems to himself and to both Charles I and Charles II. After the execution of King Charles I he went into exile. He was made a Lieutenant-General in the French army in 1651 and given command of their forces in Flanders. During Cardinal Mazarin's enforced absence from the French court, Digby tried to take his place. However, when the Cardinal was restored to power he sent Digby to Italy, having well understood his character. When Digby returned to France he was immediately informed that he was included in the list of those expelled from France as adherents of Charles II, in accordance with the treaty with Cromwell. In August 1656 he joined Charles II at Bruges, where he offered his services to Don John of Austria the Younger. He had a hand in the surrender of St Ghislain to the Spaniards in 1657. On 1 January 1657 he was appointed by Charles II as Secretary of State, but shortly afterwards, he was compelled to resign office as he had become a Roman Catholic. He was succeeded by Edward Hyde.

Another close adherent was Henry Wilmot, an officer with five years' experience in the Dutch army and who had been wounded at the siege of Breda. He served under Charles I during the Bishops' Wars, leading a cavalry

---

[*] Hyde held the post of Lord Chancellor, along with that of Chief Minister, until his fall from grace in 1667. He wrote the highly influential *History of the Rebellion* which was published in 1702. He was the maternal grandfather of two Queens, through the marriage of his daughter Anne to James, Duke of York (later James II): Queen Mary II and Queen Anne.

charge at the Battle of Newburn during which he was captured by the Scots. He represented Tamworth in the Long Parliament but was expelled after his involvement in the Army Plot of 1641. He then served Charles I throughout the First Civil War. In April 1643 he was appointed Lieutenant-General of the horse, under the command of Prince Rupert, and was created Baron Wilmot of Adderbury. Later that year he commanded a large cavalry contingent that was sent to help the western Royalist army, and on 13 July he defeated Sir William Waller at the Battle of Roundway Down, opening the way for the Royalists to solidify their position in the west. In 1644 Wilmot assumed command of the Royalist cavalry. On 29 June at the Battle of Cropredy Bridge he participated in defeating Waller for the second time, but not before he had had to lead a charge, in which he was wounded.

When his father died (in March 1644) Wilmot inherited the title of Viscount Wilmot of Athlone. Wilmot was always popular with the soldiers he commanded, being brave, friendly and a great drinker – but not with the King, for he had voted in favour of the execution of Strafford. Perhaps unwisely, he asked the King to remove Digby and the Chancellor of the Exchequer, Sir John Culpepper, which the King refused to do. Wilmot then made an unauthorised contact with the Earl of Essex, the Parliamentarian commander-in-chief, to attempt a settlement of the war, a move that the King viewed as treason. Wilmot was arrested on 8 August 1644, stripped of all his offices and gaoled in Exeter. His popularity with the army led to a petition on his behalf and eventually all charges against him were dropped on the understanding that he would retire overseas. Wilmot went to France, to join the exiled court of Queen Henrietta Maria, who had long supported him. Three years later, when Digby arrived in Paris, the two men fought a duel, which Wilmot lost.

After the execution of Charles I, Wilmot became a gentleman of the bedchamber of King Charles II, by whom he was trusted. He shared Charles's defeat at the Battle of Worcester and his exile. In 1652 he was created Earl of Rochester. On Charles's behalf he visited the Emperor Ferdinand III, Nicholas II the Duke of Lorraine and Frederick William the Elector of Brandenburg, to lobby for support. In March 1655, he led an unsuccessful attempt at a rising near York as part of the Penruddock rebellion. The uprising was put down by Colonel Robert Lilburne, Governor of York, and Wilmot fled the country once more.

In April 1656 along with the Duke of Ormonde he signed the Treaty of Brussels with the Spanish. As a consequence, in 1656, Wilmot was given command of an English foot regiment in the Royalist army in Bruges, which became the King's Guards. The unhealthy and overcrowded conditions of

Edward Hyde, Earl of Clarendon, engraved by Michael Loggan after Sir Peter Lely's portrait. (Author's collection)

the regiment's quarters in the winter of 1657–1658 caused many to fall sick, including Wilmot, who died at Sluys on 19 February.

His place as Colonel of the Guards was taken by Colonel Thomas Blagge, or Blague, who had commanded regiments of horse and foot during the Civil Wars, but later by Lord Thomas Wentworth, 5th Baron Wentworth. Like Wilmot, Wentworth had served in the Bishops' Wars and during the First English Civil War, he was the sergeant-major-general of horse in the west under Hopton and commanded the Prince of Wales's Regiment of Horse. Having seen a good deal of action, he went into exile with the Prince of Wales in the spring of 1646. He accompanied Charles II to Scotland in 1650 and after Worcester he again escaped and joined Charles in France.

These men formed the nucleus of Charles' army in exile. Subsequent to King Philip's offer to lend him 4,000 troops, Charles summoned all English, Scots and Irish officers and men serving in the French Army to join him. There were considerable numbers of Irishmen serving in the armies of both France and Spain. In the case of Spain, the Irish regiments dated from the beginning of the Eighty Years' War and provided a source of livelihood for Catholic Irishmen whose religion closed off this opportunity in the British Isles – even if they could have swallowed the idea of service to a Protestant English monarchy which since the reign of Elizabeth I had been seen as hostile. Irish recruitment to foreign service had accelerated after the defeat of the Irish Confederation in 1652, especially when Cromwell agreed that the Irish officers and men would be free to take service with a foreign power, so long as that power was not hostile to the Commonwealth. In 1652, neither France nor Spain was openly opposed to England. More than 30,000 fighting men left Ireland and by the mid 1650s, there were 17 Irish regiments in the Spanish service and eight in the French.[9]

The Duke of York was given the task of arranging the defection of the Irish from French service – a difficult mission for one who had only recently accepted the command of French troops in Italy and who had campaigned with the French for years. In his memoirs he recalled that:

> All the Irish colonels who had served in the French armies under Monsieur de Turenne and Monsieur de la Ferté, hearing of it [i.e. the summons] wrote to the Duke of York to assure him that they were ready to perform, as good subjects and men of honour, whatever he should appoint them. He thanked them and recommended … that they should keep their regiments together, as much for the service of his Majesty when there should be need of them, as for their own advantage.[10]

This summons brought in around 2,000 men, along with Charles's few household troops – not perhaps as wholehearted a response as the colonels had suggested to the Duke of York. Indeed, some regiments which had been well provided for by the French simply stayed put.[11] Hyde made such provision for the arrival of the Irish troops as he could in the town of Bruges, but there were delays in extricating the Irish from their duty to the King of France. The French, on their part, were offended by these moves, although having expelled the King from their territory in consequence of the treaty with Cromwell they can scarcely have been surprised. On 28 August, Digby told Hyde that the Marquis of Caracena, commanding the army in the Spanish Netherlands, had agreed to provide quarters and rations around Arras.[12]

The army was to be organised into six regiments of foot and two troops of horse acting as lifeguards for the King and the Duke of York. According to one captain:

> The King, by permission of Don Juan of Austria, raised three regiments, one of English under the Earl of Rochester ... the second of Scots under General Middletone; the third of Irish under Ormond. Two more were added after ... All the captaines were to be lords, knights, or colonels; at least 16 captains were ordered to be of the Scots, whereof I was one.[13]

The first of these regiments was an English regiment formed from exiles and known as the King's Own Regiment, commanded, as already described, by Henry Wilmot and then Thomas Blagge. The nominal command of this regiment appears at some point to have passed to Lord Wentworth, with William Throckmorton as Lieutenant-Colonel,[14] however the date and circumstances are unclear.

The second regiment was that of the Duke of York, which was raised in August 1656 from Irishmen in the French service in the regiments of Donagh MacCarty, 2nd Viscount Muskerry, and Sir James Darcy.[15] The Duke was nominally in command of the regiment but executive command was exercised by Muskerry. It was the largest of Charles's regiments, with about 800 men in 1656. Muskerry had commanded an Irish regiment in the French service, which, with another commanded by Sir James Darcy, formed part of the garrison of Condé. In August 1656, when Condé was taken by the Spaniards, Ormonde was sent by Charles II to persuade these Irish regiments to desert the French service. Muskerry was Ormonde's nephew, but he refused to listen to Ormonde's appeal and, while promising to join Charles II, protested that his honour as a soldier required him first to lay down his commission and to obtain permission to change his allegiance. Cardinal Mazarin refused to let the regiment go but gave him a pass for himself; Muskerry joined King Charles in the Low Countries, leaving directions to his regiment to follow him. 'He no sooner gave notice to them whither they should come,' wrote Hyde:

> but they so behaved themselves, that by sixes and sevens his whole regiment, to the number of very near 800, came to the place assigned to them, and brought their arms with them; which the Spaniard was amazed at, and – ever after very much valued him, and took as much care for the preservation of that regiment as of any that was in their service.[16]

Another Irish regiment, raised in 1657, was that of Henry, Duke of Gloucester, Charles's younger brother. Again, the executive command was held by a professional soldier, Theobald Taaffe, 2nd Viscount Taaffe, with one of the many Fitzpatricks as major.[17] There is some confusion between this regiment and that of Colonel John Fitzgerald, which joined the King after the Restoration, having remained in the Spanish service.[18]

Next came an Irish regiment, that of Colonel Lewis Farrell. Its date of formation is uncertain, but in 1653, the regiment had been sent for service against the French and had changed sides. In the winter of 1657 the regiment was in garrison, under Marshal Schomberg, in the fortress of St Ghislain, about 30 miles from Brussels. It was described as being: 'made up fore the most part of O'Farrells and their clients and followers.'[19] The fortress was invested by the Spanish in March 1657 and the Earl of Bristol, who had just deserted the French service for the Spanish, summoned other Irish troops from Taaffe's regiment in the embryonic royal army to join the besieging force, armed, paid and quartered them; Lord Newburgh's men also joined them. In April, it was reported that Bristol had: 'mounted the [siege] works and called to the Irishmen in the town "What? Are you mad, to fight against your own king?" Whereupon they threw down their arms and surrender followed.'[20] The regiment joined the King immediately afterwards and consisted of 16 companies.[21] The nominal command was given to the Earl of Bristol, with Lewis Farrell retained as Lieutenant-Colonel and Connor Farrell as major.[22] Previous research has identified Farrell's Regiment as that of William Stanley, formed in 1585, however, Stanley's Regiment was broken up in 1595 after a mutiny, and reformed in three Irish companies. These companies disappeared by 1605, and probably merged into O'Neill's Regiment (the Earl of Tyrone). This regiment dates from 1605 and had moved to Spain in 1638.

The final Irish regiment was that of Colonel Richard Grace, composed of men who had left the French service and joined the King. It was reported as being 700 strong and under the nominal command of the Marquis of Ormonde; Grace, the Lieutenant-Colonel, exercised executive command.[23] Grace had been in the Spanish service before and had transferred himself and his whole regiment to the French service when he heard that the King and the Duke of York were in France. He had accordingly gone over, but had refused to surrender his post, which he left in Spanish hands. He now changed sides a second time and seems to have brought the greater part of his regiment with him to Flanders, though at first the Spaniards – unsurprisingly – made some difficulty about receiving him again, much to the annoyance of Hyde.[24]

These four regiments were the limit of what the Spanish would support under the terms of the treaty with Charles. The Earl of Bristol reported as much in a letter to Hyde in November 1656:

> The Marquis de Caracena told me the last night, that as soon as ever the general business of the quarters with the country was settled, the four regiments promised his Majesty should also be settled, and that his Majesty might give the command of them to whom he pleased, but that he must tell me freely, that they could not give winter quarters to any more new regiments at a time when they were obliged to cashier above forty of their old ones; and that whatever men should come over to the King, as well Muskerry's as others, must be aggregated to one of those four regiments, which were ground-work enough for a body of four thousand men, which was more than they could hope to see drawn together by his Majesty this winter.[25]

CHARLES II, THE PRINCE OF CONDÉ AND THE SPANISH ARMY OF FLANDERS

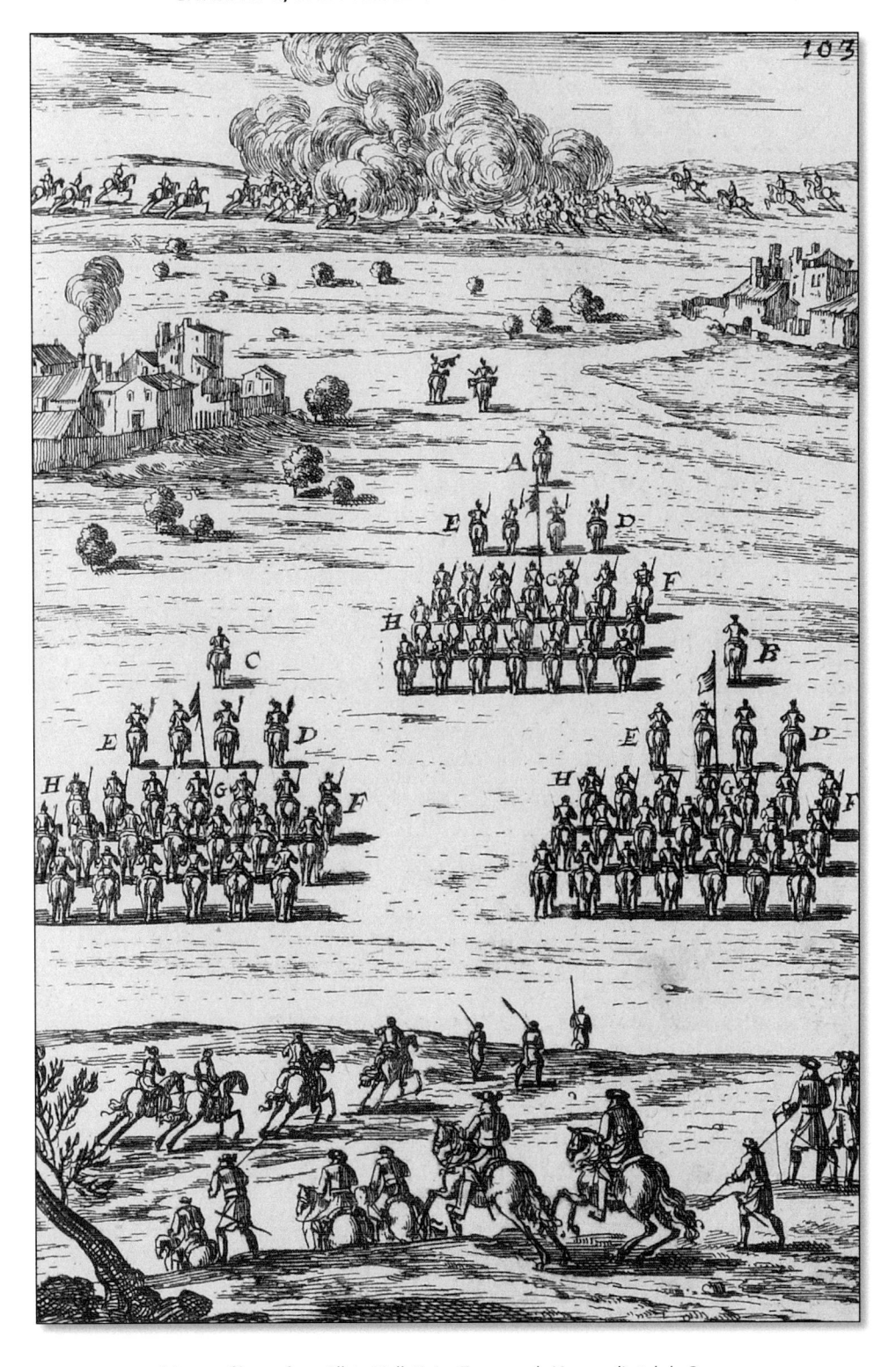

A troop of horse from Allain Mallet's *Les Traveaux de Mars, ou l'art de la Guerre*.
(<https:// digi.ub.uni-heidelberg.de> accessed 2 January 2020).

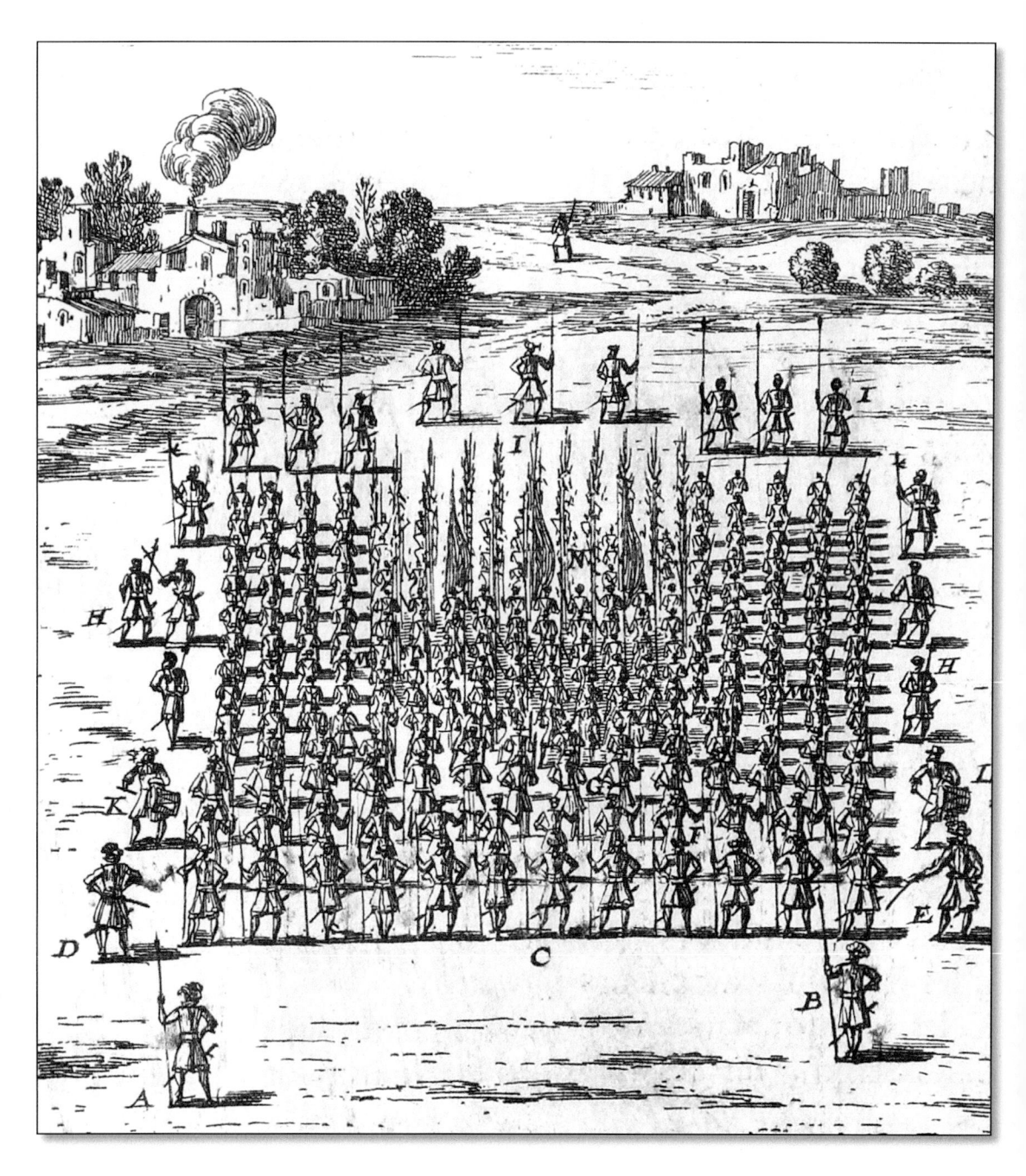

COLONIAL IRONSIDES

A company of foot from Allain Mallet, *Les Traveaux de Mars, ou l'art de la Guerre.*
(<https://digi.ub.uni-heidelberg.de> accessed 2 January 2020

The sixth regiment of foot was that of the Earl of Newburgh, raised in 1656, which was composed entirely of Scots. The Earl of Middleton was the original colonel, but he was succeeded by Newburgh in September 1656. The regiment was reported to consist of 10 companies.[26] A list of its officers, dated 4 June 1657, is given in Macray's *Ruthven Correspondence*.[27]

All these regiments of infantry were placed under the command of the Duke of York, who had managed to depart the French service, and for whom as general a troop of horse of 50 men, as a lifeguard, was raised. 'The Duke of York', wrote an English spy in June 1657, 'hath a company of fifty horse raised by the Spaniard in very good equipage for his guard; they allow him two hundred pounds per mensem during the campaign for his table.'[28] This troop of horse was commanded by Sir Charles Berkeley, who after the Restoration became Earl of Falmouth.[29]

The formation of the royal army was well known back in England, and little regarded. One spy reported that: 'The King of Scotts is at a stand, for all he hath lifted a few men; hee keeps them as yett together: they are about five hundred, of Irish the most of them are, some Scots, and some English, who rely upon him, and cannot live otherwise.'[30] Another wrote that: 'Take it upon my word, there is not in all 700, for they mutiny every day: their pay is so small, they cannot live upon it. The soldier hath but four stivers a day, and a gentleman six.'[31] Yet another said that the five regiments then raising in January 1657: 'are to consist of 20 companies each, and each company of 60 men; each soldier has seven stivers a day, and each officer 14." Another spy, writing in May, says they then numbered 4,000.[32]

What these hostile reports actually suggest is that men came in quite quickly, in spite of disorder among the Spanish following the loss of Aix-la-Chapelle. At the beginning of October 1656, the King had about 400 men, by the end of the month 800 and by April 1657 about 2,000. On 5 October, Digby reported that there were quarters for 600 in Bruges but that there was a scarcity of bread.[33] There were ambitious plans to bring Irish troops from Catalonia and Italy, and raise new regiments of horse and foot, but these came to nothing.[34] The greatest strength was probably no more than 3,000 even though rumour sometimes gave the King 5,000 or 6,000 men. Each of the six regiments ought to have numbered 1,000 or 1,200 men in 10 companies, so it is apparent that their ranks were never more than half full. One reason for this was money. The King, of course, had none and relied on the Spanish. But the Spanish exchequer was struggling. In 1656, the Spanish Netherlands was sent 900,000 *escudoes* to make good the gap between taxation and expenditure. This shrank to 500,000 in 1657 and no more than 300,000 in 1658.[35]

The English public was kept informed of the facts through the pages of *Mercurius Politicus* which on 23 April 1657 published a detailed account

---

* The stiver was worth 1/20th of a Dutch Guilder, so a soldier had less than half a guilder and an officer less than one guilder, about the same rate of pay as a labourer. These rates of pay would just about keep a man alive on bread and beer. In modern terms, a guilder in 1650 has the purchasing power today of approximately £78.00. <http://vanosnabrugge.org/docs/dutchmoney.htm> accessed 7 August 2020.

of the King's forces, naming many names.[36] Other issues gave a highly unfavourable account of the troops:

> Those English that are among them follow their old wont of vaporing and carousing, bragging to be their own carvers of other men's estates and fortunes, if ever they get but foot in England. And their old trade of lying they still follow, coyning many stories of tumults and broils at London. At present there is a feud betwixt them and the Irish, because these are best treated here, and with most respect, as being the white boys, and likest to be most true to the Spaniard, and the most keen instruments against the Puritan Roundhead rebels, which is the name they give to the Protestant party in England, Scotland, and Ireland.[37]
>
> … Of all the armies in Europe there is none wherein so much debauchery is to be seen as in these few forces which the said King hath gotten together, being so exceeding profane from the highest to the lowest. The Irish are trump among them, and bear away the bell for number and preferment, being such as are most gratefull to the Spaniard, and surest to the Stuarts' interest, because they are men implacable and irreconcilable to England.[38]

As this army was supposed to form the basis of an invading force against England, a bad press was very necessary for the Cromwellian regime. The Duke of York, however, claimed that they were 'as handsome fellows as ever I saw.'[39] James believed that more men could have been raised if the Spanish had kept their promise of paying a cash bounty – but they reneged on account of jealousy among their own men as well as the difficulties in finding money.*

The King's Army, denied the possibility of invading England, joined the Spanish Army in Flanders under the command of the viceroy and commander-in-chief, Leopold, Archduke of Austria, son of Ferdinand II. In 1656, however, Leopold was recalled to Madrid and his place was taken by Don John of Austria the Younger. Don John was born in 1629, the illegitimate son of Philip IV of Spain and Maria Calderón (rudely nicknamed La Calderona, or the boiler), a popular actress, who was forced into a convent shortly after his birth. He was brought up in secret in Leon but in 1642, the King recognised him officially as his son; thus began his career in his father's service.

In 1647 Don John was sent to Naples to support the viceroy against an insurrection, sealing off the city until the insurgents' exhaustion and the misjudgements their leader, Henry, Duke of Guise, gave him the opportunity to move in and crush the remains of the revolt. He was next sent as viceroy to Sicily, but was recalled in 1651 to complete the pacification of Catalonia, which had been in revolt since 1640. By the time Don John assumed command, most of Catalonia had been recovered and he had little to do aside from conducting the siege of Barcelona and the convention which ended the revolt in October 1652.

This far, he had played the part of a moderate which, with combined with his pleasant manners, charming personality and good looks, made him

---

* The bounty was said to be one pistole, a gold coin worth ten French *livres*, the equivalent of 10 days' pay for a labourer. A *livre* was composed of 20 *sols*, four *sols* would buy enough bread to feed a man for a day.

widely popular. In 1656, he was sent to become viceroy in Flanders. At the storming of the French camp during Battle of Valenciennes in 1656, he showed great personal courage at the head of a cavalry charge that caught the French totally by surprise and delivered victory to the Spanish.

He was not, however, the faultless paragon that most descriptions portrayed. The Duke of York pointed out his obsession with formality – probably to overcome the stigma of bastardy; his laziness, his inability to deal with detail or bother himself with the management of the army, and his inflexibility:

> Don Juan observed on campaign the same forms of gravity and reserve as if he had been in Brussels. He was everywhere difficult of access … he was imbued with qualities that could have made him a great man. But [his] scrupulous formalities ruined everything. When the army was on the march, [he] never rode at the head of it, except in the presence of the enemy. When half the troops were still out of camp, [he] would get on horseback and ride at the head of the three companies of guards straight to the quarters which had been marked out … without … taking pains to reconnoitre the ground or to know where the generals had their quarters… Don Juan was most accustomed, on arriving at his quarters, to go to bed. He supped there and did not rise until morning. When the army was not marching he seldom went out or got on horseback.[40]

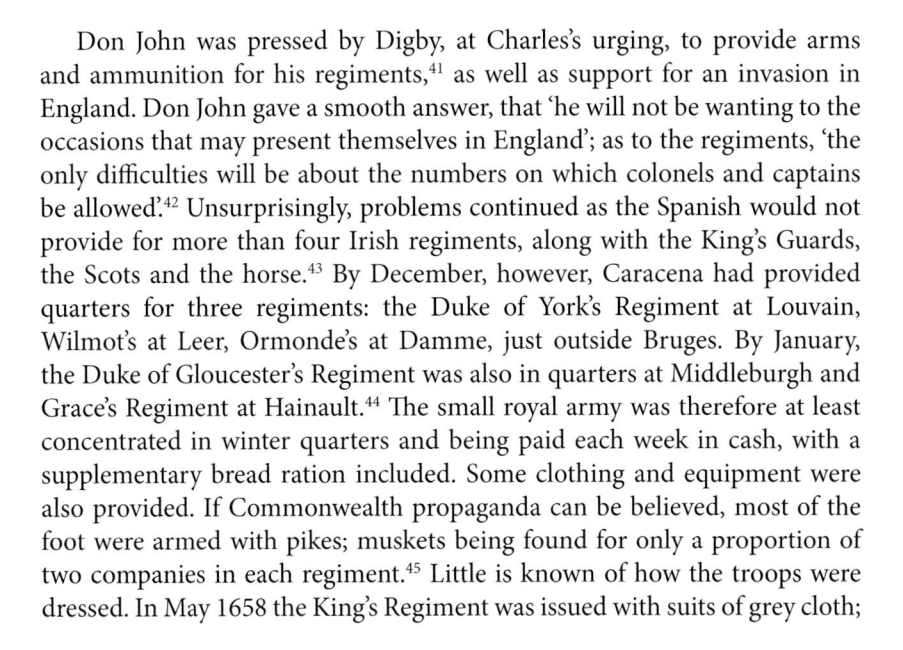

Don John of Austria the Younger, by an unknown artist.

Don John was pressed by Digby, at Charles's urging, to provide arms and ammunition for his regiments,[41] as well as support for an invasion in England. Don John gave a smooth answer, that 'he will not be wanting to the occasions that may present themselves in England'; as to the regiments, 'the only difficulties will be about the numbers on which colonels and captains be allowed'.[42] Unsurprisingly, problems continued as the Spanish would not provide for more than four Irish regiments, along with the King's Guards, the Scots and the horse.[43] By December, however, Caracena had provided quarters for three regiments: the Duke of York's Regiment at Louvain, Wilmot's at Leer, Ormonde's at Damme, just outside Bruges. By January, the Duke of Gloucester's Regiment was also in quarters at Middleburgh and Grace's Regiment at Hainault.[44] The small royal army was therefore at least concentrated in winter quarters and being paid each week in cash, with a supplementary bread ration included. Some clothing and equipment were also provided. If Commonwealth propaganda can be believed, most of the foot were armed with pikes; muskets being found for only a proportion of two companies in each regiment.[45] Little is known of how the troops were dressed. In May 1658 the King's Regiment was issued with suits of grey cloth;

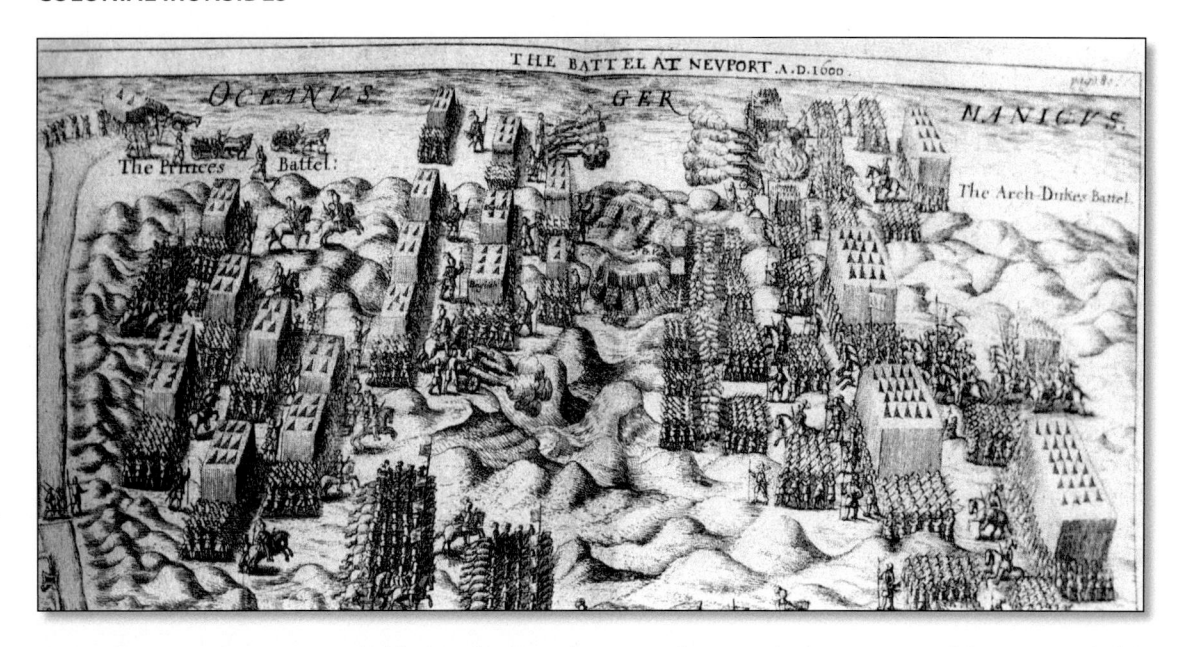

Spanish tercios and Dutch troops meet at the Battle of Nieupoort in 1600 (Francis Vere, Commentaries of the Divers Pieces of Services. Cambridge, 1657)

probably supplemented in accordance with the practice of the time with felt hats, woollen breeches and linen shirts – there was little or no uniformity of dress in the Spanish army at the time, unlike the Commonwealth troops in their red coats and grey breeches.[46] There are no records of armour being issued for the pikemen. The officers and men of the horse, being gentlemen, no doubt made their own arrangements.

But Charles's troops were but a small part of the Spanish army, so what of the rest? In 1647, the Spanish Army of Flanders numbered around 65,200 men, of whom about 11,700 were horse and the bulk of the remainder foot – with some engineers and artillery. The figures do not include the commissariat which was essentially a civilian organisation. It was a highly heterogeneous force: Geoffrey Parker, citing contemporary Spanish authorities, gives a breakdown of, in round terms, 9,700 Spaniards, 14,300 Germans, 24,100 Walloons from the Low Countries, 2,400 Italians, 2,500 from the British Isles and about 700 Burgundians.[47] An official tail of camp followers, who were given rations and lodging, numbered, in 1620, about 540. The real total would have been far larger.

The Spanish infantry was formed into four *tercios*: those of Don Gaspar de Boniface, Francesco de Meneses, Don Diego de Goni and the Marquis of Seralvo.[48] In 1647 there had also been four Italian *tercios* in Flanders – those of Naples, Lombardy, Sicily and Flanders. By 1656, those of Lombardy and Naples were engaged against the Portuguese and that of Sicily was in Lorraine.[49] This left 2,400 Italian troops in the army in the *tercio* of Flanders. There were five regiments of Germans in the army, one dispersed in garrisons, whose identities are uncertain. There were also three Walloon *tercios*: those of Flándes and Brabante and one other which cannot be identified. The 700 Burgundians formed a single small regiment. Finally the infantry included two Irish regiments: those of John Morphy, raised in 1646, with 12 companies; and George Cusack, raised in 1656.[50] The 30 companies of horse, eight or 10 to each regiment, were drawn from the Regiment, or *Tercio*, of Alcantara raised by Jean de Nestien; the Walloon Lancers; the Regiment of Farnesio, or Bateville, raised in 1649 by the Prince of Hesse-Homburg; and the *Tercio de Borbón*, raised in 1640.[51]

The command of the army under Don John was held by Luis Francisco de Benavides Carrillo de Toledo, Marquis of Caracena, born in 1608, he had served in the Spanish armies since 1629 and had been Governor of Milan since 1648. He had been sent to Flanders on the departure of Leopold to second Don John. He was, according to the Duke of York, 'a very good officer, had served for a long time, had passed through all the degrees and owed his fortune to his merit …'[52] He was, however, under the authority of Don John and seems readily to have fallen in with his ways. The captain general of the horse, the third-highest ranking officer after Don John and Caracena, was 40-year-old Claude Lamoral, Prince of Ligne, Prince of Epinoy, Marquis of Roubaix and Count of Fauquemberg, who had held the position since 1649 and was therefore an experienced soldier and diplomat.

Luis de Benavides Carrillo de Toledo, 3rd Marquis de Caracena, by Philipp Fruytiers.

Throughout the Eighty Years' War with the Dutch and after, the Spanish infantry, the backbone of her army, was organised in *tercios* of about 12 companies, commanded by a *maestro de campo*, a rank somewhere between colonel and Major-General. After 1636, a company consisted of 200 men with 11 officers and staff, 30 musketeers, 60 arquebusiers – mounted infantry or dragoons armed with a lighter weapon than the musketeers – 65 armoured pikemen and 34 unarmoured pikemen. The 11 officers and staff were a captain and his page, a lieutenant, an ensign, a sergeant, two drummers, one piper, a chaplain, a quartermaster and a barber-surgeon.[53] In the 1580s and after, Spanish troops, especially the infantry, were always regarded as the elite fighting troops of Europe, with special pay and privileges and rich rewards. Even allowing for Spanish self-congratulation, it must be acknowledged that the Spaniards of the Army of Flanders were experienced veterans, well trained and equipped. They were followed in excellence by the North Italians, English and Germans. The English and Italian troops were also organised into *tercios* on the Spanish model, while the German and Burgundian infantry were organised into regiments of 10 companies, each of 300 men. The Walloons were also formed into *Tercios* by this date, in 10 companies of around 200 officers and men. The cavalry, both light and heavy, was organised by companies and regiments but on the battlefield would be formed into squadrons.[54]

There was one additional element in the Spanish army: another foreign contingent like the English, owing loyalty to their own prince. This was the small army of Louis II of Bourbon, Prince of Condé. As Duc d'Enghien, Louis had led the French army to its great triumph at Rocroi and is generally regarded as one of the foremost generals of the early modern period. When the *Fronde* rebellion broke out, Condé was summoned by Anne of Austria. He quickly subdued the *Parlement* of Paris, and the Parliamentarian *Fronde* ended with the March 1649 Peace of Rueil. The resulting unstable balance of power between the crown and the nobility inspired Condé himself to rebel, starting the far more serious *Fronde des nobles*. In January 1650 he was arrested and imprisoned at Vincennes. Marshal Turenne and his brother the Duke of Bouillon were among those who had escaped arrest; they successfully demanded Louis' freedom, leading to a short-lived alliance between the *Fronde des nobles* and the *Fronde des parlements*. However, a shift of alliances put the Crown and *Parlement* against Condé's party of the nobility. The royal forces under Turenne defeated Condé at the Battle of the Faubourg St Antoine in July 1652, ending the *Fronde* as a serious military threat. Louis escaped with the assistance of the Duchess of Montpensier and in September 1652, he and a few loyalists defected to Spain.

Louis began recruiting troops as soon as he arrived, engaging German and Irish mercenaries under the terms of a treaty between himself and the King of Spain. There was, however, friction between Louis and the then Spanish Governor, Leopold, caused by Louis' insistence on his own autonomy and the command of his own troops.[55] By the time that Charles II's contingent had joined the Spanish army and war with England had broken out, Condé's contingent consisted of a regiment of horse and four regiments of foot: his own regiment, mostly French émigrés, formed on the basis of his original regiment of 1644; Guitard, or Guitault's, regiment of Germans; the regiment of Louis de Vaudetar, Marquis de Persan;* and a regiment variously identified as that of Collom, or Clomme, or Glommes.

This, then, was the polyglot army of Flanders, under the command of a lethargic commander, which was to face the French under one of the greatest captains of the age, Turenne, a substantial contingent of English troops who were by no means the rabble that had been sent to Hispaniola, and the powerful English fleet.

---

* Persan was Condé's *chef de l'état-major*.

Appendix to Chapter 11

Royalist Regiments in Spanish Flanders, 1656–1660

The King's Life Guard of Horse

80 gentlemen under Charles, Lord Gerard of Brandon
Lieutenant, Sir Gilbert Gerard, Bt
Cornet the Hon. Edward Stanley
Quartermaster, Colonel James Prodgiers
Chaplain, Dr Matthew Smallwood
Master Surgeon to the six regiments, Sir John Knight.[1]
Surgeon Thomas Woodall

At the Restoration this increased to 600 officers and men, having also absorbed the Duke of York's Troop of Horse Guards, of whom 200 were released and 400 returned from England to the garrison of Dunkirk as the Duke of York's Regiment of Horse; most departed to French service in 1662.

The King's Own Regiment[2]

Colonel Henry Wilmot, Earl of Rochester
Colonel Thomas Blague (October 1657)[*]
Lieutenant-Colonel Thomas Blague[3]
Lieutenant-Colonel Sir William Throckmorton[†]
Major John Beversham (killed at the Dunes)
Major Ferdinando Carey (vice Beversham 1658)
Captain John Gwynne[‡]

---

[*] Thomas Blague, or Blagge (1613–1660) was a Groom of the Bedchamber to Charles I and served the Royalist cause throughout the Civil Wars and in exile. He was colonel of a regiment of foot and another of horse (see Stuart Reid, *Officers and Regiments of the Royalist Army,* vol. 1, pp.20–21). After the Restoration he was briefly Governor of Great Yarmouth and of Landguard Fort.

[†] Mentioned by James Duke of York as having been in command of the regiment at the Battle of the Dunes. Became Knight Marshal after the Restoration and Lieutenant-Colonel of the Earl of Craven's Regiment. He does not seem to have been related to either of the Throckmorton baronetcies.

[‡] Served Charles I in Sir Thomas Salusbury's Regiment during the Civil Wars and later with Montrose. He joined Charles II in exile after Worcester. He was the author of *Military Memoirs of the Great Civil War. Being the Military Memoirs of John Gwynne,* &c., 4to,

COLONIAL IRONSIDES

Captain William Saunderson
Captain Christopher Grosse
Captain Charles Slaughter (killed at the Dunes)
Captain William Carless
Captain Matthew Wise
Captain Robert Broughton
Captain John Walters
Captain Sir Thomas Ashton
Captain Sir Richard Mauleverer
Captain John Monson
Captain John Gwillims
Captain Herbert Jefferies
Captain Thomas Cooke
Captain William Gwyn
Captain __ Farrell

Captain-Lieutenant William Barker
Lieutenant William Bayley[*]
Ensign __ Hill
Ensign George Hamilton[†]
Ensign Bevil Skelton
Ensign John Elvize[‡]

Lieutenants and Ensigns
Edward Sackville
Launcelot Stonor
Henry Crispe
Alexander Wallwynne
Anthony Coldham
Richard Richardson
Thomas Langford
Arthur Broughton
John Crofts
Anthony Thorold
William Baglio
John Carelton
Philip Paramore
Sylvanus Tomkins
Francis Hamon
Horace Slaughter
John Strode

Adjutant __ Spotswood

    Edinburgh, 1822 (reprinted by the British Library in 2011).
*   Possibly a relative of Captain Thomas Bayly who had served in Blague's Regiment of Foot in 1642.
†   Hamilton and Skelton were pages of honour to the King in exile.
‡   Cornet in the King's Life Guard of Horse in 1661.

APPENDIX TO CHAPTER 11

Quartermaster William Harwood
Physician Dr John Wiseman
Surgeon Mr Rudston
Chaplain Thomas Tyrwhitt

Mentioned by the Duke of York as having been killed at the Battle of the Dunes:[4]
Captain William Carles, or Carless[*]
Major John Beversham[†]
Captain Charles Slaughter
Captain __ Farrell
Captain Sir Thomas Ashton
Captain Thomas Cooke[‡]
Captain-Lieutenant __ Stroud[§]
Lieutenant John Elvize[¶]

Duke of York's Troop of Horse Guards

Captain Sir Charles Berkeley
Lieutenant Robert Dongan
Lieutenant William Victor
Cornet John Godolphin
Quartermaster Edward Barclay
Surgeon John Robinson

Duke of York's Regiment of Foot[5]

Colonel H.R.H. the Duke of York
Lieutenant-Colonel Donagh MacCarty, 2nd Viscount Muskerry

Captain John O'Neil	Captain Donnan (1661)	Captain Thomas Butler
Lieutenant Blaghlin Line	Lieutenant Hugh O'Keefe	Lieutenant Daniel O'Driscoll
Ensign Richard Morris	Ensign Terence O'Keefe	Ensign Sige O'Mulrean
Captain Dermot O'Brien	Captain Edmund Fitzgerald	Captain Seamus Barney
Lieutenant John Conelan	Lieutenant Edward Mandizeil	Lieutenant Pharlon O'Sulevan
Ensign Septimus Fielding	Ensign Pierce Butler	Ensign Arthur O'Keife

---

[*] William Carless or Carles (c. 1610–1689), a Catholic, had been in the original regiment of the King's Guards which disappeared in 1647, and then colonel of a regiment of horse in the Worcester campaign. He escaped to exile thereafter having assisted Charles II's flight including the episode of hiding in an oak tree. He was not killed at the Dunes but captured and later ransomed. He was later a Gentleman of the Privy Chamber.
[†] Captain in Colonel John Frescherville's Horse and major in Sir William Savile's Horse during the Civil Wars.
[‡] Formerly captain in the Queen's Lifeguard of Foot.
[§] Not identified. Possibly a mistaken identification of Ensign Stradling of the colonel's company.
[¶] An ensign, not killed at the Dunes – cornet in the King's Life Guard of Horse in 1661.

COLONIAL IRONSIDES

Captain David Danan	Captain Thomas Browne	Captain Daniel O'Sulevan
Lieutenant Morris O'Faeieren	Lieutenant Terence O'Brien	
Ensign Edmond Danan	Ensign Aulife O'Sullevan	

Captain Donal O'Driscol	Captain John Macher	Captain __ Knight[†††]
	Lieutenant Owen O'Sullevan	

The Duke of Gloucester's Regiment

Colonel H.R.H. the Duke of Gloucester
Lieutenant-Colonel Viscount Taaffe
Major __ Fitzpatrick
Lieutenant Theobald Stapleton
Ensign Cornelius Hehir

Captain Walter Phillips	Captain Lord Viscount Iveagh	Captain Mathew Rooney
Lieutenant Miles Phillipps	Lieutenant Henry Taite	Lieutenant John Flannilly
Ensign Hugh Conor	Ensign Phelim Carter	Ensign Owen O'Sulliman

Captain Colin O'Connor	Captain Dudley Costello	Captain Walter Hope
Lieutenant Robert Murett	Lieutenant Roger Conor	Lieutenant Edward Hope
Ensign John Farrell	Ensign Giles Morishove	Ensign Thomas Hope

Captain Owen O'Connor	Captain Hugh O'Connor	Captain Gerard Dillon
Lieutenant Robin Nesbitt	Lieutenant Roger O'Conor	Lieutenant Henry Nugent
Ensign Gilbert Roe	Ensign Christopher Fitzgerald	Ensign Hugo Morfi

Adjutant Roger Brennan
Chaplain Fr John MacDavid

The Earl of Bristol's Regiment (Farrell's) (1656–1661)

Colonel Lewis Farrell	Lieutenant-Colonel Conor Farrell	Major James Farrell
Captain-Lieutenant Bryan Farrell	Lieutenant Daniel Molloy	Lieutenant __ Holmes
Ensign John Donovan	Ensign James Molloy	Ensign Harry Leyes

Captain John Farrell	Captain Caspar Tuite	Captain Henry Farrell
Lieutenant Thomas Burke		
Ensign Conor Burke		

---

* Mentioned by name in *The Memoirs of James II*, p.238.

APPENDIX TO CHAPTER 11

Captain William Butler	Captain John Shea	Captain Charles Farrell
Lieutenant Roger Farrell		
Ensign Theodore Butler	Ensign Edward Farrell	
Captain Haughy Farrell	Captain Thomas Fitzpatrick	Captain James Farrell
Lieutenant Thadeus Farrell	Lieutenant Alexander Daron	Lieutenant William Farrell
Ensign Walter Reynolds	Ensign Richard Dody	Ensign James Farrell
Captain John Molloy	Captain Thomas Farrell	
Lieutenant Edward Molloy	Lieutenant Hugh Granby	
Ensign John Gilmont	Ensign Harry Dermott	

Chaplain Fr Hubert Cahill

Other Officers of Farrell's Regiment, Reduced in 1661[7]

Captains:	Lieutenants	Ensigns	Reformadoes
Bryan Lennan	Hugh Madden	Bryan Flaherty	Robert Plunkett
John Grady	Robert Farrell	Anthony Flaherty	John Tuite
Daniel Brady	Daniel McNamara	Charles Farrell	John Newman
John Flaherty	David Many	Gerrard Keigan	Murough Flaherty
James Bellings	Luke Balahide	Patrick McQuinn	
	Connor Daly	Daniel Currine	
	Fergus Hanley	Daniel Flaherty	
		James Flaherty	

Colonel Richard Grace's Regiment

Colonel the Marquis of Ormonde
Lieutenant-Colonel Richard Grace
Adjutant Brien O'Bryan
Quartermaster Marcus Browne

Captains	Lieutenants	Ranks Unknown
Robert Wagh	Richard Hogarty	Arthur Molloy
James Denny	Daniel McNamara	Edmund Burke
Dermott Lucy	Matthew Molloy	Gerard Aylmer
Gerrard Coughlin	Francis Murrough	William Stapleton
	Sherlagh Molloy	John Carroll
	Dermott Coughlin	Owen Flattry
		William Burke
		William Delany

The Earl of Newburgh's Scots Regiment.[8]

ORDER OF PRECEDENCE AMONG THE OFFICERS OF THE Scottish REGIMENT. CHARLES R. Our will and pleasure is that the respective Captaines of the regiment of our trusty and welbeloved Lieutenant Generall John Middleton be placed, and march from time to time, in the said regiment, according to the order and praecedency we have hereunder caused them to bee named, next after the superior officers of the sayd regiment, and that you signify our pleasure to every of them respectively, and cause this our order therein to bee duely and punctually observed, for such is our pleasure. Given at our Court at Bruxelles, this 4th of June, 1657.

Colonel the Earl of Middleton
Lieutenant-Colonel Viscount Newburgh
Major William Urry
Captain-Lieutenant Hamilton Wisseris
Adjutant Peter Wood (later Dermott O'Driscoll)
Quartermaster George Wills

Captains

The Earl of Kerry	The Lord Napier	Sir William Fleming
Sir William Keyth	__ Turner	__ Durham
Sir Alexander Hamilton	John Strachan	Walter Whitford
George Hamilton	Alexander Hamilton	James Lawson

Ranks Unknown

Blaine	La Grande	Doolan
Chapman	Magginis	Balfour
Higgins	Nugent	Gordon
Murray	Farquhar	Gaston
Carter	McGuire	O'Hare

NOTES

1. HMC John Eliot Hodgkin's MSS p.124.
2. TNA SP 29/20. See also for all regiments, Drenth and Riley, vol. 1, pp.86–92. The list for the Guards comes in part from Hamilton's *Origin and History*, vol. I, but he does not give sources for the names.
3. Two warrants for Blagge as Lieutenant-Colonel in the Guards are in the HMC Report on the MSS of Mr John Eliot Hodgkin, p.123.
4. *Memoirs of James II*, p.264.
5. TNA SP 44/2
6. TNA SP 29/45; SP 44/2; Jennings, various pages and notes.
7. TNA SP 29/51, f. 33 ii.
8. Rev William Dunn Macray (ed.), *Letters and Papers of Patrick Ruthven, Earl of Forth and Brentford, and of His Family: A.D. 1615–A.D. 1662. With an Appendix of Papers Relating to Sir John Urry* (London: J.B. Nichols and sons, 1868), p.165.

12

Cromwell's Expeditionary Brigade and the French Army of Flanders

Under the terms of the treaty with France, Cromwell had engaged to send a brigade of 6,000 men to join Turenne's army in Flanders. The force was to consist of six regiments of foot; no horse and no guns. Like their Spanish opponents, the French had plenty of cavalry and cannon, but were comparatively weak in infantry. The Commonwealth Navy was also to cooperate with the French army, assisting in the task of besieging and capturing coastal fortresses and maintaining supply. Sir William Lockhart remained as Cromwell's ambassador and representative to the French. Lockhart had had an unexpected encounter with the Duke of York in September 1656 while the latter was travelling from Paris to join the King:

> On his arriving at the gates of Clermont, one of [the Duke's] servants whom he had sent before to hold the horses ready, came to tell him that Lockhart, Cromwell's ambassador, was there and was lodging at the post house, which was the best in town; whereupon he gave this man orders to have his horses brought to the door of the post house. The prince on arriving had his coach stop, took out his boots, got to horseback in the street and immediately continued on his way. There was equal surprise on both sides, Lockhart feared the consequences. He knew that the duke of York was as well-liked by the people as he was held in consideration by all persons of quality in the Kingdom, and that the English of Lockhart's party were equally hated by all men. These reflections alarmed him; he caused his horses to be saddled, assembled his men in front of the inn, and made them stand on guard with their swords and pistols. He himself stood at a window of the room which looked out on the gate above the street, having beside him the principal men of his retinue who like him were uncovered. This probable that he stood thus to avoid taking off his hat and not be blamed for remaining uncovered … now the coach having stopped directly at the gate facing the window, the prince saw him, and before he could get on horseback, all the people having eagerly run up to see him, the least word from him would have made all the people fall on the Ambassador. Lockhart was afraid but his fear lasted no long time and the prince's departure reassured him.[1]

COLONIAL IRONSIDES

Left: Sir William Lockhart. (Author's collection)

Right: Major-General Sir Thomas Morgan, a contemporary image. (National Library of Wales 4671679)

This encounter should never have taken place, as Lockhart had gone to Clermont to avoid the Prince; but James had set out from Paris for Brussels earlier than expected and so the meeting that was to have been avoided happened anyway – but without any diplomatic incident.

Command of the troops was given to Major-General Sir John Reynolds as captain-general, then commissary-general of the army in Ireland. Reynolds was an experienced soldier and was an intimate of Henry Cromwell. After some initial reluctance, Reynolds accepted the post. Reynolds' lieutenant was Major-General Sir Thomas Morgan, a hard case if ever there was one in an age which did not tolerate a soft touch among military officers. Morgan was born at Llangattock Lingoed in Monmouthshire, and in spite of coming from a landed family he was all but illiterate, barely able to sign his own name. During the 1630s he began his military career in the Thirty Years' War and at the outbreak of the English Civil Wars he returned to enter the service of Parliament – unlike the majority of the Welsh nobles and gentry. He served as a captain of dragoons under Fairfax and was promoted to colonel in 1645. He served as governor of Gloucester and was active in the capture of Chepstow and Monmouth. Thereafter he served in the west of England for a time. He left military service temporarily but served under Monck in Scotland from 1651 and in 1655 was promoted to Major-General, being regarded as loyal, dependable and efficient. He was extremely coarse of manner but brave and always popular with the troops.[2] He was at this point commissary-general of the army in Scotland. Soon after his arrival in France, Morgan was visited by the two most eminent personages of the French army: Cardinal Mazarin and Marshal Turenne. What they saw was not what they expected of such a considerable military reputation:

> … whereas they thought to have found an Achillean or gigantesque person, they sawe a little man, not many degrees above a dwarfe, sitting in a hutt of turves, with his fellowe soldiers, smoking a pipe about 3 inches (or neer so) long, with a green hatt-case on. He spake with a very exile tine, and did cry-out to the soldiers, when angry with them, "Sirrah, I'le cleave your skull!" as if the words had been prolated by an eunuch.[3]

Reynolds and Morgan were each to have command of a regiment; the remaining four were to be commanded by Colonels Henry Lillingston, Roger Alsop, Samuel Clark and Sir Bryce Cochrane. Clark and his Lieutenant-Colonel, William Beadle, had both served with the Dutch before the English Civil Wars.[4] Cochrane was a Scot who had served the King during the Civil Wars but had been persuaded to change sides by Monck; he may also have served in the Dutch army.[5] His Lieutenant-Colonel, Richard Hughes had been Captain-Lieutenant in Mock's Regiment. Roger Alsop was a long-serving officer of the New Model and had been provost marshal of the army since 1650.[6] The previous career of Lillingston is unknown but he too may have been in the Dutch service, since he returned there after the Restoration.[7]

All the regiments were to be newly formed – no entire regiments were withdrawn from the standing forces of the Protectorate. The lessons of the expedition to Hispaniola seem to have been learned, however, and more care was taken over the selection of the officers and men. The nucleus of the force was provided by a draft of 1,475 men drawn from the standing regiments in England – the Lord General's, Goffe's Ingoldsby's, Lambert's, Fleetwood's, Farley's, Howard's and the Tower Regiment – and the garrisons of the fortresses.[8] The remaining 4,525 were to be volunteers. At least some of these men must have been inexperienced recruits, but many would have seen active service during the English Civil Wars, or more recently against the Scots and in Ireland.

The six regiments mustered on Blackheath on Monday, 1 May 1657, dressed in 'new red coats given them for the terrible name thereof'.[9] They were also, it seems, organised into equal numbers of pikemen and musketeers, rather than the usual two-to-one ratio of muskets to pikes:

> They were in all six regiments, stout men, and fit for action as was manifest at their appearance. Words of exhortation and encouragement were given them in a sermon by Mr Hugh Peters … This wrought upon the hearts of the soldiers so, that they declared themselves with alacrity resolved to hold up the honour and renown of England abroad. Afterwards, five hundred being drawn out of each regiment, which made up the number of thee thousand, there immediately began their march hence towards the seaside, being to embark at Dover, from thence to be transported to Calais. The other three thousand are disposed up and down in quarters, waiting further orders, which they expect some time next week, and then to follow their fellows.[10]

On the following Friday and Saturday, 5 and 6 May, the first contingent embarked, having been given a month's pay. They landed near Boulogne, rather than Calais, 'where they were met by a person of honour appointed from the King of France to receive them, as also by the Governor of Boulogne …'[11] The remainder appear to have followed soon afterwards. The whole brigade was then quartered around Boulogne, where it was expected that three months' pay would be advanced by the French authorities;* the treaty actually laid down that the French would contribute half the troops' pay and the English government the rest.

Reynold's Regiment, also known as 'the White Regiment', possibly because of its colours (although there are no details available), comprised 10 companies. There are no extant lists of the officers although the Lieutenant-Colonel was named Fenwick, possibly John Fenwick, a veteran of the New Model.[12] The Major was John Hinton, of whom nothing more is known; only one captain, Sherwin, can be identified. Morgan's Regiment, likewise, has no extant muster roll for this date. Lillingston's regiment was also referred to as 'the Blue'; its Lieutenant-Colonel was Roger Whetstone, who had served in Mandeville's Regiment in 1642. The major was Thomas Haynes, another veteran of the Civil Wars who had served in Lord Say's Regiment. Three captains can be identified: Robert Fitzwilliam, Robert Smith and Pickering.

---

* The agreed rates of pay per day were £12 for a colonel, £6 for a Lieutenant-Colonel, £5 for a major, 5 livres for a captain, 2 livres 10 sous for a lieutenant, 1 livre 5 sous for an ensign, 10 sous for a sergeant and 5 sous with ammunition bread for a soldier. Barratt, p.39.

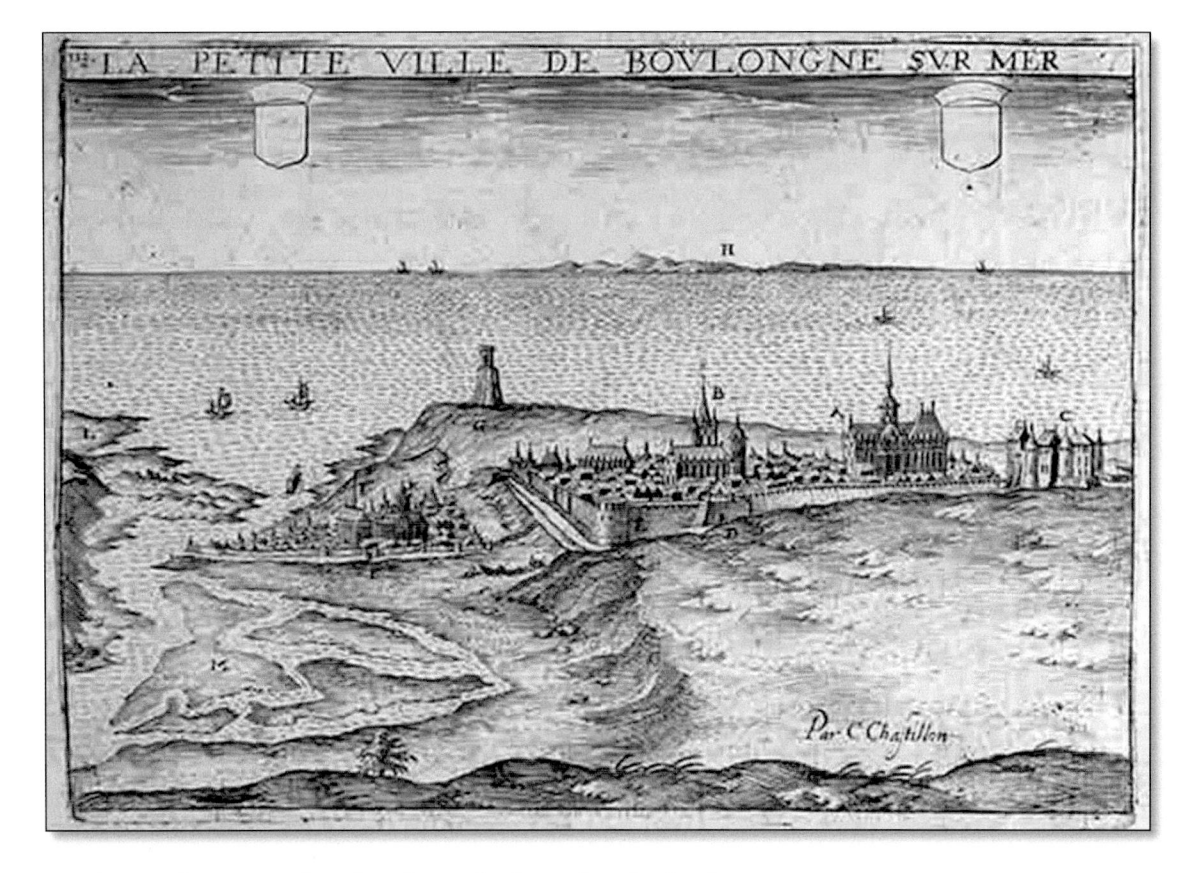

Boulogne, scene of the brigade's landing in France, about 1650. (Boulogne-sur-Mer municipal library, Portfolio 46/37.032)

Smith may have served under the Earl of Northumberland in 1640 as a young man; nothing is known of the others.[13] In Cochrane's Regiment, only Captain Roger Coates, who had served in Cole's Regiment in Ireland, can be identified.[14] In Clark's Regiment, the major was William Littleton,[15] but the lists of officers for this regiment are missing until 1659.

Correspondence from officers quoted in newspapers generally agreed that pay was regular and treatment good. The pay for a soldier was, however, less than that usually given in the English service and petitions were made for an additional threepence per day to make this good; as time went on, pay inevitably fell into arrears. Quarters were provided and the soldiers were healthy, although water was short and the men grumbled about the coarse brown bread they were given, made from bran and rye as well as wheat, which formed the bulk of the day's food in loaves of 10 ounces; there was also it seems a great shortage of cheese, which usually formed part of the ration and to which the soldiers of the Protectorate had come to see as essential – more so than meat. On the other hand, a generous ration of wine or beer was provided each day.[16] It is unclear whether the French commissariat provided all supplies, or whether, as was not unusual, contractors were employed.

The brigade marched north in easy stages from Boulogne and on or about 11 June it joined the main French army under Turenne at St Quentin. Here, on 11 June, the troops were reviewed by King Louis XIV and Cardinal Mazarin: 'they are all well-made soldiers', wrote Mazarin, 'and look as if they would do good service …'[17]

During the first half of the seventeenth century, the French regular army, which the English brigade was now to join, had grown by a factor of 15, from 55,000 in 1615 to 200,000 in 1655.[18] The organisation of the army differed from that of Spain in that the infantry was organised into regiments, each of three battalions. Each battalion had 12 companies of 50 men, armed with musket or pike. There were already some foreign units from Switzerland, Germany and Scotland, the forerunners of a much larger body of foreign troops who served in the French Army until the Revolution. The horse (including dragoons) formed between a quarter and a third of the army and was organised into squadrons of around 60 men. As in other armies, the cavalry's chief function in battle was to deliver fire from pistols at close range in volleys, breaking the cohesion of the enemy's infantry, rather than charging with the sword. French officers tended to be from the gentry and lesser nobility, although there were plenty of exceptions, such as Condé, who was a prince. The soldiers were recruited locally by a system known as *recolage*, with the permission of local authorities. Officially, enlistment was voluntary, but covert impressment and even kidnapping were not unknown. Unusually, and in common with the English, French military uniform was standardised during the 1650s and this, along with a high degree of central control and discipline, a professional officer corps and a locally recruited soldiery produced the first recognisable regimental system in a regular army, later copied across Europe.

The French army in Flanders consisted of 20,000 men of whom 12,000 were in the regiments of foot: the King's Guards; the Swiss Guards, the Queen Mother's, Turenne's own regiment, the Regiment of Picardie and the Regiment of Bretagne, with varying numbers of battalions; there were also 50 squadrons of horse and four of *gendarmes*.[19]

The final element of the Anglo-French force was the English fleet of 18 ships, commanded by General-at-Sea Edward Montagu. Of these, 11 were frigates and seven larger ships; 10 had been sent back from the Mediterranean with Montagu in July 1656 to strengthen the Channel fleet. A full list is not available but the fleet included the *London* (74), *Naseby* (80), *Newbury* (52), *Dragon* (54), *Essex* (54), *Gloucester* (50), *Speaker* (50), *Elizabeth* (50) and *Worcester* (40) and the frigates *Rose* and *Truelove*.[20] As well as providing mobility and a source of supplies, these ships represented a powerful battery of artillery capable not only of mounting a blockade, but also of helping to reduce defences during a siege.

Appendix to Chapter 12

Cromwellian Regiments of Foot in Flanders, 1657–1658

Although no lists survive from the original deployment, lists of the officers survive from the years following, up to the Restoration. These are reproduced below in composite form.

Staff[1]
Adjutant-General Anthony Mainwaring
Marshal-General Anthony Bee
Physician-General Dr John French
Apothecary Abel Clark

Sir William Lockhart's Regiment of Foot (originally Reynold's Regiment)

Captains	Lieutenants	Ensigns
Colonel Sir William Lockhart	Captain-Lieutenant Richard Baker	Christopher Monck
Lieutenant-Colonel Fenwick*	John Richardson	William James
Major John Hinton	Richard Woodward	James Hayes
__ Gargrave	James Relph	Francis Bromicham
George Fiennes†	Arthur Colcut	William Carter
John Fisher	William Cathness	Nathaniel Pamphlin
__ Devoe	Peter St Hill	
Edward Righton	Edward Leighton	Peter Rose
Thomas Ingram	John Janman	Henry Jackson
Jenkin Jones	William Beech	John Eubanke
__ Muse		

---

*   Replaced by William Fleetwood.
†   From Lillingston's Regiment. Returned 1660.

COLONIAL IRONSIDES

Staff
Surgeon Walter Scott
Chaplain J. Robinson

Roger Alsop's Regiment of Foot[3]

Captains	Lieutenants	Ensigns
Colonel Roger Alsop	Captain-Lieutenant Francis Hinton	William Hussey
Lieutenant-Colonel William Fleetwood		
Major Maurice Kingwell[‡]	Richard Lyne	Thomas Griffith
Major __ Humphreys (vice Kingwell when promoted)		
Major Richard Pease[§]	Robert Grosse	John Hemington
Richard Meautys[¶]		
John Turner	Anthony Palmer	William Fullaway
Thomas Chapman[**]		
John Withers		
__ Sherwin	Edwin Bates	Oliver Francklin
John Graham	Francis Jukes	Thomas Oxenden
William Houghton	Edward Maning	James Watkins
Nathaniel Cobham	Richard Heming	
John Giles	Edward Pope	Robert Wiles
Humphrey Atherton	Thomas Bassett	

Staff
Chaplain Ichabod Chauncey
Surgeon John Wilkinson
Quartermaster and Marshal Nicholas Tom

Henry Lillingston's Regiment of Foot

Captains	Lieutenants	Ensigns
Colonel Henry Lillingston	Captain-Lieutenant William Whittaker	William Fiennes
Lieutenant-Colonel Roger Whetstone[††]	Thomas Young	Ralph Walker

---

*   Replaced Fleetwood when he moved to Lockhart's Regiment in July 1658
†   He had served in Scotland; see John Yonge Akerman (ed.), *Letters from Roundhead Officers: Written From Scotland And Chiefly Addressed To Adam Baynes, July, 1650 To June, 1660* (London: Bannatyne, 1856) pp. 141, 144.
‡   Died before June 1659.
§   Cashiered in 1659.
¶   Replaced by Thomas Haynes.

APPENDIX TO CHAPTER 12

Major Thomas Haynes
__ Monckton
Robert Smith
Robert Laundy
Samuel Brookes
Henry Middleton
William Wandell
__ Palmer
__ Pickering
Robert Fitzwilliams

John Sherrard
Thomas Southerne
Ellis Cooper
Peter Copeland
Robert Mustian
Robert Lawrison
Lewis Powell
__ Launde

William Bressier

James Slepford
Daniel Terry
Thomas Hayne
Thomas Brereton
William Sharpe
__ Padson

Staff
Surgeon – Lindsay with two mates
Quartermaster and Marshal John Harvey

Colonel Samuel Clark's Regiment of Foot

Captains	Lieutenants	Ensigns
Colonel Samuel Clark	Captain-Lieutenant John Clark	William Chambers
Lieutenant-Colonel William Ledger	Thomas Place	Thomas Potter
Major William Littleton§§	Humphrey Howell	George Calton
John Baker	Jasper Swift	Nathaniel Smelt
Edward Claypole	Thomas Street	Ralph Erlinn
Evan Harris	Richard Bootey	Henry Bryers
William Moore	William Duckett	William Herbert
William Richardson	Evan Lewis	Nathaniel Philipps
John Manning	Francis Bolt	Thomas Berry
Edmund Geary¶¶	Richard Blake	Robert Nelson

Staff
Surgeon – Couch
Quartermaster – Thompson

---

*   Replaced by Abraham Davies.
†   Replaced by Samuel Battley.
‡   Originally in Morgan's Regiment, to Clark's in 1659.

COLONIAL IRONSIDES

Sir Bryce Cochrane's Regiment of Foot

Captains	Lieutenants	Ensigns
Colonel Sir Bryce Cochrane	Captain-Lieutenant Thomas Salusbury	William Abernethy
Lieutenant-Colonel Richard Hughes***	William Butler	Joseph Arnop
Major Francis Brockhurst	William Ufflet	William Potham
Roger Coates	Owen Hookes	Hugh Hughes
Richard Scott	Cuthbert Carr	Philip Dawley
William Cotes	Robert Ashfield	Hugh Hughes
John Tongue	Nathaniel Cole	John Shelley
George Annesley†††	Rowland Peart	Richard Pawling
William Charlton	John Blaney	John Styles
William Bassett	John Browne	James Read

Sir Thomas Morgan's Regiment of Foot[5]

Captains
Colonel Sir Thomas Morgan
Lieutenant-Colonel William Legard
George Annesley
Edmund Geary
John Hornold
John Manning
James Strangeways
Edward Witham
John Hill
John Bayley

NOTES
1 TNA CSPD Interregnum, vol. 158, August 1657.
2 TNA CSPD Interregnum, vol. 204, August 1659.
3 TNA CSPD Interregnum, vol. 204, August 1659.
4 TNA CSPD Interregnum, vol. 204, August 1659.
5 Firth and Davies, vol. ii, p. 694 from a muster prior to the regiment's return to England.

---

*   Replaced by Robert Mainwaring.
†   Originally in Morgan's Regiment.

13

Opening Moves: the Sieges of Montmédy, St-Venant and Ardres, June–September, 1657

With the English brigade now joined to his army, Turenne was ready to begin operations – somewhat later than usual in the campaigning season, for it was now mid June. Turenne had decided to send part of the army under Marshal de la Ferté[*] to lay siege to Montmédy in the Ardennes, with the aim of drawing at least a part of the Spanish field army away from Flanders; the English remained with Turenne, whose force lay between Montmédy and the coast. Reynolds wrote in some disgust to Thurloe that: 'Fighting is not the fashion of the country',[1] being unused to the system of Continental warfare focused on fixed fortifications.

The character of European war in the late sixteenth and seventeenth centuries, as distinct from the type of warfare based on pitched battles that had been the norm in Britain during the Civil Wars, was dominated by major innovation in the science of fortification. The Italians were the first to experience the new technology of gunpowder weapons at the hands of the French in the 1490s, and it was in Italy, after about 1530, that the development of fortification began to take account of it, both in mounting and resisting cannon.[†] The defensive works that resulted were built on a thick but low profile of rammed earth and rubble faced with stone and the trace, or ground plan, was designed on mathematical lines, hence the name these works were given: the *trace italienne*. Looked at from above, the ground plan resembled a star which allowed interlocking and mutually supporting fields of fire for guns that were fully casemated and thus protected from counter-battery fire; there was no cover for an attacker and the besieger's artillery could be kept at arm's length until extensive systems of entrenchments were constructed to bring fire within a range sufficient to breach the defences. Towers were remodelled

---

[*] Henri II *de la Ferté-Senneterre* (1599–1681).
[†] *The first fully mobile and effective field artillery appeared in 1494 in the train of Charles VIII of France when he invaded Italy; Fornovo in 1495 was probably the first battle where artillery played a really effective part.*

COLONIAL IRONSIDES

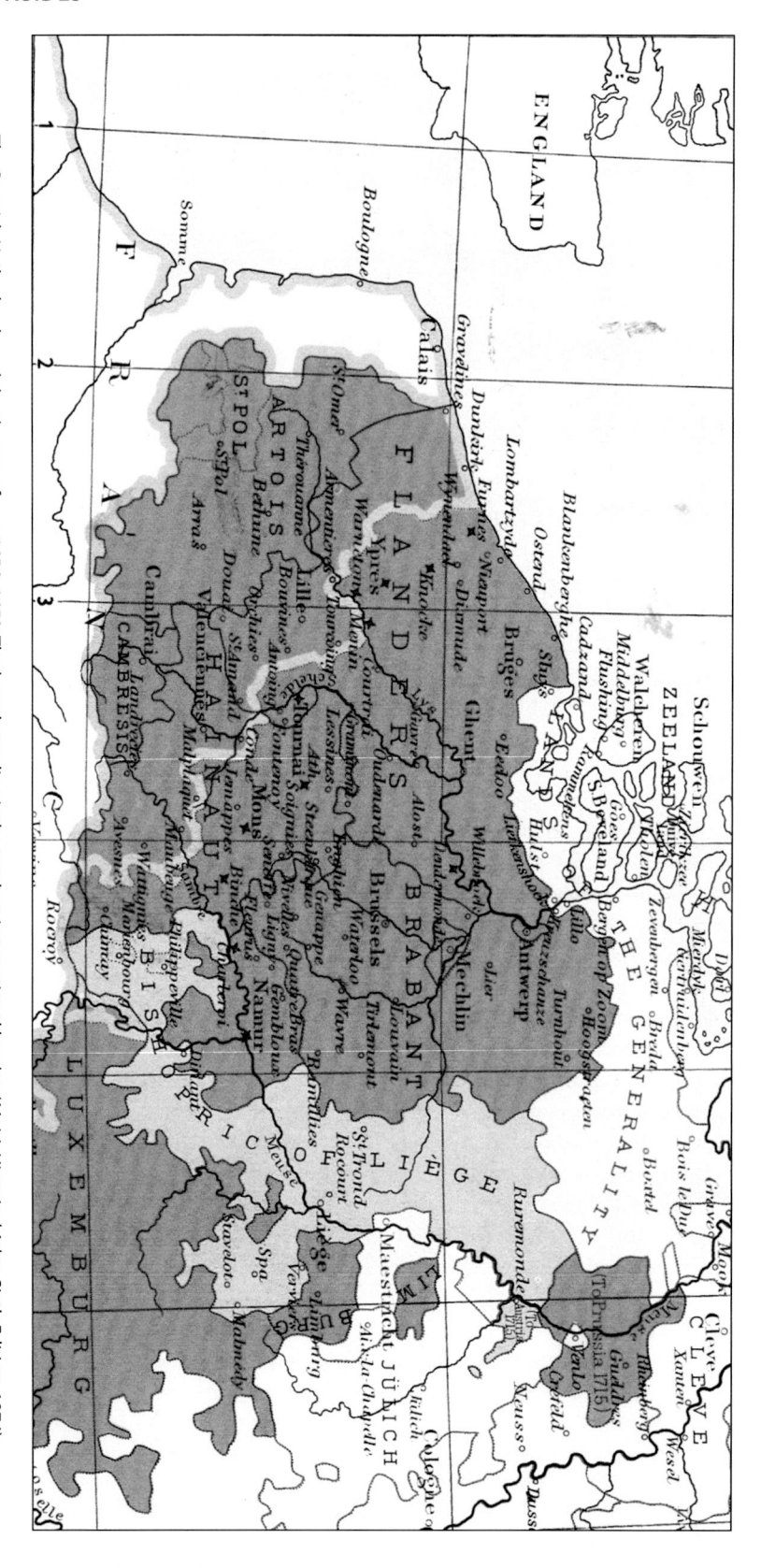

The Spanish Netherlands and the theatre of war, 1656–1659. The broad grey line is the modern international border. (*Muir's Historical Atlas*, Sixth Edition, 1974)

OPENING MOVES: THE SIEGES OF MONTMÉDY, ST-VENANT AND ARDRES, JUNE–SEPTEMBER, 1657

as pentagonal bastions, shaped to eliminate dead ground that could favour the attacker and throughout the latter decades of the sixteenth century, the defence became more and more one of depth. Deep ditches with covered ways were backed by a sloping glacis, low ramparts with bastions, and redans. Further to obstruct the attacker, bastions were supported by outworks: ravelins, hornworks, crownworks and demi-lunes – so called according to their shape – to guard the approaches.

It was the French engineer Vauban,* who combined all these developments into a single code of practice, building or remodelling some 60 fortresses during his career.[2] Vauban was Louis XIV's chief engineer and as well as developing fortification and siege techniques, he also founded the corps of engineers in the French army. Warfare thus became as much science as art and as it did so, the thinking of men like Vauban became more scientific. In the late seventeenth century, we see an increasing emphasis on observation, reconnaissance, intelligence gathering, analysis and evaluation – on rationality and calculation.[3] Vauban also developed a comprehensive scheme for the defeat of fortresses by siege warfare, for only formal sieges could break such fortifications and they needed heavy artillery, from 32- to 64-pounder, to create a breach, supported by heavy mortars to lob shells inside fortifications to kill defenders, cause fires, blow up ammunition and reduce the will to fight. Meanwhile, the attackers would dig lines of circumvallation, as they were known, for their own defence, and then open a parallel trench line opposite the area where a breach was to be made. From this first parallel, a zig-zag sap would be dug forwards until a second parallel could be opened. More sapping would advance a third parallel until the attackers were within storming distance. Usually the outworks would be taken first, and then the garrison summoned to surrender on relatively easy terms. If they refused, the main defences would be breached and the defenders summoned once more. If a garrison refused terms and the attackers then got into the town with their blood up, there would be no quarter for the enemy's soldiers and little for the civilian population. There had been sieges during the English Civil Wars, but these were mainly of towns like Oxford and Bristol which were protected by garrisons behind entrenchments, or of medieval castles like Pembroke, or fortified manor houses like Old Basing. These were small beer in comparison. The wars in the Three Kingdoms had

Seventeenth-century fortifications showing a bastion (F), ravelin (X), half-moon (Y), hornwork (2) and crownworks (3,4,5) from Allain Mallet, *Les Traveaux de Mars*, vol. i, p.67 (<https://digi.ub.uni-heidelberg.de> accessed 2 January 2020).

---

* Sébastien le Prestre de Vauban (1633–1707).

been decided by battle. The conquest of people and territory had followed the destruction of the King's field armies not the other way around.

On the Continent, by contrast, wherever war seemed likely, defences would be built – from Lombardy to the Low Countries – and the huge increase in fortification stultified warfare. In mobile operations, the ascendancy of the pike ensured an advantage to the defence and this advantage became the norm in siege warfare as well, as even a relatively small fortified town would be strong enough to resist siege, even with heavy artillery, for weeks or months provided it was well stocked with food and munitions. The heavy armoured cavalry, once the unrivalled king of the battlefield, was eclipsed by the infantry, the gunners and the sappers who were needed to form garrisons or invest forts. In 1639, for example, no less than 208 fortified areas required garrisons in the Spanish Netherlands involving over 33,000 men, from Dunkirk with its 1,000 man garrison, to a mere 10 men at La Grande Misère near Ghent;[4] and although with the end of the Eighty Years' War this total had reduced, the character of war was still defined by the possession of fortified bases.

As an example of the national investment required, each of Amsterdam's 22 bastions cost half a million florins, while Vauban took six years and five million *livres* to fortify Ath. On the other hand, the siege of La Rochelle cost 40 million *livres*.[5] This was the nub of the concept: although the initial investment was huge, fortification was cheaper than paying a large standing army. A defended, fortified town with a garrison of 1,000 men needed at least 10 times that number to reduce it. Thus, a well-designed system of fortifications could delay and obstruct an attacker at little cost. They might not be able to win wars, but they could prolong them and increase the attrition on powerful opponents. But for a field commander, it became very difficult to reach a decision by battle. Moreover, for a government, attrition caused war weariness and increased the willingness to reach a compromise peace. That said, the growth of fortification did not end pitched battles entirely, for aggressive commanders like Gustavus Adolphus, Condé and Schomberg would seek battle on favourable terms in order to reach a decision. In so doing they not only offered battle, but also accepted the risks it brought along with the costs and benefits.

While Turenne focused on laying siege to Montmédy, the Spanish had an objective of their own. Having marched to Philippeville on the Sambre, as if to raise the siege of Montmédy, Don John had then marched back to the coast. All this, according to James, Duke of York, had been designed to deceive Turenne, as the real objective was the French port of Calais, which was uncovered now that Turenne had split his army. According to James, a weak point in the defences had been identified by engineers sent to reconnoitre the place in disguise, on the seaward side of the town.[6] James, commanding a body of Spanish foot as *Maestre de Campo Generale* arrived at Arques near St-Omer on 2 July. The Prince de Ligne had gone ahead with an advanced guard of horse and from Don John who was following with the rest of the army, James received bad news. De Ligne had:

> … marched from Gravelines as soon as it was night to execute the design at low tide by seizing that part of the town which was outside the walls and adjoining

OPENING MOVES: THE SIEGES OF MONTMÉDY, ST-VENANT AND ARDRES, JUNE–SEPTEMBER, 1657

the quay, after which he could make himself master of the town in twelve hours. But he arrived half an hour too late: the water was so high that it was impossible to pass through, and he was obliged to draw off having done nothing but give a sudden alarm to the town and show the governor where the weakest point was, which the governor [Marshal d'Aumont*] then took pains to fortify and so deprive the Spaniards of any hope of being able to surprise the place.[7]

Nothing except what James described as 'useless marches' occurred until news arrived of the fall of Montmédy on 10 August. 30,000 men had besieged the town, pitted against 756 defenders. The fortress held for 57 days and the garrison only surrendered only after the death of the governor, Jean V of Allamont. Turenne, his army reunited, was known to be heading back towards the coast and on 20 August, the French laid siege to St-Venant, 30 miles south of Dunkirk. Don John and the Spanish army now marched to Calonne, only three miles east of St-Venant. Reynolds asked Turenne for 2,000 horse with which, and with the 6,000 English foot, he would assault the Spanish camp – a plan refused by Turenne. Equally, Don John thought the French position too strong to be assaulted, not least because the country was broken by a heavy network of thick hedges and drainage ditches. Instead, it was decided to intercept a major convoy of supplies, carried in 400 or 500 wagons, being brought to Turenne from Béthune. It was decided to move the army to Montbernanson, a point which the convoy would have to pass. As it was escorted by only three squadrons of horse, it could here be attacked and captured.

Because of the hedges and ditches, pioneers had to be sent ahead of the army to clear a route. It had been ordered that the army should move into position for the ambush at dawn on 22 August. The Duke of York would command the foot, the Prince de Ligne the horse on the right wing, and Condé his own troops on the left. Don John and Caracena, with their guards, marched at the head of the column and, arriving near the ambush site at about noon, immediately took their siesta.[8] James was only one hedge from the ambush site and had his men in battle formation; Ligne likewise had four or five squadrons in place. As the convoy approached, James sent to Ligne urging an immediate attack; Ligne, however, would not move without orders from Don John – who, of course, was sleeping. Even when James went personally to find Ligne and urge him to move, he would not, and so because of the strong Spanish sense of deference to authority – not to mention Don John's laziness – the opportunity was lost. The convoy, seeing the danger, speeded up and began to enter the French lines.[9]

When all but a few wagons were inside, three companies of Spanish guards arrived with orders to attack. James and Ligne sent their own guards with this body of troops which was commanded by Caracena's inexperienced nephew, the Count of Colmar. Colmar 'marched forward so hastily and in such disorder that if the enemy's three squadrons had wished to dispute the ground, they would have beaten them.'[10] The French horse had already entered their own lines but Colmar's men followed, being rapidly evicted –

---

*   Louis-Marie-Victor d'Aumont de Rochebaron (1632–1704).

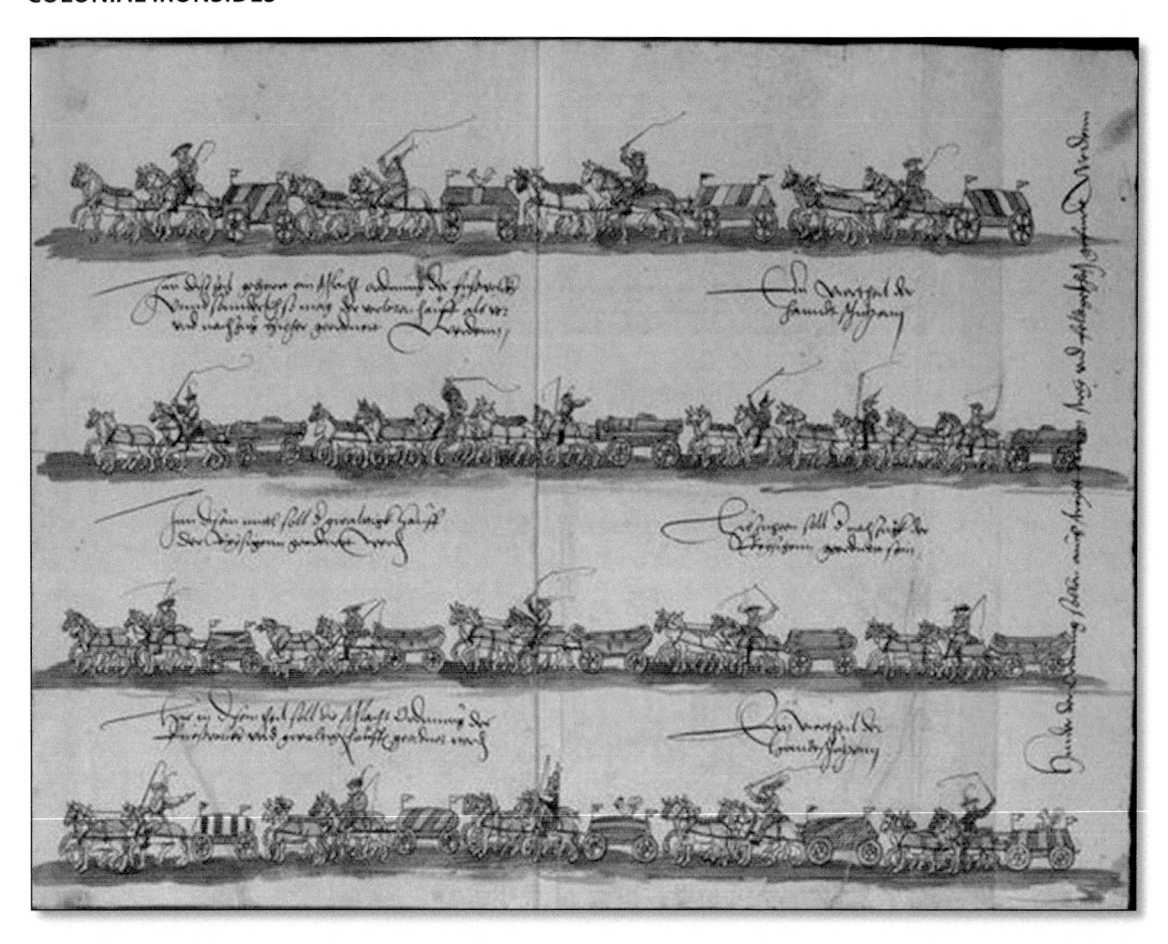

A convoy of wagons; this image dates from about 50 years before the Franco-Spanish war, but the technologies had not changed. (Universitätsbibliotek Heidelberg (<https://digi-ub.uni-heidelberg.de/digits/cpg 128/0425> accessed 19 August 2020).

'they came out more rapidly than they had gone in and fled without stopping until they had got behind Berkeley's company …' [the Duke of York's horse guards].[11] It fell to Berkeley to cover the ignominious withdrawal of the Spanish guards. The French lost not a single wagon and only a small number of killed and wounded.

The following day, the Duke of York met several French officers, including the Marquis d'Humières,* on parole – that is, under a flag of truce. With him was one of Condé's French officers, M. de Tourville,† who was to take an exposed post the next day and was sure of being heavily cannonaded. He took the opportunity to send a message to a former comrade on the other side, an artillery officer, begging that the French artillery would fire on the Spanish troops to his right. The thing was duly done, and not one shot landed among Tourville's men.

Don John and the Council of War now decided to move away and lay siege to the town of Ardres, just over the border in France and about eight miles south of Calais. The army, around 14,000 men, arrived here on Sunday

---

*   Louis de Crévant, Marquis and later Duc d'Humières (1628–1694) became a Marshal of France in 1668 and Grand Master of Artillery in 1685.

†   Presumably a relative of Anne-Hilarion de Costentin, Comte *de Tourville, a noted naval commander.*

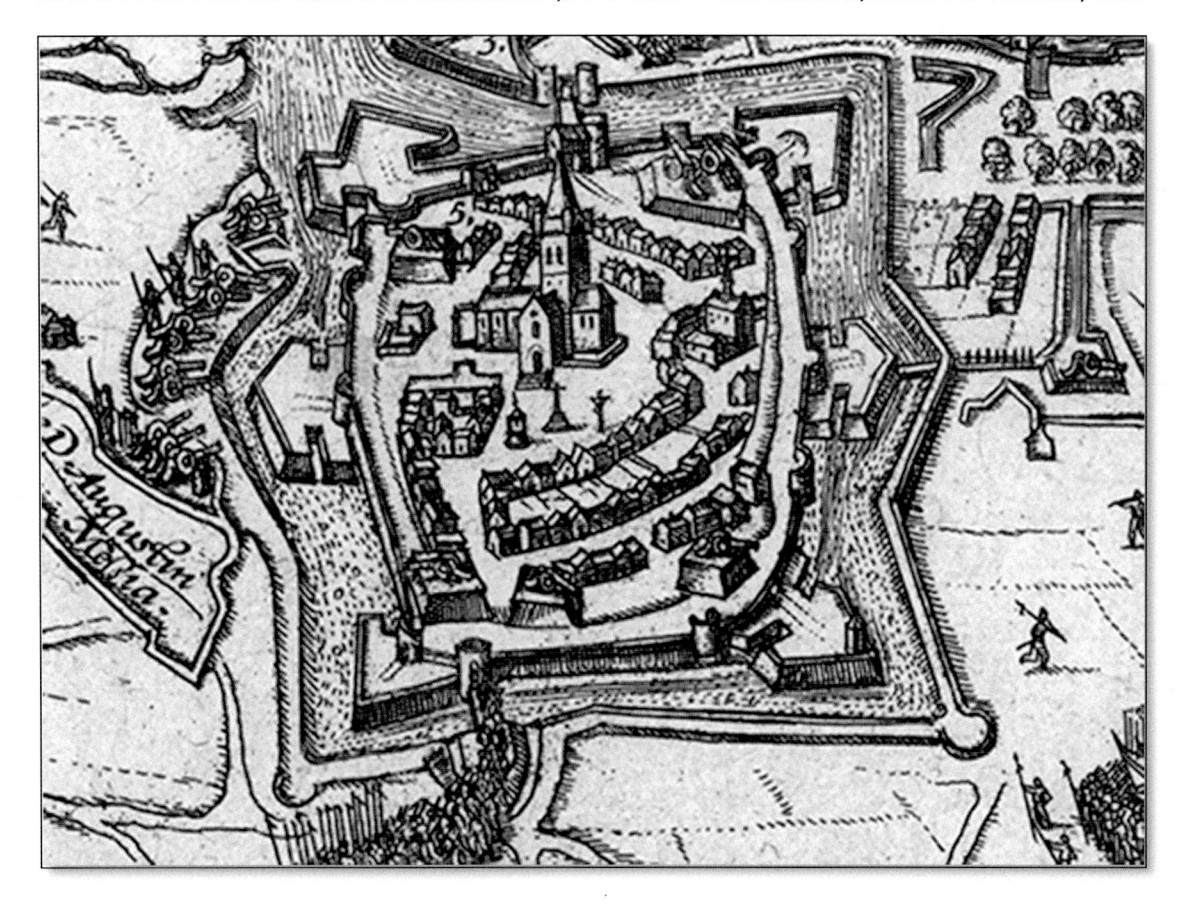

OPENING MOVES: THE SIEGES OF MONTMÉDY, ST-VENANT AND ARDRES, JUNE–SEPTEMBER, 1657

A plan of Ardres. (National Library of France, GED/6511)

26 August and found a garrison of around 400 under the governorship of M. de Rouville.[12] In 1596, Ardres had been besieged and taken by the Spaniards, following which the fortifications of the city were improved with the addition of a high walled gate, repairs to the breach in the southern rampart and the dilapidation of the hornwork. The Spanish army also took over and repaired the Governor's mansion, the King's lieutenant's house and the arsenal on the Grand-Place. The underground granaries on the eastern side of the town were also restored. The Spanish occupation ended in 1598 and the fortress was garrisoned by the French. The ramparts were modernised by the engineer Jean Errard around 1605 and strengthened further around 1630.[13] In spite of its modest garrison it was, therefore, a strong place.

The Duke of York was all for an immediate assault but, with his usual lack of urgency, Son John spent a day and a night constructing lines of circumvallation. It was initially thought that here was no rush, as St-Venant would hold out for some time, but news arrived to hasten matters, to the effect that the town was about to fall. This was brought by one of the Duke of York's men, who had spent several days as a spy in the French camp. A council of war was therefore held on 28 August, after which the Duke of York and Condé inspected the defences using telescopes, from a nearby tower. They then made a closer, personal reconnaissance. Neither Don John nor Caracena bothered themselves with such details, for it was not the Spanish custom for general officers to expose themselves, in marked contrast to the

English and French. As was customary, the town was summoned to surrender, but the governor, as he was honour bound to do, refused.[14] Preparations for the assault then went ahead. The Duke of York recorded that:

> All things being now ready, the army opened the attack as soon as it was night, on a signal from Don Juan's quarters. The besieged had no men to defend the approaches. And so the troops advanced to the edge of the ditch, where they secured a lodgement before attempting to attach the mine. For the Duke of York's attack his own regiment was employed. Lord Muskerry who commanded it had a captain and a few soldiers from other battalions to strengthen him. The Duke took care to send him fascines and everything he needed, and then went to visit the operations with the Duke of Gloucester. He found that Muskerry had ordered everything as it should be, that he had almost finished his lodgement at the edge of the ditch, facing the point of the bastion, and that he had already lodged the body of the battalion in the ditch of the ravelin which covered the point of the bastion.* The duke thought it was now time to attach the mine, but perceiving by moonlight that there was water in the bottom of the ditch, he sent a sergeant to sound it, who reported that the water was not deep enough to prevent the passage of the miners … no details will be given of the other attacks; one may simply say that [if] they had had the same success and attached their mines, it was not doubted that the place would surrender in less than 24 hours.[15]

The Cromwellian English, meanwhile, had also had ample opportunity to show their worth. Morgan was put in command of the main assault on St-Venant with his regiment. His account, which belittles the leadership of both Reynolds and Lockhart and cries up himself, gave details:

> The French King, and his Eminence the Cardinal Mazarine, came to view the six-thousand English near Charleroy; and ordered Major-General Morgan, with the said six-thousand English, to march and make conjunction with Marshal Turenne's army, who, soon after the conjunction, beleaguered a town, called St-Venant, on the borders of Flanders. Marshal Turenne having invested the town on the east side, and Major general Morgan, with his six-thousand English, and a brigade of French horse on the west, the army encamped betwixt Marshal Turenne's approaches and Major-General Morgan's; and, being to relieve Count Schomberg,† out of the approaches of the west-side of the town, Major-General Morgan marched into the approaches, with eight-hundred English. The English, at that time, being strangers in approaches, Major-General Morgan instructed the officers and soldiers to take their places by fifties, that thereby they might relieve the point to carry on the approaches, every hour …
>
> … In the evening, Count Schomberg, with six noblemen, came upon the point, to see how Major-General Morgan carried on his approaches: but there happened a

---

*   This bastion was occupied by a company commanded by Lieutenant de Bauinourt of the Regiment of Rouville (F.-J. Vaillant, p.11).

†   Friedrich Hermann von Schönberg, 1st Duke of Schomberg, 1st Count of Mertola, KG PC (1615–1690) was later a Marshal of France and a General in the English and Portuguese Armies. He was killed fighting for William III of England at the Battle of the Boyne in 1690.

little confusion, by the soldiers intermingling themselves in the approaches, so as there was never an entire fifty to be called to the point. Count Schomberg and his noblemen taking notice thereof, Major-General Morgan was much troubled, leaped upon the point, and called out fifty to take up the spades, pick-axes, and fascines, and follow him. But so it happened, that all in the approaches leaped out after him; the enemy, in the meantime, firing as fast as they could. Major-General Morgan (conceiving his loss, in bringing them again to their approaches, would be greater than in carrying them forward,) passed over a channel of water, on which there was a bridge and a turn-pike; and, the soldiers crying out, "Fall on, fall on" he fell upon the counterscarp, beat the enemy from it, and three redoubts; which caused them to capitulate; and the next morning, to surrender the town, and receive a French garrison; so as the sudden reduction thereof gave Marshal Turenne an opportunity afterwards to march and relieve Ardres.[16]

A slightly different, later, account says of Morgan's actions that:

… on the 26th following,* Providence ordered me to march into the trenches with 600 men, and to carry on the point of the trench to the barricade which entered upon the point of the counterscarp. And having lodged 80 men to work into the ground there, we had a hot dispute with the enemy. The English courage … moved them to leap out of the trenches to come up to us where we were upon plain ground, but our men shouting, firing, and calling "fall on" made me endeavour to get over the enemy's barricade and turnpike, which was soon broke open with the barrel of a musket, and so we entered within their counterscarp, and fell upon a half moon which was moated, and made the enemy quit it and enter the town, so that we wrought into a security, and our loss was 10 men killed, and not 20 wounded. Myself received a slight shot in the arm, which (blessed be God) since recovered with most of our wounded men. Marshal Turenne with most of the nobility of the army have had a high respect for us ever since.[17]

The assault hastened the surrender of the town the next day, 6 August, allowing Turenne to leave a garrison there and march to relieve Ardres. Reynolds wrote exultantly to Cromwell that: 'I rejoice to tell your lordship that the taking of St Venant and the raising of the siege of Ardres, is wholly imputed to our English forces, of whom there is so high an esteem as is scarcely credible.'[18]

On hearing the news, Don John's council of war decided to raise the siege of Ardres:

The difficulty was to withdraw the troops from the attacking positions; there had been no time to make siege works and entrenchments, so they could only drawback in the open. The operation began by bringing back the miners, which was done in the duke's position by the care of Lord Muskerry … The Duke of York on his side ordered a lieutenant with thirty horsemen, to approach the place as near as possible without exposing himself until he saw the soldiers returning from

---

* 5 August N.S.

A view of Ardres around 1650, by Matthäus Merian. (Author's collection)

the attacking position and then to … bring away any officers and men who might fall wounded … although the besieged opened a heavy fire, no officers except Captain Knight and but a few soldiers were wounded, and none died, which was as fortunate as it was extraordinary. A few miners were lost from other attacks. After the troops were everywhere drawn back with very little loss, the baggage train was sent towards Gravelines, and the whole army followed. The march was extremely painful. On arriving at the edge of the lowlands, they were obliged to halt until the cannon and baggage were on the dyke or causeway which leads from Polincour[t] to Gravelines and which heavy rain had made impossible. The rain continued without ceasing. The tempest, the darkness of the night, the road heavy with mud and the frequent halts thay had to make, distressed the troops and threw them into so great a disorder that it was impossible for the officers to prevent their breaking ranks and seeking cover where they could. In the morning there were not ten men together in one regiment.[19]

Over the next days, the army was drawn back behind the Bergues – Dunkirk canal in a strong defensive position, with the fortress of Dunkirk on the right flank and that of Mardyck as an outlying position in front of the line.

If the English, Scots and Irish troops in the Spanish army were not in a good way, it cannot be said that the English in Turenne's army were on top form. Pay was six months in arrears; Turenne had been forced to cut up

OPENING MOVES: THE SIEGES OF MONTMÉDY, ST-VENANT AND ARDRES, JUNE–SEPTEMBER, 1657

silver plate during the siege of St-Venant and pay the troops by weight. The brown ammunition bread was also not what the men were used to, and this, supplemented by fruit and water, caused a good deal of stomach trouble. Morgan commented that this had: 'brought them into a great sickness and much discouraged them, insomuch that they make all the shifts they can to get into England, notwithstanding that we take all possible care.'[20] Some men went so far as to desert to the Royalists. The result of sickness, casualties and desertion was that by early September, Reynolds told Henry Cromwell that he now had less than 4,000 effectives,[21] and begged to be recalled.

Lockhart, meanwhile, had been lobbying Mazarin for a change in the focus of the campaign, arguing that operations inland were not part of the agreement with Cromwell. If Dunkirk and Mardyck were ignored, then the English brigade would be removed. Cromwell urged him to press this line and on 31 August he was ordered to deliver an ultimatum:

> I pray you to tell the Cardinal from me, that I think, if France desires to maintain its ground, much more to get ground from the Spaniards, the performance of his treaty with us will better do it than anything yet appears to me of any design he hath. Though we cannot pretend to soldiery as those that are with him, yet we think that, we being able by sea to strengthen and secure his siege, and to reinforce it as we please by sea, the best time to besiege that place will be now …

… And therefore, if this will not be listened unto, I desire that things may be considered of to give us satisfaction for the great expense we have been at with our naval forces and otherwise, which out of an honourable and honest aim on our part hath been done, that we might answer our engagements. And that consideration may be had how our men may be put in a posture to be returned to us, whom we hope to employ to a better purpose than to have them continue where they are.[22]

Lockhart duly delivered Cromwell's message, which caused sufficient consternation for the French ambassador, Antoine de Bordeaux-Neufville, to be joined by Turenne's *Intendant*, Claude Talon.* The two represented Turenne's view that having taken St-Venant he had secured the crossings of the Lys and also taken Bourbourg, which opened the way for operations against Dunkirk. He fully intended to move against the ports, but it was now too late in the year to do more than besiege Mardyck, a necessary step towards the seizure of Dunkirk. Cromwell was far from happy, contending that Mardyck would be expensive to repair and garrison through the winter, remarking that time had been wasted in the summer. Although unsatisfied, Cromwell eventually agreed, promising 2,000 more men and an increase to 25 ships in the blockading squadron.[23] On 13 September, Reynolds informed Cromwell that Turenne was on the move and asked Montagu, commanding the Channel squadron, to blockade Mardyck and Dunkirk.[24] He also asked Cromwell for siege artillery and mortars to be shipped by sea along with his reinforcements, as well as biscuit and fodder for the horses that would draw the guns.

The Spanish, meanwhile, were preparing for the expected arrival of Turenne. On 17 September Turenne crossed the Canal de Colme and the Spanish pulled back to avoid being outflanked:[25] the native Spanish *tercios* with some of the horse went to Gravelines; the Italians were sent to Mardyck under the command of Don Tito del Prato; and the rest of the army held the line of the Bergues – Dunkirk canal, throwing up strong batteries of guns along the line of the water obstacle. Don John himself was at Dunkirk, Condé at Bergues and the Duke of York at Coudekerke. The stage was now set for the siege of Mardyck.

Frederick Hermann, 1st Duke of Schomberg, engraved by Simon Gribelin after Michael Dahl's portrait. (Author's collection)

---

* Not to be confused with Jean Talon, Count d'Orsainville (1626–1694) the first Intendant of New France.

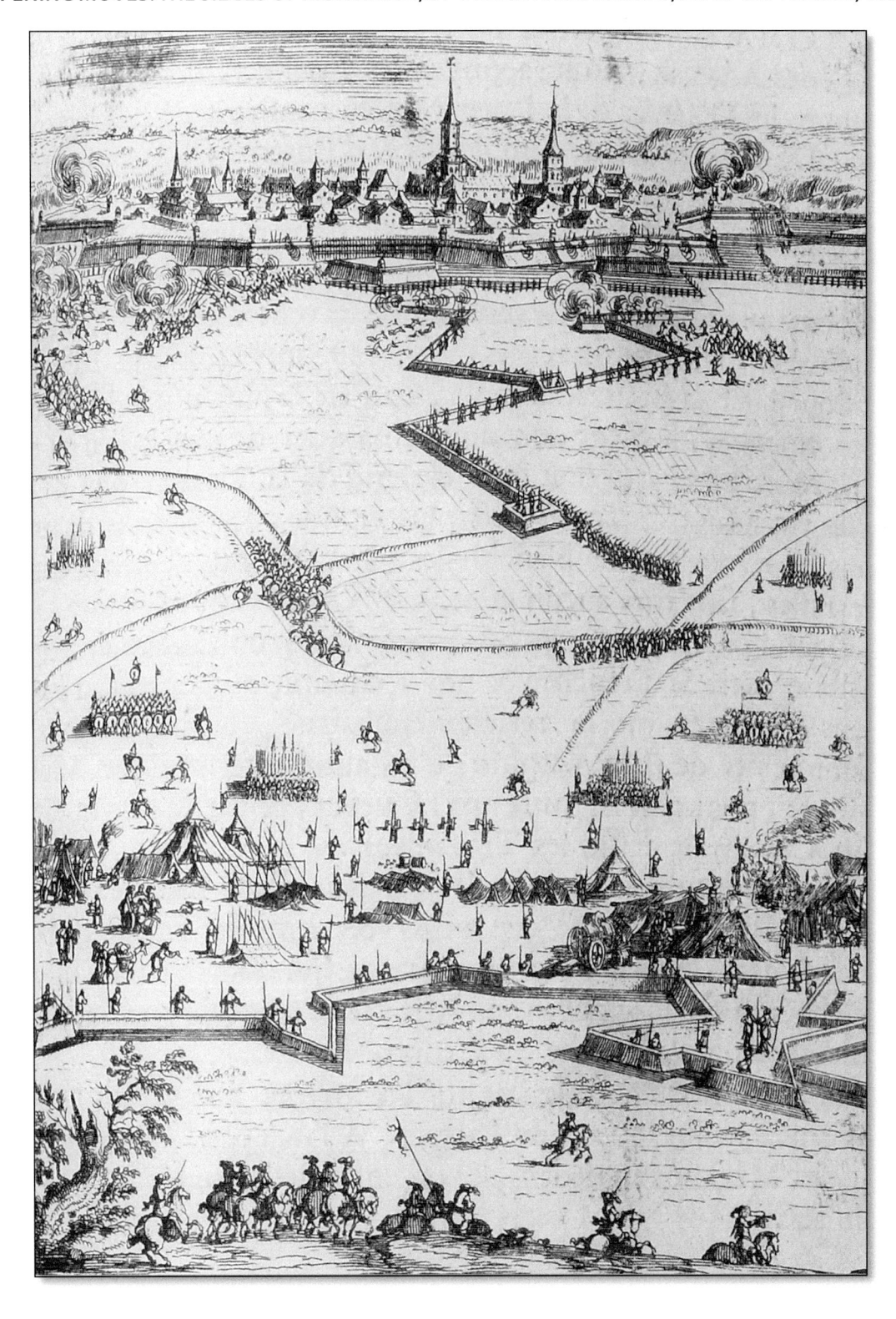

OPENING MOVES: THE SIEGES OF MONTMÉDY, ST-VENANT AND ARDRES, JUNE–SEPTEMBER, 1657

Assaulting a fortified place, from Allain Mallet, *Les Traveaux de Mars*, vol. i, p.241 (<https://digi.ub.uni-heidelberg.de> accessed 2 January 2020).

Appendix to Chapter 13

The Garrison of Ardres

Staff
Governor and Colonel: M. Rouville
Major: M. Duplessis
Adjutant: Captain de la Chaussée

Troop of Horse	**Artillery**	**Gendarmes**
M. de Baure	Captain Phillipe Damas	Le Sieur de la Guardière
40 men	Lieutenant André Damas	16 men
	Lieutenant Leger de la Gaurdière	

Company of Foot	**Company of Foot**	**Company of Foot**
Captain de Valéry	Captain Dauril	Captain Nicolas Gouge
Lieutenant de Bauincourt	Lieutenant Bourgeois (Swiss)	
100 men	100 men	100 men

14

The Siege and Occupation of Mardyck, September 1657– April 1658

In the 1650s, Mardyck had one of the best harbours on the coast and was defended by a square, four-bastioned stone and earth fort, as well as a wooden fort built on piles jutting out into the sea. It was defended by a garrison of about 700 men, with 10 guns.[1]

The French army approached Mardyck, having left behind most of the horse and the six English regiments, on Saturday 26September 1657. A line of entrenchments was constructed between Mardyck and Dunkirk, which was only five miles away, to prevent the Spanish from sending a relief force. James, Duke of York, went to observe what was happening, taking with him:

> … the Horse Guards who were outside the gates of Dunkirk and advancing to within cannon shot he left the Guards behind to secure his retreat in case he should be pursued. He then, with fifteen officers and other men well mounted, rode up so near the French army, that some officers of the Regiment of Picardy, which was on the march, advanced some way and fired on him with carbines they were carrying when on horseback. When they reached the quarter which had been assigned to them and the soldiers began to build their huts, these officers and several from other regiments rode out again to drive back the Duke. But some of them who came near the Prince recognised a big greyhound they had seen with him in France and asked if the Duke of York was there. When they were told that he was, they crie[d] out 'Sur parole', desiring to speak with him. He then stopped, and found among them several persons of the first quality who were all of old acquaintance. They alighted from their horses; the Prince did the same; and they conversed together for nearly an hour until Monsieur de Turenne ordered them to come back … This episode is related particularly that it may be observed what civility is used in that country even between enemies or persons of opposed parties, and that the Duke, although in the service of Spain, had no fewer friends in the French army.[2]

COLONIAL IRONSIDES

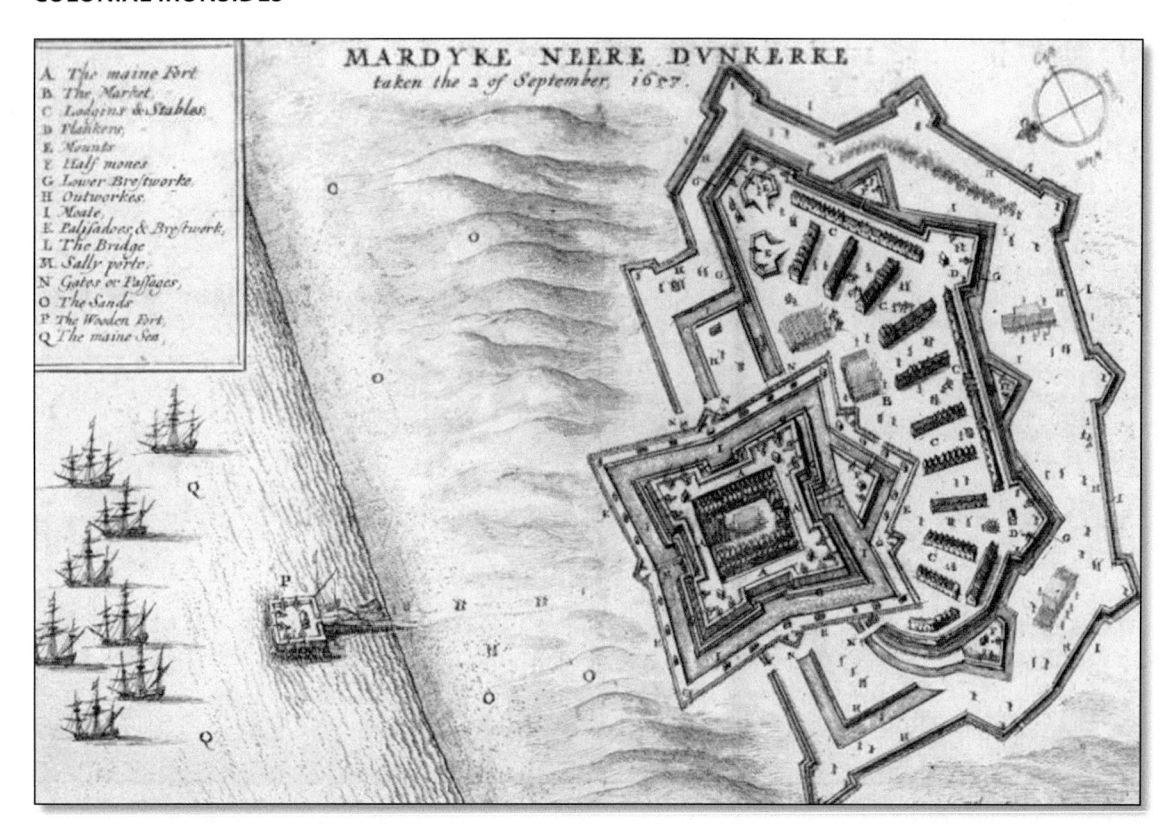

Mardyck in 1658, by Wenceslaus Hollar; the pier and wooden fort can clearly be seen. (B.M. 1872,0113.589)

The French army set to work constructing siege lines and also foraging close to the Spanish defences of Dunkirk. Three large farms, belonging to relatives of Spanish officers, had continued to operate and were even guarded – although when the French approached, the guard immediately withdrew.

> The cannon in the Spanish lines opened fire when the vanguard of the enemy approached. The Duke of York, whose quarters were only half a mile from there, galloped up and found the French were already working to get cover and entrench themselves so as to defend themselves in case of an attack.[3]

James soon met the Prince de Ligne, who was acting as *Maestre de Campo General* that day, and asked him what he intended. Not surprisingly, Ligne answered that without orders from Caracena or Don John, he would do nothing. The Duke of York answered that if nothing was done, the French would entrench themselves and then they would not be dislodged, nor could their forage be destroyed. He then told Ligne that he and his troops would attack the French and asked for support – but Ligne replied that a bridge which must be used to mount such an attack was in the hands of Spanish troops, and the Duke would not be permitted to pass.[4] And so the French foraged on, undisturbed, other than by cannon fire which killed a large number of horses. Condé also arrived, drawn by the noise of firing and the Duke told him what was happening. Condé (one can see him shrugging in that Gallic way) replied that when the Duke had been in the Spanish service as long as he had been, nothing would surprise him.

THE SIEGE AND OCCUPATION OF MARDYCK, SEPTEMBER 1657–APRIL 1658

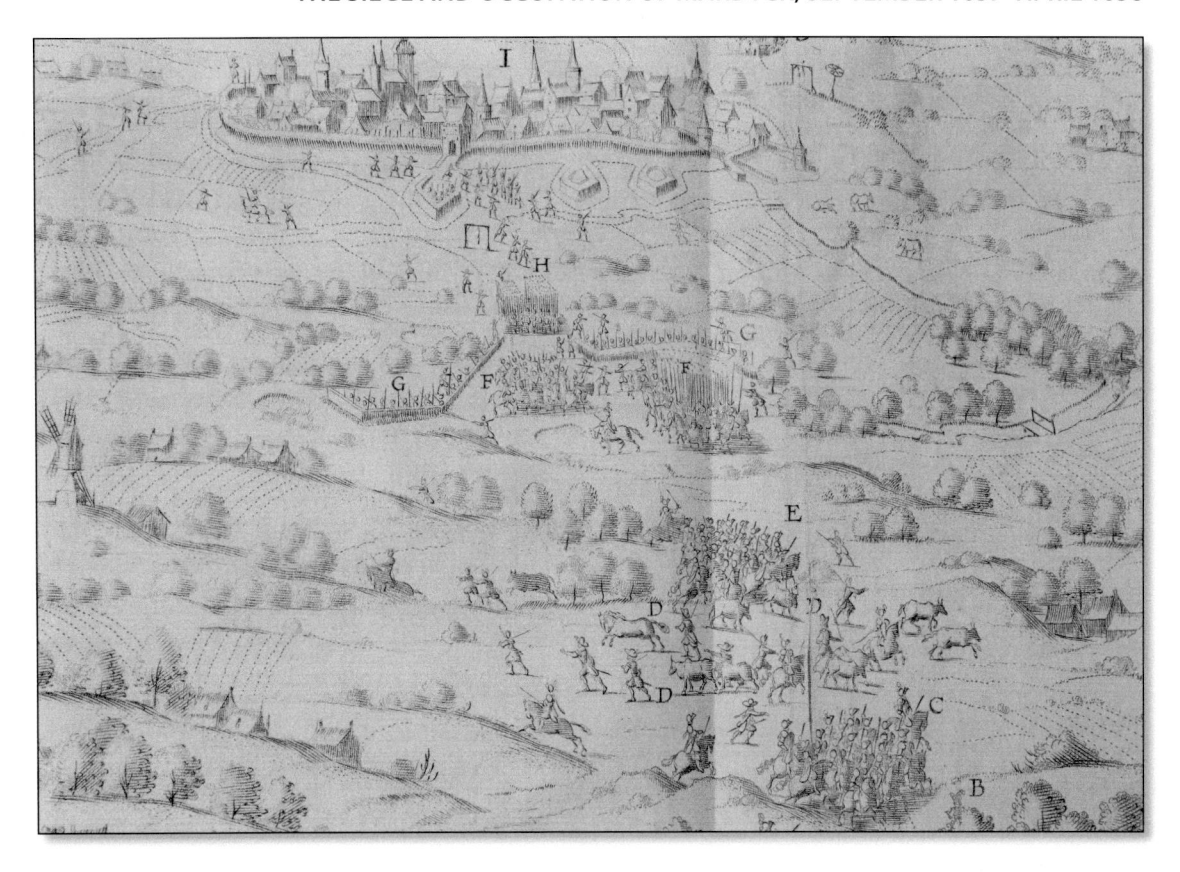

Troops foraging, from Ludovico Melzo, *Regole della cavalleri*. (© Royal Armouries RAL.08686)

On the night of Monday, 28 September, the French artillery opened an initial bombardment on the fort and pioneers began to advance the saps for an assault. Offshore, the English naval squadron under General Edward Montagu was in place, maintaining a close blockade on both Mardyck and Dunkirk.* The wooden fort was evacuated by the garrison and taken by the French almost at once. On Tuesday the 29th, the counterscarp was taken and the garrison summoned to surrender, which it did at noon on the following day, 30 September.[5] In accordance with the treaty, Mardyck was immediately handed over to the English and Colonel Francis White was appointed governor,[6] with 800 men in the garrison.

Cromwell urged that Dunkirk should immediately be attacked, offering to send another 5,000 troops, but Turenne preferred to move against the fortress of Gravelines, further away from Dunkirk. Gravelines was one of the strongest Spanish-held towns in the Low Countries, well fortified and surrounded by three tide-filling ditches. The move against it was made in early October when Morgan took a force of 400 foot and 50 horse from Mardyck, with an equal number of French troops from Bourbourg to capture and destroy two stone forts which stood nearby and a sluice controlling the water levels in the dykes. The attack was abandoned when the defenders

---

* No record of the names of the ships in the Channel squadron has survived other than the flagship, the *Naseby*.

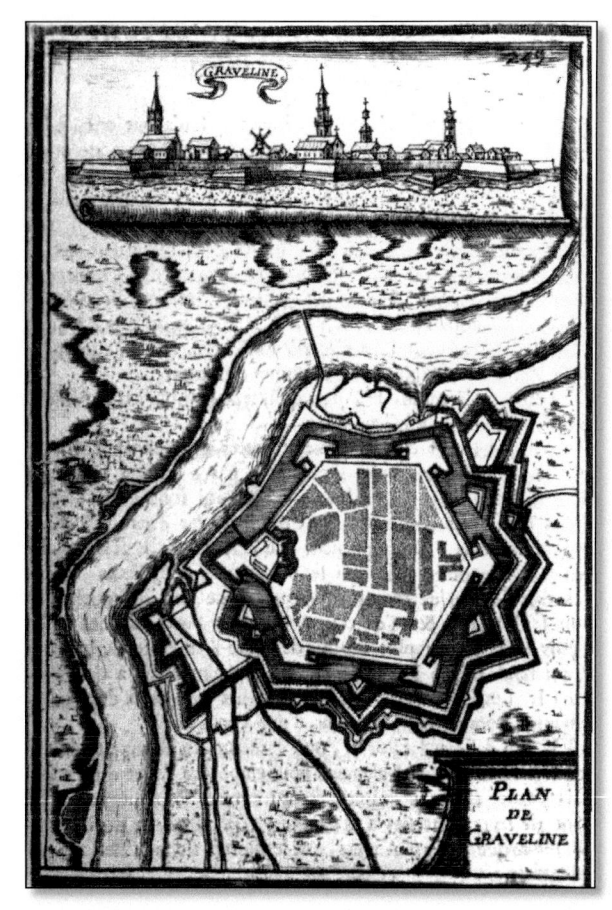

View and plan of Gravelines from Allain Mallet, *Les Traveaux de Mars,* vol. iii, p.245 (<https://digi.ub.uni-heidelberg.de> accessed 20 January 2020).

broke the dykes and flooded the surrounding country. A plan to place more of the English troops near Calais also had to be abandoned, 'as bad as the weather is, we cannot march one half day without great loss of our men',[7] and therefore it would be impossible to support Mardyck in case it was attacked in force.

Because of the problems in defending Mardyck, labour was constantly required to keep the harbour and works clear of shifting sand. On 8 December, a storm carried away part of the old wooden pier in the harbour, which meant that ships had to be unloaded into lighters offshore, further increasing the workload.[8] The fort could really only comfortably accommodate 500 men. Reynolds intended to extend the fortifications to accommodate a garrison of 2,000 horse and foot. The measures included three new bastions and accommodation for the troops. On 6 October, Reynolds reported that the fort 'may be sufficiently maintained against a storm or sudden surprise, but may easily be gained by one week's approaches', and that the work of extension would be difficult in winter not least because of the lack of timber in the area.[9]

The Duke of York reported the work at Mardyck thus: 'The English at Mardyke started repairing the old fortifications around that fortress, work which was all the easier because the ditches had not been filled in and only a small part of the parapet had been levelled.'[10] Don John was told of this and decided to march the Spanish army back to Mardyck and wreck the work. On 14 October, an agent reported to the English in Mardyck that:

> There is intelligence that the enemy have effected all their preparations in order to the storm of Mardyke and intend putting it into execution within two nights. If they do, they will be very honourably received, for there is very considerable strength in the fort and many of them men of much gallantry. It is my opinion that 20,000 will but fool themselves to make an attempt, judging it a matter of extraordinary difficulty to gain the place except they be so much masters of the field as to make their approaches by degrees, so as to force the shipping out of the Splinter, and hinder the constant supply of victuals.[11]

It was not until 22 October that Don John led a force of about 5,000 Spanish, with English and Irish Royalists and some of Condé's troops, from Dunkirk in an attempt to recapture Mardyck before the English could finish repairing and extending the fortifications. Charles II, the Duke of York and the Marquis of Ormonde accompanied the Spanish force. The attackers approached by night under torchlight, which was seen by the defenders, and

THE SIEGE AND OCCUPATION OF MARDYCK, SEPTEMBER 1657–APRIL 1658

they in turn lit beacons around their perimeter. When the attackers were within cannon shot they put out their lights and the foot began to advance. The Spaniards marched to that part of the outworks that looked towards Dunkirk (north-east), the Comte de Marsin with the Prince of Condé's foot, to the part that looks towards Gravelines (south-west); and the Duke of York, at the head of his troops, posted himself between the two:

> When they approached the fort, the enemy kept up a continual fire of cannon and musketry, and the little frigates that were in the canal did not cease firing either. The infantry suffered very little because they got straight into the shelter of the old outworks; but the balls which passed over their heads fell among the cavalry and killed men and horses. His Majesty [Charles II] having gone forward to see what the infantry were doing, the Duke of Ormonde who was with him had his horse killed under him by a cannon shot. Each corps, on arriving at its position, sent its workmen forward with soldiers to support them. But the ditch was too deep in the Duke of York's position and he was obliged to send them round to where the Spaniards were to attack. In the meantime he had the ditch filled in with fascines,* and caused a passage over to be made so that he could support them if the enemy made a sortie.
>
> While the workmen were beginning to raze the fortifications, the soldiers who had been detached in support kept up a continual fire on the enemy, and continued to do this until early dawn, when, the outworks having been razed, the army drew off in good order and arrived at Dunkirk where it was beginning to be broad daylight.
>
> The enemy were surely more surprised by the retreat than the attack, and they so little expected the Spaniards to retire so soon that they were still firing when the troops had been gone a good half-hour. There were not more than twenty horsemen, a captain of Gloucester's regiment and three or four soldiers killed; there were eight or ten wounded. The English in the fort, as was learned since, had only one man killed. And they so firmly believed that they would be besieged, that they despatched a message to monsieur de Turenne to warn him of it. He assembled his troops who were in forage quarters and began to march to their help; but on being advised that the Spaniards had drawn off, he returned to his quarters.[12]

Sir Edward Hyde later pleaded with Charles not to risk his life in such a way again: 'I am none of those that think that you are like to recover your three kingdoms without being in danger of your life, but let it be when the adventure is of use and there is some recompense in view.'[13] The upshot was that thereafter, Charles left the conduct of military operations to the Duke of York.

A second, seaward, attack came 10 days later when 12 armed shallops, small coastal craft able to carry up to a dozen men, attempted to enter the

---

* Fascines are long bundles of wooden poles or staves lashed together to make a solid but flexible tube; they were sometimes called 'sausages'. They are still in use but made of synthetic materials and are used to fill in ditches or other gaps, sometimes then faced with a road surface such as a corduroy road, for the passage of vehicles.

harbour to seize the English frigates *Rose* and *Truelove*: 'The first design had been to burn them, but this being judged too difficult, it was resolved to try to surprise the two larger ships … which mounted six or eight cannon each …'[14] Charles II and the Duke of York, with many courtiers, went along to watch the affair from the shore; however the weather turned misty. An alert seaman on one of the ships raised the alarm, calling out 'what ship's boat is that?' and receiving no reply, fired a cannon shot which injured one of the oarsmen in the nearest shallop; the attackers were then 'shamefully' frightened off by musket fire.[15]

A report sent to Cromwell added more details, stating that Don John had supported the attempt with 700 horse to draw the attention of the garrison and also employ a fireship: 'Such as came by land frighted our men so much that they quitted the counterscarp and retreated to the fosse border very unworthily which is a great trouble to us. The fault must be in some officers, for where they stand, the soldiers never flee.' The repulse of the attack had, however, heartened the men: 'Our old soldiers hath gained their old courage, and stand stoutly to their work …'[16]

Tension between the French government and Cromwell was, however, rising, for Turenne felt that Mardyck was too vulnerable to attack and should be demolished. To Cromwell, this smacked of betrayal and in spite of his earlier misgivings he warned Ambassador Bordeaux-Neufville that such a move would terminate the alliance. Cromwell further demanded that the French government bear the entire costs of the English army until Dunkirk should be taken, a demand that Mazarin, not surprisingly, rejected. A compromise was reached in that Reynolds was appointed Governor of Mardyck by Louis XIV, while money and engineering expertise would be provided to assist in extending the fortifications. In addition, 300 horse would be positioned so as to support Mardyck and Bourbourg in case of attack, along with the regiments of French and Swiss Guards at Calais and Boulogne when the army went into winter quarters in November. As a measure of goodwill, Mazarin sent some of his own guard as well as the King's musketeers to help garrison the town, with the engineers, a total of 100 men.[17] Bad feeling at high level inevitably caused tensions lower down; as late as April 1658, English soldiers killed some of the King's Guards in a fight, and allegedly were neither punished nor apprehended by Morgan.[18]

The situation of the place was, however, low-lying and unhealthy, and the soldiers were badly provided with necessaries of every kind. The regiments of the English contingent quartered there, and the 2,000 men who quartered at the town of Bourbourg, four miles away, and also the 3,000 who remained with the French army in its winter quarters on the borders of Artois, all suffered badly from sickness, probably typhus, which is spread by fleas and lice in crowded places and exhibits the symptoms described by many at the time. One report said that: 'We have abundance of sick men … It takes them with giddiness in the head, and distracts, many swellings in the legs and joints, violent fever, and agues of all sorts. Several die daily …'[19] Lieutenant Colonel Richard Hughes, of Cochrane's Regiment, reported on 4 November that: 'the sick of all the army are a very sad sight to behold … we have neither straw or covering save what we pay for.'[20] In the days before a regular commissariat supplied materials, men had to make shelter for themselves and here, the shortage of timber made the building of huts very difficult, so that around one-third of the garrison was under canvas in the damp, crowded conditions of Flanders.[21]

By the end of January around 1,000 men were sick, including officers, and death rates were around 10 per day. The English contingent was reduced from 6,000 to 3,000 men, making a total loss of about 5,000 men since its landing in Flanders; Reynolds reported that there were only 1,800 men fit for duty in Mardyck and Bourbourg.[22] Although regiments had a surgeon, few surgeons if any were physicians; and in any case the treatment of conditions like typhus was not understood. Dr John French, a chemist chiefly remembered for his works on distillation, practising as a physician at Ely, was appointed Physician General of the army in Flanders at a monthly salary of £14.[23] An apothecary, Abel Clark, also accompanied the army. French did not last long – in December 1657, his widow petitioned for a pension;[24] Dr Saltonhall succeeded him, at a greater salary, evidenced by his being given an advance of £50 on appointment.[25] Many of the sick were taken to the French hospital at St Quentin, but as death rates among the French troops were even higher than among the English, this helped but little, if at all. Many deserted in the hope of faring better with the Royalists, including one group which stole Reynolds's treasure chest. Others were taken back for care in England, their care in coastal towns in Kent and Sussex paid for in theory by the naval Sick and Hurt Board.[26]

The Royalists at Coudekerke also suffered badly, the only known physician being Dr Richard Wiseman, who had served in the Spanish navy as well as with the King in exile:[27]

Surgeons treating a wounded officer. (Wellcome Library, London)

> Few of the officers or soldiers, excepting only the natural Spaniards, escaped agues; insomuch that wee had never half our men together in a condition of doing duty. It fell most severely on those troops I commanded; for, excepting myself, there was scarcely an officer or volunteer of quality, or any of my servants, who was free from an ague. My brother the Duke of Gloucester went out of the army sick of that distemper; and the Prince of Condé was seiz'd with it to that degree that he was once given over by the phisitians.[28]

Reynolds continually wrote for reinforcements and supplies for his diminishing army. As early as November he had demanded, and perhaps obtained, 500 fresh men from England.[29] At the same time he urged Turenne to send back to Mardyck the three regiments of English serving with the French field army, which were then stationed in winter quarters near Guisnes, where they suffered little less than their comrades at Mardyck.[30] In January 1658, General D'Ormesson reported to Ambassador Bordeaux-Neufville that he had sent troops from Guisnes to Mardyck, all feeble and with very few officers; that the foot companies were only around half-strength and that the officers were claiming the pay of non-existent men, a usual practice at the time.[31] In fact estimates of troop strength varied considerably: Reynolds claimed in December 1657 that there were no more than 1,800 of his men fit for duty in the whole of Flanders;[32] another contemporary account gives 1,400 English and 700 French at Mardyck alone in December.[33] The French claimed that English strength was 3,733 in November and in Mardyck in December there were 52 officers, 1,060 men and 36 dragoons, with another 240 men sick. French numbers at Mardyck had shrunk to 38 officers and 307 men.[34]

As the garrison was within five miles of Dunkirk there were occasionally informal meetings between officers of the two English forces. At one meeting, Reynolds had met and talked to the Duke of York. Only compliments and civilities were exchanged but the meeting aroused suspicion among some of the officers at Mardyck, so that Reynolds was compelled to return to England to assure the Protector of his loyalty.[35] One correspondent, a supporter of Reynolds, told Secretary Thurloe that: 'It is given out by some of Charles Stuart's faction here, that something passed at that meeting that I know he could not be capable of …'[36]

Reynolds also felt compelled to return in order to press the matter of reinforcements, taking Francis White with him. Leave to return was arranged with the Protector by his father-in-law.[37] On 5 December 1657 the ship *Bramble*, taking him home, was wrecked on the Goodwin Sands and Reynolds, White and others were drowned.[38] He was replaced as governor and commander of the English brigade by Sir Thomas Morgan, although Cromwell superseded Morgan with Sir William Lockhart in the spring of 1658.

In an attempt to increase efficiency, Turenne demanded that the six understrength English regiments should be reduced to four, each with 1,000 men, and to make money available to raise two new regiments. There were in addition rumours of a further Spanish attack: 'For the space of four months, there was hardly a week, wherein Major-General Morgan had not two or three alarms by the Spanish army. He answered them all, and never went out of his clothes all the winter, except to change his shirt.'[39] Five companies of Colonel Robert Gibbon's Regiment, which had been raised in October 1656, were therefore sent from Kent to Mardyck.[40] Gibbon had been commissioned in the previous year to raise a regiment in Kent against a suspected Royalist uprising. Cromwell also gave warning the remainder of Gibbon's Regiment, and that of Salmon, quartered in Kent to be ready to embark at short notice.[41]

It is possible that the balance of companies from Gibbon's Regiment arrived soon afterwards, but returned to England after only a month, as the garrison now numbered 1,400 English foot, 300 French foot, 250 horse and 200 officers; their places were filled by men drawn from regiments quartered with the French.

Lockhart, wisely, did not demand further large reinforcements during the winter for Mardyck. 'I do not believe', said he, 'that the cramming it with great numbers of men will signify much for its defence.'[42] So long as the English squadron under Vice-Admiral William Goodson, commanded the approaches, the place could be well supplied and reinforced whenever the Spaniards should attack it. The English naval dominance also stopped a rumoured landing by Charles II, with 3,000 troops and arms for 12,000 more, on the English coast in January 1658.[43] Not that the Royalist army was in much of a state to make such an attempt. Irish recruits continued to come in from French service, although Lockhart regarded them as 'no better than sheep in a lion's skin'.[44] A few English also came in, some were deserters from Lockhart's brigade and perhaps 100 joined from French service.[45] There were inevitably disputes between the Commonwealth deserters and the exiled Royalists, and even more so with the Irish as the two sides detested each other. Duels were not uncommon: the Earl of Newburgh was a frequent duellist – he was not, as is sometimes reported, killed at this time as he went on to serve at the Dunes and died in 1670. In September 1657, the Duke of York's quartermaster general, Corail, attacked Taaffe with a cudgel; Corail was brought before the Duke who at a court martial sentenced him that he should: '… on his knees beg pardon of Lord Taaffe, presenting him with a stick to use as he pleases.'[46]

There had also clearly been trouble between the King's Guards and the burghers of Dixmüde, where the men were to have received quarters and an allowance for food. This seems to have been rejected by the townspeople, leading to a fight in which five soldiers had been killed. There was also a dispute about the command of the regiment between Sir William Throckmorton and Lieutenant-Colonel Thomas Blague, or Blagge – probably brought about by the merger of the two original Guards regiments into one.[47] The only real action came on 28 December [7 January 1658 N.S.] when the Spanish brought a convoy of 800 carts, escorted by 4,000 horse, to supply Gravelines. The convoy passed close enough to Mardyck to be fired on from the fort and the ships in the harbour.[48]

With no prospect of action either in Flanders or England, the Royalists too went into winter quarters, awaiting the return of good weather in the spring. That winter was hard – one report in early February 1685 stated that: 'We have had a very sharp winter here with great Frosts, which hath caused us to break the ice twice a day, to keep our moots open. The enemy is so straitned of [fire]wood, that they are forced to make use of the timber of their houses.'[49]

As for the fort of Mardyck, the improvements were reported as complete on 12 February 1659, less the stabling for the horses.[50] it remained garrisoned by English troops until 1662, of which more is said in Chapter 19. It was then sold to the French and was eventually demolished under Louis XV. Today, no trace remains of either the fort or of the old village of Mardyck. The areas of Fort Mardyck and Mardyck are now unappealing suburbs and huge industrial zones to the west of Dunkirk.

On the political front during the winter there were developments. The Anglo-French alliance was valid only for one year. In February, Lockhart urged Thurloe to make the English government's intentions clear: '… his eminence [Cardinal Mazarin] is very patient, though desirous that no more time is lost.'[51] Thurloe, on Cromwell's behalf, was guarded – perhaps wishing to avoid another situation like that of 1657 where the French, instead of moving on the coastal fortresses, had campaigned much further inland: 'They must declare their intention as to what they resolve to do this spring, and by what means and in what manner they intend to endeavour.'[52] On 16 March, Mazarin met Lockhart and the two agreed the basis for a renewal of the treaty. The French would attack Dunkirk by sea and land, between 20 April and 10 May and no other operations would take precedence. The attack on land would be supported by the English brigade and the Channel fleet would maintain the blockade by sea. Once Dunkirk was secure, both English naval and land forces would support a French advance on Gravelines.

On the English side, the most urgent requirement was to make good the losses in the brigade in time for the campaign Mazarin had been urging this for some time and in March, Lockhart stated that 4,000 more men would be needed. Mazarin provided funds for 3,000 but recruiting was slow: by mid May, 2,500 men, mostly untrained recruits, had arrived in Flanders. To bolster the strength, five companies of Gibbon's Regiment, which had been returned to England, and five of Salmon's Regiment, all under the command of Lieutenant-Colonel John Pepper, were sent from Kent.[53]

There were manoeuvrings too among the English Royalists. The Duke of York reported that the Earl of Bristol had proposed that the King should join his forces with Condé, the two together making a considerable army that would oblige the Spanish to be more open-handed – a proposal that was soon squashed.[54] As James recorded:

> All our thoughts at Bruxelles were now taken up with our preparations for the ensuing Campagne; and, as the time of action was approaching, the Spaniards applyd their greatest care in providing for those places, which they judg'd were in greatest danger … His Mty [Charles II] press'd them very much to recruit Duinkirk with a strong garrison, letting them know, that he was assured by his letters from England, and by others which he had found means to intercept from thence, That the first thing the French would undertake would be to besiege the Town …'[55]

This good warning, based on sound intelligence, was not heeded – with results that were to cost the Spanish dearly.

15

The Siege of Dunkirk and the Battle of the Dunes, June 1658

The campaign of 1658 opened at sea well before it commenced on land. On 27 February, the squadron under Goodson imposed a blockade on the port of Ostende, capturing or destroying six Dutch ships that had been hired by the Spanish to transport Charles II's invasion force to England.[1] Thurloe noted that this had caused Charles to postpone any attempts in this direction until September;[2] it was later deferred again until December. The presence of Goodson's ships also prevented the Spanish reinforcement by sea, or the supply of money, from the garrisons of Laredo, Corunna and San Sebastian, the usual routes used by the Army of Flanders.[3] The importance of the sea corridor can be judged by the fact that in My 1655, for example, the Spanish fleet transported 500,000 *escudos* in coin in May 1655 – a temporary easing of the almost constant financial crises of the Spanish Netherlands in the 1650s.[4]

In spite of the warning from Charles II, Don John was convinced that the Anglo-French army would move first on Cambrai, which was therefore strongly garrisoned. Other troops were sent into Artois and Hainault, while many of the Duke of York's men were sent to St-Omer,[5] all at the expense of Dunkirk and indeed the main field army. Moreover, the defences of Dunkirk were neglected: two forts, each with four bastions, were left unfinished on the Bergues Canal, 'which if they had been perfected and man'd, would haue render'd the Siege of Dunkirk a much more difficult piece of work.'[6] Ammunition resupply was also neglected.

Although they had undertaken to prioritise Dunkirk, the French army began operations in late April by besieging the fortress of Hesdin in Artois which, to the embarrassment of Mazarin, had gone over to Condé. The governor, Balthazar Fargues, and the Marquis de Hocquaincourt with his regiment, changed sides. Hocquaincourt had been at loggerheads with Mazarin since 1653 when Mazarin had sent him to Catalonia and attempted to have him replaced as governor of Peronne. This change of allegiance was the result of two years of secret negotiations.[7] After a short and half-hearted attempt to invest the town, Turenne was obliged to abandon the siege at the insistence of Lockhart. The French suffered another reverse at Ostende, where negotiations had been in play with Colonel Sebastian Spindler

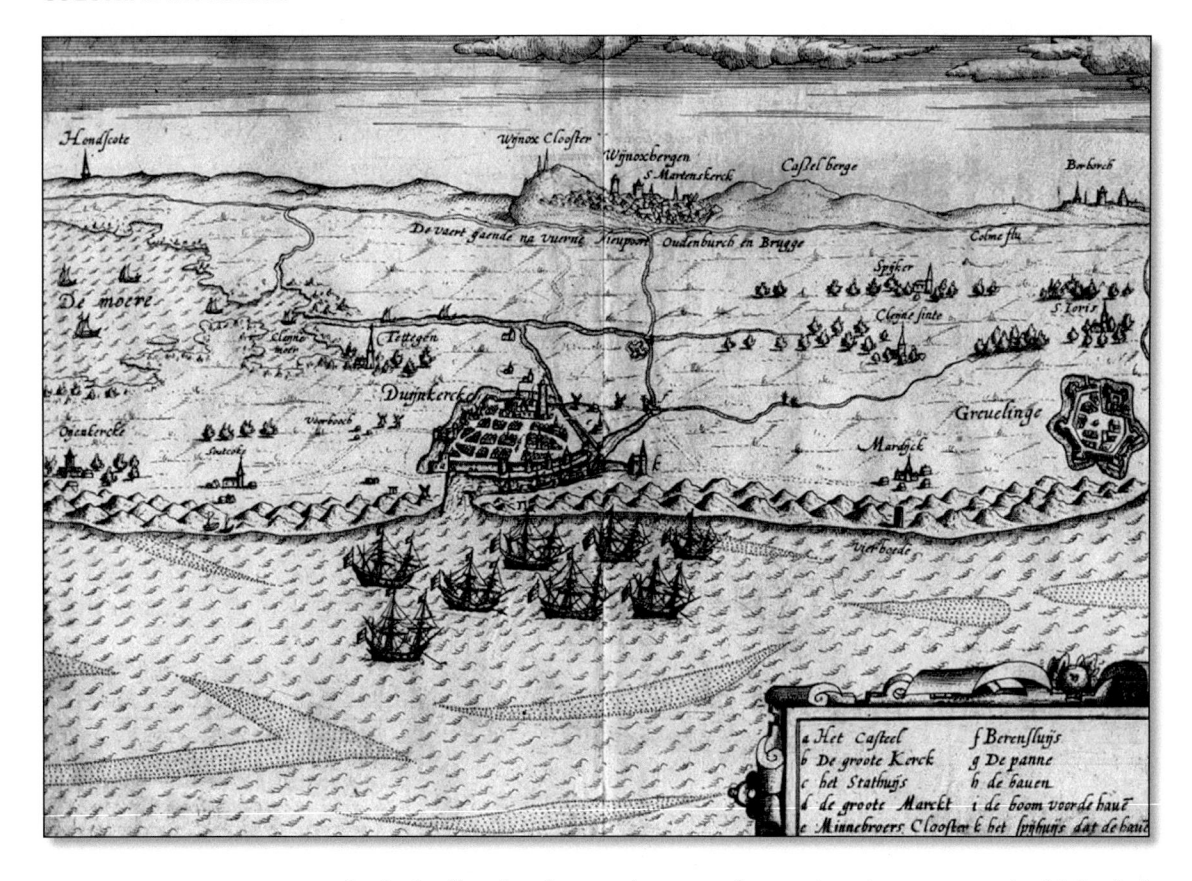

A view of Dunkirk from the sea in 1613, by Ludovico Guicciardini. This shows the town and harbour, the fort of Mardyck, the dunes, various canals and waterways and also other small towns and villages in the vicinity. (Author's collection)

who had offered to betray the town for a price. A report reached Marshal d'Aumont, the Governor of Calais, that there had been a revolt in Ostende. On 14 May he attempted to land there with 1,500 men from the Regiment of Lorraine, two companies of French Guards, some King's Musketeers and a company of English troops from Mardyck. As the force entered the town they were ambushed by Spanish troops. The French surrendered and were later marched in triumph through Brussels.[8]

Not all went against the French, however, for when in May they marched through the town of Cassel their vanguard, commanded by General François de Blanchefort, captured the entire Regiment of the Duke of Gloucester, 400 strong, which had been: 'very unadvisedly sent thither by Monsr. De Bascourt a Mareshall de battaille, under whose command were all the Troopes which acted on that side of the Country, it being a place not possibly to be defended …'[9] It is also clear that in terms of financial resources, the French were far more able to support a war than were the Spanish. As has already been noted, the funds available to the Spanish Netherlands from the central exchequer had declined by three-quarters over a period of less than five years. This was compounded by three factors: first, the lack of funds from the Holy Roman Empire, caused by the need to set aside money to assure the election of a Habsburg after the death of Ferdinand III in April 1657; secondly, the seizure of the silver fleet at Tenerife by the English (see Chapter 10); and last the inability of the Spanish provinces themselves to raise money through taxation, while in the grip of war.[10] Subsidy was required to maintain the

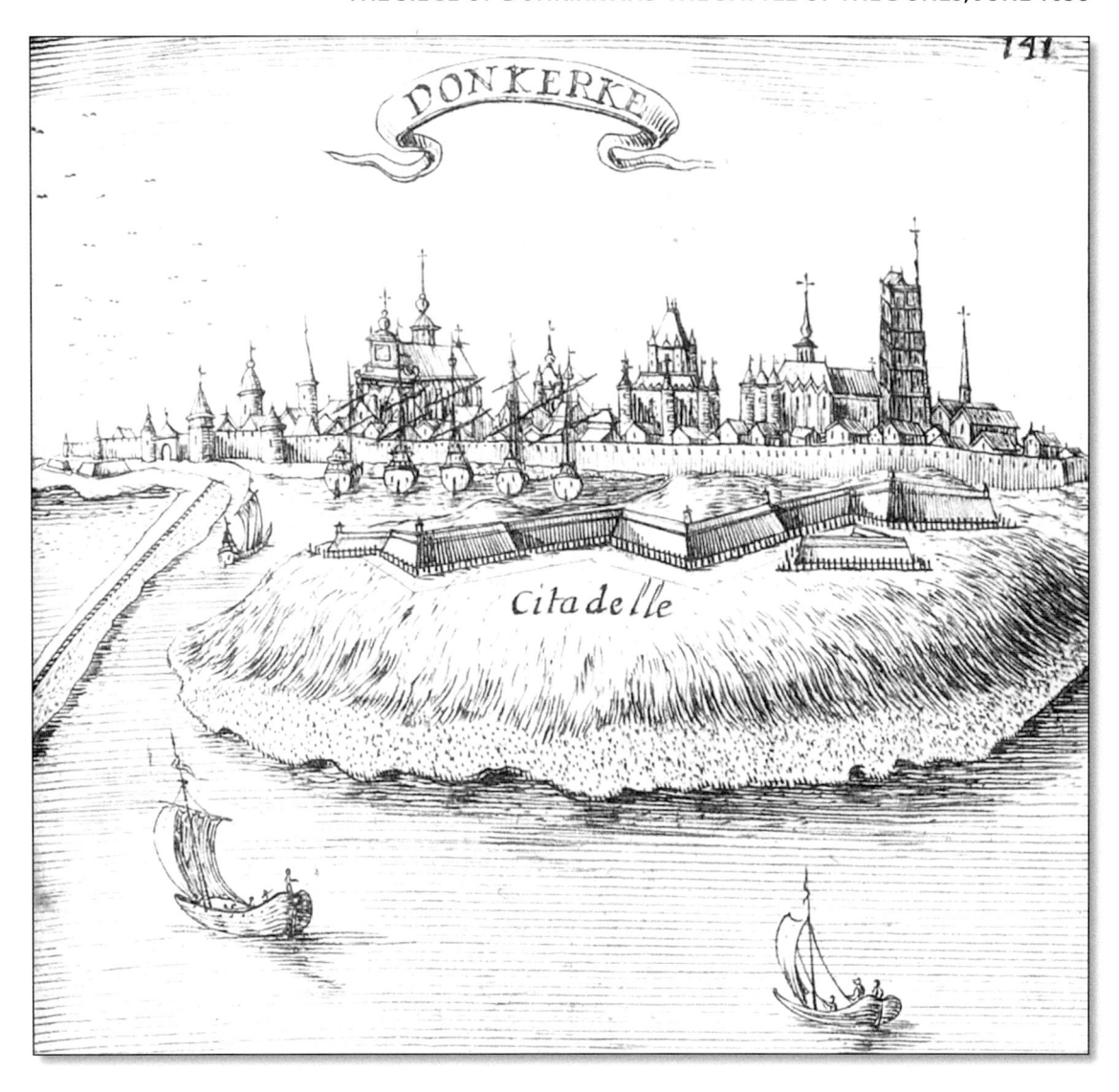

THE SIEGE OF DUNKIRK AND THE BATTLE OF THE DUNES, JUNE 1658

The city of Dunkirk, from Allain Mallet, *Art de la Guerre*, p.141 (<https://digi.ub.uni-heidelberg.de> accessed 2 January 2020).

King of England and his small army; and Condé too, even with access to his own revenues to a degree, also needed subsidy – Don John noted that in June 1657 he had been obliged to pay Condé a substantial sum to keep his army in the field. By October 1657, Don John faced a deficit of 1.5 million florins, a situation that scarcely improved as the campaign of 1658 opened, and the source of unrelenting correspondence between Don John and Madrid.[11]

The siege of Hesdin, moreover, had reinforced Spanish views that Turenne would campaign inland and they were therefore surprised when on 25 May, the Anglo-Spanish army arrived at Dunkirk, having assembled around Amiens and marched via Hesdin, Bergues and Cassel, accompanied by no less a person than King Louis XIV himself.[12] The governor, the Marquis de Leyde, only just got back from Brussels demanding men and supplies,[13] his garrison being significantly below strength. As expected, the Spanish defenders had flooded the low-lying areas around the town so that the only approaches were along the dykes bordering the canals; these two had been

A plan of the fortifications of Dunkirk, from Allain Mallet, *Art de la Guerre*, p.343 (<https://digi.ub.uni-heidelberg.de> accessed 2 January 2020).

broken in places or had strongpoints guarding them. The French therefore had to bridge the gaps with fascines and wade through deep and dirty water.

The approaches were also dominated by two forts. Fort Royal was little more than a foundation and earthwork; it was later rebuilt by the English and renamed Fort Oliver; four new bastions were completed. Another, unnamed fort, later called Fort Louis or Fort Castelnau, stood on the Canal de Bergues about two miles south of the centre of Dunkirk in the direction of Bergues. Both these forts were quickly taken. The city itself was defended by the original medieval stone wall and towers which protected the old town and the harbour. Beyond that, covering the new town and well as the old, was a considerable earthwork with a water-filled moat more than 20 feet deep. Another fort, Leon, guarded the harbour from an area of sand dunes north-west of the city; and the Fort de Bois covered the entrance to the anchorage. James Duke of York recalled that:

… the Marquis de Leyde found himself besieged in a place, the main strength of which consisted in the outworks, which were very large, all of earth, and very easy to be approached. To all this great extent of ground which was to defend, his garrison was no ways answerable, for it consisted but of a thousand foot, and eight hundred horse, and his provisions of powder and other necessaries were very scanty, even with reference to the small number of his men.[14]

Turenne established the main French army, including Condé's troops, on the north-eastern approach. Other French troops under the Marquis de Castelnau were joined by some of the English garrison from Mardyck, completing the investment of the city as Morgan recounted, but as usual giving himself rather more credit than was deserved: 'Marshal Turenne beleaguered Dunkirk on the Newport-side, and Major-General Morgan on the Mardyke-side, with his six-thousand English, and a brigade of French horse. He made a bridge over the canal, betwixt that and Bergon [Bergues], that there might be communication betwixt Marshal Turenne's camp and his.'[15] Turenne's force therefore comprised around 25,000 men. On the Mardyck side, four of Lockhart's English regiments were positioned between the Mardyck Canal and the sea; the other two were with Castelnau's 2,000 horse covering the line from the Mardyck Canal, across the Bourbourg Canal and as far as Fort Royal. Mardyck appears to have been held by the 10 companies under Pepper.

Two lines of circumvallation were opened and siege batteries erected. The first was to progress the siege and the second, outside the first, provided protection against any relief force. In addition, the beaches were barricaded with *cheveaux de frises*. At sea, Goodson was ordered to leave two ships at Gravelines and join the main fleet under Montagu off Dunkirk, making a considerable force of at least 20 ships both to bombard the seaward side of the defences and to prevent any reinforcement or resupply by sea. Logistic supply for the besiegers was organised personally by Mazarin; hospitals for the wounded were also established at Calais and Mardyck, from where the English were evacuated to Dover and other Kentish ports.[16]

This work proceeded for 10 days, largely unhampered by the Spanish but more so by the marshy terrain and the loose sand of the seashore, as Morgan recounted:

> Marshal Turenne sent a summons to the governor, the Marquis de Leda, a great captain, and brave defender of a siege; but the summons being answered with defiance, Marshal Turenne immediately broke ground, and carried on the approaches on his side, whilst the English did the same on theirs; and, it is observable, the English had two miles to march every day, upon relieving their approaches. In this manner the approaches were carried on, both by the French and English, for the space of twelve nights.[17]

On 4 June, the first assault was made. On the French side, the attack was led by the Guards and on the Mardyck side by the English, both supported by bodies of horse, all under the command of Lieutenant-General de Varenne. At the same time, the garrison made an attempt to break through the siegeworks, but this was repulsed with heavy losses.[18] Neither the French nor the English therefore made any headway – indeed the English at first retreated, but later rallied and returned to the trenches – evidence perhaps that the ranks contained many raw recruits. The next morning, however, Fort du Bois was evacuated by the Spanish.

Over the next two days, there was a series of skirmishes. The Duke of York reported that: 'They order'd all the troopes, which were at Nieuport, Dixmuyde and Furnes (of which they were jealous tho without reason, because they were all English, Scots and Irish) to march for Dunkirk (*reserving*) only the King's Regiment of foot … but these also came too late, the Town being block'd up …'[19] The approach of the troops was seen by the French on the evening of 5 June; the following night the garrison made another sortie from the Nieuport gate, but were repulsed with the loss of 10 prisoners. On the following night, a gale blew up during which, under the cover of artillery fire, the garrison launched another sortie, this time by 300 foot and six squadrons of horse advancing along the beach, wrecking the siegeworks. Badly surprised, the French threw every available man, including officers, at the attack and threw it back although with some loss. The English brigade seems to have acquitted itself well during this period: 'The action passeth for a handsome one in the report of the French, who are not over apt to flatter us. The enemy have been well satisfied with the supper they then got they have not expressed any appetite for a breakfast or any other meal of that nature.'[20] Lieutenant-Colonel Richard Hughes of Cochrane's Regiment wrote that: 'Our English soldiers behaving themselves very handsome, have gained a general applause from all the grandees of the army; the French horse, who formerly hated us, are becoming very loving and civil, and had rather engage with us than their own men.'[21]

Spanish reaction to the siege had been slow. On the night of 6 June, however, amongst all the skirmishes, Marshal Schomberg and a body of French horse intercepted letters from Caracena to the Spanish garrisons at Linck, Gravelines and Bergues, telling them that preparations were in hand to relieve Dunkirk; the majority of regular troops in these places, as well as all the militia, were to hasten to join the main army. In fact, there had been considerable alarm among the senior commanders, who had been badly caught out in their estimate of Turenne's intentions. Ypres was designated as the rendezvous for the Spanish army, but the time taken to shift the main body of the army from Artois and Hainaut meant that the final muster did not assemble until two weeks after the siege at Dunkirk had begun.

From Ypres the army marched to Furnes, arriving on 11 June. The first sign that the French and indeed the garrison had of the arrival of the relieving army occurred on 12 June, when 30 squadrons of horse under the command of Condé were seen, scouting the French lines.

According to James, Duke of York, and the account of Louis de Clerville, a further series of skirmishes ensued between Condé's squadrons and the French horse guards outside the lines of contravallation.[22] Condé seems to have made a half-hearted attempt to draw the French from their lines, hoping to slip a relief force into Dunkirk, during which the Marquis d'Hocquincourt was shot in the stomach and later died; and two other officers wounded. Meanwhile, the horse and foot regiments of the Spanish Army of Flanders assembled at Zuydcoote, a village about five miles north-east of Dunkirk, between the Furnes Canal and the sea. Condé's troops made rendezvous here after their skirmishing and by the following day, the Spanish had established a position in the natural cover of the sand dunes. James's memoirs, in which he describes Don John's council of war, imply that the encampment was intended to be a temporary affair,[23] consisting only of a hasty line of defences from the dunes on the seashore to the meadows close to the Furnes canal. Foot regiments were positioned in the line, backed by two lines of horse. The baggage train, artillery and several regiments of horse were left behind at Furnes because of the delay involved in bringing them up for what was an urgent operation. The position was weak, not least because of the lack of cannon and indeed of powder for the musketeers, but speed and surprise were judged more important than assembling the greatest number of forces. Probably, Don John and Caracena had no intention of engaging the French in a formal battle, rather preferring a rapid strike on a weak point in the lines identified by Condé, through which a relief force would force its way into the city, strengthening the garrison to such a degree that the French, faced with a reinvigorated defence and a Spanish army in their rear would be forced to lift the siege.

This intention was, however, forestalled. Turenne quickly decided to march the bulk of his force from the siegeworks and give battle to the Spanish at

THE SIEGE OF DUNKIRK AND THE BATTLE OF THE DUNES, JUNE 1658

Zuydcoote at the earliest opportunity. On the evening of 13 June Turenne gave orders for most of the English redcoats, including the regiments of Salmon and Pepper, numbering about 4,000 men, to concentrate at Dunkirk. By the early of 14 June hours – an hour before dawn according to one biographical source – the brigade had assembled north of the contravallation opposite the Spanish, along with the French horse and foot, leaving about 6,000 men in the siege lines: 'There was of the King's Army, without reckoning what remain'd in the camp, with the baggage, and in the trenches eight or nine thousand foot, and five or six thousand horse.'[24] Sources vary considerably as to the strength of horse and foot of both sides, but with a general agreement that both were about 15,000 strong. Various accounts give from 6,000 to 9,000 horse and 6,000–9,000 foot in the Anglo-French army.

Lockhart and Morgan, as usual, give rather different accounts of the events leading up to Turenne's decision. Lockhart told Thurloe that he had received word from Turenne that he had decided to give battle the next day, 14 June. Lockhart was in the grips of a painful episode of 'the stone', probably gallstones, but even so, ordered a coach (he would not have been able to ride a horse) and led the troops out[25] – he was certainly at the battle, commanding the English regiments in the first line. Morgan gives a far more colourful account, putting himself at the centre of things as the prime agent in persuading Turenne to give battle, an account that is almost certainly a fiction, since Morgan was not in command of the English brigade and during the battle was given command of the second line of English troops which was hardly engaged:

> Major-General Morgan did allege, what a dishonour it would be to the crown of France to have summoned the city of Dunkirk, and broke ground before it, and then raise the siege, and run away; and he desired the council of war would consider, that, if they raised the siege, the alliance with England would be broken, the same hour. Marshal Turenne answered, 'That, if he thought the enemy would offer that fair game, he would maintain the siege on Newport-side; and Major-General Morgan should march, and make conjunction with the French army, and leave Mardyke-side open.' Upon Marshal Turenne's reply, Major-General Morgan did rise from the board, and, upon his knees, begged a battle, and said, 'That he would venture the six-thousand English, every soul.' Upon which, Marshal Turenne consulted the noblemen that sat next him, and it was desired, that Major-General Morgan might walk a turn or two without the tent, and he should be called immediately. After he had walked two turns, he was called in: as soon as he came in, Marshal Turenne said, 'That he had considered his reasons, and that himself and the council of war resolved to give battle to the enemy, if they came on, and to maintain the siege on Newport-side; and that Major-General Morgan was to make conjunction with the French army.' Major-General Morgan then said, 'That, with God's assistance, we should be able to deal with them.'[26]

Turenne, as is shown in the detailed map by Sébastien Pontault de Beaulieu in 1698, and the accompanying key (see pp.279–281),[27] in the Duke of York's account, and in the 1735 history of Turenne's life and campaigns, drew up the army in two lines of foot, 10 battalions in the first line and six in the second with bodies of horse on their flanks, their left on the sea and their right on the canal with cavalry on each flank. On the extreme left of the first line were 14 squadrons of horse and five of the guns, supported by 400 Breton and English musketeers detached from the foot regiments. Behind them in the second line were another 10 squadrons, the whole of the horse on the left commanded by Lieutenant-General Jacques, Marquis de Castelnau with the Marquis de Varenne in command of the 14 squadrons of the first line since he was a Lorrainer, and some of these squadrons were from there.[28] The horse in the second line here was commanded by Schomberg. The centre of the first line comprised 10 battalions of foot. First on the left were the English regiments of Alsop, Cochrane, Lillingston and Lockhart,[29] under Lockhart's command. Next came the Regiment of Picardy, Turenne's, the Swiss Guards and the King's Guards on the right of the line. Another five cannon were deployed on the right of the line of infantry and slightly in advance of it. This first line of foot was commanded by General de Gadagne. In close support of the foot in the first line were four squadrons of *gendarmes* and four of light horse, under the command of Phillipe Emmanuel, Compte de Ligniville, who usually commanded the artillery of the army. The right flank of the first line was held by a further 14 squadrons of horse with 10 more behind them in the second line, all under the command of the Marquis de Créqui with Lieutenant-General Louis, Marquis de Humières, in command of the first line squadrons and the Seigneur d'Esquencourt the second line. The second line of foot was formed on the left by the regiments of Morgan and Clark and the composite regiment under Pepper, under Morgan's command; and then the battalion of Rambures and the three battalions drawn from the Regiments of the Queen Mother and of Bretagne under the Marquis de Bellesons, making seven battalions in all. Finally, there was a reserve of six squadrons of *gendarmes* under the Marquis de Richelieu, who were held at some distance behind the rest of the army.[30] The whole French army, 17 battalions of foot, 52 squadrons of horse and 10 of *gendarmes*, formed a front of more than 3,000 yards. On the seaward flank of the army, increasing the firepower, were several frigates of shallow draught, detached from Montagu's fleet.

On the opposite side, the Duke of York, by his own account, was far from easy in his mind. The army was short of powder and without its guns and was close to the enemy, an enemy and a commander that he knew well. Foraging continued as normal, however, and no word came from the indolent Don John:

> … it may be seen, how little some of our General Officers believed the French had any such intention … happening myself to be at supper that night with the Marquis de Caracena, and the company falling into discourse on the subject of our coming thither; and what the French might possibly attempt against us. I said that for my own particular I liked not our being there upon such terms as we were then … I was very confident they would give us battle the next morning. To which both the Marquis and Don Estevan de Gamarra answered that it was what they desired. To which I relied that I knew Monsieur de Turenne so well, as to assure them they should have that satisfaction.[31]

At 5.00 a.m. the next morning, the Spanish horse guards warned of movement from the French lines and the Spanish army stood to arms. James went out to the piquet line:

> I plainly saw that their whole Army was coming out of their lines. Their horse, with four small field pieces, advancing along the highway betwixt the Sand hills and the meadow grounds, and the French foot drawing out on their left hand, having thrown down some pieces of their Line, that they might march out at least a Battalion a front. And further on their left hand, which was nearer to the sea, the English were drawing out, whom I easily knew by their red coats.[32]

James returned to the encampment to report and on the way met Don John with other Spanish general officers. James told him that the French intended to fight, but Don John seemed not to believe this, being convinced that they intended only to drive in the picquet line. James replied that the French would not bring out four regiments of foot including the Guards, as well as the English, and such a great body of horse, for small a matter. At this point, the Prince de Condé arrived and gave the same view as James had done; at which point all the Spanish generals returned to their commands in order to draw up the army in a defensive line, making use of the high dunes, about three miles (five kilometres) north-east of Dunkirk and within two cannon shots of the French lines. The difficult going for an attacker in the soft sand and the security offered by the canal on their inland flank seemed to confer an advantage on the defence.

The Spanish army was significantly smaller than the French, divided between approximately 6,000 foot and 9,000 horse, although again, the authorities differ considerably. The first line of the army was formed chiefly of regiments of foot under Don John's command. On the far right, closest to the sea, were the four Spanish *tercios*. That of Boniface was nearest the sea – but shielded by the dunes from the fire of the English ships. According to some sources, Boniface's *tercio* was about 100 paces in front of the main line, on top of a high dune. Next came the *tercio* of Don Diego de Goni, commanded by Don Antonio de Cordova and then that of the Marquis de Seralvo. Slightly behind the *tercio* of Boniface was that of Francisco de Meneses, which was inclined to face the sea so as to guard against any outflanking move along the beach and as the tide was coming in, there was no prospect of stationing a body of Spanish horse on the beach, even if the English ships had not been there. The Italians and the militia are not mentioned and must have remained elsewhere in garrisons. Next came Charles II's regiments, less that of the Duke of Gloucester which had been captured at Cassell. The King's Regiment of Guards and the Earl of Bristol's Regiment together formed one battalion under the command of the Earl of Muskerry with the Duke of York's Regiment to their left. Behind them and in support was a battalion formed from the Earl of Newburgh's Scots and Richard Grace's Irish. Next came the three Walloon regiments, and two Irish regiments – those of Morphy and Cusack. Two composite battalions made up of German troops completed the line. To the left of this line of foot was the small army of the Prince de Condé: his own regiment, Guitard's Germans, that of Clomme and finally that of the Marquis of Persan. Condé's line straddled the road from Dunkirk towards Nieupoort, through the meadows as far as the canal. According to one account:

> The horse of the left wing, which was very much extended towards the canal, being uncapable of employment in that meadow, on account of the ditches, the Prince placed them in five or six lines between the Downs [i.e. the dunes] and those ditches, where neither the one nor the other could march above two or three squadrons abreast. He posted two battalions in a place somewhat covered, just before his cavalry; and afterwards going up the Downs, he placed others all along, till they join'd D. John of Austria's infantry.[33]

The Spanish horse was placed behind the foot, in two lines of perhaps 50 squadrons – James, Duke of York, considered that around half of them were not present at the battle but rather way foraging. Some of the Protectorate troops were close enough to James's foot regiments to exchange words: '… we were so near the Enemy, the Soldiers fell into great Friendship, one asking is such an Officer in your Army, another is such a Soldier in yours, and this passed on both sides.'[34] Morgan alleges that he put a stop to this – clearly a fiction, as he was back with the second line. But other authorities state that the armies were within half a musket shot of each other – no more than 50 yards, therefore.[35]

Both armies seem to have been in position around 8.00 a.m., after which there was a pause. Turenne seems to have been in no great rush:

> … the King's Army march'd leisurely on, and the enemy being pretty much puzzled to get themselves into order of battle, all the General Officers were busied therein, and we saw plainly that not one of them to their advanced Guards, who retired to the main body of their Army, without skirmishing repaired. We likewise were sensible that more diligence in marching would have been of great advantage, because expedition always deprives an enemy of an opportunity of getting into order: but when an Army is marching in battalia, it must go a certain regulated pace, and oftentimes the several corps must wait a little for each other, to be able to range into form.[36]

Fighting began when a forlorn hope from the French Guards attacked Condé's skirmishers posted in the hedges on the French right. The French artillery opened up, firing four or five rounds per gun, to which the Spanish could give no answer. Fighting began in earnest, however, when the English Protectorate regiments in the first line began to advance, led by Lockhart's Regiment. Lockhart reported that: 'necessity having no law, I ordered my own regiment to attempt it before, having some commanded foot on the strand, which were to have seconded the horse I made them attack the Spanish on the flank.'[37] The commanded foot were those detached to support the horse referred to earlier; and the flank appears to have been the *tercio* of Don Gaspar Boniface. In effect this was another forlorn hope, 'consisting of half of his excellency the Lord Ambassador's regiment, and part of that commanded by Lieutenant-Colonel Haines [from Lillingston's Regiment], and was led on by Lieutenant-Colonel [Fenwick], his excellency's Lieutenant-Colonel.'[38] Lockhart himself it seems did not lead the attack, probably on account of his illness, and Morgan therefore came up from the second line to take charge. The Spanish had fired several volleys, killing and wounding several men. Morgan sent for orders from Turenne, but:

> ... when he saw there was no hope of orders, he told them if they [all the Colonels and field officers of the regiments] would concur with him, he would immediately charge the Enemies' right wing. Heir answer was: 'They were ready whenever he gave orders.' He told them, he would try the right wing with the Blue Regiment [Lillingston's] and the four hundred firelocks which were at intervals of the French horse ... the other Five Regiments should not move from their Ground, except they saw the Blue Regiment, the White [Lockhart's], and the four hundred firelocks, shocked the enemies' right wing off of the Ground, and further showed the several Colonels what colours they were to charge ... he admonished the whole Brigade, and told them, they were to look in the face of an Enemy who had violated and endeavoured to take away their reputation, and that they had no way but to fight it out to the last man or to be killed, taken prisoner or drowned, and further, that the Honour of England did depend much upon their Gallantry and resolution that day. The Enemies' wing was posted on a Sandy Hill. And had cast up a work brat high before them. Then General Morgan did order the Blue Regiment and the four hundred firelocks to advance to the Charge.[39]

Other accounts are clear that it was Lockhart's Regiment that led the way[40] – but Morgan was never going to give Lockhart any credit, even vicariously. The Duke of York was watching this unfold from the opposite side and reported that:

> The first who engaged us were the English led up by Major General Morgan their General Lockhart (for what reason I know not) being with Major General de Castelnau at the head of their left wing. But immediately before their falling on, Don John sent, and desired me to go to our right hand, and take a particular care of that part, where he saw the English were advancing. Which I did, taking no troops along with me from the middle of the Line, where I was, excepting my own Troop of Guards. And a hundred commanded men, with two captains, and Officers proportionable out of my next battalion, to reinforce the natural Spaniards. Which Foot (from the King's Regiment of Foot) I joined to Boniface, where I judged they would make their greatest effort, and which was the greatest importance to be maintained, it being the highest of the sand hills on that side, and advanced somewhat further than the rest of them which were thereabout, commanding also those which were nearest to it.[41]

The Duke of York reported that the English came on with 'great eagerness and courage' and outpaced the French; had the Spanish sent some horse to attack them in the flank, they would have been in serious trouble – but the opportunity was lost. When Fenwick's men arrived at the bottom of the hill where the *tercio* of Boniface and the English Royalists were posted, they halted to catch their breath for two or three minutes, as the final assault would be steep and slippery. Lieutenant-Colonel Richard Hughes wrote that the ascent was so steep that the men had to climb it on their hands and knees.[42] The Duke of York went on to describe the attack:

> ... their commanded men opening to the right and left '... were continually firing at Boniface ... they began their ascent with a great shout, which was general from all their foot. But while they were scrambling up in the best manner they were able, the Lieutenant Colonel [Fenwick] fell in the middle way, being shot through the body; which yet hindered not the Major, who was called Hinton (since a Captain in the Duke of Albemarle's Regiment) from leading on his men together with the rest of the Officers, who stopped not till they came to push of pike.[43]

Hughes's account speaks of a volley as the White Regiment closed up to the Spanish. This account, that of the Duke of York, and the summoning of the detached musketeers gives a clue as to what may have happened at the top of the hill. The infantry of both armies was formed in the conventional formation of the day, sometimes known as the Dutch method: regiments in six ranks, with their pikemen in the centre to give protection against cavalry and to form the offensive arm in the advance to the 'push of pike'; musketeers on the flanks, able – at least in theory – to maintain a continuous fire as each rank discharged its weapons and was relieved in place by the next rank passing through and thus break up an enemy formation so that the pikes could push in. This alternating arrangement of blocks of pike and musket gave the battlefield of the seventeenth century a characteristic chequerboard appearance, which can be seen in the contemporary pictures of the battle. The English had adopted a variation of the Swedish methods during the Civil Wars: at very close ranges (less than 50 yards), the six ranks of muskets could be formed into three, increasing the weight of volley fire for the decisive moment. Once a heavy weight of fire had been delivered – and the weight of shot from a matchlock musket carried by the detached musketeers who are described as being armed with 'firelocks' – was around two ounces, as against 0.9 ounces from an arquebus[44] – the foot would then attack rapidly and violently with the pike, sword and clubbed muskets: the forerunner of the volley and bayonet charge which later characterised British infantry tactics on the battlefields of the eighteenth and nineteenth centuries. This tactic of fire followed by charge was also widely used in the Spanish armies of the day: the Duke of Alba had recommended opening fire at a range of a little more than two pikes' length (about 10 metres or 36 feet), especially if the opposition force was wearing armour.[45]

The Duke of York went on to say that:

> ... notwithstanding the great resistance which was made by the Spaniards, and the advantage they had of higher ground, as well as that of being well in breath, when their Enemies were almost spent with climbing, the English gained the hill and drove them off it. The Spaniards leaving dead upon the spot, seven of eleven captains who commanded in the Regiment, together with [Charles] Slaughter and Farrell, two Captains whom I had joined to that Regiment just before. Besides many of their reformed officers (their stands of pike being for the most part made

of such). Yet this ground was so well disputed, that the English besides their Lieutenant Colonel, lost several officers and soldiers.[46]

Another witness wrote of Lockhart's Regiment that: 'that regiment has done what I have never scene done before, for they charged and beate a Spanish regiment of a hill more steepe then any ascent of a breach I have seene'.[47] Lillingston's too was said to have 'had the hardest pull, where there are thirty or forty killed'.[48] Among the dead was Captain John Ward.

If the percentage of dead among the officers was replicated among the reformadoes and ordinary soldiers, then Boniface had clearly paid dearly – and the death toll supports the possibility of a devastating close-range volley of musketry rather than simply a pike duel. The English losses were much lighter. Although Lockhart wrote after the battle that: 'I have not one officer in my owne regiment, who is not dangerously wounded or ill, except one captain, and a Captain-Lieutenant, and some fewer lieutenants, ensigns and sergeants',[49] he was exaggerating. A muster of the regiment soon after the battle shows that Major John Hinton and six captains were present, as well as 728 men.[50] The remaining four English regiments suffered little.

The Duke of York attempted a counter-attack with his own troop of horse and some of Don John's horse guards but was beaten off with loss. He then found Don Gaspar de Boniface whose men were being rallied by Don John himself and Caracena. He too tried to make the men stand; as he did so he saw the English troops from the King's Regiment that he had sent to reinforce Boniface, rallied them and formed a line. This example encouraged the major of Boniface's *tercio* to rally the Spaniards too. This had scarcely been done when the Duke saw that Lillingston's and Lockhart's regiments were advancing on their right and was almost level with them. The Duke ordered Boniface's major to attack the English from the front while he with the horse attacked their flank. The Duke's attack succeeded in breaking into the foot regiments, although the Spanish failed to support him: had they done so then the advance could well have been halted. The Duke reported that:

> … I broke into them doing great execution upon them, and driving them to the edge of the Sand hill next the Strand … tis very observable that when we had broken into this Battalion, and were got amongst them, not so much as one single man of them ask'd quarter, or threw down his arms. But every one of them defended himself to the last, so that we ran as great danger by the but end of their muskets, as by the volley which they had given us. And one of them had infallibly knocked me off from my horse, if I had not prevented him when he was just ready to have discharged his blow, by a stroke I gave him with my sword over the face, which had lain him along upon the ground.[51]

An account of this from the English side admitted that the two regiments had been 'forc'd to give ground a little confusedly' when charged by the horse.[52] Morgan also said that: 'His Royal Highness the Duke of York, with a select party of horse, had got into the blue regiment [Lillingston's], by that time the white came in, and exposed his person to great danger: but we knew nobody at that time.'[53] Disengaging, the Duke became aware that the situation of the Spanish army was critical. French horse commanded by Schomberg, under cover of the English frigates offshore, had advanced along the beach: '… the regiments of horse of the left wing having speedily succour'd the English, and some of our squadrons likewise having advanced along the strand, went and placed themselves between the enemy's two lines; which put them into confusion.'[54] The Spanish position on the right wing quickly collapsed as the Spanish and Walloon *tercios* attempted to escape from the advance of the English regiments from the front and the French horse into their rear from the beach. Morgan reported that he brought the remaining English regiments up in support:

> Major-General Morgan, when he saw this opportunity, stepped to the other five regiments, which were within six score of him, and ordered them to advance, and charge immediately. But, when they came within ten pikes length, the enemy, perceiving they were not able to endure our charge, shaked their hats, held up their hand kerchiefs, and called for quarter: but the red coats cried aloud, "They had no leisure for quarter." Whereupon the enemy faced about, and would not endure our charge, but fell to run; having the English colours over their heads, and the strongest soldiers and officers clubbing them down; so that the six-thousand English carried ten or twelve-thousand horse and foot before them.[55]

French horse under the Marquis de Castelnau attacked the Duke of York's horsemen from a flank and only the intervention of Spanish troops under the Prince de Ligne saved him. The two lines of Spanish cavalry, probably only at half-strength, then began to fall back as the confusion on their left wing spread down the line. Most did not see any combat. The struggling Spanish infantry were charged in the flank by the French cavalry and they broke: 2,000 were taken prisoner; the rest were pursued as far as Nieupoort.

Meanwhile, the French had been engaged in the centre and on the inland flank. The foot regiments of the first line – those of Turenne and Picardy and the French and Swiss Guards – followed the forlorn hope. The Irish and German regiments seem to have fled after the first French volley, having probably already suffered heavy losses from the French artillery. Condé's troops halted the French Guards, but their right flank was now uncovered by the flight of Caracena's men: the Swiss Guards came through in support of the French Guards and together they broke the resistance. The flight of the foot panicked the Spanish horse to the rear, who joined their counterparts on the right in fleeing the field. Condé imposed a second check with his horse: his intention had been to attack French horse on their right, but instead, he charged the French Guards. Heavy fire brought this attempt to a halt with Condé himself narrowly avoiding capture.[56] The French horse on the right flank, like those on their left, had been reinforced with musketeers. The *History* of Turenne describes these men as being from the regiment of Montgomery; however, no such regiment existed on the French Army's order of battle at this time. The Duke of York says that they were from the Regiment de la Couronne. This regiment did not exist until 1673; at the time of the Dunes it was called the Queen Mother's and was commanded by Colonel de Montgomery; as James was writing his memoirs in France in the 1690s, he probably described the regiment by the name it then bore. One body of Spanish horse commanded by a German colonel and an officer named as 'Michel' charged Turenne's regiment. The charge was rapidly halted and the Duke of York noted that: 'Besides these two Colonels, I know not of any Spanish horse that behaved themselves well in this battle.'[57]

The English, Scots and Irish Royalists were soon also involved, but with little credit apart from the King's Regiment, as the Duke of York recounted:

> I have not yet given an account of the Battalion, which was composed of the King's Regiment and The Earl of Bristol's, and I should be very injurious to the finest of these two if I should pass them by in silence. They were posted … next to the natural Spaniards; and notwithstanding all they saw all on the right and left of them already routed and gone off, yet they continued firm (I mean that part of the Battalion that was composed of the King's Regiment) for they were all English. As for the other part of it, which was formed of My Lord of Bristol's men who were Irish, they indeed went away … Neither was it in the power of their Officers to hinder them, though they endeavoured it, but seeing their pains were to no effect, they ran for company, excepting Captain Stroud, an English Gentleman, who was Captain Lieutenant … But this was not the only discouragement which these English had, for both the Lieutenant Colonel and the Major had forsaken them before the Irish, the first on the Pretence of going for orders, the other upon an account which was not a jot more honourable… But none of these misadventures did at all daunt the King's Regiment.[58]

The French first line passed them by on the left and the Cromwellians on their right and the King's Regiment remained firm until the French second line came up. The battalion of Rambures approached and their commanding officer, seeing the Royalists isolated, offered them quarter, since the rest of the Spanish army had fled. The King's men did not at first believe this, but Captains Thomas Ashton and Thomas Cooke were conducted under parole to the top of the dunes and saw the truth of the matter. They agreed to surrender on the proviso that they would not be plundered and would not be handed over to the Cromwellians. This was agreed. Many went into captivity, although Lieutenant John Gwynne said that many of the men slipped away.[59]

The Irish and Scots battalions were confronted by the Cromwellians, as Richard Hughes recounted:

> The Duke of York's English, Middleton's Scotch and Ormond's Irish were soon beaten, the English only fighting. The Scots and Irish, as our regiment [Cochrane's] and Colonel Alsop's were coming up to them, veiled their colours, and made show of yielding, but ours judging it a defiance as they had done before we moved, gave fire at them, but it was very real, for they laid down their arms, and cried for quarter, and on our firing they struggled a little, and were soon quelled, all being killed and taken. Amongst whom it is reported my Lord Musgrave was slain and several English Gentlemen.[60]

Swift retribution waited those deserters from the English brigade who were found in the ranks of the enemy: 'Such as we met of our runaways were knock'd on the head, and such as we met amongst the French were forced from them, and intend to do justice on them.'[61]

The Duke of York realised that he would have to make his escape, or else be taken. He first tried to find Condé, with the 20 or so of his troop of horse that remained. Being a small party, they were able to slip through the French, taken at times as French themselves – as when the Duke saved one of his officers, Lieutenant William Victor, by calling out in French that Victor was 'one of our own Englishmen'. The Duke came up with the regiment of Ormonde, which was retreating in front of the French regiments of Picardy and of Turenne but found that Condé's troops had fled. Having struggled through the confusion in the village of Zuydcoote, the Duke met Don John and Caracena with whom he continued the retreat, pursued by the French as far as their own pontoon bridge.[62] The battle had lasted a little over two hours and by noon, it was over.

Most of the Spanish horse escaped – again, more than half of them never even arrived at the battle. The artillery and the baggage also escaped, having been left at Furnes. However, the foot was almost completely destroyed. The French reported around 5,000 Spanish killed, wounded and prisoners, of whom 2,000 soldiers were prisoners along with 800 officers;[63] casualties among the Spanish officers appeared to have been disproportionately high as they tried to rally their men; the Duke of York gives an account of the most notable among them and of the Royalists. Don John was left with perhaps 1,000–2,000 foot soldiers in the field army, plus those in the various garrisons. The officers and men of the Spanish *tercios* of the Army of Flanders were not allowed exchange or parole but were imprisoned:

> … the King [of France] has ordered his Commissaries that are here to pay their ransoms to those that took them and that he will not part with them, and the reason is that the King of Spain hath not now in Flanders that know the way of war in Flanders now, or that have any reputation of the country for making new levies, and that he will hardly be induced to trust the nobility of the country with military commands.[64]

Of the English Royalists, little at first remained. Most were taken prisoner although Grace's Regiment and the Duke of York's troop of horse seems to have escaped. Many of the King's Regiment escaped in small groups and later rejoined Charles and the Duke of York.[65] What was left of the Spanish army regrouped at Furnes. Things were, however, not so bad as at first appeared. Apart from the Spanish *tercios*, most of the officers and men who had been taken managed to bribe their way out of captivity; those who had been separated drifted back too and by early July, the Duke of York reported that all the regiments save the natural Spanish 'were almost as strong as when they came into the field'.[66]

In the French Army, total losses were between 300 and 400, about half of whom were English, but these figures may include some lost in the siegeworks earlier. Lockhart's regiment had borne the brunt of the fighting. Its Lieutenant-Colonel, Roger Fenwick, and two of its captains were killed, and nearly all the rest of its officers were wounded, with about 50 men killed in battle. Lillingston's lost a captain and 30 or 40 killed in battle, while the other regiments suffered only slight losses (the number of English dead rose because many died of their wounds over the next few weeks).[67]

Having rounded up the prisoners, Turenne ordered troops back to the siege lines, which took time as the troops were elated with their victory and in a mood to celebrate. At last, however, the Duc de Richelieu mustered a reasonable force and marched back to the lines. As they approached, fires could be seen in the camp: the Spanish garrison had made a sortie, killing wounded men, wrecking siegeworks and burning tents – including that of Lockhart. They were covered by five squadrons of horse and had to be forced back into Dunkirk by Richelieu. The governor, the Marquis de Leyde, still refused to surrender. On 15/16 June another sortie was made but by now the siege lines were fully manned and the attempt was stopped by heavy fire. On the following night, the attackers made an attempt to break in:

> Three days after the battle the Marquis de Créqui lodg'd himself with Turenne's regiment on the counterscarp, where we lost a great number of men, and after that, M. de Schomberg, M. de Varenne, M. d'Humières, M. de Bellesons, and M. de Gadagne advanced their approaches as far as possible: there being abundance of traverses, there was no one guard, where something very vigorous was not to be done, and that too without any cover. The English who were on the left, though they did their duty very well, could never lodge themselves on the counterscarp … After the battle, we no longer fearing to employ a good number of foot before the town, had begun an attack on that fort [Fort Leon], which serv'd rather to give a diversion than any thing else: we likewise made the enemy abandon a wooden fort, wherein they had some cannon, as also the whole length of a dyke, which advanced into the sea, from which they very much annoy'd the trenches; but they soon quitted it …[68]

A Spanish frigate from Ostende managed to slip through on the night of 19/20 June, bringing ammunition, but that same night, the Compte de Soissons with the Swiss Guards drove the defenders from the counterscarp. The governor, rallying the defenders, was shot in the shoulder and injured by a grenade and had to be carried from the walls. On 21 June, the eighteenth day of the siege, Turenne again summoned the defenders to surrender but received no reply until 23 June when it became clear that Leyde had died of his wounds.[69] Major-General de Bascourt had assumed command and, after an embassy of townspeople had negotiated terms, a truce was agreed on 23 June; that evening, French troops occupied the town:

> The King, [Louis XIV] who had been five or six days at Mardyke, came the next day with the Cardinal to M. de Turenne's quarters, where hostages being given, the capitulation was sign'd, and the garrison march'd out a day after, and was

conducted to St. Omer. There was left of them a thousand foot, the remains of seven or eight regiments,* and six or seven hundred horse.[70]

Under the terms of the treaty, the town was immediately handed over to Lockhart, although this occasioned a good deal of criticism of Mazarin among both French soldiers and civilians. Dunkirk, it was felt, might be used one day to attack France. Mazarin, however, needed English support to conclude the war with Spain and the terms of the treaty were duly honoured.[71] Lockhart's and Alsop's Regiments were placed in the garrison, the composite regiment under Pepper retaining Mardyck. In England, a day of national thanksgiving was ordered; among the army, however, it was felt that the French horse in particular had not pulled their weight and had it done so, the whole Spanish army would have been destroyed.[72]

The Dunes and the siege of Dunkirk belong to that category of battles that are truly decisive. It was not decisive in that it brought the war to an immediate close, however after it, the course of the war was set on a path that led only one way – to the inevitable defeat of Spain. The Spanish field army was now not only heavily outnumbered by the Anglo-French, but also in no moral or physical shape to engage in another pitched battle. The standing of Don John and Caracena was also badly damaged – Don John has been repeatedly criticised for his naivety in the layout of his forces and his conduct of the action. The reputation and position of the Prince de Condé had also taken a bad knock. The best that the Spanish could hope for was to tie the Anglo-French army down in a series of sieges and perhaps delay the inevitable. For Charles II, too, the outcome of the battle was disastrous: 'Charles is left without 20 men to invade England on his own', wrote Richard Hughes.[73] An exaggeration, as we have noted, but certainly any hope of a Spanish-backed Royalist invasion of England died in the Dunes. On the other hand, Turenne's reputation and standing were greatly strengthened and the dominance of the French army assured. The contribution of the English had been crucial in smashing the Spanish line, but the presence of the English fleet offshore both to blockade the port and prevent Spanish manoeuvre on the shoreline was also hugely important. After the debacle in Hispaniola, three years before, the reputation of the English redcoats was restored.

---

* Presumably, regiments of militia, since there were not this number of regular tercios left in the Spanish Army.

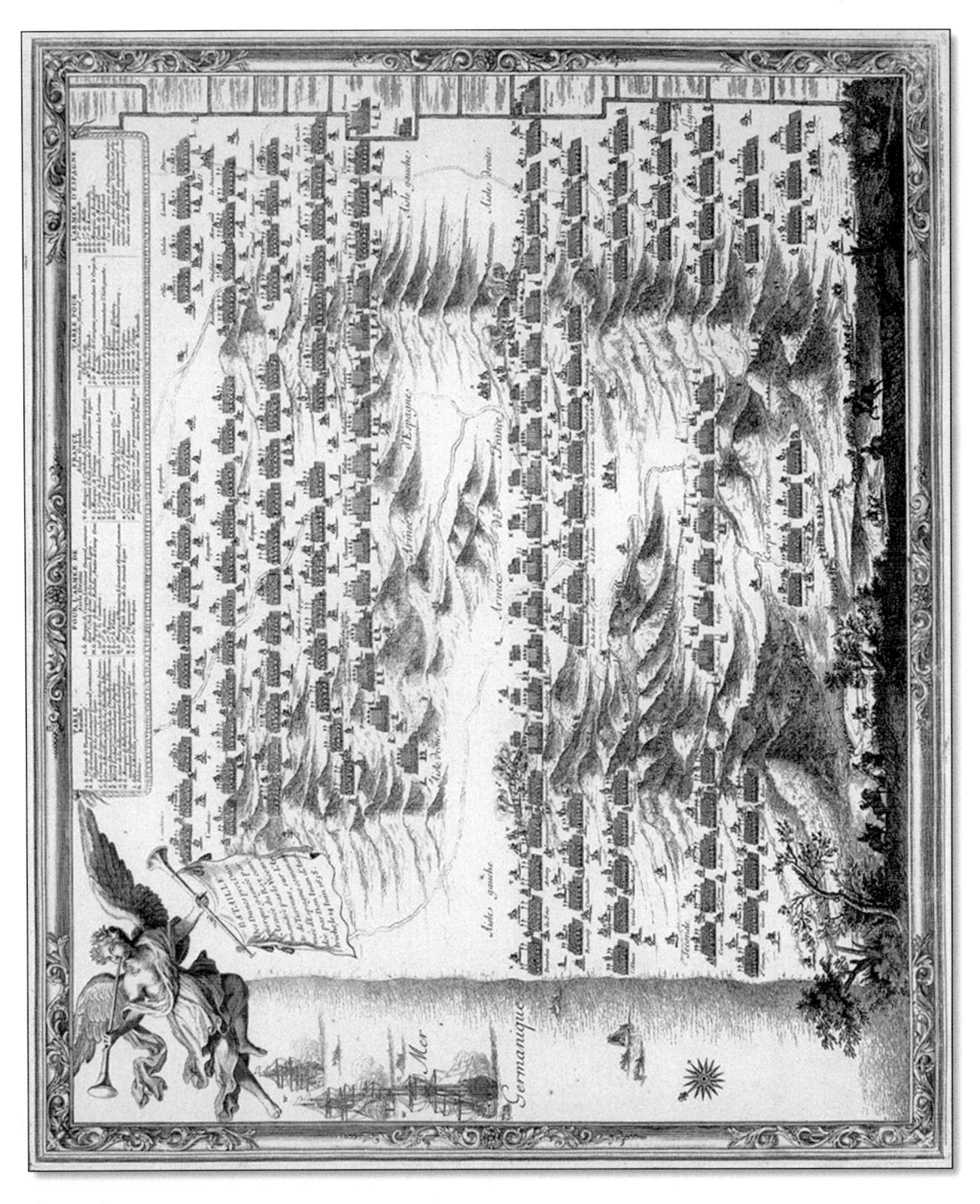

THE SIEGE OF DUNKIRK AND THE BATTLE OF THE DUNES, JUNE 1658

The Battle of the Dunes 1658 by Sebastien Pontault de Beaulieu. (Hessiches Staatsarchiv, Marburg). See key and explanatory notes overleaf.

COLONIAL IRONSIDES

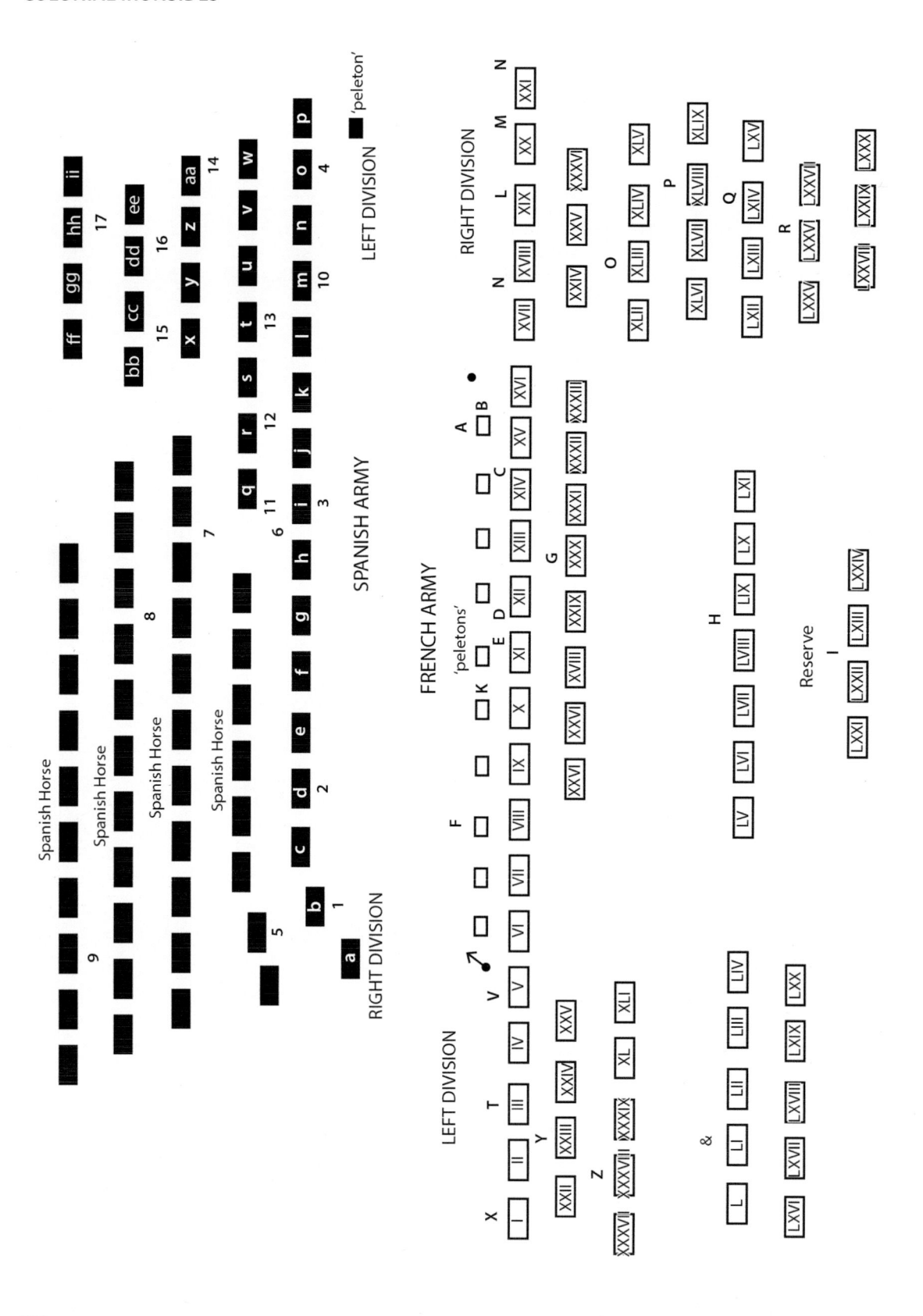

THE SIEGE OF DUNKIRK AND THE BATTLE OF THE DUNES, JUNE 1658

Key to Beaulieu's Map of the Dunes

FRENCH ARMY
A. Turenne
B. Lieutenant-General le Seigneur de Gadagne commanding the foot of the first line
C. Comte de Soissons and the Swiss Guards
D. Duc de Rouillon and Turenne's first battalion
E. Comte d'Auvergne and Turenne's second battalion
F. Lockhart
G. Le Sieur de Salle commanding the Gendarmes
H. Le Marquis de Bellefonde, Lieutenant-General commanding the foot of the second line
I. De Richelieu, commanding the reserve
J. Not used
K. 'Peletons' (platoons), forward detachments or forlorn hope

THE RIGHT DIVISION
L. Marquis de Crequi, Lieutenant-General commanding the right division of the first line
M. Marquis de Bellesons
N. Le Sieur de Garrion
O. Le Sieur d'Esparace
P. Le Sieur de Podvies
Q. Le Marquis de Humières, commanding the right division of the second line
R. Le Sieur d'Esquencourt
S. Le Sieur de Rochepierre

THE LEFT DIVISION
T. Le Marquis de Castelnau, commanding the left division of the first line
U. Not used
V. Le Marquis de Varenne
W. English frigates offshore
X. Le Comte de Ligniville commanding the Lorrainers
Y. Le Sieur de St Lieux
Z. Le Sieur de Rouvray
&. Le Comte de Schomberg, commanding the left division of the second line
• Cannon commanded by le Sieur de St Hilaire
↗ Cannon commanded by le Sieur de Letancourt

COLONIAL IRONSIDES

i	Dourches	xxvi	Queen's Regiment of heavy horse	li	St Croix and Fournier
ii	du Pace	xxvii	Dumbarton's Scots	lii	de Plessis
iii	Arberg	xxviii	Cardinal's Regiment of German heavy horse	liii	Funck
iv	Arlencourt	xxix	Cardinal's heavy horse	liv	D–
v	H–	xxx	Cardinals Guards and Gendarmes	lv	Le Marine
vi	Alsopp	xxxi	Gendarmes and heavy horse of S.A.R.	lvi	Espagny
vii	Cochrane	xxxii	King's Regiment of heavy horse	lvii	Morgan
viii	Lillingston	xxxiii	King's Gendarmes	lviii	Clark
ix	Lockhart	xxxiv	Coerlin	lix	Pepper
x	Boudebois (Picardy)	xxxv	Grammont	lx	Rambures
xi	Turenne	xxxvi	Grammont	lxi	Piedmont
xii	Turenne	xxxvii	l'Altroue	lxii	Equancourt
xiii	Baradies	xxxviii	Grand	lxiii	Canores
xiv	Swiss Guards	xxxix	Maistre	lxiv	The Queen Mother's Regiment
xv	Swiss Guards	xl	Villequier	lxv	The Queen Mother's Regiment
xvi	French Guards	xli	Castelnaut's Guards	lxvi	St Simon
xvii	Bretons	xlii	Rouillon	lxvii	Genlis
xviii	Royal	xliii	Spanish	lxviii	Torigny
xix	Peloton	xliv	Turenne	lxix	Belin
xx	Royal	xlv	Turenne	lxx	Belin
xxi	Montgomery	xlvi	Coudrey	lxxi	Nogent
xxii	Rouvray	xlvii	Villette	lxxii	Charles
xxiii	Castelnault	xlviii	Villette	lxxiii	Soissons
xxiv	Broglio	xlix	Podwies	lxxiv	Richelieu
xxv	St Lieu	l	Coarlin	lxxv	Marviller
				lxxvi	Rehen
				lxxvii	Marigine
				lxxviii	Rochep–
				lxxix	Melin
				lxxx	Roye

THE SIEGE OF DUNKIRK AND THE BATTLE OF THE DUNES, JUNE 1658

SPANISH ARMY

1. Don John of Austria
2. The Duke of York
3. The Marquis of Caracena
4. The Prince of Condé
5. The Prince de Ligne
6. The Prince d'Espinay
7. The Prince of Robec and Montmorency
8. Conde de Bergues
9. Conde de Salazar
10. Comte de Coligny
11. Marquis de Bouteville
12.
   - a. Gagne
   - b. Boniface
   - c. Marquis de Seralvo
   - d. English Guards
   - e. Duke of York's
   - f. Duke of Gloucester's
   - g. Walloons
   - h. Walloons
   - i. Morphy
   - j. Cusack
   - k. Newburgh's
   - l. Grace's
13. Signor de Guitault
14. Sieur de Meille
15. Sieur de L e f

- m. Condé
- n. Condé
- o. Clommes
- p. Persan
- q. Bouteville
- r. Guitault
- s. Persan
- t. Meille
- u. Petit Anguien
- v. Anguien
- w. Petit Condé
- x. B–

- y. Rademel
- z. Beauvais
- aa. Romanville
- bb. Rochefort
- cc. Noisfalaise
- dd. Morveuil
- ee. La Suze
- ff. Ollia
- gg. Gulsin
- hh. Limbeck
- ii. Dierne

Romainville
15. Le Marquis de Rochefort
16. Le Comte de Morveuil
17. Baron de Limbeck

SPANISH FOOT REGIMENTS/TERCIOS (HORSE NOT NAMED)

16

The Capture of Furnes, Bergues, Dixmüde and Gravelines, June–August 1658

From here on, the war would be one of sieges, for the Spanish were far too much weakened to risk another pitched battle. The Duke of York recorded that the Spanish army remained at Furnes until 26 June where it received a resupply of ammunition from Ostende, recovered its foragers and married up once more with the baggage and the artillery train. After the fall of Dunkirk, the army pulled back to Nieupoort where a council of war was called. Don John proposed defending the line of the canal from Nieupoort to Dixmüde. The Duke however argued that the army had too little infantry for the job and that morale was not good. If beaten again, he argued, all the major towns would be lost:

> I proposed that wee should divide our Army, and disperse it, as wee should judge most convenient, amongst our great places on that side of the country where wee were, a particular regard being had to those Towns, which in probability wee might expect to be next besieged; That this provision being made for their Security, what place soever should be attacked, might be in a condition of making a vigorous resistance … that when it should be taken it would be too late for the Enemy to sitt down before another; That during this siege, wee might have leasure to draw the rest of our Troopes together, and withal might watch our opportunity of attempting somewhat against the Enemy.[1]

ebate, the Duke's suggestion was adopted. He and Caracena remained at Nieupoort with about 2,000 foot and 2,000 horse, most of the foot being what remained of the English and Irish Royalist regiments; the Prince of Condé was sent with his forces to Ostende; Don John with most of the horse and some foot went to Bruges; and the remainder of the army was sent with the Prince de Ligne to Ypres. The Duke also recalled that Condé had asked him why he had argued with Don John, to which he had answered that 'I had no desire to be forced to run again, as wee had done so lately at Dunkirk.'[2]

THE CAPTURE OF FURNES, BERGUES, DIXMÜDE AND GRAVELINES, JUNE–AUGUST 1658

Meanwhile, at Dunkirk and Mardyck, as well as Lockhart's and Alsop's regiments, there were now nine companies of Gibbon's Regiment and eight of Salmon's, along with some odd companies sent from other regiments in southern England.[3] The cost of the garrisons was already beginning to mount and to cause concern in the Protector's council, in spite of the level of French subsidy. The exchequer income of England and Wales at this period was around £1,185,000 with another £143,000 for Scotland and £207,000 for Ireland. A huge slice of this was expended anyway on maintaining the armies: £638,000 per year for the army in England, £148,000 for Scotland, £104,000 for Ireland and £54,000 for the Jamaica garrison. Another £77,000 would now be needed for the garrisons of Dunkirk and Mardyck,[4] leaving the exchequer in deficit to the tune of a full year's taxation.

All the citizens of Dunkirk were immediately required to swear the oath of allegiance to the Protector and were disarmed. Those who preferred to remain Spanish citizens were allowed to leave.[5] Those who remained were concerned chiefly with the maintenance of their Catholic religion and with the discipline and good behaviour of the English troops. Lockhart was careful in both respects, giving protection to the clergy and the various religious orders which included Benedictines, Capuchins and Franciscan friars, as well as to private citizens, and issuing orders that promised severe penalties to any soldier who should: 'offer any injury or abuse to the ecclesiastics or Romish churchmen of what order soever, or condition, in the streets, in their houses, convents or churches'.[6] Even so, Lockhart had to assemble the troops and reprove them for disrespectful behaviour. It was also required of citizens that they should inform on anyone who engaged in anti-English activities; this, however, threatened the secrecy of the confessional and the priests and religious baulked at it – it seems the issue was quietly dropped, in part at least because the English had at least 700 sick and wounded men in Mardyck and Dunkirk and therefore contracted with an order of nuns to help nurse these, supplementing eight regimental hospitals that Lockhart had established.[7] This compromise with Popery brought complaints in England; but Lockhart could scarcely establish Protestantism in Flanders by himself – for there were no secular clergy and not a single chaplain with any of his regiments.

Lockhart was firmly convinced of the military and political advantages of Dunkirk and Mardyck as an English enclave on the Continent, giving full control over the Channel, leverage on the French and Dutch, a spur to the

Nieupoort, from Allain Mallet, *Les Traveaux de Mars*, p.267 (<https://digi.ub.uni-heidelberg.de> accessed 2 January 2020).

progress of Protestantism in the Low Countries and an encouragement to the Huguenots in France.[8] Further to reinforce the garrisons, Lockhart was given leave to raise a regiment of horse, of which the experienced John Hinton was to be the major.[9] He was later replaced by Tobias Bridge. Bridge served on after the Restoration in 1660, went to Tangier where he was briefly acting governor, and then went to the Barbadoes with a newly raised regiment of foot: Bridgetown is named after him. Lockhart had asked that the regiment have five or six troops, each troop consisting of at least 70 men, equipped with back and breast armour, pistols, sword and carbine; 'carabins, and good ones, are very needful to them, for wee must march for the most part betwixt dykes and watter gauges, and will be many times put to use their carabins, when their pistols are useless.'[10] The regiment was raised in June and July in London and Berkshire, from new recruits rather than drafts from the standing regiments. It appears that the men were to bring their own horses and were given an advance of three guineas, or a month's pay.[11] One notice from a troop commander detailed that the soldiers should receive: 'back, breast, headpiece, pistols, holsters … in case any horse miscarry in the said service, it shall be made good to him …'[12] It had some good officers: Captain Henry Flower, according to Lockhart, 'had given such large testimonies of his courage, good conduct, affectionate to your Highnesses [Cromwell's] interest, and love of his country in several occasions in the late siege and battle …'[13] There were others not so good: Captain Robert Broadnax for example was 'a pretty man … he seems to promise no extraordinary matters.'[14] Broadnax's troop was the first to arrive in Dunkirk in July, followed in August by Lockhart's own troops and the remaining four troops in August. Lockhart soon had cause to complain of Broadnax, who had brought his men to Flanders without arms and with an incapable lieutenant. In August, his negligence resulted in the troop being ambushed while foraging, with the loss of five men and 10 horses.[15]

In August, five supernumerary companies attached to Lillingston's Regiment were sent to Mardyck. The garrisons therefore consisted of 42 companies of foot: 10 in each of Lockhart's and Alsop's Regiments, nine in Salmon's, eight in Gibbon's and five of Lillingston's, and six troops of 100 men in the regiment of horse.[16] This translated into a garrison of 1,000 men at Mardyck, 500 at Fort Oliver, formerly Fort Royal, and around 1,500 at Dunkirk, rising to 2,000 with the arrival of Lillingston's companies. Much time and effort, however, were needed to repair and improve the fortifications. At Mardyck, shifting sands filled the defensive ditches and at Dunkirk, work was needed to repair the damage done during the siege. Worse, French soldiers had torn down the pallisadoes for firewood. The four bastions of Fort Oliver were completed and over the next year, four half-moons and a counterscarp were added.[17]

During Lockhart's frequent periods of absence on diplomatic duties, Alsop acted as governor. Alsop encouraged the trade of the town, and the toleration of Catholic practices by the inhabitants, leading to his being attacked by an anonymous informer who denounced him as 'an enemie to religion and godliness'.[18] The same informer criticised Lieutenant-Colonel

THE CAPTURE OF FURNES, BERGUES, DIXMÜDE AND GRAVELINES, JUNE–AUGUST 1658

A contemporary view of Bergues. (Author's collection)

Kingwell in similar terms; and Captains Cobham and Withers as drunkards – there were not, apparently, more than six moral officers in Alsop's regiment.

The rest of the English brigade, the regiments of Morgan, Cochrane, Clark and Lillingston, numbering perhaps 2,000 men under Morgan's command, remained in the field with Turenne,[19] who, two days after the fall of Dunkirk, on 25 June 1658, marched the army to Bergues. Here it was believed that the Spanish garrison numbered between 800 and 900 men, drawn from 'five old regiments of foot and one of horse.'[20] King Louis, who had remained at Mardyck, arrived shortly after the army began the siege, just in time to see the trenches being opened on 27 June: '… he took a ride out, and came to M. de Turenne's quarter, and he then look'd very much out of order; and indeed that very evening he was in a violent fever, and own'd he had had some symptoms of it for two days before, tho' he did not speak of it …'[21] The King had probably contracted typhus in the crowded conditions of Mardyck, the sickness not sparing anyone on account of rank. He was carried back to Calais and at one point it was feared he would die.

On the night after the trenches were opened at Bergues, the French captured a redoubt near the counterscarp, but the troops in the trenches were far too exposed to enemy fire for any further advances in daylight. However, a day later, under Schomberg's command, the counterscarp and all the outworks on that side of the town were seized and the French established themselves on the edge of the moat, which they began to fill up with fascines. Some guns were also brought forward without any cover and positioned close to the main gate: the garrison was then summoned to surrender. A parley was begun, at which Turenne told the garrison that they would not be permitted to march out with the honours of war and be granted parole, but that they would all be treated as prisoners of war. These terms caused considerable agitation among the Spanish troops and many:

> threw themselves into the Morass to get away; but they were taken by the Soldiers, and the rest threw down their arms, and forsook all the posts along the walls; and had not M. de Turenne come up, the town would have been plundered. We secured all the prisoners, both Soldiers and Officers, and sent them into France by the way of Calais.[22]

Morgan says only that: 'The next siege was Bergen St Winock [Bergues], six miles from Dunkirk, which Marshal Turenne beleaguered with the French army, and the four regiments of English; and, in four- or five-days' siege, Bergen St Winock was taken upon capitulation.'[23] The English troops taking part in the siege and suffered losses, including Lieutenant-Colonel Richard Hughes, before the town surrendered on 29 June.[24]

On the following day, as a result of intelligence either from prisoners or from his own scouts, Turenne formed the view that the Spanish were abandoning the fortress at Furnes. He therefore sent de Varenne there with 2,000 horse and foot, following himself half a day later with only a small bodyguard. The small Spanish garrison in Furnes, only a single company of 80 men, fired a few shots but were in no mood to hold out, feeling that they had been abandoned by Don John. On 3 July, Varenne sent a trumpeter to summon them to surrender, warning the townspeople that if they resisted, the town would be sacked. This was enough to make the townspeople and the garrison open the gates: Turenne rode straight in, sending the 80 men back to Don John at Nieupoort, as sending them under guard back to France would be more trouble than they were worth.[25]

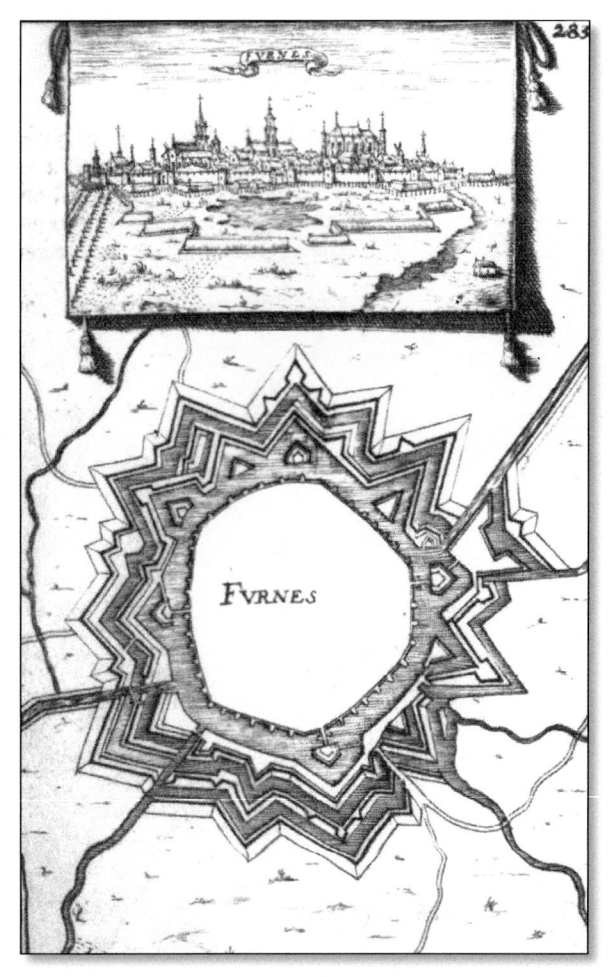

Furnes, or Veurne, from Allain Mallet, *Les Traveaux de Mars*, p.283 (<https://digi.ub.uni-heidelberg.de> accessed 2 January 2020).

Turenne remained at Furnes that night and returned very early next day, 4 July, to the camp. He had detached a body of horse under the Marquis de Créqui to a town identified as Roseburgh, on the road from Bergues to Ypres – probably Rekspoëde – and sent word to Créqui to make across country for Dixmüde while he himself marched along the dyke directly to Fintele and Kenoque, or Fort Knokke, which lay at the junction of the Iser River and the Ypres canal. After the loss of Bergues, the main Spanish army lay between Nieupoort, Dixmüde and Ypres. The canals should have provided useful delay lines to slow down the French and work had begun on a Spanish redoubt at Kenoque – there were some horse supporting this – for the best routes across Flanders were along the dykes and if the key points on these were strongly held then movement could be controlled. But Turenne's march was too fast and the Spanish were repeatedly outmanoeuvred, and dislocated. At Nieupoort, a French force under Créqui was detached by Turenne to screen the town and cut its communications with the rest of the Spanish army, while the main force moved against Dixmüde.

The French and English first made a forced march from Bergues to Kenoque, taking the unfinished redoubt, where a third of the troops swam the river to seize cattle on the far side; early next day, 6 July, the advance continued

THE CAPTURE OF FURNES, BERGUES, DIXMÜDE AND GRAVELINES, JUNE–AUGUST 1658

towards Dixmüde along the banks and dykes. This town had been greatly neglected, not being near the coast nor in any way threatened for many years. The Spanish had hurriedly begun to repair the outworks and the Prince of Condé had been overseeing the repairs. When he saw the French field army drawing close, he realised that he would not long hold the place. He drew off the main part of his forces, leaving about 400 men with orders, as was later found, to surrender if the French crossed the river.[26]

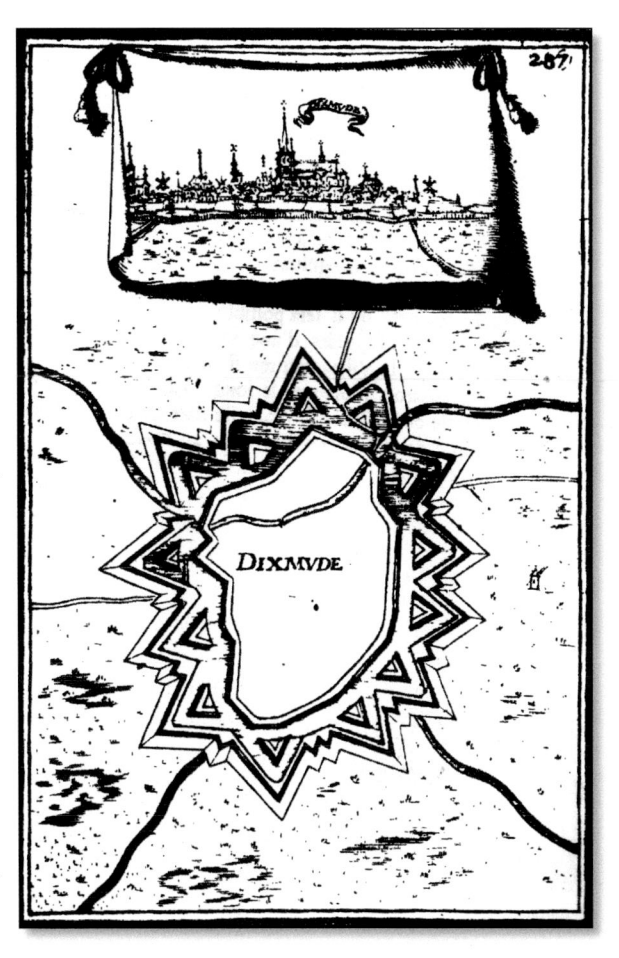

The Spanish army still lay between Dixmüde and the coast at Nieupoort, minus the large detachments of troops in the garrisons of Nieupoort and Ypres. Nor was their morale yet up to another major engagement: 'they did not think it adviseable, on account of the terror their troops were in, to make head in any place, how narrow soever it was.'[27] The French army immediately threw a pontoon bridge over the river near Dixmüde and sent a body of troops to summon the town and garrison to surrender. At this point, the Comte de Moret arrived with a message from Mazarin to the effect that the King was close to death: no further operations were to be undertaken until the outcome of the illness was known. The Cardinal also asked for some companies of the French and Swiss Guards, which were sent back under the command of the Count de Soissons. There was much anxiety over the King's health, he having no heir, and for two days he remained on the point of death until a powerful emetic was administered, which brought him back to consciousness.

The Duke of York also reported these events:

A contemporary view of Dixmüde, from Allain Mallet, *Les Traveaux de Mars*, p.287 (<https://digi.ub.uni-heidelberg.de> accessed 2 January 2020).

This was as well for the Spanish, for as the Duke of York reported: 'so careless had the Spaniards been, that … wee had not ammunition sufficient for fifteen days; so notwithstanding the great strength of our garrison, we could not have defended the Town long … But within a day or two after, wee were plentifully furnish'd with powder and shot from Ostend.'[28]

At Nieupoort, renewed preparations for a siege were underway:

… to inable ourselves the better to sustain a Siege, wee began a new Conterscarpe, and five half moons, with a langue de Serpent without the canal, which incompassed the old outworks, which wee finished in the space of eight days, and then opened our sluces to drown the Country round about us; but it had not the effect which wee expected, the ground about the town being higher than it was suppos'd …[29]

While Turenne remained outside Dixmüde and Créqui at Nieupoort, the Spanish held another council. It was decided that of Turenne should move, then Don John, Caracena and Condé would gather as large a body of troops as they could muster at Bruges in order to shadow him, while the Duke of York held Nieupoort and Ostende. On 9 July, Dixmüde surrendered and Turenne allowed the garrison to march out for Nieupoort. He himself with the Anglo-French army immediately moved off,[30] drawing in also the horse from Créqui's force. Caracena accordingly also marched off to the rendezvous with Don John. A few days later, Créqui himself with the rest of his troops also left Nieupoort to rejoin Turenne.[31] The Duke of York hurriedly assembled 600 foot and all his horse to attack the French rearguard as they withdrew. However, the foot were slow in assembling and the Duke was left with only his own troop of horse and two Spanish squadrons, not enough to take on the French.[32]

After a pause of nearly two weeks during the King's illness, Turenne turned his attention back to Gravelines, which had not been taken the previous autumn.[33] The garrison was, however, reduced to only 800 men. The town was invested on 27 July by Marshal de la Ferté with about 10,000 men, while Turenne with 3,000 foot and 7,000 horse provided a protective screen around the newly captured towns of Bergues, Furnes and Dixmüde. The English fleet provided a blockading force offshore. The trenches were opened on 7 August after preliminary operations to capture the forts Philip and Sluice.[34] The four English regiments were not involved in the siege, but two Scottish regiments in the French service, the *Garde Écossaise*, which dated from 1418, and Lord George Douglas's (later the Royal Scots) took part; so too did the young Sébastien le Prestre Vauban, who later remodelled the fortress. At one moment, a battle seemed possible when Don John and the Prince of Condé gathered a sizeable force and advanced to St-Omer with the object of raining the siege.[35] Turenne however blocked their approach and on 27 August, Gravelines surrendered: the troops were allowed to march off to Nieupoort. The three-week siege, hotly contested, had cost the French army at least 700 casualties, including Roger de Nagu, Duc de Varenne, one of Turenne's most senior lieutenants.

Appendix to Chapter 16

The Garrisons of Dunkirk and Mardyck, 1658–1659

To raise the strength of the garrison, instructions to Governor Lockhart in August 1658 stated that: 'he should call in to our garrison of Dunkirk the five supernumary companies of Englishe, which are now in the service of the King of France in the field, to complete our garrison.' The Protector's Council also allocated an additional 500 men to Lockhart, 400 to be sent from England, 50 more from each of the two regiments of Gibbon and Salmon.[1] In December, Salmon's and Gibbon's Regiments serving in Flanders were reduced to 750 men each; Gibbon's Regiment would be withdrawn and garrisoned in Sussex and Kent. Salmon's to be withdrawn and stationed in Norfolk, Suffolk and Essex.[2]

An Establishment for Dunkirk, Mardyck and Fort Oliver (formerly Fort Royal), December 1658.[3]

Staff

Engineer
Commissary of Musters
Commissary of Hay
Commissary of Provisions and a clerk
Commissary of Stores and ammunition
Assistant to above
Commissary of coals
Quartermaster of draught horses
12 Waggoners under him
Fire Master
2 firemaster's mates
6 firemaster's assistants
Master Carpenter
3 Gentlemen of the Ordnance
22 Gunners
29 Matrosses
Carpenter of the Trayne
Gunsmith
24 draught horses
Surveyor of the Works
Town Major Dunkirk
Town Major Mardike
Field and Staff Officers
Colonel
Chirurgeon
Chirurgeon's Mate
Marshall

COLONIAL IRONSIDES

Horse
Colonel's Troop of Horse:
Colonel as Captain
Lieutenant
Cornet
Quartermaster
3 trumpeters, 3 corporals, 94 troopers
Five more troops to complete a regiment of horse

Foot
Colonel
Lieutenant Colonel
Major
Preacher
Chirurgeon
Chirurgeon's Mate
Quartermaster & Marshall
Gunsmith

Company
Captain
Lieutenant
Ensign
Gentleman at Arms
2 Sergeants, 3 Corporals, 2 Drummers, 90 men
9 more companies to complete a regiment

One additional regiment as per the above

Lockhart's Regiment of Horse

Captains	Lieutenants	Cornets	Quartermasters
Col Sir William Lockhart	Captain-Lieutenant Richard Mill*	Thos Barnadiston	Robert Aske
Major John Hinton (to Aug 1659)			
Major Tobias Bridge	Nathaniel Desborrow	Matthew Wayne	William Cooke
Oliver Nicholas	Thomas Stackhouse	William Hawes	John Gilmore
Robert Broadnax†	Peter Pollins	Thomas Garthwaite	Theodore Russell
George Brett‡	William Campe	John Maitland	John Mitchell
Henry Flower	Samuel Sharpe	Wm Armstrong	John Boardman

---

*   Succeeded by Henry Flower.
†   To Gibbon's Regiment, succeeded by James Halsey
‡   Succeeded by Edward Wood

APPENDIX TO CHAPTER 16

Staff
Surgeon William Till
Marshal Humphrey Guy

Salmon's Regiment[5]

Captains	Lieutenants	Ensigns
Colonel Edward Salmon	Captain-Lieutenant Brent Ely[§]	William Turner
Lieutenant-Colonel Dennis Pepper	William Sadlington	Benjamin Waters
Major William Waters	William Carpenter	Richard Saunderson
Richard Wisdome	William Harrison	Mathew Harland
Thomas Cooke	John Person	Roger Cooke
Thomas Warde	Thomas Waters	Edmund Howson
Michael Bacon	Thomas Sprat	John Reeves
Thomas Bourchier	Moses Leniger	Thomas Dawson
Henry Watson	Gabriel Erwood	George Noble
George Wesbie	Jervice Hardstaffe	William Staniford

Staff
Chaplain Thomas Moore
Surgeon John Swadlin
Quartermaster and Marshal Allen Stileman

Gibbon's Regiment[6]

Captains	Lieutenants	Ensigns
Colonel Robert Gibbon	Captain-Lieutenant Jeremiah Masterson	Roger Rogers
Lieutenant-Colonel Henry Needler	Robert Ceely	Robert Dennison
Major John Chamberlaine	Oliver Meade	Thomas Tounge
John Gibbon	Jervase Jefferies	William Mabbison
Mark Grimes	John Haggat	Christopher Bodley
Robert Heath	William Munings	William Hamon
John Corker	John Wells	Vincent Witherley
Lyonell Lingwood	Daniel Bowker	John Lane
Robert Peacock	Nathaniel Harrison	John Taylor
Thomas Wright	Richard Gwynne[¶]	Francis Cable

---

[*] Later Captain-Lieutenant in Harley's Regiment and afterwards served in Tangier.
[†] Later served in Portugal.

COLONIAL IRONSIDES

Staff
Chaplain __ Cobb, Chaplain
Surgeon Samuell Bedford
Surgeon's Mate Robert Lloyd
Quartermaster Elias Chamberlaine

A partial list of Gibbon's Regiment is in TNA PRO 31/17/33 for December 1658:[7]

Colonel Gibbons

Captains
Robert Broadnax
Mills
Brett
Nicholas
Flower
Disbrowe

NOTES
1. TNA PRO 31/17/33, p.405.
2. TNA PRO 31/17/33, p.298, 16 December 1658.
3. TNA PRO 31/17/33, p.246, An Establishment for Dunkirk, Mardike and Fort Oliver dated 25 December 1658; TNA CSPD Interregnum, p.152, 26 August 1658
4. TNA CSPD Interregnum, vol. 204 p.151, 26 August 1659.
5. Commons Journal, vol. vii, 13 June 1659.
6. Commons Journal, vol. vii, 25 July 1659.
7. TNA PRO 31/17/33, p.397.

17

Oudenaarde, Ypres and the Defeat of the Prince de Ligne, September–October 1658

After the fall of Gravelines, Turenne returned to the main French Army which was encamped about 12 miles (19 kilometres) from Dunkirk. Here he met Lockhart, who remained at Dunkirk with the bulk of the English brigade, detaching 2,000 men under Morgan to the field army.[1] On 2 September 1658, Turenne ordered Marshal de la Ferté's troops to follow him to Dixmüde, where, leaving orders for Schomberg to assemble seven or eight regiments in the neighbourhood Dixmüde, Furnes and Bergues, he marched on with the rest of Army to the town of Tielt, which lay about halfway between Bruges and Ghent. From here, he intended to march on and secure crossings over the rivers Lys and Scheldt. His belief was that the Spanish were watching Armentières and Courtrai but that if they feared for the safety of Ghent and Bruges, they might take the field and present him with an opportunity for battle. The Spanish were mostly disposed behind the Lys but had left a strong garrison in Ypres.

On arrival at Tielt on 3 September, Turenne ordered the main body to make camp there but sent Jacob de Gassion, brother of the distinguished Marshal Jean de Gassion, with five or six regiments straight on to Deinze, about 12 miles (eight kilometres) to the east, where he knew there was a bridge over the Lys. Turenne intended, it appears, to continue immediately to the city of Oudenaarde; ordering Gassion to send scouting parties, he followed after two days with the main body, leaving the baggage train at Tielt under guard by the corps of Marshal de la Ferté. The wealthy city of Oudenaarde had been a fortified town since the tenth century with a history of siege and disputed ownership. During the Reformation, its people had adopted Protestantism and in consequence it had been besieged and captured from the Dutch by a Spanish army under Alexander Farnese, Duke of Parma, in 1581. Its medieval fortifications had been improved in 1521 but were by no means fully modernised. Its importance lay in the fact that it was situated in a loop of the Scheldt River and it therefore controlled a series of crossings over the waterway and thus the direct approach to Brussels, capital of the Spanish

The taking of Oudenaarde in 1582 (R.P. Famien Strada, Histoire de la Guerre Des Païs-Bas (Bruxelles, 1717), vol. iii, p.334.)

Netherlands. As the Duke of York put it, it was, 'a place of great importance, tho at that time of little strength'.[2]

Turenne crossed the River Lys at Deinze on 6 September, where he learned that five or six Spanish regiments had arrived at Oudenaarde. He therefore marched the same day to Gavere, a castle on the Scheldt 12 miles (18 kilometres) from Deinze and six miles (nine kilometres) north of Oudenaarde. The Spanish put a troop of 50 horse out to observe the French but could muster no more force, having not mobilised the militia:

> There was to have been a good number of peasants; but quick marches give leisure for reasoning indeed, but none at all for remedying. Of four or five thousand peasants who were order'd to be at that passage, there were not above two or three hundred and they immediately scamper'd away, all but fifty who put themselves into the castle which was on t'otherside the water.[3]

French dragoons led the way down to the river, followed by about 200 horse, all of whom forded the river. The castle immediately surrendered.

Turenne did not make immediately for Oudenaarde but moved on to Brussels, coming within about 12 miles (18 kilometres) of the city. This caused the Spanish to send some troops from Ghent and also the regiments at Oudenaarde under Don Antonio de la Cueva to protect Brussels. On 7

OUDENAARDE, YPRES AND THE DEFEAT OF THE PRINCE DE LIGNE, SEPTEMBER–OCTOBER 1658

September, Turenne threw a pontoon bridge ('a bridge of boats') over the Scheldt but made no move against Brussels. Early the next day a messenger appeared from the Spanish governor of Oudenaarde, asking for a parley, and telling Turenne that the Spanish horse had left the town. Turenne left the main army at Gavere and led 1,000 horse and 200 dragoons over the river, sending his aide-de-camp, M. de Madaillan, to warn the governor that he was about to be besieged. He was advised to remain neutral and allow the French army to cross the river there.

When Turenne approached the city, it appears that the Governor took heart at seeing so few troops and opened fire. Turenne remained three or four hours but with no foot and no artillery he could not force the city. He therefore sent word to the main army to march up, sending 300 horse under Lieutenant-Colonel De Bouillon to ford the river and prevent Spanish reinforcements from coming into the city from Courtrai. Returning himself to join the main body and leaving d'Humières in command, he sent 800 musketeers to reinforce the horse at Oudenaarde. However, not long after he had departed, the Spanish garrison made a sally and killed some of the French dragoons, burning the houses they had occupied. When he heard of this, Turenne decided that the force at Oudenaarde was vulnerable, especially if the Spanish sent a large body of troops from Tournai. He therefore sent word with the quartermaster of the horse, Martin, telling d'Humières to withdraw halfway from the town to the army.[4]

Next day, 8 September, the main army crossed its pontoon bridge, taking it up after they had passed, and moved on Oudenaarde from the direction of Courtrai, De Bouillon, at dawn, encountered two Spanish regiments of horse, forcing them to surrender; only 100 dragoons managed to break away and get into Oudenaarde. The main army, including the English regiments, was now west of the city, and d'Humières' small force to the east. Turenne crossed the river by boat to confer with d'Humières and make a reconnaissance. As he did so, three regiments of Spanish horse appeared under M. de Chamilli, which had been sent by the Prince of Condé to reinforce the city, having been told by the Governor that the approach was clear; one of the regiments was his own A small body of French dragoons under M. de Peguillain had joined Turenne and they stood fast: the Spanish took fright and drew off even though they were far superior in numbers, leaving Chamilli himself and a number of officers and men as prisoners.

From these prisoners, Turenne learned that the Spanish army was still dispersed and that he could proceed without fear of interference. The whole army therefore marched up later that day and immediately opened the siegeworks in three or four places including the approach to a demi-lune battery which was to be taken. The garrison, in the usual way, was summoned to surrender and were offered terms which included a guarantee to the citizens that the city would not be sacked and plundered. The garrison would be allowed to march out, save the horse that had arrived that morning, who must surrender themselves as prisoners.[5] These terms were accepted, and the city surrendered on 9 September. Morgan reported only that; 'there was nothing but a capitulation and a surrender presently'.[6]

Valuable as Oudenaarde was, its defences had been neglected and it was far into the Spanish Netherlands. It would have to be garrisoned strongly, but Turenne was in some doubt as to whether he should then advance on Brussels, or return to the Lys and take the town of Menin which would secure communications between Oudenaarde and Dixmüde. Another alternative would be to attempt to capture Courtrai. The issue was decided by the lack of heavy artillery, without which Brussels would not be taken. Moreover, the army was down to two or three days' provisions. Turenne therefore left only two regiments of horse and 400 foot under M. de Rochepère to garrison Oudenaarde, marching back to the Lys on 10 September. Rochepère, who was appointed governor of the city in December 1658, was described as: 'a very gallant man ... and because the place is much looked upon by the Spaniards, he is very diligent in finishing the fortifications ...'[7]

The French army marched up the right bank of the Scheldt, bringing its boats with it to give the impression that he meant to throw a bridge over the river and lay siege to Tournai. He had left de Gassion with nearly 1,500 men covering the bridge at Deinze and orders were sent to him to rejoin the army. Two hours before dawn on 11 September, the whole army was moving towards Tournai, where the Prince de Ligne was believed to been left with a body of troops by Don John, who had himself marched to Brussels. At about noon the army approached Menin and Turenne sent scouts to reconnoitre the place. Word soon came back from prisoners that the Prince de Ligne was less than five miles (eight kilometres) away with 2,000 foot and 1,500 horse, on the same side of the river as the French.

Turenne immediately sent the regiments of horse forming the advanced guard, those of the Count de Roye and Melun, to engage Ligne. Many individual officers, eager for glory, joined the attack. The Prince de Ligne had until this point been in Ypres, and as the Spanish believed Turenne to be intent on taking Brussels, Don John had sent him to Tournai from where he should then continue on to Brussels. De Ligne had halted at dawn to gather intelligence and determine which route he should take and was thus taken completely by surprise when the French horse attacked, without waiting for foot or dragoons to come up. The assault was furious and fell on the Spanish regiments of Droot and Louvigny. The Count de Roye led his regiment's charge against Louvigny and was shot twice in the legs but broke through the first Spanish squadrons. The regiments of The Queen, Rennel and Créqui followed, led by d'Humières and de Gadagne, and followed closely by de la Ferté's regiment of dragoons. The Spanish were soon in disorder; the infantry had taken cover behind hedges but put up little in the way of fire and soon began to throw down their arms and ask quarter. The horse began to retire, followed closely by the French, to a bridge on the Lys by the castle of Commines, which was in Spanish hands. There, they had left some baggage and provision waggons which had come from Lille and these further added to the confusion. The French therefore captured nearly all the Spanish foot – around 1,400 men with their arms and Colours – and around 1,000 horse. Only 300–400 escaped with Ligne back to Ypres and another 150 or so to Lille.[8]

OUDENAARDE, YPRES AND THE DEFEAT OF THE PRINCE DE LIGNE, SEPTEMBER–OCTOBER 1658

Turenne was all for besieging the castle of Commines, however prisoners revealed that Ypres was not strongly garrisoned; d'Humières therefore persuaded him that this was a far more valuable objective and must be speedily attacked. As the Duke of York put it:

> … this blow given to the Prince de Ligny, prov'd to be the worse consequence to the Spaniards, then the defeat which wee received near Dunkirk; for had it not been for this last misfortune, in all probability the French had done little during the rest of the Campagne, besides the taking of Gravelines, after the time which they were obliged to loose, while their King lay so disperatly sick at Calais; But the defeat thus given to the Prince de Ligny, put into their hands the opportunity of taking in so many Towns, as otherwise they durst not haue attempted.[9]

The capture of Oudenaarde and its aftermath is usually passed over in accounts of the campaign of 1658, but clearly at the time, it was believed to have been highly significant.

Having decided on Ypres as his next objective, Turenne warned the brigade of de Podwitz, which consisted of 10 squadrons of horse, about 1,300 men, to prepare to lead the advance. He also sent another brigade under Saint-Lieu to cut the road from Ghent to Ypres. Finally, he sent a demand for free passage to the town of Menin, where there was a bridge over the Lys about 12 miles (19 kilometres) from Ypres. The defences of Menin were in a ruinous state and the townspeople made no sort of resistance, opening their gates on 13 September. Podwitz's brigade passed through that evening appearing before Ypres on the road from Armentières by dawn the next day, 14 September. As he drew near, Podwitz observed a regiment of Spanish dragoons approaching from Armentières and attacked them, taking some prisoner and putting the rest to flight.[10]

That night, the rest of the army moved forward and camped near Menin, waiting for a body of troops which had been left near Tournai to guard the baggage train. On the following morning, 15 September, a large explosion was heard from the direction of Ypres. Turenne left 1,000 foot and 500 horse in Menin and sent orders to de Gassion, who with 800 foot and 500 horse had been sent to Deinze, to hasten to Oudenaarde and secure the army's rear, while the rest of the army made haste for Ypres. There were, however, another 1,500 men under Schomberg watching the approaches to Bergues, Furnes and Dixmüde and these were ordered to rendezvous with the army at Ypres, having left garrisons in each place. Turenne was therefore without his full army at Ypres, weakened further by having earlier detached several regiments of foot to besiege Hedin. However, he was sure of being superior in numbers and quality of troops to the Spanish garrison. This was under the command of the Prince de Ligne who had escaped there with what remained of his command. In all, the defenders numbered around 800 horse and 1,400 foot, of whom many were militia.

Without the baggage train there were no tools for digging trenches and several regiments of horse were therefore ordered to forage for picks, shovels and mattocks; Talon, the Intendant of the army, was despatched to Dunkirk to bring more, as well as timber, gabions and fascines; and also siege guns, powder and shot. There was also a severe shortage of forage for horses. Even so, the siegeworks were opened, although the early period of the siege was more of a blockade.

Turenne was uncertain about the intentions of the main Spanish army and he was therefore concerned about his communications with Oudenaarde. Accordingly, as soon as Schomberg arrived, he was sent with two regiments of foot and two of horse to secure Menin and its bridge. With his communications to Oudenaarde through Menin secured, Turenne turned his attention to Ypres. With all the various detachments and garrisons, he was short of infantry. Accordingly, he sent word to Marshal von Schulenberg, Governor of Arras, that the detachment at St-Venant, consisting of 1,200 horse, with the regiments at Hedin and 2,000 foot from the garrison of Arras, should move up to the Lys. Schulenberg's force assembled over the next days and marched first to Ypres, where he left the foot and 2,000–3,000 entrenching tools, then on to Menin with the horse.[11] Two days later, on 17 September, more entrenching tools arrived from the coast, just as the garrison made a sally, which was repulsed. Turenne then summoned the garrison to surrender, a summons that was rejected.[12]

The siege of Ypres began in earnest on 19 September with the entrenchments begun behind rising ground, about 500 yards from the outworks, which shielded the diggers and the assembled troops. Two trenches were opened, one by the French Guards and one by Marshal de la Ferté's troops. On the second day after the opening the trenches, the besiegers were approaching the counterscarp, which Turenne was determined to assault on the next day. This attack was reinforced by 500 of the English brigade under Morgan, who had taken little part in operations up to this time. Morgan's account of the preliminaries of this operation is characteristically colourful:

> Marshal Turenne turned the gentlemen of his chamber out, and shut the door himself. When this was done, he desired the Major-General to sit down by him, and the first news that he spake of, was, 'That he had certain intelligence, that the Prince of Condé and Don John of Austria were at the head of eleven-thousand horse, and four-thousand foot, within three leagues of his camp, and resolved to break through one of our quarters, to relieve the city of Ypres'; and therefore he desired Major-General Morgan, to have all the English ; 'under their arms every night at sun-set, and the French army should be so likewise.' Major-General Morgan replied, and said, 'That the Prince of Condë and Don John of Austria were great captains; and that they might dodge with Marshal Turenne to fatigue his army.' The Major-General farther said, 'That if he did keep the army three nights to that hard shift, they would not care who did knock them on the head.' Marshal Turenne replied, 'We must do it, and surmount all difficulty.' The Major-General desired to know of his Excellency, 'Whether he was certain the enemy was so near him?' He answered, 'He had two spies came just from them.' Then Major-General Morgan told him, 'His condition was somewhat desperate;' and said, 'That a desperate disease must have a desperate cure.' His Excellency asked, 'What he meant?' Major-General Morgan did offer him, to attempt the counterscarp upon an assault; and so put all things out of doubt with expedition. The Major-General had no sooner said this, but Marshal Turenne joined his hands, and looked up

through the boards towards the heavens, and said, 'Did ever my master, the King of France, or the King of Spain, attempt a counterscarp upon an assault, where there were three half-moons covered with cannon, and the ramparts of the town playing point-blank into the counterscarp?' Farther he said, 'What will the King my master think of me, if I expose his army to these hazards?'[13]

According to Morgan, Turenne and some of his senior lieutenants went forward to view the works. Morgan was all for an immediate assault, but Turenne was more cautious. Marshal Schomberg remarked that:

'My Lord, I think Major-General ... Morgan would offer nothing to your Lordship but what he thinks feasible; and he knows. He has good fighting men.' Upon this, Marshal Turenne asked Major-General Morgan, – 'How many English he would venture?' The Major-General said, 'That he would venture six-hundred common men, besides officers, and fifty pioneers.' Marshal Turenne said, 'That six-hundred of Monsieur la Ferté's army, and fifty pioneers, and six-hundred of his own army, and fifty pioneers more, would make better than two-thousand men.' Major-General Morgan replied, 'They were abundance to carry it, with God's assistance.' ... Marshal Turenne said to the Major-General, 'That he must fall into Monsieur la Ferté's approaches; and that he should take the one half of Monsieur la Ferté's men, and that he would take the other half into his own approaches.' Major-General Morgan begged his pardon, and said, 'He desired to fall on with the English entire by themselves, without intermingling them.'[14]

A discussion about possible diversionary moves followed, but these were abandoned in favour of a rapid surprise attack. Just after dusk, the English and the French Guards assembled and approached the counterscarp, the English divided into two battalions each of 300 men:

The Major-General made the English stand to their arms, and divided them into bodies; – a captain at the head of the pioneers, and the Major-General and a colonel, at the head of the two battalions: he ordered the two battalions, and the pioneers, each man to take up a long fascine upon their musquets and pikes, and then they were three small groves of wood. Immediately the Major-General commanded the two majors to go to their approaches; and that they should leap out, so soon as they should see the Major-General march between their approaches. The Major-General did order the two battalions, when they came within three-score of the stockadoes, to slip their fascines, and fall on.[15]

According to Morgan, the French, who were to move at the same time, stayed where they were until after the English attack had gone in. The English assaulted with great ferocity, throwing a great number of grenades. '... when the soldiers began to lay their hands on the stockadoes, they tore them down for the length of six-score, and leaped pell mell into the counterscarp amongst the enemy: abundance of the enemy were drowned in the moat, and many taken prisoners, with two German princes, and the counterscarp cleared.'[16]

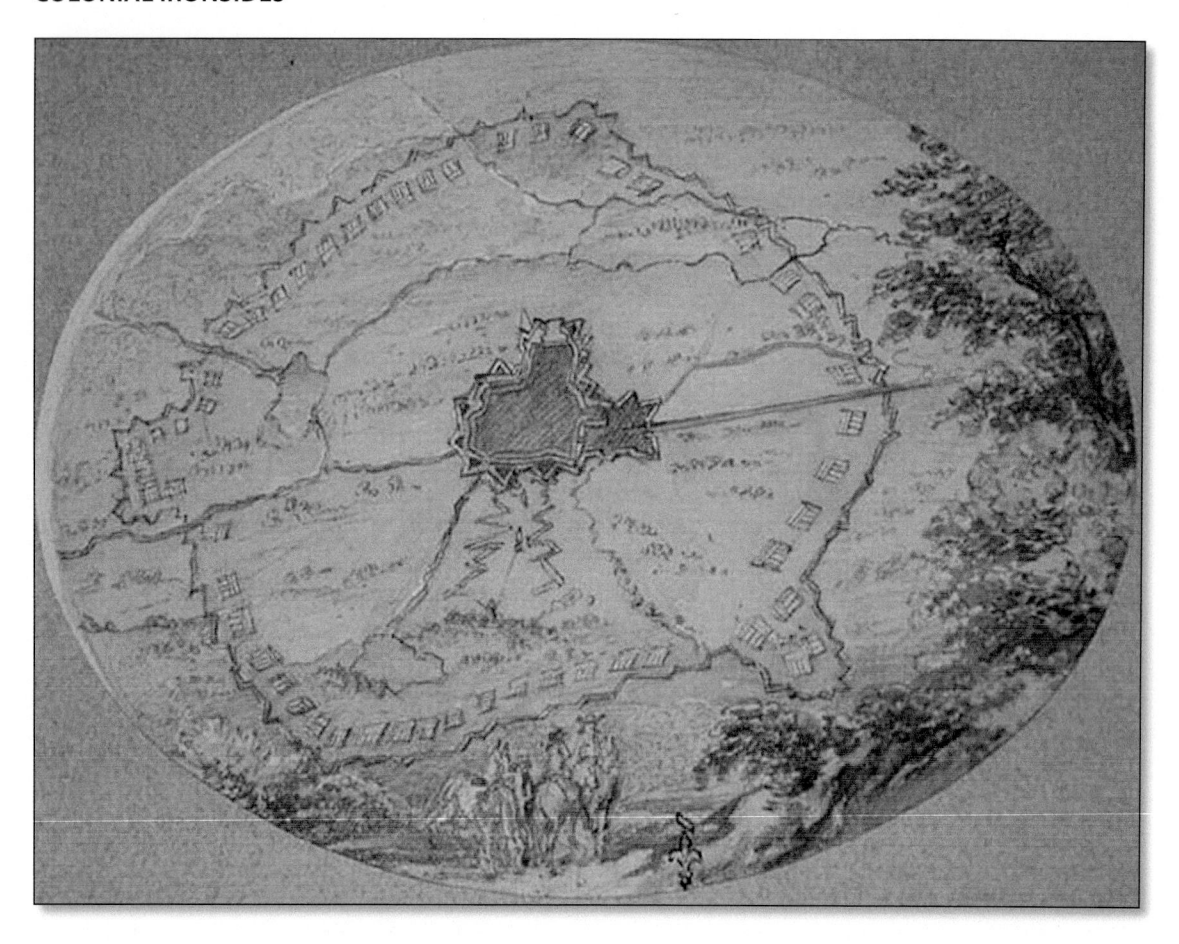

The fortifications of Ypres in 1648 (<www.fortified-paces.com/fortresses.html>, accessed 17 October 2020).

The defenders withdrew into several demi-lunes, one commanded personally by the Prince de Ligne. The French attacked one of the demi-lunes but were repulsed; the English turned several captured cannons onto the other two and carried them by assault. Morgan believed the remaining demi-lune would cause much trouble, and called on the English to carry it:

> … the redcoats cried, 'Shall we fall on in order, or happy-go-lucky?' The Major-General said, 'In the name of God, at it happy-go-lucky;' and immediately the redcoats fell on, and were on the top of it, knocking the enemy down, and casting them into the moat. When this work was done, the Major-General lodged the English on the counterscarp.[17]

Several Spanish officers were taken prisoner and the Prince only just escaped into the town, using a plank bridge over the moat.

An English captain followed Ligne into the town mistaking the escapees for his own troops and was taken prisoner. With a firm lodgement in the outworks, the attack was pressed next day by the Guards and the Regiment of Piedmont. The fourth night was spent in consolidating before them main assault on the town across the moat, which was filled with fascines carried forward by the horse. Seeing this, Ligne sent Colonel Droot, with three of the town elders, to ask for terms. Turenne sent Schomberg to conduct

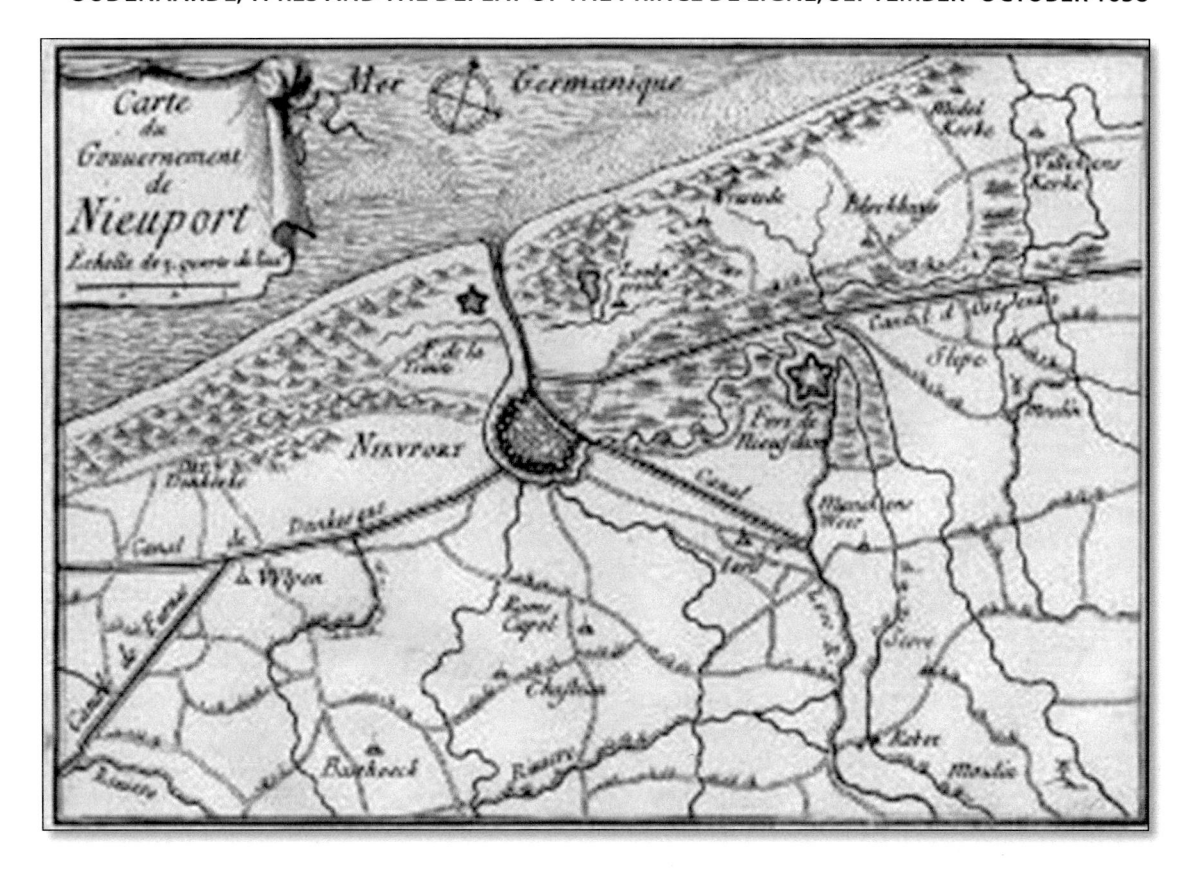

OUDENAARDE, YPRES AND THE DEFEAT OF THE PRINCE DE LIGNE, SEPTEMBER–OCTOBER 1658

A contemporary map of Nieupoort and its environs, c. 1667. (Author's collection)

the negotiations gave Ligne the honours of war and offered the city the continuation of its charter; the next day, 26 September, the Spanish garrison marched out for Courtrai with two guns, 700 horse and 1,200 foot.

The siege had lasted only five days with another eight days of blockade beforehand, but the attackers had lost 1,000 men killed and wounded. During the siege, the English lost Lieutenant-Colonel Fenwick, two captains, one lieutenant, two ensigns and 32 soldiers killed with 20 wounded. In the final assault, the English casualties were one captain, one sergeant and eight men killed, and 31 wounded. Morgan himself was slightly injured by a gunshot wound to his leg.[18]

Don John had made no attempt to interfere and had remained at Tournai, certain that the approach of autumn would oblige the French to abandon their campaign. Turenne, however, immediately returned to the reduction of the castle of Commines, sending 2,000 foot to assault it on the day of the surrender of Ypres and following up with the rest of the army a day later, after having left a garrison of 1,200 men in Ypres and sending orders for the fortification of Oudenaarde and Menin. Colonel Andrew Rutherford, later the Earl of Teviot and Governor of Dunkirk and subsequently of Tangier under Charles II, commanded the attack with his regiment, the *Garde Écossaise*, which in three days obliged the garrison of 80 men to capitulate.

On 28 September, Turenne concentrated the army at Turcoing, halfway between Tournai and Ypres. Here, a good store of corn was found for men and horses[19] and the army remained until 4 October. Marshal Schomberg returned to Arras, leaving his troops at Menin, while Turenne led the army to Epière, between Oudenaarde and Tournai. Here, he ordered that boats should be brought up from Oudenaarde for the construction of two pontoon bridges. He himself turned his full attention to the fortification and victualling of Oudenaarde, for the city was vulnerable to attack from Brussels and much in need of attention: Don John and Caracena were known to be at Brussels, but with other troops detached to cover Antwerp and Ghent, which they feared would be the next towns to be assaulted.

The Duke of York with what remained of the Royalist troops had remained at Nieupoort until Turenne was reported to be advancing, at which point he marched to Bruges, keeping the Canal d'Ostende between him and the French as he wished to avoid an unequal battle, nor let the French slip past him. Here, attacked by Lockhart with his new regiment of horse from Dunkirk – indicating perhaps that Lockhart's men were largely re-enlisted veterans, for they had had insufficient time to be transformed from raw recruits into a body capable of taking the field. Lockhart took 250 of his men and laid an ambush, taking a foraging party by surprise and capturing 500 cattle and 30 or 40 horses.[20] A week later he carried off another 1,000 head of cattle from villages around St-Omer.[21]

When Turenne was known to have moved to Oudenaarde, he returned to Bruges where on 26 September he received the news of the death of the Protector.[22] He immediately informed Don John and asked to be relieved of his command so as to join his brother. On 1 October, de Marsin was ordered to relieve him and the troops were dispersed into winter quarters. For both sides it was the end of the campaign and, as things turned out, effectively the end of the war.

18

The Peace of the Pyrenees and the Death of Cromwell, September 1658–May 1660

The close of the campaign of 1658 coincided with the arrival of news from England – news of some import: the death of the Lord Protector, Oliver Cromwell, on 3 September. He had appointed his surviving son, Richard, as his successor and the new Protector's accession was proclaimed by Lockhart and marked at Dunkirk by a salute: 'on the top of the steeple (which is of a great height) all the trumpets (belonging to the horse) sounded all the while, and afterwards sounded in every street of the town.'[1] Soon afterwards, the regiments there presented a loyal address to the new Protector.[2] The new government reappointed Lockhart as its ambassador to the French court, even though the French ambassador in England, Antoine de Bordeaux-Neufville, advised that he should remain at Dunkirk once the French army withdrew from the vicinity because of the danger of attack and the generally poor quality of the English officers: 'the enemy will find it easy enough, when the King's army is at a distance from the coast, to gain possession of the town, either by suborning the soldiers or taking them by surprise.'[3]

The English government however felt no such apprehension and at the end of December 1659, it recalled from Dunkirk the regiments of Salmon and Gibbon. Two companies of these regiments were, however, to stay at Dunkirk, and 400 old soldiers drawn from the regiments in England were to reinforce the garrison; the old soldiers designated, however, refused to embark for Dunkirk and so recruits had to be sent instead.[4] Lockhart was also instructed to recall the 'supernumerary companies of English which are now in the service of the King of France,' meaning apparently the remaining five companies of Lillingston's Regiment.[5] The five companies were accordingly sent for from their winter quarters in Amiens, travelling up the coast in ships; only half of them reached Dunkirk, as the vessel containing the rest sank. The net of these changes was that the garrison was much reduced and as the fortifications of both Dunkirk and Mardyck were in a poor condition with no money available for the work needed, Bordeaux was probably correct in

BY HIS HIGHNES COUNCIL IN SCOTLAND,

For the GOVERNMENT thereof.

WHEREAS it hath pleased the most wise GOD in His Providence, to take out of this world the most Serene and Renowned OLIVER late LORD PROTECTOR of this Commonwealth; And his said Highnesse, having in his life-time, according to the Humble Petition and Advice, Declared and appointed the most Noble and Illustrious the Lord RICHARD, eldest son of his said late Highnesse, to succeed Him in the Government of these Nations: We therefore of his Highnesse Council in Scotland, by direction of the Privy Council in England, do now hereby with one full voice and consent of tongue and heart, publish and declare the said Noble and Illustrious Lord RICHARD, to be rightfully PROTECTOR of this Commonwealth of England, Scotland and Ireland, and the Dominions and Territories thereto belonging, to whom we do acknowledge all Fidelity, and constant Obedience according to Law and the said Humble Petition and Advice, With all humble and hearty affection; Beseeching the LORD, by whom Princes rule, to blesse Him with long life, and these Nations with peace and happinesse under his Government.

And the said Council do hereby command the Sheriffs of the respective Shires, with all possible speed, to cause these Presents to be published in all the Market-Towns (except Burghs Royal) in their Sheriffdoms respectively; And do likewise command the Provost and Baylies of the respective Burghs Royal in Scotland, with all possible speed, to cause these Presents to be proclaimed in their respective Burghs, with all the Solemnity that is requisite upon such an occasion. And the said Sheriffs, Provosts and Baylies, are hereby required to make respective Returns of their Diligence herein to the Council with all expedition.

Given at Edinburgh the Ninth day of September, 1658.

George Monck,   Samuel Disbrowe,   Edward Rodes,

John Suintoune,   Nathaniel Whetham.

GOD save His Highnesse RICHARD LORD PROTECTOR.

EDINBURGH,

Printed by *Christopher Higgins*, in Harts Close, over against the Trone Church, Anno Donini, 1658.

The Proclamation of the death of Oliver Cromwell and the accession of Richard Cromwell as Lord Protector. (Beinecke Rare Book and Manuscript Library)

THE PEACE OF THE PYRENEES AND THE DEATH OF CROMWELL, SEPTEMBER 1658–MAY 1660

stating that the Governor's task was a heavy one. In Lockhart's absence, the command continued to be exercised by Alsop and Lillingston.

The war in Flanders and the rule of the Protectorate ended almost simultaneously. On 8 May 1659, in the aftermath of the French victories in Flanders during 1658, a suspension of arms was agreed upon between France and Spain, England was included as far as Dunkirk was concerned in the cessation of hostilities although England and Spain remained at war. France may have appeared ascendant, but her campaign against the Spanish territories in Lombardy had been defeated by Spanish success at Pavia and the frustration of French moves against Milan. Peace talks were convened on the Isle de Faisans in the Bidassoa River on the Spanish French border – talks in which the English were included only as observers. Peace was eventually signed on 7 November 1659 by Louis XIV of France and Philip IV of Spain with their chief ministers, Cardinal Mazarin and Don Luis Mendez de Haro. War between England and Spain was suspended in 1660 but was not finally ended until the Treaty of Madrid in 1667 which closed the English intervention in Portugal.[6]

Under the terms of the Treaty of the Pyrenees, France gained the Principality of Catalonia, which included the Roussillon, Conflet, Vallespir, the city of Perpignan and the northern half of Cerdanja. A compromise border was agreed in the debatable lands of the Basques. The French also gained the city of Montmédy, parts of the Grand Duchy of Luxembourg, Artois and territory in Flanders. This latter included the cities of Arras, Béthune, Thionville and Gravelines, but the French evacuated Oudenaarde, which returned to Spain. As part of this realignment, England, as agreed between Mazarin and Oliver Cromwell, received Dunkirk and Mardyck, its first colony on the continent of Europe since the expulsion from Calais in the reign of Queen Mary Tudor. New borders between France and Spain were fixed in the Low Countries and in the Pyrenees. Oddly, the treaty stipulated that all 'villages' north of the Pyrenees were to become part of France and therefore because it was a classed as a town, Llívia, once the capital of Cerdanja, was unintentionally left out of the settlement and became a Spanish exclave of the Spanish province of Girona. The border was not finalised in its present form until the Treaty of Bayonne in 1856. Spain was also forced to recognise officially all French gains at the Peace of Westphalia in 1648. But in exchange for Spain's losses of territory, the French abandoned their support for the rebellion in Portugal. Louis XIV also renounced his claim to the County of Barcelona which had been pursued since the revolt of the Catalans.

The treaty arranged a marriage between Louis XIV and Maria Theresa, daughter of Philip IV. Maria had to give up her claim to the throne of Spain as a condition but received a large financial settlement as part of her dowry, a settlement that was in fact never paid and which was one of the causes of the War of Devolution in 1668.

The treaty was the last major diplomatic achievement by Cardinal Mazarin. With the gains from the Peace of Westphalia, it gained for France a period of stability, both externally and internally, not least by weakening the power of both the Prince de Condé and the Crown of Spain; Condé submitted to Louis XIV and was restored to his titles and estates. However, his power as an independent prince was broken and he retired from public life. Although the Portuguese Restoration War was still in progress, most of Europe was at last at peace.

While the talks were in progress, the Long Parliament was restored in England on 17 May. It seemed probable that Lockhart's personal relations with the Cromwells, and his service to the two Protectors, would involve him in Richard's fall. But Lockhart, following the wishes of the soldiers of his garrison, accepted the change of government and submitted to the Parliament.[7] Alsop gave an account of Lockhart's speech to the officers of the garrison, a speech which was most necessary because opinion among the officers and men was divided between supporters of the Protectorate and more moderate republicans who supported the Parliament – and even some who would countenance a restoration of the monarchy:

> His excellency did then and there acquaint the officers with the transactions of things in England; and did also exhort and command the officers to a strict performance of their duty, notwithstanding the cessation made betwixt the two crowns of France and Spain, giving them good reasons to incite them thereunto; and did also acquaint them, that notwithstanding the change of government, which is now in England, that we were not to look upon particulars with the same eye, that we are bound in duty to look upon things of public concernment. And although the government were altered, the nation is still the same, and the concernment of the public also the same; for which we are immediately to act; and having through the providence of God procured this town to the use of our country, that we are to lay forth ourselves to the utmost of our power to keep and maintain it for the use aforesaid.[8]

Lockhart's first act on reassuming the government of Dunkirk, on 26 May, was to recall the three regiments still serving with the French army, those of Cochrane, Clark and Morgan. There were fears that the regiments might be detained by the Spanish, or else that the Spanish might disregard the truce and attack Dunkirk itself now that Turenne's army was removed. When they arrived at Dunkirk, they were quartered in tents just outside the walls.[9] Loyal addresses from them, and from the garrison regiments, were presented to Parliament during July: on the 19th from the regiments in French service and 27th from the garrison regiments.[10] The three regiments late in French service certainly had cause for complaint. 'They seem to be much troubled,' wrote Colonels Lillingston and Alsop, 'that no course is taken for them, by reason they are wholly forth of the French pay; and here is nothing to be got but for ready money, and that at a very dear rate.' No provision had yet been made for their pay or rations on the English establishment. However, the three regiments forming the garrison were not much better off, for though they were on the establishment they had received no pay for some time. A report presented to the Parliament on 7 April 1659, showed that the forces in Flanders and the garrison of Dunkirk cost £5,951 per month and that their pay was more than two months in arrears.

Early in June a plot had been formed among the soldiers of the garrison to pay themselves by plundering the town, but the attempt was put down without much difficulty and they appear to have been paid soon afterwards.[11] The Parliament thereafter sent over three officers to report on the state of the garrison and the fortifications, and to discover how much the town itself could be made to contribute to the support of the troops; they were Colonels William Packer and Richard Ashfield and Lieutenant-Colonel John Pearson.[12]

In August 1659, the Royalist rising led by Sir George Booth broke out in England. Parliament needed troops at once and on 4 August, Sir Bryce Cochrane was ordered to go to Dunkirk and bring back his own regiment with those of Morgan and Clark.[13] An account of the chaotic embarkation and misdirection of men from the garrison regiments is given in a disgruntled letter from Colonels Lillingston and Alsop:

> Sir Bryce Cockram came hither about four of the clock, and gave orders to the drums of the three field regiments to beat, for to ship the men away for England; which was done, but in so much confusion (notwithstanding that he carried it high, laying commands upon us to serve him much alike unto servants) that this garrison has suffered much prejudice thereby, by their carrying away near 200 of our soldiers, much to the weakening of our small number. We afforded him and the rest all the assistance imaginable. We spoke to the officers, desiring them that they would be very cautious in carrying away any of our soldiers; and they promised us that they would carry away none; but upon inquiry how many are missed out of each regiment and company we find wanting near about the number aforesaid. Indeed, it could not be well prevented by us, by reason of their being shipped by night; but by information of some of our officers we hear that many of our soldiers were disguised (in their cloaths, &c. without red coats) by some officers of those regiments, on purpose to deceive us. Our number of foot here amounteth not to above 2,500 fighting men, which is a very weak garison for this place with its forts. We made it our desires to the commissioners that there might be a recruit for these three regiments, to complete them to the number of 3,000, which will be a good ordinary garrison for this place, and with fewer we dare not promise you to keep it if we should be besieged; but with that number, and the regiment of horse, we hope, through the assistance of the Lord, we shall be able to give you such an account thereof, as may become honest men and persons fit to be intrusted with the charge of the garrison. Here are four companies (two of Colonel Salmon's and two of Colonel Gibbon's regiments) who are in a very longing condition to be relieved from hence, their regiments being in England; and the truth is, they are but weak, and daily weaker by their soldiers dropping away for England.[14]

The three regiments landed at Gravesend on or about 8 August and, as their numbers had been reduced during the campaign in Flanders, they were reorganised and reduced to two regiments, under the command of Clark and Cochrane.[15] Morgan's Regiment was broken up and the surplus officers were cashiered; Morgan himself returned to command a regiment of dragoons in Scotland.[16] Once the rebellion had been put down, the regiments were dispersed in detachments around towns in the West Country and the Midlands. They were therefore unable to play any part in the political manoeuvrings during the winter of 1659/1660. When Monck marched into

England, Clark's regiment had been concentrated and moved into billets in Yorkshire; he ordered it to Scotland to reinforce the garrisons he had left behind. It was disbanded at Leith about December 1660.[17] Cochrane's regiment was disbanded more rapidly. During the interruption of Parliament in the autumn of 1659 part of it was quartered at Gloucester, where, with his Lieutenant-Colonel, Mainwaring, 'Cochrane levied money upon the district for the support of his soldiers, and otherwise behaved in a despotic fashion.'[18] After the restoration of the authority of Parliament Cochrane was cashiered, a new colonel was appointed, and six companies of the regiment were marched first to London and then to Gravesend where they were ordered to return to Dunkirk on 14 January 1660.[19] The officers and men immediately mutinied – chiefly over continued arrears of pay – and the new colonel, whose name is not recorded, narrowly escaped death. Monck suppressed the mutiny and the regiment appears to have been disbanded shortly afterwards, in February 1660, although some of them men may have been sent back to Dunkirk to reinforce the garrison, orders having been issued for 600 men to be sent.[20]

Meanwhile, Parliament had appointed seven commissioners to review the army lists and remove all officers suspected of hostility to the republic, immorality, or religious views of a radical nature, replacing them with men who could be trusted. Around August 1659, the purge was applied to the garrison of Dunkirk. The three commissioners already there, Ashfield, Packer, and Pearson, had reported very unfavourably on the character of the garrison and its command: 'Here does want a person to command the garrison whose principle it is to encourage godliness in the power thereof. We have cause to fear that profaneness and wickedness (which do sadly abound in this place) will do more to the loss and prejudice thereof than all other enemies.'[21] Colonel Alsop, it was asserted, was 'an active man as a soldier, but an enemy to religion and godliness, especially in the sincerity of it'. Lillingston was no better: 'a mere soldier, who thinketh religion altogether useless in military discipline, or else he would not cherish such a crew of wicked officers as he doth'. Their officers too came in for severe criticism. Lillingston and Alsop became aware of these charges and what would likely follow, writing several times to the Council of State protesting strongly against falsehoods being put about by 'flatterers and designers and such as put on a cloak of religion to conceal their own unworthiness … We cannot conceal,' they wrote:

> the great regret we have to understand, that divers officers here, by some unworthy persons, have been traduced to your honours, though we know them to be men that have all along served you faithfully and cordially. We cannot believe that your honours will be ready to believe detractors, but rather to credit our testimony; for we assure you, that if we did conceive or suspect any officer of this garrison not fit for his command, either in respect of his fidelity or conversation, we should be most ready, according to our duty, to inform your honours; but truly we believe there are not in all your armies men that have demeaned themselves with more fidelity, courage, and modesty, both in England and here, wherein those that backbite them have been wanting too apparently.[22]

THE PEACE OF THE PYRENEES AND THE DEATH OF CROMWELL, SEPTEMBER 1658–MAY 1660

The various ill reports on the two seem to have had little effect and indeed, with Lockhart away on diplomatic duties once more, the burden of administering and disciplining the garrison fell squarely on these two men, who believed in the importance of the colony and were determined to uphold it: 'If we have not these supplies and the other necessaries,' says one of these letters to the Council of State:

> we cannot answer what you may perhaps expect of us, though we perish in the defence of this place, which our ambition and desire is to perpetuate to our nation, as a goad in the sides of their enemies, and to secure our footing in the Continent of Europe, lost since Queen Mary's days, and now regained; and doubtless we ought to preserve that carefully, which the Lord hath given us so graciously.[23]

They had good cause to issue such a warning, for even though the war between France and Spain was as good as over, both had designs on Dunkirk. Lockhart returned to Dunkirk in December 1659 and found the garrison loyal and under good discipline. Three weeks later, the army's attempt to rule the Three Kingdoms ended with the recall of the Long Parliament: Lockhart's letter of congratulation was read in the House of Commons on 3 January 1660.[24] There had, however, been changes as a result of the purge. In Alsop's Regiment, Captain John Withers was removed and Richard Pease was made major in place of Humphreys;[25] in Lillingston's, Captain Peter Pogson was cashiered, Major George Fiennes was reduced in rank to captain and transferred to Lockhart's Regiment with Abraham Davies made Major in his place.[26] Lockhart's own regiment seems to have been most heavily affected, with Captains Gargrave, Devoe, Muse and an unnamed fourth all cashiered.[27]

Lockhart did his best to improve the fortifications, but there was no money for other than maintenance; one small fort, Fort Manning, was built halfway between the city and Fort Oliver, but nothing now remains of it. He also commandeered the market hall as a Protestant church, although there were no clergy available until Hugh Peters, was sent over as chaplain to the army – but Peters was well known as a radical agitator. Peters did not stay long. In spite of Lockhart's general tone of toleration to the Catholic citizens, the image of the Blessed Virgin was removed from the gates and replaced with the arms of the Protector. The Sabbath was to be observed as strictly as in England, with shops forbidden to open; and penalties for the non-observance of Saints' Days were abolished.[28] Lockhart also seems to have been hopeful that English territory could be expanded to include Ostende, but this came to nothing.

Efforts were made to win Lockhart over to Charles II; Major-General John Middleton, who was well known to Lockhart, had led the attempts, but without success. Mazarin, according to Clarendon, had promised to make Lockhart a Marshal of France, and reward him financially, if he would deliver Dunkirk to the French hands.[29] Lockhart would have none of it. Increasingly, the mood at Dunkirk, as elsewhere, was that only the restoration of the monarchy would put an end to anarchy. Pepys recorded in his diary on 1 April 1660, that he was told by an officer of the garrison that 'the soldiers at Dunkirk do drink the King's health in the streets'.[30] On 8 May

1660, Lillingston presented an address to Monck on behalf of the garrison, in which they declared their acceptance of the restoration and expressed their loyalty. This closed Lockhart's government, for as soon as the King was restored, he replaced Lockhart with Sir Edward Harley.

Meanwhile, the remnants of Charles II's army continued to struggle on under the Duke of York, at Nieupoort and Nivelles. Many officers were still prisoners in France, although some managed to bribe their way to freedom. All were released in June 1659, but many had neither money nor clothes other than those they stood up in and were heavily in debt. During the winter of 1658 and the spring of 1659, the little army was reorganised and by July 1659 the King once more had six foot regiments, at least on paper: the King's Own, the Duke of York's, the Duke of Gloucester's, Lord Newburgh's, Colonel Richard Grace's, and Colonel Lewis Farrell's – as well as the two troops of horse, which were to form the basis of a regiment of horse guards.[31] The strongest was the Duke of York's, which consisted of 19 companies; the smallest that of Newburgh, which had 10. In all there were 86 companies. It appears that the Earl of Bristol lost his men to the Duke of York and then refused the offer of the Duke of Gloucester's Regiment. According to Hamilton, the King had about 2,000 men in Flanders in early 1660;[32] in May 1659, the King was reported to have said that he would bring 2,000 men with him to England.[33]

The death of Cromwell and the instability that followed gave renewed hope to the Royalists. Planning began for a general rising in England, to be supported by troops from Flanders. Booth's rising provided the opportunity the King wanted. With an eye to how the wind was blowing politically, Marshal Schomberg privately made his old comrade the Duke of York an extraordinary offer. Schomberg's own regiment of 1,200 men, with Rutherford's Scots, would cross to England with the Duke, should an attempt to invade be made in conjunction Booth's rising. With them would go six field guns, 3,000–4,000 muskets, ammunition and tools and enough flour to feed 5,000 men for six weeks. Ships to carry this force along with the Duke's own troops would be assembled at Boulogne. Should money also be needed, Schomberg would assist the Duke to pawn his plate and use as much credit as could be had.[34]

Schomberg insisted that neither the King of France nor Mazarin knew of this offer, which is hard to credit: as well as a letter of instruction to the Lieutenant-Governor of Boulogne, du Roy, Turenne produced another letter from the Governor, Marshal d'Aumont, which Queen Henrietta Maria had procured in Paris. James at once accepted. Mazarin, however, whilst permitting unofficial assistance, would sanction no overt action likely to lead to a breach with the English republic until the peace between France and Spain was finally completed. The Spanish government was also unwilling to back the Stuarts for the sake of peace with England. On returning to Brussels, the Duke found:

> ... that notwithstanding the Duke of Gloucester had delivered to the Marquis of Caracena the letters which his Royal Highness had written from Boulogne for the marching of his troops to St. Omer, yet the marquis would not permit them to

THE PEACE OF THE PYRENEES AND THE DEATH OF CROMWELL, SEPTEMBER 1658–MAY 1660

stir out of their quarters, though he was sufficiently pressed to it by the Duke of Gloucester. But he still answered, he did not believe Mr. de Turenne durst let them pass through any part of his King's dominions without order, which he knew he could not have. Nor would he suffer to draw down to the sea side, to which he was also urged by the Duke of Gloucester when he found he could not obtain his first point.[35]

It was decided that the force would land at Rye, occupy the town and then march to Rochester and Maidstone. The troops were actually *en route* to embark at Étaples when news came that Booth's rising had been defeated by Major-General Lambert; it was quickly decided to abort the invasion and await an opportunity to land Charles himself in Wales or the west of England. James and his men therefore retired once more into winter quarters. Throughout the troubles of 1659, therefore, Charles could make no use of his army, and when the Restoration took place, the force was dispersed around Flanders. After the Peace of the Pyrenees was signed, the Spanish government not unsurprisingly refused to continue their pay, referring them to their own sovereign, so that for some months their condition was harder than it had ever been. All that, however, changed with the Restoration.

19

The Restoration and Aftermath, May 1660–April 1663

Immediately upon his Restoration, in May 1660, Charles II ordered the replacement of Lockhart as Governor of Dunkirk and Mardyck by Sir Edward Harley who, although an adherent of Parliament during the Civil Wars, was a supporter of the rights of the people and an opponent of military dictatorship. Harley remained at Dunkirk until May 1661 when Andrew Rutherford, Earl of Teviot, an experienced soldier, was appointed in his place. Rutherford had spent the years of the Interregnum in the service of France and after the Restoration, Louis XIV recommended him to Charles.

Marshal Schomberg urged Charles to invest in Dunkirk, saying that he: 'had considered the place well, and he was sure it could never be taken … the holding of it would keep both France and Spain in a dependence on the king.'[1] Parliament indeed passed an act which annexed Dunkirk permanently to the English crown and the garrison was fixed at 3,600 foot and 432 horse. Service in Dunkirk was never popular, and many officers absented themselves frequently, requiring orders from Rutherford that all absentees should return to duty or face dismissal.[2]

Clarendon, however, did not agree with Schomberg, for the cost of maintaining the two fortresses as well as the new colony of Tangier, acquired through Charles's marriage to Catherine of Braganza in 1661, was too much for the exchequer to bear. The entire exchequer income of England and Wales for the year 1660 was £1,185,000 with another £143,000 for Scotland and £207,000 for Ireland. A huge slice of this was expended anyway on maintaining the armies of the Protector until they were disbanded: £638,000 per year for the army in England, £148,000 for Scotland, £104,000 for Ireland, £54,000 for the Jamaica garrison and £77,000 for the garrisons of Dunkirk and Mardyck.[3] After some negotiation, Charles agreed to sell the two fortresses to Louis XIV for five million livres, or £400,000 – £54 million in terms of real value at today's prices[4] – and withdraw what remained of the great garrisons.

During this period, therefore, Dunkirk and Mardyck acted as a holding ground for the former opponents of the two British armies in Flanders, from where, as the drawdown proceeded, the officers and men were either disbanded or sent elsewhere. Charles did not immediately call his own regiments in exile to England. They remained in Flanders and were gradually drawn to Dunkirk and were either incorporated into the garrison or otherwise given employment. The Duke of York's troop of horse was added to the establishment of Dunkirk by a vote in the House of Commons on 1 July 1660. According to the vote, the troop comprised 100 men besides officers,[5] later reduced to 50.[6] The troop remained there until the revolt of John Venner's Fifth Monarchy Men, in December 1660, when Monck recommended that the Duke of York's troop should be brought over to supplement the standing forces available for security duties. The troop was therefore added to the establishment of the army in England as one of the three troops of the Life Guards.[7] The next to be taken on to the establishment was the King's Own Regiment of Guards. On 26 August 1660, Lord Wentworth was appointed as colonel. The regiment was quartered at Nivelles and the officers at once sent Wentworth a letter explaining their parlous state:

> We are scarcely left one part of four who at Dunkirk battle entirely devoted themselves to be sacrificed for our King's sake, rather than deceive his reposed confidence in the resolve of his too few (at that time) loyal subjects. But having escaped the worst, beyond our hope, as to be prisoners, three parts of us perished with a tedious imprisonment and want of bread, and the few remainder here languish as having no allowance to live.[8]

Wentworth did not reply for some time and the regiment was moved into winter quarters at Namur. Here, they fared no better. The Marquis of Caracena sent orders to the town magistrates: 'that they were to give them no other accommodation than vacant houses upon the rampart and courts of guard, and that [they were] to expect their own subsistence from their own King, being restored to three kingdoms.'[9] The officers again wrote a petition, this time to the King, as a result of which they received orders to march to Dunkirk in early 1661. A series of warrants for arms, clothing and colours for the regiment show that it was reorganised and re-equipped at Dunkirk between March and October 1661.[10] On 20 June 1661, three months' pay was allocated for the Guards at a rate of £1,601/16s/8d per month. The regiment, now known as Lord Wentworth's Regiment of Guards, was to consist of 12 companies each of 100 men besides officers; Lord Wentworth was authorised to raise 1,100 recruits to complete it.[11] Throughout the governorship of the Earl of Teviot, it continued to form part of the garrison and seems to have lived on good terms with the former Cromwellian regiments. When Dunkirk to France in November 1662, Rutherford received orders to transport the regiment to various stations where it formed part of the English establishment. In August, Captain Robert Walters' company was sent to Guernsey and the companies of Captains Ralph Sydenham and James Jeffreys to Jersey, pending the formation of new permanent garrison companies in the islands. At the same time, Captain John Strode's company was sent to join the garrison of Dover Castle. In September Captain John Morley's company was shipped to Plymouth,[12] and in October Sydenham's company moved from Jersey to Portsmouth. In the same month, the companies of Captains Monson and Ashton were sent to Berwick-on-Tweed, Gwilliams' company to Portsmouth and Wise's to the Scilly Isles. The remaining two companies, those of the King and the Lieutenant-Colonel, went to Windsor by way of Deal.[13] Nine garrison companies had to be relocated, reformed or disbanded to find headroom in the finances to pay and accommodate the regiment: they were located in Windsor, Berwick, Portsmouth, Landguard Fort, the Scillies, Jersey, Pendennis Castle and Hull. The details are in the appendix to this chapter.[14]

On Wentworth's death on February 1665, the regiment was amalgamated with the King's Regiment of Foot Guards which Charles had raised under Colonel John Russell in England in November 1660. This regiment, consisting of 24 companies, in due course became the First or Grenadier Regiment of Foot Guards.

The four Irish regiments of foot, those of the Duke of York, the Duke of Gloucester, Colonel Grace, and Colonel Farrell, and the Scottish regiment of Lord Newburgh, probably mustered 1,700–1,800 men. They were joined by the Irish regiment of Colonel John Fitzgerald, which had until now remained in the Spanish service and which arrived from Beauvais.[15] These regiments appear to have been concentrated at Mardyck in the spring of 1661.[16] A letter from Sir Edward Harley to Monck in May described their situation and expressed some fears of an attack by the Spanish. He had consulted the Irish officers at Mardyck about moving the regiments closer to Dunkirk. Their opinion was that unless this was an urgent requirement, 'their troops will be much incommoded when they shall be in so narrow a room as they must be if they remove under the town walls, for although there are not in the troops above 1,600 effective men, yet there are many more women and children, who take up much room.' He considered that:

Sir Edward Harley, engraving by George Vertue, after Samuel Cooper, 1749. (Author's collection)

> the troops will be of more service at Mardyke to countenance the new works upon Fort Lyon side, and if the Spaniards will attempt to fall upon the Irish at Mardyke, then it is much more likely that the Spaniards will possess Mardyke, and make a quarter there; besides I must freely acquaint your Grace, that I very much doubt when the Irish and English come so near together they will not agree so well as at this distance.[17]

Intelligence reports suggested that the Spaniards were assembling troops at Nieupoort, Furnes, Hondsdroote, and Bergues, although in the event, nothing came of it. The comment about friction between the English and

THE RESTORATION AND AFTERMATH, MAY 1660–APRIL 1663

Irish is telling, reflecting both religious divisions and the remaining animosity of the Civil Wars. The remark about women and children is not surprising given the practice of the day.

During the winter of 1661–1662 the regiments were reorganised and superfluous officers were dismissed.[18] The Duke of York's Regiment of Foot, consisting of 1,200 men in 12 companies, was entered on the Dunkirk establishment by March 1662, under the command of Lord Muskerry,[19] although it was not for some time actually quartered in Dunkirk. 'I was at Mardyke,' wrote an English visitor in May 1662, 'the houses whereof being burnt down I saw not above six standing. A regiment of Irish, being the Duke of York's, keep a camp there, in huts made of sods.'[20] As the regiment was composed entirely of Irish officers and men there was no thought of incorporating it in the English army. Accordingly, in November 1662, the instructions sent to Rutherford for the disposal of the garrison of Dunkirk upon the sale of the town to France stated that the regiment was to enter the French service.[21]

The Duke of Gloucester's Regiment was, like the Duke of York's, quartered at Mardyck. When the Duke of Gloucester died in September 1660, his regiment, now commanded by William, Viscount Taaffe, had no-one to represent its interests. Forty-eight officers were dismissed during the winter of 1661–1662 and a warrant for the pay of the regiment in December 1661 shows that it nominally mustered 500 men besides officers, although its marching strength was 389.[22] After the sale to France the government forgot to issue any orders about its disposal until it sent an order to Lord Taaffe, dated 28 November 1662, ordering him to disband the regiment at once. It was accordingly broken up at Mardyck.[23]

In November 1661 the two Irish regiments of Farrell and Fitzgerald were shipped from Dunkirk to Tangier once it had been taken over from the Portuguese.[24] Farrell's was probably the regiment that had been the Earl of Bristol's; Fitzgerald's seems to have absorbed what was left of Grace's Regiment.[25] The final Royalist regiment was that of Lord Newburgh. In December 1660 it was quartered at Douai and its officers, having sold or pawned all they owned, were starving. According to their petition to Charles II, they had received neither pay nor rations of bread for the last six months except five florins each which the King had sent them.[26] The regiment was moved to Mardyck in the spring of 1661; in following December it was reduced to two companies and incorporated in one of the Irish regiments being sent to Tangier, from whence few if any men ever returned.

Alongside the old Royalists, the former Cromwellian regiments carried the major share of duties in Dunkirk. Because they were on the establishment of Dunkirk, they were not subject to the general disbandment of the army in the Three Kingdoms that followed the Restoration. In August 1660 there remained four of these regiments: Sir Edward Harley's, which had been Lockhart's; Alsop's; Lillingston's; and Colonel Robert Harley's Regiment of Horse, formerly Lockhart's. When Andrew Rutherford succeeded Sir Edward Harley as governor, Harley's Regiment of Foot passed under his command. Eighteen months later, when Dunkirk was sold to the French, the regiment was disbanded; some of its officers and an unknown number

COLONIAL IRONSIDES

Pierre Fauconnier, Bailiff of Dunkirk, raising the money for the purchase of the town. Engraving by Ternisien d'Haudricourt, c.1804. (Author's collection)

of men were sent to Tangier with Rutherford when he became governor there in February 1663.[27] The history of Lillingston's Regiment is unclear because the records are incomplete. What is known is that Lillingston was deprived of his commission in early 1661 and was succeeded in command of the regiment by Sir Robert Harley, the governor's brother.[28] In December 1661, Harley's regiment was sent to Tangier, where it landed in January 1662 with a strength of 947 men.[29] Alsop lost command of his regiment in April 1661 and was replaced by Lord Ossory and later by Lord Falkland. Alsop became Lieutenant-Colonel of the regiment and remained so for the rest of its existence. Many officers of the regiment were either replaced by Royalists and reduced in rank in order to make room for them, or else were dismissed. A petition to Monck from the officers at Dunkirk shows that they expected disbandment and only wished to be paid their arrears:

> You having been a father to your country, and more particularly to us of this garrison, God having raised you up to accomplish those things in the restoration of our Lord and master, his most sacred Majesty, to his rights, which we all constantly and passionately desired, but had not the possibility to effect but by your conduct, we implore you to mediate with the King that no officer or soldier of the troops or companies of this garrison may be cashiered or put out of their employment without first having their arrears paid. Signed by Colonel Roger Alsop, Lieutenant-Colonels Maurice Kingwell and William Fleetwood, and 47 others.[30]

Alsop himself, with some of his officers and men, accompanied Teviot to Tangier in 1663, where he became town major of the garrison. He served there until his death in 1676.

Finally, the six troops of horse raised in 1658 as Lockhart's Regiment became Sir Robert Harley's Regiment of Horse in August 1660 and then the Earl of Teviot's Regiment. Many of the officers were purged including all the Cromwellian troop commanders except Major Tobias Bridge. In April 1662 three troops of the regiment, commanded by Captain Michael Dungan, Captain William Littleton, and Major Sir William Salkeld, were paid their arrears and sent to Portugal, as part of the English expedition to support the Portuguese in their war of independence against Spain – although a condition of the Marriage Treaty when Charles II took the Infanta Catherine of Braganza as his consort, it was seen as a great insult by the Spanish after their sponsorship of the King during the last years of his exile.[31] Their numbers were made up with some volunteers from the English and Irish Royalists at Dunkirk. The three remaining troops of stayed at Dunkirk until they were disbanded in November 1662 when the place was sold to France.[32] Bridge, who was knighted about 1663, was at Tangier in command of a troop of horse in the same year and when Teviot was killed in May 1664 the surviving officers of the garrison elected Bridge acting governor, a position he held until his return to England in 1666.

The evacuation plans for Dunkirk were finalised when the sale of the fortresses was agreed with Louis' representative, Pierre Fauconnier, who became Grand Bailiff of Dunkerque, on 4 November 1662; by the spring of 1663, the French were in control. Thus ended the brief but stormy story of the only English colony on the mainland of Europe since the reign of Mary Tudor. Although Dunkirk was again briefly occupied by the British in 1712, it was the capture of Gibraltar in 1704 that began the only colonial enterprise on the Continent, if various Mediterranean islands are excluded, from that day to this.

Appendix to Chapter 19

Army Lists of the Dunkirk and Mardyck Garrisons after the Restoration, May 1660–April 1663

ʃ indicates that the officer appeared in the Indigent Officers List of 1663

Governor
Sir Edward Harley, May 1660
Andrew Rutherford, Earl of Teviot, 1 June 1661

Staff
Marshal-General Henry Gargrave
Town Major William Lloyd
Physician to the Garrison Francis Pockley
Surgeon-General Alexander Eristy

The King's Life Guard of Horse[1]

Captain Lord Gerard of Brandon

Lieutenants
Major-General Randolph Egerton
Sir Thomas Sandys, Bart.
Sir Gilbert Gerard, Bart.
Colonel Thomas Panton

Cornets
The Hon. Edward Stanley
Edward Lloyd
Captain William Dale[2]

Corporals
Colonel Francis Lovelace

APPENDIX TO CHAPTER 19

Colonel Charles Scrimshaw
Colonel Francis Berkeley
Colonel Edward Roscarrick

Staff
Chaplain Dr Mathew Smallwood
Surgeon Thomas Woodall
Quartermaster Colonel James Prodgiers
Provost Marshal Richard Llewellyn

The King's Regiment of Guards, or Lord Wentworth's Footguards (26 August 1660–October 1662)[3]

Colonel Lord Wentworth[†]	Captain-Lieutenant William Barker[‡]	Ensign Thomas Stradling ∫
	Captain-Lieutenant Thomas Stradling (12 Apr 1660)	
Lieutenant-Colonel Charles Wheeler[§]		Ensign Bevil Skelton
Major Henry Heylin		
Major John Carey (vice Heylin)	Lieutenant John Walker	
Captain (Colonel) Mathew Wise[¶]∫		
Captain (Colonel) John Morley	Lieutenant William Eaton[**]	
Captain Sir Thomas Ashton (vice Gwynn)	Lieutenant John Croft[5]	Ensign Brian Richardson
Captain John Monson	Lieutenant Anthony Thorold[††]	
Captain John Strode[‡‡]		
Captain John Gwillims, or Gwilliam		Ensign Henry Sandys[§§]
Captain Herbert Jeffries[¶¶]	Lieutenant William Sanderson (Jan 62)	
Captain Ralph Sydenham	Lieutenant Philip Paramore	

---

* Amalgamated on 16 March 1665 with Colonel John Russell's Regiment of Foot Guards, or His Majesty's Own Regiment of Foot Guards, raised in November 1660.
† Unclear as to when Wentworth actually took command from Throckmorton or Blagge. His commission is dated 26 August 1660 (Hamilton, *Origins and History*, vol. I, p.75).
‡ After the amalgamation, captain in The King's Foot Guards.
§ After the amalgamation he was appointed to command a troop of horse (Dalton, vol. I, p.61).
¶ Said to be the brother of Sir Edward Wise KG; resigned his commission 26 September 1667 as being barred from further service by the Test Acts, as a Catholic.
** After the amalgamation, captain in the King's Foot Guards.
†† Later a lieutenant in the Portsmouth garrison (Dalton, vol. I, p.127).
‡‡ 1627–1686. Later Major of the King's Foot Guards, lieutenant-governor of Dover castle and MP for Sandwich.
§§ In 1678, lieutenant in the King's Foot Guards having possibly been in the interim lieutenant in one of the additional companies raised for the Captain-General's Foot Guards.
¶¶ Captain in the garrison of York in 1670, and in 1676 commanded the Virginia battalion.

321

COLONIAL IRONSIDES

Captain Robert Walters[***]
Captain Sir Hugh Middleton[6]
Captain Stuart Walker[7]   Ensign __ Hill

Staff
Adjutant Robert Spotswood
Quartermaster and Marshal William Sanderson; William Harwood (Feb 1662)
Chaplain Timothy Boughty

Petition of the guards in Flanders for relief, not one in four of those who were att the Dunes are now in the ranks:

Captain Sylvanus Tomkins[†††]	Lieutenant Arthur Broughton[‡‡‡]	Ensign John Criefe
Captain Matthew Wyse	Lieutenant Anthony Coldham	Ensign Philip Paramore
Captain Robert Walters	Lieutenant Richard Richardson[§§§]	Ensign John Carlston
	Lieutenant John Yonge∫	Ensign Francis Hamon[¶¶¶]
	Lieutenant __ Mallinyeux	Ensign Guillamy Tomkins
	Lieutenant Thomas Langford	
	Lieutenant Henry Crispe[****]	
	Lieutenant Alexander Wallwyne	
	Lieutenant Launcelot Stanier (Stonor)	
	Lieutenant John Gwynne ∫	

Ranks Not Known
John C[urtys][††]
James Jeffreys
Anthony Thornton[‡‡]

The Duke of York's Troop of Life Guards

Captain Sir Charles Berkeley	Lieutenant Robert Dongan	Cornet John Godolphin
Corporals	**Quartermaster**	**Surgeon**
Francis Bedlow	Edward Barclay	John Robinson
James Somervill		
Thomas Davenport		

---

*   After the amalgamation, captain in the King's Foot Guards.
†   In 1673, lieutenant in the King's Foot Guards.
‡   After the amalgamation, lieutenant to Sir Francis Mackworth in the King's Foot Guards.
§   After the amalgamation, lieutenant in the King's Foot Guards, captain in 1673.
¶   Lieutenant to Robert Walters in the King's Foot Guards in 1668.
** Lieutenant to Richardson in the King's Foot Guards in 1674.
†† Served in Wentworth's Regiment of Horse in 1649.
‡‡ A Thornton had served in the Royalist army before 1649. Walter's company Jersey 1661.

Thomas Stourton

Gentleman Volunteer Nicolas Kemys

Returned to England and amalgamated with the King's Life Guard of Horse.[4]

Sir Robert Harley's, Later the Earl of Teviot's, Regiment of Horse (4th, 5th and 6th Troops to Portugal in May 1662)

1st Troop
Colonel Sir Robert Harley
Colonel Lord Rutherford, Earl of Teviot (1 Jun 1661)[*]
Captain-Lieutenant John Grant
Captain Lieutenant Henry Flower (Aug 1660)
Captain-Lieutenant Henry Fitzjames (23 Oct 1661)
Cornet Henry Willoughby
Cornet Edward Talbot (Aug 1660)
Quartermaster George Penny

2nd Troop
Major Tobias Bridge[†]
Lieutenant __ Hargrave
Lieutenant Edward Witham (4 Mar 1662)
Cornet John Brown
Quartermaster Mathew Wayne

3rd Troop
Captain Oliver Nicholas
Captain Alexander Standish (13 Jul 1662)
Lieutenant Thomas Stackhouse
Cornet Thomas Bernadiston
Quartermaster __ Laugherne

4th Troop
Captain James Halsey
Captain William Littleton (6 Jan 1662)
Lieutenant Robert Broadnax
Cornet Peter Pawlyn, or Paulinge.[‡]
Quartermaster Theodore Russell

5th Troop
Captain Edward Wood

---

[*] To Tangier as Governor in 1662, killed 1664.
[†] Later to Tangier where he became acting governor after the death of Teviot; knighted c. 1663. Later commanded the Barbadoes Regiment and was governor of the colony. Bridgetown is named after him.
[‡] Killed at Ameixial in 1663.

COLONIAL IRONSIDES

Captain Michael Dungan (9 Apr 1662)*
Lieutenant George Brett
Cornet William Ashenhurst
Quartermaster Samuel Sharp

6th Troop
Captain Sir William Salkeld (17 June 1661)†
Cornet __ Willoughby
Cornet Thomas Maddock (30 Apr 1662)

The Duke of York's Regiment of Foot (to French Service)

Colonel H.R.H. The Duke of York
Lieutenant-Colonel Lord Muskerry

Captain Edward Bennett	Lieutenant Terence O'Brien	Ensign Terence O'Higgins
Captain Daniel O'Keefe	Lieutenant Daniel O'Driscoll	Ensign Teige O'Mulligan
Captain Dermott O'Brien	Lieutenant John O'Connellan	Ensign Septimus Field
Captain Francis Huegnett	Lieutenant Donough O'Falary	Ensign Pierce Butler
Captain Philip Barry	Lieutenant Batholomew Spillman	Ensign Richard Norris
Captain Daniel Denman	Lieutenant Norris O'Hegharty	Ensign Edmund Denman
Captain Thomas Browne	Lieutenant John Burke	Ensign Anthony Snyllenan
Captain John O'Neill	Lieutenant __ Blaghlin	

The Duke of Gloucester's Regiment (Reduced, January 1662)

Colonel H.R.H. The Duke of Gloucester		Ensign Christopher Fitzgerald
Lieutenant-Colonel Viscount Taaffe		Ensign Theobald Stapleton
Major Walter Philips	Lieutenant Mayther Philips	Ensign Hugh O'Connor
Captain Hugh O'Connor	Lieutenant Robin Nisbett	Ensign Owen Snillsman
Captain the Lord Iveagh	Lieutenant Henry Tuite	Ensign Phelome Carter
Captain Dudley Costello	Lieutenant Roger O'Connor	Ensign Gilbert Roe
Captain Walter Hope	Lieutenant Edward Hope	Ensign Thomas Hope

Staff
Adjutant Roger Brenan
Chaplain Fr John MacDavid

---

* Lieutenant-Colonel of the Regiment of Horse in Portugal; killed at Ameixial in 1663.
† Old Royalist knighted in 1663. MP for Old Sarum in 1669.

Colonel Sir Edward Harley's, later the Earl of Teviot's Regiment of Foot (disbanded 1662)

Colonel Sir Edward Harley	Captain-Lieutenant Peter St Hill	Ensign Thomas Young
Colonel The Earl of Teviot (1 Jun 1661)	Captain-Lieutenant Brent Ely (March 1662)	
Lieutenant-Colonel William Fleetwood	Lieutenant Thomas Ingram	Ensign Arthur Colliot
Lieutenant-Colonel Henry Norwood (7 Sep 1661)	Lieutenant Batholomew Henderson (Mar 1662)	Ensign Benjamin Welsh (Mar 1662)
Major John Hinton	Lieutenant Richard Woodward	Ensign John Eubanke
Captain Peter St Hill (7 Sep 1661)	Lieutenant Samuel Brookes (Aug 62)	Ensign Ferdinando Carey (Aug 1662)
Major Edward Knightley (28 Feb 1662)		
Captain Francis Conway	Lieutenant John Green	Ensign William Grant
Captain __ Gladston (7 Sep 1661)	Lieutenant John Forester (Aug 1662)	Ensign John Buck (Aug 1662)
Captain Roger Cotes	Lieutenant Edward Emmes	Ensign John Eubanke (Aug 1662)
Captain Robert Needham (19 Sep 1661)		
Captain Edward Righton	Lieutenant Richard Baker	
Captain Abraham Davies	Lieutenant John Turpin	Ensign William Carter
Captain John Muse	Lieutenant William Beech	
Captain __ Coxe (7 Sep 1661)	Lieutenant Charles Daniel (7 Sep 1661)	
Captain Christopher Monk	Lieutenant Edward Layton	Ensign Henry Jackson
Captain Francis Bromwich	Lieutenant James Ralph	Ensign William Jones
Captain Ralph Emmerson		
Captain Martin Gardner (17 Dec 1661)		Ensign __ Freth (Aug 1662)

COLONIAL IRONSIDES

Captain William Langton (Aug 62)	Lieutenant William Saddlington	Ensign Thomas Blagny
Captain Sir Hugh Middleton (Aug 62)	Lieutenant William Bassett	
Captain __ Eubanke (Aug 62)		Ensign Thomas Michael

Staff
Quartermaster and Marshal-General Henry Gargrave
Surgeon Walter Scott

Colonel Roger Alsop's, Later Lord Ossory's and then Lord Falkland's, Regiment of Foot

Colonel Roger Alsop	Captain-Lieutenant John Graham	Ensign Edwin Bates
Colonel Thomas, Earl of Ossary (Apr 1661)		Ensign Charles Banks (18 Jun 1661)
Colonel Henry, Lord Falkland (Jun 1661)		
Lieutenant-Colonel Maurice Kingwell	Lieutenant John Giles	Ensign Thomas Griffith
Lieutenant-Colonel Roger Alsop (Apr 1661)		
Major John Withers	Lieutenant Francis Dukes	Ensign John Brookes
Major Henry Heylin (1 Jun 1661)	Lieutenant Francis Inches (22 Jun 1662)	Ensign Valentine Purefoy (23 Mar 1662)
Captain Thomas Chapman	Lieutenant Edward Pope	Ensign Thomas Withers
Captain James Porter (30 Dec 1661)	Lieutenant John Bultell (18 Feb 1662)	
Captain Nathaniel Cobham	Lieutenant Richard Flemming	Ensign William Hussey
Captain Richard Pease	Lieutenant Robert Grosse	Ensign Anthony Palmer
Captain John Withers (18 Jun 1661)	Lieutenant Tobias Barns (30 Sep 1661)	
Captain John Chune (26 Oct 1661)	Lieutenant Thomas Ronefossse (1662)	Ensign Zouch Tate (28 Feb 1662)
	Lieutenant John Machin (13 Jul 1662)	

APPENDIX TO CHAPTER 19

Captain Humphrey Atherton	Lieutenant Thomas Bassett	Ensign Thomas Blackat
Captain Francis Annesley	Lieutenant James Pembridge	Ensign Richard Line
Captain Rice Powell	Lieutenant Richard Dayes	Ensign Alexander Young
		Ensign George Alsop (8 May 1662)
Captain __ Scowin (1661)		
Captain Stuart Walker (18 Jun 1661)		Ensign Richard Skiep (10 Mar 1662)
Captain John Price (19 Mar 1662)		
Captain Sir Anthony Cope (18 Jun 1661)	Lieutenant William Moore (16 Sep 61)	Ensign Henry Norris (12 Jun 1661)
Captain Wm Gannock (27 Jul 1662)	Lieutenant Tobias Barns (1661)	Lieutenant Mathew Carew (30 Apr 1662)
Captain Thomas Cartwright (18 Jun 1661)	Lieutenant Edward Starsmore (31 Mar 1662)	Ensign John Chamberlain

Staff
Quartermaster and Marshal Nicholas Tom; Michael Jones (1661); Holland Simpson (4 Apr 62)
Surgeon John Wilkinson

Colonel Henry Lillingston's, later Sir Robert Harley's, Regiment of Foot[5]

Colonel Henry Lillingston	Captain-Lieutenant William Whittaker	Ensign William Fiennes
Lieutenant-Colonel Maurice Kingwell	Lieutenant Thomas Young	Ensign Ralph Walker
Lieutenant-Colonel Thomas Heynes, or Heywood		
Major George Fiennes	Lieutenant John Sherrard	Ensign Alexander Crawford
Captain Samuel Brookes	Lieutenant Robert Muschamp	Ensign Robert Myelvis
Captain Hasgrave		
Captain Lloyd[§§§§§]		
Captain Date (Dale?)		
Captain James Emmerson (Emerson)[¶¶¶¶¶]		
Captain James[******]		

---

* Possibly Thomas Lloyd who had served in Robson's Regiment until it was disbanded in Scotland in 1660.

† Had served in Hubblethorne's Regiment until its disbandment in 1660. He appears to have gone to Tangier and probably died there in 1664 (Firth and Davies, vol. ii, p.471; Davis, vol. I, p.27).

‡ Probably William James, who had served in Lockhart's Regiment in 1657.

327

COLONIAL IRONSIDES

Captain Herbert
Captain Wyerd (Wyberd?)
Captain Baullard††††††
Captain Summers

The regiment was purged of republicans and went to Tangier in January 1662:

Colonel Sir Robert Harley (8 Apr 1661)	Captain-Lieutenant William Whittaker	Ensign Thomas Mitchell
Lieutenant-Colonel Maurice Kingwell	Lieutenant Thomas Young	Ensign Ralph Walker
Major George Fiennes (Clinton)	Lieutenant John Sherrard	Ensign Alexander Crawford
Captain Robert Fitzwilliams	Lieutenant John Southerne	Ensign George Fitzwilliams
Captain Robert Smith	Lieutenant Robert Laundry	Ensign James Stopford
Captain Peter Pogson	Lieutenant Herbert Boare	Ensign William Terry
Captain Samuel Brookes	Lieutenant Robert Muschamp	Ensign Robert Mylevis
Captain William Wandes	Lieutenant Lewis Powell	Ensign Lawrence Fellow
Captain Henry Middleton	Lieutenant Robert Lawriston	Ensign Thomas Brereton
Captain John Cooke	Lieutenant William Fiennes (Clinton)	Ensign Richard Withers

Staff
Quartermaster and Marshal John Curtis
Surgeon Robert Farendit
Chaplain __ Harrison

Colonel Lewis Farrell's Regiment at Mardyck (to Tangier, 1662)

Colonel Lewis Farrell	Captain-Lieutenant Bryan Farrell	Ensign John Donovan
Lieutenant-Colonel Charles Molloy	Lieutenant Daniel Molloy	Ensign James Molloy
Major Gaspar Tuite		
Major James Bolger (1661)	Lieutenant __ Holmes	Ensign Harry Leyes
Captain Henry Farrell	Lieutenant Thomas Bourke	Ensign Conor Burke
Captain William Butler		Ensign Theodore Butler
Captain John Shaa		
Captain Charles Farrell	Lieutenant Roger Farrell	Ensign Edward Farrell
Captain Haughy Farrell	Lieutenant Thadeus Farrell	Ensign Walter Reynolds
Captain Thomas Fitzpatrick	Lieutenant Alexander Daron	Ensign Richard Dody
Captain James Farrell	Lieutenant William Farrell	Ensign James Farrell
Captain John Molloy	Lieutenant Edward Molloy	Ensign John Gilmour

---
* His commission is dated 26 June 1661.

APPENDIX TO CHAPTER 19

| Captain Thomas Farrell | Lieutenant Hugh Granby | Ensign Harry Dermott |

Staff
Quartermaster and Marshal Richard Farrell
Surgeon Cornelius Broslan
Chaplain Father Edward Nangle

Colonel John Fitzgerald's Regiment (to Tangier, 1662)

Colonel John Fitgerald	Captain-Lieutenant Mahon Mahony	Ensign Daniel Condon
Lieutenant-Colonel Edward Fitzgerald	Lieutenant James Fitzgerald	Ensign Redmond Burke
Major __ Blaggne	Captain __ Erskine	Ensign John Harbord
Captain __ Wealy	Lieutenant Kennedy Bryan	Ensign __ Roach
Captain John Walsh	Lieutenant William Roache	Ensign Hugh Maghoo
Captain Thomas Fitzmorris	Lieutenant Walter Bourke	Ensign Laughlin Hoogh
Capr Donogh McNamara	Lieutenant Hugh McSwaine	Ensign Andrew Fitzgerald
Captain David Carey	Lieutenant Edmond Carey	Ensign __ Shohand
Captain James Fitzgerald	Lieutenant __ Dullond	Ensign Patrick Fitzmorris
Captain Phiilip Bork	Lieutenant Morogh Shoohy	Ensign Murragh Mahony

Colonel Richard Grace's Regiment (disbanded and absorbed into Farrell's and Fitzgerald's Regiments)

Colonel Richard Grace		
Captain Arthur Molloy	Lieutenant John Carroll	Ensign William Delany
Captain Edmund Burke	Lieutenant Owen Flattry	Ensign Walter Waugh
Captain Gerard Aylmer	Lieutenant William Burke	Ensign Theobald Butler
Captain William Stapleton	Lieutenant Sherlagh Molloy	
Captain Robert Waugh	Lieutenant Daniel McNamara	
Captain James Denny	Lieutenant Matthew Molloy	
Captain Dermott Lucy	Lieutenant Richard Hogarty	
Captain Gerrard Coughlan	Lieutenant Dermott Coughlan	

Staff
Adjutant Brien O'Bryen
Quartermaster and Marshal Marcus Browne

The Earl of Newburgh's Scots Regiment at Mardyck (reduced to two companies in 1661 and these to Tangier in 1662)

Colonel Lord Newburgh	Captain-Lieutenant Hamilton Wisseris	Ensign __ McDonough
Lieutenant-Colonel William Urry	Lieutenant __ Blaine	Ensign __ La Grande
	Lieutenant __ Hamilton	Ensign __ Murray

COLONIAL IRONSIDES

Captain __ Strachan	Lieutenant __ Balfour	Ensign __ Farquhar
Captain __ Doolan	Lieutenant __ Higgins	Ensign __ Gaston
Captain __ Chapman	Lieutenant __ Nugent	Ensign __ Cartre
Captain __ Magginnis	Lieutenant __ Gordon	Ensign __ McGuire
Captain __ Middleton	Lieutenant __ Middleton	Ensign __ O'Hare

Staff
Captain and Adjutant Peter Wood; Denis O'Driscoll Quartermaster and Marshal George Wills

Postscript 1: Summary of the destinations of regiments and companies from Dunkirk

Regiment	Company/Troop	Destination	Notes
King's Life Guard of Horse	All	England	
Duke of York's Troop of Life Guards	All	England	Amalgamated with King's Life Guard.
Earl of Teviot's Regiment of Horse	1st (Teviot), 2nd (Witham) and 3rd (Standish)	Remained at Dunkirk	Disbanded 1662
	4th (Littleton), 5th (Dungan) and 6th (Salkeld)	Portugal	Remnants returned home and disbanded in 1668
King's Regiment of Guards. All companies added to Russell's Regiment of Guards on Wentworth's death in 1665	King's (Colonel's) and Lieutenant-Colonel's	Windsor	Company of Sir Thomas Woodcocke displaced to Hull where one company of the six there disbanded (unnamed)[7]
	Major Carey's Walters'	Landguard Fort Guernsey	Earl of Warwick's company disbanded[8]
	Sydenham's	Jersey	Later to Portsmouth where company of Captain Fincher reformed.[9]
	Jefferies'	Portsmouth	vice the company of Edward Victor which went to Jersey. Later to Jersey.[10]
	Strode's	Dover	

APPENDIX TO CHAPTER 19

Regiment	Company/Troop	Destination	Notes
	Monson's and Ashton's	Berwick-on-Tweed	Monson's vice the company of Sir Charles Stanley, disbanded; Ashton's vice the company of Sir Francis Crane, disbanded although originally noted to be moved to Pendennis or Scilly.[11]
	Gwilliams'	Portsmouth	Company of Edward Spragg disbanded at Portsmouth.
	Wise's	Pendennis	
	Morley's	Plymouth	
Duke of York's Regiment of Foot	All	to French service in 1662	
Duke of Gloucester's	All	Disbanded at Mardyck in November 1662	
Farrell's	All	to Tangier in January 1662	
Fitzgerald's	All	to Tangier in January 1662	
Grace's	All	disbanded and absorbed into Fitzgerald's	to Tangier in January 1662
Newburgh's	All	Douai; returned to Mardyck in early 1661 and reduced to two companies. Disbanded in 1662 and absorbed into Farrell's and Fitzgerald's	to Tangier in January 1662
Teviot's (formerly Edward Harley's)	All	Disbanded at Dunkirk in 1662	Teviot with some officers and men to Tangier in 1663
Lord Falkland's (Alsop's)	All	Disbanded at Dunkirk	Alsop with some officers and men to Tangier in 1663
Robert Harley's (formerly Lillingston's)	All	to Tangier in January 1662	

Postscript 2: The King's Guards after amalgamation in 1665, noting the commissions of those who had served in the Low Countries[6]

Those who had served in Wentworth's Guards are in italics. A partial list only of the 24 companies in the regiment.

Colonel John Russell	Captain-Lieutenant John Howard	Ensign James Howard
Lieutenant-Colonel Edward Grey	Lieutenant John Downing	Ensign William Bodeley
Major Edward Rolleston	Lieutenant John Colte	Ensign Basil ffieldinge
Captain John Carey	Lieutenant James Roche	
Capt Thomas Cheek, vice Carey 22 May 1665		
Captain William Barker (d. 1666)		Ensign William Harwood
Captain Sir Godfrey Lloyd, vice Barker		
Captain Sir William Leighton		
Captain Edward Scott, vice Leighton	Lieutenant Arthur Broughton	Ensign Sydney Goring
Captain William Eaton[‡‡‡‡‡‡]		
Captain Robert Walters	*Lieutenant Francis Hamon*	
Captain Sir Francis Mackworth vice Carey, 19 June 1665	*Lieutenant Arthur Broughton*	
Captain Sir John Talbot	Lieutenant Richard Barlow	Ensign Edmund Andrews
Captain (Colonel) Charles Wheeler	Lieutenant George Trip	
Captain Robert Broughton		
Captain Ralph Sydenham	Lieutenant Philip Paramore	
Captain John Gwilliam		*Ensign Henry Sandys*
Captain John Strode[§§§§§§]	Lieutenant James Wen	
Captain (Colonel) John Morley	Lieutenant William Eaton	
Captain Sir Thomas Ashton	Lieutenant John Croft	Ensign Brian Richardson
Captain John Monson	Lieutenant Anthony Thorold	
Captain (Colonel) Sir Edward Broughton	Lieutenant George Garge	Ensign William Morris
Captain Thomas Cheek, vice Broughton, 12 June 1666		
Captain (Colonel) Thomas Panton[¶¶¶¶¶¶]	Lieutenant John Hanbury	Ensign Charles Ffox
Captain Sir Thomas Daniell	Lieutenant William Lloyd	Ensign Francis Moyser
Captain John Atkins	Lieutenant Robert Warner	Ensign John Howard
Captain (Colonel) Samuel Clarke	Lieutenant Richard Bassett	Ensign Henry Taylor
Captain Edward Bennett	Lieutenant Thomas Byron	Ensign John Moyser

---

* Major in the regiment in 1684.
† Major *c.* 1666, Lieutenant-Colonel of the regiment in 1684.
‡ From the King's Life Guard of Horse.

Quartermaster John Lloyd

Unplaced:
Lieutenant Richard Richardson, captain in 1673
Lieutenant Henry Crispe, lieutenant to Richardson
Lieutenant Henry Sandys, 1678
Lieutenant Sylvanus Tomkins, 1673
*Ensign Thomas Stradling**

NOTES
1   *The Kingdom's Intelligencer*, 18 February 1661; *Mercurius Publicus*, 21 February 1661.
2   TNA CSPD 1661–1662, p.511.
3   TNA Entry Book August 1668, entry dated 28 August; Charles Dalton, vol. I, p.6; TNA CSPD 2/12 April 1660.
4   TNA CSPD 1661–1662, entry for 4 November 1662.
5   *The Kingdom's Intelligencer*, 23 December 1661 and TNA CSPD Interregnum vol. 24, August 1659.
6   Compiled from Dalton, vol. 1 and other sources as noted.
7   TNA SP 18/123; Dalton, vol. 1, pp.13–14
8   Dalton, vol.1, p.13.
9   Dalton, vol.1, p.12.
10 Dalton, vol.1, p.12.
11 Dalton, vol.1, pp.14–15

---

* Captain in the regiment in 1684.

Notes to the Text

CHAPTER 1

1. See especially J. de Vries and A. van der Woude, *The First Modern Economy. Success, Failure, and Perseverance of the Dutch Economy, 1500–1815* (Cambridge: Cambridge University Press, 1997), p.92.
2. De Vries and van der Woude, pp.93–94.
3. Jonathon Riley, *The Last Ironsides: The English Expedition to Portugal, 1662–1668* (Helion: Solihull. 2014), p.33.
4. Jorge Penim de Freitas, *A Cavalaria na Guerra da Restauração, reconstrução e evolução de uma força militar 1641–1668* (Lisbon: Prefácio, 2005), p.44.
5. Sir Roger Williams, *The Actions of the Low Countries* (New York, 1895), p.57.
6. Walter Morgan MS, ed. Duncan Caldecot-Baird, *The Expedition in Holland, 1572-4* (London: Seeley Service, 1976), p.1; Williams, *Actions*, p.xi.
7. J.P. Riley, *Continuity in the English Army, 1658–1668* (unpublished M.A. Thesis, Leeds University, 1989), p.105.
8. TNA CSP Spanish, 1585, p.553.
9. David Birmingham, *A Concise History of Portugal* (Cambridge: Cambridge University Press, 2003), p.33.
10. For a full account see J.H. Elliott, *The Revolt of the Catalans: A Study in the Decline of Spain 1598–1640* (Cambridge: Cambridge University Press, 1984). 11 See Jonathon Riley, *The Last Ironsides*.
12. De Vries and van der Woude, pp.95–96. See also Geoffrey Parker, *The Army of Flanders and the Spanish Road 1567–1659*, p.266.
13. See especially J.H. Elliott 'The Decline of Spain', in T. Aston, *Crisis in Europe 1560–1660. Essays from Past and Present* (London: Basic Books, 1965), p.176.
14. J.H. Elliott, 'The Decline of Spain', p.178.
15. John Childs, *Warfare in the Seventeenth Century* (London: Cassell, 2003), pp.110–111.
16. Lynn, p.14; see also Geoffrey Parker, pp.50–53.
17. Philip II's instructions, 5 June 1558, cited in Parker, p.129.
18. John Childs, *Warfare in the Seventeenth Century*, p.77.
19. Richard J. Bonney, 'The French Civil War, 1649–53', in *European History Quarterly*, vol. 8, no. 1 (1978), pp.71–100.

CHAPTER 2

1. *Diary of Alexander Jaffray, Provost of Aberdeen, One of the Scottish Commissioners to Charles II*, ed. John Barclay (London: Darton & Harvey, 1833), p.32.
2. H. Woolrych, *Commonwealth to Protectorate* (Oxford: Oxford University Press, 1982).
3. The establishments are listed in TNA SP 25/76A f. 199, *et seq*.
4. Timothy Venning, *Cromwell's Foreign Policy and the Western Design*, The Cromwell Association <www.olivercromwell.org> accessed 31 January 2020.
5. C.H. Firth, *Cromwell's Army. A History of the English Soldier during the civil wars, the Commonwealth and the Protectorate* (London: Methuen & Co, 1902), p.35.
6. *John Evelyn's Diary*, ed. Philip Francis (London: The Folio Society, 1963), p.110.
7. Thomas Birch (ed.), *Thurloe State Papers*, 7 vols (London: 1742), vol. i, pp.759–763.
8. Samuel Gardiner, *History of the Commonwealth and Protectorate 1649-1661*, 3 vols (London: Longmans, Green, 1901), vol. ii, pp.327–362.
9. TNA SP 31/3/89 dated 5/15 February 1649; and SP 31/3/90 dated 16/26 September 1650. Both are letters to Cardinal Mazarin on this subject.
10. Philip Knatchel, *England and the Fronde: the Impact of the English Civil War and Revolution of France* (Ithaca, NY: Cornell University Press, 1967), pp.298–300.
11. See Ambassador Antoine de Bordeaux's letters to Mazarin in TNA SP 31/3/91 dated 4/14 November 1653; and Henri de Taillefer de Barrière to Le Grand Condé, BL Additional MSS 35252 dated 5/15 December 1653.
12. TNA, CSPD Interregnum, 1652–1653, p.340.
13. Cardenas' offer of Calais is contained in TNA SP 94/43, a despatch dated 13/23 April 1653.
14. Godfroi, Compte D'Estrades to Mazarin, 15/25 February 1652, cited by M. Oppenheim, 'The Navy of the Commonwealth, 1649–1660', in *English Historical Review*, No. 11 (1896), pp.48–51.
15. J.P. Cooper, *The New Cambridge Modern History*, vol. 4: *The Decline of Spain and the Thirty Years' War, 1609–1648/49* (Cambridge: Cambridge University Press, 1979), p.236.
16. See the debate in the Council on 5 June 1654 in TNA CSPD 1654, p.201 as the first time this matter was raised, although debate and argument continued for months.
17. Timothy Venning, *Cromwell's Foreign Policy and the Western Design* (no page numbering).
18. John Milton, ed. John Carey, *The Complete Shorter Poems* (London: Evans Brothers, 1969), p.411.
19. Baas's account of his meeting with Cromwell is in TNA SP 31/3/95, dated 15/25 June 1654.
20. Gardiner, vol. ii, pp.465, 467.
21. C.H. Firth (ed.), *The Clarke Papers*, 4 vols (London: printed for The Camden Society, 1891–1901), vol. iii, pp.203–206.

22. General Venables' account in T. Park (ed.), *The Harleian Miscellany*, 12 vols (London: Printed for T. Osborne, 1807–1811), vol. iii, p.513.
23. Thurloe, vol. i, p.759.
24. Park, vol. iii, p.513.
25. BL Additional MSS. Ayscough No 6125, ff. 34–60b; Thomas Carlyle, *Oliver Cromwell's Letters and Speeches*, 2 vols (New York: Wiley & Putnam, 1845), vol. 2, part 1, pp.222–225.
26. *Clarke Papers*, vol. III, pp.207–208.
27. Thurloe, vol. iii, p.611.
28. Gardiner, vol. ii, pp.477–479.
29. Gardiner, vol. iii, pp.483–486.

CHAPTER 3

1. Hugh Chisholm (ed.), 'Blake, Robert', in *Encyclopaedia Britannica*, 11th edition (Cambridge: Cambridge University Press, 1911).
2. John Knox Laughton, 'Blake, Robert' in Stephen Leslie (ed.), *Dictionary of National Biography*, vol. 5 (London: Oxford University Press, 1886).
3. *Journal of the House of Commons*, vol. 6, 1648–1651. Entry for 5 March 1649.
4. Bernard Capp, *Cromwell's Navy: The Fleet and the English Revolution, 1648–1660* (Oxford: Oxford University Press, 1989), p.219.
5. See Julian Corbett, 'Fighting Instructions, 1530–1816', *Publications of the Navy Records Society*, vol. xxix (London: 1905).
6. R.C. Anderson, 'The Royalists at Sea in 1649', in *Mariner's Mirror*, vol. xiv (1928) and 'The Royalists at Sea, 1650' in *Mariner's Mirror*, vol. xvii (1931).
7. For more details see Roger Hainsworth, *The Swordsmen in Power. War and Politics under the English Republic 1649–1660* (Stroud: Sutton, 1997).
8. TNA CSPD Interregnum, 10 May 1651.
9. Sir Charles Firth and Godfrey Davies, *The Regimental History of Cromwell's Army*, 2 vols ((Oxford: Clarendon Press, 1940), vol. i, p.338.
10. Sir Richard Cox, *Hibernia Anglicana, or The history of Ireland, from the conquest thereof by the English, to this present time*, Chapter, 'The reign of Charles the Second' (London, 1689)
11. TNA CSPD Interregnum, 10 and 31 October 1648.
12. Hainsworth, p.52.
13. Firth and Davies, vol. ii, p.449.
14. TNA CSPD Interregnum, 20 May 1651.
15. Commons Journal, vol. vi, 11 September 1651.
16. Firth and Davies, vol. i, p.xxiv.
17. <www.measuringworth.com> accessed 24 November 2020.
18. Firth and Davies, vol. ii, pp.613, 629, 665; TNA CSPD Interregnum, 20 May 1651.
19. Hainsworth, p.53.
20. TNA CSPD Interregnum, 23 May 1651.
21. TNA CSPD Interregnum, 26 November 1651.
22. TNA CSPD Interregnum, 2 July 1651.
23. Commons Journal, vol. vi, 11 July 1651.

NOTES TO THE TEXT

24 TNA CSPD Interregnum, 7 June 1652.
25 TNA CSPD Interregnum, 2 July 1651.
26 Charles Dalton, vol. I, pp.10–11.
27 P. Draper, *The House of Stanley: Including the Sieges of Latham House* (Ormskirk: T. Hutton, 1864).
28 'Derby's Last Letter to his Lady', *A Manx Notebook* <http://www.isle-of-man.com/manxnotebook/manxsoc/msvol26/intro.htm>, accessed 18 November 2021.
29 Firth and Davies, vol. i, p.xxvi.
30 Duckenfield's account of the campaign is in *Mercurius Politicus*, 6–13 November 1651.
31 Commons Journal, vol. vi, November 1651.
32 TNA CSPD 1650–1651.
33 Historical Manuscripts Commission, Second Report, chapter 2, p.54.
34 TNA SP 25/97, 30 July 1652.
35 Clarke MSS, s.1, f.32; *Mercurius Politicus*, 4–11 September 1651.
36 *Mercurius Politicus*, cited in 'Iliam Dhone and the Manx Rebellion', *Manx Publication Society*, vol. xxvi, p.66.
37 *Mercurius Politicus*, 6–13 November 1651.
38 *Mercurius Politicus*, cited in Manx Society, vol. xxvi, p.66.
39 A list is in *Mercurius Politicus*, 6–13 November 1651.
40 TNA CSPD 1651–1652, pp.79, 110, 117, 152, 179, 184.
41 Firth and Davies, vol. i, p.xxv.
42 TNA CSPD 1651–1652, January 1652.
43 TNA CSPD 1651–1652, July 1652.
44 Commons Journal, vol. vii, 15 September 1653.
45 TNA CSPD Charles I, vol. 530, 19 March 1629.
46 TNA CSPD Charles I, vol. 530, September 1629.
47 Stuart Reid, *Officers and Regiments of the Royalist Army* (Leigh-on-Sea: Partizan Press, undated), vol. i, p.34.
48 W. Godfray, 'Beaumont Cannon', in *Annual Bulletin of the Société Jersiaise* (1947).
49 S.E. Hoskins, *Charles the Second in the Channel Islands: A contribution to his biography, and to the history of his age* (London: R. Bentley, 1854), vol. ii, p.341.
50 Commons Journal, vol. iv, 22 June 1646.
51 For details of Blake's operations see J. Uttley, *The Story of the Channel Islands* (London, Faber and Faber, 1966); F.H. Ellis, 'The Great Rebellion' in *Annual Bulletin of the Société Jersiaise* (1937); Bernard Capp, *Cromwell's Navy: The Fleet and the English Revolution, 1648–1660* (Oxford: Clarendon Press, 1989); Wienand Drenth and Jonathon Riley, *The First Colonial Soldiers: English overseas colonies and their garrisons, 1650–1714* (Eindhoven, Netherlands, 2014), vol. i.
52 TNA CSPD Interregnum, 4 December 1651.
53 TNA SP 25/97 f. 86, Letter Book 1651

CHAPTER 4
1 Drenth and Riley, vol. 2, Part 2, pp.390–395.

2 Drenth and Riley, vol. 2, part 2, p.440–442.
3 N. Darnell Davies, *The Cavaliers & Roundheads of Barbados, 1650–1652, with some account of the early history of Barbados* (Georgetown, British Guiana: Argosy Press, 1887), p.171.
4 Davies, p.166.
5 Ayscue's instructions are in TNA CSPC America and the West Indies, vol. i, 1 February 1651.
6 TNA CSPC America and the West Indies, vol. i, 19 July 1651.
7 Firth and Davies, vol. ii, p.449.
8 TNA CSPC America and the West Indies, vol. i, 11 June 1651.
9 TNA CSPC America and the West Indies, vol. i, 19 October 1651.
10 TNA, CSPC America and the West Indies, vol. i, pp.343–344; TNA Entry Book Interregnum, vol. 50, p.83.
11 Firth and Davies, vol. i, pp.382–383.
12 Davies, pp.233–236.
13 Davies, p.243.

CHAPTER 5

1 Drenth and Riley, vol. 2, Chapter 12.
2 Michael Lorenzini, 'The Dutch & the English, Part Three: Construction of the Wall, 1653–1663', N.Y.C. Department of Records and Information Services, accessed 4 November 2019.
3 William Hooke to the Protector, 3 November 1653 in *A Collection of the State Papers of John Thurloe, vol. 1, 1638–1653*, ed. Thomas Birch (London, 1742), vol. viii, p.13, *British History Online*, <http://www.british-history.ac.uk/thurloe-papers/vol 1> accessed 2 November 2019.
4 *Dictionary of Canadian Biography online*, accessed 5 November 2019.
5 Drenth and Riley, vol. 2, pp.132, 140.
6 Sedgwick to the Protector, 17 June 1654 in Thurloe, Vol. xvi, p.54; see also Rawlinson MSS Series A (Bodleian Library, Oxford), No. 16 f. 418.
7 Massachusetts Historical Society collections online, accessed 5 November 2019.
8 Oliver A. Roberts, *History of the Military Company of the Massachusetts, now called the Ancient and Honorable Artillery Company of Massachusetts, 1637–1888, 4 vols* (Boston, Mass: Mudge & Son, 1895–1901). Henry D. Sedgwick, 'Robert Sedgwick,' Colonial Society of Massachusetts *Publications*, vol. iii (1895–1897), pp.156–73.
9 Instructions to Sedgwick and Leverett by Cromwell, drafted by Thurloe and dated 8 February 1653, M.H.S. Collections online, accessed 20 November 2019.
10 TNA State Papers Colonial Series, North America and the West Indies, vol. 32, No. 8, Captain Mark Harrison of the *Church* to the Navy Commissioners, 1 July 1654.
11 TNA CSPD, vol. lxxii, p.206, 13 June 1654.
12 Richard Hildreth, *The History of the United States of America*, 6 vols (New York: Appleton & Co., 1871), vol.1, p.388.
13 TNA CSPD vol. cxxiii, p.133, 23 January 1653/4.
14 TNA CSPD vol. lxxi, p.460, 7 March 1653/4.

15. TNA CSPD vol. xxxiii, p.145, February 1652/3.
16. TNA CSPD vol. xxxv, p.256, dated 5 April 1653.
17. Firth and Davies, vol. i, p.331.
18. TNA CSP Colonial Series 1574–1660, vol. cv, Interregnum Order Books, 16 December 1656 and 10 June 1658.
19. TNA SP 46/97 f. 71A.
20. Firth and Davies, vol. i, pp.377–379.
21. TNA SP 29/61 f. 157 (State Papers online).
22. Sedgwick to the Protector, 1 July 1654, Thurloe, vol. xvi, p.7.
23. Drenth and Riley, vol. 2, pp.134, 136.
24. Firth and Davies, vol. ii, pp.417–418.
25. *Dictionary of Canadian Biography Online*, accessed 5 November 2019.
26. On the English precursor to the colonial militia, see, for example, Lindsay Boynton, *The Elizabethan Militia, 1558-1638* (London: Routledge & Kegan Paul, 1967); and J.R. Western, *The English Militia in the Eighteenth Century: The Story of a Political Issue, 1660-1802* (London: Routledge & Kegan Paul, 1965).
27. Herbert L. Osgood, *The American Colonies in the Seventeenth Century* (New York: Macmillan, 1904–07), vol. 1, pp.496–527, vol. 2, pp.375–400; Louis Morton, 'The Origins of American Military Policy,' *Military Affairs* 22 (Summer 1958), pp.75–82; Daniel Boorstin, *The Americans: The Colonial Experience* (New York: Random House, 1958), pp.343–372; John W. Shy, 'A New Look at the Colonial Militia,' *William and Mary Quarterly*, 3rd series, no. 20 (April 1963), pp.175–185; Douglas Edward Leach, *Arms for Empire: A Military History of the British Colonies in North America, 1607–1763* (New York: Macmillan, 1973), pp.1–41.
28. *Plymouth Colonial Records*, vol. 1, p.360.
29. Sedgwick to the Protector, 17 June 1654 in Thurloe, vol. xvi, p.54.
30. Sedgwick to the Protector, 17 June 1654 in Thurloe, vol. xvi, p.54. See also Leverett to the Protector, 4 July 1654 in Thurloe, vol. xvi, p.52.
31. Drenth and Riley, vol. 2, pp.43–44.
32. Drenth and Riley, vol. 2, pp.43–44.
33. W.H. Whitmore (ed.), *The Colonial Laws of Massachusetts Reprinted from the Edition of 1660, with Supplements to 1672, Containing also the Body of Liberties of 1641* (Boston: 1860), p.35.
34. Sedgwick to the Protector, 1 July 1654, Thurloe, vol.xvi, p.7; see also Rawlinson MSS Series A (Bodleian Library, Oxford), no. 16 f. 418.
35. Drenth and Riley, vol. 2, pp.44–45.
36. Sedgwick to the Protector, 17 June 1654 in Thurloe, vol. xvi, p.54.
37. Leverett to the Protector, 4 July 1654 in Thurloe, vol. xvi, p.24.
38. Papers relating to the expedition and Sedwick's correspondence are held in the Bodleian Library, Oxford, Special Collections:Richard Rawlinson MSS Series A, A16, f.7; A30, ff. 43, 175; A32, f. 143; A 34, f. 72; A37, f.19.
39. Brenda Dunn, *A History of Port Royal/Annapolis Royal, 1605-1800* (Toronto: 2004); M.A. MacDonald, *Fortune and La Tour: The civil war in Acadia* (Toronto: 1983).
40. *Dictionary of Canadian Biography online*, accessed 5 November 2019.
41. N.E.S. Griffiths, *From Migrant to Acadian: A North American Border*

> *People, 1604–1755* (Montreal: McGill University, 2005), pp.75–77; <www.measuringworth.com>, accessed 6 November 2019.

42 Harrison to the Navy Commissioners, 21 July 1654. TNA CSP Colonial Series, North America and the West Indies 1675–1676, Addendum 1654, vol. 9, p.88.
43 TNA CSPD vol. CXXIII, p.133, 23 January 1653/4
44 Harrison to the Navy Commissioners, 31 August 1654. TNA CSP Colonial Series, North America and the West Indies 1675–1676, Addendum 1654, vol. 9, p.88.
45 Harrison to the Navy Commissioners, 30 August 1654. TNA CSP Colonial Series, North America and the West Indies 1675–1676, Addendum 1654, vol. 9, p.88.
46 Sedgwick to the Protector, 9 September 1654. TNA State Papers Colonial Series, North America and the West Indies vol. 32 p.11.
47 Alaric Faulkner, 'Maintenance and Fabrication at Fort Pentagouet 1635–1654' in *Historical Archaeology.* vol., 20 No. 1 (1986), p.91.
48 TNA CSPD vol. xcix, p.1245, 15 July 1655.
49 C.E. Leverett, *A Memoir, Biographical and Genealogical of Sir John Leverett, Knt, Governor of Massachusetts* (Boston: Crosby, Nichols Co., 1856). Murdoch, *History of Nova–Scotia*, vol. I, pp.126–27, 139.
50 SP 18/136 f. 243, 13 March 1656.
51 TNA SP 29/61 f. 157 (State Papers online).
52 <www.measuringworth.com>, accessed 6 November 2019.
53 TNA CSP Colonial Series, North America and the West Indies, vol. 5, Preface.
54 Entry Book Interregnum vol. cv, pp.151–154, 29 May 1656.

CHAPTER 6

1 This chapter is largely drawn from Wienand Drenth and Jonathon Riley, *The First Colonial Soldiers. A Survey of British Colonial territories and their garrisons, 1650–1714*, vol. 2, Part 2 (Eindhoven, 2015), supplemented by other sources as noted and in particular the works of Peter Cottrell and Robert Giglio.
2 For a detailed account of this period in Virginia see Charlotte Anne Beale, 'Commonwealth and Protectorate in Virginia, 1649–1660', unpublished M.A. thesis, University of Richmond, 4 June 1940.
3 TNA, CSPC vol. 1, 1574–1660, pp.343–344; TNA Entry Book Interregnum, vol. 50, p.83.
4 TNA Entry Book Interregnum, vol. 51, pp.84–86.
5 For full details see the account in Charles Andrews, *Narratives of the Insurrections, 1675–1690* (New York: Charles Scribner's Sons, 1915).
6 TNA CSPC vol. i, 18 Nov 1656; Entry Book, Interregnum, vol. cv, p.506.
7 Carla Gardina Pestana, *The English Atlantic in an Age of Revolution, 1640–1661* (Cambridge, Mass.: Harvard University Press, 2002), pp.112–114.
8 TNA CSPC vol. i, 1 January 1650. A list of the council is in TNA CSPC vol. 1, 1 January 1652.
9 TNA CSPC vol. i, 28 June 1653.
10 Pestana, p.114.

11 Matthew Page Andrews, *History of Maryland: Province and State* (Garden City, New York: Doubleday, Doran & Co., 1929).
12 Herbert L. Osgood, *The American Colonies in the Seventeenth Century* (New York: Macmillan, 1904).
13 Montgomery J. Gambrill, *Leading Events of Maryland History* (Boston: Ginn & Co, 1904).
14 Stuart Reid, *Officers and Regiments of the Royalist Army*, vol. 2, p.100.
15 Firth and Davies, *The Regimental History of Cromwell's Army*, vol. ii, p.468.
16 See Gambrill's and Andrews' accounts for more details.
17 <https://inredcoatragsattired.com/2017/07/04/battle-of-the-severn-1655> accessed 30 September 2019.
18 For full details of the Maryland Militia in this period see Drenth and Riley, vol. 2, part 2; see also Jeffrey Rogers Humme, 'The American Militia and the origin of conscription: A Reassessment', in *Journal of Libertarian Studies*, Vol. 15, no. 4 (Fall 2001), pp.29–77.
19 Peter Cottrell, *The English Civil War in the American Colonies* (English Civil War Society of America); Robert Giglio, *English Civil War Gaming Scenarios*, vol. 3 (Leigh-on-Sea: Partizan Press, 2005).
20 George L. Beer, *The Old Colonial System, 1660-1754* (New York: Macmillan Co., 1912).

CHAPTER 7

1 Sir William Clarke, ed. C.H. Firth, *The Clarke Papers, Selections from the Papers of William Clarke, Secretary to the Council of the Army 1647–1649 and to General Monck and the Army in Scotland 1651–1660.* (London: Royal Historical Society, 1899), vol. iii, p.207.
2 *The Narrative of General Venables*, Appendix A, instructions from the Protector.
3 Undated, appended to Venables' commission as General in Thurloe, vol. iii, p.16.
4 *The Narrative of General Venables*, Appendix A.
5 Timothy Venning, 'Cromwell's Foreign Policy and the Western Design', The Cromwell Association, <www.olivercromwell.org> accessed 29 December 2019.
6 Gardiner, pp.345–346; Thurloe, vol. iii, pp.59, 62.
7 CSPD 1654, p.201.
8 *Calendar of the Clarendon Papers Preserved in the Bodleian Library*, 5 vols (Oxford: Clarendon Press, 1872–1970), vol. iii, p.379; Thurloe, vol. ii, p.414.
9 Venetian ambassador Pauluzzi to the Senate, 20/30 May and 26 May/5 June 1655, in *Calendar of State Papers Venetian 1655–6* (ed. Allen Hines), pp.60, 62–64.
10 Thurloe, vol. iii, p.16 accessed 23 December 2019; Dr Samuel Gardiner, *A History of the Commonwealth and Protectorate*, vol. ii, pp.447, 471–479 and vol. iii pp.344–346.
11 Thurloe, vol. iii, p.159.
12 Thurloe, vol. iii, pp.506–507.

13 *The Narrative of General Venables with an appendix of papers relating to the expedition to the West Indies and the conquest of Jamaica 1654–1655*, ed. C.H. Firth for the Royal Historical Society (New York: Longmans, Green and Co., 1900), Introduction, p.xxxix.
14 *The Narrative of General Venables*, Firth's introduction, p.xl.
15 Royal Museums Greenwich SIG/A (1673).
16 *The Diary of Samuel Pepys*, eds J.S. Smith and Richard, Lord Braybrooke (London: Henry Colburn, 1825), p.314.
17 Pepys, *Diary*, p.289.
18 Pepys, *Diary*, p.315.
19 Thurloe, vol. iii, p.249; *The Narrative of General Venables*, Introduction.
20 Thurloe, vol. iii, p.646.
21 *The Narrative of General Venables*, Firth's introduction, pp.14, 24, 81, 94.
22 *The Narrative of General Venables*, pp.150–152; see also *The Harleian Miscellany: A Collection of Scarce, Curious, And Entertaining Pamphlets And Tracts, as well In Manuscript As In Print, Found In The Late Earl Of Oxford's Library, Interspersed With Historical, Political, And Critical Notes* (a collection of material from the library of the Earl of Oxford and Earl Mortimer collated and edited by Samuel Johnson and William Oldys between 1744 and 1753 on behalf of the publisher Thomas Osborne), vol. iii. p.515.
23 *Report on the MSS of the Duke of Portland* (Second Report of the Royal Commission on Historical Manuscripts, London, 1871), p.88.
24 *The Narrative of General Venables*, Appendix A, instructions from the Protector.
25 Harleian Miscellany, vol. iii, p.661.
26 David Hume, *The History of England*, vol. 6 (London, 1756), p.260.
27 Gardiner, vol. ii, p.351.
28 Thurloe, vol. ii, p.661.
29 *The Narrative of General Venables*, p.6.
30 C.H. Firth, *Cromwell's Army. A History of the English Soldier during the civil wars, the Commonwealth and the Protectorate* (London: Methuen & Co., 1902), pp.69–71.
31 'The Relation of Captain Pallano', in *Spanish Narratives of the English Attack on Santo Domingo 1655*, ed. I.A. Wright for the Royal Historical Society (Camden Miscellany, vol. xiv, London, 1926), p.25.
32 Firth, pp.43–44.
33 John Dalton, *Illustrations, Historical and Genealogical: Of King James's Irish Army List* (1689) (Dublin, 1855), p.416.
34 The strengths given for all the regiments are compiled from 'A Perfect List of all the forces under the command of His Excellency General Venables, Taken at a muster March 21st 1655', an appendix to *The Narrative of General Venables*; CSP Colonial Addenda 1574–1674, p.66; and Drenth and Riley, pp.402–412.
35 CSPD 1647, p.480.
36 Thurloe, vol. iii, pp.649, 675.
37 *Calendar of the Clarendon State Papers preserved in the Bodleian Library*, ed. F.J. Routledge (Oxford: Clarendon Press, 1870), vol. I, p.332.

38 Thurloe, vol. xv, pp.115–116.
39 Drenth and Riley, pp.402–412.
40 *The Narrative of General Venables*, p.50.
41 Granville Penn, *Memorials of the Professional Life and Times of Sir William Penn*, 2 vols (London: J. Duncan, 1833), vol. ii, p.90.
42 CSPD 1654, p.414.
43 *Memorials of Penn*, vol. ii, p.67; *The Narrative of General Venables*, p.5.
44 Jonathon Riley, *Napoleon as a General* (London: Hambledon Continuum, 2007), p.118.
45 *The Narrative of General Venables*, pp.31, 122; Thurloe, vol. iii, p.514.
46 See the calculations in Martin Van Crefeld, *Supplying War* (Cambridge: Cambridge University Press, 1977), Chapter 1.
47 *The Narrative of General Venables*, pp.6, 12.
48 Letter of Major James Whistler, Fortescue's Regiment. *The Clarke Papers*, vol. iii, p.54.
49 Drenth and Riley, vol. 2, part 1, p.xxv.
50 Lieutenant-Colonel Francis Barrington's letter in the *Seventh Report of the Royal Commission on Historical Manuscripts* (London: Eyre and Spottiswoode for HMSO, 1879), p.572.
51 Thurloe, vol. iii, p.507.
52 *The Narrative of General Venables*, p.122.
53 *The Narrative of General Venables*, p.30.
54 Venables to the Protector, Rawlinson MSS A27, f. 70, Bodleian Library, Oxford.
55 Thurloe, vol. iii, p.755.
56 Barrington, *Seventh Report*, p.57.
57 *Memorials of Penn*, vol. ii, p.70.
58 *The Narrative of General Venables*, p.14.

CHAPTER 8

1 See, among many others, the accounts by: Hugh Biceno, *Elizabeth's Sea Dogs: How England's Mariners Became the Scourge of the Seas* (London: Conway, 2012); David Marley, *Historic Cities of the Americas: An Illustrated Encyclopaedia* (Santa Barbara, Calif.: ABC–CLIO, 2004), and *Wars of the Americas: A Chronology of Armed Conflict in the Western Hemisphere* (Santa Barbara, Calif.: ABC–CLIO, 2008); and John Sugden, *Sir Francis Drake* (London: Pimlico, 2004).
2 *The Narrative of General Venables*, Appendix D, p.135.
3 *The Narrative of General Venables*, Appendix D, pp.135–136.
4 *Spanish Narratives*, ed. I.A. Wright, frontispiece and notes. See also Jorge Ignacio Rubio Mañé, *Problemas de Expansión y Defensa*, UNAM (ed.) in El Virreinato, II: *Expansion y Defensa (primera parte)* (Edición 1983), p.93.
5 *The Relation of Captain Pallano*, in *Spanish Narratives*, ed. I.A. Wright, p.2. See also the Report of Count Peñalva to Gregorio de Leguia in Archives of the Indies, Seville 1634–1658, 2–5, ff. 1/28, and included in translation in *Spanish Narratives of the English Attack*, p.47.
6 Peñalva to Gregorio de Leguia, p.48.

7   *The Relation of Captain Pallano*, pp.4, 51–52.
8   *The Notorial Account*, p.52.
9   *The Notorial Account*, p.60.
10 Henry Whistler's *Journal*, Appendix E to *The Narrative of General Venables*, p.156.
11 *The Relation of Captain Pallano*, p.25.
12 Winslow to Thurloe, vol. iii, p.249.
13 *The Relation of Captain Pallano*, p.3.
14 *The Narrative of General Venables*, p.18.
15 Thurloe, vol. ii, p.755.
16 *Memorials of Penn*, vol. ii, pp.81–82, 110.
17 *The Relation of Captain Pallano*, p.34; *The Narrative of General Venables*, pp.18, 22.
18 *The Relation of Captain Pallano*, pp.34, 53, 55; see also 'The Treasurer's Report' in *Spanish Narratives*, p.66.
19 *Memorials of Penn*, vol. ii, pp.84, 93.
20 *The Narrative of General Venables*, Appendix D.
21 See, for example, *The Notorial Account*, by Francisco Facundo de Caravajal, Notary Public of Santo Domingo included in translation in *Spanish Narratives of the English Attack*, p.51; see also *The Treasurer's Report* in the same publication, p.64.
22 Peñalva to Gregorio de Leguia, p.50.
23 *The Narrative of General Venables*, pp.34, 67, 69, 102.
24 *The Narrative of General Venables*, Appendix D, p.127.
25 Venables to the Protector, Rawlinson MSS A27, f. 70, Bodleian Library, Oxford.
26 *The Relation of Captain Pallano*, p.5.
27 *The Narrative of General Venables*, Appendix D, p.128.
28 *The Narrative of General Venables*, Appendix D, p.129.
29 Peñalves to Castillo, 23 April 1655 in Archives of the Indies, Seville Book 53 File 2 f.8.
30 Nathan Mannion, 'The Irishman who became a Spanish Captain and fought Cromwell's Army', in *Irish Times*, 1 October 2019.
31 *The Relation of Captain Pallano*, p.5.
32 *The Narrative of General Venables*, p.19.
33 *The Narrative of General Venables*, pp.21, 22, 27, 27, 30.
34 *The Relation of Captain Pallano*, p.14.
35 *The Narrative of General Venables*, p.27.
36 Archives of the Indies, 53-2-8, orders from the governor.
37 Gardiner, p.363.
38 *The Relation of Captain Pallano*, p.15.
39 *The Relation of Captain Pallano*, p.6.
40 *The Notorial Account*, p.54.
41 *The Relation of Captain Pallano*, p.9.
42 Whistler's letter attached to *The Narrative of General Venables*, p.154.
43 *The Narrative of General Venables*, Annex D.
44 *The Narrative of General Venables*, Appendix D, p.134; *The Relation of Captain Pallano*, pp.12–13.

45 *The Narrative of General Venables*, Appendix D, p.132.
46 *The Relation of Captain Pallano*, p.11.
47 *The Relation of Captain Pallano*, p.14.
48 *The Relation of Captain Pallano*, p.14.
49 *The Relation of Captain Pallano*, p.13.
50 Gardiner, p.363.
51 *The Narrative of General Venables*, Appendix D, p.132.
52 Gardiner, p.364.
53 *The Relation of Captain Pallano*, p.26.
54 *The Relation of Captain Pallano*, p.21.
55 Harleian Miscellany, vol. iii, p.517.
56 *The Relation of Captain Pallano*, p.23.
57 *The Narrative of General Venables*, Appendix D, p.133.
58 Gardiner, p.364; Whistler's *Journal*, p.65.
59 Journal of Thomas White, Fortescue's Regiment, attached to *The Narrative of General Venables*, p.57.
60 The *Relation of Captain Pallano*, p.29.
61 White's *Journal*, pp.57–58.
62 *The Narrative of General Venables*, p.29. See also Gregory Butler's letter to the Protector in *Memorials of Penn*, vol. ii, p.50.
63 *The Relation of Captain Pallano*, p.27.
64 *The Relation of Captain Pallano*, p.30.
65 *The Narrative of General Venables*, Appendix D, p.134.
66 *Memorials of Penn*, vol. ii, pp.85, 87–88, 92–96, 98; Whistler's *Journal* in *The Narrative of General Venables*, pp.152, 157–159, 160.
67 *The Narrative of General Venables*, pp.32, 50, 68, 101; Thurloe, vol. iii, p.507; *Memorials of Penn*, vol. ii, p.105.
68 *The Narrative of General Venables*, p.30.
69 *The Relation of Captain Pallano*, p.30.
70 *The Narrative of General Venables*, Appendix D, p.135.
71 *The Narrative of General Venables*, p.31.
72 *Memorials of Penn*, vol. ii, pp.81, 83, 84, 85.
73 *The Relation of Captain Pallano*, p.33.
74 *The Relation of Captain Pallano*, p.1.
75 *The Narrative of General Venables*, p.xxxii; TNA CSP Colonial, Addenda 1574–1674, p.105.
76 *The Narrative of General Venables*, Appendix D, p.136.
77 Gardiner, p.368.

CHAPTER 9

1 For full descriptions see Frank Cundall and Joseph L. Pietersz (eds), *Jamaica under the Spaniards, Abstracted from the Archives of Seville* [by Irene A. Wright] (Kingston, Jamaica, 1919).
2 *The Narrative of General Venables*, Appendix E, p.169.
3 *The Narrative of General Venables*, p.47.
4 *The Narrative of General Venables*, Appendix E, p.169.
5 *The Narrative of General Venables*, p.137.
6 *The Narrative of General Venables*, p.137.

7   Gardiner, p.366; *The Narrative of General Venables*, Appendix E, p.160.
8   The Spanish accounts have been incorporated into a translation by Irene A. Wright, 'The Spanish Resistance to the Occupation of Jamaica, 1655–1660' in *Transactions of the Royal Historical Society*, vol. 13, pp.117–147 (London, 1930), pp.7, 9.
9   Stephen Saunders Webb, *The Governors-General. The English Army and the Definition of the Empire, 1569–1681* (Chapel Hill, N.C.: University of North Carolina Press, 1979), p.153.
10 *The Narrative of General Venables*, Appendix E, p.164.
11 Buller, cited in the *Seventh Report of the Historical Manuscripts Commission*, p.573.
12 Venables to Thurloe, vol. iii, p.199.
13 Barrington, 14 July 1655, Harleian Miscellany, vol. iii, p.522.
14 Barrington, *Seventh Report of the Historical Manuscripts Commission*, p.574.
15 *The Narrative of General Venables*, p.142.
16 *The Narrative of General Venables*, p.94.
17 TNA SP 25/76A ff. 154, 155 dated 10 October 1655.
18 Penn to the Protector, 31 August 1655 in *Memorials of Penn*, vol. ii, p.131.
19 Venables to Thurloe, 12 September 1655 in Thurloe, vol. iv, p.27; Venables to the Protector, 9 September 1655, Rawlinson MSS A30, f. 231, Bodleian Library Oxford.
20 *The Narrative of General Venables*, pp.71–88.
21 TNA SP 25 Interregnum, vol. 1 ff. 296, 345, 353, Council Order Books. Penn's Petition is dated 25 October 1655, TNA CSPD, vol. 101, p.76.
22 Thurloe, vol. iv, p.153.
23 Sedgwick to the Protector, 1 September [11 September N.S.] 1655 in Rawlinson MSS, Series A (Bodleian Library, Oxford, Special Collections), no. 30 f.43.
24 Sedgwick to the Protector, 5 November [15 November N.S.] 1655. Rawlinson MSS, Series A (Bodleian Library, Oxford, Special Collections), no. 32, f. 151.
25 Sedgwick to the Protector 24 January [3 February N.S.] 1655/6 in Rawlinson MSS, Series A (Bodleian Library, Oxford, Special Collections), no. 37, f. 721.
26 Saunders Webb, pp.164–165.
27 Penn, vol. ii, p.585.
28 Gardiner, vol. iii, p.457.
29 Sedgwick to the Protector, 5 November 1655 in Thurloe, vol. iv, pp.151–152.
30 Thurloe, vol. iv, p.154.
31 Thurloe, vol. iii p.751; Rawlinson MSS, Series A, No. 32, f. 151.
32 Thurloe, vol. v, pp.152–153.
33 Cromwell to Monck in Rawlinson MSS Series A Series A (Bodleian Library, Oxford, Special Collections), no. 55 f. 126.
34 Thurloe, vol. iv, p.392.
35 Saunders Webb, p.169.
36 Saunders Webb, p.153.

NOTES TO THE TEXT

37 TNA CSP Colonial Series, 1574–1661, p.431.
38 Clarke Papers, vol. iii, p.86.
39 Thurloe, vol. iv, p.457.
40 TNA CO 5/32, f. 40.
41 TNA SO 25/107.
42 Sedgwick to the Protector, 24 January [3 February N.S.] 1655/6 in Rawlinson MSS, Series A (Bodleian Library, Oxford, Special Collections), no. 37, f. 721.
43 Firth and Davies, vol. II, p.726.
44 Saunders Webb, pp.154–155.
45 Wright, p.119.
46 Thurloe, vol. iv, p.543; Wright, p.120.
47 Sedgwick to Thurloe, 24 January, 12 March, 30 April 1656 in Thurloe, vol. iv, pp.151, 454, 455, 600, 604, 748.
48 Ysassi's letters of April and June 1656 in 'The Castilla Narrative', *Camden Miscellany*, vol. XII (London: Royal Historical Society, 1924), p.22.
49 Archives of the Indies, 79–4–6 ff. 23, 54.
50 Archives of the Indies, 79–4–6 ff. 23, 28, 30, 32, 37, 41, 42, 43, 56–66.
51 Archives of the Indies, 79–4–6, f. 40 dated 30 October 1656.
52 Wright, p.124.
53 Wright, p.125.
54 Archives of the Indies, 54–3–29 dated 12 October 1656.
55 Wright, p.129.
56 Thurloe, vol. vi, p.130.
57 Archives of the Indies, 54–3–29, Ysassi to the Duke of Albuquerque, 9 July 1657.
58 Archives of the Indies, 54–3–29, Ysassi to the Duke of Albuquerque, 31 August 1675.
59 D'Oyley's *Letter on the Death of Coll. Brayne* in British Library (BL) Egerton Collection, MS 2395, 1625–1697, p.144. (Miscellaneous official papers relating to the English settlements in America and the West Indies, chiefly documents submitted to, or, issuing from, the Council of Trade and Plantations, with a few original letters; 1627–1699. A large part of the collection appears to have been formed by Thomas Povey, Secretary to the Council).
60 BL Egerton MS 2395, p.144.
61 Archives of the Indies, 54–3–29, Ysassi to Blas Ysassi Arnaldo, dated 17 July 1657.
62 Saunders Webb, p.175.
63 Saunders Webb, p.184.
64 <www.measuringworth.com>, accessed 27 January 2020.
65 Thurloe, vol. vii, p.55; Archives of the Indies, 54–3–29, various letters.
66 Archives of the Indies, 54–3–29, 20 March 1658.
67 Archives of the Indies, 54–3–29 29 October 1658.
68 D'Oyley to Thurloe, in Thurloe, vol. vii, pp.260–262 dated 12 July 1658.
69 TNA CSPC Addenda 1658, No. 305 dated 16 July 1658.
70 Edward Long, *The History of Jamaica*, BL Additional MSS No 14405, p.277.

COLONIAL IRONSIDES

71 Long, p.277.
72 Thurloe, Vol. vii, pp.260–262 dated 12 July 1658.
73 Archives of the Indies 54-3-29 dated 17 July 1658.
74 Wright, p.140.
75 Colonel Cornelius Burroughs to Robert Blackthorne, 31 January 1660 in TNA CSPC Addenda, p.134, no. 334.
76 Colonel Cornelius Burroughs to Robert Blackthorne, 31 January 1660 in TNA CSPC Addenda, p.134, no. 335.
77 Archives of the Indies, 54-3-29, Ysassi to D'Oyley, 24 March 1660.
78 Edmund Hickeringill, *Jamaica Viewed* (London, 1661), pp.75–78.
79 Firth and Davies, vol. ii, p.725.
80 TNA SP25/76A f. 152 dates 10 October 1655.
81 Gardiner, vol. iii, p.453.
82 TNA CSPC 1661–1668, p.204.
83 TNA CO 5/33 f. 52; Firth and Davies, vol. ii, p.710.

CHAPTER 10

1 For a full account of Blake's career see William Hepworth Dixon, *Robert Blake, Admiral and General at Sea, based on Family and State Papers* (London: Chapman & Hall, 1856); Frank Knight, *General-at-Sea. The Life of Admiral Robert Blake* (London: Macdonald and Co., 1971) and John Rowland Powell *Robert Blake: General-At-Sea* (London: Collins, 1972).
2 Gardiner, vol. iii, pp.372–373
3 Clarke papers, vol. iii, f. 207; Sir Julian S. Corbett, *Cromwell and the Mediterranean: A Study in the Rise and Influence of British Power Within the Straits* (London, 1917), p.246.
4 Thurloe, vol. ii, pp.724, 731; Corbett, p.247.
5 The dates are drawn from Blake's despatches and from the diary of Lieutenant Weale of the frigate *Amity* in BL Sloane MSS no. 1431.
6 Corbett, p.251.
7 Gardiner, vol. iii, p.374.
8 Blake's despatches for this period are in BL Additional MSS No. 9004.
9 BL Additional MSS No. 9300, 14 March 1655.
10 TNA SP Barbary States – Algiers, vol. ii, f. 253.
11 Corbett, p.261.
12 Corbett, p.262; Gardiner, vol. iii, p.378.
13 Thurloe, vol. iii, p.232; Gardiner, vol. iii, p.376.
14 BL Additional MSS 9304 and Thurloe, vol. iii, p.332.
15 Thurloe, vol. iii, p.390.
16 BL Sloane MSS No 3986, ff. 54, 55, observations taken in 1729.
17 Gardiner, vol. iii, p.379.
18 Corbett, pp.266–267.
19 Corbett, p.268; see also Weale's journal, f. 26.
20 Gardiner, vol. iii, p.385.
21 Gardiner, vol. iii, p.392.
22 Cromwell's orders on this point are in Thurloe, vol. iii, p.547.
23 Richard Ollard, *Cromwell's Earl. A life of Edward Montagu 1st Earl of*

Sandwich (London: HarperCollins, 1994), p.40.
24 Ollard, p.43.
25 Corbett, p.284; Montagu to Thurloe, 29 April–30 May in Thurloe, vol. v, p.67; Ollard, p.45
26 Blake to the Protector, 30 August and the Protector's reply on 13 September are in Thurloe, vol. iii, pp.719, 724.
27 Clyde L. Grose, 'The Anglo–Portuguese Marriage of 1662', in *The Hispanic American Historical Review*, 10:3 (August 1930), p.314.
28 Gardiner, vol. iii, p.474; Ollard, p.46.
29 Stayner's despatch is in Thurloe, vol. v, p.399; the Spanish account is cited in Crobett, pp.289–290.
30 <www.measuringworth.com>, accessed 25 February 2020.
31 Ollard, p.48.
32 Thurloe, vol. v, p.363.
33 John Barratt, *'Better Begging than Fighting': The Royalist Army in Exile in the War against Cromwell 1656–1660* (Helion: Solihull, 2016), pp.9–10.
34 R.C. Anderson, *Naval Wars in the Levant 1559–1853* (Princeton: Princeton University Press, 1952), p.145.
35 John Barratt, *Cromwell's Wars at Sea* (Barnsley: Pen & Sword, 2006), p.181.
36 Brian Lavery, *The Ship of the Line – Vol. 1: The Development of the Battlefleet 1650–1850* (London: Conway, 2003), p.159.
37 Cesareo Fernandez Duro, *Bosquejo biografico del Almirante D. Diego Egües y Beaumont* (Madrid: A Coruña Órbigo, 1892), pp.61–62.

CHAPTER 11

1   Gardiner, vol. iii, p.122.
2   Secretary Nicholas to Middleton 11/21 July, Nicholas papers, University of Manchester Library, GB 133 NP, vol. ii, p.78
3   Gardiner, vol. iii, p.122.
4   Gardiner, vol. iii, p.127.
5   Gardiner, vol. iii, p.426.
6   Gardiner, vol. iii, p.477.
7   Gardiner, vol. iii, p.471.
8   For full details see A. Lytton Sells (ed. and tr.), *The Memoirs of James II. His Campaigns as Duke of York* (London: Chatto & Windus, 1962).
9   For details see Brendan Jennings, *Wild Geese in Spanish Flanders* (Dublin: Stationery Office for the Irish Manuscripts Commission, 1964); John A. Lynn, *Giant of the Grand Siècle: The French Army, 1610–1715* (Cambridge: Cambridge University Press, 1997); Pierre Goulier, 'Mercenaires Irlandais en Service de la France', *Irish Sword* no. 27 (1986–1987), p.67 et seq.; Harman Murtagh, 'Irish soldiers abroad', in Thomas Bartlett and Keith Jeffery, *A Military History of Ireland* (Cambridge: Cambridge University Press, 1996), p.297; Gráinne Henry, *The Irish Military Community in Spanish Flanders, 1586–1612* (Kill Lane, Blackrock: Irish Academic Press, 1992).
10 Lytton Sells, *The Memoirs of James II*, p.219. See also P. Gouhir, 'Mercenaires Irlandais au service de la France (1635–1664)', *Revue d'Histoire Moderne & Contemporaine*, 1968, no. 15-4, pp.672–690

11 Jennings, item 2153.
12 *Calendar of the Clarendon Papers*, vol. iii, p.490.
13 Sir James Turner, *Memoirs of his Own Time* (Edinburgh: Bannatyne, 1829, from an original MS), pp.120, 130. See also *Calendar of the Clarendon Papers*, vol. iii, pp.218, 283, 307.
14 Drenth and Riley, vol. 1, p.86. Clarendon, *Rebellion*, vol. xvi, p.68; *Memoirs of James II*, p.121; *Calendar of the Clarendon Papers*, vol. iii, pp.364, 368, 379, 405. See also C.H. Firth 'Royalist and Cromwellian Armies in Flanders, 1657–1662 (1903, but published online by Cambridge University Press 17 June 2009, accessed 7 August 2020); Lt. Gen. Sir F.W. Hamilton, *Origin and History of the First or Grenadier Guards*, vol. 1 (London: J. Murray, 1874), pp.6–7.
15 Drenth and Riley, vol. 1, p.87.
16 Thomas Carte, *An History of the Life of James Duke of Ormonde* (London, 1786), vol. ii. pp.654–636; Clarendon, *History of the Rebellion*, vol. xv, pp.70–74; *Memoirs of James II*, pp.274–276, 281, 313; *Calendar of the Clarendon Papers*, vol. iii, pp.231, 232, 283.
17 Drenth and Riley, vol. 1, pp.88–89; Jennings, pp.404–408.
18 Drenth and Riley, vol. 1, p.92.
19 Thurloe, vol. i, p.514, 27 September 1653.
20 Clarendon, *Rebellion*, vol. xv, p.80; *Calendar of the Clarendon State Papers*, vol. iii, pp.256, 262, 266, 276, 790.
21 Jennings, pp.19, 621–622.
22 Jennings, pp.19–20.
23 Jennings, p.17; Drenth and Riley, vol. 1, p.91; Firth, p.70.
24 Firth, p.70; *Calendar of the Clarendon State Papers* vol. iii, p.595.
25 Bristol to Hyde, 26 November 1656 in *Calendar of the Clarendon State Papers*, vol. iii, pp.311–312.
26 Firth, pp.67–70; Drenth and Riley, vol. 1, pp.91–92; TNA SP 29/51, f. 33iv.
27 Rev William (ed.), *Letters and Papers of Patrick Ruthven, Earl of Forth and Brentford, and of His Family: A. D. 1615–A. D. 1662. With an Appendix of Papers Relating to Sir John Urry* (London: J.B. Nichols and Sons, 1868), p.165.
28 *Calendar of the Clarendon State Papers*, vol. iii, p.344.
29 *Memoirs of James II*, pp.327, 349.
30 Thurloe, vol. v, p.533.
31 Letter of intelligence, Bruges, dated 26 October (5 November N.S.) 1656 in Thurloe, vol. v, p.521.
32 *Calendar of the Clarendon State Papers*, vol. iii pp.232, 283.
33 *Calendar of the Clarendon State Papers*, vol. iii p.552.
34 *Calendar of the Clarendon State Papers*, vol. iii p.573.
35 J.J. Inglis-Jones, 'The Grand Condé in exile: Power Politics in France, Spain and the Spanish Netherlands, 1652–1659', Unpublished D.Phil Thesis, Christ Church, Oxford, 1994, p.175.
36 *Mercurius Politicus*, 16–23 April 1657, p.7750
37 *Mercurius Politicus*, 8 January 1657, p.750
38 *Mercurius Politicus*, 16–23 April 1657, p.7737

39 *Memoirs of James II*, p.297.
40 *Memoirs of James II*, pp.234–235.
41 *Calendar of the Clarendon State Papers* vol. iii, p.604.
42 *Calendar of the Clarendon State Papers* vol. iii, p.607.
43 *Calendar of the Clarendon State Papers* vol. iii, p.773.
44 *Calendar of the Clarendon State Papers* vol. iii, p.625; Thurloe, vol. v, p.533.
45 *Mercurius Politicus*, 16–23 April 1657, p.1750.
46 John Barratt, *'Better Begging than Fighting': The Royalist Army in Exile in the War against Cromwell 1656–1660* (Helion: Solihull, 2016), p.31.
47 Parker, p.272.
48 *Memoirs of James II*, p.260.
49 See Jonathon Riley, *The Last Ironsides: The English Expedition to Portugal, 1662–1668* (Helion: Solihull, 2014), for details.
50 Jennings, pp.17, 19
51 Project SYW online, accessed 9 August 2020.
52 *Memoirs of James II*, p.235.
53 Parker, p.274.
54 Parker, pp.274–275.
55 J.J. Inglis-Jones, pp.103–118.

CHAPTER 12

1 *Memoirs of James II*, pp.223–224.
2 Aubrey, *Brief Lives*, vol.ii, p.87; see also *The Dictionary of National Biography* (London, 1961).
3 Aubrey, *Brief Lives*, vol.ii, p.88.
4 Firth and Davies, vol. ii, p.683.
5 Firth and Davies, vol. ii, p.683.
6 TNA CSPD Interregnum, 1656–1657, p.94.
7 Firth and Davies, vol. ii, p.689.
8 TNA SP 25/76A, f. 199.
9 James Heath, *A Chronicle of the Late Intestine War in the Three Kingdoms* (London, 1676), p.720.
10 *Mercurius Politicus*, 30 April–7 May 1657, p.7760.
11 *Mercurius Politicus*, 30 April–7 May 1657, p.7796.
12 Peacock, p.42.
13 Firth and Davies, vol. ii, p.689.
14 Firth and Davies, vol. ii, pp.636, 686.
15 Firth and Davies, vol. ii, pp.676, 683–684.
16 *Mercurius Politicus*, 14–21 May 1657, p.7799; 21–28 May 1657, p.7890.
17 *Clarke Papers*, vol. ii, p.84.
18 Jurgen Brauer and Hubert van Tuyll, *Castles, Battles & Bombs. How Economics Explains Military History* (Chicago: University of Chicago Press, 2008), p.119; John A. Lynn, *Giant of the Grande Siècle: The French Army 1610–1715* (Cambridge: Cambridge University Press, 1997), pp.15–18.
19 *Memoirs of James II*, p.262; *The History of Henri de la Tour D'Auvergne, Viscount Turenne, Marshal-General of France*, 3 vols (London, 1735), p.184.

20 TNA CSPD Interregnum 1657–1658, vol. 156, 13 August 1657.

CHAPTER 13
1   Thurloe, vol. vi, p.289.
2   Christopher Duffy, *Fire and Stone*, p.11.
3   Brauer and Van Tuyll, p.129.
4   Parker, pp.11–12.
5   Childs, *Warfare in the Seventeenth Century*, p.113.
6   *Memoirs of James II*, p.228.
7   *Memoirs of James II*, pp.228–229.
8   *Memoirs of James II*, pp.230–231.
9   *Memoirs of James II*, pp.231–232.
10 *Memoirs of James II*, p.232.
11 *Memoirs of James II*, p.232.
12 V.-J. Vaillant, *La Siège d'Ardres en 1657 d'après une relation contemporaine inédite, ou Ardrésiens at Boulonnais* (Boulogne: Impr. de Simonnaire, 1884), p.8.
13 Michel Cabal, 'The fortifications of Ardres from the Middle Ages to the Nineteenth Century', *Publications of the Institute for Historical Research of Septentrion*, September 2018 <https://www.openedition.org/6540> accessed 18 August 2020.
14 V.-J. Vaillant, p.15.
15 *Memoirs of James II*, pp.236–237.
16 Bodleian Library, Harleian Miscellany, 'A true and just Relation of Major-General Sir Thomas Morgan's Progress in France and Flanders, with the six-thousand English, in the Years 1657 and 1658, at the Taking of Dunkirk, and other important Places; as it was delivered by the General himself.' (London, 1699), p.342.
17 *The memoirs of Major-General Morgan, Containing a true and faithful relation of his progress in France and Flanders, with the six-thousand British forces, in the years 1657 and 1658* (Glasgow, 1752), pp.1–2.
18 Thurloe, vol. vi, p.299.
19 *Memoirs of James II*, pp.237–238.
20 *Clarke Papers*, vol. iii, p.385.
21 BL Lansdowne MS 823, f. 104
22 *Clarke Papers*, vol. iii, p.119.
23 Firth, p.82; *Clarke Papers*, vol. iii, p.119; Thurloe, vol. vi, pp.522, 524.
24 Thurloe, vol. vi, p.163.
25 *Memoirs of James II*, p.238.

CHAPTER 14
1   'A Broadside on the taking of Fort Mardyck near Dunkirk and the events following until 1658'. B.M. 1872,0113.589.
2   *Memoirs of James II*, pp.239–240.
3   *Memoirs of James II*, p.241.
4   *Memoirs of James II*, p.241.
5   B.M. 1872,0113.589; *Sir Thomas Morgan's Progress in France and Flanders*, p.342.

6 Firth, p.84.
7 Thurloe, vol. vi, p.561.
8 TNA CSPD Interregnum, vol. 158, 8 December 1657.
9 Clarke Papers, vol. iii, p.176.
10 *Memoirs of James II*, p.243.
11 Thurloe, vol. vi, p.630.
12 *Memoirs of James II*, pp.243-244; see also B.M. 1872,0113.589.
13 Clarke Papers, vol. iii, p.155.
14 *Memoirs of James II*, p.244.
15 *Memoirs of James II*, p.244.
16 Clarke Papers, vol. iii, p.25.
17 *Memoirs of Major-General Morgan*, p.2; Jules Bourelly, *Cromwell et Mazarin: Deux Campagnes de Turenne en Flandres; la bataille des Dunes* (Paris: Perrin et cie, 1886), p.19.
18 Barratt, p.67.
19 Clarke Papers, vol. iii, p.25.
20 Clarke Papers, vol. iii, p.25.
21 Clarke Papers, vol. iii, p.48.
22 Clarke Papers, vol. iii, pp.21, 123, 135
23 Thurloe, vol. vi, p.275; Eric Gruber von Arni, *Justice to the Maimed Soldier. Nursing, Medical Care and Welfare for Sick Soldiers and their Families during the English Civil wars and Interregnum, 1642-1660* (Aldershot: Ashgate, 2001), p.131.
24 TNA CSPD Interregnum vol. 158, 17 December 1657.
25 Colonel G.A. Kempthorne, 'Notes on the Medical Services during the Civil War and the Interregnum, 1642-1660', in *Journal of the Royal Army Medical Corps*, vol. 10, September 1940, p.202.
26 For more details on the care of the sick and wounded at this time, see especially von Arni, pp.131-134.
27 Kempthorne, p.202; TNA CSPD Interregnum, vol. 158, 4 December 1657.
28 *Memoirs of James II*, pp.317, 322.
29 Thurloe, vol. vi, pp.637, 653.
30 Thurloe, vol. vi, p.659.
31 TNA CSPD Interregnum, vol. 158, 12 January 1658; Thurloe, vol. vii, p.651.
32 Thurloe, vol. vi, p.659.
33 B.M. 1872,0113.589.
34 Von Arni, p.133.
35 *Memoirs of James II*, pp.245-246.
36 Thurloe, vol. vi, p.665.
37 Derek P. Masserella, 'The Politics of the Army, 1647-1660', vol. ii (unpublished D. Phil thesis, University of York, 1977), p.590.
38 TNA CSPD Interregnum, vol. 158, 10 December 1657.
39 Morgan's account in the Harleian Miscellany, p.342.
40 Firth and Davies, vol. ii, p.520; Drenth and Riley, p.85; TNA CSPD 1656-1657, pp.128-129, 133, 139, 176, 245.
41 Drenth and Riley, vol. 1, p.85; Thurloe, vol. vi, pp.615, 659, 676, 677.
42 Thurloe, vol. vi, p.695.

43 *Memoirs of James II*, p.241.
44 Barratt, p.64.
45 *Calendar of the Clarendon State Papers*, vol. iii, f. 984.
46 *Calendar of the Clarendon State Papers*, vol. iii, f. 1086.
47 Two warrants for Blagge as Lieutenant-Colonel in the Guards are in the Historical Manuscripts Commission's Report on the MSS. of Mr John Eliot Hodgkin, p.123.
48 B.M. 1872,0113.589.
49 B.M. 1872,0113.589.
50 B.M. 1872,0113.589.
51 Thurloe, vol. vi, p.713.
52 Thurloe, vol. vii, p.31.
53 Firth and Davies, p.532; Clarke Papers, vol. ii pp.151, 152; Thurloe, vol. vi, p.115.
54 *Memoirs of James II*, p.251.
55 *Memoirse of James II*, pp.251–252.

CHAPTER 15

1 *Memoirs of James II*, p.251.
2 Thurloe, vol. vii, p.83.
3 Parker, p.51.
4 James Inglis–Jones, 'The Battle of the Dunes, 1658: Condé, War and Power Politics', *War in History* vol. i, no. 3, November 1994, p.257 citing R.A. Stradling, *The Armada of Flanders, Spanish Maritime Policy and European War 1568–1669* (Cambridge: Cambridge University Press, 1992), p.147.
5 *Memoirs of James II*, p.253.
6 *Memoirs of James II*, p.252.
7 Inglis–Jones, unpublished thesis, p.212.
8 Thurloe, vol. vii, pp.103, 109.
9 *Memoirs of James II*, p.253.
10 Inglis–Jones, 'Battle of the Dunes', pp.258–260.
11 Inglis–Jones, 'Battle of the Dunes', p.260.
12 M. le Duc d'Aumale, *Histoire des Princes de Condé*, vol. vii (Paris: C. Lévy, 1889), p.35; Archives de Chantilly, Correspondence du Grand Condé, Série P, vol.18, f.321: Caracena to Condé, 1 Apr. 1658; f.352; C.H. Firth, *The Last Years of the Protectorate* (London: Longmans, Green, 1909), p.183.
13 *Memoirs of James II*, p.253.
14 *Memoirs of James II*, pp.253–254.
15 Harleian Miscellany, *A true and just Relation of Major-General Sir Thomas Morgan's Progress in France and Flanders*, p.344.
16 Kempthorne, pp.199–200.
17 Harleian Miscellany, *A true and just Relation of Major-General Sir Thomas Morgan's Progress in France and Flanders*, p.343.
18 Louis Nicholas de Clerville, 'Discours fait par le Chevalier de Clerville des causes de siege de Dunkerque et de ce qui s'est passé et est notable en iceluy, 1658', in Jules Bourelly, p.289.
19 *Memoirs of James II*, pp.253–254.

NOTES TO THE TEXT

20 Thurloe, vol. vii, p.126.
21 Barratt, p.73.
22 *Memoirs of James II*, pp.254–255. Bourelly, p.296.
23 *Memoirs of James II*, p.257; Bourelly, pp.297–298.
24 *History of Henri de la Tour d'Auvergne, Viscount de Turenne*, p.184.
25 Thurloe, vol. vii, p.127.
26 Harleian Miscellany, *A true and just Relation of Major-General Sir Thomas Morgan's Progress in France and Flanders*, p.343.
27 Hessiches Staatsarchiv, Marburg.
28 *History of Henri de la Tour d'Auvergne, Viscount de Turenne, Marshal-General of FRANCE; Containing the AUTHORITIES, In THREE PARTS* (English edition, London, 1735), p.184.
29 Firth and Davies, pp.679, 686, 690, 695.
30 *History of Henri de la Tour d'Auvergne, Viscount de Turenne*, p.184; *Memoirs of James II*, p.259.
31 *Memoirs of James II*, p.258.
32 *Memoirs of James II*, p.259.
33 *History of Henri de la Tour d'Auvergne, Viscount de Turenne*, p.185.
34 Morgan, *Memoirs*, p.3.
35 Lieutenant-Colonel Richard Hughes of Cochrane's Regiment, in Clarke Papers vol. iii, p.151.
36 *History of Henri de la Tour d'Auvergne, Viscount de Turenne*, p.186.
37 Thurloe, vol. vii, p.263.
38 *Mercurius Politicus*, no. 421, 17–24 June 1658, p.619.
39 Morgan, *Memoirs*, p.5.
40 *Memoirs of James II*, p.263.
41 *Memoirs of James II*, p.263.
42 Clarke Papers, vol. iii, p.151.
43 *Memoirs of James II*, p.264.
44 Lorraine White, 'The Experience of Spain's Early Modern Soldiers: Combat, Welfare and Violence', in *War in History*, 2002, no. 9, p.11.
45 White 'Spain's Early Soldiers', p.15.
46 *Memoirs of James II*, p.264.
47 Drummond to Monck, Clarke Papers, vol. iii, p.154.
48 Drummond to Monck, Clarke Papers, vol. iii, pp.154, 157.
49 Thurloe, vol. vii, pp.155–156, 160; *Mercurius Politicus*, 17–24 June 1658, p.581.
50 Firth and Davies, p.696.
51 *Memoirs of James II*, p.267.
52 Drummond to Monck, Clarke Papers, vol. iii, p.157.
53 'A true and just Relation of Major-General Sir Thomas Morgan's Progress in France and Flanders', Harleian MSS, p.346.
54 *History of Henri de la Tour d'Auvergne, Viscount de Turenne*, p.186.
55 'A true and just Relation of Major-General Sir Thomas Morgan's Progress in France and Flanders', Harleian MSS, pp.346–347.
56 *Memoirs of James II*, p.268; Inglis–Jones, 'Battle of the Dunes', p.263; *History of Henri de la Tour d'Auvergne, Viscount de Turenne*, p.186.
57 *Memoirs of James II*, p.269.

58 *Memoirs of James II*, p.272.
59 Morgan, *Memoirs*, pp.7–8.
60 *Clarke Papers*, vol. iii, p.151.
61 *Clarke Papers*, vol. iii, p.151.
62 *Memoirs of James II*, pp.269–270.
63 Clarke Papers, vol. iii, p.151.
64 Thurloe, vol. vii, p.160.
65 *Memoirs of James II*, pp.272–273; Thurloe, vol. vii, pp.126, 156, 260; TNA CSPD Interregnum, 1658–1659, p.97.
66 *Memoirs of James II*, p.275. This is supported in the *History of Henri de la Tour d'Auvergne, Viscount de Turenne*, p.187.
67 An account of the battle and the casualties is in TNA CSPD Venetian, vol. xxxi, June 1658.
68 *History of Henri de la Tour d'Auvergne, Viscount de Turenne*, p.188.
69 *History of Henri de la Tour d'Auvergne, Viscount de Turenne*, p.188; 'A true and just Relation of Major-General Sir Thomas Morgan's Progress in France and Flanders', Harleian MSS, p.346.
70 *History of Henri de la Tour d'Auvergne, Viscount de Turenne*, p.188.
71 The surrender document and other material is contained in the Cardinal de Retz's *Remarques sur la Reddition de Dunkerque entre les mains des Anglais* (Paris, 1659).
72 Lieutenant-Colonel Richard Hughes in Clarke Papers, vol. iii, p.151.
73 Lieutenant-Colonel Richard Hughes in Clarke Papers, vol. iii, p.151.

CHAPTER 16

1 *Memoirs of James II*, pp.275–276.
2 *Memoirs of James II*, p.276.
3 Thurloe, vol. vii. p.239; Rawlinson MSS. A, vol. lix, f.87.
4 William A. Shaw, *Calendar of Treasury Books*, vol. 7, 1661–1668 (London: Institute of Historical Research, 1916).
5 Firth, *The Last Years of the Protectorate*, vol. II, p.212.
6 Thurloe, vol. vii, p.198.
7 Firth, vol. II, p.213.
8 Firth, vol. II, p.219.
9 Commons Journal, vol. vii, p.760; TNA CSPD Interregnum. 1659–1660, pp.151, 105, 143; Thurloe, vol. vii, pp.170, 239, 274. 319.
10 Thurloe, vol. vii, p.215.
11 *Mercurius Politicus*, 24 June–1 July 1658, p.650.
12 *Mercurius Politicus*, 15–22 July 1658, p.721.
13 Lockhart to Cromwell in Thurloe, vol. vii, p.201.
14 Lockhart to Cromwell in Thurloe, vol. vii, p.274.
15 Firth and Davies, vol. ii, p.673.
16 Thurloe, vol. vii, pp.170, 179, 207, 238, 239, 250, 319; Firth, vol. II, p.210. See also the appendix to this chapter.
17 Thurloe, vol. vii, p.668.
18 Firth and Davies, vol. ii, pp.679–680.
19 Thurloe, vol. vii, p.200; Firth, 'Royalist and Cromwellian Armies', p.86.
20 *History of Henri de la Tour d'Auvergne, Duc de Turenne*, p.189.

NOTES TO THE TEXT

21 *History of Henri de la Tour d'Auvergne, Duc de Turenne*, p.189.
22 *History of Henri de la Tour d'Auvergne, Duc de Turenne*, p.189.
23 Harleian Miscellany, p.347.
24 Thurloe, vol. vii, pp.187, 237, 239; *Mercurius Politicus*, 17–24 June 1658, p.634.
25 Thurloe, vol. vii, p.200; *History of Henri de la Tour d'Auvergne, Duc de Turenne*, p.190.
26 *History of Henri de la Tour d'Auvergne, Duc de Turenne*, p.190.
27 *History of Henri de la Tour d'Auvergne, Duc de Turenne*, p.191.
28 *Memoirs of James II*, pp.276–277.
29 *Memoirs of James II*, p.277.
30 Thurloe, vol. vii, pp.238, 250.
31 *Memoirs of James II*, p.277.
32 *Memoirs of James II*, p.278.
33 Firth, vol. II, pp.207–208.
34 James White, *The History of the Life and Reign of Lewis XIV, King of France and Navarre*, vol. I (London, 1742), p.317.
35 Thurloe, vol. vii, pp.250, 270, 282, 320–323, 328; Firth, vol. II, p.208.

CHAPTER 17

1 *Life of Henri de la Tour d'Auvergne*, p.196.
2 *Memoirs of James II*, p.278.
3 *Life of Henri de la Tour d'Auvergne*, p.197.
4 *Life of Henri de la Tour d'Auvergne*, p.198.
5 *Life of Henri de la Tour d'Auvergne*, p.200.
6 'A true and just Relation of Major-General Sir Thomas Morgan's Progress in France and Flanders', p.347.
7 Dr Thomas Clarges to Thurloe in Thurloe, vol. vii, December 1658.
8 *Life of Henri de la Tour d'Auvergne*, p.202.
9 *Memoirs of James II*, p.279.
10 *Life of Henri de la Tour d'Auvergne*, p.204.
11 *Life of Henri de la Tour d'Auvergne*, p.205.
12 'A true and just Relation of Major-General Sir Thomas Morgan's Progress in France and Flanders', p.347.
13 'A true and just Relation of Major-General Sir Thomas Morgan's Progress in France and Flanders', p.347.
14 'A true and just Relation of Major-General Sir Thomas Morgan's Progress in France and Flanders', p.348.
15 'A true and just Relation of Major-General Sir Thomas Morgan's Progress in France and Flanders', pp.348–349.
16 'A true and just Relation of Major-General Sir Thomas Morgan's Progress in France and Flanders', p.349.
17 'A true and just Relation of Major-General Sir Thomas Morgan's Progress in France and Flanders', p.349.
18 'A true and just Relation of Major-General Sir Thomas Morgan's Progress in France and Flanders', p.350.
19 *Life of Henri de la Tour d'Auvergne*, p.208.
20 *Mercurius Politicus*, 9–16 September 1658, p.822.

21 *Mercurius Politicus*, 9–16 September 1658, p.832.
22 *Memoirs of James II*, p.279.

CHAPTER 18

1 *Mercurius Politicus*, 16 September–14 October 1658, p.848.
2 The address is printed in *Mercurius Politicus*, 7–14 October 1659.
3 M. Guizot, tr. Andrew Scoble, *History of Richard Cromwell and the Restoration of Charles II*, English edition (London: R. Bentley, 1856), vol. i, p.235.
4 C.H. Firth, *Royalist and Cromwellian Armies in Flanders*, p.88.
5 Thurloe, vol. vii, p.579; Clarke Papers, vol. iii. p.171. See also Guizot, vol. i, p.285.
6 See Jonathon Riley, *The Last Ironsides*.
7 See Guizot, vol. I, pp.391, 398, 402, 409; Commons Journal, vol. vii, p.657 and Lockhart's own letter of 17 May 1659 in Thurloe, vol. vii, p.670.
8 Thurloe, vol. vii, p.671.
9 Commons Journal, vol. vii, p.657; Thurloe, vol. vii, pp.670, 694, 721.
10 Commons Journal, vol. vi, pp.723, 735.
11 Clarke Papers, vol. iii, p.283.
12 Thurloe, vol. vii, pp.694, 699, 712–779.
13 TNA CSPD Interregnum, 1659–1660, pp.58, 74.
14 Thurloe, vol. vii, p.722.
15 Clarke Papers, vol. iii, p.40; Commons Journal, vol. vii, pp.723, 760; TNA CSPD Interregnum 1659–1660, pp.121, 146, 195, 197.
16 Firth and Davies, vol. ii, p.694.
17 TNA CSPD Interregnum, 1659–1660, pp.307, 322, 349, 352, 368, 415, 592; Firth and Davies, vol. ii, pp.684–685.
18 C.H. Firth, *Royalist and Cromwellian Armies in Flanders*, p.92.
19 TNA CSPD Interregnum, 1659–1660, pp.300, 309, 321.
20 Guizot, vol. ii, pp.341, 343; *Public Intelligencer*, 30 January–6 February 1660, p.1068; TNA CSPD Interregnum, 1659–1660, p.343; Firth and Davies, vol. ii, pp.687–689.
21 Thurloe, vol. vii, p.695.
22 Thurloe, vol. vii, pp.723, 729, 730.
23 Thurloe, vol. vii, p.729
24 Commons Journal, vol. viii, p.803.
25 Firth and Davies, vol. ii, p.680.
26 Firth and Davies, vol. ii, p.691.
27 Firth and Davies, vol. ii, p.697; see also Derek P. Masserella, p.592.
28 Thurloe, vol. vii, p.249.
29 *Calendar of the Clarendon State Papers*, vol. xvi, p.173.
30 Pepys, *Diary*, p.104.
31 Sir Frederick Hamilton, *The origin and history of the First or Grenadier Guards. From documents in the State paper office* (London; J. Murray, 1874), vol. i, p.30.
32 Hamilton, vol. I, p.32.
33 *Calendar of the Clarendon State Papers*, vol. iii, p.472.
34 *Memoirs of James II*, p.286.

35 *Memoirs of James II*, p.279

CHAPTER 19

1 Bishop Burnet's *History of His Own Time*, vol. i, p.296.
2 TNA. CSPD, 1660–1661, p.543.
3 Shaw, *Calendar of Treasury Books*, vol. 7, 1661–1668.
4 <www.measuringworth.com> accessed 26 October 2020.
5 Commons Journal, vol. viii, pp.77, 78.
6 TNA CSPD 1662–1663, p.312.
7 *Memoirs of James II*, p.391; Dalton, *Army Lists and Commission Registers*, vol. I, p.2.
8 C.H. Firth, 'Royalist and Cromwellian Armies in Flanders', p.102.
9 C.H. Firth, 'Royalist and Cromwellian Armies in Flanders', p.102.
10 TNA CSPD 1660–1661, pp.14, 332; AO 1/203/308 and 1/216/309.
11 TNA CSPD 1660–1661, Appendix C.
12 TNA CSPD 1662–1663, p.496.
13 TNA CSPD 1662–1663, p.609.
14 TNA SP 29/61, October 1662; SP18/1236.66 (State Papers online).
15 Drenth and Riley, vol. 1, p.92.
16 TNA AO 1/203/308.
17 C.H. Firth, 'Royalist and Cromwellian Armies in Flanders', p.103.
18 TNA CSPD 1661–1662, pp.249, 287.
19 TNA AO 1/203/308; CSPD 1662–1663, p.312.
20 White Kennett, *A Register and Chronicle Ecclesiastical and Civil, with Proper Notes and References Towards Discovering and Connecting the True History of England, from the Restauration of King Charles II*, vol. i (London, 1728), p.717.
21 TNA CSPD 1660–1661, pp.545, 608, 632.
22 TNAAO 1/203/308; CSPD 1660–1661, pp.433; 1661–1662, pp. 167, 194, 249, 261, 364, 508.
23 TNA CSPD 1661–1662, pp.553, 573, 607.
24 On the decision to send the Irish to Portugal, see HMC, Portland MSS III (London, 1894), p/254. See also the Audit Office papers, TNA AO 1/203/308.
25 Drenth and Riley, vol. 1, p.92.
26 TNA CSPD 1660–1661, p.415; 1661–1662, p.2.
27 Firth and Davies, vol. ii, pp.694–698; C.H. Firth, 'Royalist and Cromwellian Armies in Flanders', pp.106–107; Riley 'Continuity in the English Army', pp.59–65.
28 C.H. Firth, 'Royalist and Cromwellian Armies in Flanders', p.108.
29 C.H. Firth, 'Royalist and Cromwellian Armies in Flanders', p.108; Drenth and Riley, vol. 1, p.81.
30 C.H. Firth, 'Royalist and Cromwellian Armies in Flanders', p.108 fn; Drenth and Riley, vol. 1, p.79.
31 See Jonathon Riley, *The Last Ironsides*, pp.50–51.
32 TNA CSPD 1662–1663, p.609.

Bibliography

Manuscripts and Original Sources

The National Archives of Great Britain (Kew)
Entry Book Interregnum vol. cv
State Papers Colonial Series, North America and the West Indies, vols i, v, xi, xxxii
Calendar of State Papers Domestic, Charles I
Calendar of State Papers Domestic, Interregnum 1647–1660
Calendar of State Papers Colonial Series, North America and the West Indies, and Addenda, 1574–1674
Calendar of State Papers Spanish, 1585
Calendar of State Papers Venetian 1655–6, 1658 (ed. Allen Hines)
State Papers of John Thurloe, Volumes ii, iii, v, vii, viii, xvi
State Papers Domestic, Interregnum, 1648–1660
Order Books; 25/76A; 25/107; 31/3/89; 31/3/90; 31/3/91;31/3/95; 49/97; 50/83; 94/43
State Papers Barbary States – Algiers, vol. ii

British Museum
'A Broadside on the taking of Fort Mardyck near Dunkirk and the events following until 1658', B.M. 1872, 0113.589

British Library
Additional MSS 35252, 9004, 9304
Ayscough No 6125
Edward Long, *The History of Jamaica*, BL Additional MSS No 14405
Sir Hans Sloane MSS, No 1431, 3986
Lansdowne MS 821–823, Original letters to Henry Cromwell when Chief Governor of Ireland, 3 vols, 1654–1659

Bodleian Library
Calendar of the Clarendon State Papers preserved in the Bodleian Library, ed. F.J. Routledge (5 vols, Oxford, 1872–1970), vols i, iii, xvi.
The Harleian Miscellany: *A Collection of Scarce, Curious, And Entertaining Pamphlets And Tracts, as well In Manuscript As In Print, Found In The Late Earl Of Oxford's Library, Interspersed With Historical, Political, And Critical Notes* (a collection of material from the library of the Earl of Oxford and Earl Mortimer collated and edited by Samuel Johnson and William Oldys between 1744 and 1753 on behalf of the publisher Thomas Osborne); in particular, 'A true and just Relation of Major-General Sir Thomas Morgan's Progress in France and Flanders, with the six–

thousand English, in the Years 1657 and 1658, at the Taking of Dunkirk, and other important Places; as it was delivered by the General himself' (London, 1699)

Second Report of the Royal Commission on Historical Manuscripts (London: Eyre & Spottiswoode for HMSO, 1871)

Seventh Report of the Royal Commission on Historical Manuscripts (London: Eyre & Spottiswoode for HMSO, 1879)

Richard Rawlinson MSS Series A:

Correspondence between the Protector and General Venables relating to the attacks on Hispaniola and Jamaica:

A21, f.118

A26, f. 459

A27, ff. 67 and 309

A30, f. 231

Admiral William Penn's account of his voyage to the West Indies:

A30, 271–278

Correspondence with Major General Robert Sedgwick concerning the attack on the French colonies in Acadia (Nova Scotia) and the Dutch in New Amsterdam:

A16, f.7

A30, ff. 43, 175

A32, f. 143

A 34, f. 721

A37, f.19

University of Manchester Library

Papers of Sir Edward Nicholas, GB 133 NP

House of Commons Library

Journal of the House of Commons, vols iv, vi, vii, viii 1648–1661

The Royal Historical Society

C.H. Firth (ed.), *The Clarke Papers* (London: The Camden Society, 4 vols, 1891–1901)

Report on the MSS. of Mr John Eliot Hodgkin

Royal Museums Greenwich

SIG/A (1673), The Duke of York's Sailing and Fighting Instructions

Letters, Journals and Diaries

John Evelyn's Diary (ed. Philip Francis) (London: The Folio Society, 1963)

The Diary of Samuel Pepys, eds J.S. Smith and Richard, Lord Braybrooke (London: Henry Colburn, 1825)

The Narrative of General Venables with an appendix of papers relating to the expedition to the West Indies and the conquest of Jamaica 1654–1655, ed. C.H. Firth for the Royal Historical Society (New York, 1900). This includes the Journals and Letters of Whistler, White and others as appendices.

American Sources

Plymouth Colonial Records, vol. 1

French Sources
Archives de Chantilly, Correspondence du Grand Condé, Série P, vol. 18

Spanish Sources
'Spanish Narratives of the English Attack on Santo Domingo 1655', ed. I.A. Wright, in *Camden Miscellany* vol. xiv (London: Royal Historical Society, 1926)

Irene A. Wright, 'The Spanish Resistance to the Occupation of Jamaica, 1655–1660', in *Transactions of the Royal Historical Society*, vol. 13, pp.117–147 (London, 1930)

'The Castilla Narrative', *Camden Miscellany* vol. XII (London: Royal Historical Society, 1924)

Archives of the Indies, Seville 1634–1658, 2–5–1/28; 53–2–8; 54–3–29; 79–4–6

Italian Sources
Ludovico Melzo, *Regolemilitari sopra il governo e servitor particolare della cavalleria* (Gioachimo Trognaesio, 1611).

Books

British and Irish
Aubrey, John, ed. Richard Barber, *Brief Lives* (Woodbridge and New York: The Folio Society, 1975)

Barratt, John, *Cromwell's Wars at Sea* (Barnsley: Pen & Sword, 2006)

Barratt, John, *'Better Begging than Fighting': The Royalist Army in Exile in the War against Cromwell 1656–1660* (Helion: Solihull, 2016)

Biceno, Hugh, *Elizabeth's Sea Dogs: How England's Mariners Became the Scourge of the Seas* (London: Conway Maritime, 2012)

Birch, Thomas (ed.), *Thurloe State Papers*, 7 vols (London, 1742)

Birmingham, David, *A Concise History of Portugal* (Cambridge: Cambridge University Press, 2003)

Burnet, Gilbert, *Bishop Burnet's History of His Own Times*, 2 vols (London, 1724–1734)

Capp, Bernard, *Cromwell's Navy: The Fleet and the English Revolution, 1648–1660* (Oxford: Oxford University Press, 1989)

Carte, Thomas, *An History of the Life of James Duke of Ormonde* (London, 1786)

Childs, John, *Warfare in the Seventeenth Century* (London: Cassell, 2003)

Clarke, Sir William, ed. C.H. Firth, *The Clarke Papers, Selections from the Papers of William Clarke, Secretary to the Council of the Army 1647–1649 and to General Monck and the Army in Scotland 1651–1660* (London: Royal Historical Society, 1899)

Clarendon, Edward Hyde Earl of, *The History of the Rebellion and Civil Wars in England, together with an historical view of the affairs of Ireland*, 15 vols (London, 1702)

Cooper, J.P., *The New Cambridge Modern History*, vol. 4: *The Decline of Spain and the Thirty Years' War, 1609–1648/49* (Cambridge: Cambridge University Press, 1979)

Corbett, Sir Julian S., *Cromwell and the Mediterranean: A Study in the Rise and Influence of British Power Within the Straits* (London, 1917)

Cox, Sir Richard, *Hibernia Anglicana, or The history of Ireland, from the conquest thereof by the English, to this present time* (London, 1689)

Crefeld, Martin van, *Supplying War* (Cambridge: Cambridge University Press, 1977)

Dalton, Charles, *English Army Lists and Commission Registers, 1661–1714*, vol. I, 1661–1685 (London: Eyre & Spottiswoode, 1892)

Dalton, John, *Illustrations, Historical and Genealogical: Of King James's Irish Army List (1689)* (Dublin, 1855)

BIBLIOGRAPHY

Darnell Davies, N., *The Cavaliers & Roundheads of Barbados, 1650–1652, with some account of the early history of Barbados* (Georgetown, British Guiana: Argosy Press, 1887)

Dictionary of National Biography (London, 1886)

Dixon, Sir William Hepworth, *Robert Blake, Admiral and General at Sea, based on Family and State Papers* (London: Chapman & Hall, 1856)

Draper, P., *The House of Stanley: Including the Sieges of Latham House* (Ormskirk: T. Hutton, 1864).

Elliott, J.H., *The Revolt of the Catalans: A Study in the Decline of Spain 1598–1640* (Cambridge: Cambridge University Press, 1984)

Encyclopaedia Britannica, 11th edition (Cambridge: Cambridge University Press, 1911)

Firth, C.H. *Cromwell's Army. A History of the English Soldier during the Civil Wars, the Commonwealth and the Protectorate* (London: Methuen & Co., 1902)

Firth, C.H., *The Last Years of the Protectorate* (London: Longmans, Green, 1909)

Firth, Sir Charles, and Godfrey Davies, *The Regimental History of Cromwell's Army*, 2 vols (Oxford: Clarendon Press, 1940)

Gardiner, Samuel, *History of the Commonwealth and Protectorate 1649–1661*, 3 vols (London: Longmans, Green, 1901)

Giglio, Robert, *English Civil War Gaming Scenarios*, vol. 3 (Leigh-on-Sea: Partizan Press, 2005)

Gruber von Arni, Eric, *Justice to the Maimed Soldier. Nursing, Medical Care and Welfare for Sick Soldiers and their Families during the English Civil Wars and Interregnum, 1642–1660* (Aldershot: Ashgate, 2001)

Hainsworth, Roger, *The Swordsmen in Power. War and Politics under the English Republic 1649–1660* (Stroud: Sutton, 1997)

Hamilton, Frederick, *The origin and history of the First or Grenadier Guards. From documents in the State paper office* (London: J. Murray, 1874)

Hexham, Henry, *Principles of the art militarie; practised in the warre of the United Netherlands* (London, 1637)

Hickeringill, Edmund, *Jamaica Viewed* (London, 1661)

Henry Gráinne, *The Irish Military Community in Spanish Flanders, 1586–1612* (Kill Lane, Blackrock: Irish Academic Press, 1992)

Hoskins, S.E., *Charles the Second in the Channel Islands*, 2 vols (London: R. Bentley, 1854)

Hume, David, *The History of England*, vol. 6 (London, 1756)

Diary of Alexander Jaffray, Provost of Aberdeen, One of the Scottish Commissioners to Charles II, ed. John Barclay (London: Darton & Harvey, 1833)

Jennings, Brendan, *Wild Geese in Spanish Flanders* (Dublin: Stationery Office for the Irish Manuscripts Commission, 1964)

Knight, Frank, *General-at-Sea. The Life of Admiral Robert Blake* (London: Macdonald & Co., 1971)

Lavery, Brian, *The Ship of the Line – Vol. 1: The Development of the Battlefleet 1650–1850* (London: Conway, 2003)

Lynn, John A., *Giant of the Grande Siècle: The French Army 1610–1715* (Cambridge: Cambridge University Press, 1997)

Macray, Rev William Dunn (ed), *Letters and Papers of Patrick Ruthven, Earl of Forth and Brentford, and of His Family: A.D. 1615–A.D. 1662. With an Appendix of Papers Relating to Sir John Urry* (London: J.B. Nichols and Sons, 1868)

The memoirs of Major-General Morgan, Containing a true and faithful relation of his progress in France and Flanders, with the six-thousand British forces, in the years 1657 and 1658 (Glasgow, 1752)

Morgan, Walter MS, ed. Duncan Caldecot-Baird, *The Expedition in Holland, 1572–4* (London: Seeley Service, 1976)

Parker, Geoffrey, *The Army of Flanders and the Spanish Road 1567-1659* (Cambridge: Cambridge University Press, 1972)

Penn, Granville, *Memorials of the Professional Life and Times of Sir William Penn*, 2 vols (London: J. Duncan, 1833)

Powell, John Rowland, *Robert Blake: General-At-Sea* (London: Collins, 1972)

Reid, Stuart, *Officers and Regiments of the Royalist Army*, vol. 2 (Leigh-on-Sea: Partizan Press, n.d.)

Riley, Jonathon, *Napoleon as a General* (London: Hambledon Continuum, 2007)

Riley, Jonathon, *The Last Ironsides: The English Expedition to Portugal, 1662-1668* (Helion: Solihull. 2014)

Sells, A. Lytton (ed. and tr.), *The Memoirs of James II. His Campaigns as Duke of York* (London: Chatto & Windus, 1962)

Shaw, William A., *Calendar of Treasury Books*, vol. 7, 1661-1668 (London: Institute of Historical Research, 1916)

Stradling, R.A., *The Armada of Flanders, Spanish Maritime Policy and European War 1568-1669* (Cambridge: Cambridge University Press, 1992)

Sugden, John, *Sir Francis Drake* (London: Pimlico, 2004)

Treharne, R.F., and Harold Fuller (eds), *Muir's Historical Atlas: Ancient Medieval and Modern*, second edition (London: G. Philip, 1974).

Turner, Sir James, *Memoirs of his Own Time* (Edinburgh: Bannatyne, 1829, from an original MS)

Uttley, J., *The Story of the Channel Islands* (London: Faber & Faber, 1966)

Vere, Sir Francis de, *The commentaries of Sr. Francis Vere being diverse pieces of service, wherein he had command/written by himself in way of commentary* (London, 1657)

Vries, J. de, and A. van der Woude, *The First Modern Economy. Success, Failure, and Perseverance of the Dutch Economy, 1500-1815* (Cambridge: Cambridge University Press, 1997)

Woolrych, H., *Commonwealth to Protectorate* (Oxford: Oxford University Press, 1982)

North American

Anderson, R.C., *Naval Wars in the Levant 1559-1853* (Princeton: Princeton University Press, 1952)

Andrews, Charles, *Narratives of the Insurrections, 1675-1690* (New York: Charles Scribner's Sons, 1915)

Andrews, Matthew Page, *History of Maryland: Province and State* (Garden City, New York: Doubleday, Doran & Co., 1929)

Beer, George L., *The Old Colonial System, 1660-1754* (New York: Macmillan & Co., 1912)

Brauer, Jurgen and Hubert van Tuyll, *Castles, Battles & Bombs. How Economics Explains Military History* (Chicago, London: University of Chicago Press, 2008)

Carlyle, Thomas, *Oliver Cromwell's Letters and Speeches*, 2 vols (New York: Wiley & Putnam, 1845)

Duffy, Christopher, *Fire and Stone. The Science of Fortress Warfare 1660-1860* (Edison, NJ: Castle Books, 1975)

Dunn, Brenda, *A History of Port-Roya/Annapolis Royal, 1605-1800* (Toronto, 2004)

Gambrill, Montgomery J., *Leading Events of Maryland History* (Boston: Ginn & Co., 1904)

Griffiths, N.E.S., *From Migrant to Acadian: A North American Border People, 1604-1755* (Montreal: McGill University, 2005)

Knatchel, Philip, *England and the Fronde: the Impact of the English Civil War and Revolution of France* (Ithaca, NY: Cornell University Press, 1967)

Leverett, C.E., *A Memoir, Biographical and Genealogical of Sir John Leverett, Knt, Governor of Massachusetts* (Boston: Crosby, Nichols Co., 1856)

MacDonald, M.A., *Fortune and La Tour: The civil war in Acadia* (Toronto, 1983)

Marley, David, *Historic Cities of the Americas: An Illustrated Encyclopaedia* (ABC-CLIO, 2004)

Marley, David, *Wars of the Americas: A Chronology of Armed Conflict in the Western Hemisphere* (ABC–CLIO, 2008)

Osgood, Herbert L., *The American Colonies in the Seventeenth Century* (New York: Macmillan, 1904)

Roberts, Oliver A., *History of the Military Company of the Massachusetts, now called the Ancient and Honorable Artillery Company of Massachusetts, 1637–1888, 4 vols* (Boston, 1895–1901)

Saunders Webb, Stephen, *The Governors–General. The English Army and the Definition of the Empire, 1569–1681* (Chapel Hill, NC: University of North Carolina Press, 1979)

White, James, *The History of the Life and Reign of Lewis XIV, King of France and Navarre*, vol. I (London, 1742)

Whitmore, W.H., ed., *The Colonial Laws of Massachusetts Reprinted from the Edition of 1660, with Supplements to 1672, Containing also the Body of Liberties of 1641* (Boston, 1860)

Williams, Sir Roger, *The Actions of the Low Countries* (New York, 1895)

French

Aumale, M. le Duc d', *Histoire des Princes de Condé*, vol. vii (Paris: C. Lévy, 1889)

Bourelly, Jules, *Cromwell et Mazarin: Deux Campagnes de Turenne en Flandres; la bataille des Dunes* (Paris: Perrin et cie, 1886)

Guizot, M., tr. Andrew Scoble, *History of Richard Cromwell and the Restoration of Charles II*, English edition (London: R. Bentley, 1856)

Mallet, Allain Manesson, *Les Travaux de Mars, ou l'art de guerre: Divisé en trois parts* (Paris, 1691)

Retz, Cardinal de, *Remarques sur la Reddition de Dunkerque entre les mains des Anglais* (Paris, 1659)

Strada, R.P. Famien, *Histoire de la Guerre Des Païs–Bas* (Bruxelles, 1717)

Turenne, *History of Henri de la Tour d'Auvergne, Viscount de Turenne, Marshal–General of France; Containing the Authorities, in Three Parts* (English edition, London, 1735)

Vaillant, V.–J., *La Siège d'Ardres en 1657 d'après une relation contemporaine inédite, ou Ardrésiens at Boulonnais* (Boulogne: Impr. de Simonnaire, 1884)

Spanish and Portuguese

Cundall, Frank, and Joseph L. Pietersz (eds), *Jamaica under the Spaniards, Abstracted from the Archives of Seville* (by Irene A. Wright) (Kingston, Jamaica, 1919)

Duro, Cesareo Fernandez, *Bosquejo biografico del Almirante D. Diego Egües y Beaumont* (Madrid: A Coruña Órbigo, 1892)

Freitas, Jorge Penim de, *A Cavalariana Guerra da Restauraçao* (Lisbon: Prefácio, 2005)

Dutch

Drenth, Wienand and Jonathon Riley, *The First Colonial Soldiers. A survey of British Colonies and their garrisons, 1650–1715* (Eindhoven, 2015). Volume 1: Europe, Africa and Asia; Volume 2 Part 1: The Americas and the Caribbean – New England and the Middle Colonies; Volume 2 Part 2: The Americas and the Caribbean – the Southern Colonies and the West Indies

Gheyn, Jacob de, *The Exercise of Arms* (Den Haag, 1607)

Papers and Academic Theses

British

Firth, C.H., 'Royalist and Cromwellian Armies in Flanders, 1657–1662', in *Transactions of the Royal Historical Society,* New Series, vol. 17 (London, 1903), pp.67–119

Inglis-Jones, J.J., 'The Grand Condé in exile: Power Politics in France, Spain and the Spanish Netherlands, 1652–1659' (unpublished D.Phil Thesis, Christ Church, Oxford, 1994)

Masserella, Derek P., 'The Politics of the Army, 1647–1660', 2 vols (unpublished D. Phil thesis, University of York, 1977)

Riley, J.P., *Continuity in the English Army, 1658–1668* (unpublished M.A. Thesis, Leeds University, 1989)

American

Cottrell, Peter, *The English Civil War in the American Colonies* (English Civil War Society of America)

Spanish

Mañé, Jorge Ignacio Rubio, *Problemas de Expansión y Defensa*, UNAM (ed.) in El Virreinato, II: *Expansion y Defensa (primeraparte)* (Edición 1983)

Articles in Journals

British and Irish

Anderson, R.C., 'The Royalists at Sea in 1649', in *Mariner's Mirror*, vol. xiv (1928) and 'The Royalists at Sea, 1650', in *Mariner's Mirror*, vol. xvii (1931)

Bonney, Richard J., 'The French Civil War, 1649–53 in *European History Quarterly*, vol. 8, no. 1 (1978)

Corbett, Julian, 'Fighting Instructions, 1530–1816', *Publications of the Navy Records Society*, Vol. XXIX (London, 1905)

Elliott, J.H., 'The Decline of Spain', in T. Aston, *Crisis in Europe 1560–1660* (London, 1965)

W. Godfray, 'Beaumont Cannon', in *Annual Bulletin of the Société Jersiaise* (1947)

James Inglis-Jones, 'The Battle of the Dunes, 1658: Condé, War and Power Politics', *War in History*, vol. i, no. 3, November 1994

Ellis, F.H., 'The Great Rebellion', in *Annual Bulletin of the Société Jersiaise* (1937)

Faulkner, Alaric, 'Maintenance and Fabrication at Fort Pentagouet 1635–1654' in *Historical Archaeology*, vol. 20, no. 1 (1986)

Kempthorne, Colonel G.A., 'Notes on the Medical Services during the Civil War and the Interregnum, 1642–1660', in *Journal of the Royal Army Medical Corps*, vol. 10, September 1940

Mannion, Nathan, 'The Irishman who became a Spanish Captain and fought Cromwell's Army', in *Irish Times*, 1 October 2019

'Iliam Dhone and the Manx Rebellion', in *Manx Publication Society*, vol. xxvi

Oppenheim, M., 'The Navy of the Commonwealth, 1649–1660', *English Historical Review*, no. 11 (1896)

White, Lorraine, 'The Experience of Spain's Early Modern Soldiers: Combat, Welfare and Violence', in *War in History*, 2002, no. 9

American

'A particular list of persons paid their first month's pay for their Respective qualities under the command of general Venables in the west indies, December 1654', *Caribbeana*, vol. II, citing TNA CO5/32

Grose, Clyde L., 'The Anglo–Portuguese Marriage of 1662', *The Hispanic American Historical Review*, 10:3 (August 1930)

Humme, Jeffrey Rogers, 'The American Militia and the origin of conscription: A Reassessment', *Journal of Libertarian Studies*, vol. 15, no. 4 (Fall 2001)

Sedgwick, Henry D., 'Robert Sedgwick,' Colonial Society of Massachusetts *Publications*, vol. iii (1895–1897)

French

Gouhier, Pierre, 'Mercenaires Irlandais en Service de la France', *Irish Sword*, no. 27 (1986–1987)

Gouhier, P., 'Mercenaires Irlandais au service de la France (1635–1664)', *Revue d'Histoire Moderne & Contemporaine*, 1968, No. 15–4.

Newspapers and Periodicals

Mercurius Politicus, 4–11 September 1651; 6–13 November 1651; 8 January 1657; 16–23 April 1657; 30April–7 May 1657; 14–21 May 1657; 21–28 May 1657; 17–24 June 1658; 9–16 September 1658; 16 September–14 October 1658; 7–14 October 1659

Public Intelligencer, 30 January–6 February 1660

Online Sources and Broadcast Material

English and American

<https//alchetron.com>

<www.britishempire.co.uk>

<https://inredcoatragsattired.com/2017/07/04/battle-of-the-severn-1655>

Dictionary of Canadian Biography online

University of Heidelberg digital collections online, <https://digi.ub.uni-heidelberg.de>

Michael Lorenzini, 'The Dutch & the English, Part Three: Construction of the Wall, 1653–1663', NYC Department of Records and Information Services

'Derby's Last Letter to his Lady', *A Manx Notebook*, < http://www.isle-of-man.com/manxnotebook/manxsoc/msvol26/intro.htm>

Massachusetts Historical Society collections online

<www.measuringworth.com>

Instructions to Sedgwick and Leverett by Cromwell, drafted by Thurloe and dated 8 February 1653, MHS Collections on-line

Timothy Venning, 'Cromwell's Foreign Policy and the Western Design', The Cromwell Association, <www.olivercromwell.org>

<https://commons.wikimedia.org>

<https://wikivisually.com>

Folger Digital Image Collections <https://luna.folger.edu>

Project SYW on-line

<www.fortified-paces.com/fortresses.html>

French

Michel Cabal, '[The fortifications of Ardres from the Middle Ages to the Nineteenth Century', Publications of the Institute for Historical Research of Septentrion, September 2018, <http://www.openedition.org/6540>

Dutch

<http://vanosnabrugge.org/docs/dutchmoney.htm>

Index

INDEX OF PERSONS

Abernathy, William, 236
Ableson, James 204
Adams, Thomas 204
Aguilar, Don Alvito de Garabito de 144, 161
Albuquerque, Franciso de Cabrera, Duke of 174, 178, 180
Aldersey, Elizabeth 117
Alfen, Martin van 169, 188
Allamont, Jean V de 241
Allen, Francis 76–7, 79
Allen, John 43, 70
Allen, Thomas 54, 131, 144
Alleyne, Richard, or Reynold 74–5, 78
Alsop, George 327
Alsop, Roger 229, 234, 268, 275, 278, 282, 285, 286–7, 307–9, 310, 311, 317–9, 326, 331
Alvarez, Don Joseph de 16, 161
Andrewes, Major 77, 79
Andrews, Edmund 332
Annesley, George 236
Añues, Don Cristobal 174–5, 178, 190
Archbould, Henry 184, 186
Archer, Captain 189
Armstrong, William 130, 292
Arnop, Joseph 236
Ashenhurst, William 324
Ashfield, Richard 309–10, 326
Ashfield Robert 236
Ashton, Lewis 130, 186
Ashton, Thomas 70, 215, 222–3, 316, 321, 331–2
Ashwood, Captain 83
Atherton, Humphrey 234
Atkins, John 332
Aumont, Marshal de 241, 262, 322
Axtell, Daniel 41
Aylmer, Gerard 225, 329

Ayscue, Sir George 35, 37–8, 39, 40, 41, 54, 55, 68, 75, 76, 77–8, 97, 124

Baas, Philippe de Castelmore, Baron 28
Bacon, Michael 293
Badiley, Richard 34, 192, 196, 198, 204
Baker, James 135
Baker, John 235
Baker, Richard 132, 233, 325
Balahide, Luke, 225
Baldwin, Richard 56, 96
Balfour, Lieutenant 330
Ballard, Lieutenant 130
Ballard, Thomas 186
Bamford, Richard 134, 184
Banks, Charles 326
Barclay, Edward 322
Barefoote, Walter 132
Barney, Septimus 223
Barns, Tobias 326
Barrell, John 130
Barrière, Henri de Taillefer de 28
Barrington, Francis 131, 166, 184, 186
Barrosco, Antonio Martin 160
Barrow, John 131
Barry, Philip 324
Barry, Samuel 133, 167, 171, 184, 187, 188
Bartlett, Henry 133, 185
Bascourt, Marshal de 262, 277
Bassett, Richard 332
Bassett, Thomas, 234
Bates, Edwin 326
Bates, James 133, 185, 234, 325
Baullard, Captain 328
Bauincourt, Lieutenant de 250

INDEX

Baure, M. de 250
Bayley, John 236
Bayley, William 77, 222
Baynard, Captain Edward (Adam) 131
Bedford, Samuell 294
Bedlington, Samuel 135, 189
Bedlow, Francis 322
Bee, Anthony 233
Beech, William, 233, 325
Bell, Philip 74–5
Bellesons, Marquis de 268, 277, 281
Bellings, James 225
Bennet, Edward 324, 332
Bennet, Richard 98
Bennet, Robert 39, 43, 69
Berkeley, Sir Charles 215, 223, 242, 322
Berkeley, William 97–8
Berkenhead, Isaac 116, 121, 131, 135, 151, 156, 167
Bernadiston, Thomas 323
Berrosano, Fr Juan 160
Berry, James 130, 184
Berry, Thomas 235
Beversham, John 223
Bingham, John 50, 186
Bingham, Brigham, Stroud 131
Birch, Thomas 45, 47, 56, 57
Birch, William 79
Bix, David 80
Blagge, Edward 125, 127
Blagge, or Blague, Thomas 210, 211, 221, 226, 259, 321
Blaggne, Major 329
Blaghlin, Lieutenant 324
Blaine, Lieutenant 329
Blake, Benjamin 127, 134, 204
Blake, Richard 136, 235
Blake, Robert 30, 32–6, 38–41, 43, 48–50, 51–3, 54, 191–202, 204
Blake, William, 61
Blanch, William 132
Blanchefort, François de 262
Bland, James 131, 134
Bland, Michael 131, 134, 151, 187
Bland, William 56
Blaney, John 236
Blenen, Peter 135
Blewfield, William 132
Blunt, Winkfield 132, 189
Boare, Herbert 328

Bodeley, William 332
Bodley, William 294
Bolger, James 329
Boniface, Don Gaspar de 218, 269–272, 283
Boone, Edward 187
Booth, Sir George 309, 312, 313
Booty, Richard 235
Bolas, Juan de 166, 181, 190
Bolt, Francis 235
Bordeaux-Neufville, Antoine de 28, 248, 256, 258, 305
Bork, Philip 329
Bossey, Thomas 129, 183
Bosvill, Edward 51–2, 62
Botsford, Edward 60
Boucher, Captain 79
Bouchier, Thomas 293
Boughty, Timothy 322
Bourgeois, Captain
Bounty, Captain 134, 155
Bounty, Mr 151
Bourke, Thomas 328
Bourke, Walter 328
Bowden, Richard 39, 68
Bowers, Nathaniel 132
Bowker, Daniel 293
Bowry, Thomas 205
Brady Daniel 225
Bramston, John 109, 187
Bramston, William 187
Brandon, Lord Gerard 320
Bray, John 185, 187
Brayne, Edward 169–171, 173, 174, 175–6
Brayne, William 183
Brennan, Roger 224
Brent, Giles 106, 114
Breres, Thomas 130, 186
Brereton, Thomas 328
Brett, George 324
Bridge, Tobias 286, 292, 319, 323
Briggs, George 80
Brigham, William 135, 186, 189
Bristol, Earl of 208, 212, 224, 259, 260, 269, 275, 312, 317
Broadnax, Robert 286, 292, 294, 323
Brockhurst, Francis 236
Bromicham, Francis 233
Bromwich, Francis 235
Brookes, John 326
Broslan, Cornelius 329

COLONIAL IRONSIDES

Broughton, Arthur 222, 322, 332
Broughton, Sir Edward 332
Broughton, Robert 332
Brown, John 323
Browne, Marcus 225
Browne, Thomas 224, 324
Bryan, Kennedy 329
Bryers, henry 235
Buck, John 325
Bueno, Francesco 151, 156, 160
Buller, Anthony 38, 68, 117, 120, 121, 131, 142, 143, 144, 148, 151, 152, 167, 171, 183, 186
Bultell, John 326
Burey, James 130, 186
Burgess, John 65
Burgess, Sir Roger 50, 53, 65
Burke, Conor 224, 328
Burke, Delany 225
Burke, Edmund 225, 329
Burke, John 324
Burke, Redmond 329
Burke, William 225, 329
Burroughs, Cornelius 186
Bushell, Theobald 132
Bustos, Pedro de 160
Butler, George 130, 157
Butler, Gregory 158, 167
Butler, James 129, 183
Butler, Theodore 225, 328, 329
Butler, Thomas 223
Butler, Pierce 223, 324
Butler, William 225, 236, 328
Byam, William 78, 79
Byron, Thomas 332

Cabiedes, Don Juan de 160
Cable, Francis 293
Cage, Thomas 130
Calderón, Juan Rodriguez de 201, 216
Calton, George 235
Calvert, (Caecilius) Cecil, 2nd Baron Baltimore 1004, 105–6, 107
Calvert, George, 1st Baron Baltimore 104, 105
Calvert, Leonard 105, 106–7, 113
Caracena, Marquis de 211–2, 217, 219, 241, 243, 252, 266, 268, 283, 284, 290, 304, 312, 315
Cardenas, Don Alonso de 27, 28, 29, 116
Carew, Matthew 327

Carey, Edmond 329
Carless, William 222
Carlston, John 322
Carman, William 133, 185
Carpenter, Philip 124, 135, 151, 156
Carpenter, William 56, 293
Carr, Cuthbert 236
Carroll, John 329
Carter, Andrew 121, 132, 143, 151, 167, 168, 171, 183, 224
Carter, Phelome 324
Carter, William 233, 325
Carteret, Sir George de 49–54, 61, 62
Carteret, Sir Philip de 52, 63
Carteret, Lady Philip de 52, 63
Cartre, Ensign 330
Cartwright, Thomas 327
Castelnau, Jacques, Marquis de 264, 268, 271, 281, 282
Castro, Don Gregorio de 160
Castro, Don Pedro de 151, 156, 160
Cathness, William 233
Catts, Captain 134, 155
Ceely, Robert 294
Chamberlaine, Elias 294
Chamberlaine, John 293
Chambers, William 235
Chandler, Job 112, 113
Chapman, Captain 330
Chapman, Thomas 234, 326, 330
Charles II, King of England, Scotland and Ireland
    Flees to the Scillies and the Channel Islands 37–8, 50, 206
    With the Scots 23–5, 43–4, 206
    Escapes after the Battle of Worcester 25, 206
In exile in France and Germany 30, 197, 206–7
In the Low Countries 286–305
Restoration 314–9
Charlton, William 236
Christian, William – see Dhone, Illiam
Chune, John 326
Claiborne, William 98, 106–7, 112, 114
Clapthorne, Giles 134
Clark, Abel 233, 257
Clarke, John, Colonel 39–41, 43, 65, 66, 68, 75–7, 79, 133, 142, 157
Clarke, John, Ensign 186, 235
Clarke, Clark Hon. Robert 112
Clarke, Samuel 53, 66, 229, 231, 268, 282, 287, 308, 309, 310, 332
Clay, Robert 205

INDEX

Claypole, Edward 235
Clayton, Thomas 132
Coates, Roger 236
Cobb, Chaplain 294
Cochrane, Sir Bryce 229, 231, 236, 256, 267–8, 275, 282, 287, 308, 309–10
Cobham, Nathaniel 196, 204, 234, 287, 326
Codrington, Christopher 71
Colbourne, Captain 132, 189
Colcut, Arthur 233
Coldham, Anthony 322
Cole, Nathaniel 236
Colleton, John 78
Collin, Henry 55
Collins, Major 61
Collins, John 61
Colliott, Arthur 325
Colmar, Count of 241
Colte, John 332
Columbus, Christopher 6, 137, 163
Condé, Louis II de Bourbon, Prince of, Duc d'Enghien 20, 21, 22, 27, 28, 211, 219, 220, 221, 232, 240, 241, 242, 248, 252, 254–5, 257, 260, 261, 2663, 264, 266, 269–70, 274, 276, 278, 283, 284, 289, 297, 300, 307
Condon, Daniel 329
Conor, Hugh 224
Conor, Roger 224
Conway, Francis, 325
Cooke, Aaron 87, 96
Cooke, John 130, 186, 328
Cooke, Roger 56, 292
Cooke, Thomas 56, 222–3, 275, 293
Cooke, William 292
Cooper, Christopher 131, 186
Cooper, Ellis 235
Cope, Anthony 327
Corbett, Vincent 131
Corker, John 294
Coronado, Don Nicolas 160
Coppain, William 128
Corail, M. 259
Costello, Dudley 224, 324
Cotes, Roger, 235
Cotes, William, 235
Couch, Surgeon 235
Coughlan, Dermott, 329
Coughlan, Gerrard 329
Cox, Mr 151, 155

Cox, John 134
Coxe, Captain 125
Coxe, Alban 50, 53, 61, 65–6
Coxe, Owen 54
Crawford, Alexander 328
Créqui, Marquis de 268, 277, 281, 288–90
Criefe, John 322
Crispin, William 127
Croft, John 332
Cromwell, Henry, Chief Governor of Ireland 121, 229, 247
Cromwell, Oliver
    Becomes protector, relations with parliament and the Council 25–6, 28
    Relations with the Dutch 26–7, 83–4, 88
    Relations with the French 27–9, 88, 197, 227, 256
    Relations with the Spanish 27–31, 115–7
    Policy in North America 83–4, 97–8, 108
    Directions and instructions to the expedition for the West Indies 73–7, 115–7, 167–8, 182
    Policy on war with Spain in Europe and the acquisition of Dunkirk 197–8, 206, 227, 253–4, 256, 258–9, 278
    Death 305
Cromwell, Richard 46fn, 306
Crowne, William 94
Cudworth, John 129, 183
Cuellar, Hernandez de 160, 174fn
Currine, Daniel 225
Curtis, Edmund 204
Curtis, Edward 98
Cusack, George 218, 269, 283
Cuttance, Roger 204, 205
Cutts, John 108, 136

Dakins, George 127
Daly, Connor 225
Daly, Luke 225
Damas, André 250
Damas, Philllipe 250
Danan, Edmond 224
Danby, Lord 49
Dane, Jeffrey 128
Daniel, Charles 325
Daniel, John 129
Daniell, Sir Thomas 332
Daron, Alexander 225, 328
Dauril, Captain de 250
Davenport, Thomas 322
Danvers, John 100

Davies, Abraham 235fn, 311, 325
Davis, Barthlomew 133, 185
Davis, Henry 130
Davis, Richard (snr) 93
Davis, Richard (jnr) 93
Dawley, Philip 236
Dawson, Thomas 293
Dayes, Richard 327
Dean, John 62, 129, 183
Deane, Richard 33, 45–6, 47, 192
Deane, William 129, 183
Debben, Lieutenant 133, 185
D'Aulnay, Charles de Menou 89
De la Tour, Charles de Saint–Étienne 89, 93
Desborough, Disbrowe, John 31, 122
Desborough, Philip 61
Denis, William 133, 185
Denman, Daniel 324
Denman, Edmund 324
Dennis, Robert 76, 97, 98, 293
Dennison, Robert 294
Denny, James 329
Dermott, Harry 225
Devoe, Captain 233, 311
Dhone, Illiam (Brown William) 44, 46, 48
D'Oyley, Edward 117, 120, 125, 130, 143, 156, 157, 167, 168, 169, 170, 171, 175–182, 183, 184
Dillon, Gerard 224
Disbrowe, Captain 294
Disney, Francis 130
Dody, Richard 225
Dolaners, John 187
Dongan, Robert 130, 186, 223
Don, Robert 185
Donovan, John 224, 328
Doolan, Captain, 329
Dorrell, James 187
Douglas, Captain 133, 185
Douglas, David 132, 185
Downing, John 332
Downing, Thomas 133, 185
Downes, Captain 131, 185
Drake, Sir Francis 29, 116, 139, 143
Draxe, James 74–5, 80
Drew, William 130
Duckenfield, Francis 59
Duckenfield, Richard 130
Duckenfield, Robert 44–7, 56–7, 130fn

Duckett, William 235
Dukes, Francis 326
Dullond, Lieutenant 329
Dungan, Michael 319, 324
Durham, Captain 226

Earning, Anthony 201, 204
Eaton, William 330, 332
Edney, Peter 8
Edwards, Obadiah 133, 185
Edwards, Thomas 133, 185
Egües, Don Diego de 202
Ellice, Thomas 78
Eltonhead, William 112
Elvize, John 223
Ely, Brent 293, 325
Emmerson, Ralph 325, 327
Emmes, Edward 325
Ennis, Christopher 169
Eristy, Alexander 320
Erlinn, Ralph 235
Erskine, Captain 329
Erwood, Gabriel 56, 293
Esquencourt, Seigneur de 268, 281
Ethon, Thomas 133, 185
Eubanke, Captain 326
Eubanke, John 233, 325
Evans, William 113, 114
Evertsen, Cornelius 41
Eyton, John 131, 186
Eyton, Phillip 57

Fagoso, Gonzalo 161
Fairfax, Francis 136
Fairfax, Sir Thomas 48, 169
Falkland, Lord 318, 326, 331
Farquhar, Lieutenant 330
Farrell, Captain 222, 223, 272
Farrell, Bryen 224, 328
Farrell, Charles 225, 328
Farrell, Connor (Conor) 212, 224
Farrell, Edward 225, 328
Farrell, Haughey 225, 328
Farrell, Henry 224, 328
Farrell, James 224, 225, 328
Farrell, John 224
Farrell, Lewis 212, 224, 312, 316, 317, 328, 331
Farrell, Richard 329

INDEX

Farrell, Robert 225
Farrell, Roger 225, 328
Farrell, Thadeus 225, 328
Farrell, Thomas 225, 329
Farrell, William, 225, 328
Farnese, Alessandro, Duke of Parma 17, 295
Farris, Lieutenant 133, 184, 187
Faulkner, George 184, 187
Fellow, Lawrence 328
Felsted, Humphrey 128
Fendall, Josias 112, 113, 114
Fenn, Captain 131
Fenn, Henry 128
Ferté, Marshal Henri de la 210, 237, 290, 295, 298, 300, 301
Fenwick (John?) 230
Fenwick Roger 233, 271, 272, 276, 303
Ferguson, John 132
Ferrobosco, Henry 186
Ffielding, Basil 332
Ffox, Charles 332
Field, Fielding, Septimus 223, 324
Fiennes (Clinton), George 233, 311, 327, 328
Fiennes, William 234, 327, 328
Figuero, Don Alonso Estevez de 161
Figueroa, Don Gabriel de Rojas Valle y 160
Filkins, John 132, 188
Finch, Symon 47, 57
Fincher, Abraham 132, 330
Fincher, Henry 65
Fisher, John 130, 184, 233
Fisher, Thomas 136
Fisher, William 130
Fitzgerald, Christopher 224
Fitzgerald, Edmund 223
Fitzgerald, George 328
Fitgerald, John 74, 120, 323
Fitzjames, henry 323
Fitz James, John 74, 120, 323
Fitzmorris, Thomas 329
Fitzwilliam, Robert 230, 235, 328
Fitzwilliams, George 328
Flaherty, Anthony 225
Flaherty, Bryan 225
Flaherty, Daniel 225
Flaherty, James 225
Flaherty, John 225
Flaherty, Murough 225
Flannilly, John 224

Flattry, Owen 329
Fleet, Thomas 128
Fleetwood, Richard 129, 183
Fleetwood, William 64, 188, 230, 233–4, 318, 325
Flemming, Fleming Richard 226 326
Flick, Nathaniel 130
Flower, Henry 286, 292, 294, 323
Forester, John 325
Forster, Josias 100, 105
Fortescue, Richard 68, 120
Fortescue, William 74, 80
Fowler, Mark 183, 129
Frampton, John 130
Francis, Benjamin 136
Francisco, Juan 161
Franco, Lazaro 157, 160, 161
Francklin, Oliver 234
Frankling, John 134, 184
Freeman, Thomas 133, 185
French, Dr John 233, 257
French, Thomas 133, 185
Freth, Ensign 325
Frias, Gonzalo de 160
Fry, Captain 186, 188
Fudge, William 134, 184
Fuenmayor, Don Fernando de Morenta y 161
Fuller, Matthew 96
Fuller, Thomas 130, 186
Fuller, William 108, 110–1, 113, 114

Gadagne, General de 268, 277, 281, 298
Gage, Thomas 116, 129
Gamarra, Don Estevan de 268
Gannock, William 327
Gardner, Martin 57, 325
Garge, George 332
Gargrave, Captain 233, 311
Gargrave, Henry 320, 326
Garrabito, Don Francisco 160
Garrett, James 127
Garrett, William 127
Garth, Ralph 131
Gathwaite, Thomas 292
Gaston, Lieutenant 330
Gaurdière, le Sieur de 250
Gaurdière, Leger 250
Geary, Edmund 235
Geraldino, Don Juan Morfa 144, 156, 160

373

COLONIAL IRONSIDES

Gerard, Sir Gilbert 320
Gibbes, Colonel 77, 79
Gibbon, Robert 53, 64, 258, 260, 285–6, 291, 293–4, 305, 309
Gibbon, Edward 114
Gibbon, John 294
Giles, John 234, 326
Gillen, Thomas 161
Gilmont, John 225
Gilmour, John 328
Gloucester, Duke of 211, 217, 224, 244, 257, 262, 283, 312–3, 316, 317, 324, 331
Goddard, Henry 130, 186
Godfrey, William 187
Godolphin, Sir Francis 37, 43, 70
Godolphin, John 223, 322
Goni, Don Diego de 218, 269
Goodfellow, Thomas 129, 183
Goodson, William 127, 134, 143, 151, 157, 167, 170, 173, 179, 258, 261, 265
Goring, Sydney 332
Gordon, Lieutenant 330
Gordward, Benjamin 133, 185
Gouge, Nicolas 250
Grace, Richard 212, 217, 225, 269, 276, 283, 312, 316, 317, 329, 331
Grady, John 225
Granby, Hugh 225
Grant, John 323
Grant, William 325
Green, John, 325
Greene, Henry 57
Greene, Samuel 131
Greene, Thomas 113, 114
Grenville, Sir John 35, 38–41, 68
Grey, Edward 332
Griffith, Thomas, 326
Grimes, Mark 294
Grosse, Robert 326
Grove, John 128
Groves, Humphrey 131, 184
Guise, Henry II, Duke of 192, 194, 216
Guitard, Guitault, Colonel 220, 269, 283
Guzman, Don Garcia 151, 156, 160
Gwilliam, Gwilliams, Gwillims, John 316, 321, 331, 332
Gwither, Nicholas 112, 113, 114
Gwyn, William 222
Gwynne, Gwyn, John 221, 275, 322
Gwynne, Richard 293

Haggat, John 294
Hale, William 93
Halford, Nicholas 132
Hall, William 132, 185
Halsey, James 292fn, 323
Hambleyne, William 132, 185
Hamilton, Lieutenant 329
Hamon, Francis 322
Hamnon, William 294
Hanbury, John 332
Hancock, Thomas 130, 157
Hangley, James 84, 95
Hanley, Fergus 225
Hannam, Willoughby 127
Hanny, Robert 132
Harbord, John 329
Hardstaff, Jervice 293
Hardwick, Ralph 133, 184, 185
Harland, 293
Harley, Sir Edward 312, 314, 316, 317, 320, 325, 331
Harley, Sir Robert 317, 318, 319, 323, 328, 331
Harman, John 201, 204
Haro, Don Luis de 307
Harris, Evan 235
Harris, Leonard 127
Harrison, Chaplain 328
Harrison, James 61, 66
Harrison, Mark 91–2, 95
Harrison, Nathaniel 293
Harrison, William 293
Harwood, William 223, 322
Hathorne, John 59
Hathorne, William 88, 92, 95
Hawkes, Samuel 128
Hayd, Edward 136
Hayes, James 233
Haynes, Thomas 230, 235
Hayward, John 127, 205
Heamans, Roger 108
Heane, Captain 135
Heane, James 39, 43, 50, 52–3, 60, 63–4, 120, 129, 133, 143, 151, 156, 157–8, 163, 167, 183
Heane, William 64, 125
Heath, Captain 63, 64
Heath, Robert 293
Heath, Thomas 55
Hehir, Cornelius 224
Hellny, Edward 84, 95

374

INDEX

Helsham, Arthur 53, 66
Henderson, Bartholomew 325
Herbert, James 132
Herbert, George 136
Herbert, William 235, 328
Heugnett, Francis
Heylin, Henry 321, 326
Hicks, Nicholas 93
Higgins, Lieutenant 330
Hill, John 136, 328
Hill, Luke 129, 183
Hill, Thomas 132, 183
Hill, William 133, 185, 204
Hilsman, John 133, 185
Hinde, Obadiah 130, 157
Hinton, Francis 234
Hinton, John 233, 272–3, 286, 292, 325
Hoare, Ezekiah 46
Hocquaincourt, Marquis de 261
Hodges, Richard 127
Hodforde, Captain 189
Hogarty, Richard 329
Holdep, Richard 17, 144, 148, 151, 168, 171, 183, 184, 187
Holland, Cornelius 101
Hooke, John 131
Hooke, Owen 236
Hooke, William 83
Hookes, Owen 236
Hope, Edward 224, 324
Hooper, Robert 79
Hopkins, William 65, 133, 184, 187
Hornold, John 236
Houghton, William, 234
Houncell, Andrew 133, 184, 187
How, Anthony 131, 186
How, Daniel 132
Howard, Captain 61
Howard, James 332
Howard, John 332
Howard, George 136
Howell, Humphrey 235
Howell, Tate 130, 185
Howell, Thomas 66, 114, 133
Howell, Thomas (jnr) 66, 185
Howell, Humphrey 235
Howlett, Captain 189
Howson, Edmund 293
Hoya, Francisco del 160

Hoyos, Juan de 201
Hubbard, John 128
Hughes, Captain 60, 63
Hughes, Hugh 236
Hughes, John 135, 155
Hughes, Thomas 122, 129, 152
Hughes, Richard 229, 236, 256, 266, 272, 275, 278, 288
Hughs, William 93
Humières, Louis, Marquis de 242, 268, 277, 281, 297–9
Humphrey, John 169, 171, 180, 183, 188
Humphreys, Major 234, 311
Hunkin, Joseph 41, 69
Hunt, John 60
Huntley, Gabriel 132
Huntley, William 133, 184, 187
Huntingdon, Major 56
Hurst, Henry 133, 185
Hussey, William, 326
Hyde, Edward 206, 208–9, 210–1, 212, 255

Inches, Francis, 326
Ingle, Richard 106–7
Ingram, Captain 57
Ingram, Thomas 233, 325
Iveagh, Lord 324

Jackson, Bartholomew 134, 184
Jackson, Henry 233, 325
Jackson, Thomas 156–7, 158
James Stuart, Duke of York 50, 118, 206, 210–2, 214, 216–7, 219, 221, 223, 227, 240–4, 248, 251–2, 254–6, 258–60, 261, 264–6, 258–60, 261, 264–76, 283, 284–90, 296, 299, 304, 312, 315, 316, 317, 322, 324, 330, 331
James, Edward 129, 183
James, William 233
Janman, John 233
Jarmin, Captain 79
Jeffereis, Herbert 222–3, 321
Jefferies, Jervase 293
Jeffrys (Jeffries), James 315, 322, 330
Jenkins, Captain 56, 57
Jenkins, John 114
Jenkins, Lasen 132
Jennings, Captain 135, 153
Jennings, James 68
Jermyn, Lord Henry 49, 53, 65
Jermyn, Sir Thomas 65

375

John of Austria, the Younger 208, 216–7, 219, 240–1, 243, 245, 248, 252, 266, 268–9, 271, 273, 276, 283, 284, 288, 290, 298, 300, 303, 304
John of Portugal 199
Johnson, Captain 135
Johnson, John 74, 80
Johnson, Peter 114
Johnson, Richard 65
Johnson, William 132, 325
Jones, Henry 121, 125, 135, 188
Jones, Jenkin 233
Jones, Michael 327
Jones, Thomas Trafford Hugh 84, 95
Jordan, Joseph 192, 204
Jordan, Thomas 87
Josse, John 135, 188
Jukes, Francis 234
Jurado, Luis Lopez 161

Keigan, Gerard 225
Kendall, William 204
Kent, Henry 133, 185
Kenne, Richard 133, 185
Kerry, Earl of 226
Ketcher, Bartholomew 127, 134
Kettell, Randall 131, 186
Keyth, Sir William 226
Kidwell, William 136
King, William 184, 187
Kirby, Francis 135
Kirby, Robert 204, 205
Knight, Captain 224, 246
Knight, John 221
Knight, Peter 113
Knightley, Edward 325

La Grande, Ensign 329
Lambert, John, General 25, 28, 29, 30, 84, 115, 119, 121, 228, 313
Lambert, John, Captain 127
Lane, John 60, 293
Lane, Nathaniel 133, 185
Langford, Thomas 322
Langton, William, 326
Larkin, Benjamin 131, 186
Larry, Patrick 93
Laundry, Robert 328
Laugherne, Quartermaster 323
Laughton, John 129, 184

La Verdure, Captain 93
Lawrence, Richard 133, 185
Lawriston, Robert 328
Lawson, James 226
Lawson, John 198, 207
Layton, Edward 325
Le Borgne, Emmanuel 89, 92
Ledger, William 235
Legard, William 236
Legatt, John 112
Leighton, Sir William 330
Le Hunt, Richard 41
Leiva, Don Francisco Cartagena de 174, 179, 190
Leniger, Moses 293
Lennan, Bryan 225
Leopold, Archduke of Austria 216, 219–20
Leverett, John 84–5, 87–8, 93, 95
Leverington, Samuel 133, 185
Lewis, Evan 235
Lewis, William 112, 113
Leyde, Marquis de 263–4, 277
Leyes, Harry 328
Ligne, Claude Lamoral, Prince de 219, 240–1, 252, 274, 283, 298–9, 301–2
Ligniville, Phillipe Emmanuel, Compte de 268, 281
Lillingston, Luke 229, 230, 234, 268, 273, 277, 283, 286, 287, 305, 307, 308–12, 317, 318, 327
Line, Blaghlin 223
Lingwood, Lionel 293
Liranso, Esteban 162
Littleton, Captain 330
Littleton, William 231, 235, 319, 323
Llewellyn, Richard 321
Lloyd, Edward 320
Lloyd, Godfrey 332
Lloyd, John 130, 204
Lloyd, Robert 294
Lloyd, Thomas 327
Lloyd, William 320
Lockhart, Sir William 30, 227–9, 233, 244, 247–8, 258–9, 261, 264, 268, 270–3, 276–8, 281, 285–6, 291, 292, 295, 304, 305–8, 311–2, 314
Louis XIV, King of France 11, 20–2, 30, 89, 192, 208, 231, 239, 256, 259, 263, 277, 287, 307, 314, 319
Lovelace, Francis 320
Lucy, Dermott 329
Ludlow, George 57
Lugg, Thomas 135, 189

INDEX

Lugo, Don Juan de 155, 160
Lydcott, Leonard 50
Lynch, Thomas 177, 184

McCarty, Donagh, Viscount Muskerry 211–2, 223, 244–5, 269, 317, 324
MacDavid, Fr John 224
McDonough, Ensign 329
McGuire, Ensign 330
McNamara, Daniel 225, 329
McNamarra, Donough 329
McSwaine, Hugh 329
Mabbison, William 294
Macher, John 224
Machin, John 326
Mackworth, Sir Francis 330
Madden, Hugh 225
Maddock, Thomas 324
Madison, Captain 131
Maginnis, Captain 330
Magoo, Laughlin, 329
Mahony, Mahon 329
Mahony, Murragh 329
Mallinson, Edward 133, 185
Mallinyeux, Lieutenant 322
Mandizeil, Edward 332
Maning, Edward 234
Manning, John 236
Manners, Roger 184
Mantilla, Pedro Velez 160
Many, David 225
Marshall, Lieutenant 184
Marsin, Comte de 255, 304
Mason, John 53, 64
Masterson, Jeremiah 294
Mattersley, Chad 130
May, Thomas 133, 185
Mazarin, Cardinal 20, 22, 27–8, 192, 201, 207–8, 211, 229, 231, 244, 247, 256, 259–61, 265, 278
Meade, Loiver 294
Mears, Lieutenant 180, 188
Meautys, Richard 234
Meneses, Francesco de 152, 160–1, 218, 269
Mercer, Francis 130, 184
Middleton, Earl of 211, 215, 275
Middleton Lt/Capt 330
Middleton, Henry 131, 186, 235, 328
Middleton, Hugh 322, 326

Middleton, John 226, 311
Middleton, Thomas 74, 80
Mills, Robert 128
Minne, John James, 131, 186
Minshin, Robert 130
Minuit, Peter 81
Mitchell, Thomas 328
Mitchell, William 47, 57, 59
Modyford, Thomas 77–8, 79, 98, 116
Molesworth, Guy 71
Molloy, Arthur 225, 329
Molloy, Daniel 328
Molloy, Edward 225, 328
Molloy, Charles 328
Molloy, James 224, 328
Molloy, John 225, 328
Molloy, Mathew 225, 329
Molloy, Sherlagh 225, 329
Monck, Christopher 233
Monck, George 53, 169, 170, 192, 202, 229, 309–12, 315–6, 318
Monckton, Captain 235
Montagu, Edward 197–9, 201–2, 232, 248, 253, 265, 268
Montijo, Don Juan Maldonaldo y 161
Monson, John 332
Montgomery, Colonel de 274, 282
Moore, John 58
Moore, Philip, 58
Moore, Robert, 58
Moore, Thomas 57, 293
Moore, William 170–1, 183, 189–90, 235, 327
Mootham, Peter 204
Morales, Don Pedro de 180
Mordaunt, William 135
More, Richard 88, 95
Morfi, Hugo 224
Morgan, Colonel 46, 56
Morgan, Henry 177
Morgan, Philip 114
Morgan, Sir Thomas 228–30, 236, 244–5, 247, 253, 256, 258, 264–5, 267–70, 273–4, 282, 287–8, 295, 297, 300–3, 308
Morla, Luis Lopez de 160
Morley, John 315, 321, 331, 332
Morphy, John 218, 269, 283
Morris, Lewis 39–40, 76–7, 79, 125, 130
Morris, Richard 223
Morris, William 332
Morrishove, Giles 224
Moyser, Francis 332

377

COLONIAL IRONSIDES

Moyser, John 332
Mucknell, John 38, 68
Munings, William 294
Murford, Mr 129, 155
Murford, Peter 136
Murray, Ensign 239
Murrett, Robert 224
Muschamp, Robert 327, 328
Muse, Captain 233, 311
Muse, John 325
Musgrave, Sir Philip 44, 46, 225
Muskerry, Lord 211–2, 223, 244–5, 275, 317
Myelvis, Robert 327, 328
Myngs, Christopher 177–8

Nangle, Fr Edward 329
Napier, Lord 226
Nash, John 96
Needham, Robert 325
Needler, Henry 294
Nelson, Robert 235
Newberry, Richard 127
Newburgh, Earl of 211, 215, 226, 259, 269, 283, 312, 316, 317, 329
Nicholas, Sir Edward 207
Nicholas, Oliver 323
Nieuchèse, Admiral 192
Nisbett, Robin 324
Noble, George 293
Noell, Captain 131, 184
Noell, Martin 171
Norman, Daniel 60, 64
Norman, Hugh 187
Norris, Henry 327
Norris, Richard 324
Norwood, Henry 325
Nugent, Lieutenant 330
Nuñez, Melchor 151, 156, 161

O'Brien, Dermott (Dermot) 223, 324
O'Bryan, Bryan 225
O'Driscoll, (O'Driscoll) Denis 224, 330
O'Driscoll, Daniel 324
O'Driscoll, Dermott 226
O'Brien, Terence 224, 324
O'Connor, Hugh 224, 324
O'Connor, Owen 224
O'Connor, Roger 324

O'Connellan, John 324
O'Fallery, Donough 324
O'Hare, Ensign 330
O'Hegarty, Norris 324
O'Higgins, Terence 324
O'Keefe, Arthur 223
O'Keefe, Daniel 223, 324
O'Keefe, Terence 223
O'Mulligan, Telge 324
O'Mulrean, Sige 223
O'Neil, John 223, 324
O'Sullevan, Aulife 224
O'Sullevan, Daniel 224
O'Sullevan, Owen 224
Ossory, Lord 318, 326
Ormesson, General de 258
Ormonde, Duke of 209, 211–2, 217, 225, 254–5, 276
Osborne, Sir Peter 50, 65
Otter, John 134
Owin, William 136
Oxenden, Thomas 234

Pack, Henry 204
Pack, Michael 55, 77–8
Packer, William 46, 57, 309, 310
Padson, Ensign 235
Paine, Matthew 186, 188
Pallano, Manuel 141–2, 152–3, 156–7, 159, 160
Palmer, Captain 235
Palmer, Anthony 234
Palmer, John 132
Pamphlin, Nathaniel 233
Panton, Sir Thomas 320
Paramore, Philip 332
Paris, Captain 130
Parrault, John 79
Parsons, George 130
Parry, Peter 131, 186
Pattison, Captain 189
Pavon, Captain 175, 190
Pawlett, Captain 122, 130, 135, 143, 151, 153, 155–7
Pawlyn, Paulinge, Peter 323
Pawling, Richard 236
Peacock, Robert 294
Peake, James 133
Pearce, Sir Richard 78
Pearson, John 56, 309, 310
Peart, Roland 236

INDEX

Pease, Richard 233, 311, 326
Pedro, John 112
Pegero, Esteban 162
Pegg, Abraham 131
Pelham, William 169, 189
Peñalva, Don Bernardino de Meneses Bracamonte y Zapata, 1st Count de 141–2, 144, 147–9, 160
Penkeville, Jonathan 131, 186
Penn, William 33, 117–9, 123–4, 126, 127, 137–8, 142–3, 152, 158–9, 163, 165–8, 191, 198
Penny, George 323
Penrose, Thomas 54, 205
Pepper, Denis 56, 293
Pepper, John 260, 264, 267–8, 278, 282, 293
Persan, Marquis de 220, 270, 283
Person, John 293
Peter, Andrew 130, 186
Peters, Hugh 230, 311
Petty, Thomas 187
Philip II, King of Spain 11, 16–17, 19, 21
Philip IV, King of Spain 20, 21, 27, 31, 173–4, 192, 207–8, 210, 216, 307
Philips, Mayther 324
Philips (Phillips), Walter 224, 324
Phillips, Miles 224
Phillipps, Miles 224
Pickering, Captain 230, 235
Pickering, Gilbert 28–9
Pimentel, Don Rodriguo 147, 161
Place, Thomas 235
Plunkett, Robert 225
Pockley, Francis 320
Pogson, Peter 311, 328
Poole, Jonas 127
Pope, Edward 234, 324, 326
Pope, Nathaniel 107
Popham, Alexander 32
Popham, Edward 33, 43
Porter, James 326
Porter, Richard 69
Potham, William 236
Potter, Henry 130, 186
Potter, Thomas 235
Poulton, John 131, 133, 185
Pound, William 93
Povey, Richard 129, 171, 183
Povey, Thomas 171, 183
Powell 93

Powell, Edward 135
Powell, Lewis 235, 238
Powell, Orwin 132
Powell, Rice 237
Prato, Don Tito del 248
Price, John 113, 114, 327
Prodgiers, James 321
Proenza, Francisco de 166, 173, 178, 190
Puerto, Marcus de 201
Purefoy, Valentine 326
Pym, Charles 78

Quiñones, Don Juan de Viloria y 161

Raleigh, Carew 53
Raleigh, George 65
Ralph, Relph, James 233, 325
Rambures, Colonel 268, 275, 282
Ramirez, Juan de Arellano 163, 166, 173, 190
Ramsey, Henry 130
Rasparu, Don Alvaro de la 190
Raymond, Edward 88, 95
Raymond, Thomas 182
Rayner, Moses 187
Read, James 236
Reade, Edmund 75, 79
Reade, John 131
Reeves, John 293
Reyes, Juan de los 174–5, 178
Reynolds, Sir John 229, 237, 241, 244–5, 247–8, 254, 256–8
Reynolds, John 56
Reynolds, Walter 225, 328
Rich, Edward 129, 143
Richardson, Brian 321
Richardson, John 233
Richardson, Richard 322, 333
Richardson, William 235
Richelieu, Marquis de 268, 278, 281–2
Righton, Edward 325
Rivers, William 133, 184
Roach, Ensign 329
Roache, William 329
Robinson, Lieutenant 180, 188
Robinson, John 223, 234, 322
Robles, Lazaro Franco de 157, 160
Roche, James 332
Rockwell, Nathaniel 84, 95
Roe, Gilbert 324

379

COLONIAL IRONSIDES

Rogers, Roger 294
Rolleston, Edward 332
Rooney, Mathew 224
Rooth, Richard 128
Rosscarrick, Edward 321
Rowe, Owen 101, 105
Rous, Thomas 74, 79
Rudiard, James 133, 185
Rudyard, John 129, 183
Rudyard, Henry 135, 167
Rupert, Prince of the Rhine 32–5, 37–8, 44, 83, 118, 197–8, 209
Russell, John 316, 332
Russell, Robert 50, 66
Russell, Theodore 292, 323
Rutherford, Andrew, Earl of Teviot 303, 312, 314–5, 317–8, 320–1
Ryley, Captain 189

St Hill, Peter, 325
Sackfield, Sackwell Edward 130, 186
Saddler, Thomas 41
Saddlington, William 293
Salkeld, Sir William 319, 324, 330
Salkield, Thomas 132
Salmon, Edward 258, 267, 286, 293, 305, 309
Salmon, Richard 84, 95,
Saltonhall, Dr 257
Salusbury, Thomas 236
Sandoval, Antonio Ortiz de 160
Sanders, Robert 127
Sanderson, William 321, 322
Sanpayo, Sebastian 161
Sandys, Henry 321, 332, 333
Sandys, Sir Thomas 320
Saunderson, Richard 293
Sayle, John 58
Sayle, William 100
Schomberg, Marshal Friedrich 212, 240, 244–5, 248, 266, 268, 274, 277, 281, 287, 295, 299–303, 312, 314
Scott, Richard 129, 184, 236
Scott, Walter 234, 326
Scotten, Edward 57, 332
Scowin, Captain 327
Scrimshaw, Charles 321
Searle, Daniel 78, 118, 124
Sedgwick, Robert 83–4, 87–9, 91–4, 95, 168–171, 173
Seeley, Robert 87, 96
Seralvo, Marquis de 218, 269, 283

Serras, Juan de 166, 190
Shaa, John 328
Sharpe, John 136
Sharpe, Samuel 292
Sharpe, William 235
Sheere, Roger 135
Shelley, Henry 29
Shelley, John 236, 237
Sherrard, John 328
Sherwin, Captain 230, 234
Shohand, Ensign 329
Shoohy, Morough 329
Silkwood, Richard 69
Silva, Don Domingo da 174–5, 178, 190
Sims, John 93
Simons, John 205
Simons, William 130, 186
Skelton, Bevil 321
Skepworth, Henry 130
Skiep, Richard 327
Slaughter, Charles 222
Smallwood, Mathew, 221, 321
Smelt, Nathaniel 235
Smith, Daniel 134, 185, 187
Smith, John 104, 114, 205
Smith, Robert 59, 131, 167, 184, 186, 188, 230–1, 235, 328
Smith, Thomas 61, 93, 131, 186
Smithsby, George 184
Smythe, Patrick 93
Snillsman, Owen 324
Snyllenan, Anthony 324
Soissons, Compte de 21, 277, 281, 282, 322
Somervill, James 289
Southerne, John 328
Spillman, Bartholomew 324
Spindler, Sebastian 261
Spotswood, Adjutant 222, 322
Sprat, Thomas 293
Sprey, Thomas 131
Spry, Edward 84, 95
Stackhouse, Thomas 323
Stagg, Thomas 98
Standish, Alexander 58, 323, 330
Standish, Myles 87, 96
Stanier (Stonor), Launcelot 322
Staniford, William 293
Stanley, Charles 331
Stanley, Charlotte, Countess of Derby 44

INDEX

Stanley, Edward 221, 320
Stanley, James, Earl of Derby 44–5, 46, 47
Stanley, Thomas 58
Stanley, William 212
Stapleton, Edward 133, 185
Stapleton, Theobald 224, 324
Stapleton, William 225, 329
Starsmore, Edward 327
Stayner, Richard 194, 199, 201–2, 204
Stephens, Robert 131
Stephenson, Stanley 135
Stevens, Richard 131, 178
Stileman Allen 293
Stokes, John 169, 204
Stone, William 107, 113, 114
Stopford, James 328
Strachan, Captain (John?) 226, 330
Stradling, Thomas 321
Strangeways, James 236
Street, Thomas 235
Strode, John 315, 321, 330
Stuyvesant, Peter 81
Styles, John 236
Summers, Captain 328
Sutton, Samuel 136
Swadlin, John 293
Swift, Jasper 235
Swinnerton, Ralph 130, 186
Sydenham, Ralph 65, 315, 321, 330, 332
Symcock, James 53, 66
Symonds, John 204

Taaffe, Theobald, Viscount 211–2, 224, 259, 317, 324
Tabor, Don Juan de 180–1, 190
Tlbot, Edward 323
Talon, Claude 248, 299
Taylor, Henry 332
Taylor, John 293
Taylor, Robert 134, 184, 186
Temple, Mr 129, 155
Temple, Benjamin 66
Temple, Thomas 93
Terrill, Robert 136
Terry, Daniel 235
Terry, James 127
Terry, William 328
Thompson, Quartermaster 235
Thompson, Thomas 58, 128

Thomson, Edward 55
Thornhill, Augustine 131, 184
Thornhill, Theobald 131
Thorold, Anthony 332
Throckmorton, William 210, 221, 259, 321fn
Throgmorton, Captain 131, 184
Thurloe, John, Secretary to Cromwell 28, 29, 83, 118, 142, 237, 258–60, 261, 267
Tickell, Thomas 128
Toleda, Fernando, Duke of Alba 16, 18
Tomkins, Guillamy 322
Tomkins, Sylvanus 222, 322, 333
Toms, Gregory 184 151, 156, 161
Tongue, John 236
Torralba, Don Juan de la Vega
Totty, Thomas 132
Tounge, Thomas 294
Tourville, M. de 242
Trimingham, John 100–1
Trip, George, 332
Tromp, Maarten 35, 38, 41, 191
Tuite, Gaspar, 328
Tuite, Henry 324
Tuite, John 225
Turenne, Henri de la Tour d'Auvergne, Marquis de 31, 208, 210, 220, 227, 229, 231–2, 237, 240–1, 244–6, 248, 251, 253, 255–8, 261, 263–9, 270–1, 274–8, 281, 282, 287–8, 290, 294–304, 308, 312–3
Turner, Captain 226
Turner, John 234
Turner, Thomas 100
Turner, William 239
Turpin, John 325
Tyrwhitt, Thomas 223
Tyson, Edward 168, 181–2, 188

Ufflet, William 236
Urry, William, 329
Usher, Captain 226

Vaca, Damian del Castillo 144, 161
Valéry, Captain de 250
Valley, Thomas 204
Vardesi, Lucas Borrero 174, 190
Varley, George 131, 183
Varenne, Duc de 265, 268, 277, 281, 288
Varvell, Thomas 55
Vauban, Sébastien le Prestre 239–40, 290

COLONIAL IRONSIDES

Vaughan, John 131, 187
Vaughan, Robert 114
Vavasser, André 64
Venables, Robert 29, 116–120, 122, 124–6, 129, 130, 137–159, 163–4, 166–8, 170, 171, 181, 183
Vera, Don Rodriguez de 174, 190
Verdugo, Don Pedro 160
Verroa, Lucas de 160
Vesey, William 127
Villafranca, Don Miguel de 162
Villanueva, Don Bayona 174–5, 178, 180

Wadeson, Robert 183
Wadeson, Thomas 129, 184
Wake, Sir Bernard 50, 65
Walded, Thomas 136
Walker, Lieutenant 180, 188
Walker, John 321
Walker, Ralph 234, 327–8
Walker, Stuart 322, 327
Walrond, Edward 74–5
Walrond, Humphrey 71, 75, 79
Walters, John 222
Walters, Robert 315, 322, 332
Walters, Thomas 133, 157, 183
Walwyne, Alexander 322
Wandell, William 133, 184, 187, 235
Wandes, William 328
Warde, (Ward) Philip 129, 183, 186
Warde, Robert 136
Warde, Thomas 56, 293
Warwick, Earl of 50, 116, 330
Waters, Benjamin 293
Waters, Thomas 293
Waters, William 293
Watkins, James 234
Watson, Henry 293
Watts, George 132
Waugh, Robert 329
Waugh, Walter 329
Wayne, Mathew 323
Wealy, Captain 329
Webley, William 187
Weld, Richard 131, 186
Wells, John 293
Wells, Richard 133, 185
Welsh, Benjamin 325
Wen, James 332

Wentworth, Lord Thomas 67, 210–1, 315, 316, 321
Wesbie, George 57, 293
Wharton, Jesse 134, 184
Wheeler, Charles 321, 332
Wheeler, Thomas 96
Whetstone, Thomas 205, 133, 185
Whetstone, Roger 230, 234
White, Andrew 105
White, Francis 56, 253, 258
White, John 127
White, George 132
White, Ralph 93
White, Thomas 133, 185
White, William 130
Whitelosse, John 95
Whitford, Walter 226
Whittaker, William 328
Wilbraham, Richard 132, 186
Wiles, Robert 234
Wilkinson, Captain 100
Wilkinson, John 234, 327
Willett, Edward 134, 184, 187
Williams, James 189
Wilmot, Henry, Earl of Rochester 208–11, 217, 221
Wilson, John 136
Willoughby, Lord Francis 75–8, 79
Willoughby, William 186
Wills, George 226, 230
Wills, Thomas 127
Winslow, Edward 118, 142, 158, 163
Winter, James 131
Wisdonme, Richard 293
Wiseman, Captain 257
Wiseman, Dr John 223
Wiseman, Dr Richard 257
Wisseris, Hamilton 329
Witham, Edward 236
Witherley, Vincent 294
Withers, John 234, 287, 311, 326
Withers, Richard 328
Withers, Thomas 326
Witteridge, Edward 55, 204
Wood, Edward 292fn, 323
Wood, Peter, 226, 370
Wood, William 187
Woodall, Thomas, 321
Woodcocke, Sir Thomas 330
Woods, Captain 57

Woodward, Richard 233, 325
Worsley, Charles 45, 47, 56, 59
Worsley, William 45
Wright, Thomas 60, 63, 64, 127, 128, 293
Wroth, Thomas 101
Wyerd (Wyberd) Captain 328
Wyse (Wise), Mathew 321, 322, 331

Young, Alexander 327
Young, Anthony 54, 305
Young, Thomas 234, 325, 327, 328
Younge, Richard 134, 184
Ysassi, Don Cristobal Arnaldo 173–5, 178–80 181, 190

Zúñiga, Francisco López de 201

INDEX OF PLACES

Acadia 84, 88–94
    Port Royal 84, 89–94
Algiers 194–7
Amiens 263, 305
Antigua 73, 75, 78, 97, 107
Ardres 243–7
Arques 240
Artois 256, 261, 266, 303
Arras 16, 30fn, 211, 300, 303

Balearic Islands
    Formentera 197
    Majorca 194
    Barbadoes
    Austin's Fort 77
    Holetown 76
    Oistins 78
    St Philip's Castle 78
    Speightstown 77
Barcelona 216, 307
Bergues 246, 248, 261, 263–6, 284–8, 290, 295, 299, 316
Bermuda – see Somers Islands
Béthune 242, 307
Blackheath 230
Bourbourg 248, 253, 256, 257, 264
Boulogne 230–1, 256, 312
Bruges 208–10, 215, 217, 284, 290, 295, 304
Brussels 206–7, 209, 212, 217, 229, 262–3, 295–8, 304, 312

Cadiz 29, 34, 192, 197–202
Cagliari 193–4, 196
Calais 27–8, 31, 230, 240, 242, 253, 256, 262, 265, 287, 299, 307
Cambrai 261
Canals
    Bergues–Dunkirk 248, 261, 264, 269–70, 284
    Bourbourg 264
    Colme 248

Furnes 266
Mardyck 255, 264
Ostende 204
Ypres 288
Canary Islands
    Santa Cruz de Tenerife 201–3, 262
Cartagena 34, 115–6, 141, 173–4, 178, 197
Cassell 269
Castellamare 193
Cerdanja 307
Channel Islands
    Alderney 48
    Castle Cornet (Guernsey) 49–50, 53, 65
    Elizabeth Castle (Jersey) 49–50, 52, 61, 62, 63–4
    Guernsey 48–53
    Jersey 48–53
    Mont Orgueil Castle (Jersey) 50, 52, 62
    St Aubin's (Jersey) 49, 62
    St Brelade (Jersey) 51, 63, 65
    St Helier (Jersey) 51–2, 62, 64
    St Ouen's (Jersey) 49, 51–2, 62, 64
    Sark 63
Chester 44–5, 47, 117fn, 168
Conflet 307
Coudekerke 248, 257
Cuba 115, 137, 141, 163, 166, 173–4, 177–181
Cumana (Brazil) 178

Deal 316
Dixmüde 259, 284, 288–90, 295, 298
Dunkirk 27–31, 65, 67, 201, 221, 240–1, 246–8, 251–6, 257, 260, 261–278, 284–8, 291–3, 295, 299, 303–4, 305–11, 314–9, 320–332

Fintele 288
Forts
    Castelnau 264

COLONIAL IRONSIDES

Du Bois 265
Leon 277
Oliver 264
Royal 264
Furnes (Veurne) 265–6, 276, 284, 288, 290, 295, 299, 316

Genoa 194
Gibraltar 198, 192, 201, 319
Gravelines 240, 246, 248, 253–5, 259–60, 265–6, 284, 289, 295, 299, 307
Gravesend 309–10
Guisnes 258

Hainault 217, 261
Hesdin 261, 263
Hispaniola
  Azua 141, 156, 161
  Baraguana 162
  La Vega 156, 163
  Pozo del Rey 153, 161
  San Domingo 115, 126, 139–40, 142–6, 151–4, 158, 163–4, 168

Jamaica
  Baycani 155, 175
  Cagway, Caguaya 173, 175, 177, 181
  Clarendon 175
  Guatibacoa 166, 175
  Liguani 174
  Las Chorreras 175, 178–9, 181
  Los Bermejelas 174–5
  Manchester 175
  Morant 163, 169, 170, 174
  Passage Fort, later Fort Cromwell 164
  Pozo de Ayron 173
  Rio Nuevo, Nuevho 179
  Santa Ana 174–5, 179
  St Catherine 175
  St Christopher 175
  St Thomas 175
  Santiago dela Vega, Spanish Town 141, 163
  Westmoreland 175

Kenoque (Fort Knokke) 288
Kinsale, Ireland 33, 38

Leer 217
Leghorn (Livorno) 191, 192, 194
Linck 266

Lisbon 33–4, 76, 199, 201
Llivia 307
Louvain 217
Luxembourg 307

Malaga 34, 194, 199
Man, Isle of
  Derby 64
  Douglas 44, 57
  Peel 43, 46, 57, 58fn
  Rushden 43–4, 46–7, 57
Mardyck, Madyke 31, 246–8, 251–60, 264–5, 267, 277–8, 285–7, 291, 305, 307, 314, 316–7, 320–331
Maryland 7, 81, 86, 97–112
Menin 298–300, 303
Montbernanson 241
Montmédy 236, 240–1
Montserrat 73, 79, 125, 129, 134, 183, 207

Nevis 29, 73, 75, 78, 97, 125, 129, 134, 169, 183
New Amsterdam 81–8
Nieuport (Nieupoort) 218, 265, 270, 2774, 284–5, 288–90, 303–4, 312, 316
Nivelles 312, 315

Ostende 261–2, 277, 284, 290, 304, 311
Oudenaarde 295–6, 298–301, 303–5, 307

Pentagouet, Maine (Pobnoscot) 92–3
Porto Farino (Ghar–al–Milh) 194–6
Philippeville 240
Providence, Maryland 107–8, 110–1
Providence Island, West Indies 73, 74fn
Puerto Cabello (Brazil) 178
Puerto Rico 115, 137, 141, 174, 190

Rivers
  Agua Dulce 144
  Bidassoa 307
  Jaina 143–4, 146–7, 148, 155, 158
  Lys 248, 295–6, 298–9, 300
  Najallo 144
  Nizao 144
  Ozama 137, 139, 143, 144, 151
  Sambre 240
  Severn (Maryland) 108–112
  Sinagua 144

INDEX

Roseburgh (Rekspoëde) 288
Rye 313

Santiago de Cuba 156, 174, 177, 179, 180, 181
St Christopher (St Kitts) 29, 73, 75–8, 97, 125, 126, 129, 134, 151, 152, 168, 169
St Ghislain 208, 212
Saint John, Acadia 84, 88–9, 92
St-Venant 241, 243, 245, 247–8, 300
Sallee 194
Scilly Isles
    Annet 36
    Bryther 35, 38, 40
    Great Ganilly 37
    Hugh Town 34, 37
    New Grimsby 37
    Northwithiel 39
    Old Grimsby 39, 40
    Tresco 35, 37–40, 68
    St Helen's 36
    St Martin's 35

St Mary's 35, 37, 38–41, 62
Star Castle 35, 37, 40
Samson 37, 40
Teän 37, 39
Somers Islands 97–100
Surinam 81, 125, 134

Tangier 17, 43, 199, 256, 293fn, 303, 314, 317–8, 319, 323fn, 327fn, 328, 329, 331
Thionville 307
Toulon 34, 192, 194
Tripoli 194
Tunis 194–5

Vallespir 307
Vigo 199
Virginia 73, 76, 81, 97–8, 102, 107, 112

Ypres 266, 284, 288–9, 295–303

Zuydcoote 266–7, 276